Professional Review Guide for the RHIA and RHIT Examinations
2014 Edition

Professional Review Guide for the RHIA and RHIT Examinations 2014 Edition

Patricia J. Schnering, RHIA, CCS
Debora J. Butts, EdD, RHIA
Debra W. Cook, MAEd, RHIA
Lauralyn Kavanaugh-Burke, DrPH, RHIA, CHTS-IM
Marjorie H. McNeill, PhD, RHIA, CCS, FAHIMA
Toni Cade, MBA, RHIA, CCS, FAHIMA
Lisa Delhomme, MHA, RHIA
Lon'Tejuana S. Cooper, PhD, RHIA, CPM
Barbara W. Mosley, PhD, RHIA
Nanette B. Sayles, EdD, RHIA, CCS, CHPS, CPHIMS, FAHIMA
Kathy C. Trawick, EdD, RHIA, FAHIMA
Charlotte McCuen, MS, RHIA
Anita Hazelwood, MLS, RHIA, FAHIMA
Carol A. Venable, MPH, RHIA, FAHIMA
Mary Teslow, MLIS, RHIA
Sheila Carlon, PhD, RHIA, FAHIMA
Leslie Moore, RHIT, CCS

CENGAGE
Learning®

Australia • Brazil • Japan • Korea • Mexico • Singapore • Spain • United Kingdom • United States

Professional Review Guide for the RHIA and RHIT Examinations, 2014 Edition
Patricia J. Schnering, RHIA, CCS

Vice President, GM Skills & Product Planning: Dawn Gerrain

Product Manager: Jadin B. Kavanaugh

Director, Development–Career and Computing: Marah Bellegarde

Product Development Manager: Juliet Steiner

Content Developer: Amy Wetsel

Product Assistant: Courtney Cozzy

Marketing Director: Michele McTighe

Marketing Manager, Special Markets: Erica Glisson

Senior Production Director: Wendy Troeger

Production Manager: Andrew Crouth

Content Project Management: Bharathi Sanjeev / S4Carlisle

Art Direction: Laurie Entringer / S4Carlisle

Media Editor: Deborah Bordeaux

Cover Image: Pgiam/E+/Getty Images

The 2014 versions of CPT, ICD-10-CM, and ICD-10-PCS were used in preparation of this product.

CPT Copyright 2013 American Medical Association. All rights reserved. CPT is a registered trademark of the American Medical Association.

For product information and technology assistance, contact us at
Cengage Learning Customer & Sales Support,
1-800-354-9706

For permission to use material from this text or product, submit all requests online at **www.cengage.com/permissions.**

Further permissions questions can be e-mailed to
permissionrequest@cengage.com

Library of Congress Control Number: 2013954421

ISBN-13: 978-1-285-73551-1
ISBN-10: 1-285-73551-X

Cengage Learning
200 First Stamford Place, 4th Floor
Stamford, CT 06902
USA

Cengage Learning is a leading provider of customized learning solutions with office locations around the globe, including Singapore, the United Kingdom, Australia, Mexico, Brazil, and Japan. Locate your local office at: **www.cengage.com/global**

Cengage Learning products are represented in Canada by Nelson Education, Ltd.

To learn more about Cengage Learning, visit **www.cengage.com**

Purchase any of our products at your local college store or at our preferred online store **www.cengagebrain.com**

Notice to the Reader

Printed in the United States of America
1 2 3 4 5 6 7 18 17 16 15 14

ABOUT THE AUTHORS

Patricia J. Schnering, RHIA, CCS

Patricia J. Schnering founded PRG Publishing, Inc. and Professional Review Guides, Inc. Mrs. Schnering is a 1995 graduate of the Health Information Management program at St. Petersburg College in St. Petersburg, Florida. In 1998, she was certified as a CCS and in 1999 she received her RHIA certification. Her education includes a Baccalaureate degree from the University of South Florida in Tampa, Florida, with a major in Business Administration. Her HIM experience includes working as Health Information Services supervisor, as an HIM consultant, and as an adjunct HIM instructor at St. Petersburg College. Pat received the Florida Health Information Management Association (FHIMA) Literary Award in 2000 and 2005.

Debora J. Butts, EdD, RHIA

Debora Butts is a graduate of Clark Atlanta University and Emory University in Atlanta, Georgia where she earned a BS degree in Health Information Management. She also holds a MA degree in Management from Webster University in St. Louis, Missouri and an Ed.D., in Higher Education Administration from Texas Southern University. Dr. Butts has worked in various positions in the academic and clinical setting in roles such as: Program Director, Center Dean, Assistant Professor, Revenue Integrity Manager, Clinical Documentation Specialist, Director of HIM and Manager of Coding and Audit. She is most passionate about the teaching and learning process and the Revenue Cycle management process as related to coding and reimbursement.

Debra W. Cook, MAEd, RHIA

Debra W. Cook is a graduate of the Medical Record Administration and the Adult Education programs at East Carolina University in Greenville, North Carolina. Her HIM experience includes five years in acute health care practice in a variety of positions, such as management, utilization management, coding, and consulting. She also has over 24 years' experience in HIM education at Alderson-Broaddus College and Marshall University in West Virginia, and Catawba Valley Community College in Hickory, North Carolina. Currently, she is the Department Head of Health Information Technology at CVCC and Director of the Workforce Development Program for Electronic Record Specialists. In addition to this, she serves on the Panel of Accreditation Reviewers for the Commission of Health Informatics and Information Management Education.

Nanette B. Sayles, EdD, RHIA, CCS, CHPS, CPHIMS, FAHIMA

Nanette Sayles is a 1985 graduate of the University of Alabama at Birmingham Medical Record Administration (now the Health Information Management) program. She earned her Master's of Science in Health Information Management (1995) and her Master's in Public Administration (1990) from the University of Alabama at Birmingham. She earned her doctorate in Adult Education from the University of Georgia (2003). She is currently Associate Professor for the Health Information Management program at East Central College in Union, Missouri. She has a wide range of health information management experience in hospitals, consulting, system development/implementation, and education. She also received the 2005 American Health Information Management Association Triumph Educator Award.

Anita Hazelwood, MLS, RHIA, FAHIMA

Anita Hazelwood is an Associate Professor in the Health Information Management Department at the University of Louisiana at Lafayette, located in Lafayette, Louisiana. She has a Bachelor's degree in Medical Record Science and a Master's degree in Library Science, and has been a credentialed Registered Health Information Administrator (RHIA) for 28 years.

Some of the courses she teaches include coding and classification systems such as ICD-9-CM and CPT coding; reimbursement methodologies such as DRGs and RBRVS; fraud and abuse; principles of health information management and alternative delivery systems. She is also the Clinical Experience Coordinator.

Anita has actively consulted in hospitals, nursing homes, clinics, facilities for the mentally retarded, and in other educational institutions. She has conducted numerous ICD-9-CM and CPT coding workshops throughout the state for hospitals and physicians' offices.

On a professional level, Anita has been a member of the American Health Information Management Association (AHIMA) for several years. She is also a member of the Society for Clinical Coding (SCC) and served on the SCC board as Secretary in 1998. Anita has been the Internet Task Force Chair for several years. She is a member of the AHIMA's Assembly on Education (AOE) and has served as Membership Chair, a member of the Nominating Committee, and on the Board of Directors.

Anita is a member of the Louisiana Health Information Management Association and was selected as its 1997 Distinguished Member.

Mary Spivey Teslow, MLIS, RHIA

Mary Spivey Teslow is a 1981 graduate of the University of Illinois at Chicago program in Health Information Management (formerly Medical Record Administration) and has been a credentialed RHIA for over 29 years. She received her first Bachelor's degree from Governors State University in Women's Studies in 1976 and her Master's degree in Library and Information Science from the University of South Florida in 1994. In 1998, Ms. Teslow was awarded an Endowed Teaching Chair in the Health Sciences. Her HIM experience includes:

- Twenty years as an HIM educator. She is currently Program Director in HIM at Western Carolina University in North Carolina.
- Fifteen years at Broward Community College in Ft. Lauderdale, Florida, where she developed and directed the Health Information Technology program.
- Seven years in HIM practice, including various management positions in acute care in both an academic medical center and a community hospital as well as managed care.
- Ongoing consulting and publication projects, including creation of the PRG Quick Notes series with Patricia Schnering, and editing and authoring several titles.

Lisa M. Delhomme, MPA, RHIA

Lisa M. Delhomme is an Instructor in the Health Information Management Department at the University of Louisiana at Lafayette located in Lafayette, Louisiana. She has a Bachelor's degree in Health Information Management and a Master's degree in Health Services Administration. She teaches several courses, including CPT coding, legal aspects for health care, and computers in health care organizations. Prior to teaching, she held a management position at a physician practice and ambulatory surgery center. Mrs. Delhomme has been an active member of the American Health Information Management Association for 12 years. In addition, she has been involved with committees and projects for the Louisiana Health Information Management Association and Louisiana Medical Group Management Association.

Toni Cade, MBA, RHIA, CCS, FAHIMA

Toni Cade is a tenured Associate Professor in the Health Information Management Department at the University of Louisiana at Lafayette. She teaches several courses including health care reimbursement methodologies (MS-DRGs, APCs, RUGs, etc.), hospital statistics, case management, performance improvement, medical terminology, and health care risk management. Mrs. Cade is also the Management Internship Site Coordinator, coordinating affiliation sites throughout the United States.

Mrs. Cade has 33 years of experience with previous positions, including Data Analyst for the QIO, Utilization Review Supervisor, and Coding Supervisor in a large acute care hospital.

She is listed in *Marquis' Who's Who in Medicine and Health Care* and serves on the Editorial Advisory Board of For the Record. She has reviewed and authored publications on topics including medical terminology, billing, reimbursement, and health care statistics.

As an independent consultant, Mrs. Cade has extensive experience conducting seminars in coding and reimbursement. She also consults at acute care hospitals and works as an expert health care data analyst and expert witness with attorneys involved in medical malpractice cases.

Mrs. Cade has served the American Health Information Management Association (AHIMA) in various positions, including Delegate, Nominating Committee member, and Fellowship Review Committee member. She was also nominated for AHIMA's Champion Award and Educator's Award.

In her state association (Louisiana Health Information Management Association), she was awarded the Distinguished Member Award and the Outstanding Volunteer Award. At the university, she received the Excellence in Teaching Award and holds the Louisiana Health Systems / BoRSF Professorship in Health Care Administration.

Charlotte McCuen, MS, RHIA

Charlotte McCuen has 30 years of experience in health information management. She currently is an independent contractor as editor and coauthor of HIM textbooks. She served as Associate Professor and Clinical Coordinator for 14 years in the Health Information Management baccalaureate and associate degree programs at Macon State College in Macon, Georgia. She also served 15 years as HIM Director of an acute care hospital and a state psychiatric / forensic acute care hospital. She has consulted for long-term care facilities, a behavioral health hospital, physician offices, and renal dialysis centers. She received her Master's degree from Mercer University in Health Care Policy and Administration and a Baccalaureate degree from the Medical College of Georgia in Medical Record Administration. She volunteers professional services to both AHIMA and Georgia Health Information Management Association (GHIMA), most recently serving on the AHIMA program committee and acting as President of GHIMA (2011–2012). She was the recipient of the Mentor Award for GHIMA in 2004.

Lon'Tejuana S. Cooper, MSHA, RHIA, CPM

Lon'Tejuana S. Cooper is a 1998 graduate of the Health Informatics and Information Management (formerly Health Information Management) program at Florida A&M University in Tallahassee, Florida. She completed the Certified Public Manager's program at Florida State University in 2002 and received her Master's of Science degree in Healthcare Administration in 2004 at Florida A&M University. Mrs. Cooper has completed 45 hours of course work toward her doctoral degree in Educational Leadership and Human Services. She has more than 8 years of experience in managing PHI in electronic format. Mrs. Cooper has developed policies and procedures on implementing HIPAA requirements, developed training modules for staff training, and designed HIPAA assessment tools. For the past 7 years, Mrs. Cooper has served as a faculty member in the Division of Health Informatics and Information Management at Florida A&M University.

Barbara W. Mosley, PhD, RHIA

Barbara W. Mosley is a 1976 graduate of the Health Information Management (formerly Medical Record Administration) program at the University of Tennessee Center for the Health Sciences in Memphis, Tennessee. She received her Master's degree in Public Administration with a concentration in Health Services Administration from the University of Memphis (formerly Memphis State University) in 1980. She earned her doctorate degree in Adult Education in 1990 from Florida State University. In 1996, Dr. Mosley was chosen Teacher of the Year at Florida A&M University. In 1998, she was chosen as the Advanced Teacher of the Year at Florida A&M University. Her experience in health information management includes:

- Twenty-six years as Health Information Management educator. Currently, she is a Professor in the Health Information Management Program and the Associate Dean for the School of Allied Health Sciences at Florida A&M University in Tallahassee, Florida.
- Nineteen years of consulting experience at several long-term care facilities in Tallahassee, Florida, and surrounding cities.
- Formerly, Assistant Director of Medical Record Department at the City of Memphis Hospital and the VA Medical Center in Birmingham, Alabama, and Director of Medical Records at the Southeast Memphis Mental Health Center.

Carol A. Venable, MPH, RHIA, FAHIMA

Carol A. Venable is a Professor and Department Head of Health Information Management at the University of Louisiana at Lafayette (ULL). She has a Bachelor's degree in Medical Record Science, a Master's degree in Public Health and Tropical Medicine, and has been a credentialed Registered Health Information Administrator (RHIA) for over 30 years. Prior to teaching at ULL, Ms. Venable held the position of Director of Medical Records at Lafayette General Medical Center and has actively consulted in hospitals, nursing homes, clinics, home health agencies, educational institutions, physicians' offices, and facilities for the mentally retarded. She has written numerous articles and coedited several coding publications. She has coauthored the books ICD-9-CM Diagnostic Coding and Reimbursement for Physician Services and ICD-10 Preview. She was coauthor of a chapter in the book, Health Information: Management of a Strategic Resource, 2nd edition. She has been a member of the Louisiana Health Information Management Association and has served as President, President-elect, Treasurer, Delegate, and a member of the Board of Directors, as well as serving on various committees and projects. Carol has also been active in the American Health Information Management Association. She has served on the Item Writing Committee, Benchmarking the Best Practices in HIM Education Project, Council on Education, and the Council on Certification's Roles and Functions Committee. She also serves as a member of the Panel of Accreditation Surveyors. In addition, Carol was awarded the Legacy Award by the American Health Information Management Association. She was elected to serve on the Assembly on Education's (AOE) Board of Directors and has served as chair of the Membership and Nomination Committees of the AOE. She also serves on the Editorial Review Board for Educational Perspectives in Health Information Management, the journal of the Assembly on Education of the American Health Information Management Association.

Sheila A. Carlon, PhD, RHIA, FAHIMA

Dr. Carlon has a PhD in Organizational Development and Systems, a Master's degree in Health Services Administration, and Bachelor's degrees in Broadcast Journalism and Health Care Management. She is a Fellow of AHIMA and received the Educator of the Year Award in 2006 and Cypress College's Distinguished Alumni Award in 2008. Dr. Carlon has been a Program Director and Degree Chair in Regis University's College for Health Professions for the past 8 years, where she administers and teaches in four-degree programs. She also has extensive hospital and physician office management experience and has been a Health Care Consultant for Deloitte, Touche International. She is a frequent meeting facilitator and speaker both locally and nationally on such topics as technology, HIPAA, the Global EHR, E- HIM, leadership and management theory and development, HIM advocacy, education trends, and organizational assessment. Dr. Carlon volunteers as an Ombudsman for the Aging Services Division of the Denver Regional Council of Governments. She serves as a Board Member of the Golden Gate Fire Department in Golden, Colorado. She is a volunteer for the Ronald McDonald House, Project Homeless, Quarters for Kids, and Project Mercy in Yetebon, Ethiopia. She is currently helping to launch the field of HIM into the country of Ethiopia.

Marjorie H. McNeill, PhD, RHIA, CCS, FAHIMA

Dr. Marjorie McNeill is Associate Professor and Director of the Division of Health Informatics and Information Management in the School of Allied Health Sciences at Florida A&M University, located in Tallahassee, Florida. She is a graduate of the Health Information Management (formerly Medical Record Administration) program at the Medical College of Georgia in Augusta. She received her MS degree in Health Education at Florida State University and her PhD in Educational Leadership at Florida A&M University.

Dr. McNeill has been credentialed as a Registered Health Information Administrator (RHIA) for 38 years and a Certified Coding Specialist (CCS) for 18 years. She is an AHIMA-approved ICD-10 trainer. Her experience in health information management includes 28 years as an HIM educator and 9 years of management and consulting experience in various health care facility practice settings (mental retardation, ambulatory surgery, nursing home, acute care hospital).

Dr. McNeill has several educational publications to her credit, including research articles in *Perspectives in Health Information Management, Journal of Allied Health,* and *Journal of the American Health Information Management Association.* She was the recipient of the 2008 Florida Health Information Management Association Distinguished Services Award and the 2010 Florida Health Information Management Association Literary Award. Dr. McNeill is a Fellow of the American Health Information Management Association.

Kathy C. Trawick, EdD, RHIA, FAHIMA

Dr. Kathy Trawick is the chairman and associate professor of the Health Information Management Department at the University of Arkansas for Medical Sciences in Little Rock, Arkansas. She is a 1985 graduate of the University of Alabama at Birmingham, Health Information Management (formerly Medical Record Administration) program. Dr. Trawick has expertise in Higher Education and in the Allied Health Sciences. Her basic research interests with keywords under the ERIC database include higher educational administration effectiveness, institutional effectiveness, and student satisfaction. Dr. Trawick has been a practitioner for 10 years in acute care facilities, as well as an HIM educator and program chairman since 1999. Topics of instruction include health care statistics, legal issues, HIM systems and the CPR, health administration, quality improvement, and cancer registry principles. She has coauthored a text (for AHIMA) on computer systems in HIT and has been a contributing author of texts on medical terminology and medical law and ethics. She has published articles in the *AHIMA Journal* and *Advance* magazine and written for Educational Perspectives in Health Information Management and the Mid-South Educational Research Association Proceedings. She is also a consultant to various types of health care facilities in Arkansas. In addition to holding offices at the state level in HIM and Cancer Registry associations, she currently serves on the CAHIIM Panel of Reviewers for HIT/HIA program accreditation.

Lauralyn Kavanaugh-Burke, DrPH, RHIA, CHTS-IM

After receiving a BS degree in Medical Record Administration with a minor in biology from York College of Pennsylvania, Dr. Burke worked in several hospitals in Virginia and Maryland in various management positions, including DRG Analyst, Assistant Director, and Director of the Medical Record / Health Information departments. During this time, her interest in pathophysiology intensified after working with several physicians in their research endeavors. She started teaching at an associate's degree Health Information Technology (HIT) program at Fairmont State College in West Virginia where she was able to strengthen her anatomy and pathophysiology skills, not only instructing HIT students, but also working with the medical laboratory and veterinary technology programs there. This position gave her the chance to complete her MS degree in Community Health Education from West Virginia University, which perfectly blended health information management and education. She achieved her Certified Health Education Specialist (CHES) credential shortly afterward. She then moved back to Pennsylvania and returned to the hospital arena as a DRG and coding consultant. Dr. Burke had the opportunity to teach at her alma mater and lay the foundation for an associate's degree program in HIT at a local community college.

Subsequent to relocating to Florida, she became a faculty member at Florida A&M University's BS degree program in Health Informatics & Information Management Division. She continued her pursuit of more training in pathophysiology, and soon after received her Doctor of Public Health (DrPH) with a concentration in epidemiology from Florida A&M University. Dr. Burke's main areas of interest are in disaster preparedness for hospitals, and bioterrorism and infectious diseases. She recently achieved certification as a Health Information Technology Implementation Manager (CHTS-IM) after completing her HITECH training through Santa Fe College.

ACKNOWLEDGMENTS

First and foremost, I wish to express my gratitude to the contributing authors who created and revised the various chapters. They are wonderful people and have graciously provided whatever is needed at the right time while the work is in process. Each of the authors is a seasoned professional and an excellent educator. I can only say that they inspire me to work harder to produce a better product for each edition. With their contributions and assistance, we have been able to provide a broad overview of content from both the RHIA and RHIT programs. I am honored to call them my friends and associates.

I have enjoyed working with the staff at Delmar Cengage Learning. They have been quite accommodating and have taught me a lot about the process of publishing. Thank you, Jadin, Amy, Lauren and the rest of the wonderful staff at Delmar Cengage Learning.

There have been very special people in my life who always knew I could do it when I was not sure I could. My late husband, Bob, always continued to keep me grounded while I would spin off in space working on the book. My mother, Emma Miller, has been my role model for perseverance leading to success. She embodied grace, courage, strength, and endurance. I will always be grateful for having had them in my life.

My thanks would not be complete without acknowledging all the HIM/HIT educators and students who support our efforts by using PRG products. I have been so fortunate in meeting such wonderful people in the HIM profession.

My reward is knowing that the materials you study here may assist you in preparing for the challenge of your examination. Thank you for the letters and words of encouragement.

Whichever credential you seek, I wish you the very best now and throughout your career.

Until we meet...

Patricia J. Schnering, RHIA, CCS

PJSPRG@AOL.COM

TABLE OF CONTENTS

Mary Spivey Teslow, MLIS, RHIA

Patricia J. Schnering, RHIA, CCS
Debra W. Cook, MAEd, RHIA
Sheila Carlon, PhD, RHIA, FAHIMA

Introduction

Patricia J. Schnering, RHIA, CCS

Introduction

Although we have no way of knowing what exactly will be on the examination, the authors tried to cover as many HIM concepts as possible. We have carefully selected questions that are generic enough to cover the broad topic categories. Researching the questions as you study should expand your knowledge such that, when you encounter similar questions, you can arrive at the correct answer. We believe this review material will jog your memory and serve to help you build on information you have already gained through your education.

With the collaboration of Health Information Administration and Technology educators, many questions have been updated and new questions added to enhance topic categories in this edition of the book. The more advanced questions for RHIA candidates are at the end of the chapters, where appropriate.

Professional Review Guide for the RHIA and RHIT Examinations by Content Areas

This review guide is arranged by content sections much as you studied in your classes. See Table I-1 for content areas and the number of questions in each content area. The number of questions does not indicate the importance of any one subject; it is merely an accounting of the questions in each section of this book. The latest timeline for launching coding ICD-10-CM/PCS on the certification examinations was given as 4/21/2014 for the RHIT Examination and 4/48/2014 for the RHIA Examination. Check the AHIMA Web site regularly for updates.

Table I-1 Professional Review Guide for the RHIA and RHIT Examinations, 2014 Edition Content Areas and Number of Questions

Professional Review Guide for the RHIA and RHIT Examinations, 2014 Edition Content Areas and Number of Questions	
Health Information Content Topic	Number of Questions
Health Data Content and Standards	98
Information Retention and Access	125
Classification Systems and Secondary Data Sources	87
Medical Billing and Reimbursement Systems	114
Medical Science	145
ICD-10-CM/PCS Coding	203
CPT Coding	217
Informatics and Information Systems	101
Health Information Privacy and Security	98
Health Statistics and Research	106
*Health Law	100
Quality and Performance Improvement	107
Organization and Management	106
Human Resources	100
Mock Examination	180
Totals	1887

Examination Content and Insights

The test uses competency categories known as domains, subdomains, and tasks that have been shown to be essential entry-level competencies for HIM practice.

Before you begin your review for the examinations, we suggest that you obtain the latest RHIA/RHIT Examination Candidate Handbook. The handbook can be downloaded from AHIMA's Web site at www.ahima.org. Visit the Certification and Credentials section of the AHIMA Web site for the latest certification information.

The entry-level tasks are grouped into six domains for the RHIA and seven domains for the RHIT examination, as shown in Table I-2.

Table I-2 Entry-Level Domains for RHIA and RHIT (Effective October 2011)

Entry-Level Domains for RHIA and RHIT	
RHIA	RHIT
1. Health Data Management	1. Data Analysis and Management
2. Health Statistics and Research Support	2. Coding
3. Information Technology and Systems	3. Compliance
4. Organization and Management	4. Information Technology
5. Privacy, Security, and Confidentiality	5. Quality
6. Legal and Regulatory Standards	6. Legal
	7. Revenue Cycle

These domains are divided further into subdomains that modify the domains. Weights for each domain and subdomain are assigned by the number of questions in the domain or subdomain. Thus, each weight correlates to the degree of emphasis, or importance, given to each domain statement as it relates to the HIM practice.

The examinations are based on the competencies. The competencies are aligned with knowledge statements. On the following pages, you will find additional information on the competencies and their corresponding knowledge statements listed for the RHIA and RHIT examinations.

Look at the differences in the level of knowledge needed for the RHIA and RHIT examinations. It may help you understand what is expected in each examination by competency. You can expect a higher level of knowledge in statistics, research, management, and information systems for the RHIA, whereas the RHIT will be focused more on Domain 1 and Domain 2 in data analysis and coding.

COMPETENCIES FOR THE RHIA EXAMINATION

The RHIA examination has 180 questions (160 questions scored and 20 that are not scored for the exam). The 160 scored questions are the basis for scoring your examination. The 20 unscored questions on the RHIA examination are to be used in obtaining statistical information to help in the construction of questions for future examinations. These 20 questions will not be identified in the exam, nor will they count toward the examination pass/fail score. Table I-3 presents the domains and equivalent weights for the RHIA examination. Review the current RHIA and RHIT Examination Candidate Handbook from AHIMA.

Table I-3 Domains and Equivalent Weights for the RHIA Certification Examination

Domains and Equivalent Weights for the RHIA Certification Examination			
Domain	Domain Name	Questions	Weight
1	Health Data Management	32	20%
2	Health Statistics and Research Support	17	11%
3	Information Technology and Systems	32	20%
4	Organization and Management	48	30%
5	Privacy, Security, and Confidentiality	21	13%
6	Legal and Regulatory Standards	10	6%
	Total	160	100%

COMPETENCIES FOR THE RHIT EXAMINATION

The RHIT examination has 150 questions (130 questions scored and 20 that are not scored for the exam). The 130 scored questions are the basis for scoring the examination. The 20 unscored questions on the RHIT examination are to be used in obtaining statistical information to help in the construction of questions for future examinations. These 20 questions will not be identified in the exam, nor will they count toward the examination pass/fail score. Table I-4 presents the domains and equivalent weights for the RHIT examination. Review the current RHIA and RHIT Examination Candidate Handbook from AHIMA to verify the competencies.

Table I-4 Domains and Equivalent Weights for the RHIT Certification Examination

Domains and Equivalent Weights for the RHIT Certification Examination			
Domain	Domain Name	Questions	Weights
1	Data Analysis and Management	26	20%
2	Coding	23	18%
3	Compliance	21	16%
4	Information Technology	16	12%
5	Quality	16	12%
6	Legal	14	11%
7	Revenue Cycle	14	11%
	Total	130	100%

In creating the review guide, we wanted to cover the competencies for both the RHIA and the RHIT. The questions in the chapters of this review guide relate to the competencies according to the breakdown of content for both the RHIA and RHIT exams.

Table I-5 provides a crosswalk between the RHIA competencies for and the number of questions in each competency by chapter.

Table I-6 provides a crosswalk of RHIT Competencies by number of questions in each Chapter.

Table I-7 shows the pass rates for the RHIA and RHIT examinations given in 2010, 2011, and 2012.

Table I-5 Crosswalk of RHIA Competencies by Chapter

Crosswalk of the RHIA Examination Competencies to Chapters								
	Domains							
Chapter	1	2	3	4	5	6		Total
Health Data Content and Standards	40	3	18	3	0	34		98
Information Retention and Access	56	3	31	14	1	20		125
Classification Systems and Secondary Data Sources	82	0	5	0	0	0		87
Medical Billing and Reimbursement Systems	114	0	0	0	0	0		114
Medical Science	145	0	0	0	0	0		145
ICD-10-CM/PCS Coding	203	0	0	0	0	0		203
CPT Coding	217	0	0	0	0	0		217
Informatics and Information Systems	0	0	101	0	0	0		101
Health Information Privacy and Security	0	0	0	0	98	0		98
Health Statistics and Research	0	106	0	0	0	0		106
*Health Law	0	0	0	0	50	50		100
Quality and Performance Improvement	0	107	0	0	0	0		107
Organization and Management	0	0	0	106	0	0		106
Human Resources	0	0	0	100	0	0		100
Mock Examination	48	40	23	36	14	19		180
Totals	905	259	178	259	163	123		1887

*Competencies for the Health Law questions fit in both domains 5 and 6.

Table I-6 RHIT Competencies by Chapter

Crosswalk of the RHIT Examination Competencies to Chapters								
	1	2	3	4	5	6	7	Total
Health Data Content and Standards	46	5	30	16	1	0	0	98
Information Retention and Retrieval	78	2	14	20	5	6	0	125
Classification Systems and Secondary Data Sources	82	0	5	0	0	0	0	87
Medical Billing and Reimbursement Systems	0	0	0	0	0	0	114	114
Medical Science	145	0	0	0	0	0	0	145
ICD-10-CM/PCS Coding	0	203	0	0	0	0	0	203
CPT Coding	0	217	0	0	0	0	0	217
Informatics and Information Systems	0	0	0	55	0	0	0	55
Health Information Privacy and Security	0	0	0	0	0	100	0	100
Health Statistics and Research	42	7	0	0	30	0	0	79
Health Law	0	0	0	0	0	100	0	100
Quality and Performance Improvement	107	0	0	0	0	0	0	107
Organization and Management	24	0	0	0	0	0	0	24
Human Resources	28	2	0	0	3	18	0	51
Mock Examination	36	32	10	16	31	17	8	150
Total RHIT Questions	588	468	59	107	70	241	122	1655

Table I-7 Passing Rates for the First-Time Test Taker for 2010, 2011, and 2012

Passing Rates for the First-Time Test Taker (2010–2012)			
*Pass Rates for First-Time Test Takers	2012	2011	2010
Registered Health Information Administrator (RHIA)	76.5%	70.9%	77.0%
Registered Health Information Technician (RHIT)	75.5%	71.3%	76.4%
*Exam pass rates are based on the calendar year.			

Source: AHIMA (AHIMA.org).

KNOWLEDGE STATEMENTS For The RHIA And RHIT

In addition to the competencies, AHIMA and the COC have identified the knowledge statements that emerged from the Roles and Function Study for the RHIA and RHIT. Mastery of these knowledge statements is necessary to successfully perform the competencies.

Table I-8 lists the knowledge statements by domain for the baccalaureate degree program (RHIA).

Table I-9 lists the knowledge statements by domain for the associate degree program (RHIT).

Table I-8 Knowledge Statements for RHIA Domains

Domain 1 Health Data Management
1. Manage health data elements and/or data sets
2. Develop and maintain organizational policies, procedures, and guidelines for management of health information
3. Ensure accuracy and integrity of health data and health record documentation
4. Manage and/or validate coding accuracy and compliance
5. Manage the use of clinical data required in reimbursement systems and prospective payment systems (PPS) in healthcare delivery
6. Code diagnosis and procedures according to established guidelines
7. Present data for organizational use (e.g., summarize, synthesize, and condense information) Health information media (paper, electronic/computer-based; e-health-personal, web-based)

Domain 2 Healthcare Statistics, Biomedical Research, and Quality Management
1. Identify and/or respond to the information needs of internal and external healthcare customers
2. Filter and/or interpret information for the end customer
3. Analyze and present information for organizational management (e.g., quality, utilization, risk)
4. Use data mining techniques to query and report from databases

Domain 3 Information Technology and Research Support
1. Implement and manage use of technology applications
2. Develop data dictionary and data models for database design
3. Manage and maintain databases (e.g., data migration, updates)
4. Apply data and functional standards to achieve interoperability of healthcare information systems
5. Apply data/record storage principles and techniques associated with the medium (e.g., paper-based, hybrid, electronic)
6. Evaluate and recommend clinical, administrative, and specialty service applications (e.g., financial systems, electronic record, clinical coding)
7. Manage master person index (e.g., patient record integration, customer–client relationship management)

Domain 4 Organization and Management
1. Develop and support strategic and operational plans for facility-wide health information management
2. Monitor industry trends and organizational needs to anticipate changes
3. Perform human resource management activities (e.g., recruiting staff, creating job descriptions, resolving personnel issues)
4. Conduct training and educational activities (e.g., HIM systems, coding, medical and institutional terminology, documentation and regulatory requirements)
5. Establish and monitor productivity standards for the HIM function
6. Optimize reimbursement through management of the revenue cycle (e.g., chargemaster maintenance)
7. Develop, motivate, and support work teams and/or individuals (e.g., coaching, mentoring)
8. Prepare and manage budgets
9. Analyze and report on budget variances
10. Determine resource needs by performing analyses (e.g., cost-benefit, business planning)
11. Evaluate and manage contracts (e.g., vendor, contract personnel, maintenance)
12. Organize and facilitate meetings
13. Advocate for department, organization, and/or profession
14. Manage projects
15. Prepare for accreditation and licensing processes (e.g., Joint Commission, Medicare, state regulators)

Table I-8 Knowledge Statements for RHIA Domains (continued)

Domain 5 Privacy, Security, and Confidentiality
1. Design and implement security measures to safeguard Protected Health Information (PHI)
2. Manage access, disclosure, and use of Protected Health Information (PHI) to ensure confidentiality
3. Investigate and resolve healthcare privacy and security issues/problems
4. Develop and maintain healthcare privacy and security training programs
Domain 6 Legal and Regulatory Standards
1. Administer organizational compliance with healthcare information laws, regulations, and standards (e.g., audit, report, and/or inform; legal health record)
2. Prepare for accreditation and licensing processes (e.g., Joint Commission, Medicare, state regulators)

Table I-9 Knowledge Statements for RHIT Domains

Domain 1 Data Analysis and Management
1. Abstract information found in health records (i.e., coding, research, physician deficiencies, etc.)
2. Analyze data (i.e., productivity reports, quality measures, health record documentation, case-mix index)
3. Maintain filing and retrieval systems for health records
4. Identify anomalies in data
5. Resolve risks and/or anomalies of data findings
6. Maintain the master patient index (i.e., enterprise systems merge/unmerge medical record numbers, etc.)
7. Eliminate duplicate documentation
8. Organize data into a useable format
9. Review trends in data
10. Gather/compile data from multiple sources
11. Generate reports or spreadsheets (i.e., customize, create, etc.)
12. Present data findings (i.e., study results, delinquencies, conclusion/summaries, gap analysis, graphical)
13. Implement workload distribution
14. Design workload distribution
15. Participate in the data management plan (i.e., determine data elements, assemble components, set time frame)
16. Input and/or submit data to registries
17. Summarize findings from data research/analysis
18. Follow data archive and backup policies
19. Develop data management plan
20. Calculate healthcare statistics (i.e., occupancy rates, length of stay, delinquency rates, etc.)
21. Determine validation process for data mapping
22. Maintain data dictionaries
Domain 2 Coding
1. Apply all official current coding guidelines
2. Assign diagnostic and procedure codes based on health record documentation
3. Insure physician documentation supports coding
4. Validate code assignment
5. Abstract data from health record
6. Sequence codes
7. Query physician when additional clinical documentation is needed
8. Review and resolve coding edits (i.e., correct coding initiative, outpatient code editor, National Coverage Determination, Local Coverage Determination, etc.)
9. Review the accuracy of abstracted data
10. Assign POA (present on admission) indicators
11. Provide educational updates to coders
12. Validate grouper assignment (i.e., MS-DRG, APC, etc.)
13. Identify HAC (hospital acquired condition)
14. Develop and manage a query process
15. Create standards for coding productivity and quality
16. Develop educational guidelines for provider documentation
17. Perform concurrent audits

Table I-9 Knowledge Statements for RHIT Domains (continued)

Domain 3 Compliance

1. Ensure patient record documentation meets state and federal regulations
2. Ensure compliance with privacy and security guidelines (HIPAA, state, hospital, etc.)
3. Control access to health information
4. Monitor documentation for completeness
5. Develop a coding compliance plan (i.e., current coding guidelines)
6. Manage release of information
7. Perform continual updates to policies and procedures
8. Implement internal and external audit guidelines
9. Evaluate medical necessity (CDMP – clinical documentation management program)
10. Collaborate with staff to prepare the organization for accreditation, licensing, and/or certification surveys
11. Evaluate medical necessity (Outpatient services)
12. Evaluate medical necessity (Data management)
13. Responding to fraud and abuse
14. Evaluate medical necessity (ISSI utilization review)
15. Develop forms (i.e., chart review, documentation, EMR, etc.)
16. Evaluate medical necessity (Case management)
17. Analyze access audit trails
18. Ensure valid healthcare provider credentials

Domain 4 Information Technology

1. Train users on software
2. Maintain database
3. Set up secure access
4. Evaluate the functionality of applications
5. Create user accounts
6. Troubleshoot HIM software or support systems
7. Create database
8. Perform end user audits
9. Participate in vendor selection
10. Perform end user needs analysis
11. Design data archive and backup policies
12. Perform system maintenance of software and systems
13. Create data dictionaries

Domain 5 Quality

1. Audit health records for content, completeness, accuracy, and timeliness
2. Apply standards, guidelines, and/or regulations to health records
3. Implement corrective actions as determined by audit findings (internal and external)
4. Design efficient workflow processes
5. Comply with national patient safety goals
6. Analyze standards, guidelines, and/or regulations to build criteria for audits
7. Apply process improvement techniques
8. Provide consultation to internal and external users of health information on HIM subject matter
9. Develop reports on audit findings
10. Perform data collection for quality reporting (core measures, PQRI, medical necessity, etc.)
11. Use trended data to participate in performance improvement plans/initiatives
12. Develop a tool for collecting statistically valid data
13. Conduct clinical pertinence reviews
14. Monitor physician credentials to practice in the facility

Table I-9 Knowledge Statements for RHIT Domains (continued)

Domain 6 Legal

1. Ensure confidentiality of the health records (paper and electronic)
2. Adhere to disclosure standards and regulations (HIPAA privacy, HITECH Act, breach notifications, etc.) at both state and federal levels
3. Demonstrate and promote legal and ethical standards of practice
4. Maintain integrity of legal health record according to organizational bylaws, rules, and regulations
5. Follow state mandated and/or organizational record retention and destruction policies
6. Serve as the custodian of the health records (paper or electronic)
7. Respond to Release of Information (ROI) requests from internal and external requestors
8. Work with risk management department to provide requested documentation
9. Identify potential health record related risk management issues through auditing
10. Respond to and process patient amendment requests to the health record
11. Facilitate basic education regarding the use of consents, healthcare Power of Attorney, Advanced Directives, DNRs, etc.
12. Represent the facility in court related matters as it applies to the health record (subpoenas, depositions, court orders, warrants)

Domain 7 Revenue Cycle

1. Communicate with providers to discuss documentation deficiencies (i.e., queries)
2. Participate in clinical documentation improvement programs to ensure proper documentation of health records
3. Collaborate with other departments on monitoring accounts receivable (i.e., unbilled, uncoded)
4. Provide ongoing education to healthcare providers (i.e., regulatory changes, new guidelines, payment standards, best practices, etc.)
5. Identify fraud and abuse
6. Assist with appeal letters in response to claim denials
7. Monitor claim denials/over-payments to identify potential revenue impact
8. Prioritize the work according to accounts receivable, patient type, etc.
9. Distribute the work according to accounts receivable, patient type, etc.
10. Maintain the chargemaster
11. Ensure physicians are credentialed with different payers for reimbursement

ADDITIONAL INSIGHTS ABOUT EXAMINATIONS

1. **Computerized exam.** The test is taken electronically in an approved testing center. You will be able to return to previously answered questions to check your answers before you close the exam file on the computer. Visit AHIMA's Web site for examples of the screens you will be using.

2. **Statistical formulas** needed to complete the questions on health statistics will be available if needed in some form so that you can see it on the screen, thus eliminating the need to memorize all the formulas. You will be expected to know basic formulas like those for average, mean, and median. However, it is critical that you know how to apply the formulas accurately. We recommend that you spend time working through as many statistical problems as possible.

3. **Math throughout.** Be aware that mathematical calculations may also be required in other types of questions (for instance, calculating FTE requirements, budget questions, etc.), so basic math skills are a must! Become proficient in making mathematical calculations on the computer by practicing on the calculator provided in the accessories folder on your computer. If math is not a strong area for you, seek out assistance and practice, practice, practice. On the examination, you will need to use the calculator function on the computer.

4. **Informatics and information systems questions are interspersed throughout the other topics.** From the workplace setting you experienced during your professional practice experiences, you know that computers are involved in almost every aspect of HIM functions, e.g., coding, record tracking, incomplete charts, release of information, etc. Therefore, it stands to reason that questions related to information systems could show up in many other categories.

5. **Legal questions are at the national level.** In reference to questions in the category of health care legal aspects, keep in mind that this is a national examination. Therefore, any state-specific laws would not be applicable. Concentrate on federal legislation, statutes, and legal issues that would be appropriate nationally in all 50 states. You can count on federal questions that relate to the HIPAA standards for privacy and security.

6. **Questions on the examinations are scrambled** and change topics from question to question. Therefore, you may have a legal question, followed by a management question, followed by a coding question, followed by a quality assurance question, etc. Be prepared to shift gears quickly throughout the exam.

7. **Quality and performance improvement focus.** Because the implementation of QA/PI is at the forefront of the health care industry, give special attention to Quality Assessment and Performance Improvement issues. Become familiar with the various QA/PI tools. Several resources for this subject are listed at the end of the Quality Assessment and Performance Improvement chapter of this book.

8. **Be sure to spend some time reviewing organization and management** functions and techniques, especially those preparing for the RHIA examination.

9. **You will not need to bring your coding books to the test.** The questions are in a narrative form and any necessary codes and/or code narratives will be supplied on the computer screen for you to choose from. Study the guidelines for coding and reporting. Review reimbursement methodologies and compliance issues as they have become more and more important in the health care arena.

10. **Application and analysis emphasis.** The questions on both the RHIA and RHIT examinations have been increasingly skewed toward application and analysis rather than recall level of question difficulty. Questions on the examination may combine several concepts into one question, increasing the level of difficulty of the question. Effective October 2011, the test specifications have been updated for the RHIT exam. The cognitive levels for this exam are as follows: 40% Recall/Understanding, 35% Application, and 25% Analysis and Higher Thinking. (Source: AHIMA.org.)

THE DAY BEFORE AND THE MORNING OF THE EXAM

1. Avoid studying the night before the exam. Last-minute studying tends to increase your anxiety level. However, you may want to spend a little time reviewing content you must memorize.

2. Organize in advance all the materials you need to take with you to the exam. Review the Candidate Handbook carefully and be sure to have all the items required, especially the admission card and appropriate proof of identity.

3. Get a good night's sleep and have a healthy meal before the exam.

4. Allow yourself plenty of time so that you arrive at the test site early. If necessary, spend the night before the examination in a hotel or motel near the exam test site.

5. Dress comfortably and plan for possible variations in room temperature. Dressing in layers may prove helpful.

TAKING THE EXAMINATION

You have stuck to your study schedule and have conditioned yourself to be in the best physical and mental shape possible. Now comes the moment of truth: the examination pops up on the screen before your eyes. Every paratrooper knows that, in addition to having a parachute, one must know how to open it. You have mastered the major topics; you have the parachute. Now you need to utilize good test-taking techniques to apply the knowledge you have gained; open the parachute!

1. Prior to starting the exam, you will be given a chance to practice taking an examination on the computer. Ten minutes will be allotted for this practice test; however, you may quit the practice test and begin the actual exam when you are comfortable with the computerized testing process.

2. Read all directions and questions carefully. Try to avoid reading too much into the questions. Be sensible and practical in your interpretation. Read ALL of the possible answers, because the first one that looks good may not be the best one.

3. Scan the computer screen quickly for the general format of the questions. Like the marathon runner, pace yourself for the distance. A good rule of thumb is 1 to 1.5 minutes per question. You may wish to keep the timer displayed on the computer to check your schedule throughout the exam. For example, at question 31, about one-half hour will have elapsed, etc.

4. Some people answer all questions that they are certain of first, and then go back through the exam a second time to answer any questions they were uncertain about. Others prefer not to skip questions but make their best choice on encountering each question and go on. Both can be good approaches; choose the one that works best for you. You can "mark" questions that you have left unanswered and/or those questions you may want to review. Before you sign off of the exam or run out of time, you have the ability to go back to those questions for a final review.

5. Answer all the questions. There are no penalties for guessing, but putting no answer is definitely a wrong answer.

6. Use deductive reasoning and the process of elimination to arrive at the most correct answer. Some questions will have more than one correct answer. You will be asked to select the "best" possible answer based on the information presented.

7. If the question is written in a scenario format, first identify the question being asked and then review the entire question for the information needed to determine the correct answer.

8. Use all the time available to recheck your answers. However, avoid changing your answers unless you are absolutely certain it is necessary. Second-guessing yourself often results in a wrong answer.

AFTER THE EXAM

Our advice is to reclaim your life and focus on your career. One good way to start is to plan a special reward for yourself at some point immediately following or shortly after the exam. Schedule a family vacation or a relaxing weekend get-away. Just find some way of being good to yourself. You certainly deserve it! You have worked hard, so relish your success.

Now Available - All New Professional Review Guide Series Online Quizzing Software

For 2014, we are providing you with new dynamic quizzing software for more effective study results. Follow the instructions on the Printed Access Card bound into this text to access the online quizzing software for this title.

Features include:
- All of the quizzes and mock exams available in the text, customizable by subject area
- Immediate feedback options by subject area and competency for better self-assessment
- Flashcards for self-review
- Case Studies available as Adobe PDF documents in the quizzing software for independent review

For Instructors:
- Ability to track student and class progress by domain or subject area in real-time for better classroom focus
- Excel ™ exporting feature for gradebooks

Go to www.cengagebrain.com to create a unique instructor user login. Contact your sales representative for more information.

I. Examination Study Strategies and Resources

Patricia J. Schnering, RHIA, CCS

FORMAT OF THE EXAMINATION

The questions developed for the examinations are based on specifications currently referred to as domains and subdomains. A complete copy of these entry-level specifications will be provided in the RHIA/RHIT Candidate Handbook provided by AHIMA.

The general format of the exams is primarily designed to engage your problem-solving and critical-thinking skills. These types of questions require that you translate what you have learned and apply it to a situation. To get a preview, you can access sample questions on AHIMA's Web site: www.ahima.org.

EXAMINATION STRATEGIES

Preparing for a major exam is similar to preparing for a marathon athletic event. The time allotted for the RHIA examination is 4 hours. The time allotted for the RHIT examination is 3½ hours. One suggestion is to use your study process to slowly build up your concentration time until you can focus your energy for the appropriate time. This is like the runner who begins jogging for 30 minutes and builds up to 1 hour, then 1½ hours, and so on, and gradually increases the endurance time to meet the demands of the race. Try this strategy; it could work for you!

Everyone has his or her own particular study style. Some people prefer to study alone and others work best in a group. Regardless of your preference, we strongly recommend that you take advantage of group study at least some of the time. Studying with others can prove very helpful when working through your weakest areas. Each member of the study team will bring strengths and weaknesses to the table, and all can benefit from the collaboration. So, even if you are a solitary learner, you may occasionally want to work with a group for those topics you find more challenging.

Theoretically, material known thoroughly after one's learning will fade predictably with time. After one day, the average person retains only 80% of what was learned; ultimately he or she will remember about 30% of it. That is why you are now relearning information you acquired over a period of years. Your aim is to achieve maximum recall through effective review.

Make your study process systematic. To facilitate this effort, we recommend that you design a 10-week study program. You should plan on spending an average of 10 to 12 hours per week studying. The idea is to study smart, not to bulldoze through tons of material in a haphazard way.

DEVELOPING YOUR STUDY HABITS

First, you must get organized. You have to be deliberate about making sure that you develop and stick to a regular study routine. Find a place where you can study, either at home or at the library.

How you schedule your study time during the week is an individual decision. However, we recommend that you avoid all-nighters and other unreasonably long study sessions. The last thing you want to do is burn yourself out by working too long and too hard at one time. Try to do a little bit at a time and maintain a steady pace that is manageable for you.

Develop your individual study program. Write the topics and subjects in a list. Outline the chapters in your HIM text. Pause at each chapter outline and recall basic points. Do you draw a blank, recall them more or less, or do you feel comfortable with your recall? Pinpoint your weakest subjects. By using this approach, you can see where you stand.

Weigh the importance of each subject. How were the topics emphasized in textbooks, in your class notes, and on previous exams (review the examination content information in the introduction of this book)? Try to pick out concepts that would make good exam questions.

Avoid trying to make a head-on attack by giving equal time and attention to all topics. Use the outlines to identify your weakest topics. Determine which topics will require a significant amount of study time and which will only require a brief review. Make a list of the topics in the order that you plan to study them.

Your list will give you a clear mental picture of what you need to do and will keep you on track. There are three additional advantages to a list:

1. It builds your morale as you steadily cross off the items that you have completed, and you can monitor your progress.

2. Glancing back at the list from time to time serves to reassure you that you are on target.

3. You can readily see that you are applying your time and effort where they are most needed.

Keep the list conspicuously in view. Carefully plan your pre-exam study time and stick to your plan. Go to the exam like a trained and disciplined runner going to a marathon event!

A SUMMARY OF TIPS FOR ORGANIZING YOUR TIME AND MATERIALS

1. **Assess your strengths and weaknesses.** Review the major topic categories and the AHIMA competency listing to help in determining where your areas of strength are and what areas are in need of improvement.

2. **Set up a realistic study schedule.** Refer to the sample schedule provided in this book and customize it to meet your needs.

3. **Focus on your weaknesses.** Spend more time and energy studying your areas of weakness, especially if these categories had a significant percentage of questions associated with them on the AHIMA competency list. Remember, every question counts toward that passing score!

4. **Organize and review all of the following items:**
   a. Course syllabi and outlines
   b. Class notes
   c. Tests and examinations
   d. Textbooks
   e. AHIMA test information and materials

5. **Take tests.** One of the best ways to study for a test is to take tests. Practice answering questions and working problems as much as possible. Work with your watch in front of you. Time yourself so that you become accustomed to taking only 1 to 1½ minutes per question. Practice using the calculator on your computer to make mathematical calculations. When you take the practice tests contained on the CD included in this book, you can practice by choosing the section and then picking the competency you want to focus on.

6. **Read the AHIMA Candidate Handbook for the Certification Examinations.** If anything in the Candidate Handbook is unclear, seek assistance from your program director or call AHIMA. You are held accountable for the important information, deadlines, and instructions addressed in this material.

SAMPLE STUDY SCHEDULE

Week 1   Health Data Contents and Standards, and Information Retention and Access

Week 2   Legal and Ethical Aspects, and Health Information Privacy and Security

Week 3   Informatics and Information Systems

Week 4   Organization and Management and Human Resources

Week 5   Classification Systems and Secondary Data Sources

Week 6   Billing and Reimbursement and Medical Science

Week 7   CPT Coding

Week 8   ICD-10-CM/PCS Coding

Week 9   Quality and Performance Improvement

Week 10   Health Statistics and Research

STUDY RESOURCES

There are three basic sources of information: books, people, and your educational program or college. If your studies become stagnant, do not sit and grind yourself down. If your text is not making the subject clear for you, don't spend time trying to memorize something you do not understand. The main issue is to understand the material so you can use the knowledge in a practical way. Search for additional information that will help make the subject clear to you.

Books and other written resources may use another style of presentation that you are more receptive to. A different textbook may be all you need to gain better insight into the subject. It can offer a fresh point of view, provide relief from boredom, and encourage critical thinking in the process of comparing the texts.

Periodical literature in the health field provides well-written articles that may open up the subject to you and turn study into an adventure in learning. AHIMA publishes authoritative and insightful information on every aspect of HIM. Sometimes an article can help put the text material into practical perspective and pull it together so that you gain a deeper understanding. With the rapidly changing health care world, HIM journals and magazines have the most current information and are frequently used as references for test questions.

Take advantage of the college library by using reserved materials set aside for your study purposes.

Professional contacts in your HIM community can also be helpful in your study effort. Most people in our field are eager to share their knowledge and are flattered by appeals for information.

Collaborating with classmates may reveal fresh viewpoints, stimulate thought by disagreement, or at least let you see that you are not alone in your quest. Organize study groups and set aside specific times to work together. This interaction can be truly beneficial in keeping you motivated and on task.

Classes, workshops, and seminars present opportunities to learn and review the subject matter in a new light. Take advantage of any examination review sessions available in your area. Talking to graduates who have recently taken the exam can also be of great assistance.

Don't overlook the power of AHIMA's Web site. In this dynamic, changing environment, the most up-to-date materials may not be available in a book. The AHIMA resources online are extensive and quite easy to access at www.ahima.org. In addition, the Communities of Practice (CoPs) are a phenomenal source of contact with HIM professionals and other students on a myriad of subjects.

In summary, some of the study resources available to you include the following:

1. HIM textbooks and Class text books: There is a large variety of textbooks for HIM and coding available on the market. Both Delmar Cengage Learning (www.cengage.com) and AHIMA (www.ahima.org) have a variety of HIM products. For example, see the partial listing of books available through Delmar Cengage Learning.
2. Review books written for the RHIA and RHIT examinations.
3. Mock exam questions on the Cengage website are available for this book for practice taking computerized tests.
4. Class notes as well as the class tests and exams.
5. Examination review sessions.
6. On-the-job experience (be cautious because the exam tests theory and not each particular practice and the test uses national laws, rules, and regulations—not state and facility practice).
7. Study groups or partners.
8. Visit various Internet sites such as www.ahima.org and www.cms.gov for the latest information on the health care industry.

AHIMA has developed a series of HIM and coding resources.

  To place an order, call (800) 335-5535.

  Visit the AHIMA Web site at http://www.ahima.org for additional resources and information about the coding certification examinations.

Optum has an array of coding, reimbursement, and compliance products.

  Contact them at 1-800-464-3649 (Choose option 1 for fastest service.).

  Visit their Web site at https://www.optumcoding.com/.

Cengage Learning has a multitude of HIM products. In addition, they have partnered with Optum so that you can order your Optum coding resources through Cengage Learning.

For additional information on these Health Information resources, visit Cengage Learning at http//www.cengage.com.

The following is a partial listing of Cengage products for Health Information:

3-2-1 Code It! (4th Edition)
  Green, Michelle A.

A Guide to Health Insurance Billing
  (Includes Optum EncoderPro Trial Printed Access Card and Premium Web Site Printed Access Card) Moisio, Marie A.

Basic Allied Health Statistics and Analysis
  Koch, G.

Case Studies for Health Information Management
  McCuen, Charlotte; Sayles, Nanette; and Schnering, Patricia

Coding Basics: Medical Billing and Reimbursement Fundamentals
  Richards, Cynthia

Coding Basics: Understanding Medical Collections
  Rimmer, Michelle

Coding for Medical Necessity in the Physician Office
  Kelly-Farwell, Deborah and Favreau, Cecile

Coding Surgical Procedures: Beyond the Basics
  Smith, Gail I.

Cengage products for Health Information (continued)

Coding Workbook for the Physician's Office
    Covell, Alice

Comparative Health Information Management
    Peden, Ann

Essentials of Health Information Management Principles and Practices (2nd Edition)
    Green, M. A. and Bowie, M. J.

Essentials of Healthcare Compliance
    Safian, Shelly

Ethics Case Studies for Health Information Management
    Grebner, Leah

Guide to Coding Compliance
    Becker, Joanne M.

Health Services Research Methods
    Shi, L.

HIPAA for Medical Office Personnel
    Krager, Dan and Krager, Carole

ICD-10: A Comprehensive Guide: Education, Planning and Implementation
    Dawlish, Carline

ICD-10-CM Diagnostic Coding System: Education, Planning and Implementation
    Dagleish, Carline

ICD-10-PCS Coding System: Education, Planning and Implementation
    Dagleish, Carline

Legal and Ethical Aspects of Health Information Management
    McWay, Dana C.

Medical Terminology for Insurance and Coding
    Moisio, Marie A.

Today's Health Information Management: An Integrated Approach
    McWay, D. C.

Understanding Health Insurance: A Guide to Billing and Reimbursement
    Green, Michelle A. and Rowell, Jo Anne

Understanding Hospital Billing and Coding: A Worktext
    Diamond, Marsha S.

Understanding ICD-9-CM: A Worktest
    Bowie, Mary Jo and Schaffer, Regina M.

Understanding ICD-9-CM Coding
    Bowie, Mary Jo and Schaffer, Regina M.

Understanding ICD-10-CM and ICD-10-PCS: A Worktext
    Bowie, Mary Jo and Schaffer, Regina M.

Understanding Medical Coding: A Comprehensive Guide
    Johnson, S. L. and McHugh, C. S.

Understanding Hospital Billing and Coding
    Diamond, M. S.

Understanding Procedural Coding: A Worktext
    Bowie, Mary Jo and Schaffer, Regina M.

Using the Electronic Health Record in the Healthcare Provider Practice
    Eichenwald Maki, Shirley and Petterson, Bonnie

II. Test-Taking Skills

Patricia J. Schnering, RHIA, CCS

Debora J. Butts, EdD, RHIA

This section of the review book is designed to provide students with techniques that will help maximize their chances for success on the RHIA and RHIT national certification examinations. Five major areas are explored in this section:

1. Becoming "test wise"
2. The "truth" about test taking
3. Characteristics of successful test takers
4. Multiple-choice test question construction
5. Practical advice for exam preparation

Health Information Administration/Technology (HIA/HIT) students may view the test-taking experience as one that causes great anxiety and concern. Test-taking does not have to be a negative experience. Students can equip themselves with an array of techniques and practical strategies to master the test-taking situation. After all, the ultimate goal of taking the exam is to pass it and move forward with one's career aspirations.

BECOMING "TEST WISE"

This section will assist the student in becoming "test wise." Becoming test wise involves a set of skills that is acquired through practice and instruction. Being test wise does not mean that one will always achieve a very high score on the exam. What it does mean is that one will learn to overcome such factors as test anxiety, which often prevent students from passing examinations. The ultimate key to being test wise is knowledge of the subject matter that will be covered on the certification examination. No amount of tips or techniques can replace adequate preparation. A colleague I know in academia often states, "Adequate preparation prevents poor performance." If one does not have thorough knowledge of the subject, no amount of test-taking knowledge or skills will improve test performance. Now, let's turn our discussion to the first topic—the "truth" about test taking.

THE "TRUTH" ABOUT TEST TAKING

It is important to be realistic about what a test really is and what it is not. The exam is not a measure of your intelligence. It is not directly a measure of your knowledge of the course material. It is not a complete picture of what you know. It is certainly not a measure of your worth as a human being. Most importantly, failing to pass the certification examination does not imply that you are in the wrong profession. Many lawyers and certified public accountants require several attempts to obtain their credentials.

Now let's look at what a test is really all about. What does it measure? A test may measure your performance on a given day. It tells you how much you know about the questions you were asked, which represent a small sampling of the material you actually covered while studying to become a health information management professional. To some degree, a test measures your skills as a test taker, such as your ability to apply reasoning and logic, as well as your critical-thinking and problem-solving skills. The test also measures your ability to recall "correct answers."

It is important as you prepare for the certification examination that you maintain a realistic perspective. The certification examination is a professionally designed test that has been developed by educators and practitioners in health information management. It will measure your ability to answer questions in the major domains.

Knowing what is expected of you in order to pass the examination and improving your test-taking skills will provide you with valuable tools to apply in your study process. If you keep the examination in the proper perspective and prepare well, you will obtain the credentials that you so rightly deserve.

Learning how to take tests will usually help you overcome inappropriate test-taking habits and allow you to demonstrate what you know to the fullest degree in the testing situation. Here are 10 truths that you should know before attempting the certification examination.

10 TRUTHS

TRUTH 1: Test-taking skills can be learned.
Good test-taking skills make the most of what you know. That's just what this chapter is focused on.

TRUTH 2: Test-taking skills make a difference.
Two people can get scores that differ greatly on the test because one person has better test-taking skills.

TRUTH 3: Good preparation reduces anxiety.
Reducing anxiety by proper preparation improves test performance.

TRUTH 4: Attitude does make a difference.
A significant percentage of success on the test will depend on your attitude toward test-taking and your general attitude about yourself. Students should strive to feel good about the test-taking experience, knowing that they have done everything possible to prepare in advance for the examination.

TRUTH 5: Always answer the easy questions first.
Avoid attempting to answer the most difficult questions first, because they will interfere with your positive attitude and confidence. Agonizing over difficult questions will result in loss of time and points.

TRUTH 6: Failure to plan to pass the exam ensures planning to fail the exam.
This might sound a bit harsh and bitter to swallow, but it is indeed the truth. Do not let poor planning and a lack of preparation hinder you from peak performance on the examination. As the saying goes, "Plan your work and work your plan."

TRUTH 7: Usually your first hunch is your best.
Changing answers after you have selected what you believe or know to be the correct answer is not recommended. Usually, your first hunch is your best, unless of course you discover or uncover information in the examination that disqualifies or nullifies your first choice.

TRUTH 8: Educated guessing is better than guessing randomly.
It is appropriate to guess after you have narrowed down the four options to two possible answers.

TRUTH 9: The only thing that stands between you and passing the exam is ...
You guessed it: "YOU." If passing the exam is your number one goal at this point in your life, then your priorities should reflect this goal. Priority number one should be to find the time to plan to be successful on the exam.

TRUTH 10: No amount of "tips and tricks" replaces content knowledge.
As mentioned previously, strong content knowledge is essential. The suggestions in this chapter are meant to make the most of what you know, not to take the place of content preparation.

CHARACTERISTICS OF SUCCESSFUL TEST TAKERS

Have you ever wondered why it seems that some people pass the exam and others do not? What are the characteristics of successful test takers? If one looks at successful people in general, you will probably find that they demonstrate these traits and habits in different aspects of their personal and professional lives. Here are some of the characteristics of successful test takers in general.

1. **Good time management.** Time is looked upon by the successful test taker as something not to be feared, but rather a medium that must be mastered and controlled in order to complete the exam with confidence. Completion of the exam with confidence means that one will be able to manage his or her time effectively and have sufficient time to attempt to answer every question without heavily depending on guessing, whether educated guessing or guessing randomly. Ultimately, if your time is not managed well, the minutes will pass whether you have completed the exam or not. Remember to avoid spending excessive time on any one question.

2. **Read questions carefully.** Read the question twice, if necessary, to fully understand the directions or to fully comprehend what exactly is being asked. In lengthy scenario questions, it may be helpful to read the question portion of the statement first. Also, have a good understanding of key terms or phrases often used in health information management, such as "confidentiality" or "skilled nursing facility." Remember, there is no substitute for knowing the facts.

3. **Take the question at face value.** In other words, avoid reading something into the question that was not intended or explicitly stated. For example, consider the following question:

   In progressive counseling, the first step in disciplining for a first offense is
   A.   termination.
   B.   suspension.
   C.   oral reprimand.
   D.   written warning.

   The student who reads into the question may decide that in order to answer this question, he or she must know more about the specific offense. However, such details are not necessary. This question assumes that the offense is one that would not require immediate termination for the first offense. Therefore, in the process of applying progressive disciplinary action, an oral reprimand (answer C) is the correct answer.

4. **Read and consider all four options carefully.** One approach in answering multiple-choice questions is to read the answers first. In using this method, you will evaluate each answer separately and equally. Look for an answer that not only seems right on its own, but completes the question statement smoothly. Statistically, the least likely correct answer on a multiple-choice question is the first option.

   If you have narrowed the options down to two that seem correct, then you must study the options and compare them with each other to see what makes them different. Using deductive reasoning and the process of elimination, you should be able to arrive at the best answer.

5. **Approach questions systematically.** Break down each question into manageable parts and proceed systematically. Consider the following question:

> For a 2-week period, the HIM department had 1,200 worked hours and 1,280 total (or paid) hours on its payroll. During this same 2 weeks, there were 375 discharges. The department's standard is 3.3 worked hours per discharge. The number of worked hours per discharge for this 2-week period was
> A. 3.0.
> B. 3.2.
> C. 3.4.
> D. 3.8.

Following the above principle of breaking down the question into component parts, what would you do to make this question more manageable? There are often several ways to arrive at the same answer. Some students may answer, "I would first pull out the number of discharges," or some may answer, "I would pull out the total hours worked." Whatever works for you to manage answering the question correctly is the right approach for you. The calculation for this question is 1,200 hours worked divided by 375 discharges equals 3.2 (answer B).

6. **Read carefully.** Reading directions thoroughly and identifying key words and phrases in the question are essential to test-taking success. For example, consider the following question:

> The health information manager exercises staff authority in the hospital when he or she
> A. abstracts a medical record.
> B. advises on a file system for the radiology department.
> C. teaches a file clerk a new procedure.
> D. writes a procedure for the correct filing of records.

The stem states "exercises staff authority." If the student did not read the question carefully, he or she may have missed these key terms, which are critical to selecting the correct answer, which is B.

7. **Avoid applying preset solutions.** The successful test taker does not try to remember solutions to similar problems; rather, he or she solves each new problem independently.

WHEN AND HOW TO GUESS

There will be questions on the exam that will be totally unfamiliar to you. Choosing the correct answer may lie in the concept of "informed guessing." In applying this technique, the test taker eliminates the absurd options and guesses on the basis of familiarity.

It is helpful to relate possible answers to the question being asked. Read all the options before selecting the correct one. Usually, you can narrow the possible answers down to two by asking yourself:

- What is the question really asking?
- What is the main idea or point of this question?
- What answer would make the most sense?
- How can I rephrase or break down the question?

Sometimes the test taker can gain information about the correct answers from cues and information from other questions. Remember, however, this is when you are in the "informed guessing" mode. There will be information in a question that is irrelevant, and it is important for you to get to the heart of the question. Don't get too preoccupied with the content or meaning of a scenario before you know what the question is asking. Use logic and common sense whenever possible.

MULTIPLE-CHOICE TEST QUESTION CONSTRUCTION

The entire multiple-choice question is called an item. Each item consists of two main parts:

- **Stem:** The first part is known as the stem. The purpose of the stem is to present a problem in a clear and concise manner. The stem should contain all the details necessary to answer the question. The stem of an item can be a complete sentence that asks a question. It can also be presented as an incomplete sentence that becomes a complete sentence when it is combined with one of the options in the item.

- **Answer options:** The second part of the item is comprised of the options or possible answers. One of the options will answer the question posed in the stem correctly. The remaining options are called *distracters*. They are referred to as distracters because they are designed to distract you from the correct answer. Consider the following sample item.

	ITEM	
Stem	In quantitative research, the formulation of the hypothesis is an activity usually associated with	
Distracter	A.	data collection.
Correct	B.	identification of the problem.
Distracter	C.	analysis.
Distracter	D.	assembling the results.

COGNITIVE LEVELS

In addition to the stem and distracters, the item may also be measuring different cognitive levels. These levels are used to identify the candidates' knowledge of subject matter at different levels needed to perform on the job (see Table 2–1). An example of each of the three levels is shown after the table.

Table 2–1 Cognitive Levels

Cognitive Levels		
Cognitive Level	**Purpose**	**Performance Required**
Recall (RE)	Primarily, to measure memory.	Identify terms, specific facts, methods, procedures, basic concepts, basic theories, principles, and processes.
Application (AP)	To measure simple interpretation of limited data.	Apply concepts and principles to new situations, recognize relationships among data, apply laws and theories to practical situations, calculate solutions to mathematical problems, interpret charts and translate graphic data, classify items, interpret information.
Analysis (AN)	To measure the application of knowledge to solving a specific problem and the assembly of various elements into a meaningful whole.	Select an appropriate solution for responsive action; revise policy, procedure, or plan; evaluate a solution, case scenario, report, or plan; compare solutions, plans, ideas, or aspects of a problem; evaluate information or a situation; perform multiple calculations to arrive at one answer.

© Cengage Learning 2015

Recall: This question is at the "recall level." The student needs to be able to recall pertinent facts.

The medical record is the property of the
    A. patient.
    B. medical facility.
    C. health information management department.
    D. attending physician.

The answer is, of course, B. This question relied on your memory of this fact.

Application: Now let's look at the second highest cognitive level, an application level question, which tests the student's ability to apply information.

The medical record is the property of the medical facility and can be removed in which of the following situations?
  A. The patient is suing the hospital and wants the original record mailed to the attorney representing his case.
  B. The attending physician wants to take the patient's original record to a professional conference for presentation.
  C. The court issues a subpoena and needs the original record in court within 24 hours.
  D. The attending physician is being sued and he wants to take the original patient record to court with him.

The correct answer in this case is C. The only instance when the original record should be removed from the hospital is in the case of the issuance of a subpoena *duces tecum*. This question requires the student to apply information about when a record can be removed from the health care facility. The application level goes beyond the student recalling the rule about who has legal ownership of the record.

Analysis (problem solving): The third and highest cognitive level utilized by test developers is the analysis level. At this level the student will demonstrate the ability to analyze familiar information in new and different situations. This is often referred to as a problem-solving or critical-thinking question.

The information below is from a transcription service in your department.
  Total average lines transcribed/month: 270,000
  Standard per person: 1,200 lines in one day
  21 workdays in a month   15% adjustment factor

The number of transcriptionists needed by this facility is
  A. 10.7.
  B. 11.7.
  C. 12.3.
  D. 16.0.

The correct answer for this question is C.

The mathematical calculation to achieve the answer is
  270,000 x 0.15 adjustment factor = 40,500
  270,000 + 40,500 = 310,500 potential lines of transcription per month
  1,200 lines x 21 days = 25,200 lines one employee can produce in one month
  310,500/25,200 = 12.3 transcriptionists

After reviewing the cognitive levels, it is clear that for both the RHIA and RHIT examinations the student must be prepared to answer questions from the lowest cognitive level (recall) to the highest cognitive level (analysis). Testing at all three levels will help ensure that students can apply their newly acquired knowledge and skills on the job.

As always, refer to the current copy of the AHIMA Candidate Handbook for a complete listing of the domains, subdomains, and task competencies.

PRACTICAL ADVICE FOR EXAM PREPARATION

As you become more proficient at applying effective test-taking techniques, you will truly understand the phrase that "knowledge is power." This is exactly what this information hopes to do, and that is to provide you with the knowledge and skills to empower you to achieve your ultimate goal—certification.

Research demonstrates that the test taker who approaches a test with physical, mental, and emotional authority is in a better position to master the testing situation and the outcome. Remember, failing to plan means planning to fail. Here are some recommendations for you to incorporate as part of your "success plan."

Recommendation 1: Follow your regular routine.
Follow your regular nightly routine the evening before and morning of the exam. Abruptly changing your schedule and habits for this testing event could throw your system off balance and negatively affect your performance.

Recommendation 2: Arrive early for the examination.
It is always better to have 15 to 30 minutes of extra time prior to the start of a major examination. By arriving early on test day, you will be able to visit the restroom, survey the situation, and collect your thoughts. Decide where you want to sit in the test area, if the seats are not assigned. By collecting your thoughts prior to the start of the exam, you can improve your mental attitude by knowing you are truly prepared for this time, this situation, and this test-taking process. Remember, you want to be in control of the test anxiety that is normal, despite all of your preparation. If you are unfamiliar with the test site, it is usually a good practice to travel to the test site in advance of the exam date. Becoming familiar with the test site will prevent you from getting lost on the exam day.

Recommendation 3: Maintain a positive mental attitude.
Perhaps you are sometimes plagued by a negative inner voice that says something like: "Well look at you… trying to pass the certification examination. Why don't you stop kidding yourself? You know you are not as smart as your classmates. They will probably all pass and you will probably fail!" Almost all of us have critical voices inside our heads. Sometimes the voice may tell us that we don't measure up to others in the class. At other times it tries to blame our performance on the test, the teacher, or some other convenient scapegoat. You can learn to replace your negative inner dialogue with positive self-talk.

Start by programming your inner voice to remind you of how long and hard you have prepared for this examination. Remind yourself that you deserve to pass because of the time and energy you have spent in school preparing for this examination. Repeat positive affirmation statements to yourself, such as "I am a wonderful, worthy person who is capable of achieving my goal of becoming an RHIA/RHIT."

Recommendation 4: Answer the questions you know first.
It is a good idea to begin the test by answering questions that build your confidence. Getting off to a good start allows you to establish a positive momentum, which will assist you when you encounter more difficult questions. Because time is critical, answering the easier questions first will assure you of getting credit for what you know.

Recommendation 5: Check your answers before exiting the computerized exam.
Make sure you have answered every question. Be careful about changing your answers. You may need to revisit any items in which you have made an educated guess or items you discovered answers to as you progressed through the questions. Submit your test knowing that you did your very best.

CONCLUSION

As you study for the exam, take a moment now and then to review the test-taking skills addressed in this section. Using these techniques will help you develop the characteristics of a successful test taker. Working through questions will help you become more and more comfortable with multiple-choice testing.

Knowing how questions are constructed and what to look for should greatly improve your correct answer ratio. A sense of the scheme of the test structure and cognitive levels will become second nature with practice.

During your exam preparation, you will find that you actually enjoy taking multiple-choice examinations as a study aid. Be sure to obtain any mock computerized test exams available online to gain experience taking the test on the computer.

This comfort zone will free you to apply your knowledge and skills effectively during the examination process. The real bonus is that you will be more focused on demonstrating your knowledge through the medium of testing than on the exam process itself.

III. Health Data Content and Standards

Debra W. Cook, MAEd, RHIA

1. In preparation for an EHR, you are conducting a total facility inventory of all forms currently used. You must name each form for bar coding and indexing into a document management system. The unnamed document in front of you includes a microscopic description of tissue excised during surgery. The document type you are most likely to give to this form is
   A. recovery room record.
   B. pathology report.
   C. operative report.
   D. discharge summary.

REFERENCE: Abdelhak, p 114
              Green and Bowie, p 167
              LaTour, Eichenwald-Maki, and Oachs, pp A32–A33
              Odom-Wesley, p 171
              Sayles, p 88

2. Patient data collection requirements vary according to health care setting. A data element you would expect to be collected in the MDS, but NOT in the UHDDS would be
   A. personal identification.
   B. cognitive patterns.
   C. procedures and dates.
   D. principal diagnosis.

REFERENCE: Abdelhak, pp 137–138, 141
              LaTour, Eichenwald-Maki, and Oachs, p 30
              Sayles, pp 147, 152

3. In the past, Joint Commission standards have focused on promoting the use of a facility-approved abbreviation list to be used by hospital care providers. With the advent of the Commission's national patient safety goals, the focus has shifted to the
   A. prohibited use of any abbreviations.
   B. flagrant use of specialty-specific abbreviations.
   C. use of prohibited or "dangerous" abbreviations.
   D. use of abbreviations in the final diagnosis.

REFERENCE: Abdelhak, p 117
              LaTour, Eichenwald-Maki, and Oachs, pp 251, 264, 672
              Odom, pp 111, 230

4. Engaging patients and their families in health care decisions is one of the core objectives for
   A. achieving meaningful use of EHRs.
   B. the Joint Commission's National Patient Safety goals.
   C. HIPAA 5010 regulations.
   D. establishing flexible clinical pathways.

REFERENCE: HealthIT.hhs.gov
              LaTour, Eichenwald-Maki, and Oachs, p 286

5. A risk manager needs to locate a full report of a patient's fall from his bed, including witness reports and probable reasons for the fall. She would most likely find this information in the
   A. doctors' progress notes.
   B. integrated progress notes.
   C. incident report.
   D. nurses' notes.

REFERENCE: Abdelhak, pp 460–461, 544–545
              Davis and LaCour, pp 378–380
              Green and Bowie, p 88
              LaTour and Eichenwald-Maki, p 861
              McWay, p 132
              Odom-Wesley, p 54
              Sayles, p 613

6. For continuity of care, ambulatory care providers are more likely than providers of acute care services to rely on the documentation found in the
   A. interdisciplinary patient care plan.
   B. discharge summary.
   C. transfer record.
   D. problem list.

REFERENCE: Abdelhak, p 136
              Davis and LaCour, pp 10–11
              Green and Bowie, p 91
              Odom-Wesley, pp 326–327
              Sayles, p 108

7. Joint Commission does not approve of auto authentication of entries in a health record. The primary objection to this practice is that
   A. it is too easy to delegate use of computer passwords.
   B. evidence cannot be provided that the physician actually reviewed and approved each report.
   C. electronic signatures are not acceptable in every state.
   D. tampering too often occurs with this method of authentication.

REFERENCE: Green and Bowie, p 78
              LaTour, Eichenwald-Maki, and Oachs, pp 174, 897

8. As part of a quality improvement study, you have been asked to provide information on the menstrual history, number of pregnancies, and number of living children on each OB patient from a stack of old obstetrical records. The best place in the record to locate this information is the
   A. prenatal record.
   B. labor and delivery record.
   C. postpartum record.
   D. discharge summary.

REFERENCE: Abdelhak, pp 114–115
              Green and Bowie, p 182
              Odom-Wesley, pp 180–186

9. As a concurrent record reviewer for an acute care facility, you have asked Dr. Crossman to provide an updated history and physical for one of her recent admissions. Dr. Crossman pages through the medical record to a copy of an H&P performed in her office a week before admission. You tell Dr. Crossman
    A. a new H&P is required for every inpatient admission.
    B. that you apologize for not noticing the H&P she provided.
    C. the H&P copy is acceptable as long as she documents any interval changes.
    D. Joint Commission standards do not allow copies of any kind in the original record.

REFERENCE: Abdelhak, p 109
               Green and Bowie, p 145
               LaTour and Eichenwald-Maki, p 196
               Odom-Wesley, p 367

10. You have been asked to identify every reportable case of cancer from the previous year. A key resource will be the facility's
    A. disease index.   C. physicians' index.
    B. number control index.   D. patient index.

REFERENCE: Abdelhak, pp 486–487
               LaTour, Eichenwald-Maki, and Oachs, pp 245, 250–251
               McWay, p 140
               Sayles, p 437

11. Joint Commission requires the attending physician to countersign health record documentation that is entered by
    A. interns or medical students.   C. consulting physicians.
    B. business associates.   D. physician partners.

REFERENCE: Davis and LaCour, pp 105, 126–127
               Green and Bowie, p 78

12. The minimum length of time for retaining original medical records is primarily governed by
    A. Joint Commission.   C. state law.
    B. medical staff.   D. readmission rates.

REFERENCE: Abdelhak, pp 196–197
               Davis and LaCour, pp 283–284
               Green and Bowie, p 93
               LaTour, Eichenwald-Maki, and Oachs, pp 311–312
               Odom-Wesley, pp 67–69
               Sayles, p 995

13. The use of personal signature stamps for authentication of entries in a paper-based record requires special measures to guard against delegated use of the stamp. In a completely computerized patient record system, similar measures might be utilized to govern the use of
    A. fingerprint signatures.   C. expert systems.
    B. voice recognition systems.   D. electronic signatures.

REFERENCE: Abdelhak, pp 117–118, 191
               Green and Bowie, pp 78–79
               LaTour, Eichenwald-Maki, and Oachs, pp 87, 100, 134, 174, 180, 258, 264, 729

14. Discharge summary documentation must include
    A. a detailed history of the patient.
    B. a note from social services or discharge planning.
    C. significant findings during hospitalization.
    D. correct codes for significant procedures.

REFERENCE: Abdelhak, pp 111, 113
               Davis and LaCour, pp 106–107
               Green and Bowie, p 144
               LaTour and Eichenwald-Maki, pp 200–201
               Odom-Wesley, pp 200–205
               Sayles, p 93

15. The performance of ongoing record reviews is an important tool in ensuring data quality. These reviews evaluate
    A. quality of care through the use of preestablished criteria.
    B. adverse effects and contraindications of drugs utilized during hospitalization.
    C. potentially compensable events.
    D. the overall quality of documentation in the record.

REFERENCE: Abdelhak, pp 130–131
               Davis and LaCour, pp 374–376
               LaTour, Eichenwald-Maki, and Oachs, pp 250–251
               Odom-Wesley, pp 251–256

16. Ultimate responsibility for the quality and completion of entries in patient health records belongs to the
    A. chief of staff.   C. HIM director.
    B. attending physician.   D. risk manager.

REFERENCE: LaTour, Eichenwald-Maki, and Oachs, p 242

17. The federally mandated resident assessment instrument used in long-term care facilities consists of three basic components, including the new care area assessment, utilization guidelines, and the
    A. UHDDS.   C. OASIS.
    B. MDS.   D. DEEDS.

REFERENCE: Peden, p 357
               Sayles, p 111

18. The foundation for communicating all patient care goals in long-term care settings is the
    A. legal assessment.   C. interdisciplinary plan of care.
    B. medical history.   D. Uniform Hospital Discharge Data Set.

REFERENCE: Abdelhak, p 109
               LaTour, Eichenwald-Maki, and Oachs, pp 31, 254
               Odom-Wesley, p 371
               Sayles, p 83

19. As the Director of a Health Information Technology Program, your community college has been selected to participate in the workforce development of electronic health record specialists as outlined by ARRA and HITECH. In order to keep abreast of changes in this program, you will need to regularly access the Web site of this governmental agency.
    A. ONC
    B. CMS
    C. OSHA
    D. CDC

REFERENCE: Sayles, pp 142, 162

20. As part of Joint Commission's National Patient Safety Goal initiative, acute care hospitals are now required to use a preoperative verification process to confirm the patient's true identity, and to confirm that necessary documents such as x-rays or medical records are available. They must also develop and use a process for
    A. including the primary caregiver in surgery consults.
    B. including the surgeon in the preanesthesia assessment.
    C. marking the surgical site.
    D. apprising the patient of all complications that might occur.

REFERENCE: Abdelhak, p 459
               LaTour, Eichenwald-Maki, and Oachs, p 672

21. In preparing your facility for initial accreditation by the Joint Commission, you are trying to improve the process of ongoing record review. All health record reviews are presently performed by a team of HIM department personnel. The committee meets quarterly and reports to a Quality Management Committee. In reviewing Joint Commission standards, your first recommended change is to
    A. have more frequent committee meetings.
    B. have the committee report to the Executive Committee.
    C. have a physician perform all the reviews.
    D. provide for record reviews to be performed by an interdisciplinary team of care providers.

REFERENCE: Abdelhak, pp 126–130
               Davis and LaCour, pp 374–376
               LaTour, Eichenwald-Maki, and Oachs, p 265
               Odom-Wesley, p 253

22. According to the Joint Commission's National Patient Safety Goals, which of the following abbreviations would most likely be prohibited?
    A. 0.4 mg Lasix
    B. 4 mg Lasix
    C. 40 mg Lasix
    D. .4 mg Lasix

REFERENCE: Odom-Wesley, pp 230–231

23. A qualitative review of a health record reveals that the history and physical for a patient admitted on June 26 was performed on June 30 and transcribed on July 1. Which of the following statements regarding the history and physical is true in this situation? Completion and charting of the H&P indicates
    A. noncompliance with Joint Commission standards.
    B. compliance with Joint Commission standards.
    C. compliance with Medicare regulations.
    D. compliance with Joint Commission standards for nonsurgical patients.

REFERENCE: Abdelhak, p 109
               LaTour, Eichenwald-Maki, and Oachs, pp 245–246, 250–251
               Odom-Wesley, p 367

24. Using the SOAP method of recording progress notes, which entry would most likely include a differential diagnosis?
    A. assessment
    B. plan
    C. subjective
    D. objective

REFERENCE: Abdelhak, pp 118–119
               Davis and LaCour, pp 41–43, 96–98
               Green, pp 91, 343
               LaTour, Eichenwald-Maki, and Oachs, pp 249, 256–257
               Odom, pp 215, 217
               Sayles, p 126

25. You have been asked by a peer review committee to print a list of the medical record numbers of all patients who had CABGs performed in the past year at your acute care hospital. Which secondary data source could be used to quickly gather this information?
    A. disease index   C. master patient index
    B. physician index   D. operation index

REFERENCE: LaTour, Eichenwald-Maki, and Oachs, p 369
               Sayles, p 437

26. The best example of point-of-care service and documentation is
    A. using an automated tracking system to locate a record.
    B. using occurrence screens to identify adverse events.
    C. doctors using voice recognition systems to dictate radiology reports.
    D. nurses using bedside terminals to record vital signs.

REFERENCE: Abdelhak, p 38
               LaTour, Eichenwald-Maki, and Oachs, p 96

27. Many of the principles of forms design apply to both paper-based and computer-based systems. For example, the physical layout of the form and/or screen should be organized to match the way the information is requested. Facilities that are scanning and imaging paper records as part of a computer-based system must give careful consideration to
    A. placement of hospital logo.   C. use of box design.
    B. signature line for authentication. D. bar code placement.

REFERENCE: Abdelhak, pp 274–275
               LaTour, Eichenwald-Maki, and Oachs, p 88

28. Which of the following is a form or view that is typically seen in the health record of a long-term care patient but is rarely seen in records of acute care patients?
    A. pharmacy consultation
    B. medical consultation
    C. physical exam
    D. emergency record

REFERENCE: Abdelhak, p 141

29. The health record states that the patient is a female, but the registration record has the patient listed as male. Which of the following characteristics of data quality has been compromised in this case?
    A. data comprehensiveness
    B. data granularity
    C. data precision
    D. data accuracy

REFERENCE: Abdelhak, pp 133–134
               Davis and LaCour, pp 356–358
               Green, pp 247–248
               LaTour, Eichenwald-Maki, and Oachs, pp 175, 229

30. The first patient with cancer seen in your facility on January 1, 2012, was diagnosed with colon cancer with no known history of previous malignancies. The accession number assigned to this patient is
    A. 13-0000/00.
    B. 13-0000/01.
    C. 13-0001/00.
    D. 13-0001/01.

REFERENCE: LaTour, Eichenwald-Maki, and Oachs, p 371
               Sayles, p 439

31. Setting up a drop down menu to make sure that the registration clerk collects "gender" as "male, female, or unknown" is an example of ensuring data
    A. reliability.
    B. timeliness.
    C. precision.
    D. validity.

REFERENCE: Abdelhak, pp 133–134
               Green and Bowie, p 258
               LaTour, Eichenwald-Maki, and Oachs, p 382

32. In determining your acute care facility's degree of compliance with prospective payment requirements for Medicare, the best resource to reference for recent certification standards is the
    A. CARF manual.
    B. hospital bylaws.
    C. Joint Commission accreditation manual.
    D. Federal Register.

REFERENCE: Abdelhak, p 441
               Green and Bowie, p 29
               LaTour, Eichenwald-Maki, and Oachs, pp 301–302, 453, 466, 915
               Odom-Wesley, p 288

33. In an acute care hospital, a complete history and physical may not be required for a new admission when
    A. the patient is readmitted for a similar problem within 1 year.
    B. the patient's stay is less than 24 hours.
    C. the patient has an uneventful course in the hospital.
    D. a legible copy of a recent H&P performed in the attending physician's office is available.

REFERENCE: Abdelhak, p 109
               Green and Bowie, p 145
               LaTour, Eichenwald-Maki, and Oachs, pp 245, 252, 925
               Odom-Wesley, p 367

34. You are developing a complete data dictionary for your facility. Which of the following resources will be most helpful in providing standard definitions for data commonly collected in acute care hospitals?
    A. Minimum Data Set
    B. Uniform Hospital Discharge Data Set
    C. Conditions of Participation
    D. Federal Register

REFERENCE: Abdelhak, pp 102–105, 134–136
               Davis and LaCour, pp 45, 61
               Green and Bowie, p 124
               LaTour, Eichenwald-Maki, and Oachs, pp 19, 213, 955
               Odom-Wesley, pp 84–85, 92–94, 310
               Sayles, p 146

35. Gerda Smith has presented to the ER in a coma with injuries sustained in a motor vehicle accident. According to her sister, Gerda has had a recent medical history taken at the public health department. The physician on call is grateful that she can access this patient information using the area's
    A. EDMS system.   C. expert system.
    B. CPOE.   D. RHIO.

REFERENCE: Green and Bowie, p 112
               LaTour, Eichenwald-Maki, and Oachs, pp 221–222, 224, 230, 944
               Sayles, p 326

36. When developing a data collection system, the most effective approach first considers
    A. the end user's needs.   C. hardware requirements.
    B. applicable accreditation standards. D. facility preference.

REFERENCE: Odom-Wesley, p 230

37. A key data item you would expect to find recorded on an ER record but would probably NOT see in an acute care record is the
    A. physical findings.   C. time and means of arrival.
    B. lab and diagnostic test results.   D. instructions for follow-up care.

REFERENCE: Abdelhak, pp 138–139
               Davis and LaCour, pp 95, 221–222
               Johns, p 93
               LaTour, Eichenwald-Maki, and Oachs, p 255
               Odom-Wesley, p 171
               Peden, p 37
               Sayles, p 107

38. A data item to include on a qualitative review checklist of infant and children inpatient health records that need not be included on adult records would be
    A. chief complaint.
    B. condition on discharge.
    C. time and means of arrival.
    D. growth and development record.

REFERENCE: Peden, p 83
               Sayles, p 110

39. You are the Director of Coding and Billing at a large group practice. The Practice Manager stops by your office on his way to a planning meeting to ask about the timeline for complying with HITECH requirements to adopt meaningful use EHR technology. You reply that the incentives began in 2011 and will end in 2014. You remind him that by 2015, sanctions for noncompliance will appear in the form of
    A. downward adjustments to Medicare reimbursement.
    B. the withdrawal of permission to treat Medicare and Medicaid patients.
    C. a mandatory action plan for implementing a meaningful use EHR.
    D. monetary fines up to $100,000.

REFERENCE: Davis and LaCour, pp 82–83
               McWay, p 305
               Sayles, pp 954, 987

40. In creating a new form or computer view, the designer should be most driven by
    A. QIO standards.
    B. medical staff bylaws.
    C. needs of the users.
    D. flow of data on the page or screen.

REFERENCE: Abdelhak, p 120
               Davis and LaCour, pp 44, 49, 52
               Green and Bowie, p 201
               LaTour, Eichenwald-Maki, and Oachs, pp 103–105, 119, 125, 148, 170, 180, 200, 213, 229, 870
               Odom-Wesley, p 230
               Sayles, p 355

41. Under which of the following conditions can an original paper-based patient health record be physically removed from the hospital?
    A. when the patient is brought to the hospital emergency department following a motor vehicle accident and, after assessment, is transferred with his health record to a trauma designated emergency department at another hospital
    B. when the director of health records is acting in response to a subpoena *duces tecum* and takes the health record to court
    C. when the patient is discharged by the physician and at the time of discharge is transported to a long-term care facility with his health record
    D. when the record is taken to a physician's private office for a follow-up patient visit postdischarge

REFERENCE: Abdelhak, pp 531–534
               Sayles, p 776

42. According to the following table, the most serious record delinquency problem occurred in which of the following months?

Record Delinquency for Second Quarter	April	May	June
Percentage incomplete records	70%	88%	79%
Percentage delinquent records	51%	43%	61%
Percentage delinquent due to missing H&P	3%	1.4%	0.5%

   A. April
   B. May
   C. June
   D. cannot determine from these data

REFERENCE: Abdelhak, pp 128–129
                    Green and Bowie, pp 99, 145

43. Using the SOAP style of documenting progress notes, choose the "subjective" statement from the following.
   A. sciatica unimproved with hot pack therapy
   B. patient moving about very cautiously, appears to be in pain
   C. adjust pain medication; begin physical therapy tomorrow
   D. patient states low back pain is as severe as it was on admission

REFERENCE: Abdelhak, pp 118–119
                    Davis and LaCour, pp 41–43, 96–98, 516–520
                    Green and Bowie, p 91
                    LaTour and Eichenwald-Maki, p 91
                    Odom-Wesley, pp 217, 331–332

44. In 1987, OBRA helped shift the focus in long-term care to patient outcomes. As a result, core assessment data elements are collected on each SNF resident as defined in the
   A. UHDDS.
   B. MDS.
   C. Uniform Clinical Data Set.
   D. Uniform Ambulatory Core Data.

REFERENCE: Abdelhak, pp 141–143
                    Davis and LaCour, p 231
                    Green and Bowie, p 253
                    LaTour, Eichenwald-Maki, and Oachs, pp 199, 435, 931
                    Peden, pp 357–360
                    Odom-Wesley, pp 365, 368–378
                    Sayles, pp 150–152

45. As the Chair of a Forms Review Committee, you need to track the field name of a particular data field and the security levels applicable to that field. Your best source for this information would be the
   A. facility's data dictionary.
   B. MDS.
   C. glossary of health care terms.
   D. UHDDS.

REFERENCE: Abdelhak, pp 502–503
                    LaTour, Eichenwald-Maki, and Oachs, pp 202, 907, C7
                    Sayles, pp 882–883

46. You notice on the admission H&P that Mr. McKahan, a Medicare patient, was admitted for disc surgery, but the progress notes indicate that due to some heart irregularities, he may not be a good surgical risk. Because of your knowledge of COP regulations, you expect that a(n) _____ will be added to his health record.
   A. interval summary
   B. consultation report
   C. advance directive
   D. interdisciplinary care plan

REFERENCE: Abdelhak, pp 111–112
               Green and Bowie, p 148
               Davis and LaCour, p 106
               Odom-Wesley, pp 117–118
               LaTour, Eichenwald-Maki, and Oachs, pp 249, 905

47. An example of objective entry in the health record supplied by a health care practitioner is the
   A. past medical history.
   B. physical assessment.
   C. chief complaint.
   D. review of systems.

REFERENCE: Abdelhak, pp 118–119
               Davis and LaCour, p 99
               Green and Bowie, p 148
               LaTour, Eichenwald-Maki, and Oachs, p 245
               Odom-Wesley, pp 217, 331–332
               Sayles, p 78

48. You have been appointed as Chair of the Health Record Committee at a new hospital. Your committee has been asked to recommend time-limited documentation standards for inclusion in the medical staff bylaws, rules, and regulations. The committee documentation standards must meet the standards of both the Joint Commission and the Medicare Conditions of Participation. The standards for the history and physical exam documentation are discussed first. You advise them that the time period for completion of this report should be set at
   A. 12 hours after admission.
   B. 24 hours after admission.
   C. 12 hours after admission or prior to surgery.
   D. 24 hours after admission or prior to surgery.

REFERENCE: Abdelhak, p 109
               Davis and LaCour, p 100
               Green and Bowie, p 145
               LaTour, Eichenwald-Maki, and Oachs, p 245
               Odom-Wesley, p 108

49. Based on the following documentation in an acute care record, where would you expect this excerpt to appear?

    "With the patient in the supine position, the right side of the neck was appropriately prepped with betadine solution and draped. I was able to pass the central line, which was taped to skin and used for administration of drugs during resuscitation."

    A. physician progress notes
    B. operative record
    C. nursing progress notes
    D. physical examination

REFERENCE: Abdelhak, pp 113–114
                Davis and LaCour, p 110
                LaTour, Eichenwald-Maki, and Oachs, p 250
                Odom-Wesley, p 164
                Sayles, p 88

50. A surgeon on the Health Record Committee voices a concern that, although he has been told that the operative report is to be dictated immediately after surgery, he has often had to deal with the problem of transcription backlog, which prevented the report from getting on the health record in a timely manner. Your advice to this doctor is that when a known backlog exists, he should
    A. provide the dictated tape to his staff.
    B. request a "stat" report.
    C. write a detailed operative note in the record.
    D. request that administration hire more transcriptionists.

REFERENCE: Abdelhak, pp 113–114
                Green and Bowie, pp 162–165
                LaTour, Eichenwald-Maki, and Oachs, p 250

51. Joint Commission standards require that a complete history and physical be documented on the health records of operative patients. Does this report carry a time requirement?
    A. Yes, within 8 hours postsurgery   C. Yes, prior to surgery
    B. No, as long as it is done ASAP   D. Yes, within 24 hours postsurgery

REFERENCE: Abdelhak, p 109
                Davis and LaCour, pp 100, 375
                Green and Bowie, p 145
                LaTour and Eichenwald-Maki, p 196
                Odom-Wesley, p 108

52. The old practices of flagging records for deficiencies and requiring retrospective documentation add little or no value to patient care. You try to convince the entire health care team to consistently enter data into the patient's record at the time and location of service instead of waiting for retrospective analysis to alert them to complete the record. You are proposing
    A. quantitative record review.   C. concurrent record analysis.
    B. clinical pertinence review.   D. point-of-care documentation.

REFERENCE: Abdelhak, p 38
                LaTour, Eichenwald-Maki, and Oachs, pp 248, 254, 263, 285, 919

53. An example of a primary data source for health care statistics is the
    A. disease index.
    B. accession register.
    C. MPI.
    D. hospital census.

REFERENCE: Abdelhak, pp 480–481
               Horton, p 4
               Koch, p 65
               LaTour, Eichenwald-Maki, and Oachs, pp 289, 368
               Odom-Wesley, p 83

54. In the computerization of forms, good screen view design, along with the options of alerts and alarms, makes it easier to ensure that all essential data items have been captured. One essential item to be captured on the physical exam is the
    A. general appearance as assessed by the physician.
    B. chief complaint.
    C. family history as related by the patient.
    D. subjective review of systems.

REFERENCE: Abdelhak, p 109
               Davis and LaCour, p 99
               Green and Bowie, p 149
               LaTour, Eichenwald-Maki, and Oachs, p 245
               Odom-Wesley, p 230
               Sayles, p 80

55. During a retrospective review of Rose Hunter's inpatient health record, the health information clerk notes that on day 4 of hospitalization there was one missed dose of insulin. What type of review is this clerk performing?
    A. utilization review
    B. quantitative review
    C. legal review
    D. qualitative review

REFERENCE: Abdelhak, pp 130–131
               Green and Bowie, p 99
               LaTour, Eichenwald-Maki, and Oachs, p 943
               McWay, p 126

56. Which of the following is least likely to be identified by a deficiency analysis technician?
    A. missing discharge summary
    B. need for physician authentication of two verbal orders
    C. discrepancy between post-op diagnosis by the surgeon and pathology diagnosis by the pathologist
    D. x-ray report charted on the wrong record

REFERENCE: Abdelhak, pp 130–131
               Green and Bowie, p 99
               McWay, p 126
               Sayles, p 351

57. The Conditions of Participation requires that the medical staff bylaws, rules, and regulations address the status of consultants. Which of the following reports would normally be considered a consultation?
    A. tissue examination done by the pathologist
    B. impressions of a cardiologist asked to determine whether patient is a good surgical risk
    C. interpretation of a radiologic study
    D. technical interpretation of electrocardiogram

REFERENCE: Abdelhak, pp 111–112
               Davis and LaCour, p 106
               Green and Bowie, p 148
               LaTour, Eichenwald-Maki, and Oachs, p 115
               Odom-Wesley, pp 117–118

58. The health care providers at your hospital do a very thorough job of periodic open record review to ensure the completeness of record documentation. A qualitative review of surgical records would likely include checking for documentation regarding
    A. the presence or absence of such items as preoperative and postoperative diagnosis, description of findings, and specimens removed.
    B. whether a postoperative infection occurred and how it was treated.
    C. the quality of follow-up care.
    D. whether the severity of illness and/or intensity of service warranted acute level care.

REFERENCE: Abdelhak, pp 113–114
               Davis and LaCour, p 374
               Green and Bowie, p 99
               LaTour, Eichenwald-Maki, and Oachs, pp 35, 655
               Odom-Wesley, pp 251–256

59. In your facility it has become critical that information regarding patients who are transferred to the oncology unit be sent to an outpatient scheduling system to facilitate outpatient appointments. This information can be obtained most efficiently from
    A. generic screens used by record abstractors.
    B. disease index.
    C. R-ADT system.
    D. indicator monitoring program.

REFERENCE: Abdelhak, pp 162–163
               LaTour, Eichenwald-Maki, and Oachs, p 944
               Sayles, p 955

60. In your facility, the health care providers from every discipline document progress notes sequentially on the same form. Your facility is utilizing
    A. integrated progress notes.   C. source-oriented records.
    B. interdisciplinary treatment plans. D. SOAP notes.

REFERENCE: Abdelhak, pp 118–119
               Green and Bowie, p 153
               LaTour, Eichenwald-Maki, and Oachs, p 248
               Odom-Wesley, pp 217–221

61. Which of the following services is LEAST likely to be provided by a facility accredited by CARF?
    A. chronic pain management
    B. palliative care
    C. brain injury management
    D. vocational evaluation

REFERENCE: Abdelhak, pp 26–29
               Green and Bowie, p 30
               LaTour, Eichenwald-Maki, and Oachs, p 254
               Sayles, p 679

62. Which method of identification of authorship or authentication of entries would be inappropriate to use in a patient's health record?
    A. written signature of the provider of care
    B. identifiable initials of a nurse writing a nursing note
    C. a unique identification code entered by the person making the report
    D. delegated use of computer key by radiology secretary

REFERENCE: Abdelhak, pp 117–118
               Green and Bowie, pp 78–79
               LaTour, Eichenwald-Maki, and Oachs, pp 258, 264, 897

63. Though you work in an integrated delivery network, not all systems in your network communicate with one another. As you meet with your partner organizations, you begin to sell them on the concept of an important development intended to support the exchange of health information across the continuum within a geographical community. You are promoting that your organization join a
    A. data warehouse.
    B. regional health information organization.
    C. continuum of care.
    D. data retrieval portal group.

REFERENCE: Abdelhak, pp 86–90
               LaTour and Eichenwald-Maki, p 51
               McWay, p 273
               Odom-Wesley, p 15

64. As a trauma registrar working in an emergency department, you want to begin comparing your trauma care services to other hospital-based emergency departments. To ensure that your facility is collecting the same data as other facilities, you review elements from which data set?
    A. DEEDS
    B. UHDDS
    C. MDS
    D. ORYX

REFERENCE: Green and Bowie, p 253
               LaTour, Eichenwald-Maki, and Oachs, p 211

65. As a new HIM manager of an acute care facility, you have been asked to update the facility's policy for a physician's verbal orders in accordance with Joint Commission standards and state law. Your first area of concern is the qualifications of those individuals in your facility who have been authorized to record verbal orders. For this information, you will consult the
    A. Consolidated Manual for Hospitals.
    B. Federal Register.
    C. Policy and Procedure Manual.
    D. Hospital Bylaws, Rules, and Regulations.

    REFERENCE: Davis and LaCour, pp 102–104
    Green and Bowie, p 154
    LaTour, Eichenwald-Maki, and Oachs, pp 26, 239–240, 242, 265–267
    Odom-Wesley, pp 111, 113, 290–291, 339
    Sayles, p 81

66. Reviewing a medical record to ensure that all diagnoses are justified by documentation throughout the chart is an example of
    A. peer review.
    B. quantitative review.
    C. qualitative review.
    D. legal analysis.

    REFERENCE: Abdelhak, pp 130–131
    Davis and LaCour, pp 374–376
    Green and Bowie, p 99
    LaTour, Eichenwald-Maki, and Oachs, pp 34–35
    McWay, p 126
    Odom-Wesley, pp 251–252

67. Accreditation by Joint Commission is a voluntary activity for a facility and it is
    A. considered unnecessary by most health care facilities.
    B. required for state licensure in all states.
    C. conducted in each facility annually.
    D. required for reimbursement of certain patient groups.

    REFERENCE: Abdelhak, pp 113–114
    LaTour, Eichenwald-Maki, and Oachs, pp 37–38
    Odom-Wesley, p 299

68. Which of the following indices might be protected from unauthorized access through the use of unique identifier codes assigned to members of the medical staff?
    A. disease index
    B. procedure index
    C. master patient index
    D. physician index

    REFERENCE: Green and Bowie, p 240
    LaTour, Eichenwald-Maki, and Oachs, pp 369–370
    Sayles, p 398

69. Which of the four distinct components of the problem-oriented record serves to help index documentation throughout the record?
    A. database
    B. problem list
    C. initial plan
    D. progress notes

    REFERENCE: Abdelhak, pp 118–119
    Davis and LaCour, pp 55–56
    Green and Bowie, p 91
    LaTour, Eichenwald-Maki, and Oachs, pp 255–256
    Odom-Wesley, pp 215–216
    Sayles, p 126

70. As supervisor of the cancer registry, you report the registry's annual caseload to administration. The most efficient way to retrieve this information would be to use
    A. patient abstracts.
    B. patient index.
    C. accession register.
    D. follow-up files.

REFERENCE: LaTour, Eichenwald-Maki, and Oachs, p 371
               Sayles, p 349

71. As the Compliance Officer for an acute care facility, you are interested in researching recent legislation designed to provide significant funding for health information technology for your next committee meeting. You begin by googling
    A. EMTALA.
    B. Health Care Quality Improvement Act.
    C. HIPAA.
    D. ARRA.

REFERENCE: LaTour, Eichenwald-Maki, and Oachs, p 17
               McWay, pp 34–35
               Sayles, pp 25, 162

72. Select the appropriate situation for which a final progress note may legitimately be substituted for a discharge summary in an inpatient medical record.
    A. Patient admitted with COPD 1/4/2013 and discharged 1/7/2013
    B. Baby Boy Hiltz, born 1/5/2013, maintained normal status, discharged 1/7/2013
    C. Baby Boy Hiltz's mother admitted 1/5/2013, C-section delivery, and discharged 1/7/2013
    D. Baby Boy Doe admitted 1/3/2013, died 1/4/2013

REFERENCE: Abdelhak, p 113
               Green and Bowie, p 142
               LaTour, Eichenwald-Maki, and Oachs, p 251
               Odom-Wesley, pp 180, 201

73. Based on the following documentation in an acute care record, where would you expect this excerpt to appear?

"Initially the patient was admitted to the medical unit to evaluate the x-ray findings and the rub. He was started on Levaquin 500 mg initially and then 250 mg daily. The patient was hydrated with IV fluids and remained afebrile. Serial cardiac enzymes were done. The rub, chest pain, and shortness of breath resolved. EKGs remained unchanged. Patient will be discharged and followed as an outpatient."

    A. discharge summary
    B. physical exam
    C. admission note
    D. clinical laboratory report

REFERENCE: Abdelhak, p 113
               Davis and LaCour, pp 106–107
               LaTour, Eichenwald-Maki, and Oachs, p 251
               Odom-Wesley, p 164
               Sayles, p 93

74. The information security officer is revising the policies at your rehabilitation facility for handling all patient clinical information. The best resource for checking out specific voluntary accreditation standards and guidelines is the
    A. Conditions of Participation for Rehabilitation Facilities.
    B. Medical Staff Bylaws, Rules, and Regulations.
    C. Joint Commission manual.
    D. CARF manual.

REFERENCE: Davis and LaCour, pp 26, 231, 351
LaTour, Eichenwald-Maki, and Oachs, p 903
Odom-Wesley, pp 191–196
Sayles, p 74

75. Stage I of meaningful use focuses on data capture and sharing. Which of the following is included in the menu set of objectives for eligible hospitals in this stage?
    A. Use CPOE for medication orders
    B. Smoking cessation counseling for MI patients
    C. Appropriate use of HL-7 standards
    D. Establish critical pathways for complex, high-dollar cases

REFERENCE: HealthIT.hhs.gov
Davis and LaCour, pp 82–84

76. Which of the following is a secondary data source that would be used to quickly gather the health records of all juvenile patients treated for diabetes within the past 6 months?
    A. disease index
    B. patient register
    C. pediatric census sheet
    D. procedure index

REFERENCE: Green and Bowie, pp 240–243
LaTour, Eichenwald-Maki, and Oachs, p 369
Sayles, p 436

77. As the Coding Supervisor, your job description includes working with agents who have been charged with detecting and correcting overpayments made to your hospital in the Medicare Fee for Service program. You will need to develop a professional relationship with
    A. the OIG.
    B. MEDPAR representatives.
    C. QIO physicians.
    D. recovery audit contractors.

REFERENCE: Green and Bowie, pp 325–326
LaTour, Eichenwald-Maki, and Oachs, pp 851, 944
Sayles, p 309

78. Using a template to collect data for key reports may help to prompt caregivers to document all required data elements in the patient record. This practice contributes to data
    A. timeliness.
    B. accuracy.
    C. comprehensiveness.
    D. security.

REFERENCE: Abdelhak, pp 133–134
Green and Bowie, p 258

79. In preparation for an upcoming site visit by Joint Commission, you discover that the number of delinquent records for the preceding month exceeded 50% of discharged patients. Even more alarming was the pattern you noticed in the type of delinquencies. Which of the following represents the most serious pattern of delinquencies? Fifteen percent of delinquent records show
    A. missing signatures on progress notes.
    B. missing discharge summaries.
    C. absence of SOAP format in progress notes.
    D. missing operative reports.

REFERENCE: Abdelhak, p 128
                Green and Bowie, pp 162–165
                LaTour, Eichenwald-Maki, and Oachs, pp 266, 652–653

80. A primary focus of screen format design in a health record computer application should be to ensure that
    A. programmers develop standard screen formats for all hospitals.
    B. the user is capturing essential data elements.
    C. paper forms are easily converted to computer forms.
    D. data fields can be randomly accessed.

REFERENCE: Abdelhak, pp 119–120, 124
                LaTour, Eichenwald-Maki, and Oachs, p 51
                McWay, pp 131–132
                Odom-Wesley, p 230
                Sayles, pp 384–385

81. A quality improvement team is focusing on the unacceptable number of unsigned doctors' orders in your facility. The most effective method for increasing the timeliness of signatures on orders and positively impacting the patient care process would be
    A. performing a retrospective review where all orders can be flagged at one time.
    B. holding a printed order sheet on the medical care unit at least 24 hours postdischarge to give the physician time to sign.
    C. developing an open-record review process.
    D. devising a signature sheet for the attending physician to sign prospectively that will apply to all orders given during the current episode of his patient's care.

REFERENCE: LaTour, Eichenwald-Maki, and Oachs, p 248

82. Before making recommendations to the Executive Committee regarding new physicians who have applied for active membership, the Credentials Committee must query the
    A. peer review organization.
    B. National Practitioner Data Bank.
    C. risk manager.
    D. Health Plan Employer Data and Information Set.

REFERENCE: Abdelhak, pp 471–472
                Green and Bowie, pp 251, 255
                LaTour, Eichenwald-Maki, and Oachs, p 16

83. A qualitative analysis of OB records reveals a pattern of inconsistent data entries when comparing documentation of the same data elements captured on both the prenatal form and labor and delivery form. The characteristic of data quality that is being compromised in this case is data
    A. reliability.
    B. accessibility.
    C. legibility.
    D. completeness.

REFERENCE: Green and Bowie, p 258
               LaTour, Eichenwald-Maki, and Oachs, pp 67, 383

84. Medicare rules state that the use of verbal orders should be infrequent and used only when the orders cannot be written or given electronically. In addition, verbal orders must be
    A. written within 24 hours of the patient's admission.
    B. accepted by charge nurses only.
    C. cosigned by the attending physician within 4 hours of giving the order.
    D. recorded by persons authorized by hospital regulations and procedures.

REFERENCES: Green and Bowie, p 154
               LaTour, Eichenwald-Maki, and Oachs, pp 247–248
               Davis and LaCour, pp 102–104
               Odom-Wesley, pp 111, 113, 290–291, 339

85. The lack of a discharge order may indicate that the patient left against medical advice. If this situation occurs, you would expect to see the circumstances of the leave
    A. documented in an incident report and filed in the patient's health record.
    B. reported as a potentially compensable event.
    C. reported to the Executive Committee.
    D. documented in both the progress notes and the discharge summary.

REFERENCE: LaTour, Eichenwald-Maki, and Oachs, pp 251, 910
               Odom-Wesley, p 446

86. Your committee is charged with developing procedures for the Health Information Services staff of a new home health agency. You recommend that the staff routinely check to verify that a summary on each patient is provided to the attending physician so that he or she can review, update, and recertify the patient as appropriate. The time frame for requiring this summary is at least every
    A. week.
    B. month.
    C. 60 days.
    D. 90 days.

REFERENCE: Abdelhak, p 143
               Peden, p 441
               Odom-Wesley, pp 401–402

87. You want to review one document in your facility that will spell out the documentation requirements for patient records, designate the time frame for completion by the active medical staff, and indicate the penalties for failure to comply with these record standards. Your best resource will be
    A. medical staff bylaws.
    B. quality management plan.
    C. Joint Commission accreditation manual.
    D. medical staff rules and regulations.

REFERENCE: Green and Bowie, p 16
               LaTour, Eichenwald-Maki, and Oachs, p 26
               Odom-Wesley, p 367

88. A quarterly review reveals the following data for Springfield Hospital:

Springfield Hospital Quarterly Statistics	
Average monthly discharges	1,820
Average monthly operative procedures	458
Number of incomplete records	1,002
Number of delinquent records	590

What is the percentage of incomplete records during this quarter?

A. 55%
B. 54%
C. 33%
D. 32%

REFERENCE: Horton, p 19
                Koch, p 48

89. Referring to the data in the previous question, determine the delinquent record rate for Springfield Hospital.

A. 55%
B. 32%
C. 33%
D. 54%

REFERENCE: Green and Bowie, p 84
                Horton, p 19
                Koch, p 48

90. Still referring to the information in the table in question 88 and the delinquent record rate shown in the answer for question 89, would the facility be out of compliance with Joint Commission standards?

A. Yes
B. No

REFERENCE: Abdelhak, p 128
                Green and Bowie, p 84
                Horton, p 19

91. In an acute care facility, the responsibility for educating physicians and other health care providers regarding proper documentation policies belongs to the

A. information security manager.
B. clinical data specialist.
C. health information manager.
D. risk manager.

REFERENCE: Green and Bowie, p 98
                LaTour, Eichenwald-Maki, and Oachs, pp 353, 762
                Odom-Wesley, pp 246–248

92. For inpatients, the first data item collected of a clinical nature is usually

A. principal diagnosis.
B. expected payer.
C. admitting diagnosis.
D. review of systems.

REFERENCE: Green and Bowie, p 140
                Davis and LaCour, p 94

93. Documentation found in acute care health records should include core measure quality indicators required for compliance with Medicare's Health Care Quality Improvement Program (HCQIP). A typical indicator for patients with pneumonia is

A. beta blocker at discharge.
B. blood culture before first antibiotic received.
C. early administration of aspirin.
D. discharged on antithrombotic.

REFERENCE: CMS, p 3

94. One record documentation requirement shared by BOTH acute care and emergency departments is
    A. patient's condition on discharge.
    B. time and means of arrival.
    C. advance directive.
    D. problem list.

REFERENCE: Abdelhak, pp 109, 133

95. In addition to diagnostic and therapeutic orders from the attending physician, you would expect every completed inpatient health record to contain
    A. standing orders.
    B. telephone orders.
    C. stop orders.
    D. discharge order.

REFERENCE: Abdelhak, p 108
               Green and Bowie, p 154
               LaTour, Eichenwald-Maki, and Oachs, p 248
               Odom-Wesley, p 115

96. As the Chair of the Forms Committee at your hospital, you are helping to design a template for house staff members to use while collecting information for the history and physical. When asked to explain how "review of systems" differs from "physical exam," you explain that the review of systems is used to document
    A. objective symptoms observed by the physician.
    B. past and current activities, such as smoking and drinking habits.
    C. a chronological description of patient's present condition from time of onset to present.
    D. subjective symptoms that the patient may have forgotten to mention or that may have seemed unimportant.

REFERENCE: Green and Bowie, p 147
               Odom-Wesley, p 331

97. Skilled nursing facilities may choose to submit MDS data using RAVEN software, or software purchased commercially through a vendor, provided that the software meets
    A. Joint Commission standards.
    B. NHIN standards.
    C. HL-7 standards.
    D. CMS standards.

REFERENCE: Peden, p 374
               Green and Bowie, p 253

98. Based on the following documentation in an acute care record, where would you expect this excerpt to appear?

"The patient is alert and in no acute distress. Initial vital signs: T 98, P 102 and regular, R 20 and BP 120/69..."

    A. physical exam
    B. past medical history
    C. social history
    D. chief complaint

REFERENCE: Abdelhak, p 107
               LaTour, Eichenwald-Maki, and Oachs, p 245
               Odom-Wesley, pp 108–109

Answer Key for Health Data Content and Standards

ANSWER   EXPLANATION

1. B   (C and D) Although a gross description of tissue removed may be mentioned on the operative note or discharge summary, only the pathology report will contain a microscopic description.

2. B   Answers A, C, and D represent items collected on Medicare inpatients according to UHDDS requirements. Only B represents a data item collected more typically in long-term care settings and required in the MDS.

3. C   The Joint Commission requires hospitals to prohibit abbreviations that have caused confusion or problems in their handwritten form, such as "U" for unit, which can be mistaken for "O" or the number "4." Spelling out the unit is preferred.

4. A   There are several core objectives for achieving meaningful use. Engaging patients and their families is one of these objectives.

5. C   Factual summaries investigating unexpected facility events should not be treated as part of the patient's health information and therefore would not be recorded in the health record.

6. D   (A, B, and C) Patient care plans, pharmacy consultations, and transfer summaries are likely to be found on the records of long-term care patients.

7. B   Auto authentication is a policy adopted by some facilities that allow physicians to state in advance that transcribed reports should automatically be considered approved and signed (or authenticated) when the physician fails to make corrections within a preestablished time frame (e.g., "Consider it signed if I do not make changes within 7 days."). Another version of this practice is when physicians authorize the HIM department to send weekly lists of unsigned documents. The physician then signs the list in lieu of signing each individual report. Neither practice ensures that the physician has reviewed and approved each report individually.

8. A   The antepartum record should include a comprehensive history and physical exam on each OB patient visit with particular attention to menstrual and reproductive history.

9. C   Joint Commission and COP allow a legible copy of a recent H&P done in a doctor's office in lieu of an admission H&P as long as interval changes are documented in the record upon admission. In addition, when the patient is readmitted within 30 days for the same or a related problem, an interval history and physical exam may be completed if the original H&P is readily available.

10. A   The major sources of case findings for cancer registry programs are the pathology department, the disease index, and the logs of patients treated in radiology and other outpatient departments. B. The number index identifies new health record numbers and the patients to whom they were assigned. C. The physicians' index identifies all patients treated by each doctor. D. The patient index links each patient treated in a facility with the health number under which the clinical information can be located.

11. A   Those who make entries in the medical record are given that privilege by the medical staff. Only house staff members who are under the supervision of active staff members require countersignatures once the privilege has been granted.

12. C   The statute of limitations for each state is information that is crucial in determining record retention schedules.

13. D   Authentication by signature stamps requires a written agreement with the facility not to delegate the use of the stamps. Similarly, in a computer-based system, it is important to ensure that personal identification codes used to authenticate entries are used only by the persons to whom they are assigned. A. Fingerprint signatures are individualized automatically.

Answer Key for Health Data Content and Standards

ANSWER   EXPLANATION

14. C A. Some reference to the patient's history may be found in the discharge summary but not a detailed history. B. The attending physician records the discharge summary. D. Codes are usually recorded on a different form in the record.

15. D A and B deal with issues directly linked to quality of care reviews. C deals with risk management. Only D points to a review aimed at evaluating the quality of documentation in the health record.

16. B Although the nursing staff, hospital administration, and the health information management professional play a role in ensuring an accurate and complete record, the major responsibility lies with the attending physician.

17. B The Minimum Data Set is a basic component of the long-term care RAI. A. UHDDS used in acute care; C. OASIS used in home health; D. DEEDS used in emergency departments.

18. C Unlike the acute care hospital, where most health care practitioners document separately, the patient care plan is the foundation around which patient care is organized in long-term care facilities because it contains the unique perspective of each discipline involved.

19. A B. Utilization review committees deal with the issues of the medical necessity of admissions and efficient utilization of facility resources. C. Risk management committees consider methods for reducing injury and financial loss. D. Joint conference committees act as a liaison between the governing body and the medical staff.

20. C The Joint Commission requires hospitals to mark the correct surgical site and to involve the patient in the marking process to help eliminate wrong site surgeries.

21. D Joint Commission suggests that HIM department, nursing, medical staff, administrative personnel, and other services participate in the record reviews.

22. D Among those abbreviations considered confusing or likely to be misinterpreted are those containing a leading decimal.

23. A Joint Commission specifies that H&Ps must be completed within 24 hours.

24. A The assessment statement combines the objective and subjective into a diagnostic conclusion, sometimes in the form of a differential diagnosis, such as "peritonitis versus appendicitis."

25. D A. The disease index is a listing in diagnostic code number order. B. The physician index is a listing of cases in order by physician name or number. C. The MPI cross-references the patient name and medical record number.

26. D A, B, and C all refer to a computer application of managing health information, but only answer D deals with the clinical application of data entry into the patient's record at the time and location of service.

27. D Most facilities use bar-coded patient identification to ensure proper indexing into the imaging system.

28. A Pharmacy consults are required for elderly patients who typically take multiple medications. These consults review for potential drug interactions and/or discrepancies in medications given and those ordered.

29. D Data accuracy denotes that data are correct values. A. Data comprehensiveness denotes that all data items are included. B. Data granularity denotes that the attributes and values of data should be defined at the correct level of detail. C. Data precision denotes that data values should be just large enough to support the application of process.

Answer Key for Health Data Content and Standards

ANSWER   EXPLANATION

30. C   In accession number 13–0001/00, "13" represents the year that the patient first entered the database; "0001" indicates that this was the first case entered that year; "00" indicates that this patient has only one known neoplasm.

31. C   Validity refers to the accuracy of data, while reliability refers to consistency of data. Timeliness refers to data being available within a time frame helpful to the user, and precision refers to data values that are just large enough to support the application of the process.

32. D   CMS publishes both proposed and final rules for the Conditions of Participation for hospitals in the daily Federal Register.

33. D   A. An interval H&P can be used when a patient is readmitted for the same or related problem within 30 days. B and C. No matter how long the patient stays or how minor the condition, an H&P is required.

34 B   A. The MDS is designed for use in long-term care facilities. C. The COP is the set of regulations that health care institutions must follow to receive Medicare reimbursement. D. The *Federal Register* is a daily government newspaper for publishing proposed and final rules of federal agencies.

35. D   With the increasing number of health care entities implementing EHR systems, the networking of electronic information between facilities has become a reality in some areas due to the establishment of regional health information organizations. A. EDMS = electronic data management system. B. CPOE = computerized provider order entry system

36. A   The needs of the end user are always the primary concern when designing systems.

37. C   Answers A, B, and D are required items in BOTH acute and ER records.

38. D   Answers A and B are items that should be documented on any inpatient record. Answer C reflects a data item you would expect to find on ER records only.

39. A   Government incentive funds for implementation of EHRs that meet meaningful use criteria expire in 2014 and the program is set to roll into sanctions on Medicare reimbursement in 2015.

40. C   The needs of the user are the primary concern in forms design.

41. B   A and C. In these situations a transfer summary or pertinent copies from the inpatient health record may accompany the patient, but the original record stays on the premises.

42. A   A recommendation for improvement from Joint Commission is indicated if the number of delinquent records is greater than 50% or if the percentage of records with delinquent records due to missing H&Ps exceeds 2% of the average monthly discharges. In the month of April, both of these delinquency problems are reflected. The percentage of incomplete records is not relevant.

43. D   A represents the assessment statement, B the objective, and C the plan.

44. B   OBRA mandates comprehensive functional assessments of long-term care residents using the Minimum Data Set for Long-Term Care.

45. A   Answers B and D are types of data sets for collecting data in long-term (MDS) and acute care (UHDDS) facilities. A data dictionary should include security levels for each field as well as definitions for all entities.

46. B   COP requires a consultation report on patients who are not a good surgical risk as well as those with obscure diagnoses, patients whose physicians have doubts as to the best therapeutic measure to be taken, and patients for whom there is a question of criminal activity.

Answer Key for Health Data Content and Standards

ANSWER   EXPLANATION

47. B The medical history, including a review of systems and chief complaint, is information supplied by the patient. A physical assessment adds objective data to the subjective data provided by the patient in the history.

48. D This meets both Joint Commission and COP standards.

49. B This entry is typical of a surgical procedure.

50. C Joint Commission requires that a detailed OP note be written in the health record when expeditious transcription of the dictated report is impossible to maintain continuity of care.

51. C Joint Commission standards require the surgeon to document the history and physical examination prior to surgery.

52. D AHIMA's Position Statement supports that point-of-care documentation raises documentation standards and improves patient care. It is defined as data entry that occurs at the point and location of service.

53. D Answers A, B, and C are examples of secondary data sources.

54. A The medical history (including chief complaint, history of present illness, past medical history, personal history, family history, and a review of systems) is provided by the patient or the most knowledgeable available source. The physical examination adds objective data to the subjective data provided by the patient. This exam begins with the physician's objective assessment of the patient's general condition.

55. D Quantitative analysis involves checking for the presence or absence of necessary reports and/or signatures, while qualitative analysis may involve checking documentation consistency, such as comparing a patient's pharmacy drug profile with the medication administration record.

56. C A, B, and D all represent common checks performed by a quantitative analysis clerk: missing reports, signatures, or patient identification. Answer C represents a more in-depth review dealing with the quality of the data documented.

57. B A, C, and D represent routine interpretations that are not normally considered to be consultations.

58. A B represents an appropriate job for the infection control officer. Answer C represents the clinical care evaluation process, rather than the review of quality documentation. Answer D is a function of the utilization review program.

59. C For tracking in-house patients who have been transferred to a specialty unit, the best source of information is the registration-admission, discharge, and transfer system.

60. A Progress notes may be integrated or they may be separated, with nurses, physicians, and other health care providers writing on designated forms for each discipline.

61. B The Commission on Accreditation of Rehabilitation Facilities is an independent accrediting agency for rehabilitation facilities. Palliative care (answer B) is most likely to be provided at a hospice.

62. D Written signatures, identifiable initials, unique computer codes, and rubber stamp signatures may all be allowed as legitimate means of authenticating an entry. However, the use of codes and stamped signatures MUST be confined to the owners and they are never to be used by anyone else.

63. B Regional health information organizations are intended to support health information exchange within a geographic region.

Answer Key for Health Data Content and Standards

ANSWER   EXPLANATION

64. A   A. Data Elements for Emergency Departments—recommended data set for hospital-based emergency departments; B. Uniform Hospital Data Set—required data set for acute care hospitals; C. Minimum Data Set—required data set for long-term care facilities; D. ORYX—an initiative of Joint Commission whereby five core measures are implemented to improve safety and quality of health care.

65. D   Although Joint Commission, CMS, and state laws may include standards for verbal orders, the specific information regarding which employees have been given authority to transcribe verbal orders in your facility should be located in your hospital's bylaws, rules, and regulations.

66. C   A. Peer review typically involves quality of care issues rather than quality of documentation issues. D. Legal analysis ensures that the record entries would be acceptable in a court of law.

67. D   A. Advantages of accreditation are numerous and include financial and legal incentives. B. State licensure is required for accreditation but not the reverse. C. Joint Commission conducts unannounced on-site surveys approximately every 3 years.

68. D   Because information contained in the physicians' index is considered confidential, identification codes are often used rather than the physicians' names.

69. B   In a POMR, the database contains the history and physical; the problem list includes titles, numbers, and dates of problems and serves as a table of contents of the record; the initial plan describes diagnostic, therapeutic, and patient education plans; and the progress notes document the progress of the patient throughout the episode of care, summarized in a discharge summary or transfer note at the end of the stay.

70. C   The accession register is a permanent log of all the cases entered into the database. Each number assigned is preceded by the accession year, making it easy to assess annual workloads.

71. D   The American Recovery and Reinvestment Act was signed into law in 2009, and included significant funding for health information technology.

72. B   A final progress note may substitute for a discharge summary in the following cases: patients who are hospitalized less than 48 hours with problems of a minor nature, normal newborns, and uncomplicated obstetrical deliveries. Answer A does not qualify because of the nature of the problem and the length of stay. Answer C describes a complicated delivery, and answer D cites a severely ill patient rather than one with a minor problem.

73. A   The excerpt clearly indicates an overall summary of the patient's course in the hospital, which is a common element of the discharge summary.

74. D   The manual published by the Commission on Accreditation of Rehabilitation Facilities will have the most specific and comprehensive standards for a rehabilitation facility.

75. A   See all objectives for Stage I of meaningful use on the HealthIT.hhs.gov website.

76. A   The disease index is compiled as a result of abstracting patient code numbers into a computer database, allowing a variety of reports to be generated.

Answer Key for Health Data Content and Standards

ANSWER   EXPLANATION

77. D The RAC program is mandated to find and correct improper Medicare payments paid to health care providers participating in the Medicare reimbursement program. (A) OIG (Office of Inspector General); (B) MEDPAR (Medicare Provider Analysis and Review); (C) QIO (Quality Improvement Organization).

78. C Data comprehensiveness refers specifically to the presence of all required data elements.

79. D Answers A and B. Both signature omissions and discharge summary reports can be captured after discharge, but history and physicals should be on the chart within 24 hours of the patient's admission. Answer C. The SOAP format is not a requirement of Joint Commission. Answer D. Institutions are given a Type I recommendation when 2% of delinquent records are due to missing history and physicals or operative reports.

80. B Both paper-based and computer-based records share similar forms and view design considerations. Among these are the selection and sequencing of essential data items.

81. C A and B. Signing orders after discharge does not affect the patient's care process. D. Although this process would speed up the signature process, it is not a legally sound method of obtaining signatures on orders.

82. B With the passage of the Health Care Quality Improvement Act of 1986, the NPDB was established. Hospitals are required to query the data bank before granting clinical privileges to physicians.

83. A Data reliability implies that data are consistent no matter how many times the same data are collected and entered into the system. Accessibility implies that data are available to authorized people when and where needed. Legibility implies data that are readable. Completeness implies that all required data are present in the information system.

84. D Only persons designated by hospital policies and procedures and state and federal law are to accept verbal orders.

85. D A. Incident reports are written accounts of unusual events that have an adverse effect on a patient, employee, or facility visitor and should never be filed with the patient's record. B. PCEs are occurrences that could result in financial liability at some future time. A patient leaving AMA does not in itself suggest a PCE. C. It is not typical to report AMAs to the Executive Committee. D. Documenting the event is crucial in protecting the legal interests of the health care team and facility.

86. C This 60-day time frame is often referred to as the patient's certification period. Recertification can continue every 62 days until the patient is discharged from home health services.

87. D Although the medical staff bylaws reflect general principles and policies of the medical staff, the rules and regulations outline the details for implementing these principles, including the process and time frames for completing records, and the penalties for failure to comply.

88. A Using the basic rate formula, calculate as follows:
Incomplete records × 100 divided by average monthly discharges, or
$$\frac{1,002 \times 100}{1820} = 55.1\%$$

89. B Using the basic rate formula, calculate as follows:
Delinquent records × 100 divided by average monthly discharges, or
$$\frac{590 \times 100}{1820} = 32.4\%$$

Answer Key for Health Data Content and Standards

ANSWER   EXPLANATION

90. B   Using the basic rate formula, the delinquent record rate is 32%. Even though the delinquent record rate is 32%, this does not exceed the Joint Commission requirement to keep this statistic below 50%.

91. C   Although all of the positions listed have an interest in proper documentation in an acute care facility, the health information manager is in the best position to keep abreast of documentation standards and advocate change where poor documentation patterns exist.

92. C   Clinical data include all health care information collected during a patient's episode of care. During the registration or intake process, the admitting diagnosis, provided by the attending physician, is entered on the face sheet. If the patient is admitted through the ED, the chief complaint listed on the ED record is usually the first clinical data collected. A. The principal diagnosis is often not known until after diagnostic tests are conducted. B. Demographic data are not clinical in nature. D. The review of systems is collected during the history and physical, which is typically done after admission to the hospital.

93 B   Answers A and C represent quality indicators for patients with acute myocardial infarction; answer D represents a quality indicator for stroke patients.

94. A   B. Time and means of arrival is required on ED records only. C. Evidence of known advance directive is required on inpatient records only. D. Problem list is required on ambulatory records by the third visit.

95. D   Although many patient health records may feasibly contain all of the orders listed, only the discharge order is required to document the formal release of a patient from the facility. Absence of a discharge order would indicate that the patient left against medical advice and this event should be thoroughly documented as well.

96. D   Answer A refers to the Physical Exam. Answer B refers to the Social History. Answer C refers to the History of Present Illness.

97. D   MDS data are reported directly to the Centers for Medicare and Medicaid Services and must conform to agency standards.

98. A   Answers B, C, and D represent components of the medical history as supplied by the patient, while the physical exam is an entry obtained through objective observation and measurement made by the provider.

REFERENCES

Abdelhak, M., Grostick, S., Hanken, M.A., (2012). *Health information: Management of a strategic resource* (4th ed.). Philadelphia: W. B. Saunders, an imprint of Elsevier.

CMS. Fiscal Year 2009 Quality Measure Reporting for 2010 Payment Update https://www.cms.gov/HospitalQualityInits/downloads/HospitalRHQDAPU200808.pdf

Davis and LaCour. (2014). *Health information technology* (3rd ed.). Maryland, MO: Elsevier (Saunders).

Green, M. A., & Bowie, J. (2011). *Essentials of health information management: Principles and practices* (2nd ed.). Clifton Park, NY: Delmar Cengage Learning.

Horton, L. (2011) *Calculating and reporting healthcare statistics* (4th ed.) Chicago: American Health Information Management Association (AHIMA).

Koch, G. (2008). *Basic allied health statistics and analysis* (3rd ed.). Clifton Park, NY: Delmar Cengage Learning.

LaTour, Eichenwald-Maki (2013). *Health information management: Concepts, principles and practice* (4th ed.). Chicago: American Health Information Management Association (AHIMA).

McWay, D. C. (2014). *Today's health information management, an integrated approach* (2nd ed.). Clifton Park, NY: Delmar Cengage Learning.

Odom-Wesley, B., Brown, D., & Meyers, C. (2009). *Documentation for medical records.* Chicago: American Health Information Management Association (AHIMA).

Peden, A. H. (2012). *Comparative health information management* (3rd ed.). Clifton Park, NY: Delmar Cengage Learning.

Sayles, N. (2013). *Health information management technology: An applied approach* (4th ed.). Chicago: American Health Information Management Association (AHIMA).

Question	RHIA Domain Competencies							RHIT Domain Competencies						
	1	2	3	4	5	6		1	2	3	4	5	6	7
1			X							X				
2	X							X						
3						X						X		
4			X							X				
5	X											X		
6	X							X						
7						X					X			
8	X							X						
9						X				X				
10	X							X						
11						X				X				
12						X							X	
13			X								X			
14	X							X						
15	X							X						
16						X						X		
17	X							X						
18	X							X						
19				X							X			
20						X						X		
21						X						X		
22						X						X		
23						X		X						
24	X							X						
25		X						X						
26			X					X						
27			X							X				
28	X							X						
29	X							X						
30	X							X						
31	X										X			
32						X				X				
33						X		X						
34	X							X						
35				X							X			
36			X					X						
37	X							X						
38	X							X						
39						X		X						
40				X							X			
41						X							X	
42						X		X						
43	X							X						
44	X									X				
45			X					X						
46						X				X				
47	X							X						
48						X				X				
49	X							X						
50						X		X						
51						X				X				
52			X					X						
53		X						X						

Question	RHIA Domain Competencies							RHIT Domain Competencies						
	1	2	3	4	5	6		1	2	3	4	5	6	7
54			X					X						
55	X							X						
56	X							X						
57						X		X						
58	X									X				
59			X								X			
60	X							X						
61						X		X						
62						X				X				
63			X								X			
64	X									X				
65						X				X				
66	X							X						
67						X				X				
68			X									X		
69	X							X						
70			X					X						
71			X								X			
72						X		X						
73	X							X						
74						X							X	
75			X							X				
76			X					X						
77			X						X					
78	X							X						
79						X				X				
80			X								X			
81		X						X						
82						X					X			
83			X					X						
84						X					X			
85	X							X						
86						X		X						
87	X							X						
88						X		X						
89						X		X						
90						X		X						
91				X					X					
92	X							X						
93						X				X				
94	X							X						
95	X							X						
96	X									X				
97						X				X				
98	X							X						

IV. Information Retention and Access

Marjorie H. McNeill, PhD, RHIA, CCS, FAHIMA

1. Which one of the following actions would NOT be included in the professional obligations of the health information practitioner that lead to responsible handling of patient health information?
   A. Educate consumers about their rights and responsibilities regarding the use of their personal health information.
   B. Extend privacy and security principles into all aspects of the data use, access, and control program adopted in the organization.
   C. Honor the patient-centric direction of the national agenda.
   D. Take a compromising position toward optimal interpretation of nonspecific regulations and laws.

REFERENCE: LaTour, Eichenwald-Maki, and Oachs, pp 346–350
Sayles, pp 33, 53, 64, 135, 230, 288, 299, 354, 402, 414, 461, 708, 829, 896, 938, 1096

2. If there is more than one patient with the identical last name, first name, and middle initial, the master patient index entries are then arranged according to the
   A. date of birth.   C. social security number.
   B. date of admission.   D. mother's maiden name.

REFERENCE: Odom-Wesley and Brown, pp 41–42, 93
Sayles, pp 329, 332

3. Which one of the following is NOT a step in developing a health record retention schedule?
   A. conducting an inventory of the facility's records
   B. determining the format and location of storage
   C. assigning all records the same retention period
   D. destroying records that are no longer needed

REFERENCE: Abdelhak, pp 196–197, 529
Green and Bowie, pp 93–94
LaTour, Eichenwald-Maki, and Oachs, pp 274–279
McWay, pp 136–139
Odom-Wesley and Brown, pp 67–69
Sayles, pp 345–346, 364, 788–789

4. What type of filing system is being used if records are filed in the following order: 12-23-75, 12-34-29, 12-35-71, 13-42-14, and 14-32-79?
   A. terminal digit   C. social security number
   B. straight numeric   D. middle digit

REFERENCE: Green and Bowie, pp 212–214
LaTour, Eichenwald-Maki, and Oachs, pp 270–271
Sayles, p 333

5. If there are 150,000 records and the HIM Department receives 3,545 requests for records within a given period of time, what is the request rate?
   A. 2.4%   C. 4.6%
   B. 3.5%   D. 5.1%

REFERENCE: LaTour, Eichenwald-Maki, and Oachs, p 484
McWay, p 204
Math Calculation

6. Which of the following is NOT an advantage of a centralized filing system?
   A. There is less transportation time and effort when a facility operates from several sites.
   B. There is less duplication of effort to create, maintain, and store records.
   C. Record control and security are easier to maintain.
   D. There is decreased cost in space and equipment.

REFERENCE: Green and Bowie, pp 214–215
               Sayles, pp 334–335

7. In a terminal digit filing system, what would be the record number immediately in front of record number 01-06-26?
   A. 00-06-26
   B. 02-06-26
   C. 03-06-26
   D. 99-99-25

REFERENCE: Abdelhak, p 225
               Green and Bowie, pp 212–214
               LaTour, Eichenwald-Maki, and Oachs, pp 270–271
               Sayles, p 333

8. The HIM Department at General Hospital has been experiencing an average 30-minute delay in the retrieval of records requested by the Emergency Department. Which one of the following corrective actions would be most effective in reducing the delay in retrieval of requested records?
   A. Offer a prize to the employee who locates the requested records first.
   B. Review and possibly reengineer the retrieval process to decrease retrieval time.
   C. Allow the requesters to retrieve the record themselves.
   D. Increase file area staff to include one additional file clerk devoted to pulling records for the emergency room.

REFERENCE: LaTour, Eichenwald-Maki, and Oachs, pp 273–274
               Sayles and Trawick, p 136

9. Which one of the following is NOT an advantage of a computerized master patient index?
   A. It allows access to data alphabetically, phonetically, or by date of birth, social security number, medical record, or billing number.
   B. It solves most space and retrieval problems.
   C. It provides other departments with immediate access to the information maintained in the master patient index.
   D. Duplication of patient registration can never occur.

REFERENCE: Green and Bowie, pp 237–239
               LaTour, Eichenwald-Maki, and Oachs, pp 226–227
               Sayles, pp 324–326

10. Color coding of record folders is used to assist in the control of
    A. record tracking.
    B. loose reports.
    C. record completion.
    D. misfiles.

REFERENCE: Green and Bowie, pp 220–221
               LaTour, Eichenwald-Maki, and Oachs, p 274
               Sayles, p 340

11. Which of the following would be considered secondary data?
    A. disease index
    B. implant registry
    C. health record
    D. National Practitioner Data

REFERENCE: Green and Bowie, p 88
LaTour, Eichenwald-Maki, and Oachs, p 368
McWay, p 139
Sayles, pp 432–433

12. Under the Patient Self-Determination Act of 1990, evidence of advance directives
    A. are required to be documented in the health record.
    B. are not required to be documented in the health record.
    C. require a doctor's approval.
    D. must be prepared by an attorney.

REFERENCE: Abdelhak, pp 13, 108
Green and Bowie, p 129
LaTour, Eichenwald-Maki, and Oachs, p 244
McWay, p 77
Sayles, p 104

13. A new Health Information Department has purchased 200 units of 6-shelf files and plans to implement a terminal digit filing system. How many shelves should be allocated to each primary number?
    A. 6
    B. 8
    C. 10
    D. 12

REFERENCE: LaTour, Eichenwald-Maki, and Oachs, p 274
Math Calculation

14. A 200-bed acute care hospital currently has 15 years of paper health records and filing space is limited. What action should be taken?
    A. Return inactive records to each individual patient.
    B. Destroy records of all deceased patients.
    C. Destroy inactive records that exceed the statute of limitations.
    D. Maintain the records indefinitely in hard copy.

REFERENCE: Abdelhak, pp 196–197
Green and Bowie, pp 93–94
LaTour, Eichenwald-Maki, and Oachs, p 276
McWay, pp 136–139

15. Which filing system would provide the most convenient method for the record retrieval of 200 patients consecutively admitted to the hospital?
    A. terminal digit
    B. unit
    C. straight numeric
    D. serial unit

REFERENCE: Green and Bowie, p 212
LaTour, Eichenwald-Maki, and Oachs, p 270

16. What is the chief criterion for determining record inactivity?
    A. Medicare's definition of inactivity
    B. amount of space available for storage of newer records
    C. efficiency of microfilming
    D. preference of the medical staff

REFERENCE: Green and Bowie, pp 93–94
                   LaTour, Eichenwald-Maki, and Oachs, p 273

17. Out of 2,543 records requested from the HIM Department, 2,375 were located. What is the filing accuracy rate?
    A. 6.61%
    B. 75.33%
    C. 89.01%
    D. 93.39%

REFERENCE: McWay, p 204
                   Math Calculation
                   Sayles, pp 358–359

18. Which set of records filed consecutively on a shelf displays terminal digit filing order?
    A. 00-79-99, 00-79-01, 99-78-99
    B. 57-78-00, 57-78-01, 56-78-99
    C. 99-05-26, 01-06-26, 49-04-02
    D. 55-55-55, 33-33-33, 44-44-44

REFERENCE: Green and Bowie, pp 212–214
                   LaTour, Eichenwald-Maki, and Oachs, pp 270–271
                   Sayles, p 333

19. In the master patient index, which is filed by last name, Jill Thomas-Jones would be
    A. J-I-L-L-T-H-O-M-A-S-J-O-N-E-S
    C. T-H-O-M-A-S-J-O-N-E-S, J-I-L-L
    B. T-H-O-M-A-S, J-I-L-L-J-O-N-E-S
    D. J-O-N-E-S, J-I-L-L-T-H-O-M-A-S

REFERENCE: Green and Bowie, p 210
                   Sayles, p 329

20. According to terminal digit filing, what would be the number of the record immediately after record number 99-99-30?
    A. 99-98-30
    B. 00-00-31
    C. 01-00-31
    D. 99-99-31

REFERENCE: Green and Bowie, pp 212–214
                   LaTour, Eichenwald-Maki, and Oachs, pp 270–271
                   Sayles, p 333

21. How many years does the CMS regulations require that health records be maintained? Medicare's Conditions of Participation for Hospitals requires that patient health records be retained for at least _____ years unless a longer period is required by state or local laws.
    A. 3
    B. 5
    C. 7
    D. 10

REFERENCE: Green and Bowie, p 93
                   LaTour, Eichenwald-Maki, and Oachs, p 275
                   Sayles, p 379

22. Your state regulations require health records to be kept for a statute of limitations period of 7 years. Federal law requires records to be retained for 5 years. The minimum retention period for health records in your facility should be
   A. 5 years.   C. 10 years.
   B. 7 years.   D. either 5 or 7 years, as determined by the facility.

REFERENCE: Abdelhak, p 526
                 LaTour, Eichenwald-Maki, and Oachs, p 275
                 McWay, p 136
                 Sayles, p 379

23. Which of the following technologies works best with automated record-tracking systems to speed the data entry process?
   A. discharge lists   C. compressible filing units
   B. bar codes   D. computerized chart-out slips

REFERENCE: Abdelhak, p 280
                 Green and Bowie, p 226
                 LaTour, Eichenwald-Maki, and Oachs, p 88
                 Sayles, pp 343, 351

24. A HIM Department, currently using 2,540 linear filing inches to store records, plans to purchase new open-shelf filing units. Each of the shelves in a new 6-shelf unit measures 36 linear filing inches. It is estimated that an additional 400 filing inches should be planned for to allow for 5-year expansion needs. How many new file shelving units should be purchased?
   A. 11   C. 13
   B. 12   D. 14

REFERENCE: Green and Bowie, p 219
                 LaTour, Eichenwald-Maki, and Oachs, p 274
                 McWay, p 135
                 Sayles, pp 337–339

25. Microfilmed records are considered
   A. inadmissible evidence.
   B. never admissible as hearsay evidence.
   C. acceptable as courtroom evidence.
   D. not admissible as secondary evidence.

REFERENCE: Sayles, p 387

26. A research request has been received by the HIM Department from the Quality Improvement Committee. The Committee plans to review the records of all patients who were admitted with CHF in the month of January 2014. Which of the following indices would be the best source in locating the needed records?
   A. master patient index   C. disease index
   B. physician index   D. operation index

REFERENCE: Green and Bowie, p 240
                 LaTour, Eichenwald-Maki, and Oachs, p 370
                 McWay, p 140
                 Sayles, pp 324, 398, 436–337

27. How many inches are recommended for aisles between file units when using stationary open-shelf files?
    A. 24
    B. 36
    C. 60
    D. 72

REFERENCE: LaTour, Eichenwald-Maki, and Oachs, p 274

28. In a manual record-tracking system, no record should be removed from the file without being replaced by a(n)
    A. 8½ × 11-inch charge-out slip.
    B. empty file folder.
    C. paddle.
    D. outguide.

REFERENCE: Green and Bowie, p 226
               Sayles, p 343

29. Which of the following should not be included in the documentation of record destruction?
    A. statement that records were destroyed in the normal course of business
    B. method of destruction
    C. signature of the individuals supervising and witnessing the destruction
    D. dates not covered in destruction

REFERENCE: AHIMA Practice Brief "Retention and Destruction of Health Information"
               Green and Bowie, pp 96–97
               LaTour, Eichenwald-Maki, and Oachs, p 279
               McWay, p 139
               Odom-Wesley and Brown, pp 69–70
               Sayles, p 346

30. If the HIM Department has purchased 100 units of 8-shelf files and plans to use the terminal digit filing system, how many shelves should be allocated to each primary number?
    A. 8
    B. 10
    C. 12
    D. 100

REFERENCE: Math Calculation

31. Which of the following is NOT a consideration when implementing a disaster plan?
    A. Include disaster training in staff orientation.
    B. Establish a plan for conducting drills.
    C. Provide staff with tools needed to implement the plan.
    D. Test the disaster plan only once.

REFERENCE: LaTour, Eichenwald-Maki, and Oachs, p 292
               McWay, pp 326–328
               Sayles, p 868

32. Which of the following lists is in correct alphabetical order?
    A. Ferlazzo, Joshua; Ferlazzo, Joshua P.; Ferlazzo, Joshua Philip; Ferlazzo, J.
    B. Ferlazzo, J.; Ferlazzo, Joshua; Ferlazzo, Joshua P.; Ferlazzo, Joshua Philip
    C. Ferlazzo, Joshua; Ferlazzo, Joshua P.; Ferlazzo, J.; Ferlazzo, Joshua Philip
    D. Ferlazzo, Joshua A.; Ferlazzo, B.; Ferlazzo, Joshua; Ferlazzo, Joshua Phillip

REFERENCE: Green and Bowie, p 210
               Sayles, p 332

33. Mary Schnering was admitted to Community Hospital on 10/3/13 and assigned a record number of 54-47-53. The patient was later admitted on 1/14/14 and assigned the number 54-88-42. Both records were eventually filed under 54-88-42. What type of numbering/filing system is being used at Community Hospital?
    A. serial-unit
    B. serial
    C. unit
    D. terminal digit

REFERENCE: Green and Bowie, p 209
               LaTour, Eichenwald-Maki, and Oachs, p 270
               McWay, p 135
               Sayles, p 327

34. Capital Health Center is moving to a new facility in December 2015. The CEO is projecting a conversion to an electronic health record system by then. This new facility will not include space for the filing of paper-based health records. Which of the following items would not be considered when planning this conversion?
    A. changing role of department functions and work flow
    B. challenges of maintaining records that are partially paper and partially electronic
    C. whether to scan older paper records
    D. relationship with the microfilm vendor

REFERENCE: LaTour, Eichenwald-Maki, and Oachs, pp 279–292
               Sayles, p 328

35. What microform should the HIM practitioner select if the records must be unitized and color-coded for filing purposes?
    A. roll microfilm
    B. cartridge
    C. jacket microfilm
    D. cassette

REFERENCE: LaTour, Eichenwald-Maki, and Oachs, pp 276–277

36. In retrieval of optical image files, cache memory
    A. decreases access time for all users on the system.
    B. increases exchange time on the jukebox.
    C. is resident on the jukebox.
    D. is a way of defragmenting a WORM platter.

REFERENCE: Sayles, p 321
               Sayles and Trawick, p 15

37. At Community Hospital the average admission will create a file that will take up 0.25 inch of file space. Each new ER record requires 0.125 inch of file space. Approximately 25,000 new patients are admitted per year and 15,000 ER patients are treated per year. The shelving cost is $1.05 per filing inch. How much money should be allocated for storage space in next year's budget?
    A. $8,531.25
    B. $8,125.00
    C. $853.25
    D. $1,875.00

REFERENCE: LaTour, Eichenwald-Maki, and Oachs, p 274
               Math Calculation
               Sayles, pp 337–339

38. On his 12/23/13 admission to Metropolitan Hospital, David Robinson was assigned the medical record number 07-23-38. The previous record number assigned to Mr. Robinson during a 9/1/13 admission was 07-10-47. In a serial numbering/filing system, how would these records be filed?
   A. Both records are combined under 07-10-47.
   B. Both records are combined under 07-23-38.
   C. Each admission is filed under its own number.
   D. Previous records are brought forward and filed under the latest number issued.

REFERENCE: Green and Bowie, pp 206–207
               LaTour, Eichenwald-Maki, and Oachs, p 270
               McWay, p 135
               Sayles, pp 337–338

39. The same patient was admitted on three different occasions and assigned a new medical record number each time. In order to correct this situation in a unit numbering system, which medical record number should be used given the following information?

Admitted 5/04/13	Patty Miller	23-33-56
Admitted 6/05/13	P. J. Miller	25-56-88
Admitted 9/27/13	Patricia Miller	27-12-12

   A. Void the first and last numbers and file all admissions under 25-56-88.
   B. Delete all previous numbers and assign a completely new number.
   C. Void the first two numbers and file all admissions under 27-12-12.
   D. Void the last two numbers and file all admissions under 23-33-56.

REFERENCE: Green and Bowie, pp 207–208
               LaTour, Eichenwald-Maki, and Oachs, p 270
               McWay, p 135
               Sayles, pp 327–328

40. The health care providers in a large teaching hospital require access to paper health records 24 hours a day, 7 days a week. To secure the area and continue to maintain accessibility, the Director of the HIM Department should
   A. staff the department with personnel 24 hours a day.
   B. be on call every evening and weekends for emergency requests.
   C. train security guards to retrieve records after the department closes.
   D. arrange for records to be retrieved at 7:00 AM every morning.

REFERENCE: Green and Bowie, pp 28–29
               LaTour, Eichenwald-Maki, and Oachs, p 723

41. As a prerequisite to phasing in a new imaging system, what process would facilitate automatic indexing?
   A. redesigning forms to include bar codes
   B. removing portions of the patient record that will not be scanned
   C. converting all microfilm to optical disk format
   D. scanning only emergency room records initially

REFERENCE: LaTour, Eichenwald-Maki, and Oachs, p 268
               McWay, p 313
               Sayles, p 1203

42. Which of the following is NOT a safety hazard in the file area of the HIM Department?
    A. tightly packed open-shelf files
    B. heavy objects placed in top file drawers
    C. stepladders that are fully open and locked in place
    D. plastic wastebasket for trash

REFERENCE: Abdelhak, p 650
               McWay, p 373

43. A HIM Department wants to buy new open-shelf filing units for its file expansion. Each of the shelves in a new 6-shelf unit measures 33 linear filing inches. There will be an estimated 1,000 records to file. The average record is 1-inch thick. How many filing units should be purchased?
    A. 2   C. 6
    B. 4   D. 8

REFERENCE: Green and Bowie, p 219
               LaTour, Eichenwald-Maki, and Oachs, p 274
               Sayles, pp 337–339

44. Which of the following microform types is the least expensive to prepare and results in the greatest storage density?
    A. microfilm jackets   C. microfiche
    B. roll microfilm   D. ultrafiche

REFERENCE: Green and Bowie, p 95
               LaTour, Eichenwald-Maki, and Oachs, pp 276–277
               Sayles, p 340

45. Brian Hills was discharged from the hospital after a 3-day hospitalization and instructed to return to the outpatient department for follow-up care. On his first visit as an outpatient, a new record was created and he was assigned a new record number. Following completion of the outpatient appointment, his outpatient record is filed permanently in the outpatient department. What is the filing system used in this situation?
    A. decentralized   C. centralized
    B. unit record   D. terminal digit

REFERENCE: Green and Bowie, pp 215–216
               LaTour, Eichenwald-Maki, and Oachs, p 221
               Sayles, p 708

46. The master patient index must, at a minimum, include sufficient information to
    A. summarize the patient's medical history.
    B. list all physicians who have ever treated the patient.
    C. uniquely identify the patient.
    D. justify the patient's hospital bill.

REFERENCE: Abdelhak, p 126
               Eichenwald-Maki and Petterson, p 81
               Green and Bowie, p 237
               LaTour, Eichenwald-Maki, and Oachs, pp 271–272
               McWay, pp 139–140
               Odom-Wesley and Brown, p 78
               Sayles, pp 322, 436

47. Dr. Gray has applied for medical staff privileges at your hospital. What database would you research to determine if he has been denied medical staff privileges at another hospital?
    A. National Practitioner Data Bank
    B. Healthcare Integrity and Protection Data Bank
    C. MEDPAR file
    D. State Administrative Data Bank

REFERENCE: Abdelhak, p 472
              Green and Bowie, pp 251, 255
              LaTour, Eichenwald-Maki, and Oachs, p 330
              Sayles, p 657

48. Which type of patient information system does the Joint Commission suggest that hospitals use?
    A. unit record
    B. computer-based patient record
    C. protocol for requesting information, whereby the request is provided to the practitioner in a timely manner
    D. any one of the above

REFERENCE: Joint Commission

49. A health information manager develops a formal plan or record retention schedule for the automatic transfer of records to inactive storage and potential destruction based on all but which one of the following factors?
    A. statute of limitations
    B. volume of research
    C. readmission rate
    D. file area staffing

REFERENCE: Green and Bowie, pp 93–94
              LaTour, Eichenwald-Maki, and Oachs, pp 276–279
              McWay, pp 136–139
              Sayles, pp 336–337

50. Which of the following is NOT a benefit of the electronic document management system in the HIM Department?
    A. online availability of information
    B. multiuser simultaneous access
    C. decreased use of computer technology
    D. system security and confidentiality

REFERENCE: Green and Bowie, p 109
              McWay, p 312
              Sayles, pp 59, 361

51. Which one of the following is an advantage of straight numeric filing over terminal digit filing?
    A. All sections of the file expand uniformly.
    B. The training period is short.
    C. Work can be evenly distributed, causing accountability for accuracy in each of the 100 sections.
    D. Inactive records can be purged evenly.

REFERENCE: Green and Bowie, pp 212–214
              LaTour, Eichenwald-Maki, and Oachs, p 270
              Sayles, p 333

52. Which one of the following is NOT an electronic document management system component?
    A. scanner
    B. file server
    C. jukebox
    D. reader-printer

REFERENCE: Sayles and Trawick, pp 161–163

53. Which of the following items is the Health Information Manager primarily concerned with when purchasing file guides?
    A. cost and color
    B. durability and visibility
    C. cost and visibility
    D. color and durability

REFERENCE: Green and Bowie, pp 224–225

54. Palm Beach Healthcare Center has been in operation for 13 years. It has 6,000 admissions per year. The facility has expanded and will allow for 200 more admissions per year from now on. There are 2,500 linear feet of filing space available and half is being used. The facility expects a 30% readmission rate. If a unit numbering/filing system is used, how many file folders will be needed for the next year?
    A. 1,800
    B. 1,860
    C. 4,340
    D. 6,200

REFERENCE: LaTour, Eichenwald-Maki, and Oachs, p 270
McWay, p 135
Math Calculation

55. As Director of the HIM Department you have become aware of instances of unauthorized access to the record file area. After considering several options to limit or restrict access to the area, you decide to
    A. install a computerized access panel.
    B. hire a security guard to monitor entrance to the file area.
    C. convert from a terminal digit filing system to serial unit filing.
    D. utilize a sign-in and sign-out log for admittance to the file area.

REFERENCE: Abdelhak, p 543
LaTour, Eichenwald-Maki, and Oachs, p 133
McWay, p 265
Sayles and Trawick, p 319

56. What technical security controls do electronic health record systems employ that are different from paper-based health record systems?
    A. audit trails
    B. data encryption protocols
    C. user-based access controls
    D. all of the above

REFERENCE: Eichenwald-Maki and Petterson, p 51
Sayles, pp 159, 753
Sayles and Trawick, pp 319–320

57. The Chief of the Medical Staff requests a report on the number of coronary artery bypass grafts performed by a particular physician in April of the previous year. Where would the health information manager look for this information?
    A. patient register
    B. disease index
    C. operation index
    D. birth defects register

REFERENCE: Green and Bowie, p 240
LaTour, Eichenwald-Maki, and Oachs, p 369
McWay, p 140
Odom-Wesley and Brown, p 79
Sayles, pp 398, 437

58. A major consideration in a hospital or facility closure is to
    A. notify all patients to pick up their original records by the date of closure.
    B. seek approval for destruction of all records with a last date of treatment over 3 years ago.
    C. ensure that authorized parties have access to the information as provided by law.
    D. arrange for donating the records to an HIA/HIT education program for student use.

REFERENCE: Green and Bowie, pp 97–98
              LaTour, Eichenwald-Maki, and Oachs, p 276
              McWay, p 138

59. What follow-up rate does the American College of Surgeons mandate for all cancer cases to meet approval requirements as a cancer program?
    A. 70%   C. 90%
    B. 80%   D. 100%

REFERENCE: American College of Surgeons' Cancer Program Manual

60. In negotiating a contract with a commercial storage company for storage of inactive records, what would be the most important issue to clarify in writing?
    A. who completes the list of what records are to be stored
    B. what are the billing terms
    C. who will purge inactive files for transfer
    D. confidentiality policies and liability concerns

REFERENCE: Green and Bowie, pp 94–95
              Sayles and Trawick, pp 127–130

61. Which index is used by the HIM department to link the patient's name and number in relation to access and retention of the clinical record?
    A. physician index   C. master patient index
    B. disease index   D. operation index

REFERENCE: Abdelhak, p 107
              LaTour, Eichenwald-Maki, and Oachs, pp 271–272
              McWay, p 139
              Sayles, pp 318, 332

62. Unless state or federal laws require longer time periods, AHIMA recommends that patient health information for minors be retained for at least how long?
    A. age of majority plus statute of limitation
    B. 10 years after the most recent encounter
    C. 10 years after the age of majority
    D. permanently

REFERENCE: AHIMA Practice Brief "Retention and Destruction of Health Information"
              Green and Bowie, p 94
              LaTour, Eichenwald-Maki, and Oachs, pp 278, 285
              McWay, p 136
              Sayles, pp 346, 383, 789

63. A health care facility has made a decision to destroy computerized data. AHIMA recommends which one of the following as the preferred method of destruction for computerized data?
    A. overwriting data with a series of characters
    B. disk reformatting
    C. magnetic degaussing
    D. overwriting the backup tapes

REFERENCE: AHIMA Practice Brief "Retention and Destruction of Health Information"
                Odom-Wesley and Brown, p 69
                Sayles, pp 346–347, 1060

64. Which of the following statements would be found in the laboratory report section of the health record?
    A. BUN reported as 20 mg
    B. Morphine sulfate gr. 1/4 q.4h. for pain
    C. IV sodium Pentothal 1% started at 9:05 AM
    D. TPR recorded q.h. for 12 hours

REFERENCE: Abdelhak, p 115
                Green and Bowie, p 170
                LaTour, Eichenwald-Maki, and Oachs, p 250
                Odom-Wesley and Brown, p 141
                Sayles, p 86

65. Which of the following is a disadvantage of terminal digit filing as compared to straight numeric filing?
    A. File personnel are crowded in the highest numbers.
    B. Inactive records are pulled from one common area.
    C. The training period is slightly longer.
    D. Files expand at the end of the number series, requiring back shifting.

REFERENCE: Green and Bowie, pp 212–214
                Sayles, p 333

66. The main advantage of phonetic filing is
    A. typographical errors are eliminated.
    B. spelling accuracy is encouraged.
    C. emphasis is placed on a foreign language.
    D. names that sound alike are filed together.

REFERENCE: Green and Bowie, p 199
                Sayles, p 323

67. Electronic health record built-in tools that can make data capture easier include all but which one of the following?
    A. data dictionaries
    B. flow process charts
    C. automated quality measures
    D. clinical decision support systems

REFERENCE: Abdelhak, pp 507–508
                LaTour, Eichenwald-Maki, and Oachs, p 172
                Sayles, p 420

68. If the file clerks are having trouble locating the terminal digit sections quickly, the filing supervisor could add more
    A. outguides.
    C. requisitions.
    B. file guides.
    D. file maintenance staff.

REFERENCE: Green and Bowie, p 224

69. The HIM Department receives a request for a certified copy of a birth certificate on a patient born in the hospital 30 years ago. The Department should
    A. issue a copy of the birth certificate from the patient's record.
    B. direct the request to the state's office of vital records.
    C. direct the request to the attending physician.
    D. issue a copy of the newborn's record.

REFERENCE: Abdelhak, p 108
               Green and Bowie, pp 134–135
               Sayles, p 455

70. A surgeon requests the name of a patient he admitted on January 11, 2013. Which of the following would be used to retrieve this information?
    A. master patient index
    C. admission register
    B. number index
    D. operation index

REFERENCE: Green and Bowie, p 244
               McWay, p 142
               Sayles, p 995

71. Which of the following is NOT a consideration in file folder size and design?
    A. reinforced top and side panels
    C. vendor location
    B. scoring on folder bottoms
    D. weight of folder

REFERENCE: Green and Bowie, pp 219–220
               Sayles, pp 339–340

72. Where in the health record would the following statement be located?

"Microscopic Diagnosis: Liver (needle biopsy), metastatic adenocarcinoma"?
    A. operative report
    C. anesthesia report
    B. pathology report
    D. radiology report

REFERENCE: Abdelhak, p 114
               Green and Bowie, pp 165–168
               LaTour, Eichenwald-Maki, and Oachs, p 250
               Odom-Wesley and Brown, p 171
               Sayles, pp 86, 92

73. The HIM Department is located in a hospital that provides health record access 24 hours a day, 7 days a week. To secure the file area and continue to maintain accessibility, the department director should
    A. be on call during the evening hours.
    B. staff the file area with file clerks on all three shifts.
    C. instruct medical staff in record retrieval.
    D. instruct nurse supervisors in record retrieval.

REFERENCE: Green and Bowie, pp 28–29
               LaTour, Eichenwald-Maki, and Oachs, pp 273–274

74. A file area has limited space, medium file activity, and two file clerks. The HIM department would benefit from choosing which type of storage equipment?
    A. compressible filing units
    B. lateral filing cabinets
    C. open shelf files
    D. motorized revolving units

REFERENCE: LaTour, Eichenwald-Maki, and Oachs, p 274
               Sayles, p 336

75. When evaluating an outside contract microfilm company, all but which of the following are important factors to rate?
    A. cost
    B. emergency returns
    C. storage after filming
    D. cache memory

REFERENCE: LaTour, Eichenwald-Maki, and Oachs, p 227
               Sayles, p 341

76. Under the HIPAA Privacy Rule, when destruction services are outsourced to a business associate, the contract must provide that the business associate will establish the permitted and required uses and disclosures and include which of the following elements?
    A. method of destruction or disposal
    B. time that will elapse between acquisition and destruction or disposal
    C. safeguards against breaches
    D. all of the above

REFERENCE: AHIMA Practice Brief "Retention and Destruction of Health Information"
               Sayles, p 347

77. The clinical laboratory department staff can use a database that allows them to see what laboratory tests were conducted and the results of those tests. By contrast, the billing department staff can only see that portion of the database that lists the laboratory tests that generate a charge, but they cannot see the test results. What kind of control is this an example of?
    A. concurrency
    B. access
    C. integrity
    D. cost

REFERENCE: McWay, p 265
               Sayles, pp 133, 188, 228
               Sayles and Trawick, p 319

78. When operating under the Health Insurance Portability and Accountability Act of 1996, what is a basic tenet in information security for health care professionals to follow?
    A. Security training is provided to all levels of staff.
    B. Patients are not educated about their right to confidentiality of health information.
    C. The information system encourages mass copying, printing, and downloading of patient records.
    D. When paper-based records are no longer needed, they are bundled and sent to a recycling center.

REFERENCE: AHIMA Practice Brief "Information Security: A Checklist for Health care
               Professionals"
               McWay, p 292
               Sayles, pp 1040, 1053

79. Which one of the following features should NOT be considered when designing screens to capture quality health data?
    A. a prompt for more information
    B. built-in alerts to notify users of possible errors
    C. the use of abbreviations on data fields
    D. left to right and bottom to top formatting

REFERENCE: Sayles, pp 125, 385–386
                Sayles and Trawick, p 177

80. When health care facilities close or medical practices dissolve, procedures for disposition of patient records should take into consideration all but which one of the following EXCEPT
    A. state laws and licensing standards.
    B. Communities of Practice requirements.
    C. needs and wishes of patients.
    D. Medicare requirements.

REFERENCE: AHIMA Practice Brief "Protecting Patient Information After a Facility Closure"
                Green and Bowie, pp 97–98
                McWay, p 138

81. Case finding methods for patients with diabetes include a review of all but which one of the following?
    A. health plans   C. billing data
    B. CPT diagnostic codes   D. medication lists

REFERENCE: LaTour, Eichenwald-Maki, and Oachs, p 373
                Sayles, pp 437, 443–444

82. What type of plan is Joint Commission-accredited facilities required to maintain to protect health information from catastrophes such as fire, flooding, bomb threats, and theft?
    A. budget   C. case management
    B. disaster   D. patient care

REFERENCE: AHIMA Practice Brief, "Disaster Planning for Health Information"
                McWay, p 326

83. Which of the following is NOT an alternative storage method for paper-based records?
    A. microfilm   C. computer
    B. optical imaging   D. outguide

REFERENCE: Green and Bowie, pp 94–96
                LaTour, Eichenwald-Maki, and Oachs, pp 273–274

84. Which of the following issues would be of LEAST concern when storing health records in off-site storage?
    A. operating hours of the storage facility
    B. safety and confidentiality procedures
    C. filing order of the records
    D. procedure for request of a record in an emergency

REFERENCE: Green and Bowie, pp 94–95
                LaTour, Eichenwald-Maki, and Oachs, p 278
                Sayles, p 1027

85. The HIM Department maintains 500,000 records and responds to 5,000 requests for records in a given period of time. What is the record usage rate?
    A. 0.01%
    C. 5%
    B. 1%
    D. 10%

REFERENCE: LaTour, Eichenwald-Maki, and Oachs, p 274
              McWay, p 204
              Math Calculation

86. Which one of the following is NOT a data retrieval tool?
    A. color
    C. point-and-click fields
    B. sound
    D. icons

REFERENCE: Sayles and Trawick, p 176

87. When engaging the services of a microfilm vendor, all but which one of the following factors should be included in the contract?
    A. who performs record preparation
    B. provision for destruction of original records
    C. type of reader or printer needed to view the microfilm
    D. confidentiality of information being filmed

REFERENCE: LaTour, Eichenwald-Maki, and Oachs, p 277
              Sayles, p 341

88. What would be the most cost-effective and prudent course of action for the storage or disposition of 250,000 records at a large teaching and research hospital?
    A. storing the records off-site at a cost of $25,000 per year
    B. microfilming all 250,000 records for the cost of $195,000
    C. purging all death records and storing them off-site
    D. destroying all records older than the time frame required by the statute of limitations

REFERENCE: Abdelhak, pp 196–197
              LaTour, Eichenwald-Maki, and Oachs, pp 276–279
              McWay, pp 136–139

89. The total number of records filed during the month is 2,500 and, upon completion of a filing accuracy study, 90 records were not found. What is the accuracy rate for filing?
    A. 1%
    C. 28%
    B. 4%
    D. 96%

REFERENCE: Johns, pp 417–418
              McWay, p 204
              Sayles, p 315
              Math Calculation

90. A quality control measure that should be established for the filing, storage, and retrieval of health records includes criteria for the
    A. accuracy of analyzing records.   C. filing of loose materials.
    B. number of incomplete records.   D. tracking of release of information requests.

REFERENCE: LaTour, Eichenwald-Maki, and Oachs, pp 273–274
              Sayles, p 358

91. According to AHIMA's recommended retention standards, which one of the following types of health information does NOT need to be retained permanently?
    A. physician index
    B. register of births
    C. register of surgical procedures
    D. register of deaths

REFERENCE: AHIMA Practice Brief "Retention and Destruction of Health Information"
                McWay, p 136
                Sayles, p 346

92. For a health care facility to meet its document destruction needs, the certificate of destruction should include all but which one of the following elements?
    A. unique and serialized transaction number
    B. location of destruction
    C. patient notification
    D. acceptance of fiduciary responsibility

REFERENCE: LaTour, Eichenwald-Maki, and Oachs, p 279
                McWay, p 139
                Odom-Wesley and Brown, pp 69–70
                Sayles, pp 346–347

93. The steps in developing a record retention program include all but which one of the following?
    A. determining the storage format and location
    B. notifying the courts of the destruction
    C. assigning each record a retention period
    D. destroying records that are no longer needed

REFERENCE: LaTour, Eichenwald-Maki, and Oachs, pp 276–279
                McWay, pp 136–139
                Odom-Wesley and Brown, pp 67–68
                Sayles, pp 343–347, 364, 380, 388–389

94. A health care facility has received a request to participate in a statewide study on cleft lip and cleft palate. This study would include data from the past year and subsequent years. Given that each of the data sources cited below contains the necessary information, the initial data would be most easily collected from the
    A. newborn records.
    B. state bureau of vital statistics.
    C. maternal records.
    D. birth defects registry.

REFERENCE: Abdelhak, pp 492–494
                LaTour, Eichenwald-Maki, and Oachs, p 373
                Sayles, pp 342–343

95. An example of a primary data source is the
    A. physician index.
    B. health record.
    C. cancer registry.
    D. hospital statistical report.

REFERENCE: Abdelhak, p 481
                LaTour, Eichenwald-Maki, and Oachs, p 368
                McWay, p 139
                Sayles, p 443

96. Which one of the following is NOT considered a challenge in the adoption of an electronic health record system?
   A. design of the work flow and processes
   B. physician willingness to adopt
   C. contribution to the quality of patient care
   D. individual state legal and regulatory issues

REFERENCE: LaTour, Eichenwald-Maki, and Oachs, p 119
                Sayles and Trawick, pp 251–252

97. Fetal monitoring strips are part of the _____ record and should be maintained_____.
   A. newborn's; 10 years past the age of majority
   B. mother's; according to the length of time required for a minor's records
   C. newborn's; according to the time period specified in the state's statute of limitations
   D. mother's; 10 years

REFERENCE: Abdelhak, p 114
                LaTour, Eichenwald-Maki, and Oachs, p 275

98. Which one of the following would NOT be a strategy when purchasing an electronic health record system?
   A. Identify stakeholders from different organizational levels and engage them appropriately.
   B. Identify return on investment or cost-benefit analysis.
   C. Identify system requirements.
   D. Broaden the vendor field and select several vendors of choice.

REFERENCE: AHIMA Practice Brief "Purchasing Strategies for EHR Systems"
                LaTour, Eichenwald-Maki, and Oachs, pp 145–146
                Sayles, p 862

99. How many years does the Food and Drug Administration require research records pertaining to cancer patients be maintained?
   A. 5   C. 30
   B. 7   D. permanently

REFERENCE: AHIMA Practice Brief "Retention and Destruction of Health Information"

100. What data cannot be retrieved from the MEDPAR?
   A. ICD-9-CM diagnosis and procedure codes
   B. Charges broken down by specific types of services
   C. Non-Medicare patient data
   D. Data on the provider

REFERENCE: LaTour, Eichenwald-Maki, and Oachs, p 377
                McWay, p 187
                Sayles, pp 145, 450–451

101. As the filing and retrieval supervisor, you are evaluating storage devices for a new health information management system. Which one of the following would you NOT consider as an option for storing health information?
   A. light pen   C. microfilm
   B. optical disc   D. magnetic disk

REFERENCE: Sayles, pp 874, 995
                Sayles and Trawick, pp 12, 20, 165

102. General Hospital utilizes various related files that include clinical and financial data to generate reports such as MS-DRG case mix reports. What application would be MOST effective for this activity?
    A. desktop publishing
    B. word processing
    C. database management system
    D. command interpreter

REFERENCE: Abdelhak, p 268
                LaTour, Eichenwald-Maki, and Oachs, pp 185–186
                Sayles, pp 153, 499, 59, 850, 879, 900, 1188

103. The Director of Health Information Management has been asked by the Board of Trustees to justify support for the use of handheld devices by the medical staff for point-of-service input. Which one of the following reasons would NOT be included in the Director's response?
    A. decreased clinical documentation errors
    B. increased work efficiency
    C. faster access to health data
    D. elimination of the need for expensive desktop computers

REFERENCE: Abdelhak, p 279
                LaTour, Eichenwald-Maki, and Oachs, p 96

104. The Assistant Director of Record Processing is evaluating software packages for a chart tracking system in the HIM Department. What is the BEST method to verify that the software will work as marketed?
    A. Visit corporate headquarters of the vendor.
    B. Perform a vendor reference check.
    C. Read consumer reports before buying.
    D. Test the software prior to purchase.

REFERENCE: Abdelhak, pp 343–345
                LaTour, Eichenwald-Maki, and Oachs, pp 146–148
                Sayles, p 862

105. Concern for health data loss and misuse within the HIM department requires that the health information practitioner evaluate
    A. security controls and access privileges of staff.
    B. policies and procedures developed to safeguard privacy and security.
    C. use of a back-up system.
    D. all of the above.

REFERENCE: LaTour, Eichenwald-Maki, and Oachs, pp 187–188
                McWay pp 290–292
                Sayles, pp 1065–1066

106. Lewis-Beck Medical Center has been collecting data on patient satisfaction for six months. It is ready to start retrieving data from the database to improve clinical services. Which tool should be used?
    A. HTML   C. XML
    B. SQL   D. data dictionary

REFERENCE: Sayles, pp 59, 876, 879–880, 886
                Sayles and Trawick, pp 177–178

107. The Assistant Director of HIM is evaluating software that would use electronic logging of the location of incomplete and delinquent records as they move through the completion process. What departmental function is this most useful for?
    A. release of information
    B. coding
    C. chart tracking
    D. transcription

REFERENCE: Green and Bowie, pp 224–226
               LaTour, Eichenwald-Maki, and Oachs, p 266
               Sayles, p 959

108. The hospital administrator is making a strategic decision by querying various institutional databases for information. What type of system is the hospital administrator using?
    A. electronic health record system
    B. results reporting system
    C. financial information system
    D. executive information system

REFERENCE: LaTour, Eichenwald-Maki, and Oachs, p 95
               Sayles, pp 885–886, 924
               Sayles and Trawick, p 213

109. University Hospital has the messaging technology to securely route an alert for a patient's possible drug interaction or abnormal lab result to the appropriate physician's pager number. Which one of the following is the medical staff using?
    A. intranet
    B. extranet
    C. Internet
    D. clinical information system

REFERENCE: LaTour, Eichenwald-Maki, and Oachs, p 90
               Sayles, pp 855–856
               Sayles and Trawick, p 226

110. The HIM practitioner's duty to retain health information by archiving and storage of health data includes
    A. strategies that consider accessibility, natural disasters, and innovations in storage technology.
    B. strategies ensuring that inactive records are as secure as active records.
    C. a retention plan for multiple volumes of records.
    D. all of the above.

REFERENCE: Abdelhak, pp 196–197
               McWay, pp 132–139
               Sayles, pp 788–789

111. As HIM director, you must ensure a means to regulate access and ensure preservation of data in the health care facility's computer system. Which of the following security measures can be implemented to prevent privacy violations in this computer system?
    A. authentication
    B. encryption
    C. disaster recovery plan
    D. all of the above

REFERENCE: LaTour, Eichenwald-Maki, and Oachs, p 133
               McWay, p 209
               Sayles, pp 883, 1038
               Sayles and Trawick, p 319

112. Health Informatics, Inc. is a vendor with a large collection of clinical information systems and hospital information systems that are designed to share data without human or technical intervention. This is a(an)
    A. interfaced system.
    B. integrated system.
    C. OLAP.
    D. standard.

REFERENCE: LaTour, Eichenwald-Maki, and Oachs, pp 132–133
              Sayles, pp 996–997
              Sayles and Trawick, pp 110–111

113. The function of a(an) _____ is limited to data retrieval.
    A. electronic health record
    B. executive information system
    C. database management system
    D. clinical data repository

REFERENCE: Abdelhak, pp 186–187
              LaTour, Eichenwald-Maki, and Oachs, p 84
              Odom-Wesley and Brown, p 225
              Sayles, p 994
              Sayles and Trawick, pp 72, 100

114. The Director of the HIM Department is explaining incentives to physicians for entering their clinical documentation in the electronic health record. Which one of the following would be the key advantage in using this type of data entry?
    A. Enhanced databases will provide information for improved clinical care.
    B. Training will be offered by the hospital.
    C. Those physicians not in compliance will be denied admitting privileges.
    D. Multiple users will not have access to the same information simultaneously.

REFERENCE: LaTour, Eichenwald-Maki, and Oachs, pp 140–142
              Odom-Wesley and Brown, p 224

115. University Hospital, a 900 bed tertiary health care organization, is undergoing an information systems development. What system would best meet its needs?
    A. application service provider model
    B. clinical workstation
    C. IBM Medical Information Systems Program
    D. legacy system

REFERENCE: Abdelhak, p 291
              LaTour, Eichenwald-Maki, and Oachs, p 140
              Sayles, pp 708, 1183
              Sayles and Trawick, p 108

116. A 16-year-old female delivers a stillborn infant in Mercy Hospital. The clinical documentation on the stillborn infant would
    A. be filed in a health record created for the infant.
    B. be filed in the mother's record.
    C. be retained in a separate file in the administrative offices.
    D. not be retained in hospital records.

REFERENCE: LaTour, Eichenwald-Maki, and Oachs, p 252
              Odom-Wesley and Brown, p 180
              Sayles, p 95

117. Which one of the following is a major management challenge in the storage and retention of electronic health record systems?
   A. Following state and federal laws and accreditation requirements when developing retention and destruction policies.
   B. Keeping technology updated in order to retrieve data.
   C. Ensuring that health information can be retrieved in a timely manner.
   D. All of the above are challenges.

REFERENCE: Abdelhak, pp 196–197
              LaTour, Eichenwald-Maki, and Oachs, pp 138–145

118. When implementing the electronic health record, what is the technical security standard that requires unique user identification, emergency access procedures, automatic log-off, and encryption and decryption of data?
   A. audit control
   B. person or entity authentication
   C. transmission security
   D. access control

REFERENCE: LaTour, Eichenwald-Maki, and Oachs, p 133
              Sayles, pp 883, 1038
              Sayles and Trawick, p 319

119. Which of the following is NOT a factor to consider when developing a record retention program?
   A. legal requirements as determined by statute of limitations
   B. record usage in the facility determined by health care provider activity
   C. reimbursement guidelines
   D. cost of space to maintain paper records

REFERENCE: LaTour, Eichenwald-Maki, and Oachs, pp 276–279
              Green and Bowie, p 94
              Sayles, pp 788–789

120. Of 750 records filed during the week, 75 were not located. What is the filing error rate?
   A. 10%
   B. 90%
   C. 0.1%
   D. 0.9%

REFERENCE: McWay, p 204
              Math Calculation

121. Which one of the following is NOT an example of document capture in the electronic document management system?
   A. scanning
   B. bar codes
   C. microfilming
   D forms recognition

REFERENCE: Sayles and Trawick, p 153

122. Which of the following statements is FALSE when addressing characteristics of the legal health record in an electronic document management system?
    A. The storage media used and the format of the scanned documents must protect data from loss and damage.
    B. The storage format must be efficient, manageable, and in compliance with laws and regulations.
    C. The backup and disaster recovery process is certified to ensure that all data can be recovered.
    D. Direct electronic interfaces from ancillary department systems to the document imaging system will not eliminate the need to scan documents and integrate the data from these ancillary systems.

REFERENCE: Sayles and Trawick, p 154

123. Which of the following is NOT a data retrieval tool?
    A. light pen
    B. SQL
    C. color, animation, sound, icons
    D. screen design

REFERENCE: Sayles and Trawick, pp 176–178

124. Messenger, pneumatic tube, dumbwaiter, and conveyor belt are all examples of
    A. record security systems.
    B. mechanical circulation systems.
    C. loose filing.
    D. filing controls.

REFERENCE: Green and Bowie, pp 228–229

125. Which item is collected and maintained in the transplant registry?
    A. vaccine manufacturer
    B. histocompatibility information
    C. cytogenetic results
    D. stage at the time of diagnosis

REFERENCE: Abdelhak, pp 495–496
                LaTour, Eichenwald-Maki, and Oachs, p 375
                Sayles, p 446

Answer Key for Information Retention and Access

NOTE: *Explanations are provided for those questions that require mathematical calculations and questions that are not clearly explained in the references that are cited.*

ANSWER EXPLANATION

1. D
2. A
3. C
4. B
5. A $(3,545 \times 100)$ divided by $15,000 = 2.36\% = 2.4\%$
6. A
7. A
8. B
9. D
10. D
11. C
12. A
13. D 200 units $\times$ 6 shelves per unit = 1,200 shelves total
1,200 shelves divided by 100 primary numbers (00–99) = 12 shelves per primary number
14. C
15. C
16. B
17. D (2,375 records retrieved from proper locations $\times$ 100) divided by 2,543 records requested = 93.39% filing accuracy
18. B
19. C
20. B
21. B
22. B
23. B
24. D $2,540 + 400 = 2,940$ inches needed
$36 \times 6 = 216$ inches per unit
2,940 (inches needed) divided by 216 (inches per unit) = 13.61 shelves
You must buy 14 units because you cannot purchase a 0.14 filing shelf.
25. C
26. C
27. B
28. D
29. D
30. A 8 shelves per unit $\times$ 100 units = 800 total shelves
800 shelves divided by 100 primary digits (00–99) = 8 shelves per primary digit
31. D
32. B
33. A
34. D
35. C
36. A

Answer Key for Information Retention and Access

	ANSWER	EXPLANATION
37.	A	25,000 inpatients × 0.25 inch/record = 6,250 inches

15,000 ER patients × 0.125 inch/record = 1,875 inches

6,250 inches + 1,875 inches = 8,125 total inches of filing space/year

8,125 total inches × $1.05/filing inch = $8,531.25 budget allocation for storage space

38. C

39. D

40. A

41. A

42. C

43. C
  33 inches per shelf × 6 shelves per unit = 198 linear filing inches per unit

  1,000 records × 1 inch per record = 1,000 inches of records to be filed

  1,000 (inches of records needed) divided by 198 inches per unit = 5.05 filing units

  In order to provide for the total expansion, 6 filing units need to be purchased.

44. B

45. A

46. C

47. A

48. D

49. D

50. C

51. B

52. D

53. B

54. C
  6,000 admissions (year currently)
  + 200 additional admissions/year
  6,200 total admissions next year

  6,200 total admissions
  × 30% readmission rate
  1,860 readmissions next year

  6,200 total admissions
  −1,860 readmissions
  4,340 new file folders needed for next year

55. A

56. D

57. C

58. C

59. C

60. D

61. C

62. A

63. C

64. A

65. C

Answer Key for Information Retention and Access

	ANSWER	EXPLANATION
66.	D	
67.	B	
68.	B	
69.	B	
70.	C	
71.	C	
72.	B	
73.	B	In a hospital where paper-based records are routinely requested 24 hours a day, it would be beneficial to have 24-hour staffing. If it were a small facility with few requests in the evenings, it could be more appropriate to have a nurse supervisor assigned responsibility for record retrieval.
74.	A	
75	D	
76	D	
77.	B	
78.	A	
79.	D	
80.	B	
81.	B	
82.	B	
83.	D	
84.	C	
85.	B	$(5,000 \times 100)$ divided by $500,000 = 1\%$
86.	C	
87.	C	
88.	B	
89.	D	$2,500 - 90 = 2,410$ $(2,410 \times 100)$ divided by $2,500 = 96.4\%$ filing accuracy
90.	C	
91.	A	
92.	C	
93.	B	
94.	D	
95.	B	
96.	C	
97.	B	
98.	D	
99.	C	
100.	C	
101.	A	
102.	C	
103.	D	
104.	D	
105	D	
106.	B	
107.	C	

Answer Key for Information Retention and Access

ANSWER   EXPLANATION

108. D
109. D
110. D
111. D
112. A
113. D
114. A
115. A
116. B
117. D
118. D
119. C
120. A
121. C
122. D
123. A
124. B
125. B

REFERENCES

Abdelhak, M., Grostick, S., and Hanken, M. (2012). *Health information: Management of a strategic resource* (4th ed.). St. Louis: Elsevier.

AHIMA Practice Briefs. All are published by the American Health Information Management Association, Chicago.

AHIMA Practice Brief: "Information Security: An Overview"

AHIMA Practice Brief: "Protecting Patient Information After a Facility Closure"

AHIMA Practice Brief: "Disaster Planning for Health Information"

AHIMA Practice Brief: "Retention and Destruction of Health Information"

AHIMA Practice Brief: "Purchasing Strategies for EHR Systems"

American College of Surgeons. (2011). *Cancer program standards 2012: Ensuring patient-centered care.* Chicago: American College of Surgeons Commission on Cancer.

Eichenwald-Maki, S., & Petterson, B. (2014). *Using the electronic health record in the health care provider practice* (2nd ed.). Clifton Park, NY: Delmar Cengage Learning.

Green, M. A., & Bowie, M. J. (2011). *Essentials of health information management: Principles and practices* (2nd ed.). Clifton Park, NY: Delmar Cengage Learning.

Joint Commission. (2013) *Comprehensive accreditation manual for hospitals: The official handbook.* Oakbrook Terrace, IL: Author.

LaTour, K., Eichenwald-Maki, S., and Oachs, P. (2013). *Health information management: Concepts, principles and practice* (4th ed.). Chicago: American Health Information Management Association.

McWay, D. C. (2014). *Today's health information management: An integrated approach* (2nd ed.). Clifton Park, NY: Delmar Cengage Learning.

Odom-Wesley, B., & Brown, D. (2009). *Documentation for medical records.* Chicago: American Health Information Management Association.

Sayles, N. (2013). *Health information management technology: An applied approach* (4th ed.). Chicago: American Health Information Management Association.

Sayles, N., & Trawick, K. (2010). *Introduction to computer systems for health information technology.* Chicago: American Health Information Management Association.

RHIA AND RHIT COMPETENCIES BY QUESTION FOR INFORMATION RETENTION AND ACCESS

Question	RHIA Domain Competencies							RHIT Domain Competencies						
	1	2	3	4	5	6		1	2	3	4	5	6	7
1					X							X		
2			X					X						
3	X											X		
4	X							X						
5	X							X						
6	X							X						
7	X							X						
8	X							X						
9			X								X			
10	X							X						
11	X							X						
12						X							X	
13	X							X						
14	X							X						
15	X							X						
16	X							X						
17	X							X						
18	X							X						
19	X							X						
20	X							X						
21						X				X				
22						X				X				
23			X								X			
24				X									X	
25						X		X						
26		X						X						
27	X							X						
28	X									X				
29						X		X						
30	X							X						
31	X							X						
32	X							X						
33	X							X						
34				X				X						
35	X							X						
36			X								X			
37	X							X						
38	X							X						
39	X							X						
40				X				X						
41			X					X						
42				X				X						
43	X							X						
44	X							X						
45	X							X						
46			X					X						
47						X					X			
48						X					X			
49						X							X	
50			X									X		
51	X							X						
52			X									X		
53	X							X						

Question	RHIA Domain Competencies							RHIT Domain Competencies						
	1	2	3	4	5	6		1	2	3	4	5	6	7
54				X				X						
55				X				X						
56				X				X						
57		X						X						
58						X							X	
59	X									X				
60				X				X						
61	X									X				
62						X				X				
63			X										X	
64	X							X						
65	X							X						
66	X							X						
67			X								X			
68	X							X						
69						X		X						
70	X							X						
71	X							X						
72	X							X						
73				X				X						
74				X				X						
75				X				X						
76						X			X					
77			X								X			
78						X				X				
79			X								X			
80						X				X				
81	X							X						
82						X				X				
83	X							X						
84	X							X						
85	X							X						
86			X					X						
87	X							X						
88				X				X						
89	X							X						
90	X							X						
91	X									X				
92						X				X				
93	X									X				
94		X						X						
95	X							X						
96			X								X			
97	X							X						
98			X								X			
99			X					X						
100			X						X					
101	X							X						
102						X		X						
103			X								X			

Table title: RHIA AND RHIT COMPETENCIES BY QUESTION FOR INFORMATION RETENTION AND ACCESS

RHIA AND RHIT COMPETENCIES BY QUESTION FOR INFORMATION RETENTION AND ACCESS

Question	RHIA Domain Competencies							RHIT Domain Competencies						
	1	2	3	4	5	6		1	2	3	4	5	6	7
104			X								X			
105				X				X						
106			X					X						
107			X					X						
108			X								X			
109			X								X			
110				X				X						
111						X					X			
112			X								X			
113			X								X			
114			X								X			
115			X								X			
116	X							X						
117			X					X						
118			X							X				
119	X									X				
120	X							X						
121			X								X			
122						X							X	
123			X									X		
124			X					X						
125	X							X						

V. Classification Systems and Secondary Data Sources

Lisa M. Delhomme, MHA, RHIA

1. Which system is a classification of health and health-related domains that describe body functions and structures, domains of activities and participation, and environmental factors that interact with all of these components?
   A. International Classification of Primary Care (ICPC-2)
   B. International Classification on Functioning, Disability, and Health (ICF)
   C. National Drug Codes
   D. Clinical Care Classification (CCC)

   REFERENCE: Latour, Eichenwald-Maki, and Oachs, p 393
                   Sayles, pp 196–197

2. A physician performed an outpatient surgical procedure on the eye orbit of a patient with Medicare. Upon searching the CPT codes and consulting with the physician, the coder is unable to find a code for the procedure. The coder should assign
   A. an unlisted Evaluation and Management code from the E/M section.
   B. an unlisted procedure code located in the eye and ocular adnexa section.
   C. a HCPCS Level Two (alphanumeric) code.
   D. an ophthalmologic treatment service code.

   REFERENCE: AMA (2014), p 63
                   Frisch, p 254
                   Green, p 384
                   Smith, p 25

3. A system of preferred terminology for naming disease processes is known as a
   A. set of categories.   C. medical nomenclature.
   B. classification system.   D. diagnosis listing.

   REFERENCE: Abdelhak, p 224
                   Green, p 9
                   Green and Bowie, p 304
                   LaTour, Eichenwald-Maki, and Oachs, pp 207–208, 348, 388–389
                   McWay, pp 149–150
                   Sayles, p 180

4. Which of the following is NOT included as a part of the minimum data maintained in the MPI?
   A. principal diagnosis   C. full name (last, first, and middle)
   B. patient medical record number   D. date of birth

   REFERENCE: Abdelhak, p 107
                   Green and Bowie, pp 237–239
                   LaTour, Eichenwald-Maki, and Oachs, pp 170, 271–272
                   McWay, pp 139–140
                   Sayles, pp 322–323

5. The Health Information Department receives research requests from various committees in the hospital. The Medicine Committee wishes to review all patients having a diagnosis of anterolateral myocardial infarction within the past 6 months. Which of the following would be the best source to identify the necessary charts?

    A. operation index   C. disease index

    B. consultation index   D. physician's index

REFERENCE: Green and Bowie, pp 240–243
                   LaTour, Eichenwald-Maki, and Oachs, pp 369–370
                   McWay, p 140
                   Sayles, pp 436–437

6. One of the major functions of the cancer registry is to ensure that patients receive regular and continued observation and management. How long should patient follow-up be continued?

    A. until remission occurs   C. for the life of the patient

    B. 10 years   D. 1 year

REFERENCE: Abdelhak, p 485
                   LaTour, Eichenwald-Maki, and Oachs, pp 370–372
                   McWay, pp 142–143
                   Sayles, pp 438–440

7. In reviewing the medical record of a patient admitted for a left herniorrhaphy, the coder discovers an extremely low potassium level on the laboratory report. In examining the physician's orders, the coder notices that intravenous potassium was ordered. The physician has not listed any indication of an abnormal potassium level or any related condition on the discharge summary. The best course of action for the coder to take is to

    A. confer with the physician and ask him or her to list the condition as a final diagnosis if he or she considers the abnormal potassium level to be clinically significant.

    B. code the record as is.

    C. code the condition as abnormal blood chemistry.

    D. code the abnormal potassium level as a complication following surgery.

REFERENCE: Bowie and Shaffer (2012), p 69
                   Green, pp 15–16
                   Johnson and Linker, pp 5–36

8. DSM-IV-TR is used most frequently in what type of health care setting?

    A. behavioral health centers   C. home health agencies

    B. ambulatory surgery centers   D. nursing homes

REFERENCE: Green, p 865
                   LaTour, Eichenwald-Maki, and Oachs, pp 394–395
                   McWay, p 152
                   Sayles, pp 208–210

9. A coder notes that a patient is taking prescription Pilocarpine. The final diagnoses on the discharge summary are congestive heart failure and diabetes mellitus. The coder should query the physician about adding a diagnosis of
   A. arthritis.
   B. glaucoma.
   C. bronchitis.
   D. laryngitis.

REFERENCE: Green, pp 15–16, 174–175
            Nobles, p 689

10. The patient is diagnosed with congestive heart failure. A drug of choice is
    A. ibuprofen.
    B. oxytocin.
    C. haloperidol.
    D. digoxin.

REFERENCE: Nobles, p 329

11. ICD-10-CM utilizes a placeholder character. This is used as a 5th character placeholder at certain 6 character codes to allow for future expansion. The placeholder character is
    A. "Z."
    B. "O."
    C. "1."
    D. "x."

REFERENCE: Bowie, p 30
            Green, p 52

12. The local safety council requests statistics on the number of head injuries occurring as a result of skateboarding accidents during the last year. To retrieve this data, you will need to have the correct
    A. CPT code.
    B. Standard Nomenclature of Injuries codes.
    C. ICD-10-CM codes.
    D. HCPCS Level II codes.

REFERENCE: Frisch, pp 150–151
            Green, pp 209–220
            Johnson and Linker, pp 16, 66–69
            McWay, pp 154–155
            Schraffenberger (2013), pp 384–385

13. All children will be entered into which of the following registries at birth, and thus will continue to be monitored by the registry in their geographic area?
    A. Birth defects registry
    B. Trauma registry
    C. Cancer registry
    D. Immunization registry

REFERENCE: Latour, Eichenwald-Maki, and Oachs, p 375
            McWay, p 141
            Sayles, pp 447–449

14. In general, all three key components (history, physical examination, and medical decision making) for the E/M codes in CPT should be met or exceeded when
    A. the patient is established.
    B. a new patient is seen in the office.
    C. the patient is given subsequent care in the hospital.
    D. the patient is seen for a follow-up inpatient consultation.

REFERENCE: AMA (2014), p 10
            Green, p 414
            Johnson and Linker, p 144

Current Procedural Terminology © 2013 American Medical Association. All Rights Reserved.

15. This registry collects data on recipients of heart valves and pacemakers.
    A. Transplant registry
    B. Implant registry
    C. Cancer registry
    D. Hypertension registry

REFERENCE: LaTour, Eichenwald-Maki, and Oachs, p 374
                         McWay, p 141
                         Sayles, pp 445–446

16. Which classification system was developed to standardize terminology and codes for use in clinical laboratories?
    A. Systematized Nomenclature of Human and Veterinary Medicine International (SNOMED)
    B. Systematized Nomenclature of Pathology (SNOP)
    C. Read Codes
    D. Logical Observation Identifiers, Names and Codes (LOINC)

REFERENCE: Abdelhak, pp 237–239
                         Latour, Eichenwald-Maki, and Oachs, pp 399–400
                         McWay, p 151

17. Which classification system is used to classify neoplasms according to site, morphology, and behavior?
    A. International Classification of Diseases for Oncology (ICD-O)
    B. Systematized Nomenclature of Human and Veterinary Medicine International (SNOMED)
    C. Diagnostic and Statistical Manual of Mental Disorders (DSM)
    D. Current Procedural Terminology (CPT)

REFERENCE: Abdelhak, p 252
                         Latour, Eichenwald-Maki, and Oachs, pp 392–393

18. According to the UHDDS, a procedure that is surgical in nature, carries a procedural or anesthetic risk, or requires special training is defined as a
    A. principal procedure.   C. operating room procedure.
    B. significant procedure.   D. therapeutic procedure.

REFERENCE: Green, p 263
                         Latour, Eichenwald-Maki, and Oachs, p 197
                         Schraffenberger (2013), p 53

19. You need to analyze data on the types of care provided to Medicare patients in your geographic area by DRG. Which of the following would be most helpful?
    A. National Practitioner Data Bank
    B. MEDPAR
    C. Vital Statistics
    D. RxNorm

REFERENCE: LaTour, Eichenwald-Maki, and Oachs, p 377
                         McWay, p 187
                         Sayles, pp 450–451

20. An encoder that prompts the coder to answer a series of questions and choices based on the documentation in the medical record is called a(n)
    A. logic-based encoder.
    B. automated codebook.
    C. grouper.
    D. automatic code assignment.

REFERENCE: LaTour, Eichenwald-Maki, and Oachs, p 444

21. Which of the following classification systems was designed with electronic systems in mind and is currently being used for problem lists, ICU unit monitoring, patient care assessments, data collection, medical research studies, clinical trials, disease surveillance, and images?
    A. SNOMED CT
    B. SNDO
    C. ICDPC-2
    D. GEM

REFERENCE: Abdelhak, pp 235–237
              LaTour, Eichenwald-Maki, and Oachs, pp 398–399
              McWay, pp 150–151

22. The Unified Medical Language System (UMLS) is a project sponsored by the
    A. National Library of Medicine.
    B. CMS.
    C. World Health Organization.
    D. Office of Inspector General.

REFERENCE: LaTour, Eichenwald-Maki, and Oachs, pp 405–406
              McWay, p 151
              Sayles, p 458

23. You have recently been hired as the Medical Staff Coordinator at your local hospital. Which database/registry will you utilize most often?
    A. Trauma Registry
    B. MEDPAR
    C. LOINC
    D. National Practitioner Data Bank (NPDB)

REFERENCE: LaTour, Eichenwald-Maki, and Oachs, p 377
              McWay, p 270
              Sayles, p 451

24. You need to retrieve information on a particular physician in your facility. Specifically, you need to know how many cases he saw during the month of May. What would be your best source of information?
    A. Healthcare Integrity and Protection Data Banks (HIPDB)
    B. Physician Index
    C. MEDLINE database
    D. National Practitioner Data Bank (NPDB)

REFERENCE: LaTour, Eichenwald-Maki, and Oachs, pp 369–370
              McWay, p 140
              Sayles, p 437

25. You just completed a process through which you reviewed a patient record and entered the required elements into a database. What is this process called?
    A. Case finding
    B. Staging
    C. Abstracting
    D. Nomenclature

REFERENCE: LaTour, Eichenwald-Maki, and Oachs, p 382
              McWay, p 140
              Sayles, p 394

26. Which system is used primarily to report services and supplies for reimbursement purposes?
    A. LOINC
    B. HCPCS
    C. NLM
    D. ASTM

REFERENCE: Green, pp 341–342
                 LaTour, Eichenwald-Maki, and Oachs, p 394
                 McWay, p 164
                 Sayles, p 182

27. You are looking at statistics for your facility that include average length of stay (ALOS) and discharge data by DRG. What type of data are you reviewing?
    A. Aggregate data
    B. Patient-identifiable data
    C. MPI data
    D. Protocol data

REFERENCE: LaTour, Eichenwald-Maki, and Oachs, p 368
                 McWay, p 208
                 Sayles, p 41

28. In which registry would you expect to find an Injury Severity Score (ISS)?
    A. Cancer Registry
    B. Birth Defects Registry
    C. Trauma Registry
    D. Transplant Registry

REFERENCE: LaTour, Eichenwald-Maki, and Oachs, p 372
                 Sayles, pp 441–442

29. A service provided by a physician whose opinion or advice regarding evaluation and/or management of a specific problem is requested by another physician is referred to as
    A. a referral.   C. risk factor intervention.
    B. a consultation.   D. concurrent care.

REFERENCE: AMA (2014), p 18–19
                 Bowie and Shaffer (2013), pp 61–63
                 Frisch, p 77
                 Green, pp 435–436
                 Johnson and Linker, pp 153–154, 644
                 Smith, pp 215–216

30. Which of the following groups maintain healthcare databases in the public and private sectors?
    A. Healthcare provider organizations
    B. Healthcare data organizations
    C. Healthcare payor organizations
    D. Healthcare supplier organizations

REFERENCE: LaTour, Eichenwald-Maki, and Oachs, p 59

31. The most widely discussed and debated unique patient identifier is the
    A. patient's date of birth.
    B. patient's first and last names.
    C. patient's social security number.
    D. Unique Physician Identification Number (UPIN).

REFERENCE: LaTour, Eichenwald-Maki, and Oachs, pp 243–244

32. A nomenclature of codes and medical terms that provides standard terminology for reporting physicians' services for third-party reimbursement is
    A. Current Medical Information and Terminology (CMIT).
    B. Current Procedural Terminology (CPT).
    C. Systematized Nomenclature of Pathology (SNOP).
    D. Diagnostic and Statistical Manual of Mental Disorders (DSM).

REFERENCE: Bowie and Schaffer (2013) pp 2, 8
               Frisch, p 5
               Green, p 10
               Johnson and Linker, p 110
               Schraffenberger and Kuehn, p 10

33. A cancer program is surveyed for approval by the
    A. American Cancer Society.
    B. Commission on Cancer of the American College of Surgeons.
    C. State Department of Health.
    D. Joint Commission on Accreditation of Healthcare Organizations.

REFERENCE: Abdelhak, p 483
               LaTour, Eichenwald-Maki, and Oachs, pp 371–372
               Sayles, p 440

34. The nursing staff would most likely use which of the following to facilitate aggregation of data for comparison at local, regional, national, and international levels?
    A. READ codes   C. SPECIALIST Lexicon
    B. ABC codes   D. LOINC

REFERENCE: Green and Bowie, p 309
               McWay, p 164

35. The Level II (national) codes of the HCPCS coding system are maintained by the
    A. American Medical Association.
    B. CPT Editorial Panel.
    C. local fiscal intermediary.
    D. Centers for Medicare and Medicaid Services.

REFERENCE: Bowie and Schaffer (2013), p 8
               Green and Bowie, p 24
               Johnson and Linker, pp 110–111

36. A patient is admitted with pneumonia. Cultures are requested to determine the infecting organism. Which of the following, if present, would alert the coder to ask the physician whether or not this should be coded as gram-negative pneumonia?
    A. pseudomonas   C. staphylococcus
    B. clostridium   D. listeria

REFERENCE: Green, pp 15–17

37. The Level I (CPT) codes of the HCPCS coding system are maintained by the
    A. American Medical Association.
    B. American Hospital Association.
    C. local fiscal intermediary.
    D. Centers for Medicare and Medicaid Services.

REFERENCE: Bowie and Schaffer (2013), pp 2, 8
                          Frisch, p 5
                          Green, p 10
                          Green and Bowie, pp 24, 307–308
                          Johnson and Linker, pp 110–111
                          McWay, p 416

38. A physician excises a 3.1 cm malignant lesion of the scalp that requires full-thickness graft from the thigh to the scalp. In CPT, which of the following procedures should be coded?
    A. full-thickness skin graft to scalp only
    B. excision of lesion; full-thickness skin graft to scalp
    C. excision of lesion; full-thickness skin graft to scalp; excision of skin from thigh
    D. code 15004 for surgical preparation of recipient site; full-thickness skin graft to scalp

REFERENCE: AMA, CPT Assistant, vol. 7, no. 9, Sept. 1997, pp 1–3
                          Green, pp 517–520, 527–529
                          Johnson and Linker, pp 222, 227–229
                          Smith, pp 61–62, 72–75

39. A patient is seen by a surgeon who determines that an emergency procedure is necessary. Identify the modifier that may be reported to indicate that the decision to do surgery was made on this office visit.
    A. −25   B. −55   C. −57   D. −58

REFERENCE: AMA (2014), pp 645–650
                          Bowie and Schaffer (2013), pp 16–25
                          Frisch, pp 18–19
                          Green, pp 387–395
                          Smith, p 212

40. A patient develops difficulty during surgery and the physician discontinues the procedure. Identify the modifier that may be reported by the physician to indicate that the procedure was discontinued.
    A. −52   B. −53   C. −73   D. −74

REFERENCE: AMA (2014), pp 645–650
                          Bowie and Schaffer (2013), pp 6–25
                          Frisch, p 18
                          Green, pp 387–395
                          Johnson and Linker, p 456
                          Smith, pp 45–49

41. A barrier to widespread use of automated code assignment is
    A. inadequate technology.   C. resistance by physicians.
    B. poor quality of documentation.   D. resistance by HIM professionals.

REFERENCE: LaTour, Eichenwald-Maki, and Oachs, pp 444–445

42. In assigning E/M codes, three key components are used. These are
   A. history, examination, counseling.
   B. history, examination, time.
   C. history, nature of presenting problem, time.
   D. history, examination, medical decision making.

REFERENCE: AMA (2014), p 9
              Bowie and Schaffer (2011), pp 39–40
              Frisch, p 12
              Green, p 414
              Johnson and Linker, p 131
              Smith, p 197

43. Mrs. Jones had an appendectomy on November 1. She was taken back to surgery on November 2 for evacuation of a hematoma of the wound site. Identify the modifier that may be reported for the November 2 visit.
   A. –58   B. –76   C. –78   D. –79

REFERENCE: AMA (2014), pp 645–650
              Bowie and Schaffer (2011), pp 22–23
              Frisch, pp 22, 240
              Green, pp 387–395
              Johnson and Linker, p 461
              Smith, pp 48–49

44. The primary goal of a hospital-based cancer registry is to
   A. improve patient care.
   B. allocate hospital resources appropriately.
   C. determine the need for professional and public education programs.
   D. monitor cancer incidence.

REFERENCE: Abdelhak, p 486
              McWay, pp 142–143

45. A secondary data source that houses and aggregates extensive data about patients with a certain diagnosis is a(n)
   A. disease index.   C. disease registry.
   B. master patient index.   D. admissions register.

REFERENCE: Green and Bowie, pp 240–243
              LaTour, Eichenwald-Maki, and Oachs, p 370

46. After reviewing the following excerpt from CPT, code 27646 would be interpreted as

27645	radical resection of tumor; tibia
27646	fibula
27647	talus or calcaneus

   A. 27646   radical resection of tumor; tibia and fibula.
   B. 27646   radical resection of tumor; fibula.
   C. 27646   radical resection of tumor; fibula or tibia.
   D. 27646   radical resection of tumor; fibula, talus or calcaneus.

REFERENCE: Bowie and Schaffer (2013), pp 4–5
              Green, p 374
              Smith, pp 19–20

Current Procedural Terminology © 2013 American Medical Association. All Rights Reserved.

47. A population-based cancer registry that is designed to determine rates and trends in a defined population is a(n)
    A. incidence-only population-based registry.
    B. cancer control population-based registry.
    C. research-oriented population-based registry.
    D. patient care population-based registry.

REFERENCE: Abdelhak, p 487
               LaTour, Eichenwald-Maki, and Oachs, p 370
               Sayles, pp 438–440

48. Given the diagnosis "carcinoma of axillary lymph nodes and lungs, metastatic from breast," what is the primary cancer site(s)?
    A. axillary lymph nodes   C. breast
    B. lungs   D. A and B

REFERENCE: Frisch, pp 142–144
               Green, pp 156–157
               Hazelwood and Venable, p 112
               Johnson and Linker, p 63
               Schraffenberger (2013), pp 93–94

49. According to CPT, in which of the following cases would an established E/M code be used?
    A. A home visit with a 45-year-old male with a long history of drug abuse and alcoholism. The man is seen at the request of Adult Protective Services for an assessment of his mental capabilities.
    B. John and his family have just moved to town. John has asthma and requires medication to control the problem. He has an appointment with Dr. You and will bring his records from his previous physician.
    C. Tom is seen by Dr. X for a sore throat. Dr. X is on call for Tom's regular physician, Dr. Y. The last time that Tom saw Dr. Y was a couple of years ago.
    D. A 78-year-old female with weight loss and progressive agitation over the past 2 months is seen by her primary care physician for drug therapy. She has not seen her primary care physician in 4 years.

REFERENCE: AMA (2014), pp 4–5
               AMA, CPT Assistant, vol. 8, no. 10, Oct. 1998
               Bowie and Schaffer (2013), pp 37–38
               Frisch, pp 49–50
               Green, pp 411–412
               Smith, pp 195–196

50. In order to use the inpatient CPT consultation codes, the consulting physician must
    A. order diagnostic tests.
    B. document his findings in the patient's medical record.
    C. communicate orally his opinion to the attending physician.
    D. use the term "referral" in his report.

REFERENCE: AMA (2014), pp 18–21
               Frisch, pp 77–78
               Green, pp 435–438
               Smith, pp 215–216

51. The attending physician requests a consultation from a cardiologist. The cardiologist takes a detailed history, performs a detailed examination, and utilizes moderate medical decision making. The cardiologist orders diagnostic tests and prescribes medication. He documents his findings in the patient's medical record and communicates in writing with the attending physician. The following day the consultant visits the patient to evaluate the patient's response to the medication, to review results from the diagnostic tests, and to discuss treatment options. What codes should the consultant report for the two visits?
    A. an initial inpatient consult and a follow-up consult
    B. an initial inpatient consult for both visits
    C. an initial inpatient consult and a subsequent hospital visit
    D. an initial inpatient consult and initial hospital care

REFERENCE: AMA (2014), pp 18–21
              Bowie and Schaffer (2013), pp 61–63
              Frisch, pp 82–86
              Green, pp 435–438
              Smith, pp 215–216

52. According to the American Medical Association, medical decision making is measured by all of the following except the
    A. number of diagnoses or management options.
    B. amount and complexity of data reviewed.
    C. risk of complications.
    D. specialty of the treating physician.

REFERENCE: AMA (2014), p 10
              Bowie and Schaffer (2013), pp 52–54
              Frisch, p 322
              Green, pp 416–417
              Johnson and Linker, pp 139–140
              Smith, pp 205–208

53. CPT provides Level I modifiers to explain all of the following situations EXCEPT
    A. when a service or procedure is partially reduced or eliminated at the physician's discretion.
    B. when one surgeon provides only postoperative services.
    C. when a patient sees a surgeon for follow-up care after surgery.
    D. when the same laboratory test is repeated multiple times on the same day.

REFERENCE: AMA (2014), pp 645–650
              Bowie and Schaffer (2013), pp 16–25
              Frisch, pp 13–23
              Green, pp 387–395
              Johnson and Linker, pp 449–464

54. The best place to ascertain the size of an excised lesion for accurate CPT coding is the
    A. discharge summary.   C. operative report.
    B. pathology report.   D. anesthesia record.

REFERENCE: Green, pp 517–520
              Johnson and Linker, pp 220–221
              Smith, pp 61–62

55. Which of the following is expected to enable hospitals to collect more specific information for use in patient care, benchmarking, quality assessment, research, public health reporting, strategic planning, and reimbursement?
    A. LOINC
    B. ICD-10-CM
    C. NDC
    D. NANDA

REFERENCE: Abdelhak, p 249
               Johnson and Linker, pp 82–89

56. Case definition is important for all types of registries. Age will certainly be an important criterion for accessing a case in a(n) _____ registry.
    A. implant   C. HIV/AIDS
    B. trauma   D. birth defects

REFERENCE: LaTour, Eichenwald-Maki, and Oachs, p 373

57. To gather statistics for surgical services provided on an outpatient basis, which of the following codes are needed?
    A. ICD-10-CM codes
    B. evaluation and management codes
    C. HCPCS Level II Codes
    D. CPT codes

REFERENCE: Green and Bowie, pp 240–243
               McWay, p 164
               Schraffenberger and Kuehn, p 10

58. The Cancer Committee at your hospital requests a list of all patients entered into your cancer registry in the last year. This information would be obtained by checking the
    A. disease index.   C. suspense file.
    B. tickler file.   D. accession register.

REFERENCE: LaTour, Eichenwald-Maki, and Oachs, p 371
               Sayles, p 439

59. The reference date for a cancer registry is
    A. January 1 of the year in which the registry was established.
    B. the date when data collection began.
    C. the date that the Cancer Committee is established.
    D. the date that the cancer program applies for approval by the American College of Surgeons.

REFERENCE: Abdelhak, p 486

60. The abstract completed on the patients in your hospital contains the following items: patient demographics; prehospital interventions; vital signs on admission; procedures and treatment prior to hospitalization; transport modality; and injury severity score. The hospital uses these data for its
    A. AIDS registry.   C. implant registry.
    B. diabetes registry.   D. trauma registry.

REFERENCE: Abdelhak, p 496
               LaTour, Eichenwald-Maki, and Oachs, pp 372–373
               Sayles, pp 441–442

61. In relation to birth defects registries, active surveillance systems
    A. use trained staff to identify cases in all hospitals, clinics, and other facilities through review of patient records, indexes, vital records, and hospital logs.
    B. are commonly used in all 50 states.
    C. miss 10% to 30% of all cases.
    D. rely on reports submitted by hospitals, clinics, or other sources.

REFERENCE: Abdelhak, p 492

62. In regard to quality of coding, the degree to which the same results (same codes) are obtained by different coders or on multiple attempts by the same coder refers to
    A. reliability.   C. completeness.
    B. validity.   D. timeliness.

REFERENCE: LaTour, Eichenwald-Maki, and Oachs, pp 442–443

63. The Healthcare Cost and Utilization Project (HCUP) consists of a set of databases that include data on inpatients whose care is paid for by third-party payers. HCUP is an initiative of the
    A. Agency for Healthcare Research and Quality.
    B. Centers for Medicare and Medicaid Services.
    C. National Library of Medicine.
    D. World Health Organization.

REFERENCE: LaTour, Eichenwald-Maki, and Oachs, pp 381, 631
               McWay, p 175

64. The coding supervisor notices that the coders are routinely failing to code all possible diagnoses and procedures for a patient encounter. This indicates to the supervisor that there is a problem with
    A. completeness.   C. reliability.
    B. validity.   D. timeliness.

REFERENCE: LaTour, Eichenwald-Maki, and Oachs, pp 442–443

65. When coding free skin grafts, which of the following is NOT an essential item of data needed for accurate coding?
    A. recipient site   C. size of defect
    B. donor site   D. type of repair

REFERENCE: Bowie and Schaffer (2013), p 110
               Green, pp 527–530
               Smith, pp 72–76

66. In CPT, Category III codes include codes
    A. to describe emerging technologies.
    B. to measure performance.
    C. for use by nonphysician practitioners.
    D. for supplies, drugs, and durable medical equipment.

REFERENCE: AMA (2014), p 629
               Bowie and Schaffer (2013), p 8
               Johnson and Linker, pp 120, 130
               Smith, p 3

67. The information collected for your registry includes patient demographic information, diagnosis codes, functional status, and histocompatibility information. This type of registry is a
    A. birth defects registry.
    C. transplant registry.
    B. diabetes registry.
    D. trauma registry.

REFERENCE: LaTour, Eichenwald-Maki, and Oachs, pp 374–375

68. Patient Jamey Smith has been seen at Oceanside Hospital three times prior to this current encounter. Unfortunately, because of clerical errors, Jamey's information was entered into the MPI incorrectly on the three previous admissions and consequently has three different medical record numbers. The unit numbering system is used at Oceanside Hospital. Jamey's previous entries into the MPI are as follows:

09/03/10	Jamey Smith	MR# 10361
03/10/11	Jamey Smith Doe	MR# 33998
07/23/12	Jamie Smith Doe	MR# 36723

The next available number to be assigned at Oceanside Hospital is 41369. Duplicate entries in the MPI should be scrubbed and all of Jamey's medical records should be filed under medical record number
    A. 10361.
    C. 36723.
    B. 33998.
    D. 41369.

REFERENCE: Green and Bowie, pp 237–240
               McWay, pp 139–140

69. The method of calculating errors in a coding audit that allows for benchmarking with other hospitals, and permits the reviewer to track errors by case type, is the
    A. record-over-record method.
    C. code method.
    B. benchmarking method.
    D. focused review method.

REFERENCE: Schraffenberger and Kuehn, p 319

70. The most common type of registry located in hospitals of all sizes and in every region of the country is the
    A. trauma registry.
    C. AIDS registry.
    B. cancer registry.
    D. birth defects registry.

REFERENCE: Green and Bowie, p 248
               McWay, p 142

71. A radiologist is asked to review a patient's CT scan that was taken at another facility. The modifier - 26 attached to the code indicates that the physician is billing for what component of the procedure?
    A. professional
    C. global
    B. technical
    D. confirmatory

REFERENCE: Bowie and Schaffer (2013), pp 17–18
               Frisch, pp 14, 16
               Green, pp 387–395
               Johnson and Linker, pp 453–454

72. When coding neoplasms, topography means
    A. cell structure and form.
    C. variation from normal tissue.
    B. site.
    D. extent of the spread of the disease.

REFERENCE: Abdelhak, p 488

73. According to CPT, antepartum care includes all of the following EXCEPT
    A. initial and subsequent history.
    B. physical examination.
    C. monthly visits up to 36 weeks.
    D. routine chemical urinalysis.

REFERENCE: Bowie and Schaffer (2013), pp 293–295
      Green, pp 687–688
      Johnson and Linker, pp 346–347
      Smith, p 146

74. The Cancer Committee at Wharton General Hospital wants to compare long-term survival rates for pancreatic cancer by evaluating medical versus surgical treatment of the cancer. The best source of these data is the
    A. disease index.
    B. operation index.
    C. master patient index.
    D. cancer registry abstracts.

REFERENCE: Abdelhak, pp 487–488
      LaTour, Eichenwald-Maki, and Oachs, pp 370–371
      McWay, pp 142–143

75. A list or collection of clinical words or phrases with their meanings is a
    A. data dictionary.
    B. language.
    C. medical nomenclature.
    D. clinical vocabulary.

REFERENCE: LaTour, Eichenwald-Maki, and Oachs, p 389

76. The main difference between concurrent and retrospective coding is
    A. when the coding is done.
    B. what classification system is used.
    C. the credentials of the coder.
    D. the involvement of the physician.

REFERENCE: Schraffenberger and Kuehn, p 30

77. A PEG procedure would most likely be done to facilitate
    A. breathing.
    B. eating.
    C. urination.
    D. none of the above.

REFERENCE: Johnson and Linker, p 89
      Schraffenberger (2013), p 253

78. CMS published a final rule indicating a compliance date to implement ICD-10-CM and ICD-10-PCS. The use of these two code sets will be effective on
    A. January 1, 2014.
    B. October 1, 2014.
    C. January 1, 2015.
    D. October 1, 2015.

REFERENCE: DeVault, Barta, and Endicott, p 3
      Bowie and Schaffer (2), p 3

79. Mappings between ICD-9-CM and ICD-10-CM were developed and released by the National Center for Health Statistics (NCHS) to facilitate the transition from one code set to another. They are called
    A. GEMS (General Equivalency Mappings).
    B. Medical Mappings.
    C. Code Maps.
    D. ICD Code Maps.

REFERENCE: DeVault, Barta, and Endicott, p 6

80. The code structure for ICD-10-CM differs from the code structure of ICD-9-CM. An ICD-10-CM code consists of
    A. five alphanumeric characters.
    B. 10 characters.
    C. three to seven characters.
    D. seven digits.

REFERENCE: DeVault, Barta, and Endicott, pp 7–8

81. The first character for all of the codes assigned in ICD-10-CM is
    A. an alphabet.
    B. a number.
    C. an alphabet or a number.
    D. a digit.

REFERENCE: DeVault, Barta, and Endicott, p 7

82. ICD-10-PCS will be implemented in the United States to code
    A. hospital inpatient procedures.
    B. physician office procedures.
    C. hospital inpatient diagnoses.
    D. hospital outpatient diagnoses.

REFERENCE: Barta, DeVault, and Endicott, p 2

83. ICD-10-PCS codes have a unique structure. An example of a valid code in the ICD-10-PCS system is
    A. L03.311.
    B. 013.2.
    C. B2151.
    D. 2W3FX1Z.

REFERENCE: Barta, DeVault, and Endicott, pp 6–10

84. ICD-10-PCS utilizes the third character in the Medical and Surgical section to identify the "root operation." The name of the root operation that describes "cutting out or off, without replacing a portion of a body part" is
    A. destruction.
    B. extirpation.
    C. excision.
    D. removal.

REFERENCE: Barta, DeVault, and Endicott, p 103

85. In ICD-10-PCS, to code "removal of a thumbnail," the root operation would be
    A. removal.
    B. extraction.
    C. fragmentation.
    D. extirpation.

REFERENCE: Barta, DeVault, and Endicott, p 111

86. In ICD-10-CM, the final character of the code indicates laterality. An unspecified side code is also provided should the site not be identified in the medical record. If no bilateral code is provided and the condition is bilateral, the ICD-10-CM Official Coding Guidelines direct the coder to
    A. assign the unspecified side code.
    B. assign separate codes for both the left and right side.
    C. not assign a code.
    D. query the physician.

REFERENCE: DeVault, Barta, and Endicott, p 24

87. An example of a valid code in ICD-10-CM is
    A. 576.212D.
    B. Z3A.34
    C. 329.6677.
    D. BJRT23x.

REFERENCE: DeVault, Barta, and Endicott, p 24

Answer Key for Classification Systems and Secondary Data Sources

NOTE: Explanations are provided for those questions that require mathematical calculations and questions that are not clearly explained in the references that are cited.

ANSWER		EXPLANATION
1.	B	
2.	B	
3.	C	
4.	A	
5.	C	
6.	C	
7.	A	A coder should never assign a code on the basis of laboratory results alone. If findings are clearly outside the normal range and the physician has ordered additional testing or treatment, it is appropriate to consult with the physician as to whether a diagnosis should be added or whether the abnormal finding should be listed.
8.	A	
9.	B	Pilocarpine is used to treat open-angle and angle-closure glaucoma to reduce intraocular pressure.
10.	D	Digoxin is used for maintenance therapy in congestive heart failure, atrial fibrillation, atrial flutter, and paroxysmal atrial tachycardia. Ibuprofen is an anti-inflammatory drug. Oxytocin is used to initiate or improve uterine contractions at term, and haloperidol is used to manage psychotic disorders.
11.	D	
12.	C	HCPCS codes (Levels I and II) would only give the code for any procedures that were performed and would not identify the diagnosis code or cause of the accident. The correct name of the nomenclature for athletic injuries is the Standard Nomenclature of Athletic Injuries and is used to identify sports injuries. It has not been revised since 1976.
13.	D	
14.	B	All three key components (history, physical examination, and medical decision making) are required for new patients and initial visits. At least two of the three key components are required for established patients and subsequent visits.
15.	B	
16.	D	
17.	A	
18.	B	
19.	B	
20.	A	
21.	A	
22.	A	
23.	D	

Answer Key for Classification Systems and Secondary Data Sources

	ANSWER	EXPLANATION
24.	B	
25.	C	
26.	B	
27.	A	
28.	C	
29.	B	
30.	B	
31.	C	
32.	B	
33.	B	
34.	B	
35.	D	
36.	A	
37.	A	
38.	B	
39.	C	
40.	B	
41.	B	
42.	D	
43.	C	
44.	A	
45.	C	
46.	B	
47.	A	
48.	C	
49.	C	
50.	B	
51.	B	
52.	D	
53.	C	
54.	C	
55.	B	
56.	D	
57.	D	
58.	D	
59.	B	
60.	D	

Answer Key for Classification Systems and Secondary Data Sources

	ANSWER	EXPLANATION
61.	A	
62.	A	
63.	A	
64.	A	
65.	B	
66	A	
67.	C	
68.	A	
69.	A	
70.	B	
71.	A	With CPT radiology codes, there are three components that have to be considered. These are the professional, technical, and global components. The professional component describes the services of a physician who supervises the taking of an x-ray film and the interpretation with report of the results. The technical component describes the services of the person who uses the equipment, the film, and other supplies. The global component describes the combination of both professional and technical components. If the billing radiologist's services include only the supervision and interpretation component, the radiologist bills the procedure code and adds the modifier -26 to indicate that he or she did only the professional component of the procedure.
72.	B	
73.	C	
74.	D	
75.	D	
76.	A	
77.	B	
78.	B	
79.	A	
80.	C	
81.	A	
82.	A	
83.	D	
84.	C	
85.	B	
86.	B	
87.	A	ICD-10-CM codes begin with an alphabetical letter. There is a decimal after the third character. Codes can consist of three to seven characters.

REFERENCES

Abdelhak, M., Grostick, S., Hanken, M.A., & Jacobs, E. (Eds.). (2012). *Health information: Management of a strategic resource* (4th ed.). St. Louis, MO: Saunders Elsevier.

American Medical Association (AMA). *CPT assistant.* Chicago: AMA, CPT Assistant, vol. 7, no. 9, Sept. 1997, pp 1–3.

American Medical Association (AMA). (2013). *Physicians' current procedural terminology (CPT) 2013, Professional Edition.* Chicago: AMA, CPT Assistant, vol. 8, no. 10, Oct. 1998.

Bowie, M. J., (2014). *Understanding ICD-10-CM and ICD-10-PCS: A worktext* (2nd ed.). Clifton Park, NY: Delmar Cengage Learning.

DeVault, K., Barta, A. & Endicott, M. (2013). *ICD-10-CM Coder Training Manual.* Chicago: American Health Information Management Association (AHIMA).

Frisch, B. (2007). *Correct coding for Medicare, compliance, and reimbursement.* Clifton Park, NY: Delmar Cengage Learning.

Green, M. (2014). *3-2-1 Code it* (4th ed.). Clifton Park, NY: Delmar Cengage Learning.

Green, M. A., & Bowie, M. J. (2011). *Essentials of health information management: Principles and practices* (2nd ed.). Clifton Park, NY: Delmar Cengage Learning.

Hazelwood, A.C., & Venable, C. A. (2013). *ICD-10-CM and ICD-9-CM diagnostic coding and reimbursement for physician services.* Chicago: American Health Information Management Association (AHIMA).

Johnson, S. L., & Linker, C. S. (2013). Understanding medical coding: A comprehensive guide (3rd ed.). Clifton Park, NY: Delmar Cengage Learning.

LaTour, K., Eichenwald-Maki, S., and Oachs, P. (2013). *Health information management: Concepts, principles and practice* (4th ed.). Chicago: American Health Information Management Association (AHIMA).

McWay, D. C. (2013). *Today's health information management: An integrated approach* (2nd ed.). Clifton Park, NY: Delmar Cengage Learning.

Nobles, S. (2002). *Delmar's drug reference for health care professionals.* Clifton Park, NY: Delmar Cengage Learning.

Sayles, N. (2013). *Health information management technology: An applied approach* (4th ed.). Chicago: American Health Information Management Association (AHIMA).

Schraffenberger, L. A. (2013). *Basic ICD-10-CM/PCS and ICD-9-CM coding.* Chicago: American Health Information Management Association (AHIMA).

Schraffenberger, L. A., & Kuehn, L. (2011). *Effective management of coding services* (4th ed.). Chicago: American Health Information Management Association (AHIMA).

Smith, G. (2012). *Basic current procedural terminology and HCPCS coding 2013.* Chicago: American Health Information Management Association (AHIMA).

Question	RHIA Domain Competencies							RHIT Domain Competencies						
	1	2	3	4	5	6		1	2	3	4	5	6	7
1	X							X						
2	X								X					
3	X							X						
4			X					X						
5	X							X						
6	X							X						
7	X								X					
8	X							X						
9	X								X					
10	X							X						
11	X							X						
12	X							X						
13	X								X					
14	X							X						
15	X							X						
16	X							X						
17	X							X						
18	X								X					
19	X								X					
20			X						X					
21			X					X						
22	X							X						
23	X							X						
24	X							X						
25	X							X						
26	X								X					
27	X							X						
28	X									X				
29	X								X					
30	X							X						
31	X								X					
32	X								X					
33	X							X						
34	X							X						
35	X							X						
36	X							X						
37	X							X						
38	X							X						
39	X								X					
40	X								X					
41	X							X						
42	X								X					
43	X								X					
44	X								X					
45			X						X					
46	X								X					
47	X								X					
48	X							X						
49	X								X					
50	X							X						
51	X								X					
52	X								X					
53	X								X					

Title: RHIA AND RHIT COMPETENCIES BY QUESTION FOR CLASSIFICATION SYSTEMS AND SECONDARY DATA SOURCES

Question	RHIA Domain Competencies							RHIT Domain Competencies						
	1	2	3	4	5	6		1	2	3	4	5	6	7
54	X								X					
55	X							X						
56	X								X					
57	X								X					
58	X								X					
59	X								X					
60	X								X					
61	X								X					
62	X								X					
63	X								X					
64			X					X						
65	X							X						
66	X							X						
67	X							X						
68	X							X						
69	X							X						
70	X							X						
71	X								X					
72	X							X						
73	X								X					
74	X								X					
75	X								X					
76	X							X						
77	X								X					
78	X								X					
79	X								X					
80	X								X					
81	X								X					
82	X								X					
83	X								X					
84	X								X					
85	X							X						
86	X							X						
87	X							X						
88	X								X					
89	X							X						
90	X								X					
91	X							X						
92	X							X						
93	X								X					
94	X								X					
95	X								X					
96	X								X					
97	X								X					
98	X								X					
99	X								X					
100	X								X					
101	X							X						
102	X								X					
103									X					

Table title: RHIA AND RHIT COMPETENCIES BY QUESTION FOR CLASSIFICATION SYSTEMS AND SECONDARY DATA SOURCES

Question	RHIA Domain Competencies							RHIT Domain Competencies						
	1	2	3	4	5	6		1	2	3	4	5	6	7
104	X								X					
105	X							X						
106	X								X					
107	X								X					
108	X								X					
109	X								X					
110	X								X					

RHIA AND RHIT COMPETENCIES BY QUESTION FOR
CLASSIFICATION SYSTEMS AND SECONDARY DATA SOURCES

VI. Medical Billing and Reimbursement Systems

Toni Cade, MBA, RHIA, CCS, FAHIMA

1. The case-mix management system that utilizes information from the Minimum Data Set (MDS) in long-term care settings is called
   A. Medicare Severity Diagnosis Related Groups (MS-DRGs).
   B. Resource Based Relative Value System (RBRVS).
   C. Resource Utilization Groups (RUGs).
   D. Ambulatory Patient Classifications (APCs).

REFERENCE: Green, p 862

2. The prospective payment system used to reimburse home health agencies for patients with Medicare utilizes data from the:
   A. MDS (Minimum Data Set).
   B. OASIS (Outcome and Assessment Information Set).
   C. UHDDS (Uniform Hospital Discharge Data Set).
   D. UACDS (Uniform Ambulatory Core Data Set).

REFERENCE: Green, p 863
               Schraffenberger and Kuehn, p 140

3. Under APCs, the payment status indicator "N" means that the payment
   A. is for ancillary services.
   B. is for a clinic or an emergency visit.
   C. is discounted at 50%.
   D. is packaged into the payment for other services.

REFERENCE: Sayles, pp 275–276

4. All of the following items are "packaged" under the Medicare outpatient prospective payment system, EXCEPT for
   A. recovery room.   C. anesthesia.
   B. medical supplies.   D. medical visits.

REFERENCE: LaTour, Eichenwald-Maki, and Oachs, p 393
               Sayles, p 330

5. Under the RBRVS, each HCPCS/CPT code contains three components, each having assigned relative value units. These three components are
   A. geographic index, wage index, and cost of living index.
   B. fee-for-service, per diem payment, and capitation.
   C. conversion factor, CMS weight, and hospital-specific rate.
   D. physician work, practice expense, and malpractice insurance expense.

REFERENCE: Green, p 867

6. The prospective payment system used to reimburse hospitals for Medicare hospital outpatients is called
   A. APGs.
   B. RBRVS.
   C. APCs.
   D. MS-DRGs.

REFERENCE: Green, p 863
               Schraffenberger and Kuehn, p 196

7. A Medicare patient was seen by Dr. Zachary, who is a nonparticipating physician. The charge for the office visit was $125. The Medicare beneficiary had already met his deductible. The Medicare Fee Schedule amount is $100. Dr. Zachary does not accept assignment. The office manager will apply a practice termed as "balance billing," which means that the patient is
   A. financially liable for the Medicare Fee Schedule amount.
   B. financially liable for charges in excess of the Medicare Fee Schedule, up to a limit.
   C. not financially liable for any amount.
   D. financially liable for only the deductible.

REFERENCE: Sayles, pp 295–297

8. The prospective payment system based on resource utilization groups (RUGs) is used for reimbursement to _____ for patients with Medicare.
   A. freestanding ambulatory surgery centers
   B. hospital-based outpatients
   C. intermediate care facilities
   D. skilled nursing facilities

REFERENCE: Schraffenberger and Kuehn, p 212

9. The _____ is a statement sent to the provider to explain payments made by third-party payers.
   A. remittance advice
   B. advance beneficiary notice
   C. attestation statement
   D. acknowledgment notice

REFERENCE: Green, p 886
               Green and Rowell, p 768

10. How many major diagnostic categories are there in the MS-DRG system?
   A. 100
   B. 2,000
   C. 80
   D. 25

REFERENCE: Scott, p 37

11. The computer-to-computer transfer of data between providers and third-party payers in a data format agreed upon by both parties is called
    A. HIPAA (Health Insurance Portability and Accountability Act).
    B. electronic data interchange (EDI).
    C. health information exchange (HIE).
    D. health data exchange (HDE).

REFERENCE: Green and Rowell, pp 76, 751

12. A computer software program that assigns appropriate MS-DRGs according to the information provided for each episode of care is called a(n)
    A. encoder.
    B. case-mix analyzer.
    C. grouper.
    D. scrubber.

REFERENCE: Casto and Forrestal, p 134

13. The standard claim form used by hospitals to request reimbursement for inpatient and outpatient procedures performed or services provided is called the
    A. UB-04.
    B. CMS-1500.
    C. CMS-1491.
    D. CMS-1600.

REFERENCE: Brown and Tyler, p 37
                Green and Rowell, p 771
                Scott, p 76

14. Under ASCs, when multiple procedures are performed during the same surgical session, a payment reduction is applied. The procedure in the highest level group is reimbursed at _____ and all remaining procedures are reimbursed at _____.
    A. 50%, 25%
    B. 100%, 50%
    C. 100%, 25%
    D. 100%, 75%

REFERENCE: Casto and Forrestal, p 192

15. The _____ refers to a statement sent to the patient to show how much the provider billed, how much Medicare reimbursed the provider, and what the patient must pay the provider.
    A. Medicare summary notice
    B. remittance advice
    C. advance beneficiary notice
    D. coordination of benefits

REFERENCE: Green and Rowell, p 762
                LaTour, Eichenwald-Maki, and Oachs, p 445
                Sayles, pp 289–290

16. Currently, which prospective payment system is used to determine the payment to the "physician" for physician services covered under Medicare Part B, such as outpatient surgery performed on a Medicare patient?
    A. MS-DRGs
    B. APCs
    C. RBRVS
    D. ASCs

REFERENCE: Green, p 867
                Schraffenberger and Kuehn, p 210

17. Which of the following best describes the situation of a provider who agrees to accept assignment for Medicare Part B services?
    A. The provider is reimbursed at 15% above the allowed charge.
    B. The provider is paid according to the Medicare Physician Fee Schedule (MPFS) plus 10%.
    C. The provider cannot bill the patients for the balance between the MPFS amount and the total charges.
    D. The provider is a nonparticipating provider.

REFERENCE: Green and Rowell, p 536

18. When the MS-DRG payment received by the hospital is lower than the actual charges for providing the inpatient services for a patient with Medicare, then the hospital
    A. makes a profit.
    B. can bill the patient for the difference.
    C. absorbs the loss.
    D. can bill Medicare for the difference.

REFERENCE: LaTour, Eichenwald-Maki, and Oachs, p 432

19. Under ASCs, bilateral procedures are reimbursed at _____ of the payment rate for their group.
    A. 50%
    B. 100%
    C. 200%
    D. 150%

REFERENCE: Casto and Forrestal, p 192

Use the following table to answer questions 20 through 23.

Plantation Hospital's TOP 10 MS-DRGs

MS-DRG	Description	Number of Patients	CMS Relative Weight
470	Major joint replacement or reattachment of lower extremity w/o MCC	2,750	1.9871
392	Esophagitis, gastroent & misc. digestive disorders w/o MCC	2,200	0.7121
194	Simple pneumonia & pleurisy w CC	1,150	1.0235
247	Perc cardiovasc proc 2 drug-eluting stent w/o MCC	900	2.1255
293	Heart failure & shock w/o CC/MCC	850	0.8765
313	Chest pain	650	0.5489
292	Heart failure & shock w CC	550	1.0134
690	Kidney & urinary tract infections w/o MCC	400	0.8000
192	Chronic obstructive pulmonary disease w/o CC/MCC	300	0.8145
871	Septicemia w/o MV 96+ hours w MCC	250	1.7484

20. The case-mix index (CMI) for the top 10 MS-DRGs above is
    A. 1.164.
    B. 1.278.
    C. 0.782.
    D. 1.097.

REFERENCE: Abdelhak, Grostick, and Hanken, p 671
               Casto and Forrestal, p 127
               Sayles, p 269

21. Which individual MS-DRGs has the highest reimbursement?
    A. 247
    B. 470
    C. 871
    D. 293

REFERENCE: Casto and Forrestal, p 127
Sayles, p 269

22. Based on this patient volume, during this time period, the MS-DRG that brings in the highest "total" reimbursement to the hospital is
    A. 470.
    B. 247.
    C. 392.
    D. 871.

REFERENCE: Casto and Forrestal, p 127
Sayles, p 296

23. Based on this patient volume, the MS-DRG that brings in the highest total profit to the hospital is
    A. 470.
    B. 247.
    C. 392.
    D. It cannot be determined from this information.

REFERENCE: Casto and Forrestal, p 127
Sayles, p 269

24. The Health Insurance Portability and Accountability Act (HIPAA) requires the retention of health insurance claims and accounting records for a minimum of ____ years, unless state law specifies a longer period.
    A. six
    B. five
    C. seven
    D. ten

REFERENCE: Green and Rowell, p 114

25. ____ is knowingly making false statements or representation of material facts to obtain a benefit or payment for which no entitlement would otherwise exist.
    A. Fraud
    B. Whistle-blowing
    C. Abuse
    D. Assault

REFERENCE: Abdelhak, Gorstick, and Hanken, p 672

26. These are assigned to every HCPCS/CPT code under the Medicare hospital outpatient prospective payment system to identify how the service or procedure described by the code would be paid.
    A. geographic practice cost indices
    B. major diagnostic categories
    C. minimum data set
    D. payment status indicator

REFERENCE: Casto and Forrestal, p 177

27. The term used to indicate that the service or procedure is reasonable and necessary for the diagnosis or treatment of illness or injury consistent with generally accepted standards of care is
    A. appropriateness.
    B. evidence-based medicine.
    C. benchmarking.
    D. medical necessity.

REFERENCE: Green and Rowell, pp 4, 146

28. This law prohibits a physician from referring Medicare patients to clinical laboratory services where the doctor or a member of his family has a financial interest.
    A. the False Claims Act
    B. the Civil Monetary Penalties Act
    C. the Federal Antikickback Statute
    D. the Stark I Law

REFERENCE: Green, p 884
               Green and Bowie, p 325

29. ____ are errors in medical care that are clearly identifiable, preventable, and serious in their consequences for patients.
    A. Sentinel events
    B. Adverse preventable events
    C. Never events
    D. Potential compensable events

REFERENCE: Green and Bowie, p 326

30. When a provider, knowingly or unknowingly, uses practices that are inconsistent with accepted medical practice and that directly or indirectly result in unnecessary costs to the Medicare program, this is called
    A. fraud.
    B. abuse.
    C. unbundling.
    D. hypercoding.

REFERENCE: Abdelhak, Gostick, and Hanken, p 672

31. What prospective payment system reimburses the provider according to prospectively determined rates for a 60-day episode of care?
    A. home health resource groups
    B. inpatient rehabilitation facility
    C. long-term care Medicare severity diagnosis-related groups
    D. the skilled nursing facility prospective payment system

REFERENCE: Green and Bowie, p 313

32. If the Medicare non-PAR approved payment amount is $128.00 for a proctoscopy, what is the total Medicare approved payment amount for a doctor who does not accept assignment, applying the limiting charge for this procedure?
    A. $140.80   C. $192.00
    B. $143.00   D. $147.20

REFERENCE: Green and Rowell, pp 64–65

33. Under the inpatient prospective payment system (IPPS), there is a 3-day payment window (formerly referred to as the 72-hour rule). This rule requires that outpatient preadmission services that are provided by a hospital up to three calendar days prior to a patient's inpatient admission be covered by the IPPS MS-DRG payment for
   A. diagnostic services.
   B. therapeutic (or nondiagnostic) services whereby the inpatient principal diagnosis code (ICD-9-CM) exactly matches the code used for preadmission services.
   C. therapeutic (or nondiagnostic) services whereby the inpatient principal diagnosis code (ICD-9-CM) does not match the code used for preadmission services.
   D. both A and B.

REFERENCE: Green, pp 858–859
               Green and Bowie, p 313
               Green and Rowell, pp 371–372

34. This initiative was instituted by the government to eliminate fraud and abuse and recover overpayments, and involves the use of _____. Charts are audited to identify Medicare overpayments and underpayments. These entities are paid based on a percentage of money they identify and collect on behalf of the government.
   A. Clinical Data Abstraction Centers (CDAC)
   B. Quality Improvement Organizations (QIO)
   C. Medicare Code Editors (MCE)
   D. Recovery Audit Contractors (RAC)

REFERENCE: Green, p 850
               Scott, p 119

35. When a patient is discharged from the inpatient rehabilitation facility and returns within three calendar days (prior to midnight on the third day) this is called a(n)
   A. interrupted stay.   C. per diem.
   B. transfer.   D. qualified discharge.

REFERENCE: Casto and Forrestal, pp 233–234
               Scott, pp 68–69

36. In a global payment methodology, which is sometimes applied to radiological and similar types of procedures that involve professional and technical components, all of the following are part of the "technical" components EXCEPT
   A. radiological equipment.   C. radiological supplies.
   B. physician services.   D. radiologic technicians

REFERENCE: Green and Rowell, p 320
               LaTour, Eichenwald-Maki, and Oachs, p 430
               Sayles, pp 263–264

37. Changes in case-mix index (CMI) may be attributed to all of the following factors EXCEPT
   A. changes in medical staff composition.
   B. changes in coding rules.
   C. changes in services offered.
   D. changes in coding productivity.

REFERENCE: Schraffenberger and Kuehn, pp 484–485

38. This prospective payment system replaced the Medicare physician payment system of "customary, prevailing, and reasonable (CPR)" charges whereby physicians were reimbursed according to their historical record of the charge for the provision of each service.
    A. Medicare Physician Fee Schedule (MPFS)
    B. Medicare Severity-Diagnosis Related Groups (MS-DRGs)
    C. Global payment
    D. Capitation

REFERENCE: Green, p 867
              Green and Rowell, pp 379–380

39. CMS-identified "Hospital-Acquired Conditions" mean that when a particular diagnosis is not "present on admission," CMS determines it to be
    A. medically necessary.
    B. reasonably preventable.
    C. a valid comorbidity.
    D. the principal diagnosis.

REFERENCE: LaTour, Eichenwald-Maki, and Oachs, pp 433–434

40. This process involves the gathering of charge documents from all departments within the facility that have provided services to patients. The purpose is to make certain that all charges are coded and entered into the billing system.
    A. precertification
    B. insurance verification
    C. charge capturing
    D. revenue cycle

REFERENCE: Diamond, p 9

41. The Correct Coding Initiative (CCI) edits contain a listing of codes under two columns titled "comprehensive codes" and "component codes." According to the CCI edits, when a provider bills Medicare for a procedure that appears in both columns for the same beneficiary on the same date of service
    A. code only the component code.
    B. do not code either one.
    C. code only the comprehensive code.
    D. code both the comprehensive code and the component code.

REFERENCE: Green, pp 395–398
              Green and Rowell, p 333

42. The following type of hospital is considered excluded when it applies for and receives a waiver from CMS. This means that the hospital does not participate in the inpatient prospective payment system (IPPS)
    A. rehabilitation hospital
    B. long-term care hospital
    C. psychiatric hospital
    D. cancer hospital

REFERENCE: Green, p 858

43. These are financial protections to ensure that certain types of facilities (e.g., children's hospitals) recoup all of their losses due to the differences in their APC payments and the pre-APC payments.
    A. limiting charge
    B. indemnity insurance
    C. hold harmless
    D. pass through

REFERENCE: Casto and Forrestal, p 176

44. LCDs and NCDs are review policies that describe the circumstances of coverage for various types of medical treatment. They advise physicians which services Medicare considers reasonable and necessary and may indicate the need for an advance beneficiary notice. They are developed by the Centers for Medicare and Medicaid Services (CMS) and Medicare Administrative Contractors. LCD and NCD are acronyms that stand for
    A. local covered determinations and noncovered determinations.
    B. local coverage determinations and national coverage determinations.
    C. list of covered decisions and noncovered decisions.
    D. local contractor's decisions and national contractor's decisions.

REFERENCE: Green, p 775
Green and Rowell, pp 418–419

Use the following table to answer questions 45 through 50.

EXAMPLE OF A CHARGE DESCRIPTION MASTER (CDM) FILE LAYOUT

Charge Service Code	Item Service Description	General Ledger Key	HCPCS Code		Charge	Revenue Code	Activity Date
			Medicare	Medicaid			
49683105	CT scan; head; w/out contrast	3	70450	70450	500.00	0351	1/1/2013
49683106	CT scan; head; with contrast	3	70460	70460	675.00	0351	1/1/2013

45. This information is printed on the UB-04 claim form to represent the cost center (e.g., lab, radiology, cardiology, respiratory, etc.) for the department in which the item is provided. It is used for Medicare billing.
    A. HCPCS
    B. revenue code
    C. charge/service code
    D. general ledger key

REFERENCE: Green, pp 870–871
Green and Rowell, pp 386–388
Schraffenberger and Kuehn, pp 225–226

46. This information is used because it provides a uniform system of identifying procedures, services, or supplies. Multiple columns can be available for various financial classes.
    A. HCPCS code
    B. revenue code
    C. general ledger key
    D. charge/service code

REFERENCE: Green, pp 780–781
Green and Rowell, pp 386–388
Schraffenberger and Kuehn, pp 226–227

47. This information provides a narrative name of the services provided. This information should be presented in a clear and concise manner. When possible, the narratives from the HCPCS/CPT book should be utilized.
    A. general ledger key
    B. HCPCS
    C. item/service description
    D. revenue code

REFERENCE: Green, pp 870–871
               Green and Rowell, pp 386–388
               Schraffenberger and Kuehn, p 225

48. This information is the numerical identification of the service or supply. Each item has a unique number with a prefix that indicates the department number (the number assigned to a specific ancillary department) and an item number (the number assigned by the accounting department or the business office) for a specific procedure or service represented on the chargemaster.
    A. charge/service code
    B. HCPCS code
    C. revenue code
    D. general ledger key

REFERENCE: Green, pp 870–871
               Green and Rowell, pp 386–388
               Schraffenberger and Kuehn, p 225

49. This information is used to assign each item to a particular section of the general ledger in a particular facility's accounting section. Reports can be generated from this information to include statistics related to volume in terms of numbers, dollars, and payer types.
    A. general ledger key
    B. charge/service code
    C. revenue code
    D. HCPCS code

REFERENCE: Green, pp 870–871
               Schraffenberger and Kuehn, p 225

50. Under APCs, the patient is responsible for paying the coinsurance amount based upon ____ of the national median charge for the services rendered.
    A. 50%
    B. 15%
    C. 20%
    D. 80%

REFERENCE: Green and Bowie, p 314

51. ____ is a joint federal and state program that provides health care coverage to low-income populations and certain aged and disabled individuals.
    A. TRICARE
    B. Medicare Part A
    C. Medicaid
    D. Medicare Part B

REFERENCE: Green, p 851

52. The DNFB report includes all patients who have been discharged from the facility but for whom, for one reason or another, the billing process is not complete. DNFB is an acronym for

    _____.
    A. diagnosis not finally balanced
    B. days not fiscally balanced
    C. dollars not fully billed
    D. discharged not final billed

REFERENCE: Schraffenberger and Kuehn, p 461

53. The limiting charge is a percentage limit on fees specified by legislation that the nonparticipating physician may bill Medicare beneficiaries above the non-PAR fee schedule amount. The limiting charge is
    A. 10%.
    B. 15%.
    C. 20%.
    D. 50%.

REFERENCE: Green and Rowell, pp 380–383

Use the following case scenario to answer questions 54 through 58.

A patient with Medicare is seen in the physician's office.
The total charge for this office visit is $250.00.
The patient has previously paid his deductible under Medicare Part B.
The PAR Medicare Fee Schedule amount for this service is $200.00.
The non-PAR Medicare Fee Schedule amount for this service is $190.00.

54. The patient is financially liable for the coinsurance amount, which is
    A. 80%.
    B. 100%.
    C. 20%.
    D. 15%.

REFERENCE: Green and Rowell, pp 380–383

55. If this physician is a participating physician who accepts assignment for this claim, the total amount the physician will receive is
    A. $200.00.
    B. $250.00.
    C. $218.50.
    D. $190.00.

REFERENCE: Green and Rowell, pp 380–383

56. If this physician is a nonparticipating physician who does NOT accept assignment for this claim, the total amount the physician will receive is
    A. $250.00.
    B. $200.00.
    C. $218.50.
    D. $190.00.

REFERENCE: Green and Rowell, pp 380–383

57. If this physician is a participating physician who accepts assignment for this claim, the total amount of the patient's financial liability (out-of-pocket expense) is
    A. $200.00.
    B. $40.00.
    C. $160.00.
    D. $30.00.

REFERENCE: Green and Rowell, pp 380–383

58. If this physician is a nonparticipating physician who does NOT accept assignment for this claim, the total amount of the patient's financial liability (out-of-pocket expense) is
    A. $66.50.
    B. $38.00.
    C. $190.00.
    D. $152.00.

REFERENCE: Green and Rowell, pp 380–383

59. A fiscal year is a yearly accounting period. It is the 12-month period on which a budget is planned. The federal fiscal year is
    A. October 1st through September 30 of the next year.
    B. January 1st through December 31.
    C. July 1st through the June 30 of the next year.
    D. April 1st through March 31 of the next year.

REFERENCE: Casto and Forrestal, p 309

60. There are times when documentation is incomplete or insufficient to support the diagnoses found in the chart. The most common way of communicating with the physician for answers is by
    A. e-mailing physicians.
    B. using physician query forms.
    C. calling the physician's office.
    D. leaving notes in the chart.

REFERENCE: Green, pp 15–17
              Scott, pp 189–199

61. Under APCs, payment status indicator "X" means
    A. ancillary services.
    B. clinic or emergency department visit (medical visits).
    C. significant procedure, multiple procedure reduction applies.
    D. significant procedure, not discounted when multiple.

REFERENCE: Casto and Forrestal, p 177
              Diamond, p 337
              LaTour, Eichenwald-Maki, and Oachs, p 436

62. Under APCs, payment status indicator "V" means
    A. ancillary services.
    B. clinic or emergency department visit (medical visits).
    C. inpatient procedure.
    D. significant procedure, not discounted when multiple.

REFERENCE: Casto and Forrestal, p 177
              Diamond, p 337
              LaTour, Eichenwald-Maki, and Oachs, p 436

63. Under APCs, payment status indicator "S" means
    A. ancillary services.
    B. clinic or emergency department visit (medical visits).
    C. significant procedure, multiple procedure reduction applies.
    D. significant procedure, multiple procedure reduction does not apply.

REFERENCE: Casto and Forrestal, p 177
              Diamond, p 337
              Green and Rowell, pp 373–374
              LaTour, Eichenwald-Maki, and Oachs, p 436

64. Under APCs, payment status indicator "T" means
    A. ancillary services.
    B. clinic or emergency department visit (medical visits).
    C. significant procedure, multiple procedure reduction applies.
    D. significant procedure, not discounted when multiple.

REFERENCE: Casto and Forrestal, p 177
              Diamond, p 337
              Green, pp 863–864
              LaTour, Eichenwald-Maki, and Oachs, p 436

65. Under APCs, payment status indicator "C" means
    A. ancillary services.
    B. inpatient procedures/services.
    C. significant procedure, multiple procedure reduction applies.
    D. significant procedure, not discounted when multiple.

REFERENCE:　　Casto and Forrestal, p 177
　　　　　　　　Diamond, p 337
　　　　　　　　LaTour, Eichenwald-Maki, and Oachs, p 436

66. This is a 10-digit, intelligence-free, numeric identifier designed to replace all previous provider legacy numbers. This number identifies the physician universally to all payers. This number is issued to all HIPAA-covered entities. It is mandatory on the CMS-1500 and UB-04 claim forms.
    A. National Practitioner Databank (NPD)
    B. Universal Physician Number (UPN)
    C. Master Patient Index (MPI)
    D. National Provider Identifier (NPI)

REFERENCE:　　Green and Rowell, pp 29, 126
　　　　　　　　Rimmer, p 30

67. In the managed care industry, there are specific reimbursement concepts, such as "capitation." All of the following statements are true in regard to the concept of "capitation," EXCEPT
    A. each service is paid based on the actual charges.
    B. the volume of services and their expense do not affect reimbursement.
    C. capitation means paying a fixed amount per member per month.
    D. capitation involves a group of physicians or an individual physician.

REFERENCE:　　Green and Rowell, p 45

68. Which of the following statements is FALSE regarding the use of modifiers with the CPT codes?
    A. All modifiers will alter (increase or decrease) the reimbursement of the procedure.
    B. Some procedures may require more than one modifier.
    C. Modifiers are appended to the end of the CPT code.
    D. Not all procedures need a modifier.

REFERENCE:　　Richards, p 147

69. This document is published by the Office of Inspector General (OIG) every year. It details the OIG's focus for Medicare fraud and abuse for that year. It gives health care providers an indication of general and specific areas that are targeted for review. It can be found on the Internet on CMS' Web site.
    A. the OIG's Evaluation and Management Documentation Guidelines
    B. the OIG's Model Compliance Plan
    C. the Federal Register
    D. the OIG's Workplan

REFERENCE:　　Sayles, p 305

70. Accounts Receivable (A/R) refers to
    A. cases that have not yet been paid.
    B. the amount the hospital was paid.
    C. cases that have been paid.
    D. denials that have been returned to the hospital.

REFERENCE: Schraffenberger and Kuehn, p 458

71. The following coding system(s) is/are utilized in the MS-DRG prospective payment methodology for assignment and proper reimbursement.
    A. HCPCS/CPT codes
    B. ICD-9-CM codes
    C. both HCPCS/CPT codes and ICD-9-CM codes
    D. none of the above

REFERENCE: Green, p 862
               Sayles, p 267

72. The following coding system(s) is/are utilized in the Inpatient Psychiatric Facilities (IPFs) prospective payment methodology for assignment and proper reimbursement.
    A. HCPCS/CPT codes
    B. ICD-9-CM codes
    C. both HCPCS/CPT codes and ICD-9-CM codes
    D. none of the above

REFERENCE: Green, p 865
               Sayles, p 285

73. An Advance Beneficiary Notice (ABN) is a document signed by the
    A. utilization review coordinator indicating that the patient stay is not medically necessary.
    B. physician advisor indicating that the patient's stay is denied.
    C. patient indicating whether he/she wants to receive services that Medicare probably will not pay for.
    D. provider indicating that Medicare will not pay for certain services.

REFERENCE: Green, p 358
               LaTour, Eichenwald-Maki, and Oachs, pp 449–450

74. CMS identified Hospital-Acquired Conditions (HACs). Some of these HACs include foreign objects retained after surgery, blood incompatibility, and catheter-associated urinary tract infection. The importance of the HAC payment provision is that the hospital
    A. will receive additional payment for these conditions when they are not present on admission.
    B. will not receive additional payment for these conditions when they are not present on admission.
    C. will receive additional payment for these conditions whether they are present on admission or not.
    D. will not receive additional payment for these conditions when they are present on admission.

REFERENCE: LaTour, Eichenwald-Maki, and Oachs, pp 433–434

75. Under Medicare Part B, all of the following statements are true and are applicable to nonparticipating physician providers, EXCEPT
    A. providers must file all Medicare claims.
    B. nonparticipating providers have a higher fee schedule than that for participating providers.
    C. fees are restricted to charging no more than the "limiting charge" on nonassigned claims.
    D. collections are restricted to only the deductible and coinsurance due at the time of service on an assigned claim.

REFERENCE: Green and Rowell, pp 380–383

76. Under Medicare, a beneficiary has lifetime reserve days. All of the following statements are true, EXCEPT
    A. the patient has a total of 60 lifetime reserve days.
    B. lifetime reserve days are usually reserved for use during the patient's final (terminal) hospital stay.
    C. lifetime reserve days are paid under Medicare Part B.
    D. lifetime reserve days are not renewable, meaning once a patient uses all of their lifetime reserve days, the patient is responsible for the total charges.

REFERENCE: Green and Rowell, pp 528–529

77. When a provider bills separately for procedures that are a part of the major procedure, this is called
    A. fraud.   C. unbundling.
    B. packaging.   D. discounting.

REFERENCE: Brown and Tyler, p 192

78. Once all data are posted to a patient's account, the claim can be reviewed for accuracy and completeness. Many facilities have internal auditing systems. The auditing systems run each claim through a set of edits specifically designed for the various third-party payers. The auditing system identifies data that have failed edits and flags the claim for correction. These "internal" auditing systems are called
    A. scrubbers.   C. groupers.
    B. pricers.   D. encoders.

REFERENCE: Casto and Forrestal, p 262

79. To compute the reimbursement to a particular hospital for a particular MS-DRG, multiply the hospital's base payment rate by the
    A. conversion factor.   C. geographic practice cost index.
    B. case-mix index.   D. relative weight for the MS-DRG.

REFERENCE: Casto and Forrestal, p 134

80. Under the APC methodology, discounted payments occur when
    A. there are two or more (multiple) procedures that are assigned to status indicator "T."
    B. there are two or more (multiple) procedures that are assigned to status indicator "S."
    C. modifier-73 is used to indicate a procedure is terminated after the patient is prepared but before anesthesia is started.
    D. both A and C.

REFERENCE: Green and Rowell, pp 373–374
               Schraffenberger and Kuehn, pp 207–209

81. This prospective payment system is for _____ and utilizes a Patient Assessment Instrument (PAI) to classify patients into case-mix groups (CMGs).
    A. skilled nursing facilities
    B. inpatient rehabilitation facilities
    C. home health agencies
    D. long-term acute care hospitals

REFERENCE: Green and Rowell, p 377
               Schraffenberger and Kuehn, p 213

82. Home Health Agencies (HHAs) utilize a data entry software system developed by the Centers for Medicare and Medicaid Services (CMS). This software is available to HHAs at no cost through the CMS Web site or on a CD-ROM.
    A. PACE (Patient Assessment and Comprehensive Evaluation)
    B. HAVEN (Home Assessment Validation and Entry)
    C. HHASS (Home Health Agency Software System)
    D. PEPP (Payment Error Prevention Program)

REFERENCE: Green and Rowell, p 367
               LaTour, Eichenwald-Maki, and Oachs, p 438
               Sayles, p 278

83. This information is published by the Medicare Administrative Contractors (MACs) to describe when and under what circumstances Medicare will cover a service. The ICD-9-CM and CPT/HCPCS codes are listed in the memoranda.
    A. LCD (Local Coverage Determinations)
    B. SI/IS (Severity of llness/Intensity of Service Criteria)
    C. OSHA (Occupational Safety and Health Administration)
    D. PEPP (Payment Error Prevention Program)

REFERENCE: Green and Rowell, pp 418–419

84. The term "hard coding" refers to
    A. HCPCS/CPT codes that are coded by the coders.
    B. HPCS/CPT codes that appear in the hospital's chargemaster and will be included automatically on the patient's bill.
    C. ICD-9-CM codes that are coded by the coders.
    D. ICD-9-CM codes that appear in the hospital's chargemaster and that are automatically included on the patient's bill.

REFERENCE: Schraffenberger and Kuehn, pp 228–229

85. This is the amount collected by the facility for the services it bills.
    A. costs
    B. charges
    C. reimbursement
    D. contractual allowance

REFERENCE: Schraffenberger and Kuehn, pp 433–434

86. Assume the patient has already met his or her deductible and that the physician is a Medicare participating (PAR) provider. The physician's standard fee for the services provided is $120.00. Medicare's PAR fee is $60.00. How much reimbursement will the physician receive from Medicare?
   A. $120.00
   B. $ 60.00
   C. $ 48.00
   D. $ 96.00

REFERENCE: Green and Rowell, pp 380–383

87. This accounting method attributes a dollar figure to every input required to provide a service.
   A. cost accounting
   B. charge accounting
   C. reimbursement
   D. contractual allowance

REFERENCE: Schraffenberger and Kuehn, p 433

88. This is the amount the facility actually bills for the services it provides.
   A. costs
   B. charges
   C. reimbursement
   D. contractual allowance

REFERENCE: Schraffenberger and Kuehn, p 433

89. This is the difference between what is charged and what is paid.
   A. costs
   B. customary
   C. reimbursement
   D. contractual allowance

REFERENCE: Schraffenberger and Kuehn, p 433

90. When appropriate, under the outpatient PPS, a hospital can use this CPT code in place of, but not in addition to, a code for a medical visit or emergency department service.
   A. CPT Code 99291 (critical care)
   B. CPT Code 99358 (prolonged evaluation and management service)
   C. CPT Code 35001 (direct repair of aneurysm)
   D. CPT Code 50300 (donor nephrectomy)

REFERENCE: Kirchoff, p 42

91. To monitor timely claims processing in a hospital, a summary report of "patient receivables" is generated frequently. Aged receivables can negatively affect a facility's cash flow; therefore, to maintain the facility's fiscal integrity, the HIM manager must routinely analyze this report. Though this report has no standard title, it is often called the
   A. remittance advice.
   B. periodic interim payments.
   C. DNFB (discharged, no final bill).
   D. chargemaster.

REFERENCE: LaTour, Eichenwald-Maki, and Oachs, p 470

92. Assume the patient has already met his or her deductible and that the physician is a nonparticipating Medicare provider but does accept assignment. The standard fee for the services provided is $120.00. Medicare's PAR fee is $60.00 and Medicare's non-PAR fee is $57.00. How much reimbursement will the physician receive from Medicare?
   A. $120.00
   B. $60.00
   C. $57.00
   D. $45.60

REFERENCE: Green and Rowell, pp 380–383

93. CMS assigns one _____ to each APC and each _____ code.
    A. payment status indicator, HCPCS
    B. CPT code, HCPCS
    C. MS-DRG, CPT
    D. payment status indicator, ICD-9-CM

REFERENCE: Kirchoff, p 11

94. All of the following statements are true of MS-DRGs, EXCEPT
    A. a patient claim may have multiple MS-DRGs.
    B. the MS-DRG payment received by the hospital may be lower than the actual cost of providing the services.
    C. special circumstances can result in a cost outlier payment to the hospital.
    D. there are several types of hospitals that are excluded from the Medicare inpatient PPS.

REFERENCE: Green and Rowell, pp 367–370
               Johns, pp 321–324
               LaTour, Eichenwald-Maki, and Oachs, pp 431–433
               Sayles, pp 266–270

95. This program, formerly called CHAMPUS (Civilian Health and Medical Program—Uniformed Services), is a health care program for active members of the military and other qualified family members.
    A. TRICARE   C. Indian Health Service
    B. CHAMPVA   D. workers' compensation

REFERENCE: Green and Rowell, p 602
               Richards, pp 116–118, 300
               Sayles, p 251

96. When health care providers are found guilty under any of the civil false claims statutes, the Office of Inspector General is responsible for negotiating these settlements and the provider is placed under a
    A. Fraud Prevention Memorandum of Understanding.
    B. Noncompliance Agreement.
    C. Corporate Integrity Agreement.
    D. Recovery Audit Contract.

REFERENCE: Brown and Tyler, p 267

97. Regarding hospital emergency department and hospital outpatient evaluation and management CPT code assignment, which statement is true?
    A. Each facility is accountable for developing and implementing its own methodology.
    B. The level of service codes reported by the facility must match those reported by the physician.
    C. Each facility must use the same methodology used by physician coders based on the history, examination, and medical decision-making components.
    D. Each facility must use acuity sheets with acuity levels and assign points for each service performed.

REFERENCE: Diamond, pp 285–287

98. CMS adjusts the Medicare Severity DRGs and the reimbursement rates every
    A. calendar year beginning January 1.
    B. quarter.
    C. month.
    D. fiscal year beginning October 1.

REFERENCE: Sayles, p 268

99. In calculating the fee for a physician's reimbursement, the three relative value units are each multiplied by the
    A. geographic practice cost indices.
    B. national conversion factor.
    C. usual and customary fees for the service.
    D. cost of living index for the particular region.

REFERENCE: Green, p 867
                Green and Rowell, pp 379–380

100. If a participating provider's usual fee for a service is $700.00 and Medicare's allowed amount is $450.00, what amount is written off by the physician?
    A. none of it is written off   C. $340.00
    B. $250.00   D. $391.00

REFERENCE: Green and Rowell, pp 380–383

101. Health plans that use _____ reimbursement methods issue lump-sum payments to providers to compensate them for all the health care services delivered to a patient for a specific illness and/or over a specific period of time.
    A. episode-of-care (EOC)   C. fee-for-service
    B. capitation   D. bundled

REFERENCE: Sayles, p 262

102. _____ offers voluntary, supplemental medical insurance to help pay for physician's services, outpatient hospital services, medical services, and medical-surgical supplies not covered by the hospitalization plan.
    A. Medicare Part A
    B. Medicare Part B
    C. Medicare Part C
    D. Medicare Part D

REFERENCE: Kirchoff, p 296

103. Commercial insurance plans usually reimburse health care providers under some type of _____ payment system, whereas the federal Medicare program uses some type of _____ payment system.
    A. prospective, retrospective   C. retrospective, prospective
    B. retrospective, concurrent   D. prospective, concurrent

REFERENCE: Green and Rowell, pp 360–361
                Sayles, pp 260–261

104. When the third-party payer refuses to grant payment to the provider, this is called a
    A. denied claim.
    B. clean claim.
    C. rejected claim.
    D. unprocessed claim.

REFERENCE: Rimmer, p 62

105. Some services are performed by a nonphysician practitioner (such as a Physician Assistant). These services are an integral yet incidental component of a physician's treatment. A physician must have personally performed an initial visit and must remain actively involved in the continuing care. Medicare requires direct supervision for these services to be billed. This is called
    A. "Technical component" billing.
    B. "Assignment" billing.
    C. "Incident to" billing.
    D. "Assistant" billing.

REFERENCE: Green and Rowell, p 385

106. When payments can be made to the provider by EFT, this means that the reimbursement is
    A. sent to the provider by check.
    B. sent to the patient, who then pays the provider.
    C. combined with all other payments from the third party payer.
    D. directly deposited into the provider's bank account.

REFERENCE: Richards, p 175

107. The following services are excluded under the Hospital Outpatient Prospective Payment System (OPPS) Ambulatory Payment Classification (APC) methodology.
    A. surgical procedures
    B. clinical lab services
    C. clinic/emergency visits
    D. radiology/radiation therapy

REFERENCE: Diamond, p 333

108. A HIPPS (Health Insurance Prospective Payment System) code is a five-character alphanumeric code. A HIPPS code is used by
    A. ambulatory surgery centers (ASC).
    B. home health agencies (HHA).
    C. inpatient rehabilitation facilities (IRF).
    D. B and C.

REFERENCE: Casto and Forrestal, p 310

109. The Centers for Medicare and Medicaid Services (CMS) will make an adjustment to the MS-DRG payment for certain conditions that the patient was not admitted with, but were acquired during the hospital stay. Therefore, hospitals are required to report an indicator for each diagnosis. This indicator is referred to as
    A. a sentinel event.
    B. a payment status indicator.
    C. a hospital acquired condition.
    D. present on admission.

REFERENCE: Casto and Forrestal, pp 293–294

110. A patient is admitted for a diagnostic workup for cachexia. The final diagnosis is malignant neoplasm of lung with metastasis. The present on admission (POA) indicator is
    A. Y = Present at the time of inpatient admission.
    B. N = Not present at the time of inpatient admission.
    C. U = Documentation is insufficient to determine if condition was present at the time of admission.
    D. W = Provider is unable to clinically determine if condition was present at the time of admission.

REFERENCE: Green, p 861
              LaTour, Eichenwald-Maki, and Oachs, pp 433–434

111. A patient undergoes outpatient surgery. During the recovery period, the patient develops atrial fibrillation and is subsequently admitted to the hospital as an inpatient. The present on admission (POA) indicator is
    A. Y = Present at the time of inpatient admission.
    B. N = Not present at the time of inpatient admission.
    C. U = Documentation is insufficient to determine if condition was present at the time of admission.
    D. W = Provider is unable to clinically determine if condition was present at the time of admission.

REFERENCE: Green, p 861
              LaTour, Eichenwald-Maki, and Oachs, pp 433–434

112. A patient is admitted to the hospital for a coronary artery bypass surgery. Postoperatively, he develops a pulmonary embolism. The present on admission (POA) indicator is
    A. Y = Present at the time of inpatient admission.
    B. N = Not present at the time of inpatient admission.
    C. U = Documentation is insufficient to determine if condition was present at the time of admission.
    D. W = Provider is unable to clinically determine if condition was present at the time of admission.

REFERENCE: Green, p 861
              LaTour, Eichenwald-Maki, and Oachs, pp 433–434

113. The nursing initial assessment upon admission documents the presence of a decubitus ulcer. There is no mention of the decubitus ulcer in the physician documentation until several days after admission. The present on admission (POA) indicator is
    A. Y = Present at the time of inpatient admission.
    B. N = Not present at the time of inpatient admission.
    C. U = Documentation is insufficient to determine if condition was present at the time of admission.
    D. W = Provider is unable to clinically determine if condition was present at the time of admission.

REFERENCE: Green, p 861
              LaTour, Eichenwald-Maki, and Oachs, pp 433–434

114. The present on admission (POA) indicator is required to be assigned to the _____ diagnosis(es) for _____ claims on _____ admissions.
    A. principal and secondary, Medicare, inpatient
    B. principal, all, inpatient
    C. principal and secondary, all, inpatient and outpatient
    D. principal, Medicare, inpatient and outpatient

REFERENCE: Green, p 861
                      LaTour, Eichenwald-Maki, and Oachs, pp 433–434

Answer Key for Medical Billing and Reimbursement Systems

ANSWER   EXPLANATION

1. C
2. B
3. A
4. D
5. D
6. C
7. B
8. D
9. A
10. D
11. B
12. C
13. A The UB-04 is used by hospitals. The CMS-1500 is used by physicians and other noninstitutional providers and suppliers. The CMS-1491 is used by ambulance services.
14. B
15. A
16. C The prospective payment system used to reimburse the "hospital" for outpatient surgery is APCs. The prospective payment used to reimburse a "free-standing surgery center" for outpatient surgery is ASCs. The prospective payment system used to reimburse the "physician" for outpatient surgery is RBRVS.
17. C Since the provider accepts assignment, he will accept the Medicare Physician Fee Schedule (MPFS) payment as payment in full.
18. C
19. D
20. B 12781.730/10,000 = 1.278

MS-DRG	Description	Number of Patients	CMS Relative Weight	Total CMS Relative Weight
470	Major joint replacement or reattachment of lower extremity w/o MCC	2,750	1.9871	5464.525
392	Esophagitis, gastroent & misc. digestive disorders w/o MCC	2,200	0.7121	1566.620
194	Simple pneumonia & pleurisy w CC	1,150	1.0235	1177.025
247	Perc cardiovasc proc 2 drug-eluting stent w/o MCC	900	2.1255	1912.950
293	Heart failure & shock w/o CC/MCC	850	0.8765	745.025
313	Chest pain	650	0.5489	356.785
292	Heart failure & shock w CC	550	1.0134	557.350
690	Kidney & urinary tract infections w/o MCC	400	0.8000	320.000
192	Chronic obstructive pulmonary disease w/o CC/MCC	300	0.8145	244.350
871	Septicemia w/o MV 96+ hours w MCC	250	1.7484	437.100
	Total	10,000		12781.730
	Case-Mix Index Total CMS Relative Weights (12781.730) divided by (10,000) patients			1.278

Answer Key for Medical Billing and Reimbursement Systems

ANSWER   EXPLANATION

21.   A   (See table on answer key under question 20.)
22.   A   (See table on answer key under question 20.)
23.   D   Total profit cannot be determined from this information alone. A comparison of the total charges on the bills and the PPS amount (reimbursement amount) that the hospital would receive for each MS-DRG could identify the total profit.

24.   A
25.   A
26.   D
27.   D
28.   D
29.   C
30.   B
31.   A
32.   D   The limiting charge is 15% above Medicare's approved payment amount for doctors who do NOT accept assignment ($128.00 × 1.15 = $147.20).

33.   D
34.   D
35.   A
36.   B
37.   D   Coding productivity will not directly affect CMI. Inaccuracy or poor coding quality can affect CMI.
38.   A   The Medicare Physician Fee Schedule (MPFS) reimburses providers according to predetermined rates assigned to services.

39.   B
40.   C
41.   C
42.   D   Cancer hospitals can apply for and receive waivers from the Centers for Medicare and Medicaid Services (CMS) and are therefore excluded from the inpatient prospective payment system (MS-DRGs). Rehabilitation hospitals are reimbursed under the Inpatient Rehabilitation Prospective Payment System (IRF PPS). Long-term care hospitals are reimbursed under the Long-Term Care Hospital Prospective Payment System (LTCH PPS). Skilled nursing facilities are reimbursed under the Skilled Nursing Facility Prospective Payment System (SNF PPS).

43.   C
44.   B
45.   B
46.   A
47.   C
48.   A
49.   A
50.   C
51.   C
52.   D
53.   B
54.   C

Answer Key for Medical Billing and Reimbursement Systems

ANSWER   EXPLANATION

55.   A   If a physician is a participating physician who accepts assignment, he will receive the lesser of "the total charges" or "the PAR Medicare Fee Schedule amount." In this case, the Medicare Fee Schedule amount is less; therefore, the total received by the physician is $200.00.

56.   C   If a physician is a nonparticipating physician who does not accept assignment, he can collect a maximum of 15% (the limiting charge) over the non-PAR Medicare Fee Schedule amount. In this case, the non-PAR Medicare Fee Schedule amount is $190.00 and 15% over this amount is $28.50; therefore, the total that he can collect is $218.50.

57.   B   The PAR Medicare Fee Schedule amount is $200.00. The patient has already met the deductible. Of the $200.00, the patient is responsible for 20% ($40.00). Medicare will pay 80% ($160.00). Therefore, the total financial liability for the patient is $40.00.

58.   A   If a physician is a nonparticipating physician who does not accept assignment, he may collect a maximum of 15% (the limiting charge) over the non-PAR Medicare Fee Schedule amount.

$190.00 = non-PAR Medicare Fee Schedule amount

$190.00 × 0.20 = $38.00 = patient liable for 20% coinsurance (patient previously met the deductible)

$190.00 × 0.80 = $152.00 = Medicare pays 80%

$190.00 × 0.15 = $28.50 = 15% (limiting charge) over non-PAR Medicare Fee Schedule amount

Physician can balance bill and collect from the patient the difference between the non-PAR Medicare Fee Schedule amount and the total charge amount. Therefore, the patient's financial liability is $38.00 (coinsurance) + 28.50 (limiting charge) = $66.50.

59.   A

60.   B

61.   A   Under the APC system, there exists a list of status indicators (also called service indicators, payment status indicators, or payment indicators). This indicator is provided for every HCPCS/CPT code and identifies how the service or procedure would be paid (if covered) by Medicare for hospital outpatient visits.

62.   B   Under the APC system, there exists a list of status indicators (also called service indicators, payment status indicators, or payment indicators). This indicator is provided for every HCPCS/CPT code and identifies how the service or procedure would be paid (if covered) by Medicare for hospital outpatient visits.

63.   D   Under the APC system, there exists a list of status indicators (also called service indicators, payment status indicators, or payment indicators). This indicator is provided for every HCPCS/CPT code and identifies how the service or procedure would be paid (if covered) by Medicare for hospital outpatient visits. Payment Status Indicator (PSI) "S" means that if a patient has more than one CPT code with this PSI, none of the procedures will be discounted or reduced. They will all be paid at 100%.

64.   C   Under the APC system, there exists a list of status indicators (also called service indicators, payment status indicators, or payment indicators). This indicator is provided for every HCPCS/CPT code and identifies how the service or procedure would be paid (if covered) by Medicare for hospital outpatient visits. Payment Status Indicator (PSI) "T" means that if a patient has more than one CPT code with this PSI, the procedure with the highest weight will be paid at 100% and all others will be reduced or discounted and paid at 50%.

Answer Key for Medical Billing and Reimbursement Systems

ANSWER   EXPLANATION

65.   B   Under the APC system, there exists a list of status indicators (also called service indicators, payment status indicators, or payment indicators). This indicator is provided for every HCPCS/CPT code and identifies how the service or procedure would be paid (if covered) by Medicare for hospital outpatient visits.

66.   D

67.   A

68.   A

69.   D

70.   A

71.   B

72.   B

73.   C

74.   B   When these conditions are not present on admission, it is assumed that it was hospital acquired and therefore, the hospital may not receive additional payment.

75.   B   Under Medicare Part B, Congress has mandated special incentives to increase the number of health care providers signing PAR (participating) agreements with Medicare. One of those incentives includes a 5% higher fee schedule for PAR providers than for non-PAR (nonparticipating) providers.

76.   C   Lifetime reserve days are applicable for hospital inpatient stays that are payable under Medicare Part A, not Medicare Part B.

77.   C

78.   A

79.   D   The relative weight is a number assigned to each MS-DRG published in the Federal Register, and it is used as a multiplier to determine reimbursement. Each hospital's prospective payment system (PPS) rate is a dollar amount based on that hospital's costs of operating as determined by several blended factors. This base payment rate is multiplied by the MS-DRG's (relative) weight to calculate that hospital's reimbursement for a given MS-DRG. Additional payments are made if applicable (such as disproportionate share, teaching hospital, cost outlier, etc.). The prospective payment system used to reimburse the "hospital" for outpatient surgery is APCs. The prospective payment used to reimburse a "free-standing surgery center" for outpatient surgery is ASCs. The prospective payment system used to reimburse the "physician" for outpatient surgery is RBRVS.

80.   D   Discounts are applied to those multiple procedures identified by CPT codes with status indicator "T" and also those CPT codes assigned with the modifier-73.

81.   B

82.   B

83.   A   Local Coverage Determinations (LCDs) were formerly called local medical review policies (LMRPs).

84.   B

85.   C

86.   C   If the physician is a participating physician (PAR) who accepts the assignment, he will receive the lesser of the "total charges" or the "PAR amount" (on the Medicare Physician Fee Schedule). Since the PAR amount is lower, the physician collects 80% of the PAR amount ($60.00) x .80 =$48.00, from Medicare. The remaining 20% ($60.00 x .20 = $12.00) of the PAR amount is paid by the patient to the physician. Therefore, the physician will receive $48.00 directly from Medicare.

Answer Key for Medical Billing and Reimbursement Systems

ANSWER   EXPLANATION

87.   A

88.   B

89.   D

90.   A   When a patient meets the definition of critical care, the hospital must use CPT Code 99291 to bill for outpatient encounters in which critical care services are furnished. This code is used instead of another E&M code.

91.   C   DNFB stands for "Discharged, Not Final Billed"

92.   D   Since the physician is a nonparticipating physician, he will receive the non-PAR fee.
The Medicare non-PAR fee is $57.00.
Medicare will pay 80% of the non-PAR fee ($57.00 x 0.80 = $45.60).
The patient will pay 20% of the non-PAR fee ($57.00 x 0.20 = $11.40).
Since the physician is accepting assignment on this claim, he cannot charge the patient any more than the 20% copayment. Therefore, the physician will receive $45.60 directly from Medicare.

93.   A

94.   A   Only one MS-DRG is assigned per inpatient hospitalization.

95.   A

96.   C

97.   A

98.   D

99.   A   The three relative value units are physician work, practice expense, and malpractice expense. These are adjusted by multiplying them by the geographical practice cost indices. Then, this total is multiplied by the national conversion factor.

100.   B   The participating physician agrees to accept Medicare's fee as payment in full; therefore, the physician would write off the difference between $700.00 and $450.00, which is 250.00.

101.   A

102.   B

103.   C

104.   A

105.   C

106.   A

107.   B

108.   D   Inpatient Rehabilitation Facilities (IRF) reports the HIPPS (Health Insurance Prospective Payment System) code on the claim. The HIPPS code is a five-digit CMG (Case Mix Group). Therefore, the HIPPS code for a patient with tier 1 comorbidity and a CMG of 0109 is B0109. Home Health Agencies (HHA) report the HIPPS code on the claim. The HIPPS code is a five-character alphanumeric code. The first character is the letter "H." The second, third, and fourth characters represent the HHRG (Home Health Resource Group). The fifth character represents what elements are computed or derived. Therefore, the HIPPS code for the HHRG C0F0S0 would be HAEJ1.

109.   D

110.   A   The malignant neoplasm was clearly present on admission, although it was not diagnosed until after the admission occurred.

111.   A   The atrial fibrillation developed prior to a written order for inpatient admission; therefore, it was present at the time of inpatient admission.

Answer Key for Medical Billing and Reimbursement Systems

ANSWER   EXPLANATION

112.   B   The pulmonary embolism is an acute condition that was not present on admission because it developed after the patient was admitted and after the patient had surgery.

113.   C   Query the physician as to whether the decubitus ulcer was present on admission or developed after admission.

114.   A

REFERENCES

Abdelhak, M., Grostick, S., and Hanken, M. (2012). *Health information management: management of a strategic resource* (4th ed.). St. Louis, MO: Elsevier Saunders.

Brown, S. and Tyler, L. (2014). *Guide to advanced medical billing: a reimbursement approach* (3rd ed.). Upper Saddle River, NJ: Pearson Education, Inc.

Casto, A. B., & Forrestal, E. (2013). *Principles of healthcare reimbursement* (4th ed.). Chicago: American Health Information Management Association (AHIMA).

CMS Web site: http://www.cms.hhs.gov/home/Medicare.asp (This Web site provides links to pages containing official informational materials on all of the Medicare Fee-For-Service Payment Systems.)

Diamond, M. S. (2012). *Understanding hospital coding and billing: A worktext* (2nd ed.).Clifton Park, NY: Delmar Cengage Learning.

Green, M. A. (2014). *3-2-1-Code It!* (4th ed.). Clifton Park, NY: Delmar Cengage Learning.

Green, M. A., & Rowell, J. C. (2013). *Understanding health insurance: A guide to billing and reimbursement* (11th ed.). Clifton Park, NY: Delmar Cengage Learning.

Green, M. A., & Bowie, M. J. (2011). *Essentials of health information management: Principles and practices* (2nd ed.). Clifton Park, NY: Delmar Cengage Learning.

Kirchoff, S. (2009). *Coding and reimbursement for hospital outpatient services.* Chicago: American Health Information Management Association (AHIMA).

LaTour, K., Eichenwald-Maki, S. and Oachs, P. (2013). *Health information management: Concepts, principles, and practice* (4th ed.). Chicago: American Health Information Management Association (AHIMA).

Richards, C. (2010). *Medical billing and reimbursement fundamentals.* Clifton Park, NY: Delmar Cengage Learning.

Rimmer, M. (2010). *Understanding medical collections.* Clifton Park, NY: Delmar Cengage Learning.

Sayles, N. (2013). *Health information management technology: An applied approach* (4th ed.). Chicago: American Health Information Management Association (AHIMA).

Schraffenberger, L. A., & Kuehn, L. (2011). *Effective management of coding services* (4th ed.). Chicago: American Health Information Management Association (AHIMA).

Scott, K. (2011). *Coding and reimbursement for hospital inpatient services* (3rd ed.). Chicago: American Health Information Management Association (AHIMA).

Medical Billing and Reimbursement Systems Competencies

Question	RHIA Domain	RHIT Domain
1–114	1	7

VII. Medical Science

Lauralyn Kavanaugh-Burke, DrPH, RHIA, CHTS-IM

1. The etiology of aplastic anemia is
   A. acute blood loss.
   B. bone marrow failure.
   C. chronic blood loss.
   D. inadequate iron intake.

   REFERENCE: Jones, pp 331, 337, 340
                  Moisio, p 213
                  Neighbors & Tannehill-Jones, p 117
                  Scott & Fong, p 250

2. The most common etiology of dementia in the United States is
   A. autism.
   B. Alzheimer's disease.
   C. alcohol abuse.
   D. anxiety disorder.

   REFERENCE: Jones, p 1084
                  Neighbors & Tannehill-Jones, p 273

3. Dr. Zambrano ordered a CEA test for Mr. Logan, a 67-year-old African American male patient. Dr. Zambrano may be considering a diagnosis of
   A. cancer.
   B. carpal tunnel syndrome.
   C. cardiomyopathy.
   D. congestive heart failure.

   REFERENCE: NLM (4)

4. The prevention of illness through vaccination occurs due to the formation of
   A. helper B cells.
   B. immunosurveillance.
   C. mast cells.
   D. memory cells.

   REFERENCE: Jones, pp 350–351
                  Scott & Fong, p 338

5. A bee stung little Bobby. He experiences itching, erythema, and respiratory distress caused by laryngeal edema and vascular collapse. In the emergency department where he is treated with an epinephrine injection, Bobby is diagnosed with
   A. allergic rhinitis.
   B. allergic sinusitis.
   C. anaphylactic shock.
   D. asthma.

   REFERENCE: Jones, pp 965, 974
                  Neighbors & Tannehill-Jones, p 69

6. Genital warts are caused by
   A. HAV.
   B. HIV.
   C. HPV.
   D. VZV.

   REFERENCE: Jones, p 716
                  Moisio, p 436
                  Scott & Fong, p 468

7. A patient's history includes the following documentation:
    - Small ulcers (chancres) appeared on the genitalia and resolved after four to six weeks
    - Elevated temperature, skin rash, and enlarged lymph nodes

    Which procedure will be used to initially diagnose the patient?
    A. bone marrow test   C. serology test
    B. chest x-ray   D. thyroid scan

    REFERENCE: Jones, p 328
                    Moisio, p 437
                    Neighbors & Tannehill-Jones, p 329

8. Which of the following cells produce histamine in a type I hypersensitivity reaction?
    A. lymphocyte   C. mast cells
    B. macrophages   D. neutrophils

    REFERENCE: Jones, p 106
                    Neighbors & Tannehill-Jones, p 47
                    Rizzo, p 104

9. Which one of the following cells produces antibodies?
    A. A cells   C. helper T cells
    B. cytotoxic T cells   D. plasma cells

    REFERENCE: Neighbors & Tannehill-Jones, p 64
                    Rizzo, pp 349, 350, 352
                    Scott & Fong, p 338

10. Which of the following conditions is NOT a predisposing risk associated with essential hypertension?
    A. age   C. low dietary sodium intake
    B. cigarette smoking   D. obesity

    REFERENCE: Jones, p 404
                    Neighbors & Tannehill-Jones, p 134
                    Scott & Fong, pp 300–301

11. A patient, who is HIV positive, has raised red or purple lesions, appearing on the skin, in the mouth, or anywhere on the body. What is the stage of his disease process in today's medical terminology?
    A. ARC   C. AZT
    B. AIDS   D. HIV positive

    REFERENCE: Jones, pp 714–715
                    Neighbors & Tannehill-Jones, p 78

12. Each of the following conditions fall under the category of COPD EXCEPT
    A. chronic bronchitis.   C. pneumonia.
    B. emphysema.   D. smoking.

    REFERENCE: Moisio, pp 238, 240
                    Neighbors & Tannehill-Jones, pp 160–161
                    Rizzo, p 407
                    Scott & Fong, p 368

13. Which of the following is a lethal arrhythmia?
    A. atrial fibrillation
    B. atrial tachycardia
    C. bradycardia
    D. ventricular fibrillation

REFERENCE: Jones, p 411
                Neighbors & Tannehill-Jones, p 144

14. The drug commonly used to treat bipolar mood swings is
    A. Lanoxin.
    B. Lasix.
    C. lithium carbonate.
    D. lorazepam.

REFERENCE: Neighbors & Tannehill-Jones, p 417
                Woodrow, pp 358, 360

15. The leading cause of blindness in the United States is a vision-related pathology caused by diabetes. It is called
    A. retinal detachment.
    B. retinoblastoma.
    C. retinopathy.
    D. rhabdomyosarcoma.

REFERENCE: Jones, pp 569, 606–607, 1075–1077
                Moisio, p 403
                Neighbors & Tannehill-Jones, pp 254–255, 289, 294–295, 300
                Scott & Fong, pp 195, 231–232

16. Penicillin is effective in the treatment of all the following diseases EXCEPT
    A. influenza.
    B. Lyme disease.
    C. strep throat.
    D. syphilis.

REFERENCE: Jones, pp 452, 070
                Neighbors & Tannehill-Jones, pp 89–90, 190, 345, 325
                Rizzo, p 459

17. Impetigo can be
    A. spread through autoinoculation.
    B. caused by *Streptococcus pyogenes.*
    C. caused by *Staphylococcus aureus.*
    D. either A or B.

REFERENCE: Jones, pp 121, 855
                Neighbors & Tannehill-Jones, pp 344, 393
                Scott & Fong, pp 78–79

18. Diagnostic testing for meningitis usually involves
    A. blood cultures.
    B. cerebrospinal fluid analysis.
    C. stool C&S.
    D. testing urine.

REFERENCE: Jones, p 292
                Neighbors & Tannehill-Jones, p 266

19. Which disease is a malignancy of the lymphatic system?
    A. cystic fibrosis
    B. Hodgkin's disease
    C. neutropenia
    D. Von Willebrand's disease

REFERENCE: Jones, p 355
                Moisio, p 216
                Neighbors & Tannehill-Jones, pp 114, 119, 121, 380
                Rizzo, p 354
                Scott & Fong, p 312

20. Which of the following is a hereditary disease of the cerebral cortex that includes progressive muscle spasticity and mental impairment leading to dementia?
    A. Huntington's disease
    B. Lou Gehrig's disease
    C. Bell's palsy
    D. Guillain–Barré syndrome

REFERENCE: Jones, pp 277–278
                Moisio, p 294
                Neighbors & Tannehill-Jones, p 280
                Scott & Fong, p 481

21. Which of the following autoimmune diseases affects tissues of the nervous system?
    A. Goodpasture's syndrome
    B. Hashimoto's disease
    C. myasthenia gravis
    D. rheumatoid arthritis

REFERENCE: Jones, pp 281–282, 356
                Neighbors & Tannehill-Jones, pp 72, 107
                Scott & Fong, p 139

22. Pain is a symptom of which of the following conditions?
    A. first-degree burn (superficial)
    B. second-degree burn (partial thickness)
    C. third-degree burn (full thickness)
    D. both A and B

REFERENCE: Jones, pp 116–117
                Neighbors & Tannehill-Jones, p 356
                Scott & Fong, pp 81–82

23. A 75-year-old patient has a sore tongue with tingling and numbness of the hands and feet. She has headaches and is fatigued. Following diagnostic workup, the doctor orders monthly injections of vitamin B_{12}. This patient most likely has which of the following conditions?
    A. aplastic anemia
    B. autoimmune hemolytic anemia
    C. pernicious anemia
    D. sickle cell anemia

REFERENCE: Jones, p 332
                Moisio, p 213
                Neighbors & Tannehill-Jones, p 116
                Scott & Fong, p 250

24. Which one of the following is NOT a pathophysiological factor in anemia?
    A. excessive RBC breakdown
    B. lack of RBC maturation
    C. loss of bone marrow function
    D. loss of spleen function

REFERENCE: Jones, pp 331–333, 338–341
                Neighbors & Tannehill-Jones, p 116
                Rizzo, p 308
                Scott & Fong, pp 250–251

25. Many bacterial diseases are transmitted directly from person to person. Which of the diseases listed below is a bacterial disease that is transmitted by way of a tick vector?
    A. Legionnaires' disease
    B. Lyme disease
    C. tetanus
    D. tuberculosis

REFERENCE: Jones, pp 228–229
               Moisio, p 434
               Neighbors & Tannehill-Jones, p 345
               Scott & Fong, p 335

26. Necrosis extending down to the underlying fascia is characteristic of a decubitus ulcer in stage
    A. one.
    B. two.
    C. three.
    D. four.

REFERENCE: Scott & Fong, p 83

27. Scabies, a highly contagious condition that produces intense pruritus and rash, is caused by
    A. pediculosis capitis.
    B. itch mites.
    C. candidiasis.
    D. ringworm.

REFERENCE: Jones, pp 124–125
               Moisio, p 108
               Neighbors & Tannehill-Jones, p 347

28. A physician prescribes a diuretic for his patient. He could be treating any of the following disorders EXCEPT
    A. congestive heart failure.
    B. mitral stenosis.
    C. pneumonia.
    D. pulmonary edema.

REFERENCE: Neighbors & Tannehill-Jones, p 162
               Scott & Fong, pp 274, 366

29. All of the following are examples of direct transmission of a disease EXCEPT
    A. contaminated foods.
    B. coughing or sneezing.
    C. droplet spread.
    D. physical contact.

REFERENCE: Neighbors & Tannehill-Jones, pp 5–6
               Scott & Fong, pp 332–336

30. _____ is the most common type of skin cancer and _____ is the most deadly type of skin cancer.
    A. Malignant melanoma, basal cell carcinoma
    B. Basal cell carcinoma, malignant melanoma
    C. Oat cell carcinoma, squamous cell carcinoma
    D. Squamous cell carcinoma, oat cell carcinoma

REFERENCE: Jones, pp 117, 122–123, 934–935, 939–940
               Neighbors & Tannehill-Jones, p 351
               Rizzo, p 132
               Scott & Fong, p 81
               Sormunen, pp 114, 115

31. John Palmer was in a car accident and sustained severe chest trauma resulting in a tension pneumothorax. Manifestations of this disorder include all of the following EXCEPT
    A. severe chest pain.
    B. dyspnea.
    C. shock.
    D. clubbing.

REFERENCE: Jones, p 454
              Neighbors & Tannehill-Jones, p 166

32. Cancer derived from epithelial tissue is classified as a(n)
    A. adenoma.
    B. carcinoma.
    C. lipoma.
    D. sarcoma.

REFERENCE: Jones, p 931
              Neighbors & Tannehill-Jones, p 26
              Rizzo, p 90
              Sormunen, p 302

33. Sex-linked genetic diseases
    A. are transmitted during sexual activity.
    B. involve a defect on a chromosome.
    C. occur equally between males and females.
    D. occur only in males.

REFERENCE: Neighbors & Tannehill-Jones, p 14
              Rizzo, p 457
              Scott & Fong, pp 480–485

34. A stapedectomy is a common treatment for
    A. atherosclerosis.
    B. multiple sclerosis.
    C. otosclerosis.
    D. scoliosis.

REFERENCE: Jones, p 630
              Moisio, pp 412–413
              Neighbors & Tannehill-Jones, p 298
              Scott & Fong, p 201

35. In systemic circulation, which of the following vessels carries oxygenated blood?
    A. right vena cava
    B. renal arteries
    C. pulmonary arteries
    D. left ventricle

REFERENCE: Jones, pp 380–382
              Moisio, pp 176–178
              Neighbors & Tannehill-Jones, p 128
              Rizzo, pp 322, 335
              Scott & Fong, pp 286–287, 295
              Sormunen, p 206

36. Which of the following sequences correctly depicts the flow of blood through the heart to the lungs in order for gas exchange to occur?
    A. right atrium, right ventricle, lungs, pulmonary artery
    B. right atrium, right ventricle, pulmonary artery, lungs
    C. right ventricle, right atrium, lungs, pulmonary artery
    D. right ventricle, right atrium, pulmonary artery, lungs

REFERENCE: Jones, pp 380–382
               Moisio, pp 176–177
               Neighbors & Tannehill-Jones, p 128
               Rizzo, pp 322, 325
               Scott & Fong, pp 286–288, 295
               Sormunen, p 206

37. Diastole occurs when
    A. cardiac insufficiency is present.   C. the ventricles contract.
    B. the atria contracts.   D. the ventricles fill.

REFERENCE: Jones, pp 384, 387
               Neighbors & Tannehill-Jones, p 130
               Rizzo, p 333
               Scott & Fong, p 295
               Sormunen, p 207

38. The most fatal type of lung cancer is
    A. adenocarcinoma.   C. small cell cancer.
    B. large cell cancer.   D. squamous cell cancer.

REFERENCE: Scott & Fong, pp 368–369

39. Gas exchange in the lungs takes place at the
    A. alveoli.   C. bronchioles.
    B. bronchi.   D. trachea.

REFERENCE: Neighbors & Tannehill-Jones, p 154
               Rizzo, pp 402–404
               Scott & Fong, p 358
               Sormunen, p 345

40. O_2 is carried in the blood
    A. bound to hemoglobin.   C. plasma.
    B. in the form of carbonic acid.   D. serum.

REFERENCE: Moisio, p 208
               Neighbors & Tannehill-Jones, p 112
               Rizzo, pp 408, 413
               Sormunen, p 247

41. Which of the following anatomical parts is involved in both the respiratory and digestive systems?
    A. larynx
    B. nasal cavity
    C. pharynx
    D. trachea

REFERENCE: Moisio, p 233
               Rizzo, p 371
               Scott & Fong, pp 355–356
               Sormunen, p 344

42. A disease of the inner ear with fluid disruption in the semicircular canal that causes vertigo is
    A. labyrinthitis.
    B. mastoiditis.
    C. Meniere's disease.
    D. both A and C.

REFERENCE: Moisio, pp 411–412
               Neighbors & Tannehill-Jones, pp 300–301
               Scott & Fong, p 201

43. Softening of the bone in children is termed _____.
    A. Raynaud's disease
    B. Reye's syndrome
    C. Rickets
    D. Rubella

REFERENCE: Neighbors & Tannehill-Jones, p 92
               Rizzo, p 147
               Scott & Fong, p 112

44. A pathological diagnosis of transitional cell carcinoma is made. The examined tissue was removed from the
    A. bladder.
    B. esophagus.
    C. oral cavity.
    D. pleura.

REFERENCE: Neighbors & Tannehill-Jones, p 235
               Rizzo, pp 102–103

45. Most carbon dioxide is carried in the
    A. blood as CO_2 gas.
    B. blood bound to hemoglobin.
    C. blood plasma in the form of carbonic acid.
    D. red blood cells.

REFERENCE: Rizzo, pp 408, 413
               Scott & Fong, p 243
               Sormunen, p 247

46. The key diagnostic finding for typical pneumonia is
    A. abnormal chemical electrolytes.
    B. elevated WBC.
    C. lung consolidation on CXR.
    D. positive sputum culture.

REFERENCE: Neighbors & Tannehill-Jones, p 162

47. The presence of fluid in the alveoli of the lungs is characteristic of
    A. COPD.
    B. Crohn's disease.
    C. pneumonia.
    D. tuberculosis.

REFERENCE: Neighbors & Tannehill-Jones, p 163
               Rizzo, p 407

48. Full-blown AIDS sets in as
    A. CD4 receptors increase.
    B. helper T-cell concentration decreases.
    C. HIV virus concentration decreases.
    D. immunity to HIV increases.

REFERENCE: Scott & Fong, pp 321–324
            Sormunen, p 271

49. Which of the following BEST describes tuberculosis?
    A. a chronic, systemic disease whose initial infection is in the lungs
    B. an acute bacterial infection of the lung
    C. an ordinary lung infection
    D. a viral infection of the lungs

REFERENCE: Neighbors & Tannehill-Jones, pp 49, 392–393
            Scott & Fong, p 366
            Sormunen, p 272

50. A treatment for sensorineural hearing loss is
    A. cochlear implants.   C. removal of impacted cerumen.
    B. myringotomy.   D. stapedectomy.

REFERENCE: Jones, p 628
            Scott & Fong, p 202

51. Mary Mulholland has diabetes. Her physician has told her about some factors that put her more at risk for infections. Which of the following factors would probably NOT be applicable?
    A. hypoxia   C. increased blood supply
    B. increased glucose in body fluids   D. both A and C

REFERENCE: Neighbors & Tannehill-Jones, pp 253–257

52. Most of the digestion of food and absorption of nutrients occur in the
    A. ascending colon.   C. small intestine.
    B. esophagus.   D. stomach.

REFERENCE: Neighbors & Tannehill-Jones, p 185
            Rizzo, pp 377–378
            Scott & Fong, pp 385–386
            Sormunen, p 374

53. The Phalen's wrist flexor test is a noninvasive method for diagnosing
    A. carpal tunnel syndrome.   C. severe acute respiratory syndrome.
    B. Down syndrome.   D. Tourette's syndrome.

REFERENCE: NINDS

54. A chronic inflammatory bowel disease where affected segments of the bowel may be separated by normal bowel tissue is characteristic of
    A. appendicitis.   C. diverticulitis.
    B. Crohn's disease.   D. Graves' disease.

REFERENCE: Moisio, p 270
            Neighbors & Tannehill-Jones, pp 193, 198
            Rizzo, p 381
            Sormunen, p 392

55. The patient's pathology report revealed the presence of Reed–Sternberg cells. This is indicative of
    A. Hodgkin's disease.
    B. leukemia.
    C. non-Hodgkin's lymphoma.
    D. sarcoma.

REFERENCE: Neighbors & Tannehill-Jones, p 119

56. The most common rickettsial disease in the United States is
    A. hantavirus.
    B. Lyme disease.
    C. Rocky Mountain spotted fever.
    D. syphilis.

REFERENCE: Moisio, pp 434–435
               Neighbors & Tannehill-Jones, p 57
               Scott & Fung, pp 331–332

57. Early detection programs apply screening guidelines to detect cancers at an early stage, which provides the likelihood of increased survival and decreased morbidity. Which of the following would NOT be a diagnostic or screening test for colorectal cancer?
    A. double contrast barium enema
    B. sigmoidoscopy
    C. fecal occult blood test
    D. upper GI x-ray

REFERENCE: American Cancer Society
               Neighbors & Tannehill-Jones, p 200
               Scott & Fong, p 399

58. Prevention programs identify risk factors and use strategies to modify attitudes and behaviors to reduce the chance of developing cancers. Which of the following would NOT be an identified risk factor for colorectal cancer?
    A. alcohol use
    B. physical inactivity
    C. high-fiber diet
    D. obesity

REFERENCE: American Cancer Society

59. In general, excessive RBC breakdown could result in
    A. Crohn's disease.
    B. elevated BUN.
    C. high bilirubin levels.
    D. peptic ulcers.

REFERENCE: Labtestsonline (1)
               Neighbors & Tannehill-Jones, p 209
               NLM (1)

60. The most common bloodborne infection in the United States is
    A. *Helicobacter pylori.*
    B. hepatitis A.
    C. hepatitis C.
    D. hemophilia.

REFERENCE: Scott & Fong, p 397

61. The first stage of alcoholic liver disease is
    A. alcoholic hepatitis.
    B. cirrhosis.
    C. fatty liver.
    D. jaundice.

REFERENCE: Neighbors & Tannehill-Jones, p 211

62. Portal hypertension can contribute to all of the following EXCEPT
    A. ascites.
    B. dilation of blood vessels lining the intestinal tract.
    C. esophageal varices.
    D. kidney failure.

REFERENCE: Mayo Clinic (1)
               Neighbors & Tannehill-Jones, pp 211–214

63. Which of the following is a liver function test?
    A. AST (SGOT)   C. ECG
    B. BUN   D. TSH

REFERENCE: Neighbors & Tannehill-Jones, pp 211–214
               Sormunen, p 389

64. Which of the following is a risk factor involved in the etiology of gallstones?
    A. being overweight   C. low-fat diets
    B. being an adolescent   D. presence of peptic ulcer

REFERENCE: Rizzo, p 215

65. A serum potassium level of 2.8 would indicate
    A. Addison disease.   C. diabetic ketoacidosis.
    B. anemia.   D. hypokalemia.

REFERENCE: Mayo Clinic (2)
               NLM (3)

66. A procedure performed with an instrument that freezes and destroys abnormal tissues (including seborrheic keratoses, basal cell carcinomas, and squamous cell carcinomas) is
    A. cryosurgery.   C. phacoemulsification.
    B. electrodesiccation.   D. photocautery.

REFERENCE: Moisio, p 110
               Rizzo, pp 81, 469

67. Which of the organs listed below has endocrine and exocrine functions?
    A. kidney   C. lung
    B. liver   D. pancreas

REFERENCE: Moisio, p 266
               Neighbors & Tannehill-Jones, p 252
               Rizzo, pp 282–283, 274
               Scott & Fong, p 386

68. Which of the following is an effect of insulin?
    A. decreases glycogen concentration in liver
    B. increases blood glucose
    C. increases the breakdown of fats
    D. increases glucose metabolism

REFERENCE: Moisio, pp 301–302, 304
               Neighbors & Tannehill-Jones, pp 244, 252–256
               Rizzo, pp 274–276, 282, 284–285
               Scott & Fong, pp 225–226, 233, 504
               Sormunen, p 554

69. The causative organism for severe acute respiratory syndrome (SARS) is a
    A. bacterium.   C. fungus.
    B. coronavirus.   D. retrovirus.

REFERENCE: Moisio, p 241
                  Neighbors & Tannehill-Jones, p 165
                  Scott & Fong, p 366

70. Before leaving the hospital, all newborns are screened for an autosomal recessive genetic disorder of defective enzymatic conversion in protein metabolism. With early detection and a protein-restricted diet, brain damage is prevented. This disease is
    A. cystic fibrosis.   C. phenylketonuria.
    B. hereditary hemochromatosis.   D. Tay–Sachs disease.

REFERENCE: Neighbors & Tannehill-Jones, p 378
                  Scott & Fong, p 481

71. Diabetic microvascular disease occurs
    A. as a direct result of elevated serum glucose.
    B. as a result of elevated fat in blood.
    C. due to damage to nerve cells.
    D. only in patients with type 1 diabetes.

REFERENCE: Neighbors & Tannehill-Jones, pp 254–255
                  Rizzo, pp 284–285
                  Scott & Fong, pp 231–232

72. Older age, obesity, and family history of diabetes are all characteristics of
    A. type 1 diabetes.   C. juvenile diabetes.
    B. type 2 diabetes.   D. IDDM.

REFERENCE: Rizzo, pp 284–285
                  Scott & Fong, p 232

73. An elevated serum amylase would be characteristic of
    A. acute pancreatitis.   C. postrenal failure.
    B. gallbladder disease.   D. prerenal failure.

REFERENCE: Neighbors & Tannehill-Jones, p 219

74. Clinical manifestations of this disease include polydipsia, polyuria, polyphagia, weight loss, and hyperglycemia. Which of the following tests would be ordered to confirm the disease?
    A. fasting blood sugar   C. glucose tolerance test
    B. glucagon   D. postprandial blood sugar

REFERENCE: Neighbors & Tannehill-Jones, pp 253–254
                  Rizzo, pp 84–85
                  Scott & Fong, pp 231, 235

75. Common kidney stone treatments that allow small particles to be flushed out of the body through the urinary system include all of the following EXCEPT
    A. extracorporeal shock wave lithotripsy.
    B. fluid hydration.
    C. ureteroscopy and stone basketing.
    D. using medication to dissolve the stone(s).

REFERENCE: Neighbors & Tannehill-Jones, p 229

76. When a decubitus ulcer has progressed to a stage in which osteomyelitis is present, the ulcer has extended to the
   A. bone.
   C. muscle.
   B. fascia.
   D. subcutaneous tissue.

REFERENCE: Neighbors & Tannehill-Jones, pp 92–93
              Scott & Fong, pp 83–84

77. The 68-year-old female patient has no visible bleeding, but remains anemic. Her physician is concerned about possible gastrointestinal bleeding. Which of the following tests might be ordered?
   A. DEXA scan
   C. Pap smear test
   B. guaiac smear test
   D. prostatic-specific antigen test

REFERENCE: Estridge & Reynolds, pp 680–681
              Sormunen, p 388

78. When a physician orders a liver panel, which of the following tests are NOT included?
   A. albumin
   C. bilirubin
   B. alkaline phosphatase
   D. creatinine

REFERENCE: Estridge & Reynolds, pp 608–609

79. Maria Giovanni is in the hospital recovering from colon resection surgery. Based on her symptoms, her doctors are concerned about the possibility that she has developed a pulmonary embolism. Which of the following procedures will provide the definitive diagnosis?
   A. chest x-ray
   C. pulmonary angiography
   B. lung scan
   D. none of the above

REFERENCE: Neighbors & Tannehill-Jones, p 168
              Scott & Fong, p 369

80. A condition that involves the fifth cranial nerve, also known as "tic douloureux," causes intense pain in the eye and forehead; lower lip, the section of the cheek closest to the ear and the outer segment of the tongue; or the upper lip, nose, and cheek.
   A. Bell's palsy
   C. trigeminal neuralgia
   B. thrush
   D. Tourette's disorder

REFERENCE: Jones, pp 283, 288
              Moisio, p 396
              Scott & Fong, p 182

81. Which of the following is a congenital condition that is the most severe neural tube defect?
   A. meningocele
   C. severe combined immunodeficiency
   B. myelomeningocele
   D. spina bifida occulta

REFERENCE: Neighbors & Tannehill-Jones, p 374

82. Which of the following tubes conveys sperm from the seminal vesicle to the urethra?
   A. ejaculatory duct
   C. oviduct
   B. epididymis
   D. vas deferens

REFERENCE: Moisio, p 332
              Neighbors & Tannehill-Jones, p 481
              Rizzo, p 444

83. The most common type of vaginitis is
    A. yeast.
    B. protozoan.
    C. viral.
    D. both A and B.

REFERENCE: Neighbors & Tannehill-Jones, p 315

84. The childhood viral disease that unvaccinated pregnant women should be prevented from because it may be passed to the fetus, causing congenital anomalies such as mental retardation, blindness, and deafness, is
    A. rickets.
    B. rubeola.
    C. rubella.
    D. tetanus.

REFERENCE: Moisio, p 435
                  Neighbors & Tannehill-Jones, p 389

85. In _____ anemia, the red blood cells become shaped like elongated crescents in the presence of low oxygen concentration.
    A. aplastic
    B. folic acid
    C. sickle cell
    D. vitamin B_{12}

REFERENCE: Jones, p 333
                  Moisio, p 213
                  Rizzo, p 308
                  Scott & Fong, pp 250–251

86. _____ is usually the first symptom of benign prostate hyperplasia.
    A. Abdominal pain
    B. Burning pain during urination
    C. Difficulty in urinating
    D. Pelvic pain

REFERENCE: Neighbors & Tannehill-Jones, pp 322–324
                  Rizzo, p 444
                  Scott & Fong, pp 467–468

87. The hypothalamus, thalamus, and pituitary gland are all parts of the
    A. brainstem.
    B. cerebellum.
    C. exocrine system.
    D. limbic system.

REFERENCE: Rizzo, pp 157–158

88. Which of the following BEST summarizes the current treatment of cervical cancer?
    A. A new three-shot vaccination series protects against the types of HPV that cause most cervical cancer cases.
    B. All stages have extremely high cure rates.
    C. Early detection and treatment of cervical cancer does not improve patient survival rates.
    D. Over 99% of cases are linked to long-term HPV infections.

REFERENCE: CDC (1)

89. Children at higher risk for sudden infant death syndrome (SIDS) include those
    A. with sleep apnea.
    B. with respiratory problems.
    C. who are premature infants.
    D. all of the above.

REFERENCE: Jones, pp 455, 867–868
                  Neighbors & Tannehill-Jones, p 395
                  Scott & Fong, p 369

90. Increasing peristalsis of intestines, increasing salivation, and slowing heart rate are examples of
    A. automatic nervous system responses.
    B. higher brain function.
    C. parasympathetic nervous system responses.
    D. sympathetic nervous system responses.

REFERENCE: Jones, p 263
               Rizzo, pp 227, 251
               Scott & Fong, pp 177–179
               Sormunen, p 585

91. Photophobia or visual aura preceding a severe headache is characteristic of
    A. malnutrition.   C. migraines.
    B. mastitis.   D. myasthenia gravis.

REFERENCE: Jones, pp 275–276
               Neighbors & Tannehill-Jones, p 271
               Scott & Fong, p 163

92. Which of the following is characteristic of Graves' disease?
    A. is an autoimmune disease.   C. usually cannot be treated.
    B. most commonly affects males.   D. usually affects the elderly.

REFERENCE: Jones, p 560
               Neighbors & Tannehill-Jones, p 248
               Rizzo, pp 280, 285
               Scott & Fong, p 228

93. A "pill-rolling" tremor of the hand is a characteristic symptom of
    A. epilepsy.   C. myasthenia gravis.
    B. Guillain–Barré syndrome.   D. Parkinson disease.

REFERENCE: Jones, pp 282–283, 1066–1067
               Neighbors & Tannehill-Jones, p 281
               Scott & Fong, pp 162–164

94. Rheumatoid arthritis typically affects the
    A. intervertebral disks.
    B. hips and shoulders.
    C. knees and small joints of the hands and feet.
    D. large, weight-bearing joints.

REFERENCE: Jones, p 230
               Moisio, p 149
               Neighbors & Tannehill-Jones, pp 71–72, 94–95
               Rizzo, p 183
               Scott & Fong, pp 110–111

95. Henry experienced sudden sharp chest pain that he described as heavy and crushing. His pain and past medical history caused Dr. James to suspect that Henry was having an acute myocardial infarction (AMI). Which of the following tests is a more specific marker for an AMI?
    A. AST   C. LDH1
    B. CK-MB   D. Troponin I

REFERENCE: Labtestsonline (2)

96. A radiological test for bone mineral density (BMD) is a useful diagnostic tool for diagnosing
    A. osteoarthritis.
    B. osteomyelitis.
    C. osteoporosis.
    D. rheumatoid arthritis.

REFERENCE: Jones, p 184
                Neighbors & Tannehill-Jones, pp 90–92
                Scott & Fong, p 113

97. A 72-year-old white male patient is on Coumadin therapy. Which of the following tests is commonly ordered to monitor the patient's Coumadin levels?
    A. bleeding time
    B. blood smear
    C. partial thromboplastin time
    D. prothrombin time

REFERENCE: Jones, p 339
                Labtestsonline (3)
                Moisio, p 219
                Neighbors & Tannehill-Jones, p 235
                NLM (2)

98. A toxic goiter has what distinguishing characteristic?
    A. iodine deficiency
    B. parathyroid involvement
    C. presence of muscle spasm
    D. thyroid hyperfunction

REFERENCE: Moisio, p 304
                Neighbors & Tannehill-Jones, pp 247–248
                Rizzo, p 280
                Sormunen, p 567

99. How can Graves' disease be treated?
    A. antithyroid drugs
    B. radioactive iodine therapy
    C. surgery
    D. all of the above

REFERENCE: Jones, pp 560–561
                Neighbors & Tannehill-Jones, pp 247–248
                Rizzo, p 285
                Sormunen, p 567

100. Fractures occur in patients with osteoporosis due to
    A. falling from loss of balance.
    B. fibrous joint adhesions tearing apart small bones.
    C. loss of bone mass.
    D. tendency to fall from lack of joint mobility.

REFERENCE: Jones, pp 174–175
                Moisio, p 149
                Neighbors & Tannehill-Jones, pp 90–92
                Scott & Fong, p 113

101. United States health care providers are concerned about a possible pandemic of avian flu because
    A. there is no vaccine currently available.
    B. it is caused by a group of viruses that mutate very easily.
    C. the causative virus is being spread around the world by migratory birds.
    D. of all of the above.

REFERENCE: CDC (2)

102. A sweat test was done on a patient with the following symptoms: frequent respiratory infections, chronic cough, and foul-smelling bloody stools. Which of the following diseases is probably suspected?
    A. cystic breast disease
    B. cystic fibrosis
    C. cystic lung disease
    D. cystic pancreas

REFERENCE: Neighbors & Tannehill-Jones, p 380

103. Margaret Vargas needs to have her mitral valve replaced. Her surgeon will discuss which of the following issues with her before the surgery?
    A. A mechanical valve will require that she take a "blood thinner" for the rest of her life.
    B. A biological valve (usually porcine) will last 10 to 15 years.
    C. A mechanical valve increases the risk of blood clots that can cause stroke.
    D. All of the above.

REFERENCE: NHLBI

104. Cervical cerclage is a procedure used to help prevent
    A. breathing restrictions.
    B. miscarriage.
    C. torsion.
    D. torticollis.

REFERENCE: Jones, pp 802, 817

105. Sam Spade has been severely injured in an MVA because he was not wearing a seat belt. The organ in his body, situated at the upper left of his abdominal cavity, under the ribs, that is part of his lymphatic system has been ruptured, and he is bleeding internally. Sam needs a surgical procedure known as
    A. sequestrectomy.
    B. sialoadenectomy.
    C. sigmoidoscopy.
    D. splenectomy.

REFERENCE: Jones, p 345
               Moisio, p 219
               Rizzo, p 346
               Sormunen, pp 275, 399

106. Henrietta Dawson presents with a chief complaint of pain and weakness in her arms and neck. After an H&P and review of diagnostic tests that include a myelogram, her doctor diagnoses a herniated nucleus pulposus at the _____ level of her spine.
    A. cervical
    B. lumbar
    C. sacral
    D. thoracic

REFERENCE: Jones, pp 160, 228, 277
               Moisio, p 147
               Neighbors & Tannehill-Jones, p 103
               Rizzo, pp 157, 170
               Scott & Fong, pp 99, 112
               Sormunen, pp 158, 161

107. Ingrid Anderson presents with a skin infection that began as a raised, itchy bump, resembling an insect bite. Within 1 to 2 days, it developed into a vesicle. Now it is a painless ulcer, about 2 cm in diameter, with a black necrotic area in the center. During the history, her doctor learns that she has recently returned from an overseas vacation and becomes concerned that she may have become infected with anthrax. He will prescribe an

    A. antibiotic.   C. antiparasitic.

    B. antineoplastic.   D. antiviral.

REFERENCE: Scott & Fong, pp 342, 366–367

108. Etiologies of dementia include

    A. brain tumors.   C. trauma.

    B. ischemia.   D. all of the above.

REFERENCE: Neighbors & Tannehill-Jones, p 414
                     Rizzo, pp 937, 946
                     Scott & Fong, p 164
                     Sormunen, p 597

109. Carpal tunnel syndrome is caused by entrapment of the

    A. medial nerve.   C. tibial nerve.

    B. radial nerve.   D. ulnar nerve.

REFERENCE: Jones, p 270
                     Moisio, p 142
                     Neighbors & Tannehill-Jones, p 104
                     NINDS
                     Rizzo, p 182
                     Sormunen, p 158

110. The organism transmitted by a mosquito bite that causes malaria is a

    A. bacteria.   C. protozoa.

    B. prion.   D. virus.

REFERENCE: Moisio, p 432
                     Neighbors & Tannehill-Jones, pp 54–55, 57
                     Rizzo, p 309
                     Scott & Fong, p 309

111. Contributing factors of mental disorders include

    A. heredity.   C. trauma.

    B. stress.   D. all of the above.

REFERENCE: Jones, pp 1008, 1010
                     Neighbors & Tannehill-Jones, p 408

112. A 13-year-old patient is brought to her pediatrician with a 2-week history of fatigue, an occasional low-grade fever, and malaise. The pediatrician indicates it is a possible infection but needs to know what type of infection. She orders a hematology laboratory test to determine the relative number and percentage of each type of leukocytes. This test is referred to as a(n)

    A. hematocrit.   C. WBC diff.

    B. CBC.   D. hemoglobin determination.

REFERENCES: Estridge & Reynolds, p 198

113. A 62-year-old female presents to her family doctor complaining of fatigue; constantly feeling cold, especially in her hands and feet; weakness; and pallor. O_2 must be transported to the cells and exchanged with CO_2, which is then transported back to the lungs to be expelled. A hematology laboratory test that evaluates the oxygen-carrying capacity of blood is referred to as a(n)
   A. hematocrit.
   B. CBC.
   C. WBC diff.
   D. hemoglobin determination.

REFERENCES: Estridge & Reynolds, pp 206–207
                Labtestsonline (15)

114. An African American couple are undergoing genetic counseling to determine the likelihood of producing children with a recessively genetic blood condition. The genetic tests reveal that the father carries the trait to produce abnormal hemoglobin, HbS, which causes crystallization in RBCs and deforms their shape when O_2 is low. This condition causes painful crises and multiple infarcts and is termed
   A. hemophilia.
   B. thalassemia.
   C. sickle cell anemia.
   D. iron-deficiency anemia.

REFERENCES: Estridge & Reynolds, pp 328–330
                Labtestsonline (4)

115. A 37-year-old female goes to her family physician complaining of dysuria, urgency, fever, and malaise. A UA is performed and upon gross examination is found to be turbid and has an unusual odor. Microscopic examination reveals a rod-shaped microorganism. A 24-hour culture produces a colony count greater than 100,000/mL of *Escherichia coli.* This would indicate a diagnosis of
   A. UTI.
   B. FUO.
   C. PID.
   D. KUB.

REFERENCES: Estridge & Reynolds, pp 751–753
                Labtestsonline (5)

116. A 57-year-old male patient is having his annual physical. Due to a family history of coronary artery disease and his sedentary lifestyle, his doctor orders a total blood cholesterol panel. What is the optimal level of total cholesterol in the blood for adults?
   A. < 200 mg/dL
   B. 200–239 mg/dL
   C. 300–339 mg/dL
   D. >500 mg/dL

REFERENCES: Estridge & Reynolds, pp 662–667
                Labtestsonline (6)

117. A pharyngeal culture is taken from a 13-year-old male patient presenting to the ER with fever, painful cervical lymph nodes, purulent tonsillar exudate, and difficulty swallowing. Blood agar culture plate shows complete hemolysis around *Streptococcus pyogenes* bacterial colonies. The patient is given a prescription for erythromycin. The diagnosis in this case is
   A. group A beta-hemolytic streptococcal throat infection.
   B. methicillin-resistant *Staphylococcus aureus* skin infection.
   C. tuberculosis with drug-resistant *Mycobacterium tuberculosis*-positive sputum.
   D. meningitis due to *Neisseria meningitidis*-positive cerebrospinal fluid.

REFERENCES: Estridge & Reynolds, pp 739–742
                Labtestsonline (7)

118. An 81-year-old male with arteriosclerosis and a long-standing history of taking Coumadin presents to his physician's office for his bi-weekly prothrombin time (PT) test. The PT test is one of the most common hemostasis tests used as a presurgery screening and monitoring Coumadin (warfarin) therapy. This test evaluates
    A. coagulation of the blood.
    B. iron-binding capacity of RBCs.
    C. oxygen-carrying capacity of RBCs.
    D. type and cross-match of blood.

REFERENCES: Estridge & Reynolds, p 394
                Labtestsonline (8)

119. A 28-year-old female presents to her general practitioner with morning nausea and vomiting, weight gain, and two missed menstrual cycles. The physician orders a pregnancy test. What chemical in the urine does this lab test detect?
    A. alpha-fetoprotein   C. carcinoembryonic antigen
    B. creatine phosphokinase   D. human chorionic gonadotropin

REFERENCES: Estridge & Reynolds, pp 471–472
                Labtestsonline (9).

120. A 19-year-old college student, who lives on campus in a dormitory, is brought to the ER by his roommates complaining of a severe headache, nuchal rigidity, fever, and photophobia. The ER physician performs an LP and orders a CSF analysis with a bacterial culture and sensitivity. The young man is admitted to the ICU with a provisional diagnosis of
    A. group A beta-hemolytic streptococcal throat infection.
    B. methicillin-resistant *Staphylococcus aureus* skin infection.
    C. tuberculosis with drug-resistant *Mycobacterium tuberculosis*-positive sputum.
    D. meningitis due to *Neisseria meningitidis*-positive cerebrospinal fluid.

REFERENCES: CDC (12)
                Labtestsonline (10)

121. Microbiological lab culture and sensitivity tests were performed on the skin scrapings of a groin lesion on a 27-year-old male patient who presented to a local health department clinic. The results confirm infection with *Treponema pallidum*. He was given a prescription for penicillin and told to return for a follow-up visit in within 2 weeks. His diagnosis is
    A. syphilis.   C. herpes.
    B. HIV.   D. HPV.

REFERENCES: CDC (13)
                Labtestsonline (11)

122. The HPV vaccine, Gardasil, is recommended for all children/young adults between the ages of 9 and 26 years. It is a quadrivalent vaccine. What is the definition of quadrivalent?
    A. It must be administered every 4 years to be effective.
    B. It is administered in a series of four shots over a 6-month period.
    C. It prevents infection from the four most prevalent types of HPV that cause cervical cancer.
    D. It reduces the risk of infection by four times.

REFERENCES: CDC (3)
               FDA (1)
               Labtestsonline (12)

123. *Mycobacterium tuberculosis* is the organism that causes tuberculosis (TB), typically a respiratory disorder. It is currently experiencing a resurgence in the United States and many other countries. What is the average time frame all patients with new, previously untreated TB must have daily antibiotic therapy?
    A. 4–7 days   C. 6–9 weeks
    B. 6–9 months   D. 4–7 years

REFERENCES: CDC (4)
               Labtestsonline (13)

124. A 63-year-old patient with terminal pancreatic cancer has started palliative chemotherapy. Palliative means
    A. alleviating or eliminating distressing symptoms of the disease.
    B. increasing the immune response to fight infections.
    C. quick destruction of cancerous cells.
    D. the combining of several medications to cure the cancer.

REFERENCES: ACS (3)
               Woodrow, pp 221–222

125. Why are there "black box warnings" on antidepressant medications regarding children and adolescents?
    A. Antidepressants increase the risk of suicidal thinking and behavior in some children and adolescents.
    B. Dosage requirements must be significantly higher in children and adolescents compared to adults.
    C. There is no established medical need for treatment of depression in children and adolescents.
    D. Antidepressants interfere with physiological growth patterns in children and adolescents.

REFERENCES: FDA (2)
               Woodrow, p 354

126. The positive belief in a drug and its ability to cure a patient's illness, even if this drug is an inactive or inert substance, typically positively influences a patient's perception of their outcome. This effect is termed
    A. synergistic effect.
    B. potentiation effect.
    C. placebo effect.
    D. antagonistic effect.

REFERENCES: Sormunen, pp 79, 92
                Woodrow, pp 34–36

127. A common cardiac glycoside medication that increases the force of the cardiac contraction without increasing the oxygen consumption, thereby increasing the cardiac output is typically given to patients with heart failure. However, a very narrow therapeutic window between effectiveness and toxicity and the patient must be monitored closely. This common cardiac medication is
    A. COX-2 inhibitor.
    B. nitroglycerin.
    C. digoxin.
    D. acetylsalicylic acid.

REFERENCES: NLM (9)
                Woodrow, pp 461–462

128. The interaction of two drugs working together to where each simultaneously helps the other achieve an effect that neither could produce alone is termed
    A. placebo effect.
    B. synergistic effect.
    C. potentiation effect.
    D. antagonistic effect.

REFERENCES: Woodrow, p 35

129. The opposing interaction of two drugs in which one decreases or cancels out the effects of the other is termed
    A. placebo effect.
    B. potentiation effect.
    C. synergistic effect.
    D. antagonistic effect.

REFERENCES: Woodrow, p 35

130. One of the most common causes of peptic ulcer disease is the consumption of aspirin and NSAIDs. Another common cause is the infection of *Helicobacter pylori,* and the usual treatment for this condition is with the use of
    A. antivirals.
    B. antibiotics.
    C. antifungals.
    D. antiemetics.

REFERENCES: NLM (10)
                Woodrow, p 254

131. A common contraceptive that is implanted in the uterus induces slight endometrial inflammation, which attracts neutrophils to the uterus. These neutrophils are toxic to sperm and prevent the fertilization of the ovum. This contraception is termed
    A. oral contraceptives.
    B. progestin injections.
    C. spermicides.
    D. IUD.

REFERENCES: Jones, pp 755–756
                Woodrow, p 447

132. There has been a significant increase in the number of cases and deaths from pertussis. Health care professionals attribute this disease trend to which of the following?
    A. A decrease in the number of people immunized with TDaP
    B. An increase in the virulence of the bacteria
    C. Drug-resistant strains of the bacteria
    D. All of the above

REFERENCES: CDC (5)

133. Which of the following is a severe, chronic, two-phased, bacterial respiratory infection that has become increasingly difficult to treat because many antibiotics are no longer effective against it?
    A. SARS
    B. MDR-TB
    C. MRSA
    D. H1N1

REFERENCES: CDC (6)

134. A new strain of influenza, H1N1, is a highly virulent strain that spread all over the world. This type of epidemiological disease pattern is referred to as a(n)
    A. cluster.
    B. outbreak.
    C. epidemic.
    D. pandemic.

REFERENCES: CDC (7)

135. Mary Smith, a 48-year-old patient, is receiving an IV mixture of four different medications to treat stage 2 invasive ductal breast carcinoma. Each of the medications acts upon a different aspect of the cancer cells. This mixture is typically termed a(n)
    A. amalgamation.
    B. cocktail.
    C. blend.
    D. mash-up.

REFERENCES: CDC (8)

136. Some immunizations, such as tetanus, require a second application, to strengthen or "remind" the immune system in response to antigens. The subsequent injections are termed
    A. alerting shots.
    B. warning shots.
    C. booster shots.
    D. unnecessary shots.

REFERENCES: CDC (9)

137. What common vitamin should be taken by pregnant women to substantially reduce the occurrence of neural tube defects, such as spina bifida, in a developing fetus?
    A. Folic acid   C. B_{12}
    B. Calcium   D. E

REFERENCES: CDC (10)

138. Why must influenza immunizations be developed and administered on an annual basis?
    A. The virus mutates significantly each year.
    B. People develop resistance to the vaccine.
    C. The immunization is only strong enough for one year.
    D. The pharmaceutical companies produce the lowest dosage possible.

REFERENCES: CDC (11)

139. Which of the following pieces of equipment records the electrical activity of the brain?
    A. EEG   C. ECG
    B. EMG   D. EKG

REFERENCES: Jones, p 290
               Moisio, 397
               NLM (5)

140. A surgical procedure that cuts into the skull to drain blood from a subdural hematoma in order to decrease the intracranial pressure is termed a(n)
    A. craniectomy.   C. angioplasty.
    B. craniotomy.   D. hemispherectomy.

REFERENCES: NLM (6)

141. A surgical procedure that is performed to realign and stabilize a fractured femur with a rod and screws is referred to as a(n)
    A. closed reduction with external fixation.
    B. closed reduction with internal fixation.
    C. osteotomy.
    D. open reduction with internal fixation.

REFERENCES: Jones, pp 180–181
               Moisio, p 152

142. Which of the following procedures is typically performed on children to facilitate the drainage of serous exudate behind the tympanic membrane in chronic otitis media?
    A. cochlear implants
    B. stapedectomy
    C. myringotomy with tympanostomy tubes
    D. cerumen evacuation

REFERENCES: Jones, p 624
               Moisio, p 413

143. Coronary arteries may become blocked, either partially or totally, due to athereosclerosis and lead to an AMI. Which of the following procedures would be used to improve the coronary blood flow by building an alternate route for the blood to bypass the blockage by inserting a portion of another blood vessel, typically the saphenous vein?
    A. PTCA   C. carotid endarterectomy
    B. CABG   D. cardiac catheterization

REFERENCES: Jones, p 1086
               Moisio, pp 185–186

144. A standard surgical procedure used for the treatment of early-stage breast cancer involves the removal of the cancerous tumor, skin, breast tissue, areola, nipple, and most of the axillary lymph nodes, but leaves the underlying chest muscles intact. This procedure is termed a(n)
    A. modified radical mastectomy.
    B. partial mastectomy.
    C. lumpectomy.
    D. incisional breast biopsy.

REFERENCES: Jones, pp 760, 936
                Moisio, p 361
                WebMD.com (1)

145. The least invasive restrictive gastric surgery used to reduce the size of the stomach to facilitate weight loss in obese patients is the
    A. gastric bypass.
    B. Roux-en-Y gastric surgery.
    C. laparoscopic gastric banding.
    D. biliopancreatic diversion.

REFERENCES: WebMD.com (2)

146. Which of the following procedures would be performed for the removal of the gall bladder due to excessive gallstone formation?
    A. ERCP
    B. cholangiography
    C. hemicolectomy
    D. cholecystectomy

REFERENCES: WebMD.com (3)
                NLM (7)

Answer Key for Medical Science

1.	B	50.	A	99.	D
2.	B	51.	C	100.	C
3.	A	52.	C	101.	D
4.	D	53.	A	102.	B
5.	C	54.	B	103.	D
6.	C	55.	A	104.	B
7.	C	56.	C	105.	D
8.	C	57.	D	106.	A
9.	D	58.	C	107.	A
10.	C	59.	C	108.	D
11.	B	60.	C	109.	A
12.	C	61.	C	110.	C
13.	D	62.	D	111.	D
14.	C	63.	A	112.	C
15.	C	64.	A	113.	D
16.	A	65.	C	114.	C
17.	D	66.	A	115.	A
18.	B	67.	D	116.	A
19.	B	68.	D	117.	A
20.	A	69.	B	118.	A
21.	C	70.	C	119.	D
22.	D	71.	A	120.	D
23.	C	72.	B	121.	A
24.	D	73.	A	122.	C
25.	B	74.	C	123.	B
26.	C	75.	C	124.	A
27.	B	76.	A	125.	A
28.	C	77.	B	126.	C
29.	A	78.	D	127.	C
30.	B	79.	C	128.	B
31.	D	80.	C	129.	D
32.	B	81.	B	130.	B
33.	B	82.	A	131.	D
34.	C	83.	D	132.	A
35.	D	84.	C	133.	B
36.	B	85.	C	134.	D
37.	D	86.	C	135.	B
38.	C	87.	D	136.	C
39.	A	88.	A	137.	A
40.	A	89.	D	138.	A
41.	C	90.	C	139.	A
42.	D	91.	C	140.	B
43.	C	92.	A	141.	D
44.	A	93.	D	142.	C
45.	D	94.	C	143.	B
46.	C	95.	B	144.	A
47.	C	96.	C	145.	C
48.	B	97.	D		
49.	A	98.	D		

REFERENCES

American Cancer Society (ACS). http://www.cancer.org

ACS (1)

http://www.cancer.org/acs/groups/cid/documents/webcontent/003096-pdf.pdf

http://www.cancer.org/Cancer/ColonandRectumCancer/DetailedGuide/colorectal-cancer-detection

ACS (3)

http://www.cancer.org/Cancer/CancerofUnknownPrimary/DetailedGuide/cancer-unknown-primary-treating-palliative-care

Centers for Disease Control and Prevention (CDC). http://www.cdc.gov/index.htm

CDC (1)

http://www.cdc.gov/std/Hpv/STDFact-HPV-vaccine-young-women.htm#why

CDC (2)

http://www.cdc.gov/flu/avian/gen-info/pdf/avian_facts.pdf

CDC (3)

http://www.cdc.gov/Features/HPVvaccine/

CDC (4)

http://www.cdc.gov/tb/topic/treatment/default.htm

CDC (5)

http://www.cdc.gov/pertussis/outbreaks-faqs.html

CDC (6)

http://www.cdc.gov/tb/topic/treatment/default.htm

CDC (7)

http://www.cdc.gov/flu/spotlights/pandemic-global-estimates.htm

CDC (8)

http://www.cdc.gov/cancer/breast/basic_info/

CDC (9)

http://www.cdc.gov/vaccines/vac-gen/default.htm

CDC (10)

http://www.cdc.gov/NCBDDD/folicacid/about.html

CDC (11)

http://www.cdc.gov/vaccines/vac-gen/default.htm

Estridge, B. H., & Reynolds, A. P. (2012). *Basic clinical laboratory techniques* (6th ed.). Clifton Park, NY: Delmar Cengage Learning.

Food and Drug Administration (FDA). http://www.fda.gov/default.htm

http://www.fda.gov/BiologicsBloodVaccines/Vaccines/ApprovedProducts/ucm094042.htm

Jones, B. D. (2011). *Comprehensive medical terminology* (4th ed.). Clifton Park, NY: Delmar Cengage Learning.

Labtestsonline. http://www.labtestsonline.org

Labtestsonline (1).

http://www.labtestsonline.org/understanding/analytes/bilirubin/glance.html

Labtestsonline (2).

http://www.labtestsonline.org/understanding/analytes/troponin/related.html

Labtestsonline (3).

http://www.labtestsonline.org/understanding/analytes/pt/test.html

Labtestsonline (4).

http://labtestsonline.org/understanding/conditions/sickle

REFERENCES (continued)

Labtestsonline (5).
http://labtestsonline.org/understanding/analytes/urinalysis/tab/test
Labtestsonline (6).
http://labtestsonline.org/understanding/analytes/cholesterol/tab/test
Labtestsonline (7)
http://labtestsonline.org/understanding/analytes/strep/tab/sample
Labtestsonline (8)
http://labtestsonline.org/understanding/analytes/pt/tab/sample
Labtestsonline (9)
http://labtestsonline.org/understanding/wellness/pregnancy/first-hcg
Labtestsonline (10)
http://labtestsonline.org/understanding/conditions/meningitis?start=3
Labtestsonline (11)
http://labtestsonline.org/understanding/analytes/syphilis/tab/glance
Labtestsonline (12)
http://www.cdc.gov/vaccines/vpd-vac/hpv/default.htm
Labtestsonline (13)
http://labtestsonline.org/understanding/conditions/tuberculosis/?start=4

Mayo Clinic. http://www.mayoclinic.com
Mayo Clinic (1).
http://www.mayoclinic.com/print/esophageal-varices/DS00820/
Mayo Clinic (2)
http://www.mayoclinic.com/health/diabetic-ketoacidosis/DS00674

Moisio, M. A. (2010). *Medical terminology for insurance and coding.* Clifton Park, NY: Delmar Cengage Learning.

National Library of Medicine. http://www.nlm.nih.gov/medlineplus/
NLM (1).
http://www.nhlbi.nih.gov/health/dci/Diseases/ha/ha_diagnosis.html
http://www.nlm.nih.gov/medlineplus/ency/article/003479.htm

NLM (2).
http://www.nlm.nih.gov/medlineplus/ency/article/003652.htm

NLM (3)
http://www.nlm.nih.gov/medlineplus/ency/article/003498.htm

NLM (4)
http://www.nlm.nih.gov/medlineplus/ency/article/003574.htm

NHLBI—National Heart Lung and Blood Institute. http://www.nhlbi.nih.gov
http://www.nhlbi.nih.gov/health/dci/Diseases/hvd/hvd_treatments.html

NINDS—National Institute of Neurological Disorders and Stroke.
http://www.ninds.nih.gov/disorders/carpal_tunnel/detail_carpal_tunnel.htm

Neighbors, M. and Tannehill-Jones, R. (2009). *Human DiseasesI* (3rd ed.). Clifton Park, NY: Delmar Cengage Learning.

Rizzo, D. C. (2006). *Fundamentals of Anatomy and Physiology* (2006). (2nd ed.) . Clifton Park, NY: Delmar Cengage Learning.

Scott, A. S., & Fong, P.E. (2009). *Body structures and functions* (11th ed.). Clifton Park, NY: Delmar Cengage Learning.

REFERENCES (continued)

Sormunen, C. (2010). *Terminology for allied health professionals* (6th ed.). Clifton Park, NY: Delmar Cengage Learning.

Woodrow, R. (2011). *Essentials of pharmacology for health occupations* (6th ed.). Clifton Park, NY: Delmar Cengage Learning.

Medical Sciences Competencies

Question	RHIA Domain	RHIT Domain
1–145	1	1

VIII. ICD-10-CM/PCS Coding

Leslie Moore, RHIT, CCS

ICD-10-CM and ICD-10-PCS

The compliance date for implementation of ICD-10-CM/PCS is October 1, 2014, for all Health Insurance Portability and Accountability Act (HIPAA)-covered entities.

ICD-10-CM, including the "ICD-10-CM Official Guidelines for Coding and Reporting," will replace ICD-9-CM Diagnosis Codes in all health care settings for diagnosis reporting with dates of service, or dates of discharge for inpatients, that occur on or after October 1, 2014.

ICD-10-PCS, including the "ICD-10-PCS Official Guidelines for Coding and Reporting," will replace ICD-9-CM Procedure Codes.

BENEFITS OF ICD-10-CM

ICD-10-CM incorporates much greater clinical detail and specificity than ICD-9-CM. Terminology and disease classification are updated to be consistent with current clinical practice. The modern classification system will provide much better data needed for:

- Measuring the quality, safety, and efficacy of care;
- Reducing the need for attachments to explain the patient's condition;
- Designing payment systems and processing claims for reimbursement;
- Conducting research, epidemiological studies, and clinical trials;
- Setting health policy;
- Operational and strategic planning;
- Designing health care delivery systems;
- Monitoring resource use;
- Improving clinical, financial, and administrative performance;
- Preventing and detecting health care fraud and abuse; and
- Tracking public health and risks.

Non-specific codes are still available for use when medical record documentation does not support a more specific code.

ICD-10-CM Diagnosis Codes:

There are 3–7 digits;

Digit 1 is alpha;

Digit 2 is numeric;

Digits 3–7 are alpha or numeric (alpha characters are not case sensitive); and a decimal is used after the third character.

Examples:

A78–Q	fever;
A69.21	Meningitis due to Lyme disease; and
S52.131A	Displaced fracture of neck of right radius, initial encounter for closed fracture.

NEW FEATURES IN ICD-10-CM

The following new features can be found in ICD-10-CM:

1) *Laterality (Left, Right, Bilateral)*
   Examples:
   C50.511 – Malignant neoplasm of lower-outer quadrant of right female breast;
   H16.013 – Central corneal ulcer, bilateral; and
   L89.012 – Pressure ulcer of right elbow, stage II.

2) *Combination Codes For Certain Conditions and Common Associated Symptoms and Manifestations*
   Examples:
   K57.21 – Diverticulitis of large intestine with perforation and abscess with bleeding;
   E11.341 – Type 2 diabetes mellitus with severe nonproliferative diabetic retinopathy with macular edema; and
   I25.110 – Atherosclerotic heart disease of native coronary artery with unstable angina pectoris.

3) *Combination Codes for Poisonings and Their Associated External Cause*
   Example:
   T42.3x2S – Poisoning by barbiturates, intentional self-harm, sequela.

4) *Obstetric Codes Identify Trimester Instead of Episode of Care*
   Example:
   O26.02 – Excessive weight gain in pregnancy, second trimester.

5) *Character "x" is Used as a 5th Character Placeholder in Certain 6 Character Codes to Allow for Future Expansion and to Fill in Other Empty Characters (For Example, Character 5 and/or 6) When a Code That is Less Than 6 Characters in Length Requires a 7th Character*
   Examples:
   T46.1x5A – Adverse effect of calcium-channel blockers, initial encounter; and
   T15.02xD – Foreign body in cornea, left eye, subsequent encounter.

6) *Two Types of Excludes Notes*
   Excludes 1 Indicates that the code excluded should never be used with the code where the note is located (do not report both codes).
   Example:
   Q03 – Congenital hydrocephalus.
       Excludes 1: Acquired hydrocephalus (**G91.-**).

   Excludes 2   Indicates that the condition excluded is not part of the condition represented by the code but a patient may have both conditions at the same time, in which case both codes may be assigned together (both codes can be reported to capture both conditions).
   Example:
   L27.2 – Dermatitis due to ingested food.
       Excludes 2: Dermatitis due to food in contact with skin (L23.6, L24.6, L25.4).

7) *Inclusion of Clinical Concepts That Do Not Exist in ICD-9-CM (For Example, Underdosing, Blood Type, Blood Alcohol Level)*

Examples:

T45.526D – Underdosing of antithrombotic drugs, subsequent encounter;

Z67.40 – Type O blood, Rh positive; and

Y90.6 – Blood alcohol level of 120 – 199 mg/100 ml.

8) *A Number of Codes Are Significantly Expanded (For Example, Injuries, Diabetes, Substance Abuse, Postoperative Complications)*

Examples:

E10.610 – Type 1 diabetes mellitus with diabetic neuropathic arthropathy;

F10.182 – Alcohol abuse with alcohol-induced sleep disorder; and

T82.02xA – Displacement of heart valve prosthesis, initial encounter.

9) *Codes for Postoperative Complications Are Expanded and a Distinction is Made Between Intraoperative Complications and Postprocedural Disorders*

Examples:

D78.01 – Intraoperative hemorrhage and hematoma of spleen complicating a procedure on the spleen; and

D78.21 – Postprocedural hemorrhage and hematoma of spleen following a procedure on the spleen.

ADDITIONAL CHANGES IN ICD-10-CM

The additional changes that can be found in ICD-10-CM are as follows:

- Injuries are grouped by anatomical site rather than by type of injury; Category restructuring and code reorganization occur in a number of ICD-10-CM chapters, resulting in the classification of certain diseases and disorders that are different from ICD-9-CM;
- Certain diseases are reclassified to different chapters or sections to reflect current medical knowledge;
- New code definitions (for example, definition of acute myocardial infarction is now 4 weeks rather than 8 weeks); and
- The codes corresponding to ICD-9-CM V codes (Factors Influencing Health Status and Contact with Health Services) and E codes (External Causes of Injury and Poisoning) are incorporated into the main classification (in ICD-9-CM they were separated into supplementary classifications).

USE OF EXTERNAL CAUSE AND UNSPECIFIED CODES IN ICD-10-CM

Similar to ICD-9-CM, there is no national requirement for mandatory ICD-10-CM external cause code reporting. Unless you are subject to a State-based external cause code reporting mandate or these codes are required by a particular payer, you are not required to report ICD-10-CM codes found in Chapter 20, External Causes of Morbidity.

If you have not been reporting ICD-9-CM external cause codes, you will not be required to report ICD-10-CM codes found in Chapter 20 unless a new State or payer-based requirement about the reporting of these codes is instituted. If such a requirement is instituted, it would be independent of ICD-10-CM implementation.

In the absence of a mandatory reporting requirement, you are encouraged to voluntarily report external cause codes, as they provide valuable data for injury research and evaluation of injury prevention strategies.

In both ICD-9-CM and ICD-10-CM, sign/symptom and unspecified codes have acceptable, even necessary, uses. While specific diagnosis codes should be reported when they are supported by the available medical record documentation and clinical knowledge of the patient's health condition, in some instances signs/symptoms or unspecified codes are the best choice to accurately reflect the health care encounter.

Each health care encounter should be coded to the level of certainty known for that encounter.
If a definitive diagnosis has not been established by the end of the encounter, it is appropriate to report codes for sign(s) and/or symptom(s) in lieu of a definitive diagnosis. When sufficient clinical information is not known or available about a particular health condition to assign a more specific code, it is acceptable to report the appropriate unspecified code (for example, a diagnosis of pneumonia has been determined but the specific type has not been determined). In fact, unspecified codes should be reported when they are the codes that most accurately reflect what is known about the patient's condition at the time of that particular encounter. It is inappropriate to select a specific code that is not supported by the medical record documentation or conduct medically unnecessary diagnostic testing to determine a more specific code. Reference: MLM Matters CMS Website

2014 release of ICD-10-CM

These files have been created by the National Center for Health Statistics (NCHS), under authorization by the World Health Organization.

These files linked below are the 2014 update of the ICD-10-CM. Content changes to the full ICD-10-CM files are described in the respective addenda files. This year in addition to PDF (Adobe) files XML format is also being made available. Most files are provided in compressed zip format for ease in downloading.

These files have been created by the National Center for Health Statistics (NCHS), under authorization by the World Health Organization.

Although this release of ICD-10-CM is now available for public viewing, the codes in ICD-10-CM are not currently valid for any purpose or use. As noted above, the effective implementation date for ICD-10-CM (and ICD-10-PCS) is October 1, 2014. Updates to this version of ICD-10-CM are anticipated prior to its implementation.

- Preface [PDF - 35 KB]
- ICD-10-CM Guidelines [PDF - 512 KB]
- Detailed List of Codes Exempt from Diagnosis Present on Admission Requirement PDF Format
- Detailed List of Codes Exempt from Diagnosis Present on Admission Requirement XLSM Format
- ICD-10-CM PDF Format
- ICD-10-CM XML Format
- ICD-10-CM List of codes and Descriptions (updated 7/3/2013)
- General Equivalence Mapping Files

To download these files go to: http://www.cdc.gov/nchs/icd/icd10cm.htm#10update
Content source: CDC/National Center for Health Statistics
Page maintained by: Office of Information Services
http://www.cdc.gov/nchs/icd/icd10cm.htm

Development of the ICD-10 Procedure Coding System (ICD-10-PCS)

Richard F. Averill, M.S., Robert L. Mullin, M.D., Barbara A. Steinbeck, RHIT, Norbert I. Goldfield, M.D, Thelma M. Grant, RHIA, Rhonda R. Butler, CCS, CCS-P

The International Classification of Diseases 10th Revision Procedure Coding System (ICD-10-PCS) has been developed as a replacement for Volume 3 of the International Classification of Diseases 9th Revision (ICD-9-CM). The development of ICD-10-PCS was funded by the U.S. Centers for Medicare and Medicaid Services (CMS).1 ICD-10-PCS has a multiaxial seven character alphanumeric code structure that provides a unique code for all substantially different procedures, and allows new procedures to be easily incorporated as new codes. ICD10-PCS was under development for over five years. The initial draft was formally tested and evaluated by an independent contractor; the final version was released in the Spring of 1998, with annual updates since the final release. The design, development and testing of ICD-10-PCS are discussed.

Introduction

Volume 3 of the International Classification of Diseases 9th Revision Clinical Modification (ICD-9-CM) has been used in the U.S. for the reporting of inpatient procedures since 1979. The structure of Volume 3 of ICD-9-CM has not allowed new procedures associated with rapidly changing technology to be effectively incorporated as new codes. As a result, in 1992 the U.S. Centers for Medicare and Medicaid Services (CMS) funded a project to design a replacement for Volume 3 of ICD-9-CM. After a review of the preliminary design, CMS in 1995 awarded 3M Health Information Systems a three-year contract to complete development of the replacement system. The new system is the ICD-10 Procedure Coding System (ICD-10-PCS).

Attributes Used in Development

The development of ICD-10-PCS had as its goal the incorporation of four major attributes:

• Completeness
There should be a unique code for all substantially different procedures. In Volume 3 of ICD-9-CM, procedures on different body parts, with different approaches, or of different types are sometimes assigned to the same code.

• Expandability
As new procedures are developed, the structure of ICD-10-PCS should allow them to be easily incorporated as unique codes.

• Multiaxial
ICD-10-PCS codes should consist of independent characters, with each individual axis retaining its meaning across broad ranges of codes to the extent possible.

• Standardized Terminology
ICD-10-PCS should include definitions of the terminology used. While the meaning of specific words varies in common usage, ICD-10-PCS should not include multiple meanings for the same term, and each term must be assigned a specific meaning.

If these four objectives are met, then ICD-10-PCS should enhance the ability of health information coders to construct accurate codes with minimal effort.

General Development Principles

In the development of ICD-10-PCS, several general principles were followed:

• *Diagnostic Information is Not Included in Procedure Description*

When procedures are performed for specific diseases or disorders, the disease or disorder is not contained in the procedure code. There are no codes for procedures exclusive to aneurysms, cleft lip, strictures, neoplasms, hernias, etc. The diagnosis codes, not the procedure codes, specify the disease or disorder.

• *Not Otherwise Specified (NOS) Options are Restricted*

ICD-9-CM often provides a "not otherwise specified" code option. Certain NOS options made available in ICD-10-PCS are restricted to the uses laid out in the ICD-10-PCS official guidelines. A minimal level of specificity is required for each component of the procedure.

• *Limited Use of Not Elsewhere Classified (NEC) Option*

ICD-9-CM often provides a "not elsewhere classified" code option.

Because all significant components of a procedure are specified in ICD-10-PCS, there is generally no need for an NEC code option. However, limited NEC options are incorporated into ICD-10-PCS where necessary. For example, new devices are frequently developed, and therefore it is necessary to provide an "Other Device" option for use until the new device can be explicitly added to the coding system. Additional NEC options are discussed later, in the sections of the system where they occur.

• *Level of Specificity*

All procedures currently performed can be specified in ICD-10-PCS. The frequency with which a procedure is performed was not a consideration in the development of the system. Rather, a unique code is available for variations of a procedure that can be performed.

ICD-10-PCS has a seven character alphanumeric code structure. Each character contains up to 34 possible values. Each value represents a specific option for the general character definition (e.g., stomach is one of the values for the body part character). The ten digits 0-9 and the 24 letters A-H, J-N and P-Z may be used in each character. The letters O and I are not used in order to avoid confusion with the digits 0 and 1.

Procedures are divided into sections that identify the general type of procedure (e.g., medical and surgical, obstetrics, imaging). The first character of the procedure code always specifies the section. The sections are shown in table 1.

Table 1: ICD-10-PCS Sections

0	Medical and Surgical
1	Obstetrics
2	Placement
3	Administration
4	Measurement and Monitoring
5	Extracorporeal Assistance and Performance
6	Extracorporeal Therapies
7	Osteopathic
8	Other Procedures
9	Chiropractic
B	Imaging
C	Nuclear Medicine
D	Radiation Oncology
F	Physical Rehabilitation and Diagnostic Audiology
G	Mental Health
H	Substance Abuse Treatment

The second through seventh characters mean the same thing within each section, but may mean different things in other sections. In all sections, the third character specifies the general type of procedure performed (e.g., resection, transfusion, fluoroscopy), while the other characters give additional information such as the body part and approach. In ICD-10-PCS, the term "procedure" refers to the complete specification of the seven characters.

ICD-10-PCS 2014 Version
Update Summary /Change Summary Table

2013 Total	New Codes	Revised Titles	Deleted Codes	2014 Total
71,920	7	0	3	**71,924**

ICD-10-PCS Code 2013 Totals, By Section

Medical and Surgical	**61,898**
Obstetrics	300
Placement	861
Administration	**1,388**
Measurement and Monitoring	339
Extracorporeal Assistance and Performance	41
Extracorporeal Therapies	42
Osteopathic	100
Other Procedures	60
Chiropractic	90
Imaging	2,934
Nuclear Medicine	463
Radiation Oncology	1,939
Rehabilitation and Diagnostic Audiology	1,380
Mental Health	30
Substance Abuse Treatment	59
Total	**71,924**

ICD-10-PCS Code Changes
Four codes added under new technology application, valid October 1, 2013

- **08H005Z** Insertion of Epiretinal Visual Prosthesis into Right Eye, Open Approach
- **08H105Z** Insertion of Epiretinal Visual Prosthesis into Left Eye, Open Approach
- **30280B1** Transfusion of Nonautologous 4-Factor Prothrombin Complex Concentrate into Vein, Open Approach
- **30283B1** Transfusion of Nonautologous 4-Factor Prothrombin Complex Concentrate into Vein, Percutaneous Approach

Three new codes added and three codes deleted, to correct body part value for temporary occlusion of abdominal aorta

- New: **04V00DJ** Restriction of Abdominal Aorta with Intraluminal Device, Temporary, Open Approach
- New: **04V03DJ** Restriction of Abdominal Aorta with Intraluminal Device, Temporary, Percutaneous Approach
- New: **04V04DJ** Restriction of Abdominal Aorta with Intraluminal Device, Temporary, Percutaneous Endoscopic Approach
- Deleted: **02VW0DJ** Restriction of Thoracic Aorta with Intraluminal Device, Temporary, Open Approach

- **Deleted: 02VW3DJ** Restriction of Thoracic Aorta with Intraluminal Device, Temporary, Percutaneous Approach
- **Deleted: 02VW4DJ** Restriction of Thoracic Aorta with Intraluminal Device, Temporary, Percutaneous Endoscopic Approach

Revised Section Title

Section title for Radiation Oncology section revised to Radiation Therapy in response to public comment. Because the phrase "Radiation Oncology" is not used in code titles, no code titles were revised as a result of the section title change.

New Index Addenda

- New file showing new, revised and deleted index entries in response to public comment
- First discussed at September 2012 Coordination and Maintenance Committee, proposed format shown at March 2013 Coordination and Maintenance Committee
- See list of updated files for details

New Definitions Addenda

- New file showing new, revised and deleted PCS definitions entries (e.g. Body Part Key) in response to public comment
- First discussed at September 2012 Coordination and Maintenance Committee, proposed format shown at March 2013 Coordination and Maintenance Committee
- See list of updated files for details

List of Updated Files
2014 Official ICD-10-PCS Coding Guidelines

- Downloadable PDF file
- Revised in response to public comment and review by the Cooperating Parties

2014 ICD-10-PCS Code Tables and Index (Zip file)

- Downloadable PDF file, file name is **PCS_2014.pdf**
- Downloadable xml files for developers, file names are:
  icd10pcs_tabular_2014.xml
  icd10pcs_index_2014.xml
  icd10pcs_definitions_2014.xml
- Accompanying schema for developers, file names are:
  icd10pcs_tabular_2014.xsd
  icd10pcs_index_2014.xsd
  icd10pcs_definitions_2014.xsd

2014 ICD-10-PCS Code Titles, Long and Abbreviated (Zip file)

- Tabular order file defines an unambiguous order for all ICD-10-CM/PCS codes
- Text file format, file name is:
  icd10pcs_order_2014.txt
  Provides a unique five-digit "order number" for each ICD-10-PCS table and code
- Accompanying documentation, file name is:
  ICD10OrderFiles.pdf

2014 ICD-10-PCS Final Addenda (Zip file)

- New code titles for FY2014 shown as ICD-10-PCS table entries, file name is: **PcsAddendaAdditionsNewLabels.pdf**
- Deleted code titles for FY2014 shown as ICD-10-PCS table entries, file name is: **PcsAddendaDeletionsOldLabels.pdf**
- Downloadable xml format for developers, file names are: **PcsAddendaAdditionsNewLabels.xml, PcsAddendaDeletionsOldLabels.xml**
- Accompanying documentation, file name is: **pcs_addenda_readme2014.pdf**
- Index addenda in downloadable PDF, file name is: **index_addenda_2014.pdf**
- PCS Definitions addenda in downloadable PDF, file name is: **definitions_addenda_2014.pdf**
- Index and Definitions addenda in machine readable text format for developers, file names are: **index_addenda_2014.txt, definitions_addenda_2014.txt**

2014 ICD-10-PCS Reference Manual (Zip file)

- Downloadable PDF file, file name is **ICD-10-PCS Reference Manual.pdf** Revised in response to public comment and internal review
- Addenda to 2014 version of reference manual specifies the changes, file name is: **pcs_ref_addenda_2014.pdf**

2014 ICD-10-PCS and ICD-9-CM General Equivalence Mappings (Zip file)

- Downloadable text format, file names are: **gem_i9pcs.txt, gem_pcsi9.txt** Contains entries for the new FY2014 ICD-9-CM and ICD-10-PCS codes and entries revised in response to public comment and internal review
- Documentation for general users and technical users, file name is: **pcs_gemguide_2014.pdf**
- Documentation for technical users, file name is: **GemsTechDoc.pdf**

2014 ICD-10 Reimbursement Mappings (Zip file)

- Downloadable text format, file names are **reimb_map_dx_2014.txt reimb_map_pr_2014.txt** FY2014 version uses the FY2014 GEM files
- Accompanying documentation includes rules used in the mapping, file name is: **reimb_map_guide_2014.pdf**

ICD-10-CM CODING SECTION

Infectious and Parasitic Diseases

1. The patient was admitted with AIDS-related Kaposi's sarcoma of the skin.
   A. B20, C46.1
   B. C46.0, B20
   C. B20, C46.7
   D. B20, C46.0

   REFERENCE: AHA I-10 Coding Handbook, p 157

2. A patient was admitted with severe sepsis due to MRSA with septic shock and acute respiratory failure with hypoxia.
   A. R65.21, A41.02, J96.02
   B. A41.02, R65.21, J96.01
   C. A49.01, R65.21, J96.01
   D. J96.01, R65.21, A41.02

   REFERENCE: AHA I-10 Coding Handbook, p 151

3. Patient was initially admitted and treated for an amebic abscess of the liver. During the stay the patient developed a "hospital acquired bacterial pneumonia."
   A. A06.4, J15.9, Y95
   B. A06.4, J15.8; Y95
   C. A06.4, J18.9, Y95
   D. A06.4, J95.89, Y95

   REFERENCE: AHA I-10 Coding Handbook, pp 153, 154

4. A patient is admitted with fever and severe headache. The physician's diagnostic statement at discharge is: Fever and severe headache probably due to viral meningitis.
   A. A87.9, R50.9, R51
   B. A87.8, R50.9, R51
   C. A87.9
   D. A87.8

   REFERENCE: AHA I-10 Coding Handbook, p 57

5. Positive HIV test in a patient who is asymptomatic and has a high-risk lifestyle for HIV infection.
   A. B20, Z20.6, Z72.89
   B. B20, Z21, Z72.89
   C. B20, Z20.6, Z72.89
   D. Z21, Z72.89

   REFERENCE: AHA I-10 Coding Handbook, p 157

6. A 32-year-old female patient presents with right arm (dominant) paralysis due to childhood poliomyelitis.
   A. A80.39
   B. A80.39, G83.21
   C. B91, G83.21
   D. A80.39, G83.3

   REFERENCE: AHA I-10 Coding Handbook, pp 6, 60, 149

Neoplasms

7. A patient is admitted for chemotherapy for treatment of breast cancer with liver metastasis. She had a mastectomy 4 months ago. Chemotherapy is given today. (Do not assign a procedure code for the chemotherapy.)
   A. C78.7, C85.3, Z51.11
   B. C85.3, C78.7, Z51.11
   C. C78.7, C85.3
   D. Z51.11, C78.7, Z85.3

   REFERENCE: AHA I-10 Coding Handbook, pp 456, 457, 459

8. A patient with a history of malignant neoplasm of the lung status post lobectomy was admitted after experiencing a violent seizure lasting more than several minutes. During the course of the hospitalization the patient has continued to have seizures. Workup revealed metastatic lesions to the brain. The patient's seizures were treated with IV Dilantin.
   A. C79.3, Z85.118, F56.9
   B. C79.31, F56.9
   C. C79.31, R56.9, Z85.118
   D. F56.9 C79.32, Z85.118

REFERENCE: AHA I-10 Coding Handbook, pp 456, 457, 458

9. A patient is admitted to the hospital for treatment of dehydration following chemotherapy as treatment for right ovarian cancer.
   A. E86.0, C56.1
   B. E86.9, C56.1
   C. C56.1, 86.9
   D. C56.1, E86.0

REFERENCE: AHA I-10 Coding Handbook, p 458

10. A patient has malignant melanoma of the skin of the back, nose, and scalp. The patient will be scheduled to undergo a radical excision of the melanoma
    A. 173.59, 86.4, 86.63
    B. C43.59, C43.31, C43.4
    C. 173.59, 86.3, 86.63
    D. 172.5, 86.3, 86.63

REFERENCE: AHA I-10 Coding Handbook, pp 443, 456, 460

11. A patient is admitted with abdominal pain. A CT and MRI of the abdomen reveal a malignant neoplasm to the head of the pancreas with metastatic disease to the peritoneal cavity.
    A. C25.1, C78.6
    B. C78.89, C78.89
    C. C25.0, C78.6
    D. D01.7, C78.6

REFERENCE: AHA I-10 Coding Handbook, pp 456–458

12. A patient to an OP Clinic with a large growth on the left side of the neck. An MRI is performed and demonstrates metastatic disease to the lymph nodes.
    A. C77.2, C80.0
    B. C77.0, C80.1
    C. C77.2, R22.1, C81.1
    D. C77.8, C80.0

REFERENCE: AHA I-10 Coding Handbook, pp 459–458, 447–44/, 452–455

Endocrine, Nutritional, and Metabolic Diseases and Immunity Disorders

13. A female, 68 years old, was admitted with type 2 diabetes mellitus with a diabetic ulcer of the left heel involving the subcutaneous layer of the skin. The patient will be scheduled for wound care with whirlpool treatments.
    A. E11.621, L97.421
    B. E11.620, I97.421
    C. E11.621
    D. L97.421, E11.621

REFERENCE: AHA I-10 Coding Handbook, p 164

14. A 67-year-old man is admitted with acute dehydration secondary to nausea and vomiting that is due to acute gastroenteritis. He is treated with IV fluids for the dehydration.
    A. K52.9, E86.0
    B. E11.2, 52.9, E86.0
    C. 86.0, E11.2, K52.9
    D. E86.0, K52.9

REFERENCE: AHA I-10 Coding Handbook, pp 30–33

15. A patient was found at home in a hypoglycemic coma. This patient had never been diagnosed as being diabetic.
    A. E16.2   C. E16.1
    B. E15   D. E16.9

REFERENCE: AHA I-10 Coding Handbook, p 167

16. A patient is admitted with aplastic anemia secondary to chemotherapy administered for multiple myeloma initial encounter.
    A. D61.1, T45.1x5A, C90.00   C. C90.00, T45.1x5A, D61.1
    B. T45.1x5A, C90.00, D61.3   D. D61.1, T45.1x5A, D61.3

REFERENCE: AHA I-10 Coding Handbook, p 459

17. A male patient is admitted with gastrointestinal hemorrhage resulting in acute blood-loss anemia. A bleeding scan fails to reveal the source of the bleed.
    A. K92, D63.8   C. K92.2, D62
    B. K92.1, D62   D. K92.2, D63.8

REFERENCE: AHA I-10 Coding Handbook, pp 191, 192–196

18. A patient is admitted with severe protein calorie malnutrition.
    A. E42   C. E46
    B. E43   D. E40

REFERENCE: AHA I-10 Coding Handbook, p 168

Diseases of the Blood and Blood-Forming Organs

19. A patient is admitted with idiopathic thrombocytopenia and purpura.
    A. D61   C. D69.49
    B. D69.3, D61   D. D69.3

REFERENCE: AHA I-10 Coding Handbook, pp 191, 199

20. A patient is admitted with sickle cell anemia with crisis.
    A. D57.00, D57.3   C. D57.1
    B. D57.00   D. D57.819

REFERENCE: AHA I-10 Coding Handbook, pp 191, 196

21. A patient is admitted with sickle cell pain crisis.
    A. D57.00   C. D57.819
    B. D57.00, D57.3   D. D57.1

REFERENCE: AHA I-10 Coding Handbook, pp 191, 196

22. A patient is readmitted for post-op anemia due to acute blood loss. Patient is 5 days status post-cholecystectomy.
    A. D62, R58   C. K91.89, D62
    B. K91.840, D62   D. D62

REFERENCE: AHA I-10 Coding Handbook, pp 199, 528

23. A patient is admitted with anemia due to end-stage renal disease. The patient is treated for anemia.
   A. N18.6, D63.8   C. D63.1, N18.5
   B. D63.1, N18.6   D. D63.1

REFERENCE: AHA I-10 Coding Handbook, p 194

24. A patient is admitted for treatment of anemia, neutropenia, and thrombocytopenia.
   A. D70.8, D69.59, D59.2   C. D70.8, D69.59, D59.2, D61.810
   B. D61.810   D. D61.818

REFERENCE: AHA I-10 Coding Handbook, p 195

Mental Disorders

25. A patient is admitted with severe recurrent major depression without psychotic features.
   A. F33.0   C. F32.2
   B. F33.3   D. F33.2

REFERENCE: AHA I-10 Coding Handbook, p 175

26. A patient is admitted with acute alcohol intoxication with a blood alcohol level of 113 mg/100 ml.
   A. Y90.5, F10.129   C. F10.129, Y90.6
   B. F10.129, Y90.5   D. F10.129, Y90.4

REFERENCE: AHA I-10 Coding Handbook, pp 12, 181

27. A patient is admitted with delirium tremens with alcohol dependence.
   A. F10.221   C. F10.121
   B. F10.222   D. F10.231

REFERENCE: AHA I-10 Coding Handbook, p 181

28. A patient is admitted with catatonic schizophrenia.
   A. F20   C. F20.2
   B. F14.221   D. F14.29

REFERENCE: AHA I-10 Coding Handbook, pp 181, 182

29. A patient with chronic paranoia due to cocaine dependence with intoxication and drug delirium.
   A. F14.129   C. F14.159
   B. F14.221   D. F14.19, F22

REFERENCE: AHA I-10 Coding Handbook, pp 181–182

30. A patient is diagnosed with psychogenic paroxysmal tachycardia.
   A. I47.9   C. I47.8, F54
   B. F54   D. I47.9, F54

REFERENCE: AHA I-10 Coding Handbook, p 179

Diseases of the Nervous System and Sense Organs

31. A patient is admitted with sensorineural deafness of the left ear. The patient was fitted for a hearing aid.
     A. H90.71   C. H90.42
     B. H90.72   D. H90.41

REFERENCE: AHA I-10 Coding Handbook, p 220

32. A patient is a type 2 diabetic with chronic kidney disease requiring dialysis.
     A. E09.29, N18.6, Z99.2   C. E11.21, N18.6, Z99.2
     B. E11.22, N18.6, Z99.2   D. E13.21, N18.6, Z99.2

REFERENCE: AHA I-10 Coding Handbook, p 265

33. A patient has intractable status epilepticus.
     A. G40.311   C. G40.31
     B. G40.301   D. G40.201

REFERENCE: AHA I-10 Coding Handbook, p 206

34. A patient is diagnosed with Alzheimer's disease and early onset dementia, and frequently wanders away from home.
     A. G30.8, F02.81, Z91.83   C. G30.0, F02.81, Z91.83
     B. F02.81, G30.0, Z91.73   D. G30.0, Z91.73

REFERENCE: AHA I-10 Coding Handbook, pp 173, 206

35. A patient is admitted with poliovirus meningitis.
     A. G02, A80.9   C. A80.3, G02
     B. A80.9, G02   D. A80.0, G02

REFERENCE: AHA I-10 Coding Handbook, p 205

36. A patient is admitted for pain control secondary to metastatic carcinoma of the spinal cord.
     A. G89.3, C79.49
     B. C79.51, C80.1, G89.3
     C. C79.49, C80.1 , G89.3
     D. G89.3, C79.49, C80.1

REFERENCE: AHA I-10 Coding Handbook, p 210

Diseases of the Circulatory System

37. A patient is admitted with a thrombosis of the right middle cerebral artery, with hemiplegia affecting the right dominant side.
     A. I66.01, I69.351   C. I63.311
     B. I63.311, I69.353   D. I63.311, I69.351

REFERENCE: AHA I-10 Coding Handbook, p 209

38. A patient is admitted with multiple problems. He has hypertensive kidney disease, CKD stage III, and acute systolic congestive heart failure.
     A. N18.3, I12.9, I50.21   C. I12.9, N18.3, I50.21
     B. I50.21, I12.9, N18.3   D. I12.9

REFERENCE: AHA I-10 Coding Handbook, pp 394, 395, 404, 405

39. A patient is admitted with acute ST Inferolateral wall myocardial infarction. Several days later during the same episode of care, the patient sustained a subsequent non-ST subendocardial myocardial infarction.
    A. I21.09, I22.8   C. I22.2, I21.02
    B. I21.02, I22.8   D. I21.19, I22.2

REFERENCE: AHA I-10 Coding Handbook, pp 389–391

40. A patient with a diagnosis of coronary artery disease with ischemic chest pain. No history of CABG.
    A. I25.119   C. I25.9
    B. I25.119, I20.9   D. I25.10, I20.9

REFERENCE: AHA I-10 Coding Handbook, p 392

41. A patient with atherosclerotic peripheral vascular disease of the left lower leg with intermittent claudication. Past surgical history is negative.
    A. I70.219   C. I70.298
    B. I70.212   D. I70.208

REFERENCE: AHA I-10 Coding Handbook, p 407

Diseases of the Respiratory System

42. A patient presents to the outpatient department for a chest x-ray. The physician's order lists the following reasons for the chest x-ray: fever and cough, rule out pneumonia. The radiologist reports that the chest x-ray is positive for double pneumonia.
    A. J18.9   C. J18.1
    B. J18.8   D. J12.9

REFERENCE: AHA I-10 Coding Handbook, pp 140, 141

43. A patient has aspiration pneumonia with pneumonia due to *Staphylococcus aureus*.
    A. J15.211   C. J69.0, J15
    B. J69.0   D. J69.0, J15.211

REFERENCE: AHA I-10 Coding Handbook, pp 224, 227, 229

44. A patient is admitted with acute respiratory failure with hypercapnia due to acute asthmatic bronchitis with status asthmaticus. Treatment consisted of IV steroids.
    A. J45.902, J96.02   C. J45.901, J96.02
    B. J96.02, J45.902   D. J45.52, J96.02

REFERENCE: AHA I-10 Coding Handbook, pp 231, 233, 235

45. A patient is admitted for treatment of influenza and pneumonia.
    A. J11.1, J18.9   C. J11.08, J11.1
    B. J11.00   D. J11.1

REFERENCE: AHA I-10 Coding Handbook, p 228

46. A patient is admitted with acute exacerbation chronic obstructive pulmonary disease with a history of tobacco dependence.
    A. J44.1, Z87.891   C. J44.0, Z87.891
    B. J44.9, Z72.0   D. J44.1, Z72.0

REFERENCE: AHA I-10 Coding Handbook, p 230

47. A patient is admitted with extrinsic asthma with status asthmaticus with bronchospasm.
    A. J45.901
    B. J45.32
    C. J45.902
    D. J45.902

REFERENCE: AHA I-10 Coding Handbook, pp 230, 231

48. A patient is admitted for infection of the tracheostomy stoma secondary to cellulitis of the neck.
    A. L03.221, J95.02
    B. J95.02, L03.221
    C. J95.03, L03.221
    D. J95.09, L03.221

REFERENCE: AHA I-10 Coding Handbook, p 230

Diseases of the Digestive System

49. A patient is admitted to the hospital for repair of a recurrent incarcerated ventral hernia. The surgery is canceled after the chest x-ray revealed lower lobe pneumonia. The patient is placed on antibiotics for treatment of the pneumonia.
    A. K43.0, J18.9, Z53.09
    B. J18.9, K43.0, Z53.09
    C. K43.6, J18.9
    D. J18.9, J43.6

REFERENCE: AHA I-10 Coding Handbook, p 253

50. A patient is admitted with acute gastric ulcer with hemorrhage and perforation.
    A. K25.0, K25.1
    B. K25.6
    C. K25.4, K25.6
    D. K25.2

REFERENCE: AHA I-10 Coding Handbook, p 246

51. A patient has diverticulitis of the large bowel with abscess. Patient was treated with IV antibiotics.
    A. K57.92
    B. K57.12
    C. K57.20
    D. K57.52

REFERENCE: AHA I-10 Coding Handbook, p 247

52. A patient is admitted with acute gangrenous cholecystitis with cholelithiasis.
    A. K80.00
    B. K80.12
    C. K81.0, K80.80
    D. K80.32

REFERENCE: AHA I-10 Coding Handbook, p 249

53. A patient is admitted with bleeding esophageal varices with alcoholic liver cirrhosis and portal hypertension. The patient is alcohol dependent.
    A. K76.6, I85.11, K70.30
    B. I85.11, K76.6, K70.30
    C. K70.30, I85.11, K76.6
    D. K70.0. I85.11, K76.6

REFERENCE: AHA I-10 Coding Handbook, p 246

54. A patient is admitted for rectal bleeding. The laboratory results reveal chronic blood-loss anemia. The CT and the Bleeding Scan results of the abdomen revealed that the rectal bleeding is due to Crohn's disease of the descending colon.
    A. K50.118, D50.0
    B. K50.111, D50.0
    C. K50.011, D50.0
    D. K50.911, D50.0

REFERENCE: AHA I-10 Coding Handbook, p 248

Diseases of the Genitourinary System

55. A patient is admitted with acute urinary tract infection due to *E. coli.*
    A. N39.0, B96.20
    B. N11.9, B96.20
    C. N30.90, B96.20
    D. N10, B96.20

REFERENCE: AHA I-10 Coding Handbook, pp 260, 261

56. A patient admitted with gross hematuria and benign prostatic hypertrophy.
    A. R31.0, N40.0
    B. R31.0, N40.1
    C. N40.0, R31.0
    D. N40.1, R31.0

REFERENCE: AHA I-10 Coding Handbook, pp 262, 270

57. A male patient presents to the ED with acute renal failure. He is also being treated for hypertension.
    A. I12.9, N17.9
    B. N17.9, I15.9
    C. N17.9, I12.9
    D. N17.9, I10

REFERENCE: AHA I-10 Coding Handbook, p 264

58. A patient is admitted with acute hemorrhagic cystitis. The patient was treated with IV antibiotics.
    A. N30.00
    B. N30.91
    C. N30.01
    D. N30.81

REFERENCE: AHA I-10 Coding Handbook, pp 260, 261

59. A patient is admitted with chronic kidney disease stage III due to hypertension and type 1 diabetes mellitus.
    A. E11.22, I12.0, N18.3
    B. E10.22, I12.0, N18.3
    C. I12.0, E11.22, N18.3
    D. E08.22, I12.0, N18.3

REFERENCE: AHA I-10 Coding Handbook, pp 263, 264, 265

60. A patient has end-stage kidney disease, which resulted from malignant hypertension.
    A. I12.0, N18.6
    B. I10, N18.6
    C. I13.11, N18.6
    D. I15.1, N18.6

REFERENCE: AHA I-10 Coding Handbook, pp 263, 264

Complications of Pregnancy, Childbirth, and the Puerperium

61. A woman has a vaginal delivery of a full-term liveborn infant after 38 weeks gestation.
    A. O80, Z37.0, Z3A.38
    B. O80, Z37.0
    C. Z3A.38, O80, Z37.0
    D. Z37.0, Z3A.38, O80

REFERENCE: AHA I-10 Coding Handbook, pp 316, 319

62. A patient is admitted with pregnancy-induced hypertension with severe edema and 24 weeks gestation.
    A. O14.12
    B. I10, Z33.1
    C. O14.12, Z3A24
    D. O14.00, 23A24

REFERENCE: AHA I-10 Coding Handbook, p 325

63. A patient is admitted with obstructed labor due to breech presentation. A single liveborn infant was delivered via Cesarean section. Do not assign the code for the procedure.
    A. O32.1xx0
    B. O32.1xx0, Z37.0
    C. 032.8xx0, Z37.0
    D. O32.6xx0, Z37.0

REFERENCE: AHA I-10 Coding Handbook, p 327

64. A patient is admitted for gestation diabetes insulin controlled 28 weeks gestation.
    A. O24.414
    B. E11.69, O09.892
    C. O24.419, Z3A28
    D. O24.414, Z3A28

REFERENCE: AHA I-10 Coding Handbook, p 325

65. A patient is seen in the ED at 22 weeks gestation who is HIV positive.
    A. B20, O98.712, Z3A.22
    B. O98.712, Z21, Z3A.22
    C. Z21, O98.712
    D. P98.712, B20

REFERENCE: AHA I-10 Coding Handbook, p 326

66. A patient is admitted who is 39 weeks gestation normal delivery single full-term newborn. During the same episode of care, patient experiences a 36-hour delayed hemorrhage following the delivery.
    A. O80, O72.2, Z37.0
    B. O72.2, Z37.0
    C. Z3A.39, O72.2, Z37.0
    D. O72.2, Z3A.39, Z37.0

REFERENCE: AHA I-10 Coding Handbook, p 319

Diseases of the Skin and Subcutaneous Tissue

67. A patient had a cholecystectomy 3 days ago and is now readmitted with cellulitis at the site of the operative incision.
    A. T81.4, K68.11, 95.61
    B. T81.4xxA, L03.311
    C. K68.11, B95.61
    D. L03.31, T81.4xxA

REFERENCE: AHA I-10 Coding Handbook, p 288

68. A patient is admitted with a wound open to the left finger with cellulitis due to a dog bite initial encounter. The patient is given IV antibiotics for treatment of the infection.
    A. L03.012
    B. L03.011
    C. S61.201A
    D. L03.012, S61.201A

REFERENCE: AHA I-10 Coding Handbook, p 288

69. A patient is admitted with Diabetes Mellitus Type II; diabetic heel ulcer with necrosis of the muscle.
    A. E11.621, L97.403
    B. E10.622, L97.403
    C. E11.622, L97.403
    D. E10.628, L97.403

REFERENCE: AHA I-10 Coding Handbook, pp 286, 287

70. A patient is admitted with dermatitis due to prescription topical antibiotic cream used as directed by a physician, initial encounter.
    A. L08.89, T49.0x5
    B. L25.1, T49.0x5A
    C. L02.91, T49.0x5
    D. T49.0x5, L25.1

REFERENCE: AHA I-10 Coding Handbook, p 284

71. A patient is admitted with a pressure ulcer left buttock stage 2.
    A. L89.322   C. L89.152
    B. L98.411   D. L03.317

REFERENCE: AHA I-10 Coding Handbook, p 287

72. A patient is admitted with a stage 1 pressure ulcer of the sacrum. During the hospitalization, the ulcer progressed to a stage 2
    A. L89.125   C. L89.152
    B. L89.151, L89.152   D. L89.153

REFERENCE: AHA I-10 Coding Handbook, p 287

Diseases of the Musculoskeletal System and Connective Tissue

73. A patient has a pathological fracture of the left femur due to metastatic bone cancer. The past medical history is significant for lung cancer.
    A. C79.51, S72.92xG, Z85.118   C. C79.51, S72.92xS, Z85.118
    B. M84.552, C79.51, Z85.118   D. C79.51, M84.552, Z85.118

REFERENCE: AHA I-10 Coding Handbook, pp 299, 300, 460, 489

74. A patient is admitted with a back pain. A myelogram demonstrated the reason for the back pain is a herniated lumbar intervertebral disc with radiculopathy.
    A. M51.26, M54.16   C. M51.26
    B. M84.552, C79.51, Z85.118   D. M51.16

REFERENCE: AHA I-10 Coding Handbook, p 296

75. A patient is admitted with pyogenic arthritis of the right hip due to Group A *Streptococcus*. Treatment consisted of IV antibiotics.
    A. M16.11, A49.1   C. M00.251
    B. M16.7, A49.1   D. M00.851

REFERENCE: AHA I-10 Coding Handbook, p 298

76. A patient is admitted with a fracture to the L1 vertebrae secondary to postmenopausal senile osteoporosis, initial encounter.
    A. M80.08   C. M80.88xA
    B. M80.88   D. M80.08xA

REFERENCE: AHA I-10 Coding Handbook, p 300

77. A patient developed a malunion of the medical condyle humeral fracture. The original injury occurred 4 months ago.
    A. S42.462K   C. S42.462P
    B. S42.462G   D. S42.462D

REFERENCE: AHA I-10 Coding Handbook, p 484

78. A patient was admitted for removal of internal pins from the left ankle. One month ago the patient sustained a displaced bimalleolar fracture to the left ankle.
    A. S82.842K   C. S82.842S
    B. S82.842D   D. S84.842G

REFERENCE: AHA I-10 Coding Handbook, p 483

Congenital Anomalies

79.   A Newborn infant is born in the hospital vaginal delivery with a unilateral hard cleft palate and cleft lip.
    A.   O37.1, Z38.00
    B.   O37.2, Z38.00
    C.   Z38.00, O37.1
    D.   Z38.00, O37.2

REFERENCE: AHA I-10 Coding Handbook, p 360

80.   A newborn is born in the hospital vaginal delivery. Physical examination demonstrates molding of the baby's scalp, which resolved prior to discharge without treatment.
    A.   Z38.00, Q82.9
    B.   Z38.00, Q82.8
    C.   Z38.00, L98.8
    D.   Z38.00

REFERENCE: AHA I-10 Coding Handbook, p 367

81.   A newborn infant is transferred to Community General Hospital for treatment of an esophageal atresia. What codes should be reported for Community General Hospital?
    A.   Z38.00, Q39.0
    B.   Q39.0
    C.   Z38.00, Q39.1
    D.   Q39.1

REFERENCE: AHA I-10 Coding Handbook, p 367

82.   A patient is admitted with cervical spina bifida with hydrocephalus.
    A.   Q76.0
    B.   Q05
    C.   Q05.0
    D.   Q05.5

REFERENCE: AHA I-10 Coding Handbook, p 359

83.   A newborn infant is born in the hospital, delivered vaginally, and sustained a fracture of the clavicle due to birth trauma.
    A.   Z38.00, P13.4
    B.   Z38.00, S42.009A
    C.   P13.4
    D.   Z38.00, P13.4, S42.009A

REFERENCE: AHA I-10 Coding Handbook

84.   A full-term infant born in hospital vaginal delivery was diagnosed with polycystic kidneys.
    A.   Z38.00, Q61.11
    B.   Z38.00, Q61.19
    C.   Z38.00, Q61.3
    D.   Z38.00, Q61.8

REFERENCE: AHA I-10 Coding Handbook, p 361

Certain Conditions Originating in the Perinatal Period

85.   A full-term newborn vaginal delivery was born in the hospital to a mother who is addicted to cocaine; however, the infant tested negative.
    A.   Z38.00, F14.10
    B.   Z38.00, F14.129
    C.   Z38.00, F14.20
    D.   Z38.00, Z03.79

REFERENCE: AHA I-10 Coding Handbook, p 373

86.   A preterm infant 34 weeks gestation is born via Cesarean section and has severe birth asphyxia.
    A.   Z38.01, P84, P07.37
    B.   Z38.01, P84, R09.01
    C.   Z38.01, P84, R09.02
    D.   Z38.01, P84, R09.2, P07.37

REFERENCE: AHA I-10 Coding Handbook, pp 368, 369

87. A preterm infant born in the hospital vaginal delivery 36 weeks gestation is treated for neonatal jaundice.
   A. Z38.00, P59.9, P07.39   C. Z38.00, P59.29, P07.39
   B. Z38.00, P59.8, P07.39   D. Z38.00, P59.3, P07.39

REFERENCE: AHA I-10 Coding Handbook, pp 367, 368

88. A 1-week-old infant is admitted to the hospital with a diagnosis of urinary tract infection contracted prior to birth. The urine culture is positive for *E. coli.*
   A. P39.3   C. P39.3, N30.90, A49.8
   B. P39.3, N39.0, A49.8   D. P39.3, A49.8

REFERENCE: AHA I-10 Coding Handbook, p 366

89. An infant has hypoglycemia and a mother with diabetes.
   A. P70.0   C. P70.1
   B. P70.2   D. P70.4

REFERENCE: AHA I-10 Coding Handbook, p 373

90. A full-term newborn vaginal delivery born in the hospital. The birth is complicated by cord compression, which affected the newborn.
   A. Z38.00, P02.5   C. Z38.00, P02.4
   B. P02.5   D. Z38.00, P02.69

REFERENCE: AHA I-10 Coding Handbook, p 367

Symptoms, Signs, and Ill-Defined Conditions

91. A patient is admitted with right lower quadrant abdominal pain. The discharge diagnosis is listed as abdominal pain due to gastroenteritis or diverticulosis.
   A. K52.9, K57.90   C. R10.31, K52.9, K57.90
   B. K57.90, K52.9   D. K52.9, K57.90, R10.31

REFERENCE: AHA I-10 Coding Handbook, p 140

92. A patient was admitted with hemoptysis; a CT of the chest revealed a lung mass.
   A. R91.8   C. R04.2
   B. R91.8, R04.2   D. R91.8, F04.1

REFERENCE: AHA I-10 Coding Handbook, pp 140–142

93. A woman has a Pap smear that detected cervical high-risk human papillomavirus (HPV). The DNA test was positive.
   A. R87.810   C. R87.820
   B. R87.811   D. R87.811

REFERENCE: AHA I-10 Coding Handbook, pp 140, 141

94. A patient is admitted with malignant ascites with widespread metastatic peritoneal lesions, primary site sigmoid colon; sigmoid colon resection 6 months ago.
   A. R18.8, C78.6, Z85.038   C. R18.0, C78.6, Z85.038
   B. R18.8, C78.6, C18.9   D. R18.0, C78.6, C18.9

REFERENCE: AHA I-10 Coding Handbook, pp 460, 461

95.   A patient is admitted with fever due to bacteremia.
       A.   R78.81   C.   R78.81, F50.81
       B.   R50.9   D.   R78.81, R50.9

REFERENCE: AHA I-10 Coding Handbook, p 150

96.   A patient is admitted that has urinary retention secondary to benign prostatic hypertrophy.
       A.   N40.0, R33.8   C.   N40.1, R33.8
       B.   N40.1, R39.11, R33.9   D.   N40.3, R33.8

REFERENCE: AHA I-10 Coding Handbook, p 270

Injury and Poisoning

97.   A patient is admitted with a nondisplaced fracture of the left medial malleolus, initial encounter.
       The fracture was treated with a cast.
       A.   S82.52xB   C.   S82.62xA
       B.   S82.52xA   D.   S82.63xA

REFERENCE: AHA I-10 Coding Handbook, p 486

98.   A patient is admitted with an anaphylactic reaction due to eating strawberries, initial encounter.
       A.   T78.04xA   C.   T78.2
       B.   T78.49   D.   T78.04

REFERENCE: AHA I-10 Coding Handbook, p 494

99.   A patient is admitted with a gunshot wound to the right upper quadrant of the abdomen, which
       involves a moderate laceration to the liver, initial encounter.
       A.   S36.118A   C.   S36.115A
       B.   S36.115A, S31.101A   D.   S36.115A, S31.600A

REFERENCE: AHA I-10 Coding Handbook, p 494

100.   A woman experienced third-degree burns to her thigh and second-degree burns to her right and
       left foot, initial encounter. She stated that the burns were from hot liquid.
       A.   T24.319A, T25.229A   C.   T24.319A, T25.222A, T25.221A
       B.   T24.31xA, T24.331A, T24.332A   D.   T24.719A, T25.222A, T25.221A

REFERENCE: AHA I-10 Coding Handbook, pp 505, 506, 507

101.   A patient is seen for a cast removal. Six weeks ago, the patient underwent open reduction
       internal fixation for a displaced fracture left radial styloid process.
       A.   S52.512D   C.   S52.515A
       B.   Z47.89   D.   Z47.2

REFERENCE: AHA I-10 Coding Handbook, p 484

102.   A patient is admitted with a left wrist laceration, with embedded glass that involved the radical
       nerve, initial encounter.
       A.   S64.22xA   C.   S61.512, S64.22xA
       B.   S62.522A   D.   S61.522A, S64.22xA

REFERENCE: AHA I-10 Coding Handbook, p 494

103. A patient is admitted with a left nondisplaced comminuted patella fracture, a displaced left spiral fracture of the shaft of the fibula, and a displaced comminuted fracture of the shaft of the left tibia, initial encounter.
   A. S82.045A, S82.442A
   B. S82.045, S82.252A
   C. S82.045A, S82.442A, S82.252A
   D. S82.045A, S82.442A, S82.255A

REFERENCE: AHA I-10 Coding Handbook, p 487

104. A patient is admitted with dizziness as a result of taking phenobarbital as prescribed, initial encounter.
   A. R42, T42.4x1A
   B. R42, T42.3x5A
   C. T42.4x2A, R42
   D. T42.4x1A, R42

REFERENCE: AHA I-10 Coding Handbook, p 518

105. A patient is admitted for control of exacerbation of chronic obstructive lung disease. The patient had stopped taking the prednisone as prescribed due to gaining weight, a known side effect for this drug.
   A. J44.1, T38.0x6A, Z91.14
   B. T38.0x6A, J44.1, Z91.14
   C. J44.0, T38.0x6A, Z91.14
   D. T38.0x6A, Z91.14, J44.0

REFERENCE: AHA I-10 Coding Handbook, pp 516, 518

106. A patient is admitted for intentional overdose of valium and acute respiratory failure with hypoxia.
   A. J96.01, T42.4x2A
   B. J96.01, T42.4x2A, R09.02
   C. T42.4x2A, J96.01
   D. T42.4x2A, J96.00, R09.02

REFERENCE: AHA I-10 Coding Handbook, p 516

Z-Codes

107. A patient is being admitted for chemotherapy for primary lung cancer, left lower lobe.
   A. Z51.11
   B. Z51.11, Z85.118
   C. C34.32, Z51.11
   D. Z51.11, C34.32

REFERENCE: AHA I-10 Coding Handbook, p 127

108. The patient presents for a screening examination for lung cancer.
   A. Z03.89
   B. C78.00
   C. Z12.2
   D. C34.90

REFERENCE: AHA I-10 Coding Handbook, p 132

109. A patient is admitted for observation for a head injury. The patient was struck while playing football. The patient also suffered a minor laceration to the forehead. Head injury was ruled out.
   A. Z71.4
   B. S01.81xA, Z71.4
   C. S01.81xA
   D. Z04.3, S01.81xA

REFERENCE: AHA I-10 Coding Handbook, pp 129–131

ICD-10-PCS Coding

Identify the correct root operation for the following:

110. Excision gallbladder
    A. Resection
    B. Excision
    C. Incision
    D. Removal

    REFERENCE: AHA I-10 Coding Handbook, p 93

111. Excision descending colon
    A. Resection
    B. Excision
    C. Incision
    D. Bypass

    REFERENCE: AHA I-10 Coding Handbook, p 93

112. Removal FB right external auditory cancel
    A. Removal
    B. Extirpation
    C. Inspection
    D. Excision

    REFERENCE: AHA I-10 Coding Handbook, p 95

113. Amputation first left toe
    A. Excision
    B. Amputation
    C. Resection
    D. Detachment

    REFERENCE: AHA I-10 Coding Handbook, p 93

114. Reduction fracture right femoral shaft
    A. Transfer
    B. Reduction
    C. Reposition
    D. Reattachment

    REFERENCE: AHA I-10 Coding Handbook, p 96

115. Colon polyp fulguration
    A. Excision
    B. Destruction
    C. Extraction
    D. Detachment

    REFERENCE: AHA I-10 Coding Handbook, p 93

116. Reattachment fourth finger
    A. Reattachment
    B. Reposition
    C. Transfer
    D. Repair

    REFERENCE: AHA I-10 Coding Handbook, p 96

117. Cystoscopy
    A. Inspection
    B. Endoscopy
    C. Insertion
    D. Drainage

    REFERENCE: AHA I-10 Coding Handbook, p 101

118. Removal deep left vein thrombosis
    A. Excision
    B. Removal
    C. Resection
    D. Extirpation

    REFERENCE: AHA I-10 Coding Handbook, p 95

119. Total left knee replacement
    A. Insertion
    B. Resection
    C. Excision
    D. Replacement

    REFERENCE: AHA I-10 Coding Handbook, p 99

120. Lysis of abdominal adhesions
    A. Excision
    B. Division
    C. Incision
    D. Release

    REFERENCE: AHA I-10 Coding Handbook, p 96

121. Percutaneous angioplasty right coronary artery
    A. Dilation
    B. Restriction
    C. Insertion
    D. Excision

    REFERENCE: AHA I-10 Coding Handbook, p 98

122. Ligation right fallopian tube
    A. Restriction
    B. Occlusion
    C. Dilation
    D. Bypass

    REFERENCE: AHA I-10 Coding Handbook, p 98

123. Removal cardiac pacemaker
    A. Change
    B. Excision
    C. Revision
    D. Removal

    REFERENCE: AHA I-10 Coding Handbook, p 99

124. Creation of arteriovenous graft brachial artery left arm for hemodialysis
    A. Bypass
    B. Creation
    C. Alteration
    D. Insertion

    REFERENCE: AHA I-10 Coding Handbook, p 98

125. Lithotripsy left ureter with removal of fragment
    A. Drainage
    B. Fragmentation
    C. Removal
    D. Extirpation

    REFERENCE: AHA I-10 Coding Handbook, p 95

126. Endometrial ablation of cervical polyps
    A. Destruction
    B. Excision
    C. Removal
    D. Extraction

    REFERENCE: AHA I-10 Coding Handbook, p 93

127. Angioplasty abdominal iliac artery
    A. Dilation
    B. Repair
    C. Angioplasty
    D. Insertion

    REFERENCE: AHA I-10 Coding Handbook, p 98

128. Radiofrequency ablation right kidney
    A. Excision
    B. Removal
    C. Destruction
    D. Ablation

    REFERENCE: AHA I-10 Coding Handbook, p 93

129. Cryoablation external genital warts
    A. Destruction
    B. Cryoablation
    C. Excision
    D. Resection

    REFERENCE: AHA I-10 Coding Handbook, p 93

130. Gastric lap band for treatment of morbid obesity
    A. Dilation
    B. Occlusion
    C. Restriction
    D. Bypass

    REFERENCE: AHA I-10 Coding Handbook, p 98

131. Excisional debridement of a chronic skin ulcer
    A. Debridement
    B. Excision
    C. Incision
    D. Resection

    REFERENCE: AHA I-10 Coding Handbook, p 93

132. Application of skin graft to the nose status post excision malignant neoplasm
    A. Transfer
    B. Creation
    C. Replacement
    D. Alteration

    REFERENCE: AHA I-10 Coding Handbook, p 99

133. Spinal fusion cervical C1-C2
    A. Arthrodesis
    B. Repair
    C. Creation
    D. Fusion

    REFERENCE: AHA I-10 Coding Handbook, p 103

134. Tracheostomy
    A. Bypass
    B. Creation
    C. Reposition
    D. Insertion

    REFERENCE: AHA I-10 Coding Handbook, p 98

135. Percutaneous needle biopsy left lung
    A. Incision
    B. Excision
    C. Drainage
    D. Resection

    REFERENCE: AHA I-10 Coding Handbook, pp 92–93

136. Extraction left intraocular lens, open
    A. Extirpation
    B. Fragmentation
    C. Extraction
    D. Excision

    REFERENCE: AHA I-10 Coding Handbook, p 93

137. Uterine dilation and curettage
   A. Extraction
   B. Dilation
   C. Excision
   D. Destruction

   REFERENCE: AHA I-10 Coding Handbook, p 94

138. Excision right popliteal artery with graft replacement, open
   A. Excision
   B. Resection
   C. Replacement
   D. Repair

   REFERENCE: AHA I-10 Coding Handbook, p 99

139. Mitral valve annuloplasty using ring, open
   A. Supplement
   B. Replacement
   C. Resection
   D. Repair

   REFERENCE: AHA I-10 Coding Handbook, p 99

140. Left common carotid endarterectomy, open
   A. Excision
   B. Resection
   C. Extirpation
   D. Release

   REFERENCE: AHA I-10 Coding Handbook, p 95

141. Excision malignant lesion skin of left ear
   A. 0HB3XZZ
   B. 0HC3XZZ
   C. 0H53XZZ
   D. 0HD3XZZ

   REFERENCE: AHA I-10 Coding Handbook, pp 92, 93, 289

142. Left below the knee amputation, proximal tibia/fibula
   A. 0YBJ0ZZ
   B. 0Y6H0ZZ
   C. 0Y6J0Z1
   D. 0Y6J0Z3

   REFERENCE: AHA I-10 Coding Handbook, pp 86, 495, 496

143. Thoracoscopic pleurodesis right side
   A. 0BBN4ZZ
   B. 0BPQ40Z
   C. 0B5N4ZZ
   D. 0BCN4ZZ

   REFERENCE: AHA I-10 Coding Handbook, pp 94, 236

144. Extraction left intraocular lens without replacement, percutaneous
    A. 08DK3ZZ
    B. 08PK3JZ
    C. 08QK3ZZ
    D. 08BK3ZZ

    REFERENCE: AHA I-10 Coding Handbook, p 94

145. Routine insertion of indwelling Foley catheter
    A. 0T9B7ZZ
    B. 0T9B70Z
    C. 0T9C80Z
    D. 0T9C8ZZ

    REFERENCE: AHA I-10 Coding Handbook, p 99

146. EGD with removal FB from duodenum
    A. 0DC98ZZ
    B. 0DF98ZZ
    C. 0D898ZZ
    D. 0D798ZZ

    REFERENCE: AHA I-10 Coding Handbook, p 95

147. Facelift, open
    A. 0WQ20ZZ
    B. 0WU20KZ
    C. 0WB20ZZ
    D. 0W020ZZ

    REFERENCE: AHA I-10 Coding Handbook, p 102

148. Normal delivery with episiotomy
    A. 0W8NXZZ
    B. 0WQNXZZ
    C. 0WBNXZZ
    D. 0WMN0ZZ

    REFERENCE: AHA I-10 Coding Handbook, p 336

149. Percutaneous endoscopic clipping cerebral aneurysm
    A. 03VG4CZ
    B. 03LG0DZ
    C. 03BG0ZZ
    D. 03CG0ZZ

    REFERENCE: AHA I-10 Coding Handbook, pp 98, 436

150. Left knee arthroscopy with reposition of the anterior horn medial meniscus
    A. 0MQP4ZZ
    B. 0MQP3ZZ
    C. 0MSP0ZZ
    D. 0MSP4ZZ

    REFERENCE: AHA I-10 Coding Handbook, pp 96, 97

151. Heart transplant using porcine heart, open
    A. 02YA0Z2
    B. 02QA0ZZ
    C. 02YA0Z0
    D. 02Y0Z1

    REFERENCE: AHA I-10 Coding Handbook, p 435

152. ESWL left ureter
    A. 0TF7XZZ
    B. 0TP930Z
    C. 0TB63ZZ
    D. 0TC63ZZ

    REFERENCE: AHA I-10 Coding Handbook, p 269

153. Reattachment severed left ear
    A. 09WJXZZ
    B. 09Q1XZZ
    C. 09M1XZZ
    D. 09S1XZZ

    REFERENCE: AHA I-10 Coding Handbook, pp 96, 97

154. Transuretheral cystoscopy with removal of right ureteral calculus
    A. 0TB68ZZ
    B. 0TJ98ZZ
    C. 0T68ZZ
    D. 0TC68ZZ

    REFERENCE: AHA I-10 Coding Handbook, p 269

155. Open reduction fracture left tibia
    A. 0QSH0ZZ
    B. 0QSH04Z
    C. 0QWH04Z
    D. 0QQH0ZZ

    REFERENCE: AHA I-10 Coding Handbook, pp 96, 97, 489, 490

156. Percutaneous insertion Greenfield IVC filer
    A. 06H03DZ
    B. 06L03DZ
    C. 06Q03ZZ
    D. 06V03DZ

    REFERENCE: AHA I-10 Coding Handbook, p 99

157. Incision and drainage external perianal abscess
    A. 0D9Q30Z
    B. 0D9RX0Z
    C. 0D9QXZZ
    D. 0D9QX0Z

    REFERENCE: AHA I-10 Coding Handbook, p 95

158. Removal FB left cornea
    A. 08B8XZZ
    B. 0858XZZ
    C. 08D8XZZ
    D. 08C9XZZ

    REFERENCE: AHA I-10 Coding Handbook, p 95

159. Percutaneous transposition left radial nerve
    A. 01X40ZZ
    B. 01S63ZZ
    C. 01Q63ZZ
    D. 01860ZZ

    REFERENCE: AHA I-10 Coding Handbook, pp 96, 97

160. Right TRAM pedicle flap reconstruction status post mastectomy, muscle only open
    A. 0KXK0Z
    B. 0KXF0ZZ
    C. 0KXK0Z6
    D. 0KXK0ZZ

    REFERENCE: AHA I-10 Coding Handbook, pp 276, 277

161. Laparotomy with exploration and adhesiolysis of the left ureter
    A. 0TN74ZZ
    B. 0TN70ZZ
    C. 0TN70ZZ
    D. 0T8N0ZZ

    REFERENCE: AHA I-10 Coding Handbook, p 96

162. Thoracentesis right pleural effusion
    A. 0W930ZZ
    B. 0W9C3ZZ
    C. 0W993ZZ
    D. 0W9C30Z

    REFERENCE: AHA I-10 Coding Handbook, p 236

163. Percutaneous radiofrequency ablation of the left vocal cord
    A. 0CBV3ZZ
    B. 0CPS30Z
    C. 0C5V3ZZ
    D. 0CYV0ZZ

    REFERENCE: AHA I-10 Coding Handbook, p 94

164. Excision malignant lesion upper lip
    A. 0CC00ZZ
    B. 0CQ00ZZ
    C. 0CT00ZZ
    D. 0CB0XZZ

    REFERENCE: AHA I-10 Coding Handbook, p 289

165. Laparoscopic appendectomy
    A. 0DBJ4ZZ
    B. 0DTJ4ZZ
    C. 0DNJ4ZZ
    D. 0DT8ZZ

    REFERENCE: AHA I-10 Coding Handbook, p 93

166. Nonexcisional debridement left heel ulcer
    A. 0HDNXZZ
    B. 0HBNXZZ
    C. 0HQNXZZ
    D. 0H5LXZZ

    REFERENCE: AHA I-10 Coding Handbook, p 94

167. Transurethral cystoscopy with fragmentation of bladder neck stones
    A. 0TBC8ZZ
    B. 0TFC8ZZ
    C. 0TFC8ZZ
    D. 0TPB8ZZ

    REFERENCE: AHA I-10 Coding Handbook, pp 95, 268

168. Laparoscopy with bilateral occlusion fallopian tubes using external clips
    A. 0UH843Z
    B. 0U774DZ
    C. 0UL74CZ
    D. 0UW84DZ

    REFERENCE: AHA I-10 Coding Handbook, pp 98, 436

169. Incision scar contracture right knee
    A. 0H8KXZZ
    B. 0HBKXZZ
    C. 0HNKXZZ
    D. 0HQKXZZ

    REFERENCE: AHA I-10 Coding Handbook, p 96

170. Colonoscopy with sigmoid colon polypectomy
    A. 0DFN8ZZ
    B. 0DBN8ZZ
    C. 0DCM8ZZ
    D. 0D5N8ZZ

    REFERENCE: AHA I-10 Coding Handbook, pp 92, 93

171. A percutaneous fascia transfer to cover defect of the anterior neck
    A. 0JX53ZZ
    B. 0JX43ZZ
    C. 0JR43ZZ
    D. 0JQ43ZZ

    REFERENCE: AHA I-10 Coding Handbook, pp 96, 97

172. Percutaneous embolization left uterine artery using coils
    A. 04VF3DZ
    B. 04QF3ZZ
    C. 04LF3DU
    D. 04LF3CZ

    REFERENCE: AHA I-10 Coding Handbook, pp 98, 436

173. Endoscopic retrograde cholangiopancreatography with lithotripsy of the pancreas
    A. 0FCD8ZZ
    B. 0FJD8ZZ
    C. 0FFD8ZZ
    D. 0FJD8ZZ

    REFERENCE: AHA I-10 Coding Handbook, pp 250, 251

174. Open left neck total lymphadenectomy
    A. 07T20ZZ
    B. 07B20ZZ
    C. 07520ZZ
    D. 07C20ZZ

    REFERENCE: AHA I-10 Coding Handbook, p 93

175. Percutaneous chest tube placement left pneumothorax
    A. 0W9B30Z
    B. 0W9D30Z
    C. 0W9B3ZZ
    D. 0W9D3ZZ

    REFERENCE: AHA I-10 Coding Handbook, p 95

176. Laparoscopy with excision old sutures from the peritoneum
    A. 0DBW4ZZ
    B. 0DNW4ZZ
    C. 0DCW4ZZ
    D. 0DPW4ZZ

    REFERENCE: AHA I-10 Coding Handbook, p 95

177. Closed reduction with percutaneous internal fixation left femoral neck fracture
    A. 0QSC34Z
    B. 0QS734Z
    C. 0QS934Z
    D. 0QS7X4Z

    REFERENCE: AHA I-10 Coding Handbook, pp 96, 97

178. Laparotomy and drain placement left lobe liver abscess
    A. 0F900ZZ
    B. 0F900ZZ
    C. 0F9030Z
    D. 0F9200Z

    REFERENCE: AHA I-10 Coding Handbook, p 95

179. Hysteroscopy with D&C, diagnostic
    A. 0UDB82X
    B. 0UDN82X
    C. 0U898ZZ
    D. 0U798ZZ

    REFERENCE: AHA I-10 Coding Handbook, p 94

180. Laparoscopy with destruction of endometriosis left ovary
    A. 0UB14ZZ
    B. 0UT14ZZ
    C. 0UP340Z
    D. 0U514ZZ

    REFERENCE: AHA I-10 Coding Handbook, p 94

181. DIP joint amputation left thumb
    A. 0X6M0Z3
    B. 0XGM022
    C. 0XGM021
    D. 0XGM020

    REFERENCE: AHA I-10 Coding Handbook, pp 86, 495

182. Removal right index fingernail
    A. 0HDQXZZ
    B. 0HPRXZZ
    C. 0HNQXZZ
    D. 0HTQXZZ

    REFERENCE: AHA I-10 Coding Handbook, p 94

183. Percutaneous drainage abdominal ascites
    A. 0W9G3ZZ
    B. 0W9G3ZZ
    C. 0W930Z
    D. 0W9H3ZZ

    REFERENCE: AHA I-10 Coding Handbook, p 95

184. Transurethral endoscopic ablation right hepatic duct
    A. 0F558ZZ
    B. 0FB58ZZ
    C. 0FT04ZZ
    D. 0FP040Z

    REFERENCE: AHA I-10 Coding Handbook, p 94

185. ERCP with balloon dilation cystic duct
    A. 0F784DZ
    B. 0F788ZZ
    C. 0F783DZ
    D. 0FT83ZZ

    REFERENCE: AHA I-10 Coding Handbook, p 98

186. Control of postoperative tonsillectomy is coded to which root operation?
  A. Revision
  B. Repair
  C. Control
  D. Change

  REFERENCE: AHA I-10 Coding Handbook, p 102

187. In the Medical Surgical Section, the third character position represents?
  A. Body System
  B. Approach
  C. Root Operation
  D. Qualifier

  REFERENCE: AHA I-10 Coding Handbook, p 72

188. In the Medical Surgical Section, the second character position represents?
  A. Body System
  B. Body Part
  C. Qualifier
  D. Approach

  REFERENCE: AHA I-10 Coding Handbook, p 70

189. In the Medical Surgical Section, the seventh character position represents?
  A. Qualifier
  B. Device
  C. Body System
  D. Approach

  REFERENCE: AHA I-10 Coding Handbook, p 80

190 In the Medical Surgical Section, the fourth character position represents?
  A. Section
  B. Body Part
  C. Body System
  D. Approach

  REFERENCE: AHA I-10 Coding Handbook, p 73

191. A complete redo of a knee replacement requiring a new prosthesis is coded to which root operation?
  A. Revision
  B. Replacement
  C. Change
  D. Insertion

  REFERENCE: AHA I-10 Coding Handbook, pp 99–100, 301

192. Reposition of a malfunctioning pacemaker lead is coded to which root operation?
  A. Change
  B. Revision
  C. Replacement
  D. Reposition

  REFERENCE: AHA I-10 Coding Handbook, pp 99–100, 416

193. Dilation of the ureter with insertion of a stent is coded to which root operation?
  A. Insertion
  B. Dilation
  C. Supplemental
  D. Inspection

  REFERENCE: AHA I-10 Coding Handbook, p 98

194. ERCP with biopsy of the common bile duct. Identify the approach.
  A. External
  B. Percutaneous Endoscopic Open
  C. Percutaneous
  D. Open

  REFERENCE: AHA I-10 Coding Handbook, p 75

195. Percutaneous insertion nephrostomy tube. Identify the approach.
    A. External
    B. Open
    C. Percutaneous
    D. Percutaneous Endoscopic

    REFERENCE: AHA I-10 Coding Handbook, p 75

196. Fulguration of anal warts. Identify the approach.
    A. Percutaneous
    B. External Endoscopic
    C. Percutaneous
    D. Open

    REFERENCE: AHA I-10 Coding Handbook, p 75

197. Percutaneous placement of pacemaker lead. Identify the approach.
    A. External
    B. Via natural or Artificial opening
    C. Percutaneous Endoscopic
    D. Percutaneous

    REFERENCE: AHA I-10 Coding Handbook, p 75

198. ESWL left ureter. Identify the approach.
    A. Percutaneous
    B. Via natural or Artificial opening
    C. External
    D. Open

    REFERENCE: AHA I-10 Coding Handbook, p 75

199. Laparoscopy with destruction of endometriosis. Identify the approach.
    A. Percutaneous
    B. Via natural/artificial opening
    C. Percutaneous Endoscopic
    D. External

    REFERENCE: AHA I-10 Coding Handbook, p 75

200. Colonoscopy. Identify the approach.
    A. Percutaneous
    B. Via natural or Artificial opening
    C. Percutaneous Endoscopic
    D. External

    REFERENCE: AHA I-10 Coding Handbook, p 75

Use this information to answer questions, pp 201–203.
Present on admission (POA) guidelines were established to identify and report diagnoses that are present at the time of a patient's admission. The reporting options for each ICD-9-CM code are

A. Y = Yes
B. N = No
C. U = Unknown
D. W = clinically undetermined
E. Unreported/Not Used (Exempt from POA) reporting

201. The physician explicitly documents that a condition is not present at the time of admission.

A. Y = Yes
B. N = No
C. U = Unknown
D. W = clinically undetermined
E. Unreported/Not Used (Exempt from POA) reporting

REFERENCE: AHA I-10 Coding Handbook, pp 571–574

202. The physician documents that the patient has diabetes that was diagnosed prior to admission.

A. Y = Yes
B. N = No
C. U = Unknown
D. W = clinically undetermined
E. Unreported/Not Used (Exempt from POA) reporting

REFERENCE: AHA I-10 Coding Handbook, pp 571–574

203. The medical record documentation is unclear as to whether the condition was present on admission.

A. Y = Yes
B. N = No
C. U = Unknown
D. W = clinically undetermined
E. Unreported/Not Used (Exempt from POA) reporting

REFERENCE: AHA I-10 Coding Handbook, pp 571–574

Answer Key for ICD-10-CM Coding

1.	D	52.	A	103.	C	155.	A
2.	B	53.	C	104.	B	156.	A
3.	A	54.	B	105.	A	157.	C
4.	C	55.	A	106.	C	158.	D
5.	D	56.	C	107.	D	159.	B
6.	C	57.	D	108.	C	160.	A
7.	D	58.	A	109.	D	161.	B
8.	C	59.	C	110.	A	162.	C
9.	A	60.	A	111.	A	163.	C
10.	B	61.	A	112.	B	164.	D
11.	C	62.	C	113.	D	165	B
12.	B	63.	B	114.	C	166.	A
13.	A	64.	D	115.	B	167.	C
14.	D	65.	B	116.	A	168.	C
15.	B	66.	D	117.	A	169.	C
16.	A	67.	B	118.	D	170.	B
17.	C	68.	D	119.	D	171.	B
18.	B	69.	A	120.	D	172.	C
19.	D	70.	B	121.	A	173.	C
20.	B	71.	A	122.	B	174.	A
21.	A	72.	C	123.	D	175.	A
22.	D	73.	B	125.	D	176.	C
23.	B	74.	D	126.	A	177.	A
24.	D	75.	C	127.	A	178.	D
25.	D	76.	D	128.	C	179.	A
26.	B	77.	C	129.	A	180.	D
27.	A	78.	B	130.	C	181.	A
28.	C	79.	C	131.	B	182.	A
29.	B	80.	D	132.	C	183.	A
30.	D	81.	B	133.	D	184.	A
31.	C	82.	C	134.	A	185.	B
32.	B	83.	A	135.	B	186.	C
33.	A	84.	B	136.	C	187.	C
34.	C	85.	D	137.	A	188.	A
35.	B	86.	A	138.	C	189.	A
36.	D	87.	A	139.	A	190.	B
37.	D	88.	D	140.	C	191.	A
38.	C	89.	C	141.	A	192.	B
39.	D	90.	A	142.	C	193.	B
40.	A	91.	C	143.	A	194.	B
41.	B	92.	B	144.	A	195.	C
42.	A	93.	A	145.	B	196.	B
43.	D	94.	C	146.	A	197.	D
44.	A	95.	D	147.	D	198.	C
45.	B	96.	C	148.	A	199.	C
46.	A	97.	B	149.	A	200.	B
47.	C	98.	A	150.	D	201.	B
48.	B	99.	D	151.	A	202.	A
49.	A	100.	C	152.	A	203.	C
50.	D	101.	A	153.	C		
51.	C	102.	D	154.	D		

REFERENCES

AHA ICD-10-CM and ICD-10-PCS Coding Handbook 2014

ICD-10-CM/PCS Chapter Competencies

Question	RHIA Domain	RHIT Domain
1–203	1	2

IX. CPT Coding

Lisa M. Delhomme, MHA, RHIA

Evaluation and Management

1. Patient is admitted to the hospital with acute abdominal pain. The attending medical physician requests a surgical consult. The consultant agrees to see the patient and conducts a comprehensive history and physical examination. The physician ordered lab work to rule out pancreatitis, along with an ultrasound of the gallbladder and abdominal x-ray. Due to the various diagnosis possibilities and the tests reviewed, a moderate medical decision was made.
   A. 99244
   B. 99222
   C. 99254
   D. 99204

   REFERENCE: AMA (7th ed.), pp 49, 54–55
   Green, pp 435–438
   Johnson and Linker, pp 153–154
   Smith, pp 213, 215–216

2. An established patient returns to the physician's office for follow-up on his hypertension and diabetes. The physician takes the blood pressure and references the patient's last three glucose tests. The patient is still running above normal glucose levels, so the physician decides to adjust the patient's insulin. An expanded history was taken and a physical examination was performed.
   A. 99213
   B. 99232
   C. 99202
   D. 99214

   REFERENCE: AMA (7th ed.), p 48
   Green, pp 428–429
   Johnson and Linker, p 149
   Smith, p 214

3. Patient arrives in the emergency room via a medical helicopter. The patient has sustained multiple life-threatening injuries due to a multiple car accident. The patient goes into cardiac arrest 10 minutes after arrival. An hour and 30 minutes of critical care time is spent trying to stabilize the patient.
   A. 99285; 99288; 99291
   B. 99291; 99292
   C. 99291; 99292; 99285
   D. 99282

   REFERENCE: AMA (7th ed.), pp 57–58
   Green, pp 439–441
   Johnson and Linker, pp 155–157
   Smith, pp 216–217

4. The physician provided services to a new patient who was in a rest home for an ulcerative sore on the hip. A problem-focused history and physical examination were performed and a straightforward medical decision was made.
   A. 99304
   B. 99325
   C. 99324
   D. 99334

   REFERENCE: AMA (7th ed.), p 55
   Green, pp 443–444
   Johnson and Linker, pp 158–159
   Smith, p 218

5. A doctor provides critical care services in the emergency department for a patient in respiratory failure. He initiates ventilator management and spends an hour and 10 minutes providing critical care for this patient.
    A. 99281, 99291, 99292, 94002
    B. 99291, 99292, 94002
    C. 99291, 94002
    D. 99291

REFERENCE: AMA (7th ed.), pp 57–58
               Green, pp 439–441
               Johnson and Linker, pp 155–157
               Smith, pp 216–217

6. Services were provided to a patient in the emergency room after the patient twisted her ankle stepping down from a curb. The emergency room physician ordered x-rays of the ankle, which came back negative for a fracture. A problem-focused history and physical examination were performed and ankle strapping was applied. A prescription for pain was given to the patient. Code the emergency room visit only.
    A. 99201   C. 99281
    B. 99282   D. 99211

REFERENCE: AMA (7th ed.), pp 47–48
               Green, pp 438–439
               Johnson and Linker, pp 155–157
               Smith, p 216

7. An established patient was seen in her primary physician's office. The patient fell at home and came to the physician's office for an examination. Due to a possible concussion, the patient was sent to the hospital to be admitted as an observation patient. A detailed history and physical examination were performed and the medical decision was low complexity. The patient stayed overnight and was discharged the next afternoon.
    A. 99214; 99234   C. 99218
    B. 99214; 99218; 99217   D. 99218; 99217

REFERENCE: AMA, 2014
               AMA (7th ed.), pp 48–49
               Green, pp 431–435
               Johnson and Linker, p 155
               Smith, pp 214–215

8. An out-of-town patient presents to a walk-in clinic to have a prescription refilled for a nonsteroidal anti-inflammatory drug. The physician performs a problem-focused history and physical examination with a straightforward decision.
   A. 99211
   B. 99201
   C. 99212
   D. 99202

   REFERENCE: AMA (7th ed.), pp 39, 48
   Frisch, pp 49–51
   Green, pp 411–412
   Johnson and Linker, p 149
   Smith, pp 195–196

9. An office consultation is performed for a postmenopausal woman who is complaining of spotting in the past 6 months with right lower quadrant tenderness. A detailed history and physical examination were performed with a low-complexity medical decision.
   A. 99242
   B. 99243
   C. 99253
   D. 99254

   REFERENCE: AMA (7th ed.), pp 39–40
   Green, pp 435–438
   Johnson and Linker, pp 153–154
   Smith, pp 215–216

Anesthesia

10. Code anesthesia for upper abdominal ventral hernia repair.
    A. 00832
    B. 00750
    C. 00752
    D. 00830

    REFERENCE: AMA (7th ed.), pp 82–83
    Green, pp 483–485
    Johnson and Linker, p 175
    Smith, pp 249–252

11. Code anesthesia for total hip replacement.
    A. 01210
    B. 01402
    C. 01230
    D. 01214

    REFERENCE: AMA (7th ed.), pp 82–83
    Green, p 487
    Smith, pp 249–252

12. Code anesthesia for vaginal hysterectomy.
    A. 00846
    B. 00944
    C. 00840
    D. 01963

    REFERENCE: AMA (7th ed.), pp 82–83
    Green, pp 484–485
    Smith, pp 249–252

13. Code anesthesia for placement of vascular shunt in forearm.
   A. 01844   C. 00532
   B. 01850   D. 01840

REFERENCE: AMA (7th ed.), pp 82–83
               Green, p 487
               Smith, pp 249–252

14. Code anesthesia for decortication of left lung.
   A. 01638   C. 00546
   B. 00542   D. 00500

REFERENCE: AMA (7th ed.), pp 82–83
               Green, p 483
               Smith, pp 249–252

15. Code anesthesia for total shoulder replacement.
   A. 01760   C. 01402
   B. 01630   D. 01638

REFERENCE: AMA (7th ed.), pp 82–83
               Green, p 487
               Smith, pp 249–252

16. Code anesthesia for cesarean section.
   A. 00840   C. 00940
   B. 01961   D. 01960

REFERENCE: AMA (7th ed.), pp 82–83
               Green, p 489
               Smith, pp 249–252

17. Code anesthesia for procedures on bony pelvis.
   A. 00400   C. 01120
   B. 01170   D. 01190

REFERENCE: AMA (7th ed.), pp 82–83
               Green, p 487
               Smith, pp 249–252

18. Code anesthesia for corneal transplant.
   A. 00144   C. 00147
   B. 00140   D. 00190

REFERENCE: AMA (7th ed.), pp 82–83
               Green, p 481
               Smith, pp 249–252

Surgery—Integumentary System

19. Patient presents to the hospital for skin grafts due to previous third-degree burns. The burn eschar of the back was removed. Once the eschar was removed, the defect size measured 10 cm x 10 cm. A skin graft from a donor bank was placed onto the defect and sewn into place as a temporary wound closure.

 A. 15002, 15130
 B. 15002, 15271, 15272, 15272, 15272
 C. 15002, 15200
 D. 15002, 15273

REFERENCE: AMA, 2014

20. Patient presents to the operating room for excision of a 4.5 cm malignant melanoma of the left forearm. A 6 cm x 6 cm rotation flap was created for closure.

 A. 14021
 B. 11606; 14020
 C. 14301
 D. 11606; 15100

REFERENCE: AMA, 2014
              AMA (7th ed.), pp 103–104, 107
              Green, pp 517–521
              Smith, pp 72–73
              Smith (2), pp 26–27

21. Female patient has a percutaneous needle biopsy of the left breast lesion in the lower outer quadrant. Following the biopsy frozen section results, the physician followed this with an excisional removal of the same lesion.

 A. 19100; 19125
 B. 19100; 19120-LT
 C. 19120-LT
 D. 19100; 19120; 19120

REFERENCE: AMA (7th ed.), p 115
              Green, pp 535–536
              Smith, p 79
              Smith (2), p 30

22. Patient presents to the emergency room with lacerations of right lower leg that involved the fascia. Lacerations measured 5 cm and 2.7 cm.

 A. 11406; 11403
 B. 12034
 C. 12032; 12031
 D. 12032

REFERENCE: AMA (7th ed.), p 107
              Smith, pp 66–68
              Smith (2), p 21

23. Ten-square-centimeters epidermal autograft to the face from the back.

 A. 15110
 B. 15115
 C. 15110, 15115
 D. 15120

REFERENCE: AMA, 2014
              AMA (7th ed.), pp 109–110
              Smith (2), p 27

24. Nonhuman graft for temporary wound closure. Patient has a 5 cm defect on the scalp.
    A. 15275, 15276
    B. 15271
    C. 15275
    D. 15271, 15272

REFERENCE: AMA, 2014

25. Patient is admitted for a blepharoplasty of the left lower eyelid and a repair for a tarsal strip of the left upper lid.
    A. 67917-E1; 15822-E2
    B. 67917-E1; 15820-E2
    C. 67917-E1
    D. 67917-E1; 15823-E2

REFERENCE: AMA (7th ed.), pp 252–253
              CPT Assistant, January 2005, p 46
              Smith (2), p 165

26. Patient presents to the emergency room with lacerations sustained in an automobile accident. Repairs of the 3.3 cm skin laceration of the left leg that involved the fascia, 2.5 cm and 3 cm lacerations of the left arm involving the fascia, and 2.7 cm of the left foot, which required simple sutures, were performed. Sterile dressings were applied.
    A. 12032; 12032-59; 12031-59; 12002-59
    B. 12002, 12002-59
    C. 12034, 12002-59
    D. 13151; 12032-59, 12032-59, 12001-59

REFERENCE: AMA (7th ed.), pp 106–108
              Green, pp 524–526
              Smith, pp 66–68
              Smith (2), p 24

27. Patient presents to the operating room for excision of three lesions. The 1.5 cm and 2 cm lesions of the back were excised with one excision. The 0.5 cm lesion of the hand was excised. The pathology report identified both back lesions as squamous cell carcinoma. The hand lesion was identified as seborrheic keratosis.
    A. 11604; 11420
    B. 11402; 11420; 11403
    C. 11403; 11642; 11642
    D. 11602; 11402

REFERENCE: AMA (7th ed.), pp 101–104
              CPT Assistant, November 2002, pp 5–6, 8
              Green, pp 517–521
              Smith, pp 61–62
              Smith (2), pp 21–22

28. Patient presents to the radiology department where a fine-needle aspiration of the breast is performed utilizing computed tomography.
    A. 19085; 77012
    B. 19100
    C. 19125
    D. 10022, 77012

REFERENCE: AMA (7th ed.), pp 270, 330–331
              CPT Assistant, November 2002, pp 2–3
              Green, p 535
              Smith (2), p 29

29. Patient presents to the operating room where a 3.2 cm malignant lesion of the shoulder was excised and repaired with simple sutures. A 2 cm benign lesion of the cheek was excised and was repaired with a rotation skin graft.
    A. 11604, 11442; 14040; 12001
    B. 14040, 11604
    C. 15002, 15120
    D. 17264, 17000; 12001

REFERENCE: AMA (7th ed.), pp 101–107
            CPT Assistant, July 1999, pp 3–4
            CPT Assistant, August 2002, p 5
            CPT Assistant, November 2002, pp 5–8
            Green, pp 517–520, 526–527
            Smith, pp 61–62, 73–75
            Smith (2), pp 26–27

30. Patient was admitted to the hospital for removal of excessive tissue due to massive weight loss. Liposuction of the abdomen and bilateral thighs was performed.
    A. 15830
    B. 15830; 15833; 15833
    C. 15877; 15879-50
    D. 15839

REFERENCE: AMA, 2014

Surgery—Musculoskeletal

31. Patient presents to the hospital with ulcer of the right foot. Patient is taken to the operating room where a revision of the right metatarsal head is performed.
    A. 28104-RT
    B. 28111-RT
    C. 28288-RT
    D. 28899-RT

REFERENCE: AMA, 2014

32. Patient presents to the emergency room following a fall. X-rays were ordered for the lower leg and results showed a fracture of the proximal left tibia. The emergency room physician performed a closed manipulation of the fracture with skeletal traction.
    A. 27532-LT
    B. 27536-LT
    C. 27530-LT
    D. 27524-LT

REFERENCE: Green, pp 565–568
            Smith, pp 84–85
            Smith (2), pp 42–44

33. Trauma patient was rushed to the operating room with multiple injuries. Open reduction with internal fixation of intertrochanteric femoral fracture; open reduction of the tibial and fibula shaft with internal fixation was performed.
    A. 27245; 27759
    B. 20690
    C. 27248; 27756
    D. 27244; 27758

REFERENCE: Green, pp 565–568
            Smith, pp 84–85
            Smith (2), pp 42–44

34. Open I&D of a deep abscess of the cervical spine.
    A. 22010
    B. 22015
    C. 10060
    D. 10140

REFERENCE: AMA, 2014

35. Patient presents to the emergency room following an assault. Examination of the patient reveals blunt trauma to the face. Radiology reports that the patient suffers from a fracture to the frontal skull and a blow-out fracture of the orbital floor. Patient is admitted and taken to the operating room where a periorbital approach to the orbital fracture is employed and an implant is inserted.

   A. 21407; 21275
   B. 21387; 61330
   C. 21390
   D. 61340; 21401

REFERENCE: Smith, pp 84–85
              Smith (2), pp 42–44

36. Patient presents with a traumatic partial amputation of the second, third, and fourth fingers on the right hand. Patient was taken to the operating room where completion of the amputation of three fingers was performed with direct closure.

   A. 26910-F6; 26910-F7; 26910-F8
   B. 26843-RT
   C. 26951-F6; 26951-F7; 26951-F8
   D. 26550-RT

REFERENCE: AMA, 2014

37. Patient is brought to the emergency room following a shark attack. The paramedics have the patient's amputated foot. The patient is taken directly to the operating room to reattach the patient's foot.

   A. 28800
   B. 28200; 28208
   C. 28110
   D. 20838

REFERENCE: AMA, 2014

38. Patient presents to the hospital with a right index trigger finger. Release of the trigger finger was performed.

   A. 26060-F7
   B. 26055-F6
   C. 26170-F6
   D. 26110

REFERENCE: AMA, 2014

39. Patient had been diagnosed with a bunion. Patient was taken to the operating room where a simple resection of the base of the proximal phalanx along with the medial eminence was performed. Kirschner wire was placed to hold the joint in place.

   A. 28292
   B. 28290
   C. 28293
   D. 28294

REFERENCE: AMA, 2014
              AMA (7th ed.), pp 93–94, 132–135
              CPT Assistant, December 1995, pp 5–7
              Smith (2), pp 47–49

Surgery—Respiratory

40. Patient has a bronchoscopy with endobronchial biopsies of three sites.

   A. 31625; 31625; 31625
   B. 31625
   C. 31622; 31625
   D. 31622; 31625; 31625; 31625

REFERENCE: AMA (7th ed.), pp 139–141
              CPT Assistant, June 2004, p 11
              Green, pp 576–577
              Smith, pp 99–100
              Smith (2), p 61

41. Patient presents to the surgical unit and undergoes unilateral nasal endoscopy, partial ethmoidectomy, and maxillary antrostomy.
    A. 31254; 31256-51   C. 31290; 31267-51
    B. 31201; 31225-51   D. 31233; 31231-51

REFERENCE: AMA (7th ed.), pp 137–138
              CPT Assistant, January 1997, pp 4–6
              Green, pp 573–574
              Smith, p 93
              Smith (2), p 59

42. Patient has been diagnosed with metastatic laryngeal carcinoma. Patient underwent subtotal supraglottic laryngectomy with radical neck dissection.
    A. 31540   C. 31365
    B. 31367   D. 31368

REFERENCE: Green, pp 574–575

43. Patient was involved in an accident and has been sent to the hospital. During transport the patient develops breathing problems and, upon arrival at the hospital, an emergency transtracheal tracheostomy was performed. Following various x-rays, the patient was diagnosed with traumatic pneumothorax and a thoracentesis with insertion of tube was performed.
    A. 31603; 31612   C. 31603; 32555
    B. 31610; 32555   D. 31603; 32555

REFERENCE: AMA, 2014

44. Patient with laryngeal cancer has a tracheoesophageal fistula created and has a voicebox inserted.
    A. 31611   C. 31395
    B. 31580   D. 31502

REFERENCE: AMA, 2014

45. Upper lobectomy of the right lung with repair of the bronchus.
    A. 32480   C. 32320
    B. 32486   D. 32480, 32501

REFERENCE: AMA (7th ed.), pp 140–141
              Green, pp 578–579
              Smith (2), pp 61–62

46. Patient with a deviated nasal septum that was repaired by septoplasty.
    A. 30400   C. 30520
    B. 30620   D. 30630

REFERENCE: AMA, 2014

47. Lye burn of the larynx repaired by laryngoplasty.
    A. 31588   C. 31360
    B. 16020   D. 31540

REFERENCE: AMA, 2014

48. Bronchoscopy with multiple transbronchial right upper and right lower lobe lung biopsy with fluoroscopic guidance.
    A. 31628-RT; 76000-RT
    B. 31717-RT; 31632-RT
    C. 32405-RT
    D. 31628-RT; 31632-RT

REFERENCE: AMA (7th ed.), pp 139–140
               CPT Assistant, March 1999, p 3
               Green, pp 576–577
               Smith, pp 99–100
               Smith (2), p 61

49. Patient has recurrent spontaneous pneumothorax which has resulted in a chemical pleurodesis by thoracoscopy.
    A. 32650
    B. 32310; 32601
    C. 32601
    D. 32960

REFERENCE: AMA, 2014

50. Laryngoscopic stripping of vocal cords for leukoplakia of the vocal cords.
    A. 31535
    B. 31540
    C. 31541
    D. 31570

REFERENCE: AMA (7th ed.), pp 137–138
               Green, pp 574–575
               Smith, p 97

Surgery—Cardiovascular System

51. Patient returns to the operating room following open-heart bypass for exploration of blood vessel to control postoperative bleeding in the chest.
    A. 35820
    B. 20101
    C. 35761
    D. 35905

REFERENCE: AMA, 2014

52. Patient undergoes construction of apical aortic conduit with an insertion of a single-ventricle ventricular assist device.
    A. 33400
    B. 33975
    C. 33977
    D. 33975; 33404

REFERENCE: CPT Assistant, January 2004, p 28

53. Patient presents to the operating room where a CABG x 3 is performed using the mammary artery and two sections of the saphenous vein.
    A. 33534; 33511
    B. 33534; 33518; 33511
    C. 33535
    D. 33533; 33518

REFERENCE: AMA (7th ed.), pp 155–158
               Green, pp 599–600
               Smith, p 108
               Smith (2), pp 74–75

54. Patient complains of recurrent syncope following carotid thromboendarterectomy. Patient returns 2 weeks after initial surgery and undergoes repeat carotid thromboendarterectomy.
    A. 33510
    B. 35301
    C. 35201
    D. 35301; 35390

REFERENCE: CPT Assistant, Winter 1993, p 3
              Smith (2), pp 78–79

55. Patient is admitted with alcohol cirrhosis and has a TIPS procedure performed.
    A. 35476; 36011; 36481
    B. 37183
    C. 37182
    D. 37140

REFERENCE: CPT Assistant, December 2003, pp 1–3

56. Eighty-year-old patient has carcinoma and presents to the operating room for placement of a tunneled implantable centrally inserted venous access port.
    A. 36558
    B. 36571
    C. 36561
    D. 36481

REFERENCE: CPT Assistant, February 1999, pp 1–5
              CPT Assistant, November 1999, pp 19–20
              Green, pp 615–618
              Smith, pp 111–112
              Smith (2), pp 79–80

57. Patient presents to the operating room and undergoes an endovascular repair of an infrarenal abdominal aortic aneurysm utilizing a unibody bifurcated prosthesis.
    A. 34800; 34813
    B. 34802
    C. 34804
    D. 35081

REFERENCE: AMA (7th ed.), pp 159–161
              CPT Assistant, September 2002, p 4
              CPT Assistant, February 2003, pp 2–4, 16
              Green, p 620
              Smith (2), pp 76–77

58. The physician punctures the left common femoral to examine the right common iliac.
    A. 36245
    B. 36246
    C. 36247
    D. 36140

REFERENCE: AMA, 2014
              AMA (7th ed.), pp 283–285

59. Patient has a history of PVD for many years and experiences chest pains. The patient underwent Doppler evaluation, which showed a common femoral DVT. Patient is now admitted for thromboendarterectomy.
    A. 35371
    B. 35372
    C. 37224
    D. 35256

REFERENCE: AMA, 2014
              Smith (2), pp 78–79

60. Patient undergoes percutaneous transluminal iliac artery balloon angioplasty.
    A. 37228
    B. 37220
    C. 37222
    D. 37224

REFERENCE: AMA, 2014
              Smith, p 114

Surgery—Hemic and Lymphatic Systems, Mediastinum, and Diaphragm

61. Patient has breast carcinoma and is now undergoing sentinel node biopsy. Patient was injected for sentinel node identification and two deep axillary lymph nodes showed up intensely. These two lymph nodes were completely excised. Path report was positive for metastatic carcinoma.
    A. 38525; 38790
    B. 38589
    C. 38308; 38790
    D. 38525; 38792

REFERENCE: CPT Assistant, November 1998, pp 15–16
              CPT Assistant, July 1999, pp 6–12
              Green, p 624

62. Patient has a history of hiatal hernia for many years, which has progressively gotten worse. The decision to repair the hernia was made and the patient was sent to the operating room where the repair took place via the thorax and abdomen.
    A. 39545
    B. 43336
    C. 43332
    D. 39503

REFERENCE: AMA, 2014

63. Patient has a bone marrow aspiration of the iliac crest and of the tibia.
    A. 38220, 38220-59
    B. 38221
    C. 38230
    D. 38220

REFERENCE: AMA (7th ed.), pp 323–324
              CPT Assistant, January 2004, p 26
              Green, pp 623–624

64. Trauma patient is rushed to the operating room with multiple injuries. The patient had his spleen removed due to massive rupture with repair of lacerated diaphragm.
    A. 38115; 39501
    B. 38120; 39599
    C. 38102; 39540
    D. 38100; 39501

REFERENCE: AMA, 2014

65. Laparoscopic retroperitoneal lymph node biopsy.
    A. 38570
    B. 38780
    C. 49323
    D. 38589

REFERENCE: AMA, 2014

66. Excision of mediastinal cyst.
    A. 11400
    B. 39200
    C. 17000
    D. 39400

REFERENCE: AMA, 2014

67. Patient diagnosed with cystic hygroma of the axilla, which was excised.
    A. 38555   C. 38550
    B. 11400   D. 38300

REFERENCE: AMA, 2014

68. Laparoscopy with multiple biopsies of retroperitoneal lymph nodes.
    A. 38570   C. 38570-22
    B. 38571   D. 38572

REFERENCE: AMA, 2014

69. Cannulation of the thoracic duct.
    A. 38794   C. 36260
    B. 36810   D. 38999

REFERENCE: AMA, 2014

70. Patient has been on the bone marrow transplant recipient list for 3 months. A perfect match was made and the patient came in and received peripheral stem cell transplant.
    A. 38242   C. 38241
    B. 38230   D. 38240

REFERENCE: Green, pp 623–624

Surgery—Digestive System

71. Laparoscopic gastric banding.
    A. 43842   C. 43770
    B. 43843   D. 43771

REFERENCE: AMA, 2014

72. Patient presents with a history of upper abdominal pain. Cholangiogram was negative and patient was sent to the hospital for ERCP. During the procedure the sphincter was incised and a stent was placed for drainage.
    A. 43260; 43262; 43264   C. 43275
    B. 43262   D. 43274

REFERENCE: CPT Assistant, Spring 1994, pp 5–7
              Smith (2), pp 92–93

73. Patient presents to the emergency room with right lower abdominal pains. Emergency room physician suspects possible appendicitis. Patient was taken to the operating room where a laparoscopic appendectomy was performed. Pathology report was negative for appendicitis.
    A. 44950   C. 44970
    B. 44950; 49320   D. 44979

REFERENCE: AMA, 2014
              AMA (7th ed.), p 176
              Smith (2), p 97

74. Morbidly obese patient comes in for vertical banding of the stomach.
    A. 43848   C. 43842
    B. 43659   D. 43999

REFERENCE: CPT Assistant, May 1998, pp 5–6

75. Patient underwent anoscopy followed by colonoscopy. The physician examined the colon to 60 cm.
    A. 46600; 45378
    B. 46600; 45378-59
    C. 45378
    D. 45999

REFERENCE: Green, pp 650–652
             Smith, pp 120–121
             Smith (2), p 93

76. Injection snoreplasty for treatment of palatal snoring.
    A. 42299
    B. 42145
    C. 42999
    D. 40899

REFERENCE: CPT Assistant, December 2004, p 19

77. Patient arrives to the hospital and has a Nissen fundoplasty done laparoscopically.
    A. 43410
    B. 43415
    C. 43502
    D. 43280

REFERENCE: AMA, 2014
             Smith (2), p 97

78. Young child presents with cleft lip and cleft palate. This is the first attempt of repair, which includes major revision of the cleft palate and unilateral cleft lip repair.
    A. 42200; 40701
    B. 42225; 40700
    C. 42220; 40720
    D. 42215; 40700

REFERENCE: AMA, 2014

79. Patient has a history of chronic alcohol abuse with portal hypertension. Patient has been vomiting blood for the past 3 days and presented to his physician's office. Patient was sent to the hospital for evaluation and an EGD was performed. Biopsy findings showed gastritis, esophagitis, and bleeding esophageal varices, which were injected with sclerosing solution.
    A. 43235; 43244; 43204
    B. 43239; 43244
    C. 43239; 43243
    D. 43239; 43243; 43204

REFERENCE: AMA (7th ed.), pp 179–180
             Green, pp 641–645
             Smith, p 118
             Smith (2), p 92

Surgery—Urinary System

80. Patient is admitted for contact laser vaporization of the prostate. The physician performed a TURP and transurethral resection of the bladder neck at the same time.
    A. 52648
    B. 52648; 52450; 52500
    C. 52450; 53500
    D. 52648; 52450

REFERENCE: AMA (7th ed.), pp 197–198
             CPT Assistant, July 2005, p 15
             Smith (2), p 122

81. Patient comes to the hospital with a history of right flank pain. Urine tests are negative. Radiology examination reveals that the patient has renal cysts. Patient is now admitted for laparoscopic ablation of the cysts.

A. 50541   C. 50280

B. 50390   D. 50920

REFERENCE: AMA (7th ed.), p 192

           CPT Assistant, November 1999, p 25

           CPT Assistant, May 2000, p 4

           CPT Assistant, October 2001, p 8

           CPT Assistant, January 2003, p 19

82. Patient has extensive bladder cancer. She underwent a complete cystectomy with bilateral pelvic lymphadenectomy and creation of ureteroileal conduit.

A. 51575; 50820   C. 51595

B. 50825; 51570; 38770   D. 51550; 38770

REFERENCE: AMA, 2014

83. Patient presents to the hospital with right ureteral calculus. Patient is taken to the operating room where a cystoscopy with ureteroscopy is performed to remove the calculus.

A. 52353   C. 51065

B. 52310   D. 52352

REFERENCE: Green, pp 664–665

           Smith, p 134

           Smith (2), pp 111–112

84. Female with 6 months of stress incontinence. Outpatient therapies are not working and the patient decides to have the problem fixed. Laparoscopic urethral suspension was completed.

A. 51992   C. 51840

B. 51990   D. 51845

REFERENCE: CPT Assistant, November 1999, p 26

           CPT Assistant, May 2000, p 4

           CPT Changes: An Insider's View, 2000

85. Patient has ovarian vein syndrome and has ureterolysis performed.

A. 58679   C. 52351

B. 58660   D. 50722

REFERENCE: AMA, 2014

86. Male patient has been diagnosed with benign prostatic hypertrophy and undergoes a transurethral destruction of the prostate by radiofrequency thermotherapy.

A. 52648   C. 52601

B. 53852   D. 53850

REFERENCE: AMA (7th ed.), pp 197–198

           CPT Assistant, November 1997, p 20

           CPT Assistant, April 2001, p 4

87. Nephrectomy with resection of half of the ureter.
    A. 50220   C. 50230; 50650
    B. 50234   D. 50546

REFERENCE: AMA (7th ed.), p 192
              Green, pp 659–660

88. Male with urinary incontinence. Sling procedure was performed 6 months ago and now the patient has returned for a revision of the sling procedure.
    A. 53449   C. 53440
    B. 53442   D. 53431

REFERENCE: AMA, 2014

89. Excision of 2.5 cm bladder tumor with cystoscopy.
    A. 51550   C. 52235
    B. 51530   D. 51060

REFERENCE: AMA (7th ed.), pp 194–195
              Green, pp 644–645
              Smith, p 131

90. Closure of ureterocutaneous fistula.
    A. 50930   C. 57310
    B. 50920   D. 50520

REFERENCE: AMA, 2014

Surgery—Male Genital System

91. Removal of nephrostomy tube with fluoroscopic guidance.
    A. 50387   C. 99212
    B. 50389   D. 99213

REFERENCE: AMA, 2014
              AMA (7th ed.), p 196

92. Patient has been diagnosed with prostate cancer. Patient arrived in the operating room where a therapeutic orchiectomy is performed.
    A. 54560   C. 55899
    B. 54530   D. 54520

REFERENCE: CPT Assistant, October 2001, p 8
              Smith (2), p 122

93. Patient undergoes laparoscopic orchiopexy for intra-abdominal testes.
    A. 54650   C. 54692
    B. 54699   D. 55899

REFERENCE: CPT Assistant, November 1999, p 27
              CPT Assistant, May 2000, p 4
              CPT Assistant, October 2001, p 8
              Smith (2), p 122

94. Scrotal wall abscess drainage.
    A. 55100
    B. 55150
    C. 54700
    D. 55110

REFERENCE: AMA, 2014

95. Hydrocelectomy of spermatic cord.
    A. 55500
    B. 55000
    C. 55041
    D. 55520

REFERENCE: CPT Assistant, October 2001, p 8

96. Patient has been followed by his primary care physician for elevated PSA. Patient underwent prostate needle biopsy in the physician office 2 weeks ago and final pathology was positive for carcinoma. Patient is admitted for prostatectomy. Frozen section of the prostate and one lymph node is positive for prostate cancer with metastatic disease to the lymph node. Prostatectomy became a radical perineal with bilateral pelvic lymphadenectomy.
    A. 55845
    B. 55815
    C. 55815; 38562
    D. 38770

REFERENCE: Green, p 665
              Smith (2), p 122

97. Male presented to operating room for sterilization by bilateral vasectomy.
    A. 55200
    B. 55400
    C. 55250
    D. 55450

REFERENCE: CPT Assistant, June 1998, p 10
              CPT Assistant, July 1998, p 10

98. Laser destruction of penile condylomas.
    A. 54057
    B. 17106
    C. 17270
    D. 54055

REFERENCE: AMA, 2014
              Smith, p 139

99. First-stage repair for hypospadias with skin flaps.
    A. 54300
    B. 54308; 14040
    C. 54322
    D. 54304

REFERENCE: AMA, 2014

100. Priapism operation with spongiosum shunt.
    A. 54450
    B. 54352
    C. 54430
    D. 55899

REFERENCE: AMA, 2014

Surgery—Female Genital System

101. Patient was admitted to the hospital with sharp pelvic pains. A pelvic ultrasound was ordered and the results showed a possible ovarian cyst. The patient was taken to the operating room where a laparoscopic destruction of two corpus luteum cysts was performed.
    A. 49321
    B. 58925
    C. 58561
    D. 58662

REFERENCE: AMA, 2014
               Smith (2), p 534

102. Patient was admitted with a cystocele and rectocele. An anterior colporrhaphy was performed.
    A. 57250
    B. 57260
    C. 57240
    D. 57110

REFERENCE: AMA, 2014

103. Patient has a Bartholin's gland cyst that was marsupialized.
    A. 54640
    B. 10060
    C. 58999
    D. 56440

REFERENCE: AMA, 2014

104. Patient is at a fertility clinic and undergoes intrauterine embryo transplant.
    A. 58679
    B. 58322
    C. 58323
    D. 58974

REFERENCE: AMA, 2014

105. Patient has been diagnosed with carcinoma of the vagina, and she has a radical vaginectomy with complete removal of the vaginal wall.
    A. 57107
    B. 57110
    C. 58150
    D. 57111

REFERENCE: AMA, 2014
               Smith (2), p 133

106. Patient has been diagnosed with uterine fibroids and undergoes a total abdominal hysterectomy with bilateral salpingo-oophorectomy.
    A. 58200
    B. 58150
    C. 58262
    D. 58150; 58720

REFERENCE: AMA (7th ed.), pp 202–203
               Green, pp 682–685
               Johnson and Linker, p 380
               Smith, pp 145–146
               Smith (2), p 133

107. Hysteroscopy with D&C and polypectomy.
    A. 58563
    B. 58558
    C. 58120; 58100; 58555
    D. 58558; 58120

REFERENCE: AMA (7th ed.), pp 203–205
             Green, pp 682–685
             Smith, p 145
             Smith (2), p 132

108. Laparoscopic tubal ligation utilizing Endoloop.
    A. 58670
    B. 58615
    C. 58671
    D. 58611

REFERENCE: AMA (7th ed.), p 204
             Green, p 685

109. Laser destruction extensive herpetic lesions of the vulva.
    A. 17106
    B. 17004
    C. 56515
    D. 56501

REFERENCE: AMA, 2014
             Smith (2), p 131

110. Patient undergoes hysteroscopy with excision uterine fibroids.
    A. 58545
    B. 58140
    C. 58561
    D. 58140; 49320

REFERENCE: AMA (7th ed.), pp 203–204
             Green, pp 683–685
             Smith, p 145
             Smith (2), p 132

Surgery—Maternity Care and Delivery

111. Attempted vaginal delivery in a previous cesarean section patient, which resulted in a repeat cesarean section.
    A. 59409
    B. 59612
    C. 59620
    D. 59514

REFERENCE: AMA (7th ed.), p 208
             Green, pp 686–690
             Smith, p 146

112. Patient is admitted to the hospital following an ultrasound at 25 weeks, which revealed fetal pleural effusion. A fetal thoracentesis was performed.
    A. 59074
    B. 32554
    C. 32555
    D. 76815

REFERENCE: AMA (7th ed.), p 206
             CPT Assistant, May 2004, pp 3–4

113. Patient in late stages of labor arrives at the hospital. Her OB physician is not able to make the delivery and the house physician delivers the baby vaginally. Primary care physician resumes care after delivery. Code the delivery.
    A. 59409
    B. 59612
    C. 59620
    D. 59400

REFERENCE: AMA (7th ed.), pp 208–209
              Green, pp 686–690
              Smith, p 143

114. Patient is 24 weeks pregnant and arrives in the emergency room following an automobile accident. No fetal movement or heartbeat noted. Patient is taken to the OB ward where prostaglandin is given to induce abortion.
    A. 59200
    B. 59855
    C. 59821
    D. 59410

REFERENCE: Green, pp 686–690

115. Patient is 6 weeks pregnant and complains of left-sided abdominal pains. Patient is suspected of having an ectopic pregnancy. Patient has a laparoscopic salpingectomy with removal of the ectopic tubal pregnancy.
    A. 59120
    B. 59200
    C. 59121
    D. 59151

REFERENCE: AMA, 2014
              AMA (7th ed.), p 206

116. Cesarean delivery with antepartum and postpartum care.
    A. 59610
    B. 59514
    C. 59400
    D. 59510

REFERENCE: AMA (7th ed.), pp 208–209
              Green, pp 686–690
              Smith, p 146

117. A pregnant patient has an incompetent cervix, which was repaired using a vaginal cerclage.
    A. 57700
    B. 57531
    C. 59320
    D. 59325

REFERENCE: AMA, 2014
              AMA (7th ed.), p 207

118. A D&C is performed for postpartum hemorrhage.
    A. 59160
    B. 58120
    C. 58558
    D. 58578

REFERENCE: AMA, 2014

119. Hysterotomy for hydatidifom mole and tubal ligation.
    A. 58285; 58600
    B. 58150; 58605
    C. 51900; 58605
    D. 59100; 58611

REFERENCE: AMA, 2014

120. D&C performed for patient with a diagnosis of incomplete abortion at 8 weeks.
   A. 59812
   B. 59820
   C. 58120
   D. 59160

REFERENCE: Green, p 690

Surgery—Endocrine System

121. Patient comes in for a percutaneous needle biopsy of the thyroid gland.
   A. 60000
   B. 60270
   C. 60699
   D. 60100

REFERENCE: CPT Assistant, June 1997, p 5

122. Laparoscopic adrenalectomy, complete.
   A. 60650
   B. 60650-50
   C. 60659
   D. 60540

REFERENCE: AMA, 2014

123. Left carotid artery excision for tumor of carotid body.
   A. 60650
   B. 60600
   C. 60605
   D. 60699

REFERENCE: AMA, 2014

124. Patient undergoes total thyroidectomy with parathyroid autotransplantation.
   A. 60240; 60512
   B. 60520; 60500
   C. 60260; 60512
   D. 60650; 60500

REFERENCE: Green, p 692

125. Unilateral partial thyroidectomy.
   A. 60252
   B. 60210
   C. 60220
   D. 60520

REFERENCE: Green, p 692

Surgery—Nervous System

126. Patient comes in through the emergency room with a wound that was caused by an electric saw. Patient is taken to the operating room where two ulna nerves are sutured.
   A. 64837
   B. 64892; 69990
   C. 64836; 64837
   D. 64856; 64859

REFERENCE: AMA, 2014
            Smith (2), p 153

127. Laminectomy and excision of intradural lumbar lesion.
   A. 63272
   B. 63267
   C. 63282
   D. 63252

REFERENCE: AMA, 2014
            Smith (2) p 149

128. Patient comes in for steroid injection for lumbar herniated disk. Marcaine and Aristocort were injected into the L2-L3 space.
     A. 64520
     B. 64483
     C. 62311
     D. 64714

REFERENCE: CPT Assistant, September 1997, p 10
               Smith, p 153
               Smith (2), p 148

129. Patient with Parkinson's disease is admitted for insertion of a brain neurostimulator pulse generator with one electrode array.
     A. 61885
     B. 61850; 61863
     C. 61888
     D. 61867; 61870

REFERENCE: AMA (7th ed.), pp 222–224
               CPT Assistant, April 2001, pp 8–9
               CPT Assistant, June 2000, pp 4, 12
               Smith (2), p 145

130. Patient has rhinorrhea, which requires repair of the CSF leak with craniotomy.
     A. 63707
     B. 63709
     C. 62100
     D. 62010

REFERENCE: AMA, 2014
               Smith (2), pp 143–144

131. Patient has metastatic brain lesions. Patient undergoes stereotactic radiosurgery gamma knife of two lesions.
     A. 61533
     B. 61500
     C. 61796; 61797
     D. 61796

REFERENCE: AMA, 2014
               AMA (7th ed.), pp 221–222

132. Patient has right sacroiliac joint dysfunction and requires a right S2-S3 paravertebral facet joint anesthetic nerve block with image guidance.
     A. 62311
     B. 64493
     C. 64490
     D. 64520

REFERENCE: AMA, 2014
               Smith (2), pp 152–153

133. Patient requires repair of a 6 cm meningocele.
     A. 63700
     B. 63709
     C. 63180
     D. 63702

REFERENCE: AMA, 2014
               Smith (2), pp 151–152

134. Patient comes in through the emergency room with a laceration of the posterior tibial nerve. Patient is taken to the operating room where the nerve requires transposition and suture.
    A. 64856
    B. 64831; 64832; 64876
    C. 64840; 64874
    D. 64834; 64859; 64872

    REFERENCE: AMA, 2014
                  Smith (2), p 153

Surgery—Eye and Ocular Adnexa

135. Patient returns to the physician's office complaining of obscured vision. Patient has had cataract surgery 6 months prior. Patient requires laser discission of secondary cataract.
    A. 66821
    B. 66940
    C. 67835
    D. 66830

    REFERENCE: AMA (7th ed.), p 297
                  Smith, pp 157–158
                  Smith (2), pp 162–163

136. Patient undergoes enucleation of left eye and muscles were reattached to an implant.
    A. 65135-LT
    B. 65105-LT
    C. 65730-LT
    D. 65103-LT

    REFERENCE: AMA, 2014
                  Smith (2), p 161

137. Patient suffers from strabismus and requires surgery. Recession of the lateral rectus (horizontal) muscle with adjustable sutures was performed.
    A. 67340; 67500
    B. 67314; 67320
    C. 67332; 67334
    D. 67311; 67335

    REFERENCE: AMA, 2014
                  AMA (7th ed.), p 253
                  CPT Assistant, Summer 1993, p 20
                  CPT Assistant, March 1997, p 5
                  CPT Assistant, November 1998, p 1
                  CPT Assistant, September 2002, p 10
                  Smith, p 160
                  Smith (2), p 165

138. Radial keratotomy.
    A. 92071
    B. 65855
    C. 65767
    D. 65771

    REFERENCE: Green, pp 706–711
                  Smith (2), pp 162–163

139. Correction of trichiasis by incision of lid margin.
    A. 67840
    B. 67830
    C. 67835
    D. 67850

    REFERENCE: AMA, 2014
                  Smith (2), p 165

140. Patient undergoes ocular resurfacing construction utilizing stem cell allograft from a cadaver.
    A. 67320
    B. 66999
    C. 68371
    D. 65781

REFERENCE: CPT Assistant, May 2004, pp 9–11
              Smith (2), pp 162–163

141. Aphakia penetrating corneal transplant.
    A. 65755
    B. 65730
    C. 65750
    D. 65765

REFERENCE: AMA, 2014
              AMA (7th ed.), pp 247–248
              Smith (2), pp 162–163

142. Lagophthalmos correction with implantation using gold weight.
    A. 67912
    B. 67911
    C. 67901
    D. 67121

REFERENCE: CPT Assistant, May 2004, p 12
              Smith (2), p 165

143. Lacrimal fistula closure.
    A. 68760
    B. 68761
    C. 68700
    D. 68770

REFERENCE: AMA, 2014
              AMA (7th ed.), pp 255–256
              Smith (2), pp 165–166

Surgery—Auditory

144. Patient comes into the office for removal of impacted earwax.
    A. 69210
    B. 69200
    C. 69222
    D. 69000

REFERENCE: AMA (7th ed.), p 257
              Green, pp 712–713
              Smith (2), p 120

145. Patient with a traumatic rupture of the eardrum. Repaired with tympanoplasty with incision of the mastoid. Repair of ossicular chain not required.
    A. 69641
    B. 69646
    C. 69642
    D. 69635

REFERENCE: AMA, 2014
              AMA (7th ed.), pp 258–259
              Smith (2), p 173

146. Patient came in for excision of a middle ear lesion.
    A. 11440
    B. 69540
    C. 69552
    D. 69535

REFERENCE: AMA, 2014
              Smith (2), p 173

147. Patient with chronic otitis media requiring eustachian tube catheterization.
    A. 69400
    B. 69424
    C. 69421
    D. 69405

REFERENCE: AMA, 2014
              AMA (7th ed.), p 258
              Smith (2), p 173

148. Modified radical mastoidectomy.
    A. 69511
    B. 69505
    C. 69635
    D. 69641

REFERENCE: AMA, 2014
              Smith (2), p 173

149. Decompression internal auditory canal.
    A. 69979
    B. 69915
    C. 69970
    D. 69960

REFERENCE: AMA, 2014
              Smith (2), pp 172–173

150. Myringoplasty.
    A. 69620
    B. 69635
    C. 69610
    D. 69420

REFERENCE: AMA (7th ed.), p 258
              CPT Assistant, March 2001, p 10

151. Insertion of cochlear device inner ear.
    A. 69711
    B. 69949
    C. 69930
    D. 69960; 69990

REFERENCE: AMA, 2014
              AMA (7th ed.), p 259
              Smith (2), p 173

152. Patient with Bell's palsy requiring a total facial nerve decompression.
    A. 64742
    B. 64771
    C. 69955
    D. 64864

REFERENCE: AMA, 2014
              Smith (2), p 173

153. Drainage of simple external ear abscess.
    A. 69000
    B. 69100
    C. 10060
    D. 69020

REFERENCE: CPT Assistant, October 1997, p 11
              CPT Assistant, October 1999, p 10
              Smith (2), p 173

Radiology

154. Administration of initial oral radionuclide therapy for hyperthyroidism.
    A. 78015
    B. 77402
    C. 78099
    D. 79005

REFERENCE: Green, pp 753–761

155. Patient comes into the outpatient department at the local hospital for an MRI of the cervical spine with contrast. Patient status post automobile accident.
    A. 72156
    B. 72142
    C. 72149
    D. 72126

REFERENCE: AMA (7th ed.), pp 277–278
              Smith, pp 175–176

156. Obstetric patient comes in for a pelvimetry with placental placement.
    A. 74710
    B. 76946
    C. 76805
    D. 76825

REFERENCE: AMA, 2014

157. Patient comes into his physician's office complaining of wrist pain. Physician gives the patient an injection and sends the patient to the hospital for an arthrography. Code the complete procedure.
    A. 73115
    B. 73100
    C. 73110
    D. 25246; 73115

REFERENCE: AMA, 2014
              AMA (7th ed.), pp 278–279

158. Patient has carcinoma of the breast and undergoes proton beam delivery of radiation to the breast with a single port.
    A. 77523
    B. 77432
    C. 77520
    D. 77402

REFERENCE: AMA (7th ed.), p 299
              Green, pp 753–761
              Smith, pp 178–180

159. CT scan of the head with contrast.
    A. 70460
    B. 70542
    C. 70551
    D. 70470

REFERENCE: AMA (7th ed.), p 274
              Smith, pp 175–176

160. Patient undergoes x-ray of the foot with three views.
    A. 73620
    B. 73610
    C. 73630
    D. 27648; 73615

REFERENCE: Smith, pp 175–176

161. Unilateral mammogram with computer-aided detection with further physician review and interpretation.
    A. 77055, 77032
    B. 77055-22
    C. 77056-52, 77051
    D. 77055, 77051

REFERENCE: AMA, 2014
AMA (7th ed.), pp 291–292
Green, pp 751–752

162. Pregnant female comes in for a complete fetal and maternal evaluation via ultrasound.
    A. 76856
    B. 76805
    C. 76811
    D. 76810

REFERENCE: AMA (7th ed.), pp 286–287
Green, p 750

163. Ultrasonic guidance for the needle biopsy of the liver. Code the complete procedure.
    A. 47000; 76942
    B. 47000; 76937
    C. 47000; 76999
    D. 47000; 77002

REFERENCE: AMA (7th ed.), p 281
Green, p 750

Pathology and Laboratory

164. What code is used for a culture of embryos less than 4 days?
    A. 89251
    B. 89272
    C. 89268
    D. 89250

REFERENCE: AMA (7th ed.), p 336
CPT Assistant, April 2004, p 2
CPT Assistant, May 2004, p 16
CPT Assistant, June 2004, p 9
Green, pp 790–791

165. Basic metabolic panel (calcium, total) and total bilirubin.
    A. 80048; 82247
    B. 80053
    C. 80100
    D. 82239; 80400; 80051

REFERENCE: AMA (7th ed.), p 309
Green, p 778
Smith, p 188

166. Huhner test and semen analysis.
    A. 89325
    B. 89258
    C. 89310
    D. 89300

REFERENCE: CPT Assistant, November 1997, p 36
CPT Assistant, July 1998, p 10
CPT Assistant, October 1998, p 1
CPT Assistant, April 2004, p 3

167. Chlamydia culture.
   A. 87110
   B. 87106
   C. 87118
   D. 87109; 87168

REFERENCE: Green, pp 785–786

168. Partial thromboplastin time utilizing whole blood.
   A. 85732
   B. 85730
   C. 85245
   D. 85246

REFERENCE: AMA (7th ed.), p 323
             Smith, p 190

169. Pathologist bills for gross and microscopic examination of medial meniscus.
   A. 88300
   B. 88302; 88311
   C. 88325
   D. 88304

REFERENCE: AMA (7th ed.), p 334
             Green, pp 789–790
             Smith, p 190

170. Cytopathology of cervical Pap smear with automated thin-layer preparation utilizing computer screening and manual rescreening under physician supervision.
   A. 88175
   B. 88148
   C. 88160; 88141
   D. 88161

REFERENCE: AMA (7th ed.), p 329
             CPT Assistant, July 2003, p 9
             CPT Assistant, March 2004, p 4
             Green, pp 786–787

171. Pathologist performs a postmortem examination including brain of an adult. Tissue is being sent to the lab for microscopic examination.
   A. 88309
   B. 88025
   C. 88099
   D. 88028

REFERENCE: Green, p 486
             Smith, p 190

172. Clotting factor VII.
   A. 85220
   B. 85240
   C. 85362
   D. 85230

REFERENCE: Smith, p 190

Medicine Section

173. IV push of one antineoplastic drug.
   A. 96401
   B. 96409
   C. 96411
   D. 96413

REFERENCE: AMA (7th ed.), pp 418–419
             Green, pp 825–828
             Smith, pp 240–242

174. One-half hour of IV chemotherapy by infusion followed by IV push of a different drug.
    A. 96413
    B. 96413; 96411
    C. 96413; 96409
    D. 96409; 96411

REFERENCE: AMA (7th ed.), pp 417–418
            Green, pp 825–828
            Smith, pp 240–242

175. Caloric vestibular test using air.
    A. 92543; 92700
    B. 92543; 92543
    C. 92700
    D. 92543

REFERENCE: AMA (7th ed.), p 361
            CPT Assistant, November 2004, p 10

176. Patient presents to the emergency room with chest pains. The patient is admitted as a 23-hour observation. The cardiologist orders cardiac workup and the patient undergoes left heart catheterization via the left femoral artery with visualization of the coronary arteries and left ventriculography. The physician interprets the report. Code the heart catheterization.
    A. 93452; 93455
    B. 93452; 93458
    C. 93458
    D. 93459

REFERENCE: AMA, 2014

177. Patient with hematochromatosis had a therapeutic phlebotomy performed on an outpatient basis.
    A. 99195
    B. 36522
    C. 36514
    D. 99199

REFERENCE: AMA (7th ed.), p 307
            CPT Assistant, June 1996, p 10

178. A physician performs a PTCA with drug-eluting stent placement in the left anterior descending artery and angioplasty only in the right coronary artery.
    A. 92928-LD; 92929-RC
    B. 92928-LD; 92920-RC
    C. 92928-LD; 92920-RC
    D. 92920-RC; 92929-LD

REFERENCE: AMA (7th ed.), pp 366–367
            CPT Assistant, April 2005, p 14
            Smith, pp 231–234

179. Transesophageal echocardiography (TEE) with probe placement, image, and interpretation and report.
    A. 93307
    B. 93303; 93325
    C. 93312; 93313; 93314
    D. 93312

REFERENCE: AMA (7th ed.), pp 374–375
            CPT Assistant, December 1997, p 5
            CPT Assistant, January 2000, p 10

180. Which code listed below would be used to report an esophageal electrogram during an EPS?
    A. 93600
    B. 93615
    C. 93612
    D. 93616

REFERENCE: CPT Assistant, April 2004, p 9
             Smith, p 237

181. Cardioversion of cardiac arrhythmia by external forces.
    A. 92961
    B. 92950
    C. 92960
    D. 92970

REFERENCE: CPT Assistant, Summer 1993, p 13
             CPT Assistant, November 1999, p 49
             CPT Assistant, June 2000, p 5
             CPT Assistant, November 2000, p 9
             CPT Assistant, July 2001, p 11

182. Osteopathic manipulative treatment to three body regions.
    A. 98926
    B. 98941
    C. 97110
    D. 97012

REFERENCE: Green, p 830

183. Patient presents to the Respiratory Therapy Department and undergoes a pulmonary stress test. CO_2 production with O_2 uptake with recordings was also performed.
    A. 94450
    B. 94620
    C. 94002
    D. 94621

REFERENCE: CPT Assistant, November 1998, p 35
             CPT Assistant, January 1999, p 8
             CPT Assistant, August 2002, p 10

For the following questions, you will be utilizing the codes provided for the scenarios. You will need to code appropriate CPT-4 codes only.

184. Patient presents to the hospital for debridement of a diabetic ulcer of the left ankle. The patient has a history of recurrent ulcers. Medication taken by the patient includes Diabeta and the patient was covered in the hospital with insulin sliding scales. The decubitus ulcer was debrided down to the bone.

11043	Debridement, muscle and/or fascia (includes epidermis, dermis, and subcutaneous tissue, if performed); first 20 cm² or less
11044	Debridement, bone (includes epidermis, dermis, subcutaneous tissue, muscle and/or fascia, if performed); first 20 cm² or less
+11046	each additional 20 cm² thereof (List separately in addition to code for primary procedure.) (Use 11046 in conjunction with 11043.)
+11047	each additional 20 cm², or part thereof (List separately in addition to code for primary procedure.) (Use 11047 in conjunction with 11047.)

A. 11043, +11047   C. 11044
B. 11043, +11046   D. 11044, +11047

REFERENCE: AMA, 2014

185. Patient presents to the emergency room following a fall from a tree. X-rays were ordered for the left upper arm, which showed a fracture of the humerus shaft. The emergency room physician performed a closed reduction of the fracture and placed the patient in a long arm spica cast. Code the diagnoses and procedures, excluding the x-ray.

24500	Closed treatment of humeral shaft fracture; without manipulation
24505	Closed treatment of humeral shaft fracture; with manipulation, with or without skeletal traction
24515	Open treatment of humeral shaft fracture with plate/screws, with or without cerclage
29065	Application, cast; shoulder to hand (long arm)
LT	Left side

A. 24505-LT
B. 24515-LT
C. 24505-LT, 29065
D. 24500-LT

REFERENCE: AMA (7th ed.), pp 115, 134–135
                        Green, p 563
                        Smith, pp 84–85

186. Patient was admitted with hemoptysis and underwent a bronchoscopy with transbronchial lung biopsy. Following the bronchoscopy the patient was taken to the operating room where a left lower lobe lobectomy was performed without complications. Pathology reported large cell carcinoma of the left lower lobe.

31625	Bronchoscopy with bronchial or endobronchial biopsy, with or without fluoroscopic guidance
31628	Bronchoscopy with transbronchial lung biopsy, with or without fluoroscopic guidance
32405	Biopsy, lung or mediastinum, percutaneous needle
32440	Removal of lung, total pneumonectomy
32480	Removal of lung, other than total pneumonectomy, single lobe (lobectomy)
32484	Removal of lung, other than total pneumonectomy, single segment (segmentectomy)

A. 31625

B. 31628, 32480

C. 32405, 32484

D. 32440

REFERENCE: AMA (7th ed.), pp 140–141
                    CPT Assistant, June 2001, p 10
                    CPT Assistant, June 2002, p 10
                    CPT Assistant, September 2004, p 9
                    Green, pp 576–580
                    Smith, p 100

187. Patient was admitted for right upper quadrant pain. Workup included various x-rays that showed cholelithiasis. Patient was taken to the operating room where a laparoscopic cholecystectomy was performed. During the procedure, the physician was unable to visualize through the ports and an open cholecystectomy was elected to be performed. Intraoperative cholangiogram was performed. Pathology report states acute and chronic cholecystitis with cholelithiasis.

47605	Cholecystectomy with cholangiography
47563	Laparoscopy, surgical; cholecystectomy with cholangiography

A. 47563

B. 47563, 47605

C. 47605

REFERENCE: AMA (7th ed.), p 187
                    Green, p 654

188. Patient presents to the emergency room complaining of right forearm/elbow pain after racquetball last night. Patient states that he did not fall, but overworked his arm. Past medical history is negative and the physical examination reveals the patient is unable to supinate. A four-view x-ray of the right elbow is performed and is negative. The physician signs the patient out with right elbow sprain. Prescription of Motrin is given to the patient.

73040	X-ray of shoulder, arthrography radiological supervision and interpretation
73070	X-ray of elbow, two views
73080	X-ray of elbow, complete, minimum of three views
99281	E/M visit to emergency room—problem-focused history, problem-focused exam, straightforward medical decision
99282	E/M visit to emergency room—expanded problem-focused history, expanded problem-focused exam, and medical decision of low complexity
-25	Significant, separately identifiable evaluation and management service by the same physician on the same day of the procedure or other service

A. 73080
B. 99281, 73070
C. 73080, 99282, 73040
D. 99281-25, 73080

REFERENCE: AMA, 2014
AMA (7th ed.), pp 56–57, 275, 276
Smith, pp 175–176, 216

189. A physician orders a lipid panel on a 54-year-old male with hypercholesterolemia, hypertension, and a family history of heart disease. The lab employee in his office performs and reports the total cholesterol and HDL cholesterol only.

80061	Lipid panel; this panel must include the following: Cholesterol, serum, total (82465); Lipoprotein, direct measurement, high density cholesterol (HDL cholesterol) (83718); Triglycerides (84478)
82465	Cholesterol, serum or whole blood, total
83718	Lipoprotein, direct measurement; high density cholesterol (HDL cholesterol)
84478	Triglycerides
52	Reduced services

A. 80061
B. 80061-52
C. 82465, 83718
D. 82465, 84478

REFERENCE: AMA (7th ed.), p 308
Green, p 788
Smith, pp 188–189

190. Chronic nontraumatic rotator cuff tear. Arthroscopic subacromial decompression with coracoacromial ligament release, and open rotator cuff repair.

23410	Repair of ruptured musculotendinous cuff (e.g., rotator cuff); open, acute
23412	Repair of ruptured musculotendinous cuff (e.g., rotator cuff) open; chronic
29821	Arthroscopy, shoulder, surgical; synovectomy, complete
29823	Arthroscopy, shoulder, surgical; debridement, extensive
+29826	Arthroscopy, shoulder, surgical; decompression of subacromial space with partial acromioplasty, with coracoacromial ligament release (List separately in addition to code from primary procedure.)
29827	Arthroscopy, shoulder, surgical; with rotator cuff repair
-59	Distinct procedural service

A. 29823

B. 23412, 29826-59

C. 29826, 29821

D. 23410

REFERENCE: AMA (7th ed.), pp 135, 498
Smith, p 88

191. The patient is on vacation and presents to a physician's office with a lacerated finger. The physician repairs the laceration and gives a prescription for pain control and has the patient follow up with his primary physician when he returns home. The physician fills out the superbill as a problem-focused history and physical examination with straightforward medical decision making. Also checked is a laceration repair for a 1.5 cm finger wound.

99201	New patient office visit with a problem-focused history, problem-focused examination and straightforward medical decision making
99212	Established patient office visit with a problem-focused history, problem-focused examination and straightforward medical decision making
12001	Simple repair of superficial wounds of scalp, neck, axillae, external genitalia, trunk and/or extremities (including hands and feet); 2.5 cm or less
13131	Repair, complex, forehead, cheeks, chin, mouth, neck, axillae, genitalia, hands and/or feet; 1.1 cm to 2.5 cm

A. 99212; 13131

B. 12001

C. 99212; 12001

D. 99201; 12001

REFERENCE: AMA (7th ed.), pp 107, 447–448
Green, pp 428–429, 524–526
Smith, pp 66–68, 195–196

192. A 69-year-old established female patient presents to the office with chronic obstructive lung disease, congestive heart failure, and hypertension. The physician conducts a comprehensive history and physical examination and makes a medical decision of moderate complexity. Physician admits the patient from the office to the hospital for acute exacerbation of CHF.

99212	Established office visit for problem-focused history and exam, straightforward medical decision making
99214	Established office visit for a detailed history and physical exam, moderate medical decision making
99222	Initial hospital care for comprehensive history and physical exam, moderate medical decision making
99223	Initial hospital care for comprehensive history and physical exam, high medical decision making

    A. 402.91; 496; 99214   C. 428.0; 496; 401.9; 99222

    B. 428.0; 496; 401.1; 99223   D. 402.91; 496; 401.1; 99212

REFERENCE: AMA (7th ed.), p 48
                       Green, pp 432–435
                       Smith, pp 214–215

193. Established 42-year-old patient comes into your office to obtain vaccines required for his trip to Sri Lanka. The nurse injects intramuscularly the following vaccines: hepatitis A and B vaccines, cholera vaccine, and yellow fever vaccine. As the coding specialist, what would you report on the CMS 1500 form?

    A. office visit, hepatitis A and B vaccine, cholera vaccine and yellow fever vaccine

    B. office visit, intramuscular injection; HCPCS Level II codes

    C. office visit; administration of two or more single vaccines; vaccine products for hepatitis A and B, cholera, and yellow fever

    D. administration of two or more single vaccines; vaccine products for hepatitis A and B, cholera, and yellow fever

REFERENCE: Green, pp 802–804
                       Smith, p 226

194. Patient presents to the operating room where the physician performed, using imaging guidance, a percutaneous breast biopsy utilizing a rotating biopsy device.

19000	Puncture aspiration of cyst of breast
19103	Biopsy, breast, with placement of breast localization device(s), when performed, and imaging of the biopsy specimen, when performed, percutaneous; first lesion, including stereotactic guidance
19120	Excision of cyst, fibroadenoma, or other benign or malignant tumor, aberrant breast tissue, duct lesion, nipple or areolar lesion (except 19300), open, male or female, one or more lesions
19125	Excision of breast lesion identified by preoperative placement of radiological marker, open; single lesion
19283	Placement of breast localization device(s) (ed clip, metallic pellet, wire/needle, radioactive seeds), percutaneous; first lesion, including stereotactic guidance

A. 19081
B. 19125; 19283

C. 19120
D. 19000

REFERENCE: AMA (7th ed.), p 115
CPT Assistant, January 2001, pp 10–11
Green, pp 835–837
Smith, pp 79–80

195. Facelift utilizing the superficial musculoaponeurotic system (SMAS) flap technique.

15788	Chemical peel, facial; epidermal
15825	Rhytidectomy; neck with platysmal tightening (platysmal flap, P-flap)
15828	Rhytidectomy; cheek, chin, and neck
15829	Rhytidectomy; SMAS flap

A. 15825
B. 15788

C. 15829
D. 15828

REFERENCE: AMA, 2014
Green, pp 531–532

196. Tracheostoma revision with flap rotation.

31613	Tracheostoma revision; simple, without flap rotation
31614	Tracheostoma revision; complex, with flap rotation
31750	Tracheoplasty; cervical
31830	Revision of tracheostomy scar

A. 31830
B. 31750

C. 31614
D. 31613

REFERENCE: AMA, 2014

197. Blood transfusion of three units of packed red blood cells.

36430	Transfusion, blood or blood components
36455	Exchange transfusion; blood, other than newborn
36460	Transfusion, intrauterine, fetal

A. 36430
B. 36430; 36430; 36430

C. 36460
D. 36455

REFERENCE: AMA, 2014

198. Two-year-old patient returns to the hospital for cleft palate repair where a secondary lengthening procedure takes place.

40720	Plastic repair of cleft lip/nasal deformity; secondary, by re-creation of defect and reclosure
42145	Palatopharyngoplasty
42220	Palatoplasty for cleft palate; secondary lengthening procedure
42226	Lengthening of palate and pharyngeal flap

A. 40720
B. 42220

C. 42226
D. 42145

REFERENCE: AMA, 2014

199. Tonsillectomy on a 14-year-old.

42820	Tonsillectomy and adenoidectomy; under age 12
42821	Tonsillectomy and adenoidectomy; age 12 or over
42825	Tonsillectomy, primary or secondary; under age 12
42826	Tonsillectomy, primary or secondary; age 12 or over

A. 42820
B. 42821

C. 42825
D. 42826

REFERENCE: Green, p 640

200. Laparoscopic repair of umbilical hernia.

49580	Repair umbilical hernia, under age 5 years, reducible
49585	Repair umbilical hernia, age 5 years or over, reducible
49652	Laparoscopy, surgical, repair, ventral, umbilical, spigelian or epigastric hernia (includes mesh insertion when performed); reducible
49654	Laparoscopy, surgical, repair, incisional hernia (includes mesh insertion when performed); reducible

A. 49580
B. 49654

C. 49585
D. 49652

REFERENCE: AMA, 2014
                       AMA (7th ed.), p 189

201. Ureterolithotomy completed laparoscopically.

50600	Ureterotomy with exploration or drainage (separate procedure)
50945	Laparoscopy, surgical ureterolithotomy
52325	Cystourethroscopy; with fragmentation of ureteral calculus
52352	Cystourethroscopy, with urethroscopy and/or pyeloscopy; with removal or manipulation of calculus (ureteral catheterization is included)

A. 52352   C. 50600
B. 52325   D. 50945

REFERENCE: CPT Assistant, November 1999, p 26
       CPT Assistant, May 2000, p 4
       CPT Assistant, October 2001, p 8

202. Patient undergoes partial nephrectomy for carcinoma of the kidney.

50220	Nephrectomy, including partial ureterectomy, any open approach including rib resection
50234	Nephrectomy with total ureterectomy and bladder cuff; through same incision
50240	Nephrectomy, partial
50340	Recipient nephrectomy (separate procedure)

A. 50234   C. 50340
B. 50220   D. 50240

REFERENCE: AMA (7th ed.), p 193
       Green, pp 659–660

203. Patient presents to the operating room for fulguration of bladder tumors. The cystoscope was inserted and entered the urethra, which was normal. Bladder tumors measuring approximately 1.5 cm were removed.

50957	Ureteral endoscopy through established ureterostomy, with or without irrigation, instillation, or ureteropyelography, exclusive of radiologic service; with fulguration and/or incision, with or without biopsy
51530	Cystotomy; for excision of bladder tumor
52214	Cystourethroscopy, with fulguration of trigone, bladder neck, prostatic fossa, urethra, or periurethral glands
52234	Cystourethroscopy, with fulguration (including cryosurgery or laser surgery) and/or resection of small bladder tumor(s) (0.5 up to 2.0 cm)

A. 52234   C. 52214
B. 50957   D. 51530

REFERENCE: AMA (7th ed.), pp 193–194
       Green, pp 664–665
       Smith, p 134

204. Excision of Cowper's gland.

53220	Excision or fulguration of carcinoma of urethra
53250	Excision of bulbourethral gland (Cowper's gland)
53260	Excision or fulguration; urethral polyp(s), distal urethra
53450	Urethromeatoplasty, with mucosal advancement

A. 53250
B. 53450

C. 53260
D. 53220

REFERENCE: AMA, 2014

205. Placement of double-J stent.

52320	Cystourethroscopy (including ureteral catheterization); with removal of ureteral calculus
52330	Cystourethroscopy; with manipulation, without removal of ureteral calculus
52332	Cystourethroscopy with insertion of indwelling ureteral stent (e.g., Gibbons or double-J type)
52341	Cystourethroscopy, with treatment of ureteral stricture (e.g., balloon dilation, laser electrocautery, and incision)

A. 52341
B. 52320

C. 52330; 52332
D. 52332

REFERENCE: AMA (7th ed.), pp 193–195
Green, pp 664–665
Smith, p 134

206. Litholapaxy, 3 cm calculus.

50590	Lithotripsy, extracorporeal shock wave
52317	Litholapaxy, simple or small (< 2.5 cm)
52318	Litholapaxy, complicated or large (over 2.5 cm)
52353	Cystourethroscopy, with ureteroscopy and/or pyeloscopy; with lithotripsy

A. 52353
B. 50590

C. 52318
D. 52317

REFERENCE: AMA, 2014

207. Patient presented to the operating room where an incision was made in the epigastric region for a repair of ureterovisceral fistula.

50520	Closure of nephrocutaneous or pyelocutaneous fistula
50525	Closure of nephrovisceral fistula, including visceral repair; abdominal approach
50526	Closure of nephrovisceral fistula, including visceral repair; thoracic approach
50930	Closure of ureterovisceral fistula (including visceral repair)

A. 50526
B. 50930

C. 50520
D. 50525

REFERENCE: AMA, 2014

208. Amniocentesis.

57530	Trachelectomy, amputation of cervix (separate procedure)
57550	Excision of cervical stump, vaginal approach
59000	Amniocentesis, diagnostic
59200	Insertion of cervical dilator (separate procedure)

A. 59000
B. 59200
C. 57550
D. 57530

REFERENCE: AMA, 2014
AMA (7th ed.), p 206

209. Patient is admitted to the hospital with facial droop and left-sided paralysis. CT scan of the brain shows subdural hematoma. Burr holes were performed to evacuate the hematoma.

61150	Burr hole(s) or trephine; with drainage of brain abscess or cyst
61154	Burr hole(s) with evacuation and/or drainage of hematoma, extradural or subdural
61156	Burr hole(s); with aspiration of hematoma or cyst, intracerebral
61314	Craniectomy or craniotomy for evacuation of hematoma, infratentorial; extradural or subdural

A. 61156
B. 61314
C. 61154
D. 61150

REFERENCE: Green, p 695

210. Spinal tap.

62268	Percutaneous aspiration, spinal cord cyst or syrinx
62270	Spinal puncture, lumbar diagnostic
62272	Spinal puncture, therapeutic, for drainage of cerebrospinal fluid (by needle or catheter)
64999	Unlisted procedure, nervous system

A. 62272
B. 64999
C. 62268
D. 62270

REFERENCE: AMA, 2014
AMA (7th ed.), p 445

211. Injection of anesthesia for nerve block of the brachial plexus.

64413	Injection, anesthetic agent; cervical plexus
64415	Injection, anesthetic agent; brachial plexus, single
64510	Injection, anesthetic agent; stellate ganglion (cervical sympathetic)
64530	Injection, anesthetic agent; celiac plexus, with or without radiologic monitoring

A. 64415
B. 64413
C. 64530
D. 64510

REFERENCE: AMA (7th ed.), p 448
Green, p 703

212. SPECT bone imaging.

77080	Dual energy x-ray absorptiometry (DXA), bone density study, one or more sites; axial skeleton (e.g., hips, pelvis, spine)
76977	Ultrasound bone density measurement and interpretation, peripheral site(s), any method
78300	Bone and/or joint imaging; limited area
78320	Bone and/or joint imaging; tomographic (SPECT)

A. 76977   C. 77080
B. 78320   D. 76977

REFERENCE: AMA, 2014
                        AMA (7th ed.), pp 303–304
                        CPT Assistant, June 2003, p 11

213. Vitamin B_{12}.

82180	Ascorbic acid (vitamin C), blood
82607	Cyanocobalamin (vitamin B_{12})
84590	Vitamin A
84591	Vitamin, not otherwise specified

A. 84590   C. 84591
B. 82180   D. 82607

REFERENCE: AMA (2014)
                        Green, p 782
                        Smith, p 190

214. Hepatitis C antibody.

86803	Hepatitis C antibody
86804	Hepatitis C antibody; confirmatory test (e.g., immunoblot)
87520	Infectious agent detection by nucleic acid (DNA or RNA); hepatitis C, direct probe technique
87522	Infectious agent detection by nucleic acid (DNA or RNA); hepatitis C, quantification

A. 86804   C. 87522
B. 86803   D. 87520

REFERENCE: AMA (2014)
                        Green, p 784

215. Creatinine clearance.

82550	Creatine kinase (CK), (CPK); total
82565	Creatinine; blood
82575	Creatinine; clearance
82585	Cryofibrinogen

A. 82550
B. 82565
C. 82575
D. 82585

REFERENCE: Green, p 782
Smith, p 190

216. Comprehensive electrophysiologic evaluation (EPS) with induction of arrhythmia.

93618	Induction of arrhythmia by electrical pacing
93619	Comprehensive electrophysiologic evaluation with right atrial pacing and recording, right ventricular pacing and recording, His bundle recording, including insertion and repositioning of multiple electrode catheters, without induction or attempted induction of arrhythmia
93620	Comprehensive electrophysiologic evaluation including insertion and repositioning of multiple electrode catheters with induction or attempted induction of arrhythmia; with right atrial pacing and recording, right ventricular pacing and recording, His bundle recording
+93623	Programmed stimulation and pacing after intravenous drug infusion (list separately in addition to code for primary procedure)
93640	Electrophysiologic evaluation of single- or dual-chamber pacing cardioverter-defibrillator leads including defibrillation threshold evaluation (induction of arrhythmia, evaluation of sensing and pacing for arrhythmia termination) at time of initial implantation or replacement

A. 93618; 93620
B. 93620
C. 93640; 93623
D. 93619; 93620

REFERENCE: AMA (7th ed.), p 149
CPT Assistant, Summer 1994, p 12
CPT Assistant, August 1997, p 9
CPT Assistant, October 1997, p 10
CPT Assistant, July 1998, p 10

217. Patient presents to the hospital for a two-view chest x-ray for a cough. The radiology report comes back negative. What would be the correct codes to report to the insurance company?

71010	Radiologic examination, chest; single view, frontal
71020	Radiologic examination, chest, two views, frontal and lateral
71035	Radiologic examination, chest, special views

A. 71010
B. 71020
C. 71035

REFERENCE: AMA, 2014
Schraffenberger, pp 338–339

Answer Key for CPT-4 Coding

1.	C	
2.	A	
3.	B	
4.	C	
5.	D	
6.	C	
7.	D	
8.	B	
9.	B	
10.	C	
11.	D	
12.	B	
13.	A	
14.	B	
15.	D	
16.	B	
17.	C	
18.	A	
19.	D	The supply of skin substitutes graft(s) should be reported separately.
20.	C	
21.	C	
22.	B	
23.	B	
24.	C	The supply of skin substitutes graft(s) should be reported separately.
25.	B	
26.	C	
27.	A	See Principles of CPT Coding 7th edition, pages 103–104. If two lesions are removed with one excision, only one excision code would be reported
28.	D	
29.	B	
30.	C	
31.	D	
32.	A	
33.	D	
34.	A	Codes 10060 and 10140 are used for I&Ds of superficial abscesses.
35.	C	
36.	C	
37.	D	
38.	B	
39.	A	
40.	B	
41.	A	
42.	D	

43.	C	
44.	A	
45.	D	
46.	C	
47.	A	
48.	D	
49.	A	
50.	B	
51.	A	
52.	B	
53.	D	
54.	B	
55.	C	
56.	C	
57.	C	
58.	A	
59.	A	
60.	B	
61.	D	
62.	B	
63.	A	
64.	D	
65.	A	
66.	B	
67.	C	
68.	A	
69.	A	
70.	D	
71.	C	
72.	D	Radiology codes would be used for the supervision and interpretation.
73.	C	
74.	C	
75.	C	
76.	A	
77.	D	
78.	D	
79.	C	
80.	A	
81.	A	
82.	C	
83.	D	
84.	B	
85.	D	
86.	B	
87.	A	
88.	B	
89.	C	
90.	B	
91.	B	

Answer Key for CPT-4 Coding

92.	D	137.	D
93.	C	138.	D
94.	A	139.	B
95.	A	140.	D
96.	B	141.	C
97.	C	142.	A
98.	A	143.	D
99.	D	144.	A
100.	C	145.	D
101.	D	146.	B
102.	C	147.	D
103.	D	148.	B
104.	D	149.	D
105.	D	150.	A
106.	B	151.	C
107.	B	152.	C
108.	C	153.	A
109.	C	154.	D
110.	C	155.	B
111.	C	156.	A
112.	A	157.	D
113.	A	158.	C
114.	B	159.	A
115.	D	160.	C
116.	D	161.	D
117.	C	162.	C
118.	A	163.	A

119. D When tubal ligation is performed at the same time as hysterotomy, use 58611 in addition to 59100

		164.	D
		165.	A
		166.	D
		167.	A
120.	A	168.	B
121.	D	169.	D
122.	A	170.	A
123.	C	171.	B
124.	A	172.	D
125.	B	173.	B
126.	C	174.	B

175. C Code 92543 is for use when an irrigation substance is used.

127.	A		
128.	C		
129.	A	176.	C
130.	C	177.	A
131.	C	178.	B
132.	B	179.	D
133.	D	180.	B
134.	C	181.	C
135.	A	182	A
136.	B		

Answer Key for CPT-4 Coding

183.	D	
184.	C	
185.	A	Casting is included in the surgical procedure.
186.	B	
187.	C	
188.	D	
189.	C	In order to use the code for the panel, every test must have been performed.
190.	B	Code both the arthroscopic procedure and the open procedure. Both need to be reported because there were two separate procedures. Modifier -59 must be added to code 29826 because it is a component of the comprehensive procedure 23412. That is allowed if an appropriate modifier is used per NCCI edits.
191.	D	
192.	C	According to CPT guidelines, when a patient is admitted to the hospital on the same day as an office visit, the office visit is not billable. Code rules do not allow the use of 402.91 because the scenario given does not state that the patient has hypertensive heart disease.

193.	D	According to the CPT coding guidelines for vaccines, only a separate identifiable Evaluation and Management code may be billed in addition to the vaccine. In this scenario, the patient was seen only for his vaccines. This guideline immediately eliminates all the other answers.
194.	A	
195.	C	
196.	C	
197.	A	Report this code only once no matter how many units were given.
198.	B	
199.	D	
200.	D	
201.	D	
202.	D	
203.	A	
204.	A	
205.	D	
206.	C	
207.	B	
208.	A	
209.	C	
210.	D	
211.	A	
212.	B	
213.	D	
214.	B	
215.	C	
216.	B	
217.	B	

REFERENCES

American Medical Association (AMA). *CPT assistant*. Chicago: Author.

American Medical Association (AMA). (2013). *Principles of CPT coding* (7th ed.). Chicago: Author.

American Medical Association (AMA). (2013). *Physician's current procedural terminology (CPT) 2014, Professional Edition*. Chicago: Author.

Green, M. (2014). *3-2-1 Code It!* (4th ed.). Clifton Park, NY: Delmar Cengage Learning.

Hazelwood, A., & Venable, C. (2013). *ICD-9-CM and ICD-10-CM coding and reimbursement for physician services*. Chicago: American Health Information Management Association (AHIMA).

Johnson, S. L., & Linker, R. (2013). *Understanding medical coding: A comprehensive guide* (3rd ed.). Clifton Park, NY: Delmar Cengage Learning.

Smith, G. (2012). *Basic current procedural terminology and HCPCS coding, 2013 edition*. Chicago: American Health Information Management Association (AHIMA).

Smith, G. (2) (2011). *Coding surgical procedures: Beyond the basics*. Clifton Park, NY. Delmar Cengage Learning.

ICD-10-CM/PCS Competencies

Question	RHIA Domain	RHIT Domain
1–203	1	2

X. Informatics and Information Systems

Nanette B. Sayles, EdD, RHIA, CCS, CHPS, CPHIMS, FAHIMA

Special Note

The Information Technology and Systems domains are very different for the RHIA and RHIT Examinations. Questions with only an RHIA competency begin at question 56. We advise that RHIT students should also study these questions. It is always better to know more than less.

1. Which of the following is primary storage?
   A. RAM
   B. USB drive
   C. CD
   D. external hard drive

REFERENCE: Glandon, Smaltz, and Slovensky, p 138

2. Your release of information system has part of the computing on the workstation and part on the file server. What type of technology is being used?
   A. Internet
   B. client server
   C. LAN
   D. operating system

REFERENCE: Eichenwald-Maki and Petterson, pp 29–30, 288
               Marreel and McLellan, pp 8, 191
               Sayles, p 999

3. Dr. Smith is entering a medication order in a CPOE. A window pops up with the following message:

   Patient is on beta-blocker, which is a contraindication for this medication. Do you want to order this medication? Yes or No.

   This is an example of a(n)
   A. reminder.
   B. alert.
   C. allergy.
   D. structured entry.

REFERENCE: Eichenwald-Maki and Petterson, pp 128, 130, 131–133, 287
               Marreel and McLellan, p 16

4. Barbara is being seen at a physician's office that she has never been to before. This physician practice is independently owned and is not associated with a hospital or other physician practice. She did not have to request copies of her medical records, but the physician has everything that she needs. The physician must be part of a(n)
   A. integrated health network.
   B. corporation.
   C. health information exchange.
   D. electronic health record.

REFERENCE: McWay, pp 272–273
               Sayles, pp 983–984

5. What types of software provide a front-end structure/interface that presents information in a familiar format leading to a natural style of interaction through the use of icons and a mouse?
   A. graphical user interface
   B. fiber optics
   C. assembly level language
   D. machine language

REFERENCE: Abdelhak, p 126
              Marreel and McLellan, p 196
              Sayles, p 877

6. With data exchange standards, the ability to transfer data from one system to another system is called
   A. data sets.
   B. messaging standards.
   C. interfaces.
   D. interoperability.

REFERENCE: Eichenwald-Maki and Petterson, p 3
              LaTour, Eichenwald-Maki, and Oachs, p 116
              Marreel and McLellan, pp 75–76, 199
              Sayles, p 919

7. Which of the following would be a foreign key in the patient table?
   A. last name
   B. addres
   C. medical record number
   D. billing number

REFERENCE: Sayles and Trawick, p 91

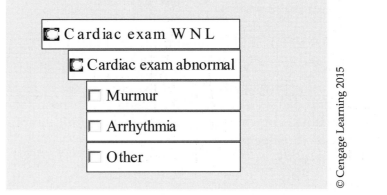

8. Review the simplistic screen above. This is an example of how _____ data can be entered.
   A. unstructured
   B. structured
   C. nomenclature
   D. template

REFERENCE: Amatayakul, p 248
              Eichenwald-Maki and Petterson, pp 35–37, 108

9. Why would the database administrator add a foreign key to one of the tables?
   A. the data element refers to ethnicity
   B. to indicate that it is a primary key in another table
   C. to ensure that each row is unique
   D. to separate two tables

REFERENCE: LaTour, Eichenwald-Maki, and Oachs, p 916
               Sayles, p 881

10. The information systems manager is testing what the system can handle with regard to passing large amounts of data. This is called
    A. volume testing.   C. rigorous testing.
    B. acceptance testing.   D. final testing.

REFERENCE: Abdelhak, p 331

11. You need to identify some patterns in our database. What technology should you use?
    A. reminders   C. data mining
    B. alerts   D. clinical guidelines

REFERENCE: Amatayakul, p 30
               Green and Bowie, p 258
               LaTour, Eichenwald-Maki, and Oachs, p 86
               McWay, p 268

12. The vendor has provided an update to their software. With this update, the system has new functions. This is known as a
    A. fix.
    B. version.
    C. release.
    D. link.

REFERENCE: McWay, p 287

13. Which application design is used in a computer-assisted coding (CAC)?
    A. electronic data interchange   C. message standards
    B. intraoperability   D. natural language processing

REFERENCE: Eichenwald-Maki and Petterson, p 160
               LaTour, Eichenwald-Maki, and Oachs, p 86
               McWay, p 158
               Sayles, p 218

14. Mary is designing a computer screen that will be used to collect patient demographic information. What input design should be utilized for the state field?
    A. an icon
    B. a dialog box
    C. the drop-down menu
    D. free form text

REFERENCE: Abdelhak, p 126
               Eichenwald-Maki and Petterson, pp 33–35

15. One of the coders is out on medical leave unexpectedly. At this facility, electronic workflow is used to distribute work. The supervisor needs the work normally sent to her to be distributed among the other coders. Which of the following statements is true?
    A. The supervisor will have to get a programmer to make the change.
    B. Each chart will have to be rerouted manually.
    C. The supervisor can change the established criteria.
    D. The vendor will have to be contacted to make the change.

REFERENCE: Sayles and Trawick, p 167

16. Which of the following tests determines how well new systems being implemented work with existing systems?
    A. volume test
    B. system test
    C. unit test
    D. integration test

REFERENCE: Abdelhak, p 331

17. You are working with a database that is created from multiple databases being stored in a single database. This is a(n)
    A. electronic health record.
    B. personal health record.
    C. clinical data repository.
    D. health information exchange.

REFERENCE: Green and Bowie, p 108
               Marreel and McLellan, p 175
               McWay, p 267

18. When entering the URL in a browser, the user types an "S" at the end of the http. This indicates the use of which of the following?
    A. World Wide Web
    B. domain name
    C. firewall
    D. digital certificate

REFERENCE: McWay, p 289

19. The data on the hard drive were erased by a corrupted file that had been attached to an e-mail message. Which software would be used to prevent this?
    A. productivity
    B. utility
    C. virus checker
    D. encryption

REFERENCE: Marreel and McLellan, pp 156–157
               McWay, p 290

20. In selecting a messaging standard for use in a picture archival communication system, the BEST choice would be
    A. Consolidated Health Informatics Initiatives.
    B. National Drug Code.
    C. HL7.
    D. DICOM.

REFERENCE: LaTour, Eichenwald-Maki, and Oachs, p 132

21. You have just inserted data contained in a spreadsheet into your word processed document. This is an example of a(n) _____ system.
    A. integrated
    B. interfaced
    C. mapped
    D. graphical user interface

REFERENCE: Glandon, Smaltz, and Slovensky, p 144
                      Marreel and McLellan, pp 74–75
                      McWay, p 110

22. What Medicare program requires the use of a certified electronic health record?
    A. meaningful use
    B. prospective payment
    C. health information exchange
    D. data standards

REFERENCE: McWay, p 305

23. The health care facility uses both a centralized system and the Internet to access information. What is this known as?
    A. a virtual private network
    B. cloud computing
    C. security
    D. meaningful use

REFERENCE: McWay, p 302

24. In the RFP, you have asked for information regarding the amount of time that a vendor has been in business and the number of installations of the product under consideration. If you want to review this information, you would go to the _____ section.
    A. functional specifications
    B. organizational profile
    C. vendor information
    D. licensing and contractual details

REFERENCE: Abdelhak, p 340
                      Amatayakul, p 385
                      Marreel and McLellan, pp 109–110
                      McWay, p 401
                      Murphy, p 135

25. A facility wants to purchase a system that will use barcodes on all drug and biological products to help in ensuring patient safety. Which system should the facility purchase?
    A. BC-MAR
    B. EMAR
    C. CPOE
    D. EHR

REFERENCE: Amatayakul, p 27

26. One of the ways that an EHR is distinguished from a clinical data repository is that the EHR
    A. has clinical decision support capabilities.
    B. has data from multiple information systems.
    C. can have digital images.
    D. aggregates data.

REFERENCE: Green and Bowie, pp 114–116
                McWay, p 126

27. You have been asked to give an example of a clinical information system. Which one of the following would you cite?
    A. laboratory information system   C. billing system
    B. financial information system   D. Admission, Discharge, Transfer

REFERENCE: McWay, pp 302–303

28. Which of the following systems would provide a snapshot of information about the patient's condition?
    A. EHR   C. personal health record
    B. continuity of care record   D. SMART card

REFERENCE: Sayles and Trawick, p 243

29. You are entering orders into an information system. This system prevented you from ordering a duplicate radiology test and prevented you from ordering a medication that the patient was allergic to. What system are you using?
    A. order entry/results reporting   C. clinical provider order entry
    B. electronic health record   D. decision support system

REFERENCE: Sayles, p 961

30. Buying and selling information is known as
    A. a business record exception.   C. information brokering.
    B. business intelligence.   D. marketing.

REFERENCE: McWay, p 311

31. You are developing a list of functions needed by users of a release of information system. You are also evaluating the current system to see what opportunities there are to improve the system. Which stage of the system developmental life cycle stages are you in?
    A. analysis
    B. implementation
    C. design
    D. obsolescence

REFERENCE: Johns, pp 858–860
               LaTour, Eichenwald-Maki, and Oachs, pp 105–106
               Marreel and McLellan, pp 62–64, 317–319
               McWay, pp 286–287

32. Which of the following can be used to check on a patient who is homebound?
    A. interactive voice recognition
    B. digital imaging
    C. radio frequency identification
    D. natural language processing

REFERENCE: McWay, p 312

33. In performing a "what if" query to determine if the facility should expand the emergency department, which of the following systems would be used?
    A. decision support system
    B. financial information system
    C. clinical decision support system
    D. knowledge based system

REFERENCE: Abdelhak, p 40
               Sayles, p 854

34. What type of system would be purchased to provide information on the census, update the master patient index, and distribute demographic data?
    A. Admission, Discharge, Transfer
    B. executive information system
    C. clinical information system
    D. financial information system

REFERENCE: McWay, p 313

35. As HIM Department Director, you are on the implementation team for the new MPI. You have been assigned the responsibility of looking at every data element stored in the system and establishing criteria for the use of each. An example of what you are doing is shown below.

Name	Last name
Description	This field is for the patient's last name
Number of characters	30
Alphanumeric	Alpha
Acceptable characters	a–z
Responsible person	HIM Director
Used in reports	Admissions list, discharge list, transfer list, health record number list, UB-92, CMS-1500

You are responsible for the
A. data flow diagram.
B. decision tree.
C. data dictionary.
D. rules based algorithms.

REFERENCE: Amatayakul, p 270
Eichenwald-Maki and Petterson, p 27
Green and Bowie, pp 250, 253
Marreel and McLellan, pp 79–81, 191
McWay, p 262
Sayles, pp 882–884

36. A milestone is
A. the distance between the users and the data center.
B. a step in the path to the implementation of a system such as the EHR.
C. a project plan.
D. a module of an information system such as the EHR.

REFERENCE: Amatayakul, p 120

37. A common language used in data definition and data manipulation is
A. unified modeling language.
B. metadata.
C. HTML.
D. SQL.

REFERENCE: Marreel and McLellan, p 207
McWay, p 171
Sayles and Trawick, p 177

38. You are trying to ensure a patient's name, but the entire name will not fit in the field. Only the first eight characters will fit. This is a problem with which of the following?
A. the data model
B. policy and procedure
C. the data dictionary
D. data mapping

REFERENCE: Sayles and Trawick, p 94

39. Differentiate between the physical and logical data models.
    A. The physical data model shows how the logical model will be created, and the logical data model shows the technology plan to be used.
    B. The logical data model shows what the system should do, and the physical data model shows how the logical data model will be created.
    C. The logical data model uses DFDs, and the physical data model uses entity relationship models.
    D. The physical data model uses DFDs, and the logical uses entity relationship model.

REFERENCE: Sayles and Trawick, p 196

40. The administrator has asked us to develop a patient satisfaction database internally. This database will be used to collect data that can be used to improve our services. He does not want this to be a long, drawn-out process. Which of the following could speed up this process?
    A. RFI
    B. RFP
    C. prototyping
    D. functional requirements

REFERENCE: Sayles and Trawick, p 130

41. Disease management is an example of which of the following?
    A. clinical information
    B. information brokering
    C. radio frequency device
    D. e-health

REFERENCE: McWay, p 311

42. The medical staff wants a speech recognition system where the staff dictates and then the editing of the dictation is done by editors. What type of speech recognition is this?
    A. key-word spotting
    B. hidden Markov model
    C. back-end speech recognition
    D. front-end speech recognition

REFERENCE: Sayles and Trawick, p 284

43. The EHR system implementation team is using simulated patients and simulated patient information to add progress notes, nurses' notes, and so on, to the EHR prior to implementation. Which phase is the team involved in?
    A. conversion
    B. testing
    C. analysis
    D. site preparation

REFERENCE: Abdelhak, p 331
               LaTour, Eichenwald-Maki, and Oachs, p 107
               Sayles, p 886

44. You are interested in performing some data analysis on patients with cardiac problems. You have downloaded the data that you need on the cardiology patients from the data warehouse into a smaller database that you can work with. You are using a
    A. data mart.
    B. clinical data repository.
    C. specialized data warehouse.
    D. executive information system.

    REFERENCE: Abdelhak, p 293
                          Amatayakul, p 274
                          LaTour, Eichenwald-Maki, and Oachs, p 94
                          McWay, p 268
                          Sayles, p 925

45. The laboratory system was installed 3 years ago. It is running well and meeting the needs of the department. In which stage of the IS life cycle is the lab system?
    A. initiation
    B. development
    C. implementation
    D. operations (maintenance)

    REFERENCE: Abdelhak, p 304
                          Johns, pp 891-892
                          LaTour, Eichenwald-Maki, and Oachs, p 107
                          Marreel and McLellan, pp 62–64, 317–319
                          McWay, p 287

46. Drop boxes, radio buttons, and pick lists are used in
    A. structured data entry.
    B. free text.
    C. natural language processing.
    D. unstructured data entry.

    REFERENCE: Amatayakul, p 321

47. The facility Hospital Information System team has been researching network topologies and has decided on one that combines the attributes of bus, ring, and star topologies. What topology has the team chosen?
    A. hybrid network
    B. network protocol
    C. physical topology
    D. TCP/IP

    REFERENCE: Sayles and Trawick, p 28

48. The hospital utilizes the best of breed model for its information systems. The hospital is able to exchange data between the information systems from the various vendors seamlessly. This concept is
    A. interoperability.
    B. networks.
    C. transparency.
    D. EDI.

    REFERENCE: Sayles and Trawick, p 265

49. Which of the following is the term used to identify who made an entry in the health record?
    A. access control
    B. authentication
    C. authorship
    D. accessibility

    REFERENCE: McWay, p 304

System Evaluation: Chart Location System							
Requirement	Priority	System A	System B	System C	System A Weighted	System B Weighted	System C Weighted
Ad hoc reporting	2	1	3	2	2	6	4
Check-out chart	3	3	3	3	9	9	9
Mass check out of chart	3	3	3	3	9	9	9
Unlimited locations	1	2	2	1	2	2	1
Password security	2	2	3	2	4	6	4
User-friendly	3	3	2	3	9	6	9
Check-in chart	3	1	3	3	3	9	9
Total					38	47	45

50. The EHR system selection committee evaluated three systems on a scale of 1–3 with a score of 3 being the best. The priority is ranked on a scale of 1–3 with 3 being the highest. Based on the evaluation above, which of the following systems should be purchased?
   A. System A
   B. System B
   C. System C
   D. none of the above

REFERENCE: Sayles and Trawick, pp 126–127

51. Upon final review of the RFP that is to be sent out to prospective vendors, you notice that there is content that should not be included in the operational requirement section of the document. Which of the following information should be deleted from this section?
   A. response time
   B. data architecture
   C. data conversion
   D. data analysis tools

REFERENCE: Amatayakul, p 386
              Marreel and McLellan, pp 90–100
              McWay, p 401

52. Which of the following is an example of a peripheral?
   A. monitor
   B. scanner
   C. central processing unit
   D. hard drive

REFERENCE: McWay, p 282

53. Maria has received a request to update a patient's insurance number. What system should she use?
   A. executive information system
   B. clinical decision support system
   C. admission-discharge-transfer system
   D. laboratory information system

REFERENCE: Abdelhak, p 179
               Green and Bowie, pp 237–240
               Marreel and McLellan, pp 8, 187
               Sayles, pp 912–913

54. If the database will store video and audio, which of the following database models should be considered?
   A. relational
   B. object oriented
   C. network
   D. hierarchical

REFERENCE: LaTour, Eichenwald-Maki, and Oachs, p 172
               McWay, p 263

55. To enter the results of a CBC into the computer system, you would use a(n)
   A. laboratory system.
   B. radiology system.
   C. pharmacy system.
   D. order entry/results reporting system.

REFERENCE: Sayles and Trawick, p 99

The following questions represent advanced competencies.

56. In developing your Information Systems Strategic Plan, which of the following should be the basis for the plan?
   A. business plan
   B. previous IS strategic plan
   C. consultant's recommendations
   D. previous IS budgets

REFERENCE: Sayles, p 857

57. The vendor that you work for has decided to get into the EHR market. What standard should you suggest using in developing the functions performed by the EHR?
   A. DICOM
   B. LOINC
   C. HL7 EHR functional model
   D. IEEE 1073

REFERENCE: Abdelhak, p 70
               Sayles, p 953

58. When negotiating an information system contract, which of the following would be an example of a performance warranty specified in the contract?
   A. remedies
   B. operational practices
   C. insurances
   D. uptime

REFERENCE: Amatayakul, p 420

59. Critique the following statement:

> The EHR utilizes existing source systems to supply data.

   A. This is true because the EHR uses many source systems to populate the data.
   B. This is false because the EHR is a stand-alone system.
   C. This is false because the EHR requires the latest and greatest system, thus eliminating legacy systems.
   D. This is true because the EHR obtains information SOLELY from the source documents.

REFERENCE: Amatayakul, p 417

60. You have been asked how to handle versioning of documents in the EDMS. Which of the following should be your response?
   A. Delete the first version and retain the second.
   B. Display the second version but identify that a previous version exists.
   C. Do not allow edits to the system.
   D. Display both versions side by side.

REFERENCE: Abdelhak, p 202

61. The physician will be called automatically when a lab result is at the panic level. This is an example of a
   A. data-driven rule.   C. clinical guideline.
   B. database.   D. reminder.

REFERENCE: Murphy, p 338

62. The chief financial officer has decided that he wants to drop bills 36 hours after patient discharge. What would have to be updated?
   A. prototype   C. code
   B. interface   D. setting configuration

REFERENCE: Sayles and Trawick, p 132

63. Dr. Smith accesses the EHR in his office to see what patients are ready to be seen and what calls he needs to make. This functionality is called
   A. checkout   C. registration
   B. the in-basket function   D. the patient summary

REFERENCE: Amatayakul, p 515

64. Which one of the following is necessary during the strategic planning process for the EHR?
    A. gauging the user's readiness for the EHR
    B. writing the request for proposal to be used in selecting the EHR
    C. selecting the EHR to be used
    D. creating a newsletter to keep users informed of the status of EHR

REFERENCE: Amatayakul, p 77

65. The hospital is undergoing the development of an information system strategic plan. The part of the process where changes in the community, legislation, and other factors are monitored is called
    A. health information exchange.   C. environmental scanning.
    B. alerts.   D. critical path analysis.

REFERENCE: Glandon, Smaltz, and Slovensky, pp 124–125
               McWay, p 325

66. You are logging into a system and there is a string of characters that you have to enter. These characters are distorted. What kind of access control is this?
    A. CAPTCHA   C. token
    B. biometrics   D. two-factor authentication

REFERENCE: Sayles, p 1039

Patient
Last name
First name
Middle initial
Street address
City
State
Zip
Medical record number
Date of birth

67. You are developing an entity relationship diagram. In the entity of the patient shown above, which of the attributes is the primary key?
    A. last name
    B. combination of last and first names
    C. street address
    D. medical record number

REFERENCE: McWay, pp 263–264
               Sayles and Trawick, p 96

68. A preliminary step prior to issuing a formal RFP, which allows the facility to narrow down the field of potential vendors for procurement of a new hospital-wide computer system, would be to
    A. select the system to be purchased.
    B. create a Gantt chart to monitor project progress.
    C. issue a request for information (RFI) to potential vendors.
    D. initiate contract negotiations.

REFERENCE: LaTour, Eichenwald-Maki, and Oachs, p 106
                 Marreel and McLellan, pp 88–90
                 McWay, p 401

69. Administration has asked the clinical provider order-entry task force to select the method of implementation that will reduce risk to the hospital. What method should they choose?
    A. Implement all modules across the entire organization.
    B. Implement one module in one unit while running the current system in parallel.
    C. Implement all modules across the entire organization while running the current system in parallel.
    D. Implement one module in one unit while shutting down the existing system.

REFERENCE: Sayles, p 867

70. The information system has just notified you that someone has attempted to access the system inappropriately. This process is known as
    A. integrity   C. intrusion detection
    B. intrusion protocol   D. cryptography

REFERENCE: Sayles, p 1043

71. You recently installed a new computer system and you just learned that the vendor does not have the right to use one portion of the system. Another company owns the rights to the information contained in this portion of the system. What clause in your contract would you review to see if you are protected from being sued by the other company?
    A. warranties   C. support
    B. indemnification   D. force majeure

REFERENCE: Abdelhak, p 347
                 Marreel and McLellan, p 103

72. Your facility has implemented the clinical systems needed to support the EHR. The knowledge-based and decision support systems will be installed next. Your team has a firm plan to indicate the direction you should take and the expected timeframe. This is called a
    A. cost-benefit analysis.   C. critical path.
    B. migration path.   D. value realization.

REFERENCE: Amatayakul, p 162

73. Which of the following is an example of two-factor authentication?
    A. user name and password
    B. token and smart card
    C. fingerprint and retinal scan
    D. password and token

REFERENCE: Abdelhak, p 287
               LaTour, Eichenwald-Maki, and Oachs, p 134
               McWay, p 290
               Sayles, p 1039
               Sayles and Trawick, p 322

74. As Director of Health Information Services, you are negotiating a contract to purchase a new computerized dictation system that will be used across three satellite ambulatory clinics. What element is most critical in the contract negotiation to ensure use of the software in multiple environments?
    A. delivery terms
    B. scope and term of warranties
    C. price and payment terms
    D. license grant

REFERENCE: Abdelhak, p 347

75. The most secure model of signatures used in information systems is
    A. digital signature.
    B. electronic signature.
    C. digitized signature.
    D. there is no difference in the level of security between these models.

REFERENCE: Sayles and Trawick, p 253

76. Which of the following situations would be an appropriate use of a DSS?
    A. determining the number of staff needed on the nursing unit
    B. establishing the productivity standard for the organization
    C. generating a report that aggregates data from multiple information system, including both clinical and financial data
    D. determining whether or not to purchase a new MRI machine so that there are two instead of just one

REFERENCE: LaTour, Eichenwald-Maki, and Oachs, p 194

77. You need a report that includes only Medicare patients. What operation enables you to generate this report?
    A. filtering
    B. sorting
    C. grouping
    D. calculations

REFERENCE: Sayles and Trawick, p 174

78. Which of these functions is found in an ambulatory EHR but not in an acute care EHR?
    A. results review
    B. online documentation
    C. eMAR
    D. registration

REFERENCE: Amatayakul, p 511

79. Which of the following is a risky practice in the EHR?
    A. copy and paste
    B. data reuse
    C. free text
    D. graphical user interface

REFERENCE: Amatayakul, p 321

80. Which of the following would be considered unsecured e-PHI?
    A. encrypted data on a portable device
    B. encrypted data on a file sever
    C. a hard drive that has been degaussed
    D. a hard drive that has had the data deleted

REFERENCE: Sayles, pp 1059–1060

81. The facility is implementing a new PACS. They know that the volume of data that will be passing over the Internet will significantly increase. As a result, they have updated their network. They want to determine if the updated network can handle the amount of data that is expected to be sent across the system. Which type of testing would they use?
    A. conversion
    B. functionality
    C. interface
    D. load or volume

REFERENCE: Abdelhak, p 331
                Amatayakul, p 419

© Cengage Learning 2015

82. Which of the following relationships does the diagram above demonstrate?
    A. one to one
    B. many to many
    C. one to many
    D. one and only one

REFERENCE: Abdelhak, p 316

83. There was an unexpected hardware failure for our EHR. It is expected to be up and operational in 3 hours. Until then, which of the following plans would you need to initiate?
    A. information system strategic plan
    B. implementation plan
    C. business continuity plan
    D. project planning

REFERENCE: Glandon, Smaltz, and Slovensky, p 191
                Sayles and Trawick, pp 173–174

84. You have been asked to develop scenarios that will be used to design and program a new release of information system. These scenarios will include the processes to be used in detail. What are you designing?
  A. strategic plan
  B. functional requirements
  C. use cases
  D. request for proposal

REFERENCE: Abdelhak, p 319
               Sayles and Trawick, p 258

85. Mountaintop Hospital has decided to use the "best of breed" philosophy. Because of this, they need a(n) _____ to manage the sharing of data.
  A. DBMS
  B. RFP
  C. consultant
  D. interface engine

REFERENCE: Amatayakul, p 375
               Marreel and McLellan, p 198

86. The HIM supervisor is evaluating software that would utilize electronic logging and monitoring of requests for copies of patient information and develop an accounting of disclosure. What department function is this most useful for?
  A. release of information/disclosure management
  B. record completion
  C. record location/tracking
  D. transcription

REFERENCE: Green and Bowie, pp 296–298
               Sayles and Trawick, p 182

87. You have been asked to identify and display the existing record processing workflow with the paper record. After you finish this, you will redesign the process and display the new process. What tool should you use?
  A. policy and procedure
  B. data dictionary
  C. data flow diagram
  D data mapping

REFERENCE: Abdelhak, p 310
               Sayles and Trawick, p 97

88. Installation of a new electronic document management system is scheduled for the HIM department. The department director calls a meeting of the HIM supervisors to coordinate plans for training the HIM staff. What key factors must be taken into consideration as part of the training preparation process?
  A. the total storage capacity and price of the new system
  B. collecting the results of the RFP responses and vendor selection process used during the selection process
  C. presentation content and scheduling to accommodate all employee shifts
  D. scheduling training times and locations for all physicians and hospital personnel who will use the system

REFERENCE: Abdelhak, p 330
               LaTour, Eichenwald-Maki, and Oachs, p 107

89. The patient's blood pressure is automatically being recorded. This is an example of what type of clinical information system?
    A. patient monitoring system
    B. medical documentation
    C. nursing applications
    D. patient registration

REFERENCE: Green and Bowie, p 115

90. You have been asked to establish guidelines on screen design that will be used in all of your information system projects. Which of the following standards would be included in your guidelines?
    A. The screen should read right to left.
    B. Eliminate all hyperlinks.
    C. Provide instructions on how to complete the screen.
    D. Use red and green to flag key data.

REFERENCE: Abdelhak, p 121

91. You are entering the valid choices for each of the data elements, defining each data element and more. You must be managing the
    A. functional requirement.
    B. data dictionary.
    C. system analysis.
    D. data flow diagram.

REFERENCE: Abdelhak, p 121
               LaTour, Eichenwald-Maki, and Oachs, p 172
               McWay, p 262
               Sayles, p 884

92. Your department must send information electronically to the state health department every day. Currently this is taking a significant amount of time. What technology can be used to automatically send this information without human intervention?
    A. electronic data interchange
    B. LAN
    C. Internet
    D. network interface card

REFERENCE: Glandon, Smaltz, and Slovensky, p 159
               LaTour, Eichenwald-Maki, and Oachs, p 90
               Marreel and McLellan, pp 4, 55–60
               McWay, p 266
               Sayles, p 895

93. Which of the following is an example of Wen 2.0 technologies?
    A. a blog
    B. a chat room
    C. web pages
    D. an extranet

REFERENCE: LaTour, Eichenwald-Maki, and Oachs, p 99

94. The three components of a security program are protecting the privacy of data, ensuring the integrity of data, and ensuring the _____.
    A. validity of data
    B. availability of data
    C. security of hardware
    D. security of data

REFERENCE: Sayles, p 1026

95. You have had a problem with duplicate medical record numbers in your facility's MPI. Now you are joining a health information exchange, so you will need to clean up your database and prevent the duplicates from happening again. If you want to find near matches as well as identical matches in your MPI, you should implement a _____ algorithm.
    A. probabilistic
    B. deterministic
    C. fuzzy
    D. none of the above

REFERENCE: Gudea, p 51
Sayles and Trawick, p 217

96. Juan has been asked to investigate e-health companies. Which of the following would NOT be included in his investigation?
    A. Health Data: a company that stores patient identifiable health information online.
    B. HealthInfo: a company that provides medical references to patients.
    C. Physician Services: a company that provides medical references to physicians.
    D. Café Services: a company that provides cafeteria services to the hospital.

REFERENCE: Fuller, p 50
McWay, p 311

97. If your network was graphed, it would show a hub in the middle with nodes surrounding it. What type of network is it and why would you choose it?
    A. Star, ease of adding computers
    B. Ring, operates over high distance
    C. Bus, ease of adding computers
    D. Ring, does not go down much

REFERENCE: Glandon, Smaltz, and Slovensky, p 158

98. Dr. Smith has a practice in Macon, Georgia. He is treating a patient who is physically located in Soperton, Georgia, which is about 70 miles away. What technology is required for Dr. Smith to treat the patient?
    A. EHR
    B. clinical data repository
    C. telehealth
    D. cloud computing

REFERENCE: LaTour, Eichenwald-Maki, and Oachs, p 97

99. The patient has been on medication X for several years. A physician ordered medication Y. The information system immediately sends the physician a message that says that medication Y is contraindicated due to medication X. What technology is being used?
    A. point-of-care system
    B. clinical decision support systems
    C. EHR
    D. order entry results reporting

REFERENCE: Abdelhak, p 182
               Glandon, Smaltz, and Slovensky, p 222
               Sayles and Trawick, p 249

100. The new computer hardware arrived and the technical staff was not able to install it because there was not enough space in the computer room. Which of the following implementation steps was not properly executed?
    A. system evaluation   C. site preparation
    B. conversion   D. user preparation

REFERENCE: Abdelhak, p 331
               Sayles and Trawick, p 132

101. You are considering three vendors for your new encoder. Your facility wants to purchase the system from a stable company. After reviewing the vendor profile information below, which of the vendors would you eliminate from consideration?

Topic	Vendor A	Vendor B	Vendor C
Number of years in business	2	10	3
Number of installations	72	135	5
Number of installation staff	3	4	1
Age of product	2	6	3
Financial standing	Good	Excellent	Fair

    A. Vendor A   C. Vendor C
    B. Vendor B   D. You cannot eliminate any of the vendors.

REFERENCE: Marreel and McLellan, pp 101–106
               Sayles and Trawick, p 126

Answer Key for Informatics and Information Systems

1.	A	43.	B
2.	B	44.	A
3.	B	45.	D
4.	C	46.	A
5.	A	47.	A
6.	D	48.	A
7.	D	49.	C
8.	B	50.	B
9.	B	51.	C
10.	A	52.	B
11.	C	53.	C
12.	B	54.	A
13.	D	55.	A
14.	C	56.	A
15.	C	57.	C
16.	D	58.	D
17.	C	59.	A
18.	D	60.	B
19.	C	61.	A
20.	D	62.	D
21.	A	63.	B
22.	A	64.	A
23.	B	65.	C
24.	C	66.	A
25.	A	67.	D
26.	A	68.	C
27.	A	69.	B
28.	B	70.	C
29.	C	71.	B
30.	C	72.	B
31.	A	73.	D
32.	C	74.	D
33.	A	75.	A
34.	B	76.	D
35.	C	77.	A
36.	B	78.	D
37.	D	79.	A
38.	D	80.	D
39.	B	81.	D
40.	C	82.	A
41.	D	83.	C
42.	C	84.	C

Answer Key for Informatics and Information Systems

85. A   Although the facility may benefit from the services of a consultant and they will need a DBMS to manage the database for the new systems, it is the interface engine that will be needed to manage communication between the various systems.

86. A
87. C
88. C
89. A

90. A
91. B
92. A
93. A
94. B
95. A
96. D
97. A
98. C
99. B
100. C
101. C

REFERENCES

Abdelhak, M., Grostick, S., Hanken, M. A., & Jacobs, E. (2012). *Health information: management of a strategic resource* (4th ed.). Philadelphia: W. B. Saunders.

Amatayakul, M. K. (2012). *Electronic health records: A practical guide for professionals and organizations* (5th ed.). Chicago: American Health Information Management Association.

Eichenwald-Maki, S., & Petterson, B. (2008). *Using the electronic health record.* Clifton Park, NY: Delmar Cengage Learning.

Fuller, S. (2000). To "E" or not to "E": HIM and the dawn of e-health. *Journal of AHIMA, 71*(4), 50–53. Chicago: American Health Information Management Association (AHIMA).

Glandon, G., Smaltz, D., & Slovensky, D. (2008). *Information systems for healthcare management.* Chicago: Health Administration Press.

Green, M. A., & Bowie, M. J. (2011). *Essentials of health information management* (2nd ed.). Clifton Park, NY: Delmar Cengage Learning.

Gudea, S. (2005). Deterministic, probabilistic, or fuzzy? A primer on the search algorithms that drive MPI quality. *Journal of AHIMA, 76*(8), 5–54. Chicago: American Health Information Management Association (AHIMA).

LaTour, K., Eichenwald-Maki, S., and Oachs, P. (2013). *Health information management: Concepts, principles, and practice* (3rd ed.). Chicago: American Health Information Management Association (AHIMA).

Mahoney, M. E. (1997). Document imaging and workflow technology in health care today. *Journal of AHIMA, 68*(4), 28–36. Chicago: American Health Information Management Association (AHIMA).

Marreel, R., & McLellan, J. (1999). *Information management in health care.* Clifton Park, NY: Delmar Cengage Learning.

McWay, D. (2014). *Today's health information management: An integrated approach* (2nd ed.). Chicago: Delmar Cengage Learning.

Murphy, G. F., Hanken, M. A., & Waters, K. (1999). *Electronic health records: Changing the vision.* Philadelphia: W. B. Saunders.

Sayles, N. B. (2013). *Health information management technology: An applied approach* (4th ed.). Chicago: AHIMA Press.

Sayles N. B., & Trawick, K. (2010). *Introduction to computer systems for health information technology.* Chicago: American Health Information Management Association.

Sheridan, C. (2001). Do you need an ASP ASAP? *Journal of AHIMA, 72*(8), 38–42. Chicago: American Health Information Management Association (AHIMA).

Informatics and Information Systems Chapter Domains

Question	RHIA Domain	RHIT Domain
1–101	3	
1–55		4

XI. Health Information Privacy and Security

Nanette B. Sayles, EdD, RHIA, CCS, CHPS, CPHIMS, FAHIMA

1. As Chief Privacy Officer for Premier Medical Center, you are responsible for which of the following?
   A. backing up data
   B. developing a plan for reporting privacy complaints
   C. writing policies on protecting hardware
   D. writing policies on encryption standards

   REFERENCE: Green and Bowie, p 42
                           Hjort (2001), p 64B
                           Krager and Krager, pp 11–12, 41
                           McWay (2014), p 39
                           Sayles, p 829

2. Which of the following situations violate a patient's privacy?
   A. The hospital sends patients who are scheduled for deliveries information on free childbirth classes.
   B. The physician on the quality improvement committee reviews medical records for potential quality problems.
   C. The hospital provides patient names and addresses to a pharmaceutical company to be used in a mass mailing of free drug samples.
   D. The hospital uses aggregate data to determine whether or not to add a new operating room suite.

   REFERENCE: Amatayakul (2001b), p 16B
                           Green and Bowie, p 294
                           Krager and Krager, p 39
                           Sayles, p 827

3. The patient has the right to control access to his or her health information. This is known as
   A. security.
   B. confidentiality.
   C. privacy.
   D. disclosure.

   REFERENCE: McWay (2014), p 71

4. Mary processed a request for information and mailed it out last week. Today, the requestor, an attorney, called and said that all of the requested information was not provided. Mary pulls the documentation, including the authorization and what was sent. She believes that she sent everything that was required based on what was requested. She confirms this with her supervisor. The requestor still believes that some extra documentation is required. Given the above information, which of the following statements is true?
   A. Mary is not required to release the extra documentation because the facility has the right to interpret a request and apply the minimum standard rule.
   B. Mary is required to release the extra documentation because the requestor knows what is needed.
   C. Mary is required to release the extra documentation because, in the customer service program for the facility, the customer is always right.
   D. Mary is not required to release the additional information because her administrator agrees with her.

REFERENCE: Hughes (2002b), p 56A
              Krager and Krager, pp 34–35, 41
              McWay (2010), pp 73–74
              McWay (2010), p 204
              Sayles, p 799

5. Mountain Hospital has discovered a security breach. Someone hacked into the system and viewed 50 medical records. According to ARRA, what is the responsibility of the covered entity?
   A. ARRA does not address this issue.
   B. All individuals must be notified within 30 days.
   C. All individuals must be notified within 60 days.
   D. ARRA requires oral notification.

REFERENCE: Rhodes (2009a), p 10
              Sayles, pp 826–827
              U.S. DHHS 2

6. Physical safeguards include

   1. tools to monitor access
   2. tools to control access to computer systems
   3. fire protection
   4. tools preventing unauthorized access to data

   A. 1 and 2 only   C. 2 and 3 only
   B. 1 and 3 only   D. 2 and 4 only

REFERENCE: Green and Bowie, p 282
              Hartley and Jones, pp 168–170
              Krager and Krager, pp 92–93
              McWay (2010), pp 290–292
              Sayles, p 1055

7. You are reviewing your privacy and security policies, procedures, training program, and so on, and comparing them to the HIPAA and ARRA regulations. You are conducting a
   A. policy assessment.
   B. risk assessment.
   C. compliance audit.
   D. risk management.

   REFERENCE: Hjort (2001), p 64A
   Krager and Krager, pp 86–87, 105
   McWay (2010), pp 258–259

8. Which of the following can be released without consent or authorization?
   A. summary of patient care
   B. de-identified health information
   C. personal health information
   D. protected health information

   REFERENCE: Mcway (2014), p 72

9. Kyle, the HIM Director, has received a request to amend a patient's medical record. The appropriate action for him to take is
   A. make the modification because you have received the request.
   B. file the request in the chart to document the disagreement with the information contained in the medical record.
   C. route the request to the physician who wrote the note in question to determine appropriateness of the amendment.
   D. return the notice to the patient because amendments are not allowed.

   REFERENCE: Green and Bowie, pp 84–85
   Krager and Krager, pp 44–45
   McWay (2014), p 104
   Sayles, p 803
   Thieleman, p 46

10. An employee in the admission department took the patient's name, Social Security number, and other information and used it to get a charge card in the patient's name. This is an example of
    A. identity theft.
    B. mitigation.
    C. disclosure.
    D. release of information.

REFERENCE: McWay (2010), p 219

11. A patient has submitted an authorization to release information to a physician office for continued care. The release of information clerk wants to limit the information provided because of the minimum necessary rule. What should the supervisor tell the clerk?
    A. Good call.
    B. The patient is an exception to the minimum necessary rule, so process the request as written.
    C. The minimum necessary rule was eliminated with ARRA.
    D. The minimum necessary rule only applies to attorneys.

REFERENCE: McWay (2010), p 204
McWay (2014), p 73

12. Patricia is processing a request for medical records. The record contains an operative note and a discharge summary from another hospital. The records are going to another physician for patient care. What should Patricia do?
    A. Notify the requestor that redisclosure is illegal and so he must get the operative and discharge summary records from the original source hospital.
    B. Include the documents from the other hospital.
    C. Redisclose when necessary for patient care.
    D. Redisclose when allowed by law.

REFERENCE: Green and Bowie, pp 295–296
Hughes (2001b), p 72B
Krager and Krager, pp 127–128
Sayles, p 799

13. Before a user is allowed to access protected health information, the system confirms that the patient is who he or she says they are. This is known as
    A. access control.
    B. notification.
    C. authorization.
    D. authentication.

REFERENCE: McWay (2014), p 290

14. Contingency planning includes which of the following processes?
    A. data quality   C. disaster planning
    B. systems analysis   D. hiring practices

REFERENCE: McWay (2014), p 290

15. Which of the following disclosures would require patient authorization?
    A. law enforcement activities
    B. workers' compensation
    C. release to patient's family
    D. public health activities

REFERENCE: Green and Bowie, pp 291–294
               Hartley and Jones, pp 103–198
               LaTour, Eichenwald-Maki, and Oachs, p 316

16. Your department was unable to provide a patient with a copy of his record within the 30-day limitation. What should you do?
    A. Call the patient and apologize.
    B. Call the patient and let him know that you will need a 30-day extension.
    C. Write the patient and tell him that you will need a 30-day extension.
    D. Both write and call the patient to tell him you need a 30-day extension.

REFERENCE: Green and Bowie, p 295

17. I have been asked if I want to be in the directory. The admission clerk explains that if I am in the directory,
    A. my friends and family can find out my room number.
    B. my condition can be discussed with any caller in detail.
    C. my condition can be released to the news media.
    D. my condition can be released to hospital staff only.

REFERENCE: Krager and Krager, pp 35–36, 40, 124–125
               Roach, p 172
               Sayles, p 907

18. Which of the following techniques would a facility employ for access control?

    1. automatic logoff
    2. authentication
    3. integrity controls
    4. unique user identification

    A. 1 and 4 only   C. 2 and 4 only
    B. 1 and 2 only   D. 3 and 4 only

REFERENCE: Green and Bowie, pp 282–283
               Hartley and Jones, pp 170–171
               Krager and Krager, pp 96–98
               Sayles, p 1037

19. Which of the following statements is true about the Privacy Act of 1974?
    A. It applies to all organizations that maintain health care data in any form.
    B. It applies to all health care organizations.
    C. It applies to the federal government.
    D. It applies to federal government except for the Veterans Health Administration.

REFERENCE: LaTour, Eichenwald-Maki, and Oachs, p 310

20. Which of the following statements is true about a requested restriction?
    A. ARRA mandates that a CE must comply with a requested restriction.
    B. ARRA states that a CE does not have to agree to a requested restriction.
    C. ARRA mandates that a CE must comply with a requested restriction unless it meets one of the exceptions.
    D. ARRA does not address restrictions to PHI.

REFERENCE: Rhodes (2009a), p 13
               Sayles, p 807

21. Which of the following is an example of administrative safeguards under the security rule?
    A. encryption
    B. monitoring the computer access activity of the user
    C. assigning unique identifiers
    D. monitoring traffic on the network

REFERENCE: McWay (2014), p 291

22. Someone accessed the covered entity's electronic health record and sold the information that was accessed. This person is known as which of the following?
    A. malware
    B. a virus
    C. a hacker
    D. a cracker

REFERENCE: McWay (2014), p 290

23. Intentional threats to security could include
    A. a natural disaster (flood).
    B. equipment failure (software failure).
    C. human error (data entry error).
    D. data theft (unauthorized downloading of files).

REFERENCE: Sayles, pp 1029–1030

24. Which of the following would be a business associate?
    A. release of information company
    B. bulk food service provider
    C. childbirth class instructor
    D. security guards

REFERENCE: Krager and Krager, p 42
               McWay (2010), p 215
               McWay (2014), p 68

25. Which of the following statements demonstrates a violation of protected health information?
    A. "Can you help me find Mary Smith's record?"
    B. A member of the physician's office staff calls centralized scheduling and says, "Dr. Smith wants to perform a bunionectomy on Mary Jones next Tuesday."
    C. "Mary, at work yesterday I saw that Susan had a hysterectomy."
    D. Dr. Jones tells a nurse on the floor to give Ms. Brown Demerol for her pain.

REFERENCE: Krager and Krager, pp 19, 29–30
              McWay (2014), p 72
              Roach, p 45
              Sayles, p 799

26. Mark, a patient of Schnering Hospital, has asked for an electronic copy of his medical record to go to his physician. According to ARRA, what is the CE's obligation to Mark?
    A. None, as this is prohibited by HIPAA.
    B. None, as this is prohibited by ARRA.
    C. Mark has a right to an electronic copy, but it has to go to him, not a third party.
    D. Mark has a right to an electronic copy or to have it sent to someone else.

REFERENCE: Rhodes (2009a), p 16

27. Margot looked up PHI on her ex-sister-in-law. A routine audit discovered the violation. Which statement is true under ARRA?
    A. Margot cannot be prosecuted since she is not a covered entity.
    B. Margot cannot be prosecuted since she is not a covered entity or business associate.
    C. Margot cannot be prosecuted since she did not sell the PHI.
    D. Margot can be prosecuted.

REFERENCE: Rhodes (2009a), p 18

28. You are defining the designated record set for South Beach Healthcare Center. Which of the following would be included?
    A. quality reports
    B. psychotherapy notes
    C. discharge summary
    D. information compiled for use in civil hearing

REFERENCE: Amatayakul and Waymack, p 16A
              Krager and Krager, p 31
              LaTour, Eichenwald-Maki, and Oachs, p 314
              Sayles, pp 798–799

29. You have been asked to provide examples of technical security measures. Which of the following would you include in your list of examples?
    A. locked doors   C. minimum necessary
    B. automatic logout   D. training

REFERENCE: Green and Bowie, p 283
              Krager and Krager, pp 90–100
              McWay (2014), p 292

30. Which security measure utilizes fingerprints or retina scans?
    A. audit trail
    B. biometrics
    C. authentication
    D. encryption

REFERENCE: Abdelhak, p 288
Fuller, p 40
Green and Bowie, p 283
Krager and Krager, pp 96–97
Sayles, p 1038

31. Ms. Thomas was a patient at your facility. She has been told that there are some records that she cannot have access to. These records are most likely
    A. psychotherapy notes.
    B. alcohol and drug records.
    C. AIDS records.
    D. mental health assessment.

REFERENCE: Green and Bowie, pp 278, 294–295
Hughes (2001a), p 90
Krager and Krager, pp 38–39
Sayles, p 800

32. Your organization is sending confidential patient information across the Internet using technology that will transform the original data into unintelligible code that can be re-created by authorized users. This technique is called
    A. a firewall.
    B. validity processing.
    C. a call-back process.
    D. data encryption.

REFERENCE: Abdelhak, p 289
Green and Bowie, p 283
Krager and Krager, pp 99–100
McWay (2014), p 290
Sayles, p 1042

33. When patients are able to obtain a copy of their health record, this is an example of which of the following?
    A. a required standard
    B. an addressable requirement
    C. a patient right
    D. a preemption

REFERENCE: McWay (2014), p 69

34. Which of the following should the record destruction program include?
    A. the method of destruction
    B. the name of the supervisor of the person destroying the records
    C. citing the laws followed
    D. requirement of daily destruction

REFERENCE: Green and Bowie, pp 96–97
                LaTour, Eichenwald-Maki, and Oachs, p 279
                McWay (2014), p 136
                Sayles, pp 346–347

35. You are looking for potential problems and violations of the privacy rule. What is this security management process called?
    A. risk management
    B. risk assessment
    C. risk aversion
    D. business continuity planning

REFERENCE: Green, p 281

36. The administrator states that he should not have to participate in privacy and security training as he does not use PHI. How should you respond?
    A. "All employees are required to participate in the training, including top administration."
    B. "I will record that in my files."
    C. "Did you read the privacy rules?"
    D. "You are correct. There is no reason for you to participate in the training."

REFERENCE: Hartley and Jones, p 84
                Krager and Krager, p 90
                Sayles, p 829

37. The surgeon comes out to speak to a patient's family. He tells them that the patient came through the surgery fine. The mass was benign and they could see the patient in an hour. He talks low so that the other people in the waiting room will not hear but someone walked by and heard. This is called a(n)
    A. privacy breach.   C. incidental disclosure.
    B. violation of policy.   D. privacy incident.

REFERENCE: Krager and Krager, pp 19, 36
                Sayles, p 819

38. The HIPAA security rule does not require specific technologies to be used but rather provides direction on the outcome. The term used to describe this philosophy is
    A. technology free.
    B. technology neutral.
    C. administrative rules.
    D. generic technology.

REFERENCE: Krager and Krager, p 101
               Roach, p 460

39. A mechanism to ensure that PHI has not been altered or destroyed inappropriately has been established. This process is called
    A. entity authentication.
    B. audit controls.
    C. access control.
    D. integrity.

REFERENCE: Green, p 283

40. America LTD. has developed a PHR. According to ARRA, the health information that they store is
    A. not protected.
    B. protected.
    C. mandated to be de-identified.
    D. subject to security, but not privacy, requirements.

REFERENCE: Rhodes (2009a), p 2
               U.S. DHHS 6

41. The hospital has received a request for an amendment. How long does the facility have in order to accept or deny the request?
    A. 30 days   C. 14 days
    B. 60 days   D. 10 days

REFERENCE: Green and Bowie, pp 84–85
               Krager and Krager, pp 23–24, 44
               Roach, p 233
               Sayles (2013), p 804

42. You work for a 60-bed hospital in a rural community. You are conducting research on what you need to do to comply with HIPAA. You are afraid that you will have to implement all of the steps that your friend at a 900-bed teaching hospital is implementing at his facility. You continue reading and learn that you only have to implement what is prudent and reasonable for your facility. This is called
    A. scalable.
    B. risk assessment.
    C. technology neutral.
    D. access control.

REFERENCE: Krager and Krager, p 87
               McWay (2014), p 291

43. Barbara, a nurse, has been flagged for review because she logged in to the EHR in the evening when she usually works the day shift. Why should this conduct be reviewed?
    A. This is a privacy violation.
    B. This needs to be investigated before a decision is made because there may be a legitimate reason why she logged in at this time.
    C. This is not a violation since Barbara, as a nurse, has full access to data in the EHR.
    D. No action is required.

REFERENCE: Sayles and Trawick, p 324

44. Alisa has trouble remembering her password. She is trying to come up with a solution that will help her remember. Which one of the following would be the BEST practice?
    A. using the word "password" for her password
    B. using her daughter's name for her password
    C. writing the complex password on the last page of her calendar
    D. creating a password that utilizes a combination of letters and numbers

REFERENCE: Amatayakul and Walsh, p 16C
               Krager and Krager, pp 88–89, 97
               Sayles, p 1038

45. Which statement is true about when a family member can be provided with PHI?
    A. The patient's mother can always receive PHI on their child.
    B. The family member lives out of town and cannot come to the facility to check on the patient.
    C. The family member is a health care professional.
    D. The family member is directly involved in the patient's care.

REFERENCE: Green & Bowie, p 273

The following questions represent advanced competencies.

46. HIPAA states that release to a coroner is allowed. State law says that the coroner must provide a subpoena. Which of the following is a correct statement?
    A. Follow the HIPAA requirement since it is a federal law.
    B. Follow the state law since it is stricter.
    C. You can follow either the state law or the HIPAA rule.
    D. You must request a ruling from a judge.

REFERENCE: McWay (2014), p 70

47. The computer system containing the electronic health record was located in a room that was flooded. As a result, the system is inoperable. Which of the following would be implemented?
    A. SWOT analysis
    B. information systems strategic planning
    C. request for proposal
    D. business continuity processes

REFERENCE: Green and Bowie, pp 28–282
               Krager and Krager, pp 91–92
               Sayles, p 1044

48. You have been given the responsibility of destroying the PHI contained in the system's old server before it is trashed. What destruction method do you recommend?
    A. crushing
    B. overwriting data
    C. degaussing
    D. incineration

REFERENCE: Sayles and Trawick, p 317

49. You are walking around the facility to identify any privacy and security issues. You walk onto the 6W nursing unit and from the desk where you are standing you are able to watch the nurse entering confidential patient information. How can you best improve the privacy of the patient's health information?
    A. Ask the nurse to type the data on another computer.
    B. Turn the computer screen so that the public cannot see it.
    C. Give the nurse additional training.
    D. None of the above.

REFERENCE: Amatayakul (2002a), p 16A-C
              Krager and Krager, pp 86–87, 104–105

50. In conducting an environmental risk assessment, which of the following would be considered in the assessment?
    A. placement of water pipes in the facility
    B. verifying that virus checking software is in place
    C. use of single sign-on technology
    D. authentication

REFERENCE: Dennis, p 18
              McWay (2014), p 327
              Sayles, p 1034

51. Which of the following documents is subject to the HIPAA security rule?
    A. document faxed to the facility
    B. copy of discharge summary
    C. paper medical record
    D. scanned operative report stored on CD

REFERENCE: Krager and Krager, pp 6, 84–85
              McWay (2014), p 291
              Roach, p 459

52. A hacker recently accessed our database. We are trying to determine how the hacker got through the firewall and exactly what was accessed. The process used to gather this evidence is called
    A. forensics.   C. security event.
    B. mitigation.   D. incident.

REFERENCE: Sayles and Trawick, p 310

53. As Chief Privacy Officer, you have been asked why you are conducting a risk assessment. Which reason would you give?
    A. to get rid of problem staff
    B. to change organizational culture
    C. to prevent breach of confidentiality
    D. to learn about the organization

REFERENCE: Dennis, p 36
               Krager and Krager, pp 86–87, 105
               McWay (2014), p 326

54. Which of the following situations would require authorization before disclosing PHI?
    A. releasing information to the Bureau of Disability Determination
    B. health oversight activity
    C. workers' compensation
    D. public health activities

REFERENCE: Green & Bowie, p 291

55. A covered entity
    A. is exempt from the HIPAA privacy and security rules.
    B. includes all health care providers.
    C. includes health care providers who perform specified actions electronically.
    D. must utilize business associates.

REFERENCE: Krager and Krager, pp 10–11, 13
               McWay (2014), p 68
               Roach, pp 141–142
               Sayles, p 794

56. Which of the following is an example of a security incident?
    A. Temporary employees were not given individual passwords.
    B. An employee took home a laptop with unsecured PHI.
    C. A handheld device was left unattended on the crash cart in the hall for 10 minutes.
    D. A hacker accessed PHI from off site.

REFERENCE: Sayles and Trawick, p 310

57. Protected health information includes
   A. only electronic individually identifiable health information.
   B. only paper individually identifiable health information.
   C. individually identifiable health information in any format stored by a health care provider.
   D. individually identifiable health information in any format stored by a health care provider or business associate.

REFERENCE: Green and Bowie, pp 272–273
               Krager and Krager, pp 6–8, 28–29
               LaTour, Eichenwald-Maki, and Oachs, p 313
               McWay (2014), p 69
               Roach, p 105
               Sayles, p 797

58. The HIM director received an e-mail from the technology support services department about her e-mail being full and asking for her password. The director contacted tech support and it was confirmed that their department did not send this e-mail. This is an example of what type of malware?
   A. phishing   C. denial of service
   B. spyware   D. virus

REFERENCE: Sayles and Trawick, p 326

59. You have been asked to create a presentation on intentional and unintentional threats. Which of the following should be included in the list of threats you cite?
   A. hard drive failures
   B. data deleted by accident
   C. data loss due to electrical failures
   D. a patient's Social Security number being used for credit card applications

REFERENCE: Sayles and Trawick, p 301

60. The supervisors have decided to give nursing staff access to the EHR. They can add notes, view, and print. This is an example of what?
   A. the termination process
   B. an information system activity review
   C. spoliation
   D. a workforce clearance procedure

REFERENCE: Green and Bowie, p 281

61. The information systems department was performing their routine destruction of data that they do every year. Unfortunately, they accidently deleted a record that is involved in a medical malpractice case. This unintentional destruction of evidence is called
    A. mitigation.
    B. spoliation.
    C. forensics.
    D. a security event.

REFERENCE: Sayles and Trawick, p 310

62. Mark is an HIM employee who utilizes six different information systems as part of his job. Each of these has a different password. In order to keep up with the password for each system, Mark has written them all on paper and taped it to the back of his wife's picture on his desk. What technology could be used to eliminate this problem for Mark and other employees in the same situation?
    A. role-based access   C. SSO
    B. user-based access   D. DAC

REFERENCE: Krager and Krager, pp 88–89, 97
               Miller and Gregory, p 40

63. Cindy, Tiffany, and LaShaundra are all nurses at Sandyshore Health Care. They all have access to the same functions in the information system. It is likely that this facility is using
    A. user-based access.   C. DAC.
    B. role-based access.   D. MAC.

REFERENCE: Krager and Krager, pp 88–89, 105
               Miller and Gregory, p 49

64. You will be choosing the type of encryption to be used for the new EHR. What are your choices?
    A. symmetric and conventional   C. symmetric and asymmetric
    B. asymmetric and public key   D. public key and integrity

REFERENCE: Stallings, p 651

65. You have been given some information that includes the patient's account number. Which statement is true?
    A. This is de-identified information because the patient's name and social security are not included in the data.
    B. This is not de-identified information, because it is possible to identify the patient.
    C. These data are individually identified data.
    D. These data are a limited data set.

REFERENCE: McWay, pp 72, 242, 244

66. Which of the following is an example of a trigger that might be used to reduce auditing?
    A. A patient has not signed their notice of privacy practices.
    B. A patient and user have the same last name.
    C. A nurse is caring for a patient and reviews the patient's record.
    D. The patient is a Medicare patient.

REFERENCE: Sayles and Trawick, p 323

67. Bob submitted his resignation from Coastal Hospital. His last day is today. He should no longer have access to the EHR and other systems as of 5:00 PM today. The removal of his privileges is known as
    A. terminating access.
    B. isolating access.
    C. password management.
    D. sanction policy.

REFERENCE: Green and Bowie, p 281

68. The company's policy states that audit logs, access reports, and security incident reports should be reviewed daily. This review is known as
    A. a data criticality analysis.
    B. a workforce clearinghouse.
    C. an information system activity review.
    D. a risk analysis.

REFERENCE: Green and Bowie, p 281

69. If an authorization is missing a Social Security number, can it be valid?
    A. yes
    B. no
    C. only if the patient is a minor
    D. only if the patient is an adult

REFERENCE: McWay (2014), p 75

70. If the patient has agreed to be in the directory, which of the following statements would be true?
    A. The patient has given up the right to privacy.
    B. The patient's condition can be described in detail with family members but not others.
    C. The patient's condition can be described in general terms like "good" and "fair."
    D. The number of visitors is limited to people on the approved visitor list.

REFERENCE: LaTour, Eichenwald-Maki, and Oachs, p 316

71. Your system just crashed. Fortunately, you have established a site that holds computer processors but not data. This site can be converted to meet our needs quickly. This is a
    A. hot site.   C. redundant site.
    B. cold site.   D. backup site.

REFERENCE: NIST, chap. 11, p 5

72. The purpose of the notice of privacy practices is to
    A. notify the patient of uses of PHI.
    B. notify the patient of audits.
    C. report incidents to the OIG.
    D. notify researchers of allowable data use.

REFERENCE: Green and Bowie, pp 273–278
                Krager and Krager, p 43
                McWay (2014), pp 72–73
                Sayles, p 808

73. You have been asked what should be done with the notice of privacy practice acknowledgment when the patient had been discharged before it was signed. Your response is to
    A. shred it.
    B. try to get it signed, and if not, to document the action taken.
    C. keep trying to get the document signed until you succeed, even if you must go to the patient's home.
    D. File the blank form in the chart.

REFERENCE: LaTour, Eichenwald-Maki, and Oachs, p 314

74. Our Web site was attacked by malware that overloaded it. What type of malware was this?
    A. phishing   C. denial of service
    B. virus   D. spyware

REFERENCE: Sayles & Trawick, p 326

75. Mabel is a volunteer at a hospital. She works at the information desk. A visitor comes to the desk and says that he wants to know what room John Brown is in. What should Mabel do?
    A. Look the patient up and give the room number to the visitor.
    B. Look the patient up to see if John has agreed to be in the directory. If he has, then give the room number to the visitor.
    C. Look the patient up to see if the patient signed a notice of privacy practice. If so, then give the visitor the room number.
    D. Look the patient up in the system to determine if the patient has agreed to TPO usage, and then give the room number to the visitor if he had.

REFERENCE: LaTour, Eichenwald-Maki, and Oachs, p 316
                Sayles, p 815

76. Which of the following is a true statement about symmetric encryption?
    A. Symmetric encryption uses a private and public key.
    B. Symmetric encryption is also known as secure socket layer.
    C. Symmetric encryption assigns a public key to data.
    D. Symmetric encryption assigns a secret key to data.

REFERENCE: Roach, pp 466–468

77. The facility had a security breach. The breach was identified on October 10, 2013. The investigation was completed on October 15, 2013. What is the deadline that the notification must be completed?
    A. 60 days from October 10
    B. 60 days from October 15
    C. 30 days from October 10
    D. 30 days from October 15

REFERENCE: Sayles, pp 826–827
                U.S. Department of Health and Human Services (n.d.)

78. Miles has asked you to explain the rights he has via HIPAA privacy standards. Which of the following is one of his HIPAA-given rights?
    A. He can review his bill.
    B. He can ask to be contacted at an alternative site.
    C. He can discuss financial arrangements with business office staff.
    D. He can ask a patient advocate to sit in on all appointments at the facility.

REFERENCE: LaTour, Eichenwald-Maki, and Oachs, pp 314–315
                McWay (2014), p 104
                Sayles, p 802
                U.S. Office of Civil Rights (n.d.), pp 1–2

79. The following is a sentence from the notice of privacy practices. What problem do you identify?

The party of the first part vows to mitigate breaches should a security incident occur.

    A. None, because that is the responsibility of a covered entity.
    B. None, because that is the responsibility of a business associate.
    C. It is not the responsibility of a covered entity.
    D. It is not written in plain English.

REFERENCE: Krager and Krager, p 31
                U.S. Department of Health and Human Services Office for Civil Rights

80. HIPAA workforce security requires
    A. a criminal background check.
    B. a two-factor authentication.
    C. that access to PHI be appropriate.
    D. the use of card keys.

REFERENCE: Krager and Krager, pp 88–89
                Roach, p 463

81. To prevent our network from going down, we have duplicated much of our hardware and cables. This duplication is called
    A. emergency mode plan.
    B. redundancy.
    C. contingency plan.
    D. business continuity planning.

REFERENCE: Sayles & Trawick, p 313

82. Richard has asked to view his medical record. How long does the facility have to provide this record to him?
    A. 30 days
    B. 60 days
    C. 14 days
    D. 10 days

REFERENCE: Sayles, p 801
                U.S. Department of Health and Human Services Office for Civil Rights

83. A patient authorizes Park Hospital to send a copy of a discharge summary for the latest hospitalization to Flowers Hospital. The hospital uses the discharge summary in the patient's care and files it in the medical record. When Flowers Hospital receives a request for records, a copy of Park Hospital's discharge summary is sent. This is an example of
    A. a privacy violation.
    B. redisclosure.
    C. satisfactory assurance.
    D. inappropriate release.

REFERENCE: Abdelhak, p 540
                Green and Bowie, pp 295–296
                Krager and Krager, pp 127–128
                Servais, pp 345–349

84. You have to decide which type of firewall you want to use in your facility. Which of the following is one of your options?
    A. packet filter
    B. secure socket layer
    C. CCOW
    D. denial of service

REFERENCE: Abdelhak, p 289

85. A data use agreement is required when
    A. a complaint has been filed.
    B. a limited data set is used.
    C. a notice of disclosure is requested.
    D. information is provided to a business associate.

REFERENCE: McWay, p 272

86. What type of digital signature uses encryption?
    A. digitized signature
    B. electronic signature
    C. digital signature
    D. encryption is not a part of digital signatures

REFERENCE: Sayles and Trawick, p 253

87. The police came to the HIM Department today and asked that a patient's right to an accounting of disclosure be suspended for two months. What is the proper response to this request?
    A. "I'm sorry officer, but privacy regulations do not allow us to do this."
    B. "I'm sorry officer but we can only do this for one month."
    C. "Certainly officer. We will take care of that right now."
    D. "Certainly officer. We will be glad to do that as soon as we have the request in writing."

REFERENCE: Green and Bowie, p 296

88. Which of the following set(s) is an appropriate use of the emergency access procedure?
    A. A patient is crashing. The attending physician is not in the hospital, so a physician who is available helps the patient.
    B. One of the nurses is at lunch. The nurse covering for her needs patient information.
    C. The coder who usually codes the emergency room charts is out sick and the charts are left on a desk in the ER admitting area.
    D. A and B.

REFERENCE: Green and Bowie, pp 273, 275, 278
               Krager and Krager, pp 89, 105
               U.S. HHS OCR, 1

89. Today is August 30, 2013. When can the training records for the HIPAA privacy training being conducted today be destroyed?
    A. August 30, 2017
    B. August 30, 2018
    C. August 30, 2019
    D. August 30, 2020

REFERENCE: Hjort (2002), p 60 A–G
                         Krager and Krager, p 90

90. We have just identified that an employee looked up his own medical record. Which of the following actions should be taken?
    A. Notify his or her supervisor because this is a minor incident and therefore not subject to the incident response procedure.
    B. Follow the incident response procedure.
    C. Terminate the employee on the spot.
    D. Notify OCR.

REFERENCE: U.S. HHS, OCR, 2

91. Your facility just learned that one of its business associates is out of compliance with your contract and with the privacy rule. What should your response be according to ARRA?
    A. Educate the business associate and conduct an audit in 30 days.
    B. Educate the business associate. Request that the problem be corrected by the business associate within 60 days.
    C. Request that the problem be corrected by the business associate within 60 days.
    D. Request that the business associate correct the problem or stop doing business with the organization.

REFERENCE: Rhodes and Rode, p 39

92. You have been assigned the responsibility of performing an audit to confirm that all of the workforce's access is appropriate for their role in the organization. This process is called
    A. risk assessment.
    B. information system activity review.
    C. workforce clearance procedure.
    D. information access management.

REFERENCE: Sayles and Trawick, p 305

93. A data use agreement allows the organization receiving the data to
    A. use the non-PHI data any way they want.
    B. use PHI data any way they want.
    C. use data only within the bounds of the agreement.
    D. conduct business for the organization.

REFERENCE: U.S. Department of Health and Human Services Office for Civil Rights (2003), p 31

94. Which of the following is subject to the HIPAA security rule?
    A. x-ray films stored in radiology
    B. paper medical record
    C. faxed records
    D. clinical data repository

REFERENCE: Roach, p 459

95. You work for an organization that publishes a health information management journal and provides clearinghouse services. What must you do?
    A. Have the same security plan for the entire organization.
    B. Separate the e-PHI from the noncovered entity portion of the organization.
    C. Train the journal staff on HIPAA security awareness.
    D. Follow the same rules in all parts of the organization.

REFERENCE: Sayles and Trawick, p 306

96. Robert Burchfield was recently caught accessing his wife's medical record. The system automatically notified the staff of a potential breach due to the same last name for the user and the patient. This was an example of a
    A. trigger.
    B. biometrics.
    C. telephone callback procedures.
    D. transmission security.

REFERENCE: Sayles and Trawick, p 323

97. Your facility just learned that some PHI was posted to the Internet in error. The PHI was online for 2 days before the problem was found. Unfortunately, there were people who visited the Web page during this time. Four hundred patients were impacted. Which of the following applies?
    A. The media must be notified.
    B. Patients as well as Health and Human Services must be notified.
    C. Health and Human Services must be notified within 60 days.
    D. The media and Health and Human Services must be notified.

REFERENCE: U.S. Department of Health and Human Services (n.d.)

98. An organization that is a covered entity, that performs functions that are covered and noncovered by HIPAA, and that specifies the portion of the organization that will be subject to HIPAA is called a(n)
    A. hybrid entity.
    B. affiliated covered entity.
    C. organized health care arrangement.
    D. business associate.

REFERENCE: Roach, p 149

99. The facility can release information to which of the following requesters without a patient authorization?
    A. the public health department
    B. the nurse caring for the patient
    C. a court with a court order
    D. a business associate

REFERENCE: Green and Bowie, p 289

100. Researchers can access patient information if it is
    A. protected health information.
    B. a limited data set.
    C. patient specific.
    D. related to identity theft.

REFERENCE: McWay (2010), p 231

Answer Key for Health Information Privacy and Security

ANSWER   EXPLANATION

1. B
2. C   The release of childbirth information is acceptable because it is related to the reason for admission. The mass mailing of samples violates giving out confidential information to outside agencies.
3. C
4. A
5. C
6. C
7. B
8. B
9. C   The person who recorded the documentation in question should be the one who authorizes the change. While these references may not explicitly state this, it does state that the form should have a place for the provider's signature and comments.
10. A
11. B
12. B
13. D
14. C
15. C
16. C
17. A
18. A
19. C
20. C
21. B
22. D
23. D   Natural disasters, equipment failure, and human error are usually unintentional threats to security. Data theft is intentional.
24. A
25. C
26. D
27. D
28. C
29. B
30. B
31. A
32. D
33. C
34. A
35. B
36. A
37. C
38. B
39. D
40. B
41. B   The request must be acted on within 60 days after receipt; however, the response may be extended once by 30 days, with a written statement with reason and response date.
42. A
43. B
44. D
45. D
46. B
47. D
48. C
49. B
50. A
51. D
52. A
53. C
54. A
55. C
56. D
57. D
58. A
59. D
60. D
61. B
62. C
63. B
64. C
65. B
66. B

Answer Key for Health Information Privacy and Security

ANSWER   EXPLANATION

67. A		
68. C		
69. A		
70. C		
71. B		
72. A		
73. B		
74. C		
75. B		
76. D		
77. A		
78. B		
79. D	The Notice of Privacy must be written in plain English so that it can be understood.	
80. C		
81. B		
82. A		
83. B		

84. B		
85. B		
86. C		
87. D		
88. D		
89. C		
90. B		
91. D		
92. C		
93. C		
94. D	The security rule only applies to e-PHI.
95. B		
96. A		
97. B		
98. A		
99. C		
100. B		

REFERENCES

Abdelhak, M., Grostick, S., Hanken, M. A., & Jacobs, E. (2012). *Health information: Management of a strategic resource* (4th ed.). Philadelphia: W. B. Saunders.

Amatayakul, M. (2001a). HIPAA on the job series: Five steps to reading the HIPAA rules. *Journal of AHIMA, 72*(8), 16A–C.

Amatayakul, M. (2001b). HIPAA on the job series: Managing individual rights requirements under HIPAA privacy. *Journal of AHIMA, 72*(6), 16A–D.

Amatayakul, M. (2002a). HIPAA on the job: A reasonable approach to physical security. *Journal of AHIMA, 73*(4), 16A–C.

Amatayakul, M. (2002b). United under HIPAA: A comparison of arrangements and agreements. *Journal of AHIMA, 73*(8), 24A–D.

Amatayakul, M. (2012). *Electronic health records a practical guide for professionals and organizations* (5th ed.). Chicago: American Health Information Management Association.

Amatayakul, M., & Walsh, T. (2001). Selecting strong passwords (HIPAA on the job series). *Journal of AHIMA, 72, 40.9,* 16A–D.

Amatayakul, M., & Waymack, P. (2002). What's your designated record set? *Journal of AHIMA, 73*(6), 16A–C.

Cassidy, B. S. (2000). HIPAA on the job: Understanding chain of trust and business partner agreements. *Journal of AHIMA, 71*(9), 16A–C.

Cassidy, B. S. (2001). HIPAA on the job: The next challenge: Employee training on privacy, security. *Journal of AHIMA, 72*(1), 16A–C.

Dennis, J. C. (2000). *Privacy and confidentiality of health information.* San Francisco: Jossey-Bass.

Dougherty, M. (2001). Practice brief: Accounting and tracking disclosure of protected health information. *Journal of AHIMA, 72*(10), 72E–H.

Fuller, S. (1999). Implementing HIPAA security standards—are you ready? *Journal of AHIMA, 70*(9), 38–44.

Green, M. A., & Bowie, M. J. (2011). *Essentials of health information management* (2nd ed.). Clifton Park, NY: Delmar Cengage Learning.

Hartley, C. P., & Jones, III, E. D. (2011). *HIPAA plain and simple: A compliance guide for health care professionals* (2nd ed). Chicago: American Medical Association.

Hjort, B. (2001). AHIMA practice brief: A HIPAA privacy checklist. *Journal of AHIMA, 72*(6), 64A–C.

REFERENCES (continued)

Hjort, B. (2002). Privacy and security training. *Journal of AHIMA, 73*(4), 60A–G.

Hjort, B. (2011). *Practice brief: Security audits.*
Retrieved September 28, 2013, from http://ahima.org
http://library.ahima.org/xpedio/groups/public/documents/ahima/bok1_048702.hcsp?dDocName=bok1_048702

Hughes, G. (2001a). Managing exceptions to HIPAA's patient access rule. *Journal of AHIMA, 72*(9), 90–92.

Hughes, G. (2001b). Practice briefs: Redisclosure of PHI. *Journal of AHIMA, 72*(8), 72A, 72B.

Hughes, G. (2002a). Practice briefs: Notice of information practices (updated). *Journal of AHIMA,* 72(5), 64I–M.

Hughes, G. (2002b). Practice brief: Understanding the minimum necessary standard. *Journal of AHIMA, 73*(1), 56A–B.

Hughes, G. (2002c). Simple steps to tracking disclosures. *Journal of AHIMA, 73*(7), 68–70.

Hughes, G. (2002d). Understanding the privacy rule's amendments. *Journal of AHIMA, 73*(10), 64–66.

Krager, D., & Krager, C. (2008). *HIPAA for health care professionals.* Clifton Park, NY: Delmar Cengage Learning.

LaTour, K. M., Eichenwald-Maki, S., and Oachs, P. K. (2013). *Health information management: Concepts, principles, and practice* (4th ed.). Chicago: American Health Information Management Association.

McWay, D.C. (2014). *Today's health information management: An integrated approach* (2nd ed.). Clifton Park, NY: Delmar Cengage.

McWay, D. C. (2010). *Legal and ethical aspects of health information management.* (3rd ed.). Clifton Park, NY: Delmar Cengage.

Miaoulis, W. M. (2010). Access, use, and disclosure: HITECH's impact on the HIPAA touchstones. *Journal of AHIMA, 81*(3), 38–39, 64.

Miller, L., & Gregory, P. (2002). *CISSP for dummies.* New York: Wiley.

National Institute of Standards and Technology (NIST). (2005). *Special Publication 800-12: An Introduction to Computer Security – The NIST Handbook.* Printed from http://csrc.nist.gov/publications/nistpubs/800-12/800-12-html/

Roach, M. (2001). HIPAA compliance questions for business partner agreements. *Journal of AHIMA,* 72(2), 45–51.

REFERENCES (continued)

Roach, W., Hoban, R., Broccolo, B., Roth, A., & Blanchard, T. (2006). *Medical records and the law.* Sudbury, MA: Jones and Bartlett.

Rhodes, H. (2009a). *Analysis of health care confidentiality, privacy, and security provisions of The American Recovery and Reinvestment Act of 2009, Public Law 111–5.* Retrieved from http://library.ahima.org/xpedio/groups/public/documents/ahima/bok1_044016.pdf.

Rhodes, H. (2009b). Accounting of disclosures: ARRA's impact. *2009 AHIMA Convention Proceedings.*

Rhodes, H., & Rode, D. (2010). HIPAA, too: Many ARRA privacy provisions amend HIPAA, not create new regulations. *Journal of AHIMA, 81*(1), 38–39.

Sayles, N. B. (2013), *Health information technology: An applied approach* (4th ed.). Chicago: AHIMA Press.

Sayles, N. B., & Trawick, K. (2010*). Introduction to computer systems for health information technology.* Chicago: AHIMA Press.

Servais, C., Olderman, N., & Trahan, K. (2008). *The legal health record.* Chicago: American Health Information Management Association.

Stallings, W. (2000). *Data and computer communication* (6th ed.). Upper Saddle River, NJ: Prentice-Hall.

Sullivan, T. (2002). Mind your business associate access: Six steps. *Journal of AHIMA, 73*(9), 92, 94, 96.

Thieleman, W. (2002). A patient friendly approach to the record amendment process. *Journal of AHIMA, 73*(5), 46–47.

U.S. Department of Health and Human Services. (n.d.). Breach notification rule. Retrieved from http://www.hhs.gov/ocr/privacy/hipaa/administrative/breachnotificationrule/index.html

U.S. DHHS 45 CFR Parts 164 and 164. Breach Notification for Unsecured Protected Health Information; Interim Final Rule. Retrieved from http://edocket.access.gpo.gov/2009/pdf/E9-20169.pdf

    U.S. DHHS 1, p. 42768/Section 164.404 (c) Implementation Specifications: Contents of Notification

    U.S. DHHS 2, p. 42768/Section 164.404(a)

    U.S. DHHS 3, p. 42767/Section 164.103 Definitions

    U.S. DHHS 4. p. 42743/Supplementary Information: 1. Background

    U.S. DHHS 5, p. 42760/Summary of Costs and Benefits, 1.a. Affected Entities

    U.S. DHHS 6, p. 42743/Supplementary Information: IV 1. Definitions-Section 164.402

    U.S. DHHS 7, p. 42757/Section V. Impact Statement and Other Required Analyses A Introduction

REFERENCES (continued)

U.S. Department of Health and Human Services Office for Civil Rights. *Standards for Privacy of Individually Identifiable Health Information Security Standards for the Protection of Electronic Protected Health Information General Administrative Requirements, Including Civil Money Penalties: Procedures for Investigations, Imposition of Penalties, and Hearings Regulation Text* 45 CFR Parts 160 and 164 (Unofficial version, as amended through February 16, 2006). Retrieved from http://www.hhs.gov/ocr/privacy/hipaa/administrative/privacyrule/adminsimpregtext.pdf
    U.S. HHS OCR, 1, Section 164.306(a) (1)
    U.S. HHS OCR, 2, Section 164.308(6) (i)

U.S. Office of Civil Rights. (n.d.). *For consumers.* Retrieved from http://www.hhs.gov/ocr/privacy/hipaa/understanding/consumers/index.html

Health Information Privacy and Security

Chapter Competencies

Question	RHIA Domain	RHIT Domain
1–100	5	6

XII. Health Law

Barbara W. Mosley, PhD, RHIA

Lon'Tejuana S. Cooper, MSHA, RHIA, CPM

CASE STUDY #1

Dr. Roberts, an orthopedic surgeon, and Nurse Parrish, head nurse on the orthopedic surgery unit, have had an acrimonious working relationship for years. While making rounds on the unit, Dr. Roberts discovered that the physical therapy evaluation he had ordered for one of his patients had not been performed and became outraged. Even though he did not have proof, Dr. Roberts placed the blame for the missed evaluation with Nurse Parrish. Dr. Roberts wrote in the patient's medical record that Nurse Parrish failed to properly order the physical therapy evaluation because she was incompetent and could not be trusted to carry out even the simplest order. After having read Dr. Roberts's note, Nurse Parrish countered by making a disparaging remark about Dr. Roberts to the medical personnel at the nurses' station. Nurse Parrish stated that Dr. Roberts was the one who was incompetent and was responsible for the needless suffering of countless patients over the years.

1. Referring to Case Study #1, the written statement by Dr. Roberts about Nurse Parrish's professional competence in the patient's medical record can constitute
    A. libel.
    C. perjury.
    B. slander.
    D. defamation.

REFERENCE: Brodnik, pp 76–77
               LaTour, Eichenwald-Maki, and Oachs, p 305
               McWay (2010), pp 80, 411
               Pozgar, pp 47–48, 580
               Roach, p 401

2. Referring to Case Study #1, the oral statement by Nurse Parrish about Dr. Roberts's professional practices at the nurses' station can constitute
    A. libel.
    C. perjury.
    B. slander.
    D. defamation.

REFERENCE: Brodnik, pp 76–77
               LaTour, Eichenwald-Maki, and Oachs, p 305
               McWay (2010), pp 80, 415
               Pozgar, p 600
               Roach, p 401

3. Referring to Case Study #1, what should Dr. Roberts be reminded of regarding his notation in the patient's chart about Nurse Parrish?
    A. It is against the law to mention names of persons who are not actively attending to his patient.
    B. His action violates the 1974 Privacy Act.
    C. The medical record must not be used as a battleground against another professional.
    D. He should erase his note about Nurse Parrish because it is malicious.

REFERENCE: Brodnik, pp 6–8
               Pozgar, pp 283, 297
               Roach, pp 291–292

4. Which type of law is constituted by rules and principles determined by legislative bodies?
    A. statutory law   C. common law
    B. administrative law   D. case law

REFERENCE: Brodnik, pp 14–15
                Green and Bowie, pp 265–267
                LaTour, Eichenwald-Maki, and Oachs, pp 301, 950
                McWay (2010), pp 8–10
                McWay (2014), pp 50, 522
                Pozgar, pp 16, 19, 582
                Roach, pp 6–7

5. Which of the following elements of negligence must be present in order to recover damages?
    A. duty of care; breach of duty of care; value attached to injury is greater than a certain value (ordinarily $1,000); provisions of the HIPAA privacy rule have been met
    B. duty of care; breach of the duty of care; suffered an injury; value attached to injury is greater than a certain value (ordinarily $1,000)
    C. duty of care; breach of duty of care; suffered an injury; defendant's conduct caused the plaintiff harm
    D. breach of duty of care; suffered an injury; value attached to injury is greater than a certain value (ordinarily $1,000); provision of HIPAA privacy rule have been met

REFERENCE: Brodnik, pp 70–71, 75–76, 79
                Green and Bowie, p 267
                LaTour, Eichenwald-Maki, and Oachs, p 304
                McWay (2014), p 65

6. When the physician failed to give the patient the lips of the famous actress as promised, the physician engaged in which of the following?
    A. slander   C. libel
    B. a breach of contract   D. invasion of privacy

REFERENCE: LaTour, Eichenwald-Maki, and Oachs, pp 307–308
                McWay (2010), p 83
                McWay (2014), p 64
                Pozgar, p 87

7. Laws that limit the period during which legal action may be brought against another party are known as
    A. case law.   C. statutes of limitations.
    B. summons.   D. common law.

REFERENCE: Brodnik, pp 81–83
                Green and Bowie, pp 94, 267
                McWay (2010), pp 84–85, 416
                McWay (2014), p 136
                Pozgar, pp 90, 130, 582
                Roach, pp 43–44

8. The protection of a patient's health information is addressed in each of the following EXCEPT
   A. Health Insurance Portability and Accountability Act.
   B. Privacy Act.
   C. Drug Abuse and Treatment Act.
   D. U.S. Patriot Act.

REFERENCE: Brodnik, pp 238–242, 247–248, 256, 263–264
               Green and Bowie, pp 284–285
               McWay (2010), pp 47, 285, 292
               Pozgar, pp 26–27, 279–280
               Roach, pp 104–106

9. In a court of law, Attorney A, the attorney for Sun City Hospital, introduces the medical record from the hospital as evidence. However, Attorney B, the attorney for the defendant, objects on the grounds that the medical record is subject to the hearsay rule, which prohibits its admission as evidence. Attorney B's objection is overridden. Why?
   A. The medical record does not belong to the hospital; therefore, the hospital has no right to release the medical record as evidence.
   B. It would violate physician–patient privilege, even though the patient signed a proper release of information form.
   C. The doctrine of *res ipsa loquitur* prevails; therefore, reference to the medical record is moot.
   D. The medical record may be admitted as business records or as an explicit exception to hearsay rule.

REFERENCE: Brodnik, pp 57–58, 125, 127
               Green and Bowie, pp 270–271
               McWay (2010), pp 50–51, 409
               Pozgar, pp 120–122
               Roach, pp 383–384

10. Medical record information may be exempt from the Freedom of Information Act requirements if the request for information meets the test of being an unwarranted invasion of personal privacy. Which of the following is NOT one of the conditions of the test?
   A. The information must be contained in a personal, medical, or similar file.
   B. The information is generated from federally funded research conducted by a private health care organization.
   C. Disclosure of the information constitutes an invasion of personal privacy.
   D. The severity of the invasion must outweigh the public's interest in disclosure.

REFERENCE: Brodnik, pp 154, 254
               Green and Bowie, p 284
               LaTour and Eichenwald-Maki, pp 310–311
               McWay (2010), p 177
               Roach, pp 123–127

11. The doctrine that the decisions of the court should stand as precedents for future guidance is
    A. res ipsa loquitur.   C. stare decisis.
    B. respondeat superior.   D. statute of limitations.

REFERENCE: Brodnik, p 17
                Green and Bowie, p 257
                McWay (2010), pp 12–13, 15, 18, 415
                Pozgar, pp18, 1582
                Roach, pp 16–18

12. The body of law founded on custom, natural justice and reason, and sanctioned by usage and judicial decision is known as
    A. common law.   C. constitutional law.
    B. lien law.   D. statutory law.

REFERENCE: Brodnik, pp 17, 20
                Green and Bowie, pp 265–267
                LaTour and Eichenwald-Maki, pp 300–301, 903
                McWay (2010), pp 12, 405
                McWay (2014), p 50
                Pozgar, pp 16–19, 578
                Roach, pp 10, 545

CASE STUDY #2

You are the Director of the Health Information Management Department for Bayshore Hospital. A former patient of the hospital, Barbara Masters, is suing the hospital for negligent care of an infected decubitus ulcer. You are asked by Barbara's attorney to provide sworn verbal testimony and/or written answers to questions.

13. Referring to Case Study #2, Barbara Masters is the _____ in this case.
    A. appellant   C. defendant
    B. appellee   D. plaintiff

REFERENCE: Brodnik, p 35
                Green and Bowie, pp 265, 267
                LaTour and Eichenwald-Maki, pp 302–303, 939
                McWay (2010), pp 31, 413
                McWay (2014), p 60
                Pozgar, pp 108, 531, 581

14. Referring to Case Study #2, Bayshore Hospital is the _____ in this case.
    A. appellant   C. defendant
    B. appellee   D. plaintiff

REFERENCE: Brodnik, p 35
                Green and Bowie, pp 265, 337
                LaTour and Eichenwald-Maki, pp 302–303, 909
                McWay (2010), pp 31, 406
                McWay (2014), p 60
                Pozgar, pp 108, 578

15. Referring to Case Study #2, the sworn verbal testimony you are asked to provide is called a(n)
    A. interrogatory.
    B. deposition.
    C. physical and mental examination.
    D. court order.

REFERENCE: Brodnik, p 28
              Green and Bowie, pp 265, 337
              McWay (2010), pp 34, 39, 57, 406
              Pozgar, p 578

16. Referring to Case Study #2, the written answers to questions you have been asked to provide are known as a(n)
    A. interrogatory.
    B. deposition.
    C. physical and mental examination.
    D. court order.

REFERENCE: Brodnik, pp 29, 41
              Green and Bowie, pp 265, 342
              LaTour and Eichenwald-Maki, pp 303, 925
              McWay (2010), pp 34, 40, 57, 410
              Pozgar, p 580
              Roach, p 375

17. Referring to Case Study #2, what phase of the lawsuit are you involved in?
    A. pretrial conference   C. discovery
    B. trial   D. appeal

REFERENCE: Brodnik, p 35
              Green and Bowie, pp 265, 338
              LaTour and Eichenwald-Maki, p 325
              McWay (2010), pp 34, 57, 263, 407
              McWay (2014), pp 62–63
              Pozgar, pp 110–111, 579
              Roach, pp 374–375

18. Which of the following claims of negligence fits into the category of *res ipsa loquitur*?
    A. incorrect administration of anesthesia
    B. failure to refer patient to a specialist
    C. leaving a foreign body inside a patient
    D. improper use of x-rays

REFERENCE: Brodnik, pp 71–72
              Green and Bowie, pp 267, 350
              McWay (2010), pp 75–76, 414
              Pozgar, pp 56, 115–117, 582

19. The failure to obtain the written consent of the patient before performing a surgical procedure may constitute

A.	battery.	C.	libel.
B.	contempt.	D.	malpractice.

REFERENCE: Brodnik, pp 115–116
                         Green and Bowie, p 333
                         LaTour and Eichenwald-Maki, p 305
                         McWay (2010), pp 80, 404
                         McWay (2014), p 64
                         Pozgar, pp 43–44, 577

20. The fee paid for reimbursement for expenses incurred from providing health information whether for subpoena or reproduction by health care providers is determined by the
    A. American Health Information Management Association.
    B. hospitals and lawyers.
    C. statute or court rules.
    D. plaintiff and defendant lawyers.

REFERENCE: Brodnik, pp 262–263
                         McWay (2010), p 209

21. Who determines the retention period for health records?
    A. state and federal governments
    B. medical staff
    C. city and state governments
    D. commercial storage vendors

REFERENCE: Brodnik, pp 52, 140–146
                         Green and Bowie, p 93
                         LaTour and Eichenwald-Maki, pp 274–275
                         McWay (2010), pp 159–161, 163, 414
                         McWay (2014), pp 53, 136, 400, 520
                         Pozgar, p 282
                         Roach, pp 40–41

22. The extent to which the HIPAA privacy rule may regulate an individual's rights of access is not meant to preempt other existing federal laws and regulations. This means that if an individual's rights of access
    A. are less under another existing federal law, HIPAA must follow the directions of that law.
    B. are refused by a federal facility, HIPAA must also refuse the individual of the access.
    C. are greater under another applicable federal law, the individual should be afforded the greater access.
    D. are greater under another existing federal law, HIPAA can obstruct freedoms of the other federal law when using electronic health records.

REFERENCE: Brodnik, pp 186, 271
                         LaTour and Eichenwald-Maki, p 283

CASE STUDY #3

A 73-year-old male was admitted to the Sunset Nursing Facility with senility, cataracts, and S/P cerebrovascular accident with right-side hemiplegia. On his second day at the facility, the resident was discovered to have extensive thermal burns on his buttocks and legs by one of the facility's attendants.

23. Referring to Case Study #3, the resident's family brought legal action against the nursing facility for
   A. medical abandonment.
   B. vicarious liability.
   C. assault and battery.
   D. negligence.

REFERENCE: Brodnik, pp 69–71
                Green and Bowie, pp 267, 345
                LaTour and Eichenwald-Maki, pp 304–305, 933
                McWay (2010), pp 71–72, 412
                McWay (2014), p 65
                Pozgar, pp 32–40, 150–152, 581

24. Referring to Case Study #3, which of the following can the attorney of the resident's family also use as a basis for the lawsuit and why?
   A. The doctrine of *res ipsa loquitur* because it allows the plaintiff to shift the burden of proof to the defendant because direct evidence is available.
   B. The doctrine of charitable immunity because the nursing facility is a private institution and is shielded from liability for any torts committed on its property.
   C. The Good Samaritan Statutes because they protect the Director of Nursing, an employee of the nursing facility, who was not present when the injury occurred.
   D. The failure to warn theory because the doctor did not inform the resident's family that the resident was in danger at the nursing facility.

REFERENCE: Brodnik, pp 71–72
                Green and Bowie, pp 267, 350
                McWay (2010), pp 75–76, 414
                McWay (2014), p 65
                Pozgar, pp 56, 115–117, 582

25. In a negligence or malpractice case, all of the following elements must be present in order to shift the burden of proof onto the defendant EXCEPT the
   A. event would not normally have occurred in the absence of negligence.
   B. health care facility does not have a risk management program.
   C. defendant had exclusive control over the instrumentality that caused the injury.
   D. plaintiff did not contribute to the injury.

REFERENCE: Brodnik, pp 70–71
                LaTour and Eichenwald-Maki, pp 304–305
                McWay (2010), pp 71–75
                McWay (2014), p 65
                Pozgar, pp 33–41

26. When a health care facility fails to investigate the qualifications of a physician hired to work as an independent contractor in the emergency room and is accused of negligence, the health care facility can be held liable under
    A. respondeat superior.
    B. corporate negligence.
    C. contributory negligence.
    D. general negligence.

REFERENCE: Brodnik, p 74
               LaTour and Eichenwald-Maki, pp 329–330
               McWay (2010), pp 77–78
               McWay (2013), p 66
               Pozgar, pp 150–152

27. What source or document is considered the "supreme law of the land"?
    A. Bill of Rights
    B. Supreme Court decisions
    C. presidential power
    D. Constitution of the United States

REFERENCE: Brodnik, pp 14–15
               LaTour and Eichenwald-Maki, p 300
               McWay (2014), p 50
               Pozgar, p 19

28. Hospitals that destroy their own medical records must have a policy that
    A. ensures records are destroyed and confidentiality is protected.
    B. notifies the physicians when the records of their patients are destroyed.
    C. states that all records are destroyed annually.
    D. ensures that the type of equipment to be used for destruction of records is properly maintained.

REFERENCE: Brodnik, p 147
               Green and Bowie, pp 96–97, 349
               LaTour and Eichenwald-Maki, p 276
               McWay (2010), pp 164–166
               McWay (2014), pp 36–139
               Roach, pp 49–50

29. A written authorization from the patient releasing copies of his or her medical records is required by all of the following EXCEPT
    A. the patient's attorney.
    B. a physician requesting copies from another physician.
    C. an insurance company.
    D. the hospital attorney for the facility where the patient is treated.

REFERENCE: Brodnik, pp 163–164
               Green and Bowie, p 291
               LaTour and Eichenwald-Maki, pp 312–324
               McWay (2010), pp 207–208

30. Traditionally, the medical record is accepted as being the property of the
    A. patient's guardian.   C. institution.
    B. court.   D. patient.

REFERENCE: Brodnik, pp 239–241
                Green and Bowie, pp 72–73
                LaTour and Eichenwald-Maki, p 312
                McWay (2010), pp 194–196
                McWay (2014), pp 73–75
                Pozgar, p 279

31. The ownership of the information contained in the physical medical/health record is considered to belong to the
    A. patient.   C. physician.
    B. hospital.   D. insurance company.

REFERENCE: Green and Bowie, pp 72–73
                LaTour and Eichenwald-Maki, p 312
                McWay (2010), pp 194–196
                McWay (2014), pp 73–76
                Pozgar, p 279

32. When developing a record retention policy, the HIM professionals should consider all of the following EXCEPT
    A. current storage space.
    B. uses of and need for information.
    C. all applicable statutes and regulations.
    D. the thickness of the records.

REFERENCE: Brodnik, pp 52, 146–147, 149
                Green and Bowie, p 94
                LaTour and Eichenwald-Maki, pp 276–280
                McWay (2010), pp 160–163
                McWay (2014), pp 53, 136, 400, 520
                Pozgar, pp 282–283

33. If the patient record is involved in litigation and the physician requests to make a change to that record, what should the HIM professional do?
    A. Refer request to legal counsel.
    B. Allow the change to occur.
    C. Notify the patient.
    D. Say the record is unavailable.

REFERENCE: Brodnik, pp 138–140
                Green and Bowie, pp 84–85
                McWay (2010), pp 157–158
                Pozgar, pp 287–288

34. One of the greatest threats to the confidentiality of health data is
    A. when medical information is reviewed as a part of quality assurance activities.
    B. disclosure of information for purposes not authorized in writing by the patient.
    C. lack of written authorization by the patient.
    D. when medical information is used for research or education.

REFERENCE: Green and Bowie, p 271
              McWay (2010), pp 202–208
              McWay (2014), pp 71–72

35. All of the following are areas in which electronically stored information, for example, the electronic health record, differs from paper-based information EXCEPT
    A. volume.
    B. metadata.
    C. variety of sources.
    D. confidentiality.

REFERENCE: Brodnik, p 46
              McWay (2010), pp 34–35
              McWay (2014), p 62

36. Spoliation is the term that refers to the wrongful destruction of evidence or the failure to preserve property, which addresses which of the following methods of discovery?
    A. interrogatories
    B. deposition
    C. e-discovery
    D. request for admissions

REFERENCE: Brodnik, pp 50–51
              LaTour, Eichenwald-Maki, and Oachs, p 325
              McWay (2010), pp 34–35

37. What type of testimony is inappropriate for a health information manager serving as custodian of the record when he or she is called to be a witness in court?
    A. whether the record is in the practitioner's possession
    B. title and position held in the health care facility
    C. whether the medical record was made in the usual course of business
    D. interpretation of documentation in the record

REFERENCE: Brodnik, pp 29–31

38. Internal disclosures of patient information for patient care purposes should not be granted
    A. to the facility's legal counsel.
    B. to the attending physician.
    C. on a need to know basis.
    D. to a family member who is a registered nurse at the facility.

REFERENCE: Green and Bowie, pp 271, 275
              McWay (2014), pp 69–75

Case Study #4

William is a 16-year-old male who lives at home with his parents and works part-time as a dishwasher at one of the local restaurants. While emptying the dishwasher, William is severely scalded and rendered unconscious. He is taken to the emergency room of the local acute care hospital for emergency treatment.

39. Referring to Case Study #4, given the emergency of the situation, who should the health care provider seek consent from in order to provide treatment to William?
    A. the employer
    B. the parents
    C. the patient
    D. no consent is needed for emergency care

REFERENCE: Brodnik, pp 99–100
               LaTour, Eichenwald-Maki, and Oachs, pp 317–319
               McWay (2010), pp 187–188
               Pozgar, pp 312, 314
               Roach, pp 89–91

40. Referring to Case Study #4, in order to release information to his employer, the hospital must receive a
    A. consent signed by the patient.
    B. court order.
    C. consent signed by the doctor.
    D. consent signed by the patient's parent.

REFERENCE: Brodnik, pp 244–245, 255
               LaTour, Eichenwald-Maki, and Oachs, p 317
               McWay (2010), p 186
               Pozgar, p 314

41. A valid authorization for the disclosure of health information should not be
    A. dated prior to discharge of the patient.
    B. in writing.
    C. addressed to the health care provider.
    D. signed by the patient.

REFERENCE: Brodnik, pp 259–260
               LaTour, Eichenwald-Maki, and Oachs, p 317

42. Internal disclosures of patient information for patient care purposes should be granted
    A. to legal counsel.
    B. on a need to know basis.
    C. to any physician on staff.
    D. to a family member who is an employee.

REFERENCE: Brodnik, pp 176–177
               Green and Bowie, p 275
               LaTour, Eichenwald-Maki, and Oachs, p 319
               McWay (2010), pp 99, 102, 203–204
               McWay (2014), pp 69–75

43. According to AHIMA's Position on Transmission of Health Information, the health information manager should engage in all of the following to ensure that information is properly sent via facsimile transmission EXCEPT
    A. to always follow up by sending the original record by mail.
    B. to preprogram into the machine the number of destination sites.
    C. encrypt the data if public channels are used for electronic transmittal.
    D. ask the sender to contact the recipient prior to and after transmission.

REFERENCE: Brodnik, p 261
              Roach, pp 492–495

44. All of the following need a proper authorization to access a patient's health information EXCEPT
    A. local and state law enforcement officers.
    B. IRS agents.
    C. medical examiners or coroners.
    D. FBI agents.

REFERENCE: Green and Bowie, p 289
              LaTour, Eichenwald-Maki, and Oachs, pp 312–324
              McWay (2010), pp 200–201

45. One best practice to follow in order to establish safeguards for the security and confidentiality of a patient's information when a person makes a request for his or her records in person is to
    A. ask the requester for identification and the request in writing.
    B. refuse the request.
    C. refer the requester to the facility's attorney.
    D. charge an exorbitant fee.

REFERENCE: Brodnik, pp 258–260
              Roach, pp 239–241

46. Which of the following acts was passed to stimulate the development of standards to facilitate electronic maintenance and transmission of health information?
    A. Health Insurance for the Aged
    B. Health Insurance Portability and Accountability Act
    C. Conditions of Participation
    D. Hospital Survey and Construction Act

REFERENCE: Brodnik, pp 155–156
              Green and Bowie, pp 10, 320
              LaTour, Eichenwald-Maki, and Oachs, pp 151–152, 309–310
              McWay (2010), p 161
              McWay (2014), pp 68–70
              Pozgar, pp 27, 282

47. The premise that charitable institutions could be held blameless for their negligent acts is known as
    A. doctrine of respondeat superior.
    B. doctrine of *res ipsa loquitur*.
    C. doctrine of charitable immunity.
    D. negligence factor.

REFERENCE: Brodnik, pp 291–292
               McWay (2010), pp 85, 405
               Pozgar, pp 151, 578
               Roach, pp 10–11

48. Under traditional rules of evidence, a medical/health record is considered _____ and is _____ into evidence.
    A. hearsay; admissible   C.   reliable; admissible
    B. hearsay; inadmissible   D.   reliable; inadmissible

REFERENCE: Brodnik, pp 56–58
               Green and Bowie, pp 270–271
               LaTour, Eichenwald-Maki, and Oachs, p 324
               McWay (2010), pp 50–51, 409
               Roach, pp 383–385

49. Substance abuse records cannot be redisclosed by a receiving facility to another health care facility unless the
    A. patient expires at the receiving facility.
    B. charge nurse signs the release form.
    C. physician signs the DNR form.
    D. patient gives written consent.

REFERENCE: McWay (2010), pp 232–233

50. Who is legally responsible for obtaining the patient's informed consent for surgery?
    A. the admissions clerk
    B. the surgeon performing the surgery
    C. the nurse
    D. medical records personnel

REFERENCE: Brodnik, pp 116
               Green and Bowie, pp 129, 132
               McWay (2010), pp 188–189
               McWay (2014), pp 76–77
               Pozgar, pp 199–200
               Roach, p 74

51. With regard to confidentiality, when HIM functions are outsourced (i.e., record copying, microfilming, or transcription), the HIM professional should confirm that the outside contractor's
    A. costs are not prohibitive, thus compromising confidentiality.
    B. hours of operation permit easy access by all health care providers.
    C. is contractually bound to handle confidential information appropriately by means of a signed business associate agreement.
    D. is located in an easy to find place.

REFERENCE: Brodnik, pp 158–159
               McWay (2010), pp 215–216

52. A 21-year-old employee of National Services was treated in an acute care hospital for an illness unrelated to work. A representative from the personnel department of National Services calls to request information regarding the employee's diagnosis. What would be the appropriate course of action?
    A. Request that the personnel office send an authorization for release of information that is signed and dated by the patient.
    B. Require parental consent.
    C. Release the information because the employer is paying the patient's bill.
    D. Call the patient to obtain verbal permission.

REFERENCE: Brodnik, pp 244–245, 255
               Green and Bowie, pp 291–292
               LaTour, Eichenwald-Maki, and Oachs, pp 316–317

53. *Darling v. Charleston Community Memorial Hospital* is considered one of the benchmark cases in health care because it was with this case that the doctrine of _____ was eliminated for nonprofit hospitals.
    A. charitable immunity
    B. corporate negligence
    C. professional negligence
    D. contributory negligence

REFERENCE: Brodnik, pp 291–292
               Green and Bowie, p 267
               McWay (2010), p 77
               Pozgar, pp 150–152

54. All of the following are elements of a contract EXCEPT
    A. offer/communication.   C. price/consideration.
    B. duty.   D. acceptance.

REFERENCE: Brodnik, p 83
               LaTour, Eichenwald-Maki, and Oachs, pp 307–308
               McWay (2010), p 5
               Pozgar, pp 87–88

55. A valid authorization for release of information contains
    A. the name, agency, or institution to which the information is to be provided.
    B. the name of the hospital or provider who is releasing the medical information.
    C. the date and signature of the patient or the patient's authorized representative.
    D. all of the above.

REFERENCE: Brodnik, pp 259–262
               LaTour, Eichenwald-Maki, and Oachs, p 317
               McWay (2010), pp 202–203

56. In which of the following circumstances would release of information without the patient's authorization be permissible?
    A. release to an attorney
    B. release to third-party payers
    C. release to state workers' compensation agencies
    D. release to insurance companies

REFERENCE: Brodnik, pp 170–175, 281–282
                       Green and Bowie, p 291
                       LaTour, Eichenwald-Maki, and Oachs, p 318
                       McWay (2010), pp 202–209

57. Who decides whether all or portions of the medical record will be received in evidence in a court of law?
    A. presiding judge/court   C. clerk of the court
    B. subpoenaing attorney   D. defendant

REFERENCE: Brodnik, p 44
                       McWay (2010), p 42

58. Which of the following health care systems have to comply with the requirements of the Freedom of Information Act?
    A. private hospitals   C. veterans' hospitals
    B. physicians' offices   D. single-day surgery clinics

REFERENCE: Brodnik, p 157
                       LaTour, Eichenwald-Maki, and Oachs, p 310
                       McWay (2010), p 177
                       Roach, p 123

59. Which of the following measures should a health care facility incorporate into its institution-wide security plan to protect the confidentiality of the patient record?
    A. verification of employee identification
    B. locked access to data processing and record areas
    C. use of unique computer passwords, key cares, or biometric identification
    D. all of the above

REFERENCE: Brodnik, pp 199–200
                       Green and Bowie, pp 282–283
                       LaTour, Eichenwald-Maki, and Oachs, p 188
                       McWay (2010), pp 289, 291–295
                       Roach, pp 462–470

60. A signed consent for release of information dated December 1, 2010, is received with a request for the chart from the patient's admission of 12/5/2010. Indicate the appropriate response from the options below.
    A. Request another authorization that is dated closer but prior to the admission date.
    B. Request another authorization dated after the discharge date.
    C. Release the requested information.
    D. Call the patient for a verbal authorization.

REFERENCE: Brodnik, pp 168–171
                       LaTour, Eichenwald-Maki, and Oachs, p 317
                       McWay (2010), p 204

61. Willful disregard of a subpoena is considered
    A. breach of contract.
    B. abuse of process.
    C. contributory negligence.
    D. contempt of court.

REFERENCE: Brodnik, p 30
               McWay (2010), p 204
               McWay (2014), pp 77–78
               Pozgar, p 115
               Roach, p 322

62. HIM personnel charged with the responsibility of bringing a medical record to court would ordinarily do so in answer to a
    A. personal subpoena.
    B. deposition.
    C. subpoena duces tecum.
    D. judgment.

REFERENCE: Brodnik, p 31
               Green and Bowie, p 289
               McWay (2010), pp 40–41, 54, 416
               McWay (2014), p 77
               Pozgar, p 115
               Roach, p 317

63. HIPAA requires that certain covered entities provide every patient a Notice of Privacy Practices that sets forth all of the following EXCEPT
    A. covered entities provide every patient with its annual business report.
    B. how covered entities may use and disclose PHI.
    C. patient's rights regarding the covered entities' uses and disclosures.
    D. covered entities' obligations for protecting the patient's PHI.

REFERENCE: Brodnik, pp 165–166
               Green and Bowie, p 273
               LaTour, Eichenwald-Maki, and Oachs, pp 244, 314
               McWay (2010), pp 196–205
               McWay (2014), pp 72–73, 274, 441–450
               Roach, pp 218–222

64. A record that has been requested by subpoena duces tecum is currently located at an off-site microfilm company. By contacting the microfilm provider, you learn that the microfilm is ready and the original copy of the record still exists. What legal requirement would compel you to produce the original record for the court?
    A. best evidence rule   C. motion to quash
    B. hearsay rule   D. subpoena instanter

REFERENCE: Brodnik, pp 56–57
               Roach, pp 487–488

65. Under which category of law would Marleana Harrison bring a cause of action against Dr. Billy Ray for disclosing information regarding her previous physical examination to his wife, Jana Ray, who is Ms. Harrison's hairstylist?
    A. administrative law
    B. criminal law
    C. private law
    D. procedural law

REFERENCE: Brodnik, p 14
                McWay (2010), pp 45–46
                McWay (2014), pp 49–50
                Pozgar, pp 15–16
                Roach, p 2

66. As a general rule, a person making a report in good faith and under statutory command (e.g., on child abuse, communicable diseases, births, deaths, etc.) is
    A. not protected from liability claims.
    B. subject to penalties imposed by federal law.
    C. subject to penalties imposed by state law.
    D. protected.

REFERENCE: Brodnik, pp 67–68
                Green and Bowie, p 288
                LaTour, Eichenwald-Maki, and Oachs, p 313
                McWay (2010), pp 217–218
                Pozgar, pp 323–324
                Roach, pp 247–248

67. According to AHIMA and AHA guidelines, which of the following would be an acceptable authorization for release of information from the medical record of an adult, mentally competent patient hospitalized from 4/16/2011 to 5/10/2011? An authorization dated
    A. 7/10/2013 and presented 7/15/2013
    B. 5/09/2013 and presented 1/15/2014
    C. 3/10/2013 and presented 5/15/2013
    D. 2/15/2013 and presented 1/10/2013

REFERENCE: Brodnik, pp 168–170
                Green and Bowie, pp 122, 124–125
                McWay (2010), pp 96–98, 203
                McWay (2014), p 73

68. Which would be the better "best practice" for handling fax transmission of a physician's orders?
    A. Treat faxed orders like verbal orders and require authentication of the orders by appropriate medical staff within the required period.
    B. Faxed orders should be placed on the patient's chart immediately upon receipt after the head nurse signs the orders.
    C. Wait 24 hours before placing faxed orders on the patient's chart to ensure that the orders are legitimate.
    D. Faxed orders should never be accepted.

REFERENCE: Brodnik, pp 131, 386
                Green and Bowie, p 81
                Roach, p 494

69. The *Darling v. Charleston Community Memorial Hospital* case established the following doctrine for hospitals to observe and changed the way hospitals dealt with liability.
    A. doctrine of respondeat superior
    B. doctrine of continuing wrong
    C. doctrine of *res ipsa loquitur*
    D. doctrine of corporate negligence

REFERENCE: Brodnik, pp 291–292
Green and Bowie, p 257
LaTour, Eichenwald-Maki, and Oachs, pp 329–330
McWay (2010), pp 50–51
Pozgar, p 150

70. HIM professionals have a duty to maintain health information that complies with
    A. state statutes.
    B. federal statutes.
    C. accreditation standards.
    D. all of the above.

REFERENCE: Brodnik, p 128
Green and Bowie, p 273
LaTour, Eichenwald-Maki, and Oachs, p 328
McWay (2010), pp 147, 201
McWay (2014), pp 70–71
Roach, pp 40–41

71. In general, which of the following statements is correct?
    A. When federal and state laws conflict, valid federal laws supersede state laws.
    B. When federal and state laws conflict, valid state laws supersede federal laws.
    C. When federal and state laws conflict, valid local laws supersede federal and state laws.
    D. When federal and state laws conflict, valid corporate policies supersede federal and state laws.

REFERENCE: Brodnik, p 128
LaTour, Eichenwald-Maki, and Oachs, p 300
McWay (2010), p 201
McWay (2014), p 70

72. Which of the following statements is correct regarding HIPAA preemption analysis?
    A. If the state law that recognizes a patient's right to health care information privacy is more stringent than the HIPAA federal rule, then the state law prevails.
    B. State law regarding a patient's right to health care information privacy can never prevail over the HIPAA federal rule.
    C. If a state law that recognizes a patient's right to health care information privacy is more stringent than the HIPAA federal rule, then the courts must decide which shall prevail.
    D. Even if the state law that recognizes a patient's right to health care information privacy is more stringent than the HIPAA federal rule, the HIPAA federal rule will still prevail.

REFERENCE: Brodnik, pp 186, 271
Green and Bowie, p 283
LaTour, Eichenwald-Maki, and Oachs, p 313
McWay (2010), p 201
McWay (2014), p 70
Roach, pp 100–101

73. The minimum record retention period for patients who are minors is
    A. age of majority.
    B. age of majority plus the statute of limitations.
    C. 5 years past treatment.
    D. 2 years past treatment.

REFERENCE: Brodnik, pp 141–146
               Green and Bowie, p 94
               McWay (2014) pp 53, 136, 400, 520
               Roach, pp 43–44

74. In which type of facility does the Privacy Act of 1974 permit patients to request amendments to
    their medical record?
    A. private proprietary health care facility
    B. mental health and chemical dependency facility
    C. university-based teaching facility
    D. Department of Defense health care facility

REFERENCE: Brodnik, p 157
               Green and Bowie, p 285
               LaTour, Eichenwald-Maki, and Oachs, p 310
               Pozgar, pp 279–280

75. What advice should be given to a physician who has just informed you that she just discovered
    that a significant portion of a discharge summary she dictated last month was left out?
    A. Squeeze in the information omitted by writing in available spaces such as the top, bottom,
       and side margins.
    B. Dictate the portion omitted with the heading "Discharge Summary—Addendum" and make
       a reference to the addendum with a note that is dated and signed on the initial Discharge
       Summary (e.g., "9/1/11—See Addendum to Discharge Summary"—Signature).
    C. Redictate the discharge summary and replace the old one with the new one.
    D. Inform the physician that nothing can be done about the situation.

REFERENCE: Brodnik, pp 138–140
               Green and Bowie, pp 84–85
               McWay (2010), p 177
               Roach, p 70

76. While performing routine quantitative analysis of a record, a medical record employee finds an incident report in the record. The employee brings this to the attention of her supervisor. Which best practice should the supervisor follow to deal with this situation?
    A. Remove the incident report and send it to the patient.
    B. Tell the employee to leave the report in the record.
    C. Remove the incident report and have nursing personnel transfer all documentation from the report to the medical record.
    D. Refer this record to the Risk Manager for further review and removal of the incident report.

REFERENCE: Brodnik, pp 295–297
                Green and Bowie, p 88
                LaTour, Eichenwald-Maki, and Oachs, p 335
                McWay (2010), pp 262–263
                McWay (2014), p 132
                Pozgar, pp 329–330
                Roach, p 393

77. Which of the following is considered confidential information if the patient is seeking treatment in a substance abuse facility?
    A. patient's name   C. patient's diagnosis
    B. patient's address   D. all of the above

REFERENCE: Brodnik, pp 247–250
                Green and Bowie, pp 284–285

78. In electronic health records, authentication may be achieved by
    A. handwritten signature.   C. verbal statement.
    B. digital signature.   D. all the above.

REFERENCE: Brodnik, pp 133–135
                Green and Bowie, pp 26, 278
                LaTour, Eichenwald-Maki, and Oachs, p 87
                McWay (2010), p 286
                McWay (2014), p 125

79. It is common practice to forgo patient authorization for the release of information when the
    A. patient is an employee.
    B. patient is a physician.
    C. patient has a direct transfer from the hospital to a long-term care facility.
    D. patient is incompetent.

REFERENCE: LaTour, Eichenwald-Maki, and Oachs, p 319

80. Many states have recognized a minor's right to seek treatment without parental consent in all of the following situations EXCEPT a(n)
    A. minor seeking treatment for breast reduction.
    B. minor seeking treatment for a sexually transmitted disease.
    C. minor seeking treatment for alcohol and substance abuse.
    D. emancipated minor seeking treatment for breast enlargement.

REFERENCE: Brodnik, pp 113–115
                Pozgar, pp 313–314
                Roach, pp 89–90

81. When a health information professional (record custodian) brings the medical record to court in response to a subpoena duces tecum, it is his or her responsibility to
    A. confirm whether or not the record is complete, accurate, and made in the ordinary course of business.
    B. present the case favorably for the patient involved.
    C. leave the original record in the possession of the plaintiff's attorney.
    D. explain details of the medical treatment given to the patient.

REFERENCE: Brodnik, pp 30–31, 54–55
              McWay (2010), p 52

82. When substituting a photocopy of the original record in response to legal process, which of the following can be helpful in convincing the court to accept the photocopy as a true and exact copy of the original?
    A. certificate of authentication
    B. consent from the patient
    C. consent from the hospital administrator
    D. correspondence from the attending physician

REFERENCE: Brodnik, pp 33–34, 54–55

83. Which of the following should be required to sign a confidentiality statement before having access to patients' medical information?
    A. nursing students   C. HIM students
    B. medical students   D. all of the above

REFERENCE: Brodnik, pp 158, 215, 442
              Green and Bowie, pp 43–48
              Pozgar, pp 290–292

84. All of the following have laws and regulations addressing medical records EXCEPT
    A. accrediting agencies.   C. state laws.
    B. corporate law.   D. federal laws.

REFERENCE: Brodnik, pp 156–158
              Green and Bowie, p 265

85. The proper method for correcting a documentation error in a medical record is for the author to
    A. draw an "X" through the incorrect documentation.
    B. draw a single line through the incorrect information, date and initial the change.
    C. white it out, date and initial the change.
    D. remove the form from the chart and add a revised form.

REFERENCE: Brodnik, pp 138–140
              Green and Bowie, pp 84–85
              McWay (2010), p 157
              Pozgar, p 297
              Roach, p 70

86. Dr. Vincent Orangeburg performed a cesarean on Mrs. Greentree, who later returned to the emergency room 5 days after the surgery with abdominal pain. An x-ray performed revealed that a sponge was left in the lower abdominal cavity from the cesarean. Which case law principle can be used in a lawsuit against Dr. Orangeburg?
    A. res gestae
    B. star decis
    C. res ipsa loquitur
    D. res judicata

REFERENCE: Brodnik, pp 71–72
               Green and Bowie, p 267
               McWay (2010), p 75
               McWay (2014), pp 65–66
               Pozgar, pp 56, 115–117

87. To be admitted into court as evidence, medical records or health information are introduced as
    A. torts or contracts.
    B. privileged information.
    C. business records or exception to hearsay rule.
    D. product liability.

REFERENCE: Brodnik, pp 44–45
               Green and Bowie, pp 270–271
               LaTour, Eichenwald-Maki, and Oachs, p 333
               McWay (2010), p 51
               Roach, pp 383–386

88. A health care organization's compliance plans should not only focus on regulatory compliance, but also have a
    A. strong personnel component that reduces the rapid turnover of nursing personnel.
    B. coding compliance program that prevents fraudulent coding and billing.
    C. component that increases the security of medical records.
    D. substantial program that increases the availability of clinical data.

REFERENCE: Brodnik, pp 316–318
               Green and Bowie, p 323
               LaTour, Eichenwald-Maki, and Oachs, pp 453–454
               McWay (2010), p 318
               McWay (2014), pp 81, 158
               Pozgar, pp 332–333

89. A written consent from the patient is required from which of the following entities in order to learn a patient's HIV status?
    A. insurance companies
    B. emergency medical personnel
    C. spouse or needle partner
    D. health care workers

REFERENCE: Brodnik, pp 250–251
                Green and Bowie, p 292
                McWay (2010), pp 181–183
                McWay (2014), pp 78, 109
                Pozgar, pp 358–559
                Roach, pp 352–362

90. Dr. Sam Vineyard improperly performed a knee replacement surgery, which caused the patient to develop an infection that lead to the amputation of the leg and thigh. The best term to describe the action performed is
    A. misfeasance.
    B. malpractice.
    C. nonfeasance.
    D. malfeasance.

REFERENCE: Brodnik, p 70
                LaTour, Eichenwald-Maki, and Oachs, p 304
                Pozgar, p 33

91. The ideal consent for medical treatment obtained by the physician is
    A. expressed.   C. implied.
    B. informed.   D. verbal.

REFERENCE: Brodnik, pp 96–99
                Green and Bowie, pp 129, 132, 134
                McWay (2010), p 173
                McWay (2014), pp 76–77
                Pozgar, pp 302–303
                Roach, pp 78–81

92. Which of the following is an example of the breach of confidentiality?
    A. a nurse speaking with the physician in the patient's room
    B. staff members discussing patients in the elevator
    C. the admission clerk verifying over the phone that the patient is in-house
    D. the hospital operator paging code blue in room 3 north

REFERENCE: Brodnik, pp 78–79
                Pozgar, p 52
                Roach, pp 406–408

93. Which of the following would be an inappropriate procedure for the custodian of the medical record to perform prior to taking a medical record from a health care facility to court?
    A. Number each page of the record in ink.
    B. Document in the file folder the total number of pages in the record.
    C. Remove any information that might prove detrimental to the hospital or physician.
    D. Prepare an itemized list of sheets contained in the medical record.

REFERENCE: Brodnik, pp 33–34
               Pozgar, pp 284–287

94. Which of the following agencies is empowered to implement the law governing Medicare and Medicaid?
    A. Centers for Medicare and Medicaid Services (CMS) formerly known as Health Care Financing Administration (HCFA)
    B. Joint Commission
    C. Institutes of Health
    D. Department of Health and Human Services

REFERENCE: Brodnik, p 128
               Green and Bowie, p 65
               LaTour, Eichenwald-Maki, and Oachs, p 37
               McWay (2010), p 12
               McWay (2014), pp 12, 52, 56–57
               Pozgar, pp 25–28

95. Consent forms may be challenged on all the following grounds EXCEPT
    A. wording was too technical.
    B. the treating physician obtained the patient's signature.
    C. it is written in a language that the patient could not understand.
    D. the signature was not voluntary.

REFERENCE: Brodnik, pp 115–118
               Green and Bowie, pp 129, 132, 134
               Roach, p 97

96. Mandatory reporting requirements for vital statistics generally
    A. do not require authorization by the patient.
    B. require authorization by the physician.
    C. require authorization by the payer.
    D. do not apply to health care facilities.

REFERENCE: Brodnik, pp 172–175
               Green and Bowie, p 277
               McWay (2010), p 301
               McWay (2014), p 202
               Pozgar, p 330

97. The responsibility of obtaining an informed consent for a surgical or invasive procedure rests with the
    A. patient.   C. physician.
    B. nurse.   D. hospital.

REFERENCE: Brodnik, pp 115–118
                Green and Bowie, pp 129, 132, 134
                Pozgar, pp 302–303
                Roach, pp 91–94

98. Courts have released adoption records based on
    A. the request of the adoptee.
    B. the request of the biological parent(s).
    C. the Freedom of Information Act.
    D. a court order for good cause.

REFERENCE: Brodnik, pp 152–153
                McWay (2010), p 218
                Roach, p 301

99. The legislation that required all federally funded facilities to inform patients of their rights under state law to accept or refuse medical treatment is known as
    A. advance directives.
    B. living wills.
    C. Patient Self-Determination Act.
    D. durable power of attorney.

REFERENCE: Brodnik, p 105
                Green and Bowie, p 129
                McWay (2010), pp 114, 142, 186–187
                McWay (2014), p 77
                Pozgar, pp 316–317, 424, 430
                Roach, p 97

100. An improper disclosure of patient information to unauthorized individuals, agencies, or news media may be considered a(n)
    A. invasion of privacy.
    B. libel.
    C. slander.
    D. defamation.

REFERENCE: Green and Bowie, p 271
                McWay (2010), p 81
                McWay (2014), p 64
                Pozgar, p 52
                Roach, pp 406–407, 410

Answer Key for Health Law

1.	A	35.	B	69.	D
2.	B	36.	C	70.	D
3.	C	37.	D	71.	A
4.	A	38.	D	72.	A
5.	C	39.	D	73.	B
6.	B	40.	D	74.	D
7.	C	41.	A	75.	B
8.	D	42.	B	76.	D
9.	D	43.	A	77.	D
10.	B	44.	C	78.	B
11.	C	45.	A	79.	C
12.	A	46.	B	80.	A
13.	D	47.	C	81.	A
14.	C	48.	B	82.	A
15.	B	49.	D	83.	D
16.	A	50.	B	84.	B
17.	C	51.	C	85.	B
18.	C	52.	A	86.	C
19.	A	53.	A	87.	C
20.	C	54.	B	88.	B
21.	A	55.	D	89.	A
22.	C	56.	C	90.	A
23.	D	57.	A	91.	B
24.	A	58.	C	92.	B
25.	B	59.	D	93.	C
26.	B	60.	B	94.	A
27.	D	61.	D	95.	B
28.	A	62.	C	96.	A
29.	D	63.	A	97.	C
30.	C	64.	A	98.	D
31.	A	65.	C	99.	C
32.	D	66.	D	100.	A
33.	A	67.	A		
34.	B	68.	A		

REFERENCES

Brodnik, M. S., McCain, M. C., Rinehart-Thompson, L. A., Reynolds, R. B. et al. (2009). *Fundamentals of law for health informatics and information management.* Chicago: American Health Information Management Association.

Green, M. A., & Bowie, M. J. (2011). *Essentials of health information management: Principles and practices.* Clifton Park, NY: Delmar Cengage Learning.

LaTour, K., Eichenwald-Maki, S., and Oachs, P. (2013). *Health information management: Concepts, principles, and practice* (4th ed.). Chicago: American Health Information Management Association (AHIMA).

McWay, D. C. (2010). *Legal and ethical aspects of health information management* (3rd ed.). Clifton Park, NY: Delmar Cengage Learning.

McWay, D. C. (2014). *Today's health information management: An integrated approach* (2nd ed.). Clifton Park, NY: Delmar Cengage Learning.

Pozgar, G. D. (2013). *Legal aspects of health care administration* (12th ed.). Sudbury, MA: Jones & Bartlett.

Roach, W. H. (2006). *Medical records and the law* (4th ed.). Sudbury, MA: Jones & Bartlett.

Health Law Competency Domains

Question	RHIA Domain	RHIT Domain
1–100	5–6	
1–100		6

XIII. Health Statistics and Research

Kathy C. Trawick, EdD, RHIA

As noted in the main Introduction section, you will be able to access some statistical formulas on the computer to use during the exam. You may not find them in any set location—be prepared to look around for them a little. Of course, there are some formulas, (for example: mean, median, and average) you will be responsible for knowing. When preparing for the exam, practice using the calculator located in the program accessories bar on your computer and the formulas that are provided in this text.

Although some questions are included from the Commonly Computed Rates and Percentages for Hospital Inpatients, you will often be asked to interpret everyday data and/or solve questions that have more to do with common sense and good math skills than with memorized formulas. To help you distinguish among the types of questions you might expect, and to make sure you realistically evaluate your skills in this area, this chapter has been divided into four sections:
1. Statistical basics
2. Commonly computed rates
3. Data display and interpretation
4. Research and financial statistics

According to the breakdown of content for both the RHIA and RHIT exams, the health statistics questions have been included in Domain II. This section not only covers statistics and research, but also may include data collection, interpretation, and presentation as well as knowledge of registries, specialized databases, and the Institutional Review Board (IRB). You should also be prepared to analyze and interpret statistical charts and graphs. Some questions will refer to a graphical representation of data when asking for the answer. Refer to the specific details of these items in the domain and subdomain competencies found in the Certification Guide.

You will want to work with statistical formulas from this chapter, from your formal courses, and from previous textbooks until you get your speed up. Sometimes the length of time it takes in calculating formulas and mathematical computations can make or break you on the entire examination as far as your testing time. Thus, increasing your speed by practicing formulas can really help you at exam time.

Most answers in this section should be rounded to the first decimal point. On the national examination, let the answers provided in the test be your guide, or follow the examination instructions in order to round correctly.

Do not let the word problems throw you off. Some of these are quite long; look for the pertinent data.

Do not panic—approach word problems just as you did in your formal classes. You will have the formulas provided for you as appropriately required on the exam. For problems that you may not have a formula for, try the memory device of—"what did happen divided by what could have happened." Here, the "what did happen" is always the numerator (top number) and the "what could have happened" is always the denominator (bottom number).

We recommend that you review the textbooks listed at the end of this chapter as you study for this section of your exam.

Health Statistics Definitions and Formulas

There are a number of important things to think about when you tackle census and occupancy statistics. First, remember that when it comes to occupancy, beds and bassinets are counted separately. This means newborn discharges are separated from the discharges of adults and children. Next, remember not to be fooled by beds set up temporarily to meet unusual admission needs; all occupancy statistics should be calculated based on approved, permanent beds only. The common rates used for census and occupancy statistics are as follows:

Census Statistics

Daily Inpatient Census	Total number of patients treated during a 24-hour period
Inpatient Service Day	Services received by one inpatient in one 24-hour period
Total Inpatient Service Days	Sum of all inpatient service days for each of the days in the period
FORMULA: Average Daily Census	<u>Total inpatient service days for a period (excluding newborns)</u> Total number of days in the period

Length of Stay

Length of Stay (LOS)	Number of calendar days from admission to discharge
Total Length of Stay	Sum of the days' stay of any group of inpatients discharged during a specific period
FORMULA: Average LOS	<u>Total length of stay (discharge days)</u> Total number of discharges

Bed Count

Inpatient Bed Count	Number of available hospital beds, both occupied and vacant, on any given day
Inpatient Bed Count Day	Counts the presence of one inpatient bed (occupied or vacant) that is set up and staffed for use in one 24-hour period
Total Inpatient Bed Count Day	Sum of inpatient bed count days for each of the days in a period

Percentage of Occupancy

FORMULA:	<u>Total number of inpatient service days for a period × 100</u> Total inpatient bed count days × number of days in the period

Bed Turnover Rate

Direct Formula:

$$\frac{\text{Total number of discharges for a period}}{\text{Average bed count for the same period}}$$

Indirect Formula:

$$\frac{\text{Percentage of occupancy} \times \text{Days in the period} \times 100}{\text{Average length of stay}}$$

NOTE: The indirect formula must be used in cases where the bed count changes during the period in question.

Death (Mortality) Rates

Anesthesia Death Rate	$\dfrac{\text{Total number of deaths caused by an anesthetic agent} \times 100}{\text{Total number of anesthetics administered}}$
Fetal Death Rate (Stillbirth Rate)	$\dfrac{\text{Total number of intermediate and late fetal deaths} \times 100}{\text{Total number of births (plus intermediate and late fetal deaths)}}$
Gross Hospital Death Rate	$\dfrac{\text{Total number of inpatient deaths (including newborns)} \times 100}{\text{Total number of discharges (including deaths and newborns)}}$
Net Hospital Death Rate	$\dfrac{\text{Number of inpatient deaths (including NB) minus deaths <48 hours of admission} \times 100}{\text{Total discharges (including deaths and NB, minus deaths <48 hours)}}$
Maternal Death Rate	$\dfrac{\text{Total number of maternal deaths for a period} \times 100}{\text{Total number of obstetrical discharges}}$
Neonatal Death Rate (Infant Mortality Rate)	$\dfrac{\text{Total number of newborn (NB. deaths for a period} \times 100)}{\text{Total number of newborn (NB. Discharges)}}$
Postoperative Death Rate	$\dfrac{\text{Number of deaths within 10 days of surgery} \times 100}{\text{Total number of patients operated on}}$

Autopsy Rates

Newborn (NB) Autopsy Rate	$\dfrac{\text{Number of autopsies on NB deaths} \times 100}{\text{Total number of NB deaths}}$
Fetal Autopsy Rate	$\dfrac{\text{Number of autopsies on intermediate and late fetal deaths} \times 100}{\text{Total number of intermediate and late fetal deaths}}$
Gross Autopsy Rate	$\dfrac{\text{Total inpatient autopsies for a period} \times 100}{\text{Total inpatient deaths for the period}}$
Net Autopsy Rate	$\dfrac{\text{Total inpatient autopsies for a period} \times 100}{\text{Total inpatient deaths minus unautopsied coroner's or medical examiner's cases for the period}}$
Hospital Autopsy Rate (Adjusted)	$\dfrac{\text{Total hospital autopsies} \times 100}{\text{Number of deaths of hospital patients whose bodies are available for hospital autopsy}}$

The hospital patients whose bodies after death are available for hospital autopsy include inpatients, unless the bodies are removed from the hospital by legal authorities. However, in any such case, if the hospital pathologist or delegated physician of the medical staff performs an autopsy while acting as an agent for the coroner, the autopsy is included in the numerator and the death in the denominator.

In addition, other hospital patients (including hospital home care patients, outpatients, and previous hospital patients who have died elsewhere) whose bodies have been made available for the performance of hospital autopsy, the autopsy is included in the numerator and the death in the denominator.

Infection (Morbidity) Rates

Total Hospital (Morbidity) Infection Rate	$$\frac{\text{Total number of hospital infections} \times 100}{\text{Total number of discharges}}$$
Nosocomial Infection Rate	$$\frac{\text{Number of hospital acquired infections} \times 100}{\text{Total number of discharges (including deaths)}}$$
Community-Acquired Infection Rate	$$\frac{\text{Number of community-acquired infections} \times 100}{\text{Total number of discharges}}$$
Postoperative Infection Rate	$$\frac{\text{Number of postoperative infections for a period (within 10 days postoperatively)} \times 100}{\text{Total number of operations performed}}$$

Other Rates

Cesarean Section Rate	$$\frac{\text{Total number of cesarean sections performed in a period} \times 100}{\text{Total number of deliveries in the period}}$$
Consultation Rate	$$\frac{\text{Total number of consultations for a period} \times 100}{\text{Total number of discharges for the period}}$$
Delinquent Medical Record Rate	$$\frac{\text{Total number of delinquent records} \times 100}{\text{Average number of discharges during a completion period}}$$
Incomplete Medical Record Rate	$$\frac{\text{Total number of incomplete records} \times 100}{\text{Total number of discharges during the completion period}}$$
Percentage of Medicare Patients	$$\frac{\text{Total number of Medicare discharges} \times 100}{\text{Total number of adult and children discharges}}$$
Percentage of Medicare Discharge Days	$$\frac{\text{Total number of Medicare discharge days} \times 100}{\text{Total number of discharge days for adults and children}}$$
Readmission Rate	$$\frac{\text{Number of readmissions for a period} \times 100}{\text{Number of total admissions (including readmissions)}}$$

Generic Formulas

Percentage Rates	$$\frac{\text{Total number of times events actually happened} \times 100}{\text{Total number of times events could have happened}}$$
Mean	Add all the available values and divide the sum by the total number of values involved. Example: Average length of stay or average daily inpatient census.
Median	The midpoint of an ordered series of numbers arranged in numerical order from highest to lowest or vice versa.
Mode	The most frequently recurring value in a set of numbers is the mode.

Section I—Math and Statistical Basics

The basics include mathematical and statistical terminology as well as the measures of central tendency and variations around those measures. It is unlikely that you will get instructions for calculating the measures of central tendency, so they are supplied along with the statistical formulas at the beginning of this chapter.

1. Sandy Beach Hospital reports 1,652 discharges for September. The infection control report documents 21 nosocomial infections and 27 community-acquired infections for the same month. What is the community-acquired infection rate?
   A. 1.3
   B. 1.4
   C. 1.6
   D. 2.9

REFERENCE: Koch, p 179
               Sayles, p 497

2. Physicians at South Seas Clinic are expected to see six patients per hour on average. The physicians with the highest productivity each week are exempted from on-call responsibilities for the weekend. Which physician will get the weekend off this week?

SOUTH SEAS CLINIC PHYSICIAN PRODUCTIVITY Week 1 January 2014		
PHYSICIAN NAME	NUMBER OF HOURS WORKED	NUMBER OF PATIENTS SEEN
Robinson	32	185
Beasley	30	161
Hiltz	35	200
Wolf	26	157

   A. Robinson
   B. Beasley
   C. Hiltz
   D. Wolf

REFERENCE: Abdelhak, pp 368–369
               Horton, pp 147–148
               Koch, pp 56–57
               LaTour, Eichenwald-Maki, and Oachs, p 807
               McWay, pp 221–222

3. If there are 150,000 medical records and the Health Information Department receives 3,545 requests for records in a week, what percentage of the records are requested weekly?
   A. 2.4%
   B. 3.5%
   C. 4.6%
   D. 5.1%

REFERENCE: Abdelhak, pp 368–369
               Horton, pp 14, 19–20
               Koch, p 49
               LaTour, Eichenwald-Maki, and Oachs, pp 484–485
               McWay, p 204

4. You are conducting a study on the pain associated with a specific illness. For the purpose of your study, you classify pain level as follows:

CODE	PAIN LEVEL (as described by the patient)
01	None
02	Little or Minimal
03	Moderate
04	Heavy
05	Severe

These data are best described as

A. discrete.

B. continuous.

C. nominal.

D. ordinal.

REFERENCE: Abdelhak, pp 380–385
Horton, pp 196–199
Koch, pp 12–13
LaTour, Eichenwald-Maki, and Oachs, pp 482–483
McWay, p 212

5. You are choosing restaurants where you might eat while you are in Chicago at the AHIMA Leadership Conference. You have collected the following information about four possible lunch restaurants that are all located within easy walking distance of the meeting site. The data are displayed below.

RESTAURANT NAME	MEAN LUNCH COST	STANDARD DEVIATION
Bon Appetite	$8.00	0.75
Mario's	$7.50	1
Au Courant	$9.00	1.25
The Windy City Grill	$7.50	1.5

You want to stay within the reimbursement rate allowed by your Component State Association, so it is important to you that you have at least a 95% chance of eating a lunch that costs no more than $10.00. Therefore, when lunchtime comes, you head to

A. Bon Appetite or Mario's.

B. Mario's or Au Courant.

C. Au Courant or The Windy City Grill.

D. The Windy City Grill or Bon Appetite.

REFERENCE: Horton, pp 184–186
Koch, pp 246–247
McWay, p 206

6. Organizations collect statistics to increase their knowledge of a specified population. The knowledge does not come automatically—it is developed in the following sequence:

A. data → facts → information → knowledge.

B. data → information → facts → knowledge.

C. facts → data → information → knowledge.

D. facts → information → data → knowledge.

REFERENCE: Horton, pp 2–3

Questions 7 and 8 are based on the study and data below.

The coding supervisor at Bayside Hospital regularly has the coders recode records from the previous week in an effort to improve and monitor coding consistency. The supervisor has collected the data displayed below on four coders.

Coder	Records Under Review	Same Code on Self-Coding Review	Same Code on Peer Coding Review
Coder A	28	22	20
Coder B	18	16	16
Coder C	45	42	43
Coder D	17	15	16

7. The data in the column on the far right were collected when the coders traded records for recoding. This is a common practice used to check
   A. interrater reliability.
   B. intrarater reliability.
   C. interrater validity.
   D. intrarater validity.

REFERENCE: Abdelhak, pp 410–412
               Sayles, pp 574–575
               Shi, p 299

8. The coder with the highest overall accuracy rating will get the day after Thanksgiving off. Which coder will get to spend the day after Thanksgiving off rather than coding?
   A. Coder A
   B. Coder B
   C. Coder C
   D. Coder D

REFERENCE: Abdelhak pp 368–369
               Koch, p 48
               Horton, pp 14, 19–20
               Sayles, pp 475–476

9. Which of the following interactions fits the definition of a patient encounter?

   Phyllis saw Dr. Holland during a scheduled office visit. Dr. Holland prescribed a new medication.

   Jean called Dr. Holland with a question about her medication. Dr. Holland returned the telephone call and answered Jean's question.

   Howard was seen by Dr. Holland in the hospital emergency department after having a reaction to his medication.

   The pharmacy received telephone approval from Dr. Horton for a refill on Jackson's prescription.

   A. Phyllis, Jean, Howard, and Jackson
   B. Jackson, Howard, and Jean
   C. Jean, Phyllis, and Howard
   D. Phyllis and Howard

REFERENCE: Abdelhak, p 138
               Horton, pp 4, 148
               LaTour, Eichenwald-Maki, and Oachs, p 498

10. A small portion of the form you are using for a research study is reproduced below.

Male	1
Female	2

This is an example of

A. ordinal data.
B. ranked data.
C. nominal data.
D. discrete data.

REFERENCE: Abdelhak, pp 380–385
                        Horton, pp 196–199
                        Koch, pp 12–13
                        LaTour, Eichenwald-Maki, and Oachs, pp 482–483
                        McWay, p 212

11. You have made a list of the advantages and disadvantages of a measure of central tendency.

ADVANTAGES	DISADVANTAGES
Easy to obtain and interpret	May not be descriptive of the distribution
Not sensitive to extreme observations in the frequency distribution	May not be unique
Easy to communicate and explain to others	Does not provide information about the entire distribution

The measure of central tendency you are describing is the

A. mean.
B. median.
C. range.
D. mode.

REFERENCE: Abdelhak, pp 385–387
                        Horton, pp 175–181
                        Koch, pp 234–237
                        LaTour, Eichenwald-Maki, and Oachs, pp 518–520
                        McWay, pp 205–206
                        Sayles, pp 538–541

The following data were collected in your physician office practice from one morning's visits. Use the data for questions 12, 13, and 14.

Office Visit ID Number	Minutes with the Physician	Physician
508-123	5	Robinson
508-124	9	Robinson
508-125	8	Beasley
508-126	12	Wolf
508-127	6	Beasley
508-128	7	Beasley
508-129	5	Wolf
508-130	10	Baumstark
508-131	7	Baumstark
508-132	9	Robinson
508-133	11	Wolf

12. The median number of minutes with the physician (considering all physicians) is
    A. 7 minutes.
    B. 8 minutes.
    C. 8.4 minutes.
    D. 9 minutes.

REFERENCE: Abdelhak, pp 385–387
              Horton, pp 175–181
              Koch, pp 234–237
              McWay, pp 205–206
              Sayles, pp 538–541
              Shaw, p 56

13. The mean number of minutes with the physician (considering all physicians) is
    A. 7 minutes.
    B. 8 minutes.
    C. 8.4 minutes.
    D. 9 minutes.

REFERENCE: Abdelhak, pp 385–387
              Horton, pp 175–181
              Koch, pp 234–237
              McWay, p 194
              Sayles, pp 538–541
              Shaw, pp 53–54

14. Which physician spent the longest average time with patients on that day?
    A. Beasley
    B. Wolf
    C. Baumstark
    D. Robinson

REFERENCE: Abdelhak, pp 385–387
              Koch, pp 234–237
              Sayles, pp 538–541
              Shaw, pp 53–54

Use this portion of the discharges printout below to answer questions 15 and 16.

Discharge List					
Patient #	Admit Date	Service	Physician ID	Room #	LOS
12-32-21	1/02/14	MED	212	44-A	13
12-32-22	1/02/14	SURG	218	32	13
12-32-85	1/14/14	PEDS	214	23-B	1
11-99-94	1/12/14	MED	212	46-A	3
10-93-23	1/10/14	MED	212	45	5
12-35-94	1/11/14	SURG	218	33	4
10-85-14	1/01/14	PEDS	214	23-A	14

15. Without even performing any complex calculations, you can get a quick, simple measure of dispersion in the LOS for yesterday's discharges by computing the
    A. range of the data set.
    B. mean of the data set.
    C. variance of the data set.
    D. coefficient of variation of the data set.

REFERENCE: Abdelhak, pp 385–389
               Horton, pp 175–182
               Koch, pp 234–243
               Sayles, pp 538–542

16. Looking more closely at the LOS for these patients, when you calculate the standard deviation on the data, you would expect
    A. a large standard deviation because the dispersion is large.
    B. a small standard deviation because the dispersion is small.
    C. a large standard deviation because the dispersion is small.
    D. a small standard deviation because the dispersion is large.

REFERENCE: Abdelhak, pp 387–389
               Horton, pp 183–186
               Koch, pp 246–247
               McWay, pp 206–204
               Sayles, p 542
               Shaw, pp 54–56

17. Englewood Health Center collected the following data on patients discharged on January 1, 2013. Which measure of central tendency would be most affected by Mallory's extremely long LOS?

Patient Name	Length of Stay
Ben	1
Josh	2
Emma	3
Bryan	4
Mallory	29
Taylor	2
Matthew	3
Aiden	2
Trevor	4
Tyler	2

A. variance
B. median
C. mean
D. mode

REFERENCE: Abdelhak, pp 385–387
Horton, pp 175–181
Koch, pp 234–243
LaTour, Eichenwald-Maki, and Oachs, pp 518–520
McWay, pp 205–206
Sayles, pp 538–541
Shaw, pp 53–56

CASE NUMBER	BRIEF DESCRIPTION
101-43-26	A 32-year-old female was admitted through the ED following an automobile accident. She spontaneously delivered a 720 g fetus that showed no sign of life.
101-44-23	A 22-year-old female was admitted in labor. Following an uneventful course, she delivered a 7 lb 4 oz term male. The child developed sudden and unexpected respiratory distress. All attempts at resuscitation failed; the baby was pronounced dead less than 2 hours after delivery.
101-48-69	A 19-year-old female spontaneously delivered a 475 g fetus following a fall down the stairs at home.
101-56-29	A 28-year-old female was admitted for a late-term therapeutic abortion. The procedure was completed without complication; product of conception weighed 728 g.

18. The OB/GYN Department reported the information in the table shown above to the Quality Management/Statistics Committee. When the committee considers these adverse outcomes from the OB/GYN Department, which of the cases will be included in the numerator of the facility's fetal death rate?
A. 101-43-26
B. 101-43-26 and 101-44-23
C. 101-43-26 and 101-48-69
D. 101-43-26 and 101-56-29

REFERENCE: Abdelhak, pp 368–372
Horton, pp 88–89
Johns, pp 557–559
Koch, pp 147–148
LaTour, Eichenwald-Maki, and Oachs, p 492

19. Which of the cases listed in the table above will have an impact on the facility's gross death rate?
    A. 101-43-26
    B. 101-44-23
    C. 101-48-69
    D. 101-56-29

REFERENCE: Abdelhak, pp 368–373
              Horton, pp 72–74
              Koch, p 120
              LaTour, Eichenwald-Maki, and Oachs, p 490
              Sayles, p 489

20. Patients in the pediatrics ward were studied to determine their favorite color. The survey results are listed below. The results of the favorite color study are reported in a

REPORTED FAVORITE COLOR OF PEDIATRIC PATIENTS AZURE TIDES HOSPITAL JANUARY 18, 2014	
FAVORITE COLOR	NUMBER OF RESPONDENTS
RED	12
GREEN	14
BLUE	22
YELLOW	18
ORANGE	16

    A. frequency polygon.
    B. line graph.
    C. frequency distribution.
    D. systematic fashion.

REFERENCE: Abdelhak, pp 382–385
              Horton, pp 202–212
              Koch, pp 260–284
              McWay, pp 212–215
              Sayles, pp 522–533
              Shi, pp 359–360

21. All of the following items mean the same thing, EXCEPT
    A. inpatient service day.
    B. daily inpatient census.
    C. daily census.
    D. inpatient census.

REFERENCE: Abdelhak, pp 378–379
              Horton, pp 24–27
              Koch, pp 64–67
              LaTour, Eichenwald-Maki, and Oachs, pp 510–516
              McWay, pp 201–216

22. Pasadena Bay Hospital reports an average LOS in February of 3.7 days with a standard deviation of 20. This tells us that
    A. most patients had an LOS of 3–4 days.
    B. there was a small variation in the LOS.
    C. patients at Pasadena Bay stay longer than average.
    D. there was a large variation in the LOS.

REFERENCE:　　Abdelhak, pp 385–388
　　　　　　　　Horton, pp 184–186
　　　　　　　　Koch, pp 246–247
　　　　　　　　LaTour, Eichenwald-Maki, and Oachs, pp 520–521
　　　　　　　　McWay, pp 206–207
　　　　　　　　Sayles, pp 542–545
　　　　　　　　Shaw, pp 54–56

23. Jason collected data on the length of stay (LOS) for 10 patients and then determined the median LOS as follows:

1	
2	
4	
3	
1	← median
3	
2	
4	
2	
8	

What is wrong with Jason's determination of the median?
    A. There is nothing wrong with Jason's determination of the median.
    B. Jason forgot to put the numbers in sequential order before determining the median.
    C. It is not possible to determine the median on such a small number of data points.
    D. It is not possible to determine the median on an even number of data points.

REFERENCE:　　Abdelhak, pp 383–389
　　　　　　　　Horton, pp 175–181
　　　　　　　　Koch, pp 234–237
　　　　　　　　McWay, pp 204–206
　　　　　　　　Sayles, pp 538–541
　　　　　　　　Shaw, p 54

Section II—Commonly Computed Rates and Percentages for Hospital Inpatients

24. All Women's Hospital reports the following statistics:

Single births	
Vaginal	40
C-section	0
Twin births	
Twins—vaginal	12 (6 sets)
Twins—C-section	8 (4 sets)
Other multiple births	0
Intermediate fetal deaths	
Vaginal	5
C-section	0
Late fetal deaths	
Vaginal	2
C-section	0

How many deliveries occurred?
A. 50
B. 57
C. 60
D. 67

REFERENCE: Horton, pp 124–125
                      Koch, p 140

25. The inpatient census at midnight is 67. Two patients were admitted in the morning; one died 2 hours later; the second patient was transferred to another facility that same afternoon. The inpatient service days for that day will be
A. 65.
B. 67.
C. 68.
D. 69.

REFERENCE: Abdelhak, pp 378–380
                      Horton, pp 27–32
                      Koch, pp 68–69
                      LaTour, Eichenwald-Maki, and Oachs, pp 486–487
                      Sayles, p 481

26. Bayside Hospital has 275 adult beds, 30 pediatric beds, and 40 bassinets. In a nonleap year, inpatient service days were 75,860 for adults, 7,100 for pediatrics, and 11,800 for newborns. What was the average daily census for the year?
A. 227
B. 208
C. 207
D. 259

REFERENCE: Abdelhak, pp 378–380
                      Horton, pp 38–42
                      Koch, pp 75–77
                      LaTour, Eichenwald-Maki, and Oachs, pp 486–487
                      Sayles, pp 481–482

27. In order to derive the total inpatient service days for any given day, you would need to
    A. subtract intra hospital transfers from the inpatient census.
    B. add same-day admits and discharges to the inpatient census.
    C. add intra hospital transfers to the inpatient census.
    D. subtract same day admits and discharges from the inpatient census.

REFERENCE: Abdelhak, pp 378–380
Horton, pp 27–32
Koch, pp 68–69
LaTour, Eichenwald-Maki, and Oachs, p 487

28. Mr. McDonaldson was admitted to your hospital at 10:45 PM on January 1. He died at 4:22 AM on January 3. How many inpatient service days did Mr. McDonaldson receive?
    A. 1   C. 3
    B. 2   D. 4

REFERENCE: Abdelhak, pp 382–384
Horton, pp 27–32
Koch, pp 68–69
LaTour, Eichenwald-Maki, and Oachs, pp 486–487
McWay, p 209
Sayles, p 481

29. A patient admitted to the hospital on January 24 and discharged on February 9 has a length of stay of
    A. 16 days.   C. 17 days.
    B. 15 days.   D. 14 days.

REFERENCE: Abdelhak, pp 378–380
Horton, pp 58–61
Koch, pp 102–106
McWay, p 209
Sayles, pp 485–487

Use the data in the table below to answer the next two questions.

Royal Palm Hospital has 500 beds and 55 bassinets. In February of a nonleap year, it reported the following statistics:

Inpatient service days:	
Adult and pediatric	12,345
Newborn	553
Discharges:	
Adult and pediatric	1,351
Newborn	77
Discharge days:	
Adult and pediatric	9,457
Newborn	231

30. What was the percentage of occupancy for adults and pediatrics in February?
    A. 84.8%
    B. 88.2%
    C. 79.6%
    D. 80.5%

REFERENCE: Abdelhak, pp 378–380
               Koch, pp 86–90
               Horton, pp 46–48
               LaTour, Eichenwald-Maki, and Oachs, p 488
               Sayles, pp 483–484

31. What was the average length of stay at Royal Palm Hospital in February?
    A. 6.8 days
    B. 7 days
    C. 9 days
    D. 9.1 days

REFERENCE: Abdelhak, pp 378–380
               Koch, pp 106–110
               Horton, pp 63–65
               LaTour, Eichenwald-Maki, and Oachs, p 490
               McWay, p 209
               Sayles, p 490

32. You are responsible for calculating and reporting average length of stay (ALOS) for your hospital each month. This month, there were 92 discharges, and the total discharge days equal 875. One of the patients discharged this month had a total of 428 discharge days, so the ALOS is distorted by this unusually long stay. In this situation, you should report an ALOS of
   A. 9.51 days— no further information is necessary.
   B. 9.61 days and make a note that the one patient with an unusually long LOS was subtracted prior to making the calculation.
   C. 4.86 days and make a note that one unusually long LOS was subtracted prior to making the calculation.
   D. 4.91 days and make a note that the data on one patient with an unusually long LOS were subtracted prior to making the calculation.

REFERENCE: Abdelhak, pp 378–380
                Horton, pp 63–65
                Koch, pp 106–110
                McWay, p 209
                Sayles, pp 489–488, 487–788
                Shaw, pp 46–48

33. A hospital reported the following statistics during a nonleap year. Calculate the percentage of occupancy for the entire year.

Time Period	Bed Count	Inpatient Service Days
January 1–May 31	200	28,690
June 1–October 15	250	27,400
October 16–December 31	275	19,250

   A. 85.2%   C. 90.0%
   B. 88%   D. 91.2%

REFERENCE: Abdelhak, pp 378–380
                Horton, pp 46–48
                Koch, pp 86–90
                LaTour, Eichenwald-Maki, and Oachs, p 488
                Sayles, pp 483–484

34. Lake City Health Center has 200 beds and 20 bassinets. In a nonleap year, Styles Hospital admitted 16,437 adults and children; 16,570 adults and children were discharged. There were 1,764 live births and 1,798 newborns discharged. The bed turnover rate for the year was
   A. 82.2.   C. 82.9.
   B. 82.7.   D. 93.5.

REFERENCE: Abdelhak, pp 378–380
                Horton, pp 52–53
                Koch, pp 185–187
                LaTour, Eichenwald-Maki, and Oachs, pp 488–489
                Sayles, p 484

35. Sea Crest Hospital has 200 beds and 20 bassinets. There was a sudden spurt in the birth rate in the town in November. The hospital set up five additional bassinets for the entire month. Total bed count days for Sea Crest Hospital in a nonleap year would be
    A. 73,000.
    C. 80,450.
    B. 80,300.
    D. 80,455.

REFERENCE: Abdelhak, pp 378–380
Horton, p 45
Koch, pp 84–85
LaTour, Eichenwald-Maki, and Oachs, p 488
Sayles, pp 483–484

36. Use the statistics provided in the table to compute the fetal death rate at All Women's Hospital for March.

All Women's Hospital March Statistics	
Live births	225
Intermediate and late fetal deaths	5
Early fetal deaths	4
Newborn discharges	235

    A. 4.0%
    C. 2.2%
    B. 1.78%
    D. 1.77%

REFERENCE: Abdelhak, pp 372–373
Horton, pp 88–89
Koch, pp 147–149
LaTour, Eichenwald-Maki, and Oachs, p 492
Sayles, pp 490–491

The following obstetrical statistics were collected for the month of October. Use the data in the table below to answer the next two questions.

DELIVERED		TOTAL	DELIVERED BY C-SECTION
Live			
	Single infant	50	15
	Twins	3 sets	1 set
Dead			
	Early fetal	1	0
	Late fetal	1	1

37. The number of births in the facility in October is
    A. 53.
    C. 56.
    B. 55.
    D. 58.

REFERENCE: Horton, pp 124–125
Koch, pp 209–210
Sayles, pp 509–511

38. The number of deliveries in the facility in October is
    A. 53.
    C. 56.
    B. 55.
    D. 58.

REFERENCE: Horton, pp 124–125
              Koch, p 140

39. Ocean View Healthcare Center recorded six fetal deaths during the last year; details are listed below.

Fetal Death Information		
ID	WEIGHT	GESTATIONAL AGE
A	526 g	22 weeks
B	405 g	18 weeks
C	817 g	26 weeks
D	1,023 g	30 weeks
E	629 g	24 weeks
F	1,113 g	29 weeks

How should these deaths be counted in the hospital death rates?
    A. All the deaths except B will be included in the gross death rate.
    B. Deaths D and F will be included in the gross death rate.
    C. Deaths C, D, and F will be included in the gross death rate.
    D. None of these deaths will be included in the gross death rate.

REFERENCE: Abdelhak, p 372
              Horton, pp 72–74
              Johns, p 556
              Koch, p 120
              LaTour, Eichenwald-Maki, and Oachs, pp 490–492
              Sayles, pp 488–489

40. William Rumple was pronounced dead on arrival (DOA). The hospital pathologist performed an autopsy on Mr. Rumple's body. This statistical event would be counted in the
    A. net death rate.
    C. net autopsy rate.
    B. gross death rate.
    D. hospital autopsy rate.

REFERENCE: Abdelhak, pp 375–376
              Horton, pp 72–76, 95–105
              Koch, pp 119–121, 162–170
              LaTour, Eichenwald-Maki, and Oachs, pp 490–495
              Sayles, pp 488–496

Tampa Bay Health Center discharged 6,069 adults/children and 545 newborns last year. A total of 1,648 adults/children and 1,279 newborns were seen in the emergency department. Information on the deaths at Happy Valley last year is listed below. Use the data to answer the next two questions.

INPATIENT DEATHS		
Adult/child	245 < 48 hr	105 > 48 hr
Newborn	8 < 48 hr	3 > 48 hr

OUTPATIENT (ED) DEATHS		
Adult/child	2	
Newborn	0	

FETAL DEATHS		
Early	1	
Intermediate	3	
Late	2	

41. What was the gross (hospital) death rate at Tampa Bay Health Center last year?
    A. 3.8%   C. 5.5%
    B. 5.4%   D. 5.6%

REFERENCE: Abdelhak, pp 369–371
             Horton, pp 72–74
             Koch, p 120
             LaTour, Eichenwald-Maki, and Oachs, p 490
             Sayles, p 489

42. What was the net death rate at Tampa Bay Health Center last year?
    A. 1.6%   C. 1.8%
    B. 1.7%   D. 1.9%

REFERENCE: Abdelhak, pp 369–371
             Horton, pp 75–76
             Koch, pp 120–121
             LaTour, Eichenwald-Maki, and Oachs, p 492
             Sayles, p 489

43. During the month of September, Superior Health Care Center had 1,382 inpatient discharges, including 48 deaths. There were 38 deaths over 48 hours. Statistics also show 4 fetal deaths, 3 DOAs, and 4 inpatient coroner's cases. Which of the following calculations is correct to figure the net death rate?
    A. (48 × 100) / (1,382 – 10)
    B. (48–10 × 100) / (1,382 – 10)
    C. (1,382 × 100) / (48 – 10)
    D. (1,382 – 10) × 100 / (48 – 10)

REFERENCE: Abdelhak, pp 369–373
             Horton, pp 75–76
             Koch, pp 120–121
             LaTour, Eichenwald-Maki, and Oachs, p 492
             Sayles, p 489

44. The best form/graph for demonstrating trends over time would be
    A. frequency polygon.   C. pie chart.
    B. line graph.   D. histogram.

REFERENCE: Horton, p 212
                 Koch, pp 273–274
                 McWay, p 201
                 Shaw, pp 49–51, 57–63

45. Joseph Woodley has been on a third floor nursing unit since October 2012 and was finally discharged to a nursing home in December 2013. When the average length of stay is calculated for the year 2013, this very long length of stay will
    A. have little impact on the average length of stay.
    B. result in a special cause variation in the average length of stay.
    C. result in a small variation in the average length of stay.
    D. result in a common cause variation in the average length of stay.

REFERENCE: Abdelhak, pp 385–388
                 Horton, pp 62–64
                 Koch, pp 106–110
                 Sayles, pp 486–488
                 Shaw, pp 44–46

46. Still thinking about Mr. Woodley and his long stay, if you were to graph the ALOS for the facility for 2013, which of the following graphs would you expect to see?

A.   C.

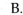

B.   D.

REFERENCE: Abdelhak, pp 387–389
                 Horton, pp 187–189
                 Koch, pp 238–240
                 LaTour, Eichenwald-Maki, and Oachs, pp 510–516
                 Shaw, pp 44–46

47. The New Beginnings Maternity Center recorded the following statistics in December:

FETAL DEATHS:	
EARLY	240
INTERMEDIATE	40
LATE	32
BIRTHS	980
DELIVERIES	994
NEWBORN DISCHARGES	1,008

What was the fetal death rate at New Beginnings Maternity Center in December?
A. 6.8%   C. 7.4%
B. 7.3%   D. 31.8%

REFERENCE: Abdelhak, pp 369–372
                Horton, pp 88–89
                Koch, pp 147–149
                LaTour, Eichenwald-Maki, and Oachs, p 492
                Sayles, pp 490–491

48. The statistics reported for a 300-bed hospital for 1 year were 20,932 discharges with 136,651 discharge days and 3,699 consultations performed. What was the consultation rate for the year?
A. 16.5%   C. 17.7%
B. 17.0%   D. 18.0%

REFERENCE: Horton, pp 126–127
                Koch, pp 182–183
                Sayles, pp 498–499

Section III—Data Display

You have already practiced reading tables in many of the preceding questions. Data display—the selection, interpretation, and construction of data—is an important part of HIM practice. Therefore, a number of data display questions should be expected. Examples of these kinds of questions follow.

© Cengage Learning 2015

49. Look at the graph grid displayed above. If you want to follow accepted principles for graph construction, you will follow the three-quarter-high rule. That means the
    A. height of the graph should be three-fourths the length of the graph.
    B. length of the graph should be three-fourths the height of the graph.
    C. height of the graph should display three-fourths of the data in the graph.
    D. length of the graph should display three-fourths of the data in the graph.

REFERENCE: Horton, p 207
              LaTour, Eichenwald-Maki, and Oachs, p 510
              Sayles, p 522

50. You are preparing data from a series of weight loss studies for display. The data collected during the study are as follows:

POUNDS LOST	NUMBER IN GROUP A WITH THIS WEIGHT LOSS	NUMBER IN GROUP B WITH THIS WEIGHT LOSS
7.5–9.4	1	2
9.5–11.4	3	2
11.5–13.4	6	5
13.5–15.4	5	4
15.5–17.4	8	7
17.5–19.4	2	3

If you want to allow the reader to compare the results of Group A with those of Group B on one graphic display, your best choice would be to construct a

A. bar chart.
B. line graph.
C. histogram.
D. frequency polygon.

REFERENCE: Abdelhak, pp 382–385
Horton, pp 207–212
Koch, pp 264–284
LaTour, Eichenwald-Maki, and Oachs, pp 510–513
McWay, pp 213–215
Sayles, pp 522–529
Shaw, pp 48–51, 57–63

51. A distribution is said to be positively skewed when the mean is
A. bimodal.
B. multimodal.
C. shifted to the left.
D. shifted to the right.

REFERENCE: Horton, pp 187–189
Koch, pp 238–240
Shaw, pp 56–58

52. You want to graph the number of patients admitted to three different medical staff services on each day of the last month. Because you have a large number of observations (one for each day of the month) and you want to be able to compare the observations for each of the three services on one data display, your best choice is a
A. table.
B. bar chart.
C. line graph.
D. histogram.

REFERENCE: Horton, pp 207–212
Koch, pp 264–284
LaTour, Eichenwald-Maki, and Oachs, pp 510–516
McWay, pp 201–206
Sayles, pp 522–533
Shaw, pp 48–51, 57–63

53. You have just constructed the chart displayed below.

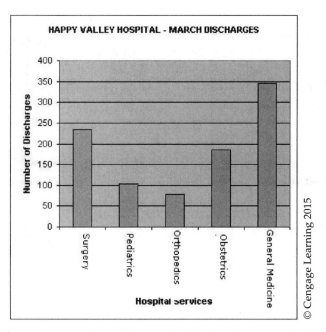

The names of the hospital services are hard to read. The best way to deal with this problem would be to

A. construct a line graph instead of a bar chart.
B. use a column chart instead of a bar chart.
C. plot your primary variable along the *x*-axis.
D. divide the data into two charts.

REFERENCE: Horton, pp 206–209
               Koch, pp 264–273
               LaTour, Eichenwald-Maki, and Oachs, pp 508–509
               Sayles, pp 520–522

54. The display below is a

A. bar chart, which is commonly used to display continuous data.
B. bar chart, which is commonly used to display discrete data.
C. histogram, which is commonly used to display continuous data.
D. histogram, which is commonly used to display discrete data.

REFERENCE: Horton, pp 207–212
               Koch, pp 264–283
               LaTour, Eichenwald-Maki, and Oachs, pp 510–513
               McWay, pp 213–214
               Sayles, pp 522–528
               Shaw, pp 48–51, 57–63

55. The data display below is a

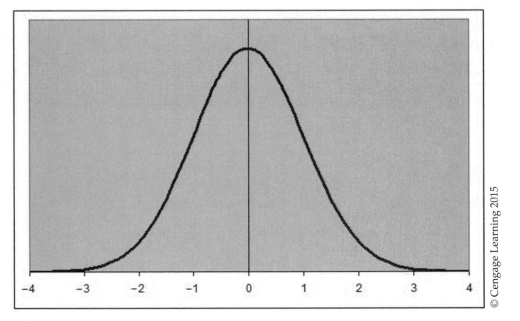

A. normal distribution or curve.
B. positive skewed curve.
C. negative skewed curve.
D. heterogeneous curve.

REFERENCE: Horton, pp 187–189
               Koch, pp 238–240
               McWay, pp 219–220
               Shaw, pp 56–58
               Shi, p 359

56. What conclusion can you make from the pie graph below?

NUMBER OF PATIENTS DISCHARGED IN MARCH
BY SERVICE

- Surgery
- Pediatrics
- Orthopedics
- Obstetrics
- General Medicine
- Newborn Nursery
- PICU
- Gerentology
- Psychiatry
- Rehabilitation

© Cengage Learning 2015

    A. A pie graph should not be used, because there are too many categories for effective display.
    B. A pie graph should not be used, because the data are representational instead of quantitative.
    C. A pie graph should not be used, because the data are qualitative instead of quantitative.
    D. A pie graph is a good choice and is often used to display this kind of data.

REFERENCE: Abdelhak, pp 382–383
                 Horton, pp 210–211
                 Koch, pp 273–274
                 LaTour, Eichenwald-Maki, and Oachs, pp 510–511
                 McWay, pp 213–214
                 Sayles, p 525
                 Shaw, pp 48–51, 57–63

57. You are trying to improve communication with your staff by posting graphs of significant statistics on the employee bulletin board. You recently calculated the percentage of time employees spend on each of six major tasks. Because you would like the employees to appreciate each task as a percentage of their whole day, you will post these figures using a
    A. line graph.   C. scatter diagram.
    B. bar graph.   D. pie graph.

REFERENCE: Abdelhak, pp 382–385
                 Horton, pp 207–216
                 Koch, pp 264–274
                 LaTour, Eichenwald-Maki, and Oachs, pp 510–514
                 McWay, pp 213–215
                 Sayles, pp 522–531
                 Shaw, pp 48–51, 57–63

58. The graph below can best be described as

A. sequential.
B. multimodal.

C. substitutional.
D. erratic.

REFERENCE: Koch, pp 241–243
              Horton, pp 187–189

59. Looking at the data represented in the scatter diagram below, you would conclude that there is

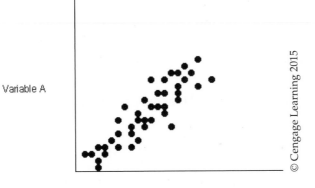

A. no correlation between Variable A and Variable B.
B. a positive correlation between Variable A and Variable B.
C. a negative correlation between Variable A and Variable B.
D. a cause and effect relationship between Variable A and Variable B.

REFERENCE: Horton, pp 216–219
              LaTour, Eichenwald-Maki, and Oachs, pp 513–514
              McWay, pp 219–220
              Sayles, pp 544–545

60. The data displayed in the histogram below could best be described as

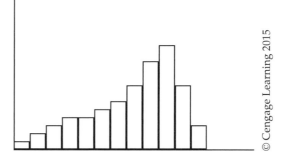

© Cengage Learning 2015

   A. negatively skewed.
   B. positively skewed.
   C. evenly distributed.
   D. normally distributed.

REFERENCE: Horton, pp 187–189
               Koch, pp 238–240
               LaTour, Eichenwald-Maki, and Oachs, pp 513–514
               Sayles, pp 544–545
               Shaw, pp 56–58

61. You want to construct a data display for a frequency distribution. You will use a
   A. frequency polygon or histogram.
   B. frequency polygon or bar chart.
   C. line graph or histogram.
   D. line graph or bar chart.

REFERENCE: Abdelhak, pp 382–385
               Horton, pp 207–212
               LaTour, Eichenwald-Maki, and Oachs, pp 510–513
               McWay, pp 213–215
               Sayles, pp 522–529
               Shaw, pp 48–51, 57–63

62. Look at the graph below. It is an example of a

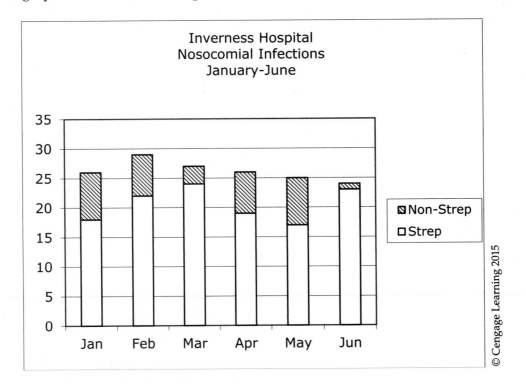

A. stacked bar chart; it is well constructed.
B. histogram; it is well constructed.
C. comparison bar chart; it is not well constructed.
D. frequency polygon; it is not well constructed.

REFERENCE: Abdelhak, pp 382–385
Koch, pp 264–285
McWay, pp 213–215
Sayles, pp 522–529

Use the historical graph below to answer questions 63 and 64.

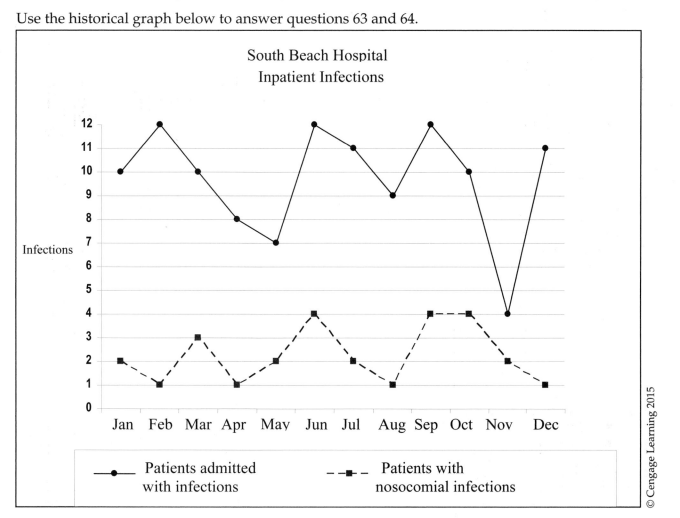

63. The total number of infections at South Beach Hospital during the first quarter (January–March) was
    A. 6.
    B. 12.
    C. 22.
    D. 38.

REFERENCE: Abdelhak, pp 382–385
              Horton, pp 212–214
              Koch, pp 274–278
              LaTour, Eichenwald-Maki, and Oachs, pp 495–496
              McWay, pp 210–211
              Sayles, pp 497–498

64. Look again at the graph you used for the last question. From this graph, you can assume that more people
    A. were admitted to the facility with infections than without infections.
    B. were admitted to the facility with infections than is typical for U.S. hospitals.
    C. were admitted to the facility with infections than acquired infections in the hospital.
    D. acquired infections in the hospital than were admitted with infections.

REFERENCE: Abdelhak, pp 382–385
              Horton, pp 212–214
              Koch, pp 274–278
              McWay, pp 213–214

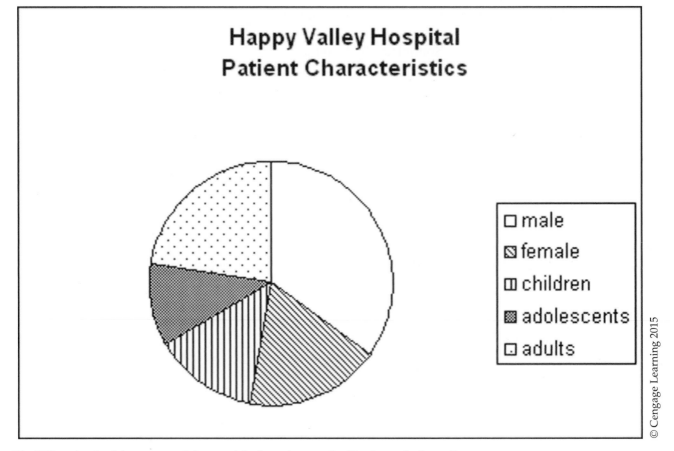

**Happy Valley Hospital
Patient Characteristics**

- □ male
- ⊠ female
- ⊞ children
- ▨ adolescents
- □ adults

© Cengage Learning 2015

65. What is the biggest problem with the pie graph displayed above?
   A. There is not enough variation in the patterns to clearly distinguish between females and children.
   B. The total males and females do not equal the total children, adolescents, and adults.
   C. There are no definitions for children, adolescents, and adults.
   D. There is more than one variable displayed on the chart.

REFERENCE: Horton, pp 210–211
               Koch, pp 273–274
               LaTour, Eichenwald-Maki, and Oachs, pp 510–511
               McWay, pp 213–214

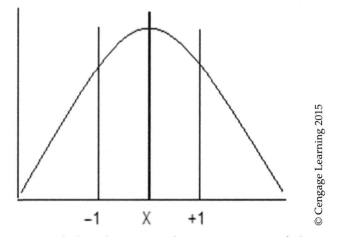

© Cengage Learning 2015

66. The chart above shows a normal distribution. What percentage of the cases fall within the two lines showing the standard distribution between –1 and +1 on either side of the mean?
    A. 68%   C. 95%
    B. 75%   D. 99%

REFERENCE: Horton, pp 184–186
                Koch, pp 238–243
                LaTour, Eichenwald-Maki, and Oachs, pp 520–521
                Shaw, pp 54–56

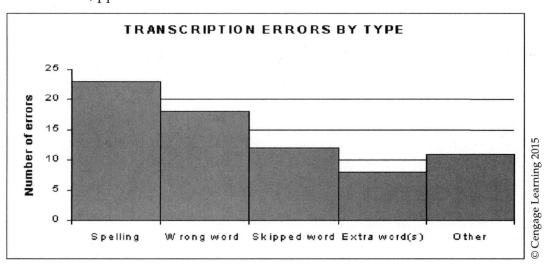

© Cengage Learning 2015

67. A transcription supervisor collected the data displayed above. What kind of data display is it? And how many errors are attributed to skipped words?
    A. This is a Pareto diagram; twelve (12) errors were due to skipped words.
    B. This is a bar chart; eighteen (18) errors were due to skipped words.
    C. This is a Pareto diagram; eighteen (18) errors were due to skipped words.
    D. This is a bar chart; twelve (12) errors were due to skipped words.

REFERENCE: Abdelhak, pp 382–385
                LaTour, Eichenwald-Maki, and Oachs, p 510
                McWay, p 213
                Shaw, pp 48–51, 57–63

68. A fetal death occurring during the 21st week of pregnancy, weighing 1,000 g is considered to be a(n)
   A. early fetal death.
   B. preterm neonate.
   C. intermediate fetal death.
   D. late fetal death.

REFERENCE: Horton, p 88
            Koch, pp 142–144
            LaTour, Eichenwald-Maki, and Oachs, p 492
            Sayles, pp 490–491

Section IV—Research, Financial Statistics, Etc.

You will use your statistics skills for a number of HIM functions. As usual, you must be prepared for that nebulous category we call "other." For these questions, use your basic problem-solving skills along with the terminology you learned in your statistics class. Many of these questions deal primarily with research and budgeting matters, so they are typically considered more appropriate for the RHIA than the RHIT. The RHIA questions are listed last and are so labeled.

69. Harry H. Potter was admitted to your hospital to receive a second round of chemotherapy for an invasive tumor. Four days after admission, Harry complained of a sore throat and developed a fever. Harry's throat culture was positive for strep. His strep throat will be
    A. added to the denominator of the hospital's nosocomial infection rate.
    B. added to the numerator of the hospital's community-acquired infection rate.
    C. considered separately because Harry H. Potter is immune suppressed from chemotherapy.
    D. added to the numerator of the hospital's nosocomial infection rate.

REFERENCE: Abdelhak, pp 376–378
               Horton, pp 116–117
               Koch, p 179
               LaTour, Eichenwald-Maki, and Oachs, p 495
               McWay, pp 201–211
               Sayles, p 497

70. Twelve new cases of a certain disease occurred during the month of August. If 4,000 persons were at risk during August, then the
    A. prevalence was 3 per 1,000 persons.
    B. prevalence was 6 per 1,000 persons.
    C. incidence was 3 per 1,000 persons.
    D. incidence was 6 per 1,000 persons.

REFERENCE: Abdelhak, pp 376–378
               Koch, p 205
               LaTour, Eichenwald-Maki, and Oachs, p 506
               Layman and Watzlaf, pp 131–132, 138
               McWay, p 210
               Sayles, pp 516–517

71. The primary difference between an experimental (randomized) clinical trial and other observational study designs in epidemiology is that in an experimental trial, the
    A. study is prospective.
    B. investigator determines who is and who is not exposed.
    C. study is case controlled.
    D. study and control maps are selected on the basis of exposure to the suspected causal factor.

REFERENCE: Abdelhak, pp 424–427
               Horton, pp 232–234
               Layman and Watzlaf, pp 44–46, 48–49
               McWay, pp 234–237
               Shi, pp 166–167, 182–186

72. The ability to obtain the same results from different studies using different methodologies and different populations is
    A. reliability.
    B. validity.
    C. confidence.
    D. specificity.

REFERENCE: Abdelhak, pp 410–412
               Horton, pp 232–233
               LaTour, Eichenwald-Maki, and Oachs, pp 573–575
               Layman and Watzlaf, pp 221–222
               McWay, pp 240–241
               Shi, pp 291, 297–300

73. You have been conducting productivity studies on your coders and find that 20% of their time is devoted to querying physicians about missing or unclear diagnoses. Assuming your coders work a 7-hour day, how many minutes do they spend per day querying physicians?
    A. 21
    B. 56
    C. 84
    D. 140

REFERENCE: Horton, pp 147–148
               Koch, pp 56–57

Use these data to calculate answers to questions 74 and 75.

Venice Bay Health Center collected the data displayed below concerning its four highest volume MS-DRGs.

MS-DRG A		MS-DRG B		MS-DRG C		MS-DRG D	
CMS WEIGHT	NUMBER PATIENTS WITH THIS MS-DRG	CMS WEIGHT	NUMBER PATIENTS WITH THIS MS-DRG	CMS WEIGHT	NUMBER PATIENTS WITH THIS MS-DRG	CMS WEIGHT	NUMBER PATIENTS WITH THIS MS-DRG
2.023	323	0.987	489	1.925	402	1.243	386

74. The MS-DRG that generated the most revenue for Venice Bay Health Center is
    A. MS-DRG A.
    B. MS-DRG B.
    C. MS-DRG C.
    D. MS-DRG D.

REFERENCE: Horton, pp 158–159
               LaTour, Eichenwald-Maki, and Oachs, pp 496–497
               Sayles, p 269

75. CMS has increased the weight for MS-DRG A by 14%, increased the weight for MS-DRG B by 20%, and decreased the weight for MS-DRG D by 10%. Given these new weights, which MS-DRG generated the most revenue for Venice Bay Health Center?
    A. MS-DRG A
    B. MS-DRG B
    C. MS-DRG C
    D. MS-DRG D

REFERENCE: Horton, pp 158–159
               Sayles, p 269

Use these data to answer questions 76 and 77.

Sea Side Clinic (SSC) provides episode of care service for four insurance companies. Data on services provided and reimbursement received are provided below.

COMPANY	UNITS OF SERVICE A	REIMBURSEMENT FOR SERVICE A	UNITS OF SERVICE B	REIMBURSEMENT FOR SERVICE B	TOTAL REIMBURSEMENT
Lifecare	259	31,196.55	812	163,577.40	194,773.95
Get Well	786	100,859.52	465	96,929.25	197,788.77
SureHealth	462	54,631.50	509	107,093.60	161,725.10
Be Healthy	219	26,991.75	417	89,425.65	116,417.40

76. It would be most profitable for Sea Side Clinic to increase episode of care service with
    A. Lifecare.
    B. Get Well.
    C. SureHealth.
    D. BeHealthy.

REFERENCE: Horton, pp 175–180
               Koch, pp 234–237
               LaTour, Eichenwald-Maki, and Oachs, pp 518–520
               Sayles, pp 538–541

77. The most profitable insurance company for the units of services Sea Side Clinic performs is
    A. service A with Lifecare.
    B. service B with GetWell.
    C. service A with SureHealth.
    D. service B with BeHealthy.

REFERENCE: Horton, pp 175–180
               Koch, pp 234–237
               LaTour, Eichenwald-Maki, and Oachs, pp 518–520
               Sayles, pp 538–541

Use these statistics to calculate answers to questions 78 and 79.

The physicians at Sunset Shore Clinic reported the following statistics last Tuesday.

PHYSICIAN	SERVICE A	SERVICE B	SERVICE C
Truba	10	18	14
Wooley	14	22	9
Howe	18	5	6
Masters	12	20	7

78. The physician who performed the highest number of services overall last Tuesday was Doctor
    A. Truba.
    B. Wooley.
    C. Howe.
    D. Masters.

REFERENCE: Horton, pp 147–148
                  Koch, pp 56–57

79. It takes twice as long to perform Service C, so the doctors decided Service C should count as two services for the purpose of calculating workload. If Service C counts twice as much as Service A or Service B, then the physician who provided the most services was Doctor
    A. Truba.
    B. Wooley.
    C. Howe.
    D. Masters.

REFERENCE: Horton, pp 147–148
                  Koch, pp 56–57

The following questions begin advanced competencies.

80. Your facility conducted a study of patient satisfaction, but you question the reliability of the questionnaire you used. The high degree of patient satisfaction expressed on the questionnaire just does not match the large number of complaints you have been receiving. You decide to try switching to an investigative strategy that will give you an immediate opportunity to review patient responses and correct errors. You have decided to use
    A. samples.
    B. interviews.
    C. observations.
    D. questionnaires.

REFERENCE: Horton, pp 232–233
               LaTour, Eichenwald-Maki, and Oachs, pp 562–564
               Shaw, pp 91–103

The next five questions are based on this study and the data collected for it.

The American Health Information Management Association conducted a study on job stress and job satisfaction in HIM professionals with more than 5 years of experience. The data they collected are displayed below.

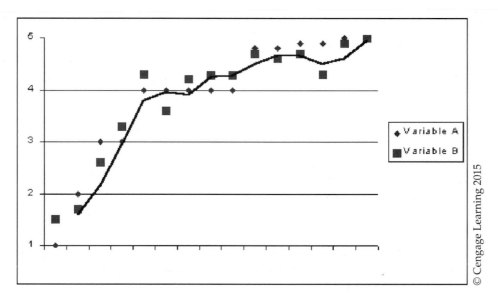

81. The researchers at AHIMA started by assuming there was no relationship between job stress and job satisfaction. This statement is generally called the
    A. study statement.
    B. false assumption.
    C. null hypothesis.
    D. correlation statement.

REFERENCE: Abdelhak, pp 389–391
               Horton, pp 231–232
               LaTour, Eichenwald-Maki, and Oachs, pp 570–571
               Layman and Watzlaf, pp 28–34
               McWay, p 239

82. Based on the data displayed in the graph AHIMA created,
    A. you can assume there is a positive relationship between variable A and variable B.
    B. you can assume there is a negative relationship between variable A and variable B.
    C. you can assume there is a causal relationship between variable A and variable B.
    D. you cannot make any assumptions without additional data.

REFERENCE: Horton, pp 216–219
               Johns, p 632
               Koch, pp 238–240
               LaTour, Eichenwald-Maki, and Oachs, pp 513–514
               Layman and Watzlaf, pp 28–31
               McWay, pp 219–220
               Sayles, pp 544–545

Very Dissatisfied	Somewhat Dissatisfied	Neutral	Somewhat Satisfied	Very Satisfied
1	2	3	4	5

83. The researchers at AHIMA who had professionals with 5 or more years' HIM experience rate their stress on a scale of 1–5, as shown in the chart above. Both job satisfaction and job stress are continuous variables. If the AHIMA researchers want to assess both the direction and the degree of the relationship between these two continuous variables, they may choose to compute the
    A. variable correlation coefficient.
    B. Pearson correlation coefficient.
    C. continuous correlation coefficient.
    D. Danbury correlation coefficient.

REFERENCE: Abdelhak, p 393
               Layman and Watzlaf, pp 28–31
               McWay, pp 215–216
               Shi, pp 366–367

84. There were some HIM professionals who refused to participate in a job stress/job satisfaction study. This is of great concern to the AHIMA researchers, who worry about the introduction of
    A. recall bias.   C. interviewer bias.
    B. selection bias.   D. nonresponse bias.

REFERENCE: Abdelhak, pp 412–414
               LaTour, Eichenwald-Maki, and Oachs, p 583
               Layman and Watzlaf, pp 228, 230
               Shi, p 382

85. A researcher has repeated the same study 10 times. Each time the study is repeated, the p value decreases. As the p value approaches zero, the
    A. size of the sample increases.
    B. value of the study decreases.
    C. chance that the results are due to a sampling error decreases.
    D. chance that the results are due to a sampling error increases.

REFERENCE: Abdelhak, pp 389–391
               Horton, pp 250–253
               LaTour, Eichenwald-Maki, and Oachs, pp 527–528

86. You and your colleague are designing a study to try to determine the ideal mean cost for a discretionary service. You will market your service to a very large population. Your colleague thinks you will get the best data if you take lots of small samples. You think the data will be more reliable if you take one or two very large samples.
    A. Your colleague is right—the mean of multiple samples will yield more reliable results.
    B. You are right—the means of a few large samples will yield more reliable results.
    C. You are equally correct—there is little difference in the reliability of these sampling methods.
    D. You are equally wrong—unless you use stratified sampling, you cannot expect reliable results.

REFERENCE: Abdelhak, pp 396–398
                Horton, pp 241–242
                LaTour, Eichenwald-Maki, and Oachs, pp 528–530
                Layman and Watzlaf, pp 68–69, 237–238
                Shi, pp 279–280, 282–284

87. You are conducting a patient satisfaction survey in your outpatient clinic using interviewers who administer a questionnaire. Because you typically see about 300 people per day in the clinic, you decide to have the interviewers administer the questionnaire on every tenth patient. You are using
    A. systematic sampling.   C. variable sampling.
    B. stratified sampling.   D. convenience sampling.

REFERENCE: Abdelhak, pp 396–398
                Horton, pp 242–246
                LaTour, Eichenwald-Maki, and Oachs, pp 578–580
                Layman and Watzlaf, pp 68, 235–238
                Shi, pp 272–274

88. The people of Treasure Island Beach have been struck with a rash that seems to be infecting almost everyone in town. The staff of the hospital is working to design a study of this mysterious disease. They decide to do a cross-sectional study because cross-sectional or prevalence studies are known for
    A. quickly identifying cause and effect relationships that can serve as a basis for treatment.
    B. concurrently describing characteristics and health outcomes at one specific point in time.
    C. providing the information necessary to test for the most effective treatment of an illness or condition.
    D. supplying entire populations with therapeutic interventions on an epidemiologically sound basis.

REFERENCE: Abdelhak, pp 413–414
                Koch, p 205
                LaTour, Eichenwald-Maki, and Oachs, pp 622–626
                Layman and Watzlaf, pp 129–133
                McWay, pp 237–238
                Shi, p 61

89. You are planning a prospective study to try to prove a cause and effect relationship between dipping snuff and throat cancer. First, you identify subjects who regularly dip snuff and who are free of any signs of throat cancer. Next, you need to identify subjects who
   A. dip snuff regularly and who currently have throat cancer.
   B. dip snuff regularly and who currently have significant signs of throat cancer.
   C. do not dip snuff and who currently have significant signs of throat cancer.
   D. do not dip snuff and who are free of any signs of throat cancer.

REFERENCE: Abdelhak, pp 420–423
               LaTour, Eichenwald-Maki, and Oachs, pp 622–624
               Layman and Watzlaf, pp 130–131, 134, 138–139
               McWay, p 237
               Shi, pp 15–16, 371–374

90. Your administrator is concerned about the snuff study (see question 88). The administrator would like to consider using a case–control study model rather than the prospective one you are planning. One of the biggest reasons the administrator is promoting the case–control model is because case–control is
   A. more likely to be free of design errors than a prospective study.
   B. the best way to analytically test the hypothesis of cause and effect.
   C. more likely to decrease recall bias errors than prospective studies.
   D. less expensive than prospective studies because it uses existing records.

REFERENCE: Abdelhak, pp 420–422
               LaTour, Eichenwald-Maki, and Oachs, pp 622–624
               McWay, p 237

91. You point out to your administrator that the study model generally accepted to be the best method to determine the magnitude of risk in the population with the characteristic or suspected risk factor is the
   A. descriptive study design.   C. prospective study design.
   B. analytic study design.   D. case–control study design.

REFERENCE: Abdelhak, pp 420–426
               LaTour, Eichenwald-Maki, and Oachs, pp 622–624
               Layman and Watzlaf, pp 130–131, 134, 138–139
               McWay, p 237

92. Investigator A claims that his results are statistically significant at the 10% level. Investigator B argues that significance should be announced only if the results are statistically significant at the 5% level. From this we can conclude that
   A. if investigator A has significant results at the 10% level, they will never be significant at the 5% level.
   B. it will be more difficult for investigator A to reject statistical null hypotheses if he always works at the 10% level compared with investigator B who works at the 5% level.
   C. if investigator A has significant results at the 10% level, they will also be significant at the 5% level.
   D. it will be less difficult for investigator A to reject statistical null hypotheses if he always works at the 10% level compared with investigator B who works at the 5% level.

REFERENCE: Abdelhak, pp 389–391
               LaTour, Eichenwald-Maki, and Oachs, pp 571–573
               Layman and Watzlaf, p 210
               McWay, pp 215–220
               Shi, p 371

93. John Parker surveyed members of AHIMA's student COP regarding the relationship between clinical experiences and job opportunities. All respondents were seniors in HIA programs and each one expected to graduate and take the national exam within the next 6 months. Fifteen of the 18 respondents indicated that at least one clinical rotation had resulted in a job offer. Based on this information, Parker expects to be offered a job during senior clinical rotations. John is basing this expectation on
   A. scientific inquiry.   C. inductive reasoning.
   B. empiricism.   D. deductive reasoning.

REFERENCE: LaTour, Eichenwald-Maki, and Oachs, pp 548–549
               Shi, pp 6, 35

Use the formula below as a resource to answer questions 94 and 95.

FORMULA FOR CALCULATING SAMPLE SIZE
$$n = \dfrac{Np\,(1-p)}{(N-1)\,\dfrac{(B^2)}{4} + (p)\,(1-p)}$$

94. If population size (N) = 1,200 and the proportion of subjects needed (p) = 0.5 and the acceptable amount of error (B) = 0.05, then sample size (n) =
   A. 200.   C. 400.
   B. 300.   D. 600.

REFERENCE: Abdelhak, pp 396–398
               LaTour, Eichenwald-Maki, and Oachs, pp 579–580
               Layman and Watzlaf, p 210
               Shi, pp 279–280, 282–283

95. After the researchers see the number of subjects they will have to interview, they reexamine their criteria. The researchers could decrease the number of subjects while having the least impact on the reliability of the study by
   A. increasing p and decreasing B.
   B. increasing p or decreasing B.
   C. decreasing p and increasing B.
   D. decreasing p or increasing B.

REFERENCE: Abdelhak, pp 396–398
               LaTour, Eichenwald-Maki, and Oachs, pp 571–573
               Layman and Watzlaf, p 210
               Shi, pp 279–280, 282–283

96. Which statistical analysis would be the best technique to use on the following problem?

A study compared the effects of retesting on the scores of students who failed a writing test. Students who did not pass on their first attempt were allowed to retest. Results showed that students had higher mean scores at retest whether they attended additional training before retesting or not.

   A. descriptive stats   C. regression
   B. ANOVA   D. T test

REFERENCE: Abdelhak, pp 389–394
               Horton, pp 250–257
               McWay, pp 215–220

97. The name given to the error committed when the null hypothesis is rejected and it is actually true is
   A. type II error.
   B. selection bias.
   C. type I error.
   D. alternative hypothesis.

REFERENCE: Abdelhak, pp 389–391
               LaTour, Eichenwald-Maki, and Oachs, pp 571–572
               McWay, pp 224, 241

98. The major purpose of random assignment in a clinical trial is to
    A. reduce selection bias in allocation of treatment.
    B. help ensure that study subjects are representative of the general population.
    C. facilitate double-blinding.
    D. ensure that the study groups are comparable on baseline characteristics.

REFERENCE: Abdelhak, pp 422–426
               LaTour, Eichenwald-Maki, and Oachs, pp 624–625
               McWay, pp 235–237
               Shi, pp 155–157

99. In statistics, the notation "ΣXY" means
    A. summed all the values of the X variable and then multiplied this result times the values of the Y variable.
    B. summed all the values of the X variable, all the values of the Y variable, then multiplied all of these results.
    C. multiplied each pair of the X and Y scores, then summed their values.
    D. variation of the X and Y variable is multiplied then squared.

REFERENCE: Horton, p 183
               Koch, p 234
               LaTour, Eichenwald-Maki, and Oachs, p 518
               Sayles, p 538

100. A major disadvantage of cross-sectional studies is that
     A. the time sequence of exposure and disease is usually not known.
     B. they are usually more expensive and can take a long time to complete.
     C. prevalence rates cannot be calculated.
     D. they cannot provide information on both exposure and disease status in the same individual.

REFERENCE: Abdelhak, pp 313–315
               LaTour, Eichenwald-Maki, and Oachs, pp 622–623
               Layman and Watzlaf, p 132
               Shi, pp 75, 131, 191

101. A study found that liver cancer rates per 100,000 males among cigarette smokers and nonsmokers in a major U.S. city were 48.0 and 25.4, respectively. The relative risk of developing liver cancer for male smokers compared to nonsmokers is
A. 1.89.
B. 15.6.
C. 22.6.
D. 48.0.

REFERENCE: Abdelhak, pp 420–422
LaTour, Eichenwald-Maki, and Oachs, p 625
Layman and Watzlaf, p 138
McWay, p 251
Shi, pp 371–373

102. The standard deviation of a particular set of measures was found to be 20.00. The sample variance would then be:
A. 20
B. 5
C. 400
D. 10

REFERENCE: Horton, pp 182–185
Koch, pp 246–247
LaTour, Eichenwald-Maki, and Oachs, p 520
Shi, p 361

103. If a constant is added to all measurements within a sample
A. the mean remains the same.
B. the standard deviation remains the same.
C. both A and B are true.
D. both A and B are false.

REFERENCE: Horton, pp 182–185
Koch, pp 246–247
LaTour, Eichenwald-Maki, and Oachs, pp 518–520

104. Measurements within sample A are assumed to be more variable than measurements within sample B when
A. sample A and sample B have the same mean.
B. individuals within sample A are more alike than individuals within sample B.
C. individuals within sample A differ more from one another than individuals within sample B.
D. sample A and sample B have the same standard deviation.

REFERENCE: Horton, pp 182–185
Koch, pp 246–247
LaTour, Eichenwald-Maki, and Oachs, pp 518–520

105. _____ refers to the flatness or peakedness of one distribution in relation to another distribution.
    A. Skewness
    B. Correlation
    C. Central tendency
    D. Kurtosis

REFERENCE: Horton, pp 187–189
              Koch, pp 238–243
              LaTour, Eichenwald-Maki, and Oachs, p 521

106. Given a positively skewed frequency distribution
    A. the frequencies are identical between the mean, median, and mode.
    B. larger frequencies are concentrated at the low end of the variable.
    C. larger frequencies are concentrated at the high end of the variable.
    D. largest frequencies occur at both low and high ends of the variable.

REFERENCE: Horton, pp 187–189
              Koch, pp 238–243
              LaTour, Eichenwald-Maki, and Oachs, p 521

Answer Key for Health Statistics and Research

ANSWER   EXPLANATION

1. C $(27 \times 100) / 1{,}652 = 1.6\%$

2. D   Calculate the answer as follows:

PHYSICIAN NAME	NUMBER OF HOURS WORKED	NUMBER OF PATIENTS SEEN	NUMBER OF PATIENTS SEEN PER HOUR WORKED
Robinson	32	185	185/32 = 5.78
Beasley	30	161	161/30 = 5.37
Hiltz	35	200	200/35 = 5.71
Wolf	26	157	157/26 = 6.04

3. A   3,545 requested records × 100 / 150,000 total records = 354,500/150,000 = 2.36 = 2.4%.

4. D

5. A   Calculations: 95% of the observations fall within two standard deviations of the mean, so the cost of a lunch at Bon Appetite will be between $6.50
$[8 - (2 \times 0.75)]$ and $9.50 $[8 + (2 \times 0.75)]$.
Lunch at Mario's will be between $5.50 $[7.5 - (2 \times 1)]$ and $9.50 $[7.5 + (2 \times 1)]$.
Lunch at Au Courant will cost too much $[\$9 + (2 \times 1.25) = \$11.50]$.
As will the Windy City Grill $[\$7.50 (2 \times 1.5) = \$10.50]$.

6. B

7. A

8. C   Calculations:

	Records under Review	Same Code on Self-Coding Review	Intrarater Reliability Percentage	Same Code on Peer-Coding Review	Interrater Reliability Percentage	Mean Reliability Percentage
Coder A	28	22	78.57	20	71.43	75.00
Coder B	18	16	88.89	16	88.89	88.89
Coder C	45	42	93.33	43	95.56	94.44
Coder D	17	15	88.24	16	94.12	91.18

9   D

10. C

11. D

12. B

13. B   Calculation: 5 + 9 + 8 + 12 + 6 + 7 + 5 + 10 + 7 + 9 + 11 = 89 / 11 = 8.09

14. B   Calculate the mean time each physician spent with patients as follows:

PHYSICIAN	TIMES WITH PATIENTS	AVERAGE (MEAN) TIME WITH PATIENTS
Beasley	8, 6, 7	7
Robinson	5, 9, 9	7.7
Baumstark	10, 7	8.5
Wolf	12, 5, 11	9.3

15. A

16. A

Answer Key for Health Statistics and Research

ANSWER   EXPLANATION

17. C

18. A

19. B

20 C

21. D

22. D

23. B

24. B $40 + 10 + 5 + 2 = 57$

25. D $67 + 2 = 69$ admissions/discharges same day

(Transfers to other facilities and deaths are forms of discharge.)

26. A $(75,860 + 7,100) / 365 = 227$

(Note: Average daily census includes adult and pediatrics, but NOT newborns.)

27. B

28. B   The day of admission is counted as an inpatient service day, but the day of discharge is not.

29. A $1/24 - 31 = 8$ days $+ 2/1$ through $2/8 = 8$ days so $8 + 8 = 16$
(Count the day of admission but not discharge.)

30. B $(12,345 \times 100) / (500 \times 28) = 88.2\%$

31. B   9,457 discharge days/1,351 discharges = 7 days
(Count the day of admission but not discharge.)

32. D   Only two answers, A and D, are correctly calculated. Should you choose to include the unusually long LOS, you should make a note to avoid confusing readers, which makes the answer "A" a poor choice. Should you choose to eliminate the potentially confusing LOS, you must subtract both the patient from the total discharges and the discharge days from the total discharge days.

33. B $\dfrac{(28,690 + 27,400 + 19,250) \times 100}{(151 \times 200) + (137 \times 250) + (77 \times 275)} = 88.0 = 88\%$

34. C   Use the direct method, bed turnover.
16,570 adult and peds discharges/200 adult and peds beds = 82.85 = 82.9%

35. A   200 beds × 365 days in a nonleap year = 73,000 (Note: Bassinets are excluded.)

36. C $\dfrac{(5 \times 100)}{(225 + 5)} = 2.2\%$

37. C   50 + (3 sets of twins × 2 births per set) = 56 births

38. B   Multiple births are one delivery; fetal deaths are counted as deliveries
$50 + 3 + 1 + 1 = 55$

39. D

40. D

41. C   Calculations: 361 total inpatient deaths × 100/6614 total discharges = 5.45 = 5.5%
Fetal deaths and outpatient deaths are not included in this calculation.

Answer Key for Health Statistics and Research

ANSWER   EXPLANATION

42. B   Calculations:

$$\frac{(108 \text{ total inpatient deaths} >48 \text{ hours}) \times 100}{(6{,}614 \text{ total discharges} - 253 \text{ deaths} <48 \text{ hours})} = \frac{10800}{6{,}361} = 1.697 = 1.7\%$$

43. B   48 – 38 deaths over 48 hours = 10 deaths less than 48 hours. $\dfrac{(48 - 10)\ (100)}{(1{,}382 - 10)}$

44. B

45. B

46. C   LOS would increase through the year and drop when patient is discharged.

47. A $\dfrac{(72 \text{ intermediate and late fetal deaths} \times 100)}{(980 \text{ births} + 72 \text{ intermediate and late fetal deaths})} = \dfrac{7{,}200}{1{,}052} = 6.8\%$

48. C   (3,699 × 100) / 20,932 = 17.7%

49. A

50. C

51. D

52. C

53. B

54. C

55. A

56. A

57. D

58. B

59. B

60. A

61. A

62. A

63. D

64. C

65. D

66. A

67. A

68. D

69. D

70. C

71. B

72. A

73. C   7 hours per day × 60 minutes per hour = 420 minutes per day. 20% of 420 = 84

Answer Key for Health Statistics and Research

ANSWER   EXPLANATION

74. C   Calculations:
- MS-DRG A = 2.023 × 323 = 653.43
- MS-DRG B = 0.987 × 489 = 482.64
- MS-DRG C = 1.925 × 402 = 773.85
- MS-DRG D = 1.243 × 386 = 479.80

75. C   Calculations:
- MS-DRG A = 2.023 × 0.14 = 0.283;   0.283 + 2.023 = 2.306 × 323 = 744.84
- MS-DRG B = 0.987 × 0.20 = 0.197;   0.987 + 0.197 = 1.184 × 489 = 578.98
- MS-DRG C = 1.925 × 402 = 773.85
- MS-DRG D = 1.243 × 0.10 = 0.124;   1.243 – 0.124 = 1.119 × 386 = 431.93

76. D   Arrive at the answer by calculating the reimbursement per unit for each service and averaging those answers, as shown below.

INSURANCE COMPANY	UNITS OF SERVICE A	REIMBURSE-MENT FOR SERVICE A	REIMBURSE-MENT PER UNIT FOR SERVICE A	UNITS OF SERVICE B	REIMBURSE-MENT FOR SERVICE B	REIMBURSE-MENT PER UNIT FOR SERVICE B	TOTAL REIMBURSE MENT	AVERAGE REIMBURSE-MENT PER UNIT OF SERVICE
Lifecare	259	31,196.55	120.45	812	163,577.40	201.45	194,773.95	160.95
Get-Well	786	100,859.52	128.32	465	96,929.25	208.45	197,788.77	168.39
SureHealth	462	54,631.50	118.25	509	107,093.60	210.40	161,725.10	164.33
Be-Healthy	219	26,991.75	123.25	417	89,425.65	214.45	116,417.40	168.85

77. D   Reference the table above.

78. B   Calculate by adding total services.

PHYSICIAN	SERVICE A	SERVICE B	SERVICE C	TOTAL SERVICES
Truba	10	22	10	42
Wooley	14	22	9	45
Howe	18	5	6	29
Masters	12	20	7	39

79. A   Double Service C in the table above.

80. B

81. C

82. A

83. C

84. D

85. C

86. B

87. A

88. B

89. D

90. D

91. C

Answer Key for Health Statistics and Research

ANSWER   EXPLANATION

92. B

93. C

94. B

$$n = \frac{(1200)\,(0.5)\,(1 - 0.5)}{(1200 - 1)\,\dfrac{(0.05^2)}{4} + (0.5)\,(1 - 0.5)}$$

$$n = \frac{300}{(1199)\,(0.000625) + 0.25}$$

$$n = \frac{300}{0.749 + 0.25} = \frac{300}{1} = 300$$

95. D

96. D

97. C

98. A

99. C

100. A

101. A   RR = risk exposed divided by risk not exposed = 48 divided by 25.4 = 1.89

102. C

103. B

104. C

105. D

106. B

REFERENCES

Abdelhak, M., Grostick, S., Hanken, M. A., & Jacobs, E. (Eds.). (2011). *Health information: Management of a strategic resource* (4th ed.). St. Louis, MO: Saunders Elsevier.

Horton, L. (2012). *Calculating and reporting health care statistics* (4th ed.). Chicago: American Health Information Management Association (AHIMA).

Koch, G. (2008). *Basic allied health statistics and analysis* (3rd ed.). Clifton Park, NY: Delmar Cengage Learning.

LaTour, K., Eichenwald-Maki, S. and, Oachs, P. (2013). *Health information management: Concepts, principles, and practice* (4th ed.). Chicago: American Health Information Management Association (AHIMA).

Layman, E. J., & Watzlaf, V. J. (2009). *Health informatics research methods, principles and practice*. Chicago: American Health Information Management Association (AHIMA).

McWay, D. C. (2014). *Today's health information management: An integrated approach* (2nd ed.). Clifton Park, NY: Delmar Cengage Learning.

Sayles, N. B. (2013). *Health information management technology: An applied approach* (4th ed.). Chicago: AHIMA Press.

Shaw, P., Elliot, C., Isaacson, P., & Murphy, E. (2012). *Quality and performance improvement in health care* (5th ed.). Chicago: American Health Information Management Association (AHIMA).

Shi, L. (2008). *Health services research methods* (2nd ed.). Clifton Park, NY: Delmar Cengage Learning.

Health Statistics and Research Competency Domains

COMPETENCIES FOR HEALTH STATISTICS AND RESEARCH							
Question		RHIA Domain Competencies					
	1	2	3	4	5	6	
1–106		X					

COMPETENCIES FOR HEALTH STATISTICS AND RESEARCH								
Question		RHIT Domain Competencies						
	1	2	3	4	5	6	7	
1	X							
2	X							
3					X			
4					X			
5					X			
6	X							
7	X							
8	X							
9	X							
10					X			
11					X			
12	X							
13	X							
14	X							
15	X							
16	X							
17	X							
18	X							
19	X							
20	X							
21	X							
22	X							
23	X							
24	X							
25	X							
26	X							
27	X							
28	X							
29	X							
30	X							
31	X							
32	X							
33	X							
34	X							
35	X							
36	X							
37	X							
38	X							
39	X							
40	X							
41	X							
42	X							
43	X							
44					X			
45					X			

Question		RHIT Domain Competencies							
	1	2	3	4	5	6	7	
46					X			
47	X							
48	X							
49					X			
50	X							
51					X			
52					X			
53					X			
54					X			
55					X			
56					X			
57					X			
58					X			
59					X			
60					X			
61					X			
62					X			
63					X			
64					X			
65					X			
66					X			
67					X			
68	X							
69					X			
70					X			
71					X			
72					X			
73		X						
74		X						
75		X						
76		X						
77		X						
78		X						
79		X						

XIV. Quality and Performance Improvement

Charlotte McCuen, MS, RHIA

1. What process assists a health care facility in continuously looking at the ways that problems develop and seeking ways to prevent problems from happening in the future?
    A. risk management
    B. quality control
    C. utilization management
    D. performance improvement

    REFERENCE: Abdelhak, pp 438, 447, 460, 462
                    Davis and LaCour, pp 359–360
                    LaTour, Eichenwald-Maki, and Oachs, pp 650–652
                    McWay, pp 172, 187–189
                    Sayles, pp 595–598
                    Shaw, p 4

2. The current hospital policy time frame for authenticating verbal orders adheres to the CMS COP that requires the ordering physician, or another health care practitioner responsible for the care of the patient, to write orders according to hospital policy and authenticate
    A. based on federal and state law.
    B. within 48 hours if a state law time frame doesn't exist.
    C. within 24 hours if a state law time frame doesn't exist.
    D. both A and B

    REFERENCE: Federal Register, pp 17–18
                    AHIMA (2012a)

3. The Blood Usage Review Committee has a quality monitor established to review all blood transfusion reaction cases. The HIM Director will be working with the committee to identify and abstract patient outcome information for committee evaluation. What data should be collected?
    A. effects of transfusion reaction (e.g., rash, death, etc.)
    B. type and cross-match accuracy
    C. justification for the transfusion
    D. all of the above

    REFERENCE: LaTour, Eichenwald-Maki, and Oachs, pp 665–666
                    Shaw, pp 136–137

4. As supervisor of the record completion function of the HIM department, you are asked for record completion statistics for specific physicians who are being evaluated for reappointment to the medical staff. Which of the following information elements would you report for each physician?
    A. physician education and training
    B. number of delinquent records
    C. state licensure expiration date
    D. prior physician malpractice claims history

    REFERENCE: Abdelhak, pp 468–469
                    Davis and LaCour, p 130
                    LaTour, Eichenwald-Maki, and Oachs, pp 267, 330
                    McWay, p 24
                    Shaw, p 296

5. The Recovery Audit Contractor (RAC) program identifies improper payments for
   A. Medicaid claims.
   B. Medicare claims.
   C. both B and D
   D. collection of overpayments.

REFERENCE: Davis and LaCour, pp 208, 354–355
               LaTour, Eichenwald-Maki, and Oachs, pp 855–856
               McWay, p 71
               Sayles, p 310

6. A document requirement of health facilities pursuant to HIPAA legislation, that informs patient
   how a covered entity intends to use and disclose protected health information is called
   A. Notice of Privacy Practices (NPP).
   B. informed consent.
   C. incident report.
   D. periodic performance review (PPR).

REFERENCE: Davis and LaCour, p 389
               LaTour, Eichenwald-Maki, and Oachs, pp 244, 314
               McWay, pp 72–73
               Sayles, pp 102–103
               Shaw, p 432

7. Clinical privileges are granted to the physician for an interval specified in the medical staff by
   laws, but not longer than
   A. 6 months.   C. 2 years.
   B. 1 year.   D. 3 years.

REFERENCE: LaTour, Eichenwald-Maki, and Oachs, p 331
               Sayles, pp 102–103, 451
               Shaw, p 296

8. The hospital implemented an electronic query system to allow more effective communication
   with physicians and other health practitioners to improve clinical documentation in the patient
   record. This program is known as
   A. core measure reporting.
   B. clinical documentation improvement (CDI).
   C. tumor registry (TR).
   D. evidence-based medicine.

REFERENCE: AHIMA (2012b)
               Davis and LaCour, pp 191–192
               LaTour, Eichenwald-Maki, and Oachs, p 442
               Sayles, pp 120–121

9. The person or group who is overall responsible and accountable for maintaining the quality and safety of patient care is the
A. Chief Nursing Officer (CNO).
B. Board of Directors (BOD) or governing body.
C. Chief Executive Officer (CEO).
D. Quality Improvement Director.

REFERENCE: LaTour, Eichenwald-Maki, and Oachs, p 663
Sayles, pp 597, 674
Shaw, p 318

10. What quality indicator would prove useful in tracking customer satisfaction in the correspondence/release of information function?
A. the number of medical record personnel required to perform the function
B. the amount of overtime necessary to stay current
C. the number of charts pulled for correspondence requests
D. the turnaround time from the date a request is received to the date the information is provided to the requester

REFERENCE: LaTour, Eichenwald-Maki, and Oachs, pp 653, 815
Shaw, pp 118–119

11. Most acute care facilities use this type of screening criteria for utilization review purposes to determine the need for inpatient services and justification for continued stay.
A. severity of illness/intensity of service criteria (SI/IS)
B. critical pathways
C. Joint Commission defined and developed criteria
D. Health Plan Employer Data & Information (HEDIS) measures

REFERENCE: Abdelhak, pp 463–465
Davis and LaCour, p 377
Sayles, p 610
Shaw, p 119

12. The improvement process of comparing the collection and coding of POA indicators at your facility with those of comparable departments of superior performance of other health care facilities is referred to as
A. focused review.   C. peer review.
B. benchmarking.   D. occurrence screening.

REFERENCE: Abdelhak, pp 446–447, 613
Davis and LaCour, pp 65, 363
LaTour, Eichenwald-Maki, and Oachs, pp 653, 808
McWay, pp 179, 183
Sayles, pp 594, 625, 1122
Shaw, p 16

13. With the passage of Medicare (Title XVIII of the Social Security Act) in 1965, which of the following functions became mandatory?

A. quality improvement
B. risk management
C. quality assessment
D. utilization review

REFERENCE: Abdelhak, p 462
LaTour, Eichenwald-Maki, and Oachs, pp 15–16
McWay, pp 192–195
Sayles, pp 654–655
Shaw, p xxv

14. An ophthalmologist has requested permission to perform specialized laser procedures within the hospital. His request is evaluated by the Credentials Committee through a process to determine the specific procedures and services this physician can perform. This is known as

A. discharge planning.
B. medical staff evaluation.
C. delineation of privileges.
D. reappointment.

REFERENCE: Abdelhak, pp 23, 467
LaTour and Eichenwald-Maki, pp 330–331
McWay, pp 23–24
Sayles, p 834
Shaw, p 294

15. Major responsibilities of the Risk Manager generally include

A. loss prevention and reduction.
B. liability claims management.
C. participating in safety and security programs.
D. all of the above.

REFERENCE: Abdelhak, pp 460–461
LaTour and Eichenwald-Maki, pp 860–863
McWay, pp 189–191
Sayles, pp 613–620
Shaw, pp 189, 196–200

16. Needlesticks, patient or employee falls, medication errors, or any event not consistent with routine patient care activities would require risk reporting documentation in the form of an

A. operative report.
B. emergency room report.
C. incident report.
D. insurance claim.

REFERENCE: Abdelhak, p 653
Davis and LaCour, pp 378–379
LaTour and Eichenwald-Maki, pp 860–863
McWay, p 189
Sayles, pp 613–620
Shaw, p 189

17. The responsibility for performing quality monitoring and evaluation activities in a departmentalized hospital is delegated to the
    A. director of utilization management.
    B. chairman of the board of trustees.
    C. clinical chairpersons of medical staff committees or ancillary department directors.
    D. chief executive officer.

REFERENCE: LaTour and Eichenwald-Maki, pp 860–863
              Sayles, pp 613–620
              Shaw, pp 318, 320

18. What criterion is critical in selecting performance indicators for a health information management department?
    A. The indicators must include the most important aspects of performance.
    B. Indicators must correlate with Deming's 14 points.
    C. Identify at least 25 indicators that are reflective of all department functions.
    D. Select only indicators that reflect positively on the department.

REFERENCE: LaTour and Eichenwald-Maki, pp 652–653, 807
              Sayles, p 358
              Shaw, pp 6–7

19. In the Act phase of the PDSA method, what step can assist in implementing change in a department?
    A. incorporating changes into a policy statement or new standard
    B. distributing new policies and procedures to people affected by the changes and explaining the rationale for the changes
    C. informing all affected parties about the changes
    D. all of the above

REFERENCE: Abdelhak, p 447
              Davis and LaCour, pp 359–361
              LaTour and Eichenwald-Maki, p 820
              McWay, pp 173–175
              Sayles, pp 613–620

20. What feature distinguishes the Nominal Group Technique (NGT) from brainstorming?
    A. NGT can be accomplished by mail.
    B. NGT uses a visual device like a flip chart to keep track of responses.
    C. NGT draws responses from a large group of people.
    D. NGT determines the importance of responses through a rating system.

REFERENCE: Abdelhak, p 450
              LaTour and Eichenwald-Maki, p 822
              McWay, p 179
              Sayles, pp 593–594
              Shaw, pp 20–21

21. When the policy and procedures manual no longer reflect current practices, it creates a situation that becomes a risk management issue because
    A. supervisory time and effort will be wasted to correct the manual.
    B. training of new personnel will not be standardized.
    C. broad and permissive policy statements cannot commit the organization to a course of action.
    D. policy and procedures should represent the normal course of business.

REFERENCE: LaTour and Eichenwald-Maki, pp 560, 804–805
                  Sayles, p 807
                  Shaw, p 189

22. The medical malpractice crisis of the 1970s prompted the development of _____ in health care facilities.
    A. utilization management   C. quality improvement programs
    B. financial analysis programs   D. risk management

REFERENCE: Abdelhak, p 461
                  LaTour and Eichenwald-Maki, pp 44, 860–861
                  McWay, p 189
                  Shaw, p 426

23. The following legislation requires that patient-identifiable health information remains confidential and protected against unauthorized disclosure, alteration, or destruction.
    A. HIPAA Security Rule   C. Privacy Act of 1974
    B. Patient Care Act   D. Workman's Compensation Act

REFERENCE: LaTour and Eichenwald-Maki, p 208
                  McWay, pp 11, 69, 291–293
                  Sayles, pp 170, 833, 1026–1027

24. The hospital Quality Department adopted the Lean Management quality model using JIT, which ensures required process items and resources are
    A. available at the right place and the right time.
    B. for the correct patient, using the correct procedure, at the correct site.
    C. always kept stocked in Central Processing.
    D. automatically restocked to maintain a surplus.

REFERENCE: LaTour, Eichenwald-Maki, and Oachs, pp 742, 829

25. The Utilization Review Coordinator reviews inpatient records at regular intervals to justify necessity and appropriateness of care to warrant further hospitalization. Which of the following utilization review activities is being performed?
    A. admission review   C. retrospective review
    B. preadmission   D. continued stay review

REFERENCE: Abdelhak, p 463
                  LaTour, Eichenwald-Maki, and Oachs, p 464
                  McWay, pp 191–193
                  Sayles, p 113
                  Shaw, p 113

26. The Joint Commission recently surveyed an acute care hospital. The hospital just received the survey report and the accreditation decision. Which of the following categories should the hospital leaders address first?
    A. Requirements for Improvement
    B. Grid Elements
    C. Written Progress Reports
    D. Triennial Exception Rules

REFERENCE: Shaw, p 341

27. What feature is a trademark of an effective PI program?
    A. a one-time cure—all for a facility's problems
    B. an unmanageable project that is too expensive
    C. a cost-containment effort
    D. a continuous cycle of improvement projects over time

REFERENCE: Davis and LaCour, p 359
               LaTour, Eichenwald-Maki, and Oachs, pp 650–653, 808
               McWay, pp 172, 187–189
               Sayles, p 595
               Shaw, pp 4–5

28. What quality improvement (QI) tool uses criteria to weigh different alternatives? This display would assist in viewing all relevant information at the same time.
    A. the PDSA method
    B. a decision matrix
    C. a flowchart
    D. a customer satisfaction survey

REFERENCE: Abdelhak, p 451
               Davis and LaCour, pp 369–370
               LaTour, Eichenwald-Maki, and Oachs, p 695

29. The QI plan for your hospital requires each coder maintain a minimum of 94.5% accuracy in coding. You manage the coding department, and the past year's average accuracy rating was 95.3%. The QI plan allows a standard deviation (SD) of ±2 against best practices of 97% accuracy. Did your coding staff's overall average meet within standard deviation range?
    A. Yes, within ±2 below SD
    B. Yes, within ±2 above SD
    C. No, because it is >±2 below SD
    D. No, because it is >±2 above SD

REFERENCE: Abdelhak, pp 448–449
               LaTour, Eichenwald-Maki, and Oachs, pp 520–521
               Shaw, p 442

30. Surgical case review includes all the following EXCEPT
    A. determination of surgical justification based on clinical indication(s) in cases where no tissue has been removed.
    B. cases with elements missing in the preoperative anesthesia consultation.
    C. cases where there is a significant discrepancy between preoperative, postoperative, and pathological diagnoses.
    D. cases with serious surgical complications or surgical mortalities.

REFERENCE: LaTour, Eichenwald-Maki, and Oachs, p 665

31. What federal legislation passed in 1986 confers liability to individuals and health facilities for any peer review process activities conducted?
    A. Healthcare Quality Improvement Act
    B. Utilization Review Act
    C. Patient Protection and Affordable Care Act (PPACA)
    D. Health Insurance Portability and Accountability Act (HIPAA)

REFERENCE: Davis and LaCour, p 353
               LaTour, Eichenwald-Maki, and Oachs, p 16
               Sayles, pp 605–606
               Shaw, p 430

32. The credentialing process requires healthcare facilities to
    A. query the NPDB to collect and report malpractice judgement and settlements.
    B. review and approve the appointment of medical staff and other licensed independent practitioners.
    C. create a mechanism to report adverse licensure activity to the Secretary HHS.
    D. all of the above

REFERENCE: LaTour, Eichenwald-Maki, and Oachs, p 330
               McWay, pp 22–24
               Sayles, p 451

33. A plantiff must establish which burden of proof to recover damages for medical negligence or malpractice?
    1. A breach of the duty to care by the defendant.
    2. Damages or injury resulted from the defendant's negligence.
    3. A duty of care relationship between the defendant and patient.
    4. Causation existed for harm to the plantiff from the defendant's conduct.

    A. Only 1   C. 1, 2, 3, and 4
    B. 1 and 3   D. 2 and 4

REFERENCE: LaTour, Eichenwald-Maki, and Oachs, p 304
               Sayles, p 783
               Shaw, p 427

34. Reporting the monthly average turnaround time for the release of information (ROI) over a 6-month period using a run or line chart will reflect
    A. the quality of informed consents.
    B. trends and detect if improvements were made.
    C. the quality of appropriate authorized consents.
    D. the number of denied requests.

REFERENCE: Abdelhak, pp 452–453, 453f
               LaTour, Eichenwald-Maki, and Oachs, p 824
               McWay, pp 180, 213
               Sayles, p 581

35. As an HIM coding supervisor, you are asked to compare the current coding process with a proposed concurrent coding process. What visual tool would be the best to identify all the logical steps and sequence of each procedure?
    A. decision matrix
    B. cause and effect diagram
    C. flowchart
    D. checksheet

REFERENCE: Abdelhak, pp 450–451, 618
                LaTour, Eichenwald-Maki, and Oachs, pp 804–805
                McWay, pp 348–349
                Sayles, p 585
                Shaw, pp 166–172

36. Physicians who are members of the Surgery Committee meet to review surgical cases referred for quality issues and deviations from standard care norms. This type of review in which a physician's record is reviewed by his or her professional colleagues is known as
    A. concurrent review.
    B. clinical pertinence review.
    C. incident screening.
    D. peer review.

REFERENCE: Abdelhak, p 407
                LaTour, Eichenwald-Maki, and Oachs, pp 804–805
                Sayles, p 585
                Shaw, pp 324–325

37. Patient mortality, infection and complication rates, adherence to living will requirements, adequate pain control, and other documentation that describe end results of care or a measurable change in the patient's health are examples of
    A. outcome measures.
    B. threshold level.
    C. sentinel events.
    D. incident reports.

REFERENCE: Abdelhak, p 442
                LaTour, Eichenwald-Maki, and Oachs, pp 628–631, 670
                McWay, pp 127–128, 183
                Sayles, pp 600, 604
                Shaw, pp 14, 16

38. In quality review activities, departments are directed to focus on clinical processes that are
    A. high volume.
    B. high risk.
    C. problem prone.
    D. all of the above

REFERENCE: LaTour, Eichenwald-Maki, and Oachs, p 652
                Shaw, pp 6, 17

39. The HIM department frequently experiences a backlog in loose report filing. A quality improvement team is assembled to identify the outcome variables and the major or root causes. What visual QI tool is helpful to report the findings?
    A. PDCA method
    B. run chart
    C. fishbone (cause and effect) diagram
    D. scatter diagram

REFERENCE: Abdelhak, p 451
                Davis and LaCour, p 356
                LaTour, Eichenwald-Maki, and Oachs, pp 822–823
                McWay, p 179
                Sayles, p 587

40. According to the HIPAA Privacy Rule, the following persons must adhere to the minimum necessary standard when releasing patient-specific information.
    A. physicians
    B. employees
    C. volunteers
    D. all of the above

REFERENCES: Davis and LaCour, p 391
LaTour, Eichenwald-Maki, and Oachs, p 133
McWay, pp 73, 515
Sayles, p 799

41. As the new Coding Manager, you met with the coding staff to encourage feedback on ways to increase coding accuracy to meet established benchmarks. The coders provided feedback through brainstorming that you compiled on flipcharts and organized into categories. This is known as a(n)
    A. affinity diagram.
    B. cause-and-effect diagram.
    C. flow process chart.
    D. nominal group technique.

REFERENCE: Abdelhak, p 450
LaTour, Eichenwald-Maki, and Oachs, p 822
McWay, pp 347, 349
Sayles, p 593
Shaw, pp 20–21

42. You sit on the quality improvement team for the Nursing department that meets to generate ideas to address verbal order documentation problems about the "Read Back Verbal Order" policy. What QI tool would prove useful in sharing input and various recommendations for solving this problem?
    A. flowchart
    B. scatter diagram
    C. check sheet
    D. brainstorming

REFERENCE: Abdelhak, p 450
Davis and LaCour, p 366
LaTour, Eichenwald-Maki, and Oachs, pp 821–822
McWay, pp 179, 346
Sayles, pp 592–593
Shaw, p 20

43. A histogram is a valuable tool for representing
    A. the solution to a problem.
    B. priorities in problem solving.
    C. a frequency distribution with continuous-interval data.
    D. the root causes of a problem.

REFERENCE: Abdelhak, pp 386, 452
Davis and LaCour, pp 309–310
LaTour, Eichenwald-Maki, and Oachs, pp 513, 824
McWay, pp 180–181
Sayles, pp 527–528

44. Eighty (80) requests for records to be pulled for the emergency room were processed in January. From the histogram provided above, what was the most frequent amount of time taken to process a request?
    A. 1–10 minutes
    B. 11–20 minutes
    C. 21–30 minutes
    D. 31–40 minutes

REFERENCE: Abdelhak, p 386
               LaTour, Eichenwald-Maki, and Oachs, pp 513, 824
               McWay, pp 180–181
               Sayles, pp 527–528
               Shaw, pp 57–58

45. Which quality management theorist focused on zero defects as the goal of performance improvement efforts?
    A. Kaizen
    B. Crosby
    C. Peters
    D. Deming

REFERENCE: Davis and LaCour, p 347
               LaTour, Echenwald-Maki, and Oachs, p 650
               McWay, pp 172–173
               Sayles, pp 563, 565
               Shaw, p xxvii

46. As Director of the HIM department, you are asked to chair a committee that will review, select, and implement a CPOE system. The information has been collected, and you bring your committee together to prioritize their suggestions. This method of working with information is known as
    A. force field analysis.
    B. Delphi process.
    C. nominal group process.
    D. correlation analysis.

REFERENCE: LaTour, Eichenwald-Maki, and Oachs, p 822
               McWay, pp 179, 347
               Sayles, pp 593–594
               Shaw, pp 20–21

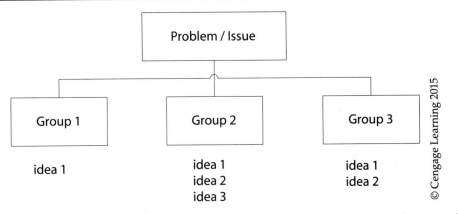

© Cengage Learning 2015

47. The performance tool shown above is used to provide structure by classifying information into smaller groups. What is the name of this chart/diagram?
   A. flowchart
   B. matrix
   C. affinity diagram
   D. arrow diagram

REFERENCE: Abdelhak, p 450
               LaTour, Eichenwald-Maki, and Oachs, p 822
               McWay, pp 179, 347, 349, 500
               Sayles, p 593
               Shaw, pp 20–21

48. Which quality management theorist believed that merit raises, formal evaluations, and quotas established through benchmarking hinder worker productivity and growth?
   A. Brian Joiner
   B. Philip Crosby
   C. Joseph Juran
   D. W. Edwards Deming

REFERENCE: Davis and LaCour, p 347
               LaTour, Eichenwald-Maki, and Oachs, pp 687–688
               Sayles, p 564
               Shaw, p xxvii

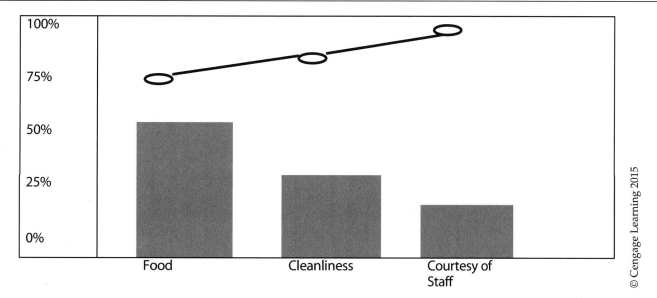

49. As head of the Performance Improvement Department, you are asked to evaluate patient satisfaction and offer recommendations for action. The performance tool shown above is used to graphically display the results. What is the name of this chart?
    A. Pareto chart
    B. line chart
    C. bar chart
    D. run chart

REFERENCE: Abdelhak, p 453
              LaTour, Eichenwald-Maki, and Oachs, p 823
              McWay, pp 179–180
              Sayles, pp 591–592
              Shaw, pp 58–59

50. Based on the previous graphic chart, which two areas should you recommend be acted upon first in order to address 80% of the patients' complaints?
    A. food and cleanliness
    B. food and courtesy of staff
    C. cleanliness and courtesy of staff
    D. not enough information to determine

REFERENCE: LaTour, Eichenwald-Maki, and Oachs, p 823
              McWay, pp 179–180
              Sayles, pp 591–592
              Shaw, pp 58–59

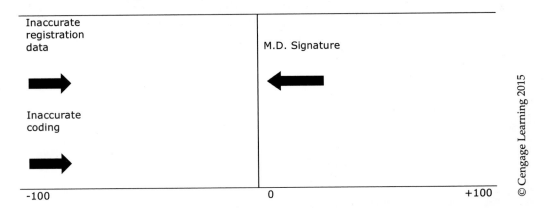

51. As Director of the HIM department, it is your responsibility to reduce the turnaround time for your organization's accounts receivable balance. The performance improvement tool shown above was used to add weights in order to prioritize ideas. What is it called?
    A. fishbone diagram
    B. precision matrix
    C. flowchart
    D. force field analysis

REFERENCE: Abdelhak, p 452
              LaTour, Eichenwald-Maki, and Oachs, p 823
              McWay, p 347
              Sayles, p 588

52. Which of the following processes is mandatory for health care facilities?
    A. accreditation
    B. certification
    C. AHA registration
    D. licensure

REFERENCE: Abdelhak, p 12
              Davis and LaCour, p 23
              LaTour, Eichenwald-Maki, and Oachs, p 37
              McWay, p 17
              Shaw, p 330

53. A surgeon left a clamp in a patient, resulting in a return to the operating room. In an integrated organizational quality management model, all of the following entities would receive data about the investigation EXCEPT the
    A. Tissue Committee.
    B. Credentials Committee.
    C. Risk Management Program.
    D. Pharmacy and Therapeutics Committee.

REFERENCE: LaTour, Eichenwald-Maki, and Oachs, pp 249, 664–666, 860–861
              Sayles, pp 27, 435, 451, 612–621
              Shaw, p 198

54. The Joint Commission requires health care facilities manage the environment of care by implementing seven (7) various safety plans, which must be evaluated at least
   A. monthly.
   B. quarterly.
   C. biannually.
   D. annually.

REFERENCE: Sayles, p 73
                      Shaw, p 271

55. The type of indicator about the placement and number of fire extinguishers would be a(n)
   A. process.
   B. outcome.
   C. structure.
   D. regulation.

REFERENCE: Abdelhak, p 442
                      Sayles, p 568
                      Shaw, pp xxviii, 14

56. The Joint Commission has a standard stating that a hospital must plan and design information management processes to meet _____ information needs.
   A. internal
   B. external
   C. both internal and external
   D. patient record

REFERENCE: Abdelhak, pp 128–129
                      Shaw, p 366
                      http://www.jointcommission.org

57. HEDIS gathers data in which of the following areas?
   A. measures of access (e.g., at least one visit to a provider within 3 years)
   B. measures of quality (e.g., cholesterol screenings)
   C. measures of member satisfaction (e.g., cost per member)
   D. all of the above

REFERENCE: Abdelhak, pp 692–693
                      Davis and LaCour, p 241
                      LaTour, Eichenwald-Maki, and Oachs, pp 200, 426–427
                      McWay, p 412
                      Sayles, p 254
                      Shaw, pp 332–333

58. If administrators of a home health agency wanted to measure the outcomes of adult patients receiving their agency's services, which tool would they use?
    A. OASIS
    B. HEDIS
    C. ORYX
    D. QAI

REFERENCE: Abdelhak, pp 137–138
                 LaTour, Eichenwald-Maki, and Oachs, pp 199, 438
                 McWay, pp 10, 186, 270
                 Sayles, pp 278–279
                 Shaw, p 151

59. Your hospital is required by the Joint Commission and CMS to participate in national benchmarking on specific disease entities for quality of care measurement. This required collection and reporting of disease-specific data is considered
    A. an environment of care.
    B. a group of sentinel events.
    C. a series of core measures.
    D. risk assessment.

REFERENCE: LaTour, Eichenwald-Maki, and Oachs, pp 201, 382, 670–671
                 Sayles, pp 156, 968
                 Shaw, pp 132, 359

60. Continuous quality improvement is best described by the following statements EXCEPT
    A. corrective action targets clinicians more so than processes.
    B. standards are defined, measured, and systematically applied.
    C. monitoring is ongoing with periodic feedback.
    D. all personnel support quality improvement efforts, including top management and the governing body.

REFERENCE: Abdelhak, pp 441–442
                 LaTour, Eichenwald-Maki, and Oachs, pp 35, 294, 442, 650, 658–659, 663, 687, 818,
                 825, 833, 852, 905
                 McWay, p 142
                 Sayles, pp 583–584, 565–568, 598, 684
                 Shaw, pp 4–9

61. Which of the following is a disadvantage of retrospective data collection?
    A. Data are all available.
    B. Fewer data collectors are required.
    C. Deficiencies in documentation can effect reimbursement.
    D. Reviewer bias is reduced.

REFERENCE: Davis and LaCour, pp 336–337
                 LaTour, Eichenwald-Maki, and Oachs, p 624
                 McWay, pp 208, 521
                 Sayles, pp 262, 350, 396

62. According to current theory in the quality management field, should concurrent data collection or retrospective data collection be utilized?
    A. Concurrent and retrospective data collection methods are both necessary in order to effect meaningful interventions and contain costs.
    B. Concurrent data collection methods alone are meaningful because they emulate health practitioner training.
    C. Concurrent data collection methods alone are meaningful because interventions must always be immediate.
    D. Retrospective data collection methods alone are appropriate in the reimbursement realities of this decade.

REFERENCE: Davis and LaCour, pp 336–337
              LaTour, Eichenwald-Maki, and Oachs, p 624
              McWay, pp 208, 521
              Sayles, pp 262, 350, 396

63. You are determining the sample size for a quality study. Which of the following factors should you consider first?
    A. cost
    B. personnel
    C. size of the target population
    D. confidentiality of the record

REFERENCE: Abdelhak, pp 399–400
              LaTour, Eichenwald-Maki, and Oachs, p 455
              Shaw, p 46

64. The Anesthesia Department is adding a new indicator to its plan. The Chief Anesthesiologist has come to you, the Director of Quality Management, to help her design a data collection methodology. The two of you are now considering who will be doing the data collection. All of the following are factors in your deliberations EXCEPT
    A. quality management organizational model of the institution.
    B. Joint Commission standards and required characteristics.
    C. the location of data.
    D. the expertise of the staff.

REFERENCE: McWay, pp 124–125
              Shaw, pp 46–47

65. The manager of the utilization review department wants to monitor and evaluate the prevention of inappropriate admissions. When would the manager need to collect data?
    A. prospective review
    B. concurrent review
    C. retrospective review
    D. long-term care review

REFERENCE: Abdelhak, p 463
              Davis and LaCour, pp 173–175, 377
              LaTour, Eichenwald-Maki, and Oachs, pp 28–29, 331, 430, 464
              McWay, p 227
              Sayles, pp 610–611

66. The manager of the Quality Department is listing various sources of data. Which of the following data sources would be an example of an external source?
    A. emergency room logs
    B. incident reports
    C. patient registration and admission, discharge, transfer (ADT) information
    D. quality improvement organization (QIO) information

REFERENCE: Abdelhak, p 438
              Davis and LaCour, pp 290–292
              LaTour, Eichenwald-Maki, and Oachs, pp 189, 368
              McWay, pp 142, 160
              Sayles, p 433
              Shaw, p 46

67. The primary advantage of concurrent quality data collection is that
    A. multiple chart reviews eliminate collector bias.
    B. patient care problems can be remedied immediately.
    C. practitioners receive immediate feedback about patient processes and outcomes.
    D. staffing is decreased.

REFERENCE: Davis and LaCour, pp 128, 337, 427–428
              LaTour, Eichenwald-Maki, and Oachs, pp 248, 254, 263, 266, 899
              McWay, pp 107–209
              Sayles, pp 350, 1188

SUMMARY OF SELECTED BLOOD PRODUCT REVIEW

Monitoring Element	Packed Red Blood Cells		Fresh Frozen Plasma		Platelets	
(N = 295)	(N = 256)		(N = 29)		(N = 10)	
	Met N (%)	Unmet N (%)	Met N (%)	Unmet N (%)	Met N (%)	Unmet N (%)
Indications	232 (91%)	24 (9%)	7 (24%)	22 (76%)	10 (100%)	0 (0%)

68. Refer to the Summary of Selected Blood Product Review table shown above. Which blood component or derivative had the most units reviewed?
    A. packed red blood cells   C. platelets
    B. fresh frozen plasma   D. unable to determine from the table

REFERENCE: Abdelhak, pp 384, 386
              Davis and LaCour, pp 367–368
              LaTour, Eichenwald-Maki, and Oachs, pp 508, 523, 589–590
              McWay, p 229
              Sayles, pp 518, 520, 557
              Shaw, pp 53–54

69. Refer to the Summary of Selected Blood Product Review table shown above. Which quality improvement function would prompt the production of the table?
    A. pharmacy and therapeutics function
    B. drug usage evaluation
    C. medical record review
    D. blood usage review

REFERENCE: LaTour, Eichenwald-Maki, and Oachs, pp 665–666

70. Refer to the Summary of Selected Blood Product Review table shown above. What percent of the fresh frozen plasma units met indications?
    A. 7%   C. 22%
    B. 24%   D. 76%

REFERENCE: Abdelhak, pp 384, 386
               McWay, pp 192–193, 218
               Shaw, pp 53–54, 119

71. Refer to the Summary of Selected Blood Product Review table shown above. Based on the results reported in the table, which blood component or derivative should first be the topic of an in-depth study?
    A. packed red blood cells   C. platelets
    B. fresh frozen plasma   D. unable to determine from the table

REFERENCE: Abdelhak, pp 384, 386, 452
               Davis and LaCour, pp 367–368
               LaTour, Eichenwald-Maki, and Oachs, pp 508, 523, 589–590
               Sayles, pp 518, 520, 557
               Shaw, pp 47–48, 57

CASE STUDY #1

Upon employment at your facility, all new employees read, demonstrate understanding, and sign Confidentiality Statements. Disclosure of confidential information is grounds for immediate dismissal. Each year, during the annual performance evaluation, every employee again reads, demonstrates understanding, and signs the Confidentiality Statement.

You are the Director of the Quality Department. Your department has found that the femoral-popliteal bypass failure rate of one of your vascular surgeons, Dr. Z, is twice that of the national average. Members of the surgery department have reviewed that vascular surgeon's performance both by reading the medical records and by watching videos of her surgery. The Surgery Department and the Executive Committee have decided to deny reappointment for this surgeon.

Lucille X, the mother of one of your quality coordinators, has severe peripheral vascular disease. She was admitted to your facility and had an angiogram. The angiogram shows that she should have a femoral-popliteal bypass. She had told you that she would be in your facility and asked you to visit her. You are now fulfilling that promise and are also bringing her flowers. While pausing to knock on her door, you hear your employee, Mary G, vehemently state to her mother, "Mom, Dr. Z is a quack; half of her bypass surgeries fail. You must have Dr. DoGood!"

72. Referring to Case Study #1, what do you do as Director of the Quality Department?
    A. Seek the advice of the facility's legal counsel.
    B. Immediately dismiss Mary G upon her arrival back in the department.
    C. Walk into Lucille's room and state that Dr. Z is a fine surgeon and also advise Mary G to lower her voice.
    D. Upon Mary G's arrival back in the department, give her a written warning.

REFERENCE: Abdelhak, pp 521, 534–536
              LaTour, Eichenwald-Maki, and Oachs, pp 775–776
              McWay, p 378
              Sayles, pp 1033, 1103

73. Referring to Case Study #1, are the meeting minutes about the decisions regarding Dr. Z of the Department of Surgery and of the Executive Committee admissible in court?
    A. Yes, federal amendments to the Medicare Act require release of peer review.
    B. Yes, state laws allow discovery of medical review committee records.
    C. No, the federal Freedom of Information Act and state "sunshine laws" protect peer review.
    D. No, under state laws, records of medical review committees are not subject to introduction into evidence.

REFERENCE: Abdelhak, pp 534–536
              LaTour, Eichenwald-Maki, and Oachs, p 665
              Shaw, p 429

CASE STUDY #2

You are helping the nursing department to write indicators to determine appropriate formulas for ratios and to determine data collection time frames. One important aspect of care is the documentation of education of patients. More specifically, the nursing department would like to assess its documentation of education on colostomy care for patients with new colostomies.

74. Referring to Case Study #2, what would be the most cost-effective and appropriate data collection time frame?
    A. prospective
    B. concurrent
    C. retrospective
    D. long-term care review

REFERENCE: Davis and LaCour, pp 336–337
               LaTour, Eichenwald-Maki, and Oachs, pp 331–332, 470, 624, 658
               McWay, pp 237, 531
               Sayles, pp 53, 350–361, 968

75. Referring to Case Study #2, which of the following ratios would you recommend?
    A. Number of records with documentation of colostomy-care teaching
       Total number of patients on surgery unit
    B. Number of records with documentation of teaching
       Total number of discharges
    C. Number of records with documentation of colostomy-care teaching
       Total number of patients with new colostomy
    D. Number of records reviewed with documentation of colostomy-care teaching
       Total number of records reviewed

REFERENCE: Abdelhak, p 373
               Davis and LaCour, pp 310–311
               LaTour, Eichenwald-Maki, and Oachs, pp 540–541
               McWay, pp 204, 519
               Sayles, pp 472, 474–475, 478
               Shaw, p 119

76. A culture and sensitivity report was returned to the inpatient unit of Brian Hospital. The sensitivity showed bacterial resistance to the current antibiotic the patient was receiving. The patient continued on the same antibiotic without improvement. A generic quality screen identified this case for review. At a minimum, which committee should review this case?
    A. Surgical Case Review
    B. Safety Committee
    C. Information Management Committee
    D. Pharmacy and Therapeutics Committee

REFERENCE: Sayles, p 647
               Shaw, p 219

77. The outpatient coding staff has been working to improve coding accuracy. The standard for the number of cases that must be coded has been raised four times in the past year. The staff said, "the more cases that must be coded, the greater the error rate will be for the corresponding time period." The department keeps statistics on both the numbers of cases coded and the corresponding error rate. What is the best QI tool for testing the coding staff's theory?
    A. control chart
    B. Pareto chart
    C. run chart
    D. scatter diagram

REFERENCE: LaTour, Eichenwald-Maki, and Oachs, pp 513–514, 537
               McWay, pp 180–181, 184, 210–211
               Sayles, pp 589, 591

78. The health information reception desk is experiencing a huge influx of phone calls on Monday, Tuesday, and Wednesday mornings. This is creating a problem in getting requested patient information out within an acceptable time frame. The reception staff work group has agreed to start recording the reason for the phone calls for the next 4 weeks. They want to focus on solving the response-time problem by reducing the turnaround time for the largest category of phone calls. Which QI tool best supports this goal?
    A. control chart
    B. Pareto chart
    C. run chart
    D. scatter diagram

REFERENCE: Abdelhak, p 453
                LaTour, Eichenwald-Maki, and Oachs, p 823
                McWay, pp 179–180, 347, 349
                Sayles, pp 591–592
                Shaw, pp 58–59

79. The board of directors of a 400-bed women's hospital receives a report of key quality indicator results on a periodic basis. The report always includes the quarterly cesarean section rate. This reporting period, they see a rise in the rate and want to know if it is a significant increase. What is the best QI tool for this purpose?
    A. control chart
    B. Pareto chart
    C. run chart
    D. scatter diagram

REFERENCE: Abdelhak, p 453
                LaTour, Eichenwald-Maki, and Oachs, p 825
                McWay, pp 148–151
                Sayles, pp 581–582
                Shaw, pp 62–63

80. What is the best tool for differentiating between common cause variation and special cause variation?
    A. control chart
    B. Pareto chart
    C. run chart
    D. scatter diagram

REFERENCE: Abdelhak, pp 453–454
                LaTour, Eichenwald-Maki, and Oachs, p 825
                McWay, pp 211–212
                Sayles, pp 581–582
                Shaw, pp 62–63

81. Which department will most likely be responsible for taking corrective action regarding the following quality indicator?

> QUALITY INDICATOR:
> Ninety-five percent (95%) of physician appointments/reappointments will be completed within 90 days of receipt of all required materials.

    A. Admissions
    B. Business Office
    C. Health Information Department
    D. Medical Staff Office

REFERENCE: Abdelhak, pp 443, 467–468
                Davis and LaCour, pp 370–372
                LaTour, Eichenwald-Maki, and Oachs, p 26
                Sayles, p 834
                Shaw, p 294

82. Which department will most likely be responsible for taking corrective action regarding the following quality indicator?

> QUALITY INDICATOR:
> The number of DRG validation changes made by the QIO will not exceed 2%.

A. Admissions
B. Business Office
C. Health Information Department
D. Medical Staff Office

REFERENCE: Abdelhak, pp 442, 659

83. All of the following are among the Joint Commission's initial core measure sets for hospitals EXCEPT
A. acute myocardial infarction.
B. diabetes.
C. pneumonia.
D. surgical infection prevention.

REFERENCE: LaTour, Eichenwald-Maki, and Oachs, pp 201, 670–671
Sayles, pp 156, 578–579
Shaw, pp 131–132

84. Which department will most likely be responsible for taking corrective action regarding the following quality indicator?

> QUALITY INDICATOR:
> Number of insurance claims requiring resubmission due to errors (not related to coding) will not exceed 3%.

A. Admissions
B. Business Office
C. Health Information Department
D. Medical Staff Office

REFERENCE: Abdelhak, p 657

85. What quality indicator would identify improvement needs in hospital electronic transmission of health care claims and remittances to allow interoperability with ICD-10 codes?
A. an increase in requests for operative reports
B. denied requests for medical record copies for continued care
C. an increase in hospital-acquired infections
D. an increase in 5010 rejections

REFERENCE: AHIMA (2010)

86. Historic accomplishments impacting quality in medical care include all EXCEPT
A. ensuring competent practitioners.
B. *Darling v. Charleston Community Hospital.*
C. implementation of OTRA.
D. medical education reform (Flexner report findings).

REFERENCE: Abdelhak, pp 7–8, 438–439
LaTour, Eichenwald-Maki, and Oachs, pp 9, 626
McWay, p 238
Sayles, pp 641–642

87. An accreditation agency counterpart to the Joint Commission for managed care organizations is the
    A. AHRQ.
    B. AHCPR.
    C. IOM.
    D. NCQA.

REFERENCE: LaTour, Eichenwald-Maki, and Oachs, pp 135, 200
               McWay, pp 52–53, 177–178, 247, 271, 412, 439
               Sayles, pp 74–75, 254, 952
               Shaw, p 145

88. The PQRS is a reporting system established by the federal government for physician practices who participate in Medicare for
    A. monetary incentives.
    B. meaningful use incentives.
    C. quality measure reporting.
    D. all of the above

REFERENCE: LaTour, Eichenwald-Maki, and Oachs, p 129
               Sayles, p 968

89. Which data bank is a result of HIPAA legislation?
    A. Fraud and Abuse Data Bank
    B. Health Care Integrity and Protection Data Bank
    C. National Practitioner Data Bank
    D. Privacy Information Breach Data Bank

REFERENCE: Abdelhak, p 468
               LaTour, Eichenwald-Maki, and Oachs, pp 377–378
               McWay, p 71
               Sayles, pp 451–452
               Shaw, p 295

90. The following "sentinel events" must be available for Joint Commission review EXCEPT
    A. infant abduction.
    B. petechiae due to adverse drug reaction.
    C. rape.
    D. surgery on wrong patient or wrong body part.

REFERENCE: Abdelhak, pp 456, 459
               LaTour, Eichenwald-Maki, and Oachs, pp 672–673, 862
               McWay, pp 190, 521
               Sayles, pp 621–622
               Shaw, pp 187–188

Year 2012 Month	Percent Patients with Unacceptable Waiting Time (%)
January	5
February	4
March	3
April	5
May	3
June	10
July	5
August	2
September	1
October	2
November	1
December	3

91. Use the information shown in the table above. Calculate the average percentage of patients for the entire year who waited longer than an acceptable amount of waiting time. (The sample size for each month's data is 100.)
    A. 3.1%
    B. 3.6%
    C. 3.7%
    D. 4.0%

REFERENCE: Abdelhak, pp 389–390
              McWay, p 204
              Sayles, p 538

92. Which of the following is incorrect about the use of control charts?
    A. Control charts can be used to measure key processes over time.
    B. The upper and lower control limits are always ± 2 standard deviations.
    C. The lower control limits are always ± 2 standard deviations.
    D. The upper control limits are always ± 1.8 standard deviations.

REFERENCE: LaTour, Eichenwald-Maki, and Oachs, pp 825, 950
              McWay, pp 180, 223–224
              Sayles, pp 581–582
              Shaw, pp 62–63

93. The average percent of patients exceeding acceptable waiting time was 3.7% (see table for question 91). The calculated UCL (upper control limit) is 9.4. When you plot the upper and lower limits, what would you suggest as the reason for the June variation?
    A. common cause variation
    B. root cause variation
    C. special cause variation
    D. unable to determine with the data given

REFERENCE: LaTour, Eichenwald-Maki, and Oachs, pp 825, 950
              McWay, pp 180, 223–224
              Sayles, pp 581–582
              Shaw, p 62

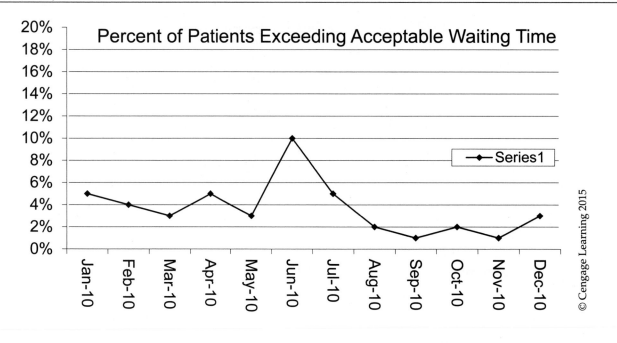

94. Adding the UCL (upper control limit) and LCL (lower control limit) to the chart above (from question 93) creates a
    A. control chart.   C. run chart.
    B. frequency distribution.   D. variation graph.

REFERENCE: Abdelhak, pp 452–454
                  LaTour, Eichenwald-Maki, and Oachs, pp 825, 950
                  McWay, pp 180, 223–224
                  Sayles, pp 581–582
                  Shaw, pp 62–63

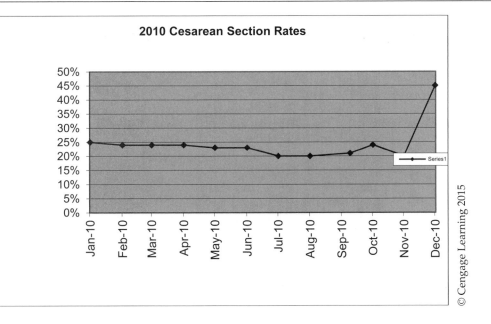

95. You are the Quality Coordinator for the medical staff. Analyze the chart above and determine the steps to be taken next.
    A. Plot the control limits, check the indicator threshold, and take the December charts to the OB/GYN Committee if the threshold is exceeded.
    B. Plot the control limits and take the December charts to the OB/GYN Committee if the December data point exceeds UCL.
    C. Plot the control limits, pull the charts for December, and do a focused review screening.
    D. Plot the control limits and refer to the Medical Executive Committee for variation review.

REFERENCE: Abdelhak, pp 386, 453–454
               LaTour, Eichenwald-Maki, and Oachs, pp 825, 950
               McWay, pp 130, 223–224
               Sayles, pp 581–582
               Shaw, pp 62–63

96. The U.S. federal government's CMS substitutes compliance of its Conditions of Participation requirements to hospitals that already have accreditation awarded by various other agencies that include the Joint Commission, CARF, AOA, or AAAHC. This is known as
    A. deemed status.   C. contingent statutory.
    B. due process.   D. waiver status.

REFERENCE: Abdelhak, p 12
               LaTour, Eichenwald-Maki, and Oachs, pp 37–38, 309, 909
               McWay, p 52
               Sayles, pp 72–74, 404, 687–688, 1200
               Shaw, p 334

97. Dr. Jeremy is establishing a clinical trial research study for his patients with lung cancer wishing to participate in a chemotherapy clinical trial. As Assistant Director, you are responsible for clinical abstract of data and advise him to first seek approval of research involving human subjects through the
    A. medical staff.
    C. institutional review board (IRB).
    B. governing board.
    D. Office of National Coordinator (ONC).

REFERENCE: Abdelhak, pp 521–522
               Davis and LaCour, pp 298–299
               LaTour, Eichenwald-Maki, and Oachs, pp 321, 580, 610–611, 620–621, 923
               McWay, pp 214–248, 512
               Sayles, p 752
               Shaw, p 92

98. The Joint Commission on-site survey process incorporates tracer methodology, which emphasizes surveyor review by means of
    A. patient tracers.
    C. both system tracers and patient tracers.
    B. system tracers.
    D. policy and procedure manual reviews.

REFERENCE: Davis and LaCour, p 375
               LaTour, Eichenwald-Maki, and Oachs, pp 671, 953
               McWay, pp 10–11, 524
               Sayles, pp 404, 604–605, 628
               Shaw, pp 336–337

99. Storyboards are a method used in health care that
    A. graphically display a performance improvement project conducted.
    B. serve as a documentation format in patient records.
    C. serve as a teaching tool for customers and staff.
    D. both A and C

REFERENCE: Shaw, pp 74–75

100. The Six Sigma methodology differs from other quality improvement models by defining improvement opportunities using
    A. scientific management.
    C. nonvalue activities/processes.
    B. critical quality tree.
    D. brainstorming.

REFERENCE: Abdelhak, pp 448–449
               Davis and LaCour, pp 362–363
               LaTour, Eichenwald-Maki, and Oachs, pp 820, 828–829
               McWay, p 175
               Sayles, pp 625–626
               Shaw, p 443

101. The FOCUS PDCA model used in performance improvement is best known for its change strategy technique of
    A. Business Process Engineering.
    B. Plan, Do, Study, Act.
    C. Input, Through-Put, Output.
    D. Cause and Effect Diagramming.

REFERENCE: Abdelhak, p 447
               Davis and LaCour, pp 356–361
               LaTour, Eichenwald-Maki, and Oachs, pp 819–820
               McWay, pp 173–175, 183, 185, 346
               Sayles, p 1237

102. The quality review process of invasive and noninvasive procedures to ensure performance of appropriate procedure, preparation of patient, monitoring and postoperative care, and education of patient describes

A. universal protocol.
B. infection review.
C. surgical review.
D. blood and blood component usage.

REFERENCE: Abdelhak, p 465
                LaTour, Eichenwald-Maki, and Oachs, p 665

103. The Institute of Medicine (IOM) published report titled *To Err Is Human: Building a Safer Health System*, heightened concern by the U.S. government and accrediting agencies. This led the Joint Commission to place emphasis on improving patient safety and sentinel event occurrences through its safety program, known as

A. ORYX Initiative Set.
B. National Patient Safety Goals (NPSG).
C. Health Care Quality Improvement Program (HCQIP).
D. Health Plan Employer Data & Information (HEDIS).

REFERENCE: Abdelhak, pp 454–455
                Davis and LaCour, p 215
                LaTour, Eichenwald-Maki, and Oachs, pp 663, 672–674
                Sayles, pp 604, 622, 666, 1228
                Shaw, pp 138–139, 185–188

104. When a decision is made to restrict or deny clinical privileges during the recredentialing or reappointment process to a medical staff member, a _____ must be offered.

A. privilege suspension
B. revocation of license
C. due process
D. crisis intervention

REFERENCE: Abdelhak, pp 467–468
                LaTour, Eichenwald-Maki, and Oachs, p 634
                McWay, pp 22–24
                Sayles, p 834
                Shaw, p 296

105. A patient satisfaction survey conducted after discharge is a method of quality measurement through

A. prospective indicator.
B. structure indicator.
C. process indicator.
D. outcomes indicator.

REFERENCE: Abdelhak, pp 489–490
                LaTour, Eichenwald-Maki, and Oachs, pp 653–656
                Sayles, p 568
                Shaw, pp 14, 95–96

106. The Joint Commission's emphasis on improving quality of patient care for a participating facility is exemplary through the required self-assessment process tool known as
    A.   total quality management (TQM).
    B.   focused standards asessment.
    C.   intracycle monitoring.
    D.   both B and C

REFERENCE: Joint Commission

107. During the Utilization Review Committee meeting, a case presented for discussion involved a surgical case resulting in unexpected loss of lower extremity below the knee due to complications requiring extended length of stay. Being a sentinel event, the committee requested that an investigation and reporting was required to identify the cause and prevention of future occurrences. This investigation and required reporting to the Joint Commission is known as
    A.   root cause analysis.   C.   medication review.
    B.   potential compensable event.   D.   report card.

REFERENCE: Abdelhak, pp 458–459, 704–705
                LaTour, Eichenwald-Maki, and Oachs, pp 672–673
                McWay, pp 190, 251
                Sayles, p 587
                Shaw, pp 146, 157, 187–189

Answer Key for Quality and Performance Improvement

1. D
2. D
3. D
4. B
5. D
6. D
7. C
8. B
9. B
10. D
11. A Definition: HEDIS is Health Plan Employer Data and Information Set
12. B
13. D
14. C
15. D
16. C
17. C
18. A
19. D
20. D
21. D
22. D
23. D
24. A
25. D
26. A
27. D
28. B
29. C
30. B
31. C
32. D
33. C
34. B
35. C
36. D
37. A
38. D
39. C
40. D
41. C
42. D
43. C
44. B
45. B
46. C

47. C
48. D
49. A
50. A
51. D
52. D
53. D
54. D
55. C
56. C
57. D
58. A
59. C
60. A
61. C
62. A
63. C
64. B
65. A
66. D
67. B
68. A
69. D
70. B
71. B
72. B
73. D
74. C
75. C Number of times an event occurred divided by number of times the event could have occurred
76. D
77. D
78. B
79. A
80. A
81. D
82. C
83. B
84. B
85. D
86. C
87. D
88. C
89. B
90. B

Answer Key for Quality and Performance Improvement

91. C $(5 + 4 + 3 + 5 + 3 + 10 + 5 + 2 + 1 + 2 + 1 + 3) \div 12 = 3.66 = 3.7$

92. D

93. C Data points that lie outside the upper or lower control limits may signal special cause variation.

94. A

95. A

96. A

97. C

98. C

99. D

100. B

101. B

102. C

103. B

104 C

105. D

106. C

107. A

REFERENCES

Abdelhak, M., Grostick, S., Hanken, M. A., & Jacobs, E. (2012). *Health information: Management of a strategic resource* (4th ed.). Philadelphia: W. B. Saunders.

AHIMA. (2010, September). Three short years organizations lagging in 5010 and ICD-10 progress. *Journal of AHIMA, 80*(9). Retrieved from http://AHIMA.org

AHIMA. (2012a, August 15). *Book of knowledge—Practice brief, verbal/telephone order authentication and time frames (Updated).* Retrieved from http://AHIMA.org

AHIMA. (2012b, October 2). *Book of knowledge—Practice brief, electronic documentation templates support ICD-10-CM/PCS.* Retrieved from http://AHIMA.org

CMS Federal Register. (n.d.). Retrieved from http://www.gpo.gov/fdsys/pkg/CFR-2011-title42-vol5/pdf/CFR-2011-title42-vol5.pdf.

Joint Commission. (n.d.). Retrieved from http://www.jointcommission.org/AboutUs/Fact_Sheets/PPR_QA.htm

LaTour, K., Eichenwald, S. and Oachs, P. (2013). *Health information management: Concepts, principles, and practice* (4th ed.). Chicago: American Health Information Management Association (AHIMA).

McWay, D. (2013). *Today's health information management: An integrated approach* (2nd ed.). Clifton Park, NY: Delmar Cengage Learning.

Sayles, N. B. (2013). *Health information management technology: An applied approach* (4th ed.). Chicago: American Health Information Management Association (AHIMA).

Shaw, P. (2010). *Quality and performance improvement in health care: A tool for programmed learning* (4th ed.). Chicago: American Health Information Management Association (AHIMA).

Quality and Performance Improvement Competencies

Question	RHIA Domain	RHIT Domain
1–107	2	5

XV. Organization and Management

Anita Hazelwood, MLS, RHIA, FAHIMA

Carol A. Venable, MPH, RHIA, FAHIMA

1. The manager of a Health Information Department has many training and development methods available for the departmental and nondepartmental staff. Consider the following situation. The department's working hours are 8:00 AM to 6:00 PM. After 6:00 PM, if a record is needed in the emergency room for a possible readmission, the ER clerk has access to the HID in order to retrieve the record. On the occasions when the ER clerk has retrieved a record, she has left the department open, the records have been pulled and not replaced, and it appears as if the clerk was viewing records unnecessarily. What would be the best training or development method for the ER clerk in order to rectify this situation?
   A. receive training by an ER coworker
   B. receive training by an expert in record documentation
   C. attend an outside workshop or seminar
   D. receive training by the supervisor of files

REFERENCE: Abdelhak, pp 607–608
              LaTour, Eichenwald-Maki, and Oachs, pp 743, 745–748
              McWay, pp 364–365

2. Strong lateral relationships within a facility are most likely when
   A. vertical relationships are less than adequate.
   B. individual departments cooperate together to achieve organizational goals.
   C. individual departments are only interested in their internal goals.
   D. individual departments avoid one another.

REFERENCE: LaTour, Eichenwald-Maki, and Oachs, pp 688–694

3. The Director of the Health Information Services Department has asked that the supervisor of coding institute a method to monitor the accuracy of coding. What method would be the most effective approach?
   A. Perform a 100% review of one of the employees' work each day.
   B. Review a sample of each employee's work annually.
   C. Review a random sample of each employee's work monthly.
   D. Have each employee check each other's work and report any problems to the supervisor.

REFERENCE: Abdelhak, pp 619–621
              LaTour, Eichenwald-Maki, and Oachs, pp 806–809
              McWay, pp 364–365

4. You are the Coding Supervisor and wish to know the amount of time spent on coding by eight employees this month. You have the following productivity log. What percentage of time was spent on coding?

Productivity Log January			
Number of Employees	Charts Coded	Standard	Hours Worked
8	725	12 minutes per chart	1,280

   A. 14.7%   C. 8.8%
   B. 6.8%   D. 11.3%

REFERENCE: Abdelhak, pp 619–621
              Davis and LaCour, pp 425, 443
              McWay, pp 221–223

5. The Director of Health Information Services has asked the supervisor over files to determine productivity standards for the file clerks. In initiating this process, the supervisor has determined that the best way to institute work standards is to
   A. determine which employee can work the fastest.
   B. perform time and motion studies.
   C. improve employee morale.
   D. develop standards based on professional standards and industry benchmarks.

REFERENCE: Abdelhak, pp 619–621
               Davis and LaCour, pp 441–443
               McWay, pp 221–223

6. A new health information management clerk has been on staff for 2 days. She has thus far analyzed charts incorrectly, sent out confidential information improperly, and used the copy machine inappropriately. Evaluate this situation and determine the best resolution.
   A. Review the job description and job procedure with the clerk and follow up with an in-service.
   B. Review the job procedure with the clerk and have the analysis supervisor monitor her progress.
   C. Review the job description and job procedure with the clerk and follow up with a merit evaluation.
   D. Review job procedures with the clerk and follow up with an in-service.

REFERENCE: Abdelhak, p 608
               LaTour, Eichenwald-Maki, and Oachs, pp 730–739
               McWay, pp 364–365

7. "Qualified employees should be given priority when vacancies within the organization occur" is an example of
   A. a policy of the organization.
   B. an objective for the organization.
   C. a rule for the organization.
   D. a procedure for the organization.

REFERENCE: Abdelhak, p 646
               Davis and LaCour, pp 435–436
               LaTour, Eichenwald-Maki, and Oachs, pp 724–725
               McWay, p 326

8. A rule is helpful to both managers and the employees in the decision-making process. A rule
   A. allows judgments to be made.
   B. requires interpretation.
   C. predecides issues.
   D. provides the necessary details.

REFERENCE: Davis and LaCour, p 49
               LaTour, Eichenwald-Maki, and Oachs pp 722–731
               McWay, pp 23, 49

9. Which of the following statements describes a method of following a procedure?
   A. Medical records requested by the emergency room will be retrieved and delivered within 30 minutes.
   B. Multiple-page discharge summaries are stapled together in the left-hand corner.
   C. Transcription turnaround time is established as 24 hours following completion of dictation by the physician.
   D. Only HIM personnel have access to the medical record filing area.

REFERENCE: Abdelhak, pp 623–624
               Davis and LaCour, pp 435–436
               LaTour, Eichenwald-Maki, and Oachs, pp 724–725
               McWay, p 240

10. The supervisor of retention and retrieval was receiving frequent complaints from the file clerks regarding the discharge clerk's job performance. The file clerks stated that it was becoming difficult to maintain their productivity levels because the discharge clerk was not processing the requisition slips in a timely manner. In order to get a clearer understanding of the situation, the supervisor asked the file clerks and the discharge clerk to complete a task list for a 2-week period. The supervisor is constructing a
    A. flow process chart.
    B. movement diagram.
    C. work distribution chart.
    D. procedure flowchart.

REFERENCE: Abdelhak, pp 614–619
               LaTour, Eichenwald-Maki, and Oachs, pp 800–801
               McWay, pp 335, 525

11. Choose the system below that is the type of identification system in which the patient is issued a different number for each admission or encounter for care and the records of past episodes of care are brought forward to be filed under the last number issued.
    A. serial unit numbering   C. family numbering system
    B. unit numbering system   D. serial-unit number system

REFERENCE: Davis and LaCour, pp 255–256
               LaTour, Eichenwald-Maki, and Oachs, p 270

12. The standard for record retrieval is 200 work units per month. Based on the table below, what is the variance from standard for the month of May?

May Productivity Report—Chart Retrieval			
Week 1	Week 2	Week 3	Week 4
30	40	25	35

   A. 75%   C. 53%
   B. 65%   D. 15%

REFERENCE: McWay, pp 398–399

13. Ms. Wolf, supervisor of coding and abstracting, would like to determine the coders' accuracy. Which type of management tool would provide her with the information she needs?
    A. a stopwatch study
    B. a coding audit
    C. an employee-reported log
    D. a time log

REFERENCE: Davis and LaCour, pp 441–443
            LaTour, Eichenwald-Maki, and Oachs, pp 808–811
            McWay, pp 338–339

14. After a work sampling study was completed, it was found that 20% of a coder's time was devoted to pulling records for physicians with missing diagnoses. How many minutes of a 7-hour day are taken up with this activity?
    A. 140
    B. 84
    C. 21
    D. 56

REFERENCE: Abdelhak, pp 619–621
            LaTour, Eichenwald-Maki, and Oachs, pp 808–811
            McWay, pp 339–340

15. Written documents that assist an organization in achieving its objectives and carrying out its mission statement are known as
    A. strategic plans.
    B. game plans.
    C. tactical plans.
    D. operational plans.

REFERENCE: Abdelhak, pp 636–637
            Davis and LaCour, p 429
            LaTour, Eichenwald-Maki, and Oachs, pp 866–867
            McWay, pp 324–325
            Shortell and Kaluzny, pp 460–461

16. Anna Kathryn is attending budget training for new supervisors. The representative from Finance explains that _____ costs will vary in direct proportion to changes in the volume of care provided.
    A. fixed
    B. periodic
    C. variable
    D. semivariable

REFERENCE: Abdelhak, p 675
            LaTour, Eichenwald-Maki, and Oachs, pp 781–782
            McLean, p 129

17. The organizing process determines how the work in a particular department will be divided and accomplished. In order to be in the best position to organize the work effectively, the manager must first engage in which management function?
    A. staffing
    B. directing
    C. planning
    D. controlling

REFERENCE: Davis and LaCour, pp 429–430
            LaTour, Eichenwald-Maki, and Oachs, p 690
            McWay, p 323

18. The director of a Health Information Department has discovered that the department's policy regarding the usage of the copy machine has been consistently abused by the majority of the staff. To put an end to this inappropriate use of the copy machine, the director should institute a department
    A. method.
    B. rule.
    C. objective.
    D. procedure.

REFERENCE: LaTour, Eichenwald-Maki, and Oachs, pp 724–725
              McWay, p 49

19. The average number of transcribed lines per month at Bent Tree Hospital is 142,500. The daily production standard is 950 lines per day. With 20 workdays in the month, calculate the minimum number of FTEs needed for this volume.
    A. 13
    B. 8
    C. 6
    D. 7.5

REFERENCE: Davis and LaCour, pp 415–416
              LaTour, Eichenwald-Maki, and Oachs, pp 806–807

20. The supervisor of release of information in a Health Information Department is preparing a work distribution chart in the hopes of identifying some problem areas. Although the work distribution chart can provide the supervisor with a great deal of information concerning the work performed by her staff, it will not indicate
    A. if a task is divided among employees disproportionately.
    B. the solution to a specific problem area.
    C. if the skills of each employee are utilized appropriately.
    D. the appropriate method of work division.

REFERENCE: Abdelhak, pp 614–619
              LaTour, Eichenwald-Maki, and Oachs, pp 800–801

21. Emma Grace is a transcriptionist. Her productivity level, as determined by line count per day, has dropped significantly over the past 2 weeks. As a result, there is a backlog in transcription of history and physical reports and surgical reports. Several doctors and the operating room supervisor have complained. An appropriate initial course of action for the Supervisor of Transcription is to
    A. counsel the transcriptionist privately.
    B. fire the transcriptionist immediately.
    C. refer the matter to the Human Resources Department.
    D. suspend the transcriptionist without pay for 3 days.

REFERENCE: LaTour, Eichenwald-Maki, and Oachs, pp 815–816
              McWay, p 379

22. The Director of the Health Information Services Department has determined that an in-service for department supervisors on improving productivity levels in their respective areas is needed. As an outcome of this in-service, the director would like the supervisors to understand that when setting productivity levels, a supervisor must
   A. tailor any training needs to each individual employee to achieve the productivity levels.
   B. direct training needs to the most efficient employee within the department in order to achieve the productivity levels.
   C. determine the productivity standards for each area and job function.
   D. consider only quantity and not quality.

REFERENCE: Davis and LaCour, pp 466–470
LaTour, Eichenwald-Maki, and Oachs, pp 806–811
McWay, p 365

23. The coding supervisor reviewed the productivity logs of four newly hired coders after their first month. The report below illustrates each coder's output. Based on analysis of this report, which employee will require additional assistance in order to meet the coding standards?

PRODUCTIVITY REPORT Coding Standard: 20 charts per day				
Coder	Week 1	Week 2	Week 3	Week 4
1	90	100	95	100
2	100	105	105	95
3	70	75	90	85
4	85	85	90	100

   A. Coder 1
   B. Coder 2
   C. Coder 3
   D. Coder 4

REFERENCE: Davis and LaCour, pp 426–427, 443–445
LaTour, Eichenwald-Maki, and Oachs, pp 811–817
Sayles, pp 546–547

24. Which of the following statements best describes the scalar or chain of command principle?
   A. Effective organization is made up of people who perform the work assigned.
   B. There is a clear flow of authority from superior to subordinate throughout the organization.
   C. The objectives of a business or a group of functions within the business must be clearly defined and understood.
   D. The number of subordinates under the immediate supervision of the supervisor should be limited.

REFERENCE: LaTour, Eichenwald-Maki, and Oachs, pp 686, 690
McWay, pp 417–418

The following questions represent advanced competencies.

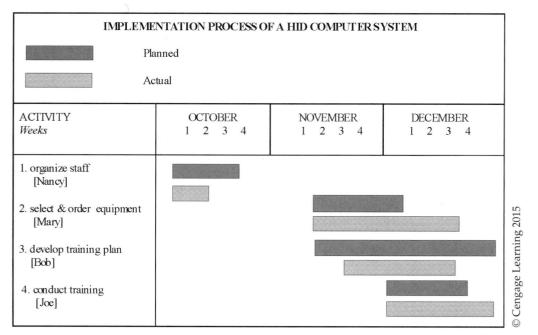

IMPLEMENTATION PROCESS OF A HID COMPUTER SYSTEM

Planned

Actual

ACTIVITY *Weeks*	OCTOBER 1 2 3 4	NOVEMBER 1 2 3 4	DECEMBER 1 2 3 4
1. organize staff [Nancy]			
2. select & order equipment [Mary]			
3. develop training plan [Bob]			
4. conduct training [Joe]			

© Cengage Learning 2015

25. Based on the Gantt chart shown above, which planned activities can be done simultaneously?
    A. activities 1 and 2
    B. activities 3 and 4
    C. activities 1, 3, and 4
    D. activities 2 and 3

REFERENCE: LaTour, Eichenwald-Maki, and Oachs, p 847
              McWay, p 179

26. In order to improve efficiency and productivity, which of the following sequence of steps is the most effective?
    A. Break down the work into component activities, assign personnel, and delegate authority.
    B. Delegate authority, assign personnel, and define individual job duties.
    C. Know the objective; assign personnel and group activities into proper organizational units.
    D. Know the objective; break down the work into component activities, and the group activities into proper organizational units.

REFERENCE: LaTour, Eichenwald-Maki, and Oachs, pp 107, 811–813, 847

27. Amelia Claire is a CNA and an RHIA who is a clinical documentation trainer for a large health system. The results of a quality improvement study indicated that an informed consent was not obtained for 25% of the surgical procedures performed. Amelia has discussed the problem with the director of the Health Information Department and they have decided to begin corrective action by providing an in-service. The most important participants who should attend this in-service are
    A. nurses and unit clerks.
    B. medical record and quality improvement personnel.
    C. physicians and residents.
    D. administrators.

REFERENCE: Davis and LaCour, pp 466–467
              LaTour, Eichenwald-Maki, and Oachs, p 731
              McWay, pp 364–365

28. The Director of Health Information Services has recently received approval to purchase the necessary equipment to place all inactive records on optical disc. The director plans to redo the department layout to accommodate the equipment and to ensure that the equipment is placed in the most appropriate area of the department. Which of the following tools will best assist the director with this new layout?

A. proximity chart
B. frequency chart

C. Gantt chart
D. replacement chart

REFERENCE: Abdelhak, p 647

29. One of your first tasks as the new Manager of Health Information Services is to review the department policy and procedure manual. You have determined that several policy statements are incongruent with appropriate current employee practices. Proper management conventions require

A. leaving the policy as written in the manual.
B. contacting the hospital attorney to decide what action to take.
C. enforcing the existing policy.
D. revising the policy appropriately and documenting the date of the change.

REFERENCE: Davis and LaCour, pp 436–437
LaTour, Eichenwald-Maki, and Oachs, p 723
McWay, p 326

30. Elizabeth Home is the Chief Executive Officer (CEO) at St. Augustine Medical Center. At the beginning of each fiscal year, she begins a formal planning cycle. Her annual planning process should begin with which of the following?

A. revising the institutional mission
B. developing strategic plans
C. establishing the annual organizational objectives
D. developing strategic goals

REFERENCE: Davis and LaCour, pp 429–443
LaTour, Eichenwald-Maki, and Oachs, p 690
McWay, pp 323–329

31. Which of the following statements is false in regard to departmental reengineering?

A. It is mainly done to reduce departmental costs.
B. It is intended to make small or minor changes in order to improve a function or process.
C. It is intended to improve departmental productivity.
D. It is intended to ensure satisfied customers.

REFERENCE: Davis and LaCour, pp 346–348
LaTour, Eichenwald-Maki, and Oachs, pp 695, 825–826
McWay, pp 96, 395

32. In preparing a capital budget request, the first priority will be to document

A. the specific type of equipment requested.
B. where the new equipment will be located.
C. the need for the new equipment.
D. the cost of the new equipment.

REFERENCE: Davis and LaCour, p 330
McLean, p 152
McWay, p 398

33. Based on the information displayed in the decision matrix below, which vendor would you recommend for the purchase of a copy machine?

Criteria	Weight	Vendor A Rating	Vendor B Rating	Vendor C Rating	Vendor D Rating
Quality	5	4	3	3	3
Speed	4	3	1	3	2
Service	2	3	3	5	2

A. Vendor A   C. Vendor C
B. Vendor B   D. Vendor D

REFERENCE: Davis and LaCour, pp 336–338
              LaTour, Eichenwald-Maki, and Oachs, p 695
              McWay, pp 94, 390

34. As the Director of the Health Information Department, you are preparing a request for approval for the purchase of an encoding system. Because this is considered a capital request, you are required to submit the cost–benefit ratio. The software and license cost $6,000, hardware maintenance is $1,500, and the training of two employees will cost $500. It is expected that the encoding system will increase reimbursement by $10,000. The cost–benefit ratio is
A. 0.8.   C. 1.25.
B. 1.7.   D. 1.33.

REFERENCE: Abdelhak, p 332
              McWay, pp 94, 390

35. What two types of budgets are often prepared by managers of health information departments?
A. capital budget and the finance budget
B. capital budget and the operational or revenue and expense budget
C. profit and loss budget and the finance budget
D. finance budget and the revenue and expense budget

REFERENCE: Davis and LaCour, pp 430–431
              McLean, pp 151–152

36. Both Mary and Sue are employed as medical transcriptionists at All Children's Hospital. They are able to set their own work hours provided the department is covered by one of them during regular office hours. This kind of work arrangement is referred to as
A. compressed work week.   C. flex time.
B. job sharing.   D. telecommuting.

REFERENCE: LaTour, Eichenwald-Maki, and Oachs, pp 727–728

37. The most important consideration in planning the office layout for a Health Information Services department is the
A. number of employees.   C. types of furniture to be purchased.
B. cost.   D. workflow.

REFERENCE: Davis and LaCour, p 454
              LaTour, Eichenwald-Maki, and Oachs, pp 796–797

38. Allison has conducted a timely performance evaluation for one of her employees and awarded the employee a 4% merit increase. She is currently completing the paperwork to submit to Human Resources. If the employee's hourly salary is presently $7.10, what will the hourly salary be with this increase?
    A. $7.33
    B. $7.38
    C. $7.80
    D. $7.54

REFERENCE: Abdelhak, pp 594–595

39. The span of control in an organization refers to the
    A.   number of supervisors for each functional area.
    B.   amount of space assigned to one supervisor.
    C.   amount of work expected of an employee.
    D.   number of people who report to one supervisor.

REFERENCE: Davis and LaCour, p 419
              LaTour, Eichenwald-Maki, and Oachs, p 690

40. A work environment that is not ergonomically sound could lead to
    A.   injuries.
    B.   conflict among departments.
    C.   employee arguments.
    D.   increases in department equipment budgets.

REFERENCE: Davis and LaCour, pp 454–456
              LaTour, Eichenwald-Maki, and Oachs, pp 799–800
              McWay, pp 335–336

41. Jessica is the leader of a project team working on the definition of the women's health service line. Several departments are so enthusiastic about the progress that they ask for additions to the project. This is not uncommon, and is known as
    A.   add-ons.
    B.   scope creep.
    C.   effort expansion.
    D.   deliverable increase.

REFERENCE: LaTour, Eichenwald-Maki, and Oachs, pp 836–837

42. The transcription production for February was 225,333 lines. The total work hours for all transcriptionists for the same period was 2,000. The average hourly cost was $13.50. Determine the cost per line for operating this service for this month.
    A. $1.20
    B. $0.24
    C. $2.40
    D. $0.12

REFERENCE: Abdelhak, pp 619–621

HEALTH INFORMATION DEPARTMENT MONTHLY BUDGET JANUARY		
Items	Budget	Actual
Supplies	495	675
Travel	300	150
Rental Equipment	1,250	1,250
Service Contracts	900	1,130

43. Based on the budget illustrated above, what is the monthly budget variance percent for supplies?
   A. 13.6%
   B. 36%
   C. 26.6%
   D. 11.9%

REFERENCE: Davis and LaCour, pp 430–443
               LaTour, Eichenwald-Maki, and Oachs, pp 785–787
               McLean, pp 156–157
               McWay, p 398

44. The most realistic approach that could encourage increased productivity in the tedious record file/retrieval area is to
   A. shorten the workday by 1 hour.
   B. vary and rotate the work assigned to each file clerk.
   C. have all the file clerks work on a part-time basis.
   D. arrange for all the file clerks to have flex time.

REFERENCE: McWay, pp 221–223

45. The HIM Department of a local hospital will experience a 20% increase in the number of discharges processed per day as the result of a merger with a smaller facility. This 20% increase is projected as 120 additional records per day. The standard time for coding a record is 15 minutes. Compute the number of FTEs required to process this increased volume in coding based on an 8-hour day.
   A. 3.75
   B. 2.8
   C. 6.5
   D. 5.25

REFERENCE: Davis and LaCour, pp 415–416
               LaTour, Eichenwald-Maki, and Oachs, pp 724, 806–807

46. Cheryl is the Director of the Health Information Services Department and Suzanne is the Assistant Director. Cheryl notices one of Suzanne's subordinates leaving the department for an unscheduled break. When the employee returns, Cheryl immediately asks the employee to step into her office and begins discussing the unauthorized break. Which organizational principle is this director violating?
   A. organizational function
   B. grievance procedure
   C. span of control
   D. unity of command

REFERENCE: Davis and LaCour, p 419
               LaTour, Eichenwald-Maki, and Oachs, p 690

47. As the Director of Health Information Services, you manage the department with the assistance of four supervisors. One day you observe a coder coding charts from the face sheet without reviewing the record for additional documentation. The most appropriate course of action would be to
   A. discuss your concerns with the Supervisor of Coding and direct her to address this issue immediately.
   B. discuss the problem with the CFO.
   C. discuss the matter directly with the coder and instruct him to review the entire record for correct assignment of codes.
   D. do nothing because the coding area is extremely productive.

REFERENCE: Davis and LaCour, p 419
LaTour, Eichenwald-Maki, and Oachs, p 690

48. During the month of May, there were 800 discharge abstracts processed at a cost of $0.90 per abstract for a total of $720.00. In June, 732 discharge abstracts were processed for a total cost of $658.80. This type of cost is known as
   A. semivariable.   C. fixed.
   B. adjustable rate.   D. variable.

REFERENCE: McLean, p 129

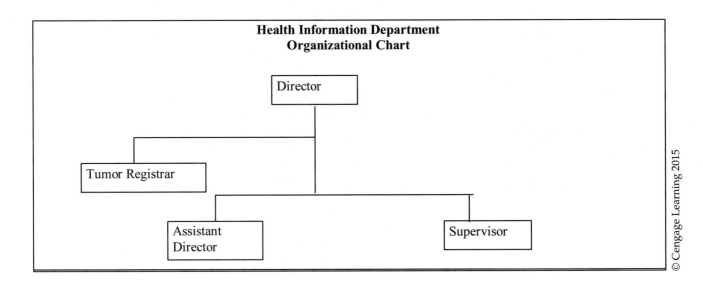

49. Which statement is an inaccurate description of the organization chart shown above?
   A. The director has authority over others in the department.
   B. The director has subordinates.
   C. The assistant director and the supervisor have a lateral relationship.
   D. The tumor registrar has authority over the assistant director.

REFERENCE: Davis and LaCour, pp 417–418
LaTour, Eichenwald-Maki, and Oachs, pp 690–691
McWay, pp 331–333

50. The Director of a Health Information Department has received the quarterly variance budget report. The report indicates the "overtime" category is unfavorable. The director is required to justify this overtime expense. Which of the following would be considered an acceptable explanation for this expenditure? Overtime is unfavorable this quarter due to
    A. the annual purging of inactive files.
    B. a chronic backlog in transcription.
    C. a decrease in admissions this quarter.
    D. a lack of supervision in the file area.

REFERENCE: Davis and LaCour, pp 430–431
LaTour, Eichenwald-Maki, and Oachs, pp 786–788
McWay, pp 398–399

51. The director of a Health Information Department has asked the department supervisors to review and revise all job descriptions. Missy Harris, the supervisor over coding and analysis, has determined that the job description for the senior coders must be revised. Ms. Harris' decision to revise the job description is probably due to a change in the
    A. number of coders.
    B. recruitment practices for coders.
    C. scope of coding responsibilities.
    D. method in which the coders' performance is evaluated.

REFERENCE: Davis and LaCour, p 437
LaTour, Eichenwald-Maki, and Oachs, pp 723–724
McWay, p 334

52. Which of the following is false in regard to budget variances?
    A. Variances are often calculated on the monthly budget report.
    B. Permanent budget variances do not resolve during the current fiscal year.
    C. A variance analysis identifies whether the variance is favorable or unfavorable.
    D. Temporary budget variances are expected to continue in subsequent months.

REFERENCE: Davis and LaCour, pp 430–431
LaTour, Eichenwald-Maki, and Oachs, pp 786–788
McWay, pp 389–399

53. The expense budget is also known as the
    A. production budget.
    B. operating budget.
    C. contract budget.
    D. profit and loss budget.

REFERENCE: Davis and LaCour, pp 430–431
LaTour, Eichenwald-Maki, and Oachs, pp 785–786

54. The Supervisor of a Health Information Department has aspirations of becoming the HID director. She works very long hours so that she can address all department issues herself rather than relying on her staff to assist her. Which type of management skills is she in need of improving in order to attain her goal of department director?
    A. delegating skills
    B. leadership skills
    C. motivating skills
    D. political skills

REFERENCE: Davis and LaCour, pp 419–420
LaTour, Eichenwald-Maki, and Oachs, p 754
McWay, pp 334, 392

55. The supervisor over release of information has requested a meeting with her superior, the Director of Health Information Services. She begins the meeting by describing how overwhelmed she is feeling. She is extremely behind in her work and she does not know what she can do to change the situation. In advising the supervisor, the director suggests that perhaps she should begin addressing her problem by attending a management workshop. Which of the following workshop topics is more likely to help the supervisor with her problem?
    A. "Leadership Styles for Women Managers and Supervisors"
    B. "The Nature of Delegation"
    C. "Understanding Your Employee"
    D. "Writing Skills for the Release of Information Supervisor"

REFERENCE: Davis and LaCour, pp 419–420
              LaTour, Eichenwald-Maki, and Oachs, p 754
              McWay, pp 334, 392

56. The Director of the Health Information Services Department is developing a plan to convert their existing filing system to a terminal digit filing system. The tool that is most useful to the director in displaying the steps and completion schedule for each phase of the conversion is a
    A. work distribution chart.   C. procedure flowchart.
    B. Gantt chart.   D. flow process chart.

REFERENCE: LaTour, Eichenwald-Maki, and Oachs, p 847
              McWay, p 329

57. Mr. Beasley determined that the rate of absenteeism with three of his employees was 15%. He felt that this was unacceptable and decided that there were two different ways he could handle this situation. He evaluated these alternatives and thought the best thing to do would be to suspend all three for 2 days. Once he implemented this idea, he analyzed the consequences. How would you label this process?
    A. decision making   C. crisis management
    B. planning   D. communicating

REFERENCE: LaTour, Eichenwald-Maki, and Oachs, pp 695–696
              McWay, pp 336–337

58. The Project Manager is responsible for all of the following functions, EXCEPT
    A. approval of the budget for the project.   C. recruitment of project team.
    B. creation of project plan.   D. recommending plan revisions.

REFERENCE: LaTour, Eichenwald-Maki, and Oachs, pp 840–842
              McWay, pp 345–346

59. A basic concept of office layout and workflow is that the
    A. paper and employee move to a predetermined location.
    B. employee moves to the paper.
    C. office layout and workflow should be revised frequently.
    D. paper moves to the employee.

REFERENCE: Davis and LaCour, p 442
              LaTour, Eichenwald-Maki, and Oachs, pp 796–798
              McWay, p 335

60. Which of the following tasks is the most appropriate for the Health Information Services Director to delegate to the Supervisor of Record Processing and Statistics?
    A. formulating a record retention policy for the entire facility
    B. reviewing monthly statistical reports to verify accuracy
    C. interviewing applicants for the position of Tumor Registrar
    D. completing a performance rating on the Assistant Director of the department

REFERENCE: Davis and LaCour, pp 419–420
LaTour, Eichenwald-Maki, and Oachs, p 754
McWay, pp 334, 392

61. When interviewing a prospective employee, which question would be inappropriate to ask?
    A. "Can you type?"
    B. "Where may we contact you?"
    C. "What language other than English can you speak or write?"
    D. "Do you own a home?"

REFERENCE: Davis and LaTour, pp 448–451
LaTour, Eichenwald-Maki, and Oachs, pp 720–721

62. If the budgeted payroll expense was $24,300 and the actual payroll expense was $25,800, what is the percentage of cost variance?
    A. 6.0%
    B. 0.58%
    C. 6.17%
    D. 6.7%

REFERENCE: LaTour, Eichenwald-Maki, and Oachs, pp 786–788
McLean, pp 156–157
McWay, pp 398–399

63. Which of the following actions illustrates the use of a participative management style?
    A. discussing suggested approaches of improving productivity and performance with employees
    B. basing decisions on information found in the manual of operations
    C. providing supervision only when requested by employees
    D. micromanaging all aspects and functions performed in the department

REFERENCE: Davis and LaCour, p 419
LaTour, Eichenwald-Maki, and Oachs, p 687
McWay, pp 344, 380

64. In deciding to purchase or lease a new dictation system, the Director of Health Information Services calculated the payback period and rate of return on the investment. The hospital's required payback period is 3 years with a required rate of return of 20%. If the equipment costs $32,000 and generates $8,000 per year in savings, what would the payback period for this equipment be?
    A. 2 years
    B. 5 years
    C. 3 years
    D. 4 years

REFERENCE: LaTour, Eichenwald-Maki, and Oachs, p 791
McWay, p 390

65. The Director of a Health Information Department prepared a document in which the following information could be obtained: job title, reporting line, span of control, and routes of promotion. The document she was preparing was a(n)
    A. job description.
    B. organizational chart.
    C. work distribution chart.
    D. job procedure.

REFERENCE: Davis and LaCour, pp 418–422
LaTour, Eichenwald-Maki, and Oachs, pp 690–691
McWay, pp 330–333

66. The Director of the Health Information Department had to resign immediately due to a family crisis requiring her to leave the country. Her superior, the Administrator of Support Services, must appoint an Acting Director as soon as possible but is questioning who might be the best individual for this temporary role. What tool would assist the administrator with this decision?

A. staffing table
B. replacement chart
C. proximity chart
D. frequency chart

REFERENCE: Abdelhak, pp 584–585

67. The file section supervisor is preparing the staffing budget for the coming fiscal year. Presently, the staff is filing approximately 500 charts per day. By the time the fiscal year begins, this is expected to increase to 650 charts per day. Currently, it takes nine FTEs to file 500 charts. The supervisor should project an FTE increase for the coming year's budget of

A. 13%.
B. 76%.
C. 23%.
D. 55%.

REFERENCE: Calculation

68. Lizzie O'Leary, Director of the Health Information Services Department, is writing a memo about a recent problem the department has had with a contracted copy service when she is notified of an emergency, hospital-wide department-head meeting. Because it is necessary that the memo be completed by the end of the day, it is most appropriate for the director to delegate its completion to the supervisor of

A. storage and retrieval.
B. transcription.
C. coding and abstracting.
D. release of information.

REFERENCE: LaTour, Eichenwald-Maki, and Oachs, p 690
McWay, pp 334, 392

69. Of the following, which is NOT considered justification to approve overtime? Overtime is not justified

A. for unpredictable fluctuations in volume.
B. when there is unusually high absenteeism.
C. when there is a temporary change of work methods.
D. for employees who want to supplement their wages.

REFERENCE: LaTour, Eichenwald-Maki, and Oachs, pp 786–788

70. A job analysis includes the

A. summation of the qualifications needed in a worker for a specific job.
B. collection of data to determine the content of a job.
C. title of the job and summary of the basic tasks making up a job.
D. goals to be achieved by a worker over a specified period.

REFERENCE: Abdelhak, pp 586–587
Davis and LaCour, pp 440–441
LaTour, Eichenwald-Maki, and Oachs, p 731
McWay, p 333

71. The Director of the Health Information Services Department is preparing the department's budget for the coming year. She has included the costs for the coding staff to attend at least two workshops in the budget. What portion of the department's budget will the cost of the workshops be allocated to?
    A. staffing budget
    B. revenue budget
    C. personnel budget
    D. expense budget

REFERENCE: McLean, p 152

72. The manager of a transcription agency is preparing December's staffing schedule. Because this month has several holidays, there are more requests for vacation and personal days than usual. Additionally, it is apparent to the supervisor that she will not be able to approve all requests for time off. It will be best for the supervisor to construct the schedule by
    A. processing requests based on seniority.
    B. granting requests on a first-come basis.
    C. adhering to the hospital and department policy regarding requests for time off.
    D. not approving any time off, thus eliminating any conflicts.

REFERENCE: LaTour, Eichenwald-Maki, and Oachs, p 802
McWay, p 326

73. The supervisor over the file section has discovered an enormous backlog of loose lab reports. The first step that the supervisor should take in attempting to resolve this matter is to
    A. analyze possible courses of action.
    B. gather relevant data regarding the problem.
    C. identify and clarify the problem.
    D. choose the best course of action.

REFERENCE: LaTour, Eichenwald-Maki, and Oachs, pp 695–696

74. New equipment has just been purchased for a Health Information Services Department. Prior to its arrival and placement in the department, it is important for the manager to adhere to the rules and regulations governed by
    A. FDA.
    B. OSHA.
    C. CMS.
    D. SSA.

REFERENCE: Davis and LaCour, pp 216–217
LaTour, Eichenwald-Maki, and Oachs, p 722
McWay, p 368

75. The best source for obtaining data for a job analysis is the
    A. department director.
    B. supervisor of the job.
    C. the person who performs the job.
    D. procedures manual.

REFERENCE: Abdelhak, pp 586–587
McWay, p 333

76. Mike is an information specialist in the Department of Information Technology. He has been asked to assist with the Joint Commission survey process, which accounts for approximately 75% of his time. He also receives project assignments from the HIM director, his immediate supervisor, as well as the overall project manager. This refers to what type of authority relationship?
    A. functional
    B. parallel
    C. matrix
    D. divisional

REFERENCE: Shortell and Kaluzny, p 77

77. The department director is responsible for budget costs that are controllable. Which of the following costs would be out of the director's control?
    A. equipment purchases
    B. fringe benefit cost per employee
    C. supply requisitions
    D. overtime authorizations

REFERENCE: Davis and LaCour, pp 730–731
               LaTour, Eichenwald-Maki, and Oachs, p 781
               McWay, pp 397–398

78. Kim Khoury is planning a luncheon for the team members and stakeholders on the CPOE implementation to celebrate reaching a major milestone. Which of the following is true?
    A. Acknowledging accomplishments and milestones motivates teams.
    B. Budgets rarely permit these extra expenses.
    C. Celebrations are only appropriate at the close of a project.
    D. Professionals are self-motivated, making celebrations unnecessary.

REFERENCE: LaTour, Eichenwald-Maki, and Oachs, p 850
               McWay, pp 345–346

79. Beth Huber, Director of Health Information, has been selected to participate in a strategic planning retreat for her health system. In preparation, she refreshes her understanding of strategic planning. Which of the following will likely be included in the retreat?

    A. improvement of existing programs and services
    B. opportunities to review internal structures and systems
    C. enhancing customer and patient satisfaction
    D. focus on the organization's fit with the external environment

REFERENCE: LaTour, Eichenwald-Maki, and Oachs, pp 866–867
               McWay, pp 323–325

80. The project definition justifies the need for the new project. What would you expect to see in the project justification?
    A. project scope, resources needed, and amount of time required
    B. project scope, resources needed, and developing the solution
    C. resources needed, amount of time required, and preparing supporting documentation for the system chosen
    D. amount of time required, alternative analysis, and implementation review

REFERENCE: LaTour, Eichenwald-Maki, and Oachs, pp 841–842
               McWay, pp 345–346

81. Roberta Little Eagle is the new HIM supervisor at a large South Dakota reservation clinic. In order to become familiar with the specific steps currently used in record processing, she uses which graphic tool?
    A. force field analysis   C. fishbone analysis
    B. histogram   D. flowchart

REFERENCE: Davis and LaCour, pp 370–371
               LaTour, Eichenwald-Maki, and Oachs, p 822
               McWay, pp 335–336

82. Megan is the new Director of Health Information at Blue Ridge Rehabilitation Associates, a large multispecialty clinic. Her initial assessment of the department's functioning is that there is considerable duplication of effort. To collect information on the systems used in the current functions and to analyze and improve the process, she chose to use a
    A. work process flowchart.
    B. systems diagram.
    C. decision tree.
    D. Pareto chart.

REFERENCE: LaTour, Eichenwald-Maki, and Oachs, p 821
               McWay, p 338

83. Which of the following would NOT be a scientific method of establishing standards?
    A. stopwatch studies
    B. work sampling
    C. personal experience
    D. time-log studies

REFERENCE: LaTour, Eichenwald-Maki, and Oachs, pp 806–807
               McWay, pp 339–340

84. Lucy Ann manages a claims review unit for an insurance company. Her staff keys a high volume of data daily. She has scheduled a staff physical therapist to do the annual ergonomics presentation to help prevent repetitive strain injuries. All of the following would be included EXCEPT
    A. using a footrest.
    B. wrists should be elevated.
    C. monitor placed directly in front and elevated.
    D. lumbar support provided.

REFERENCE: Davis and LaCour, pp 454–456
               LaTour, Eichenwald-Maki, and Oachs, p 799
               McWay, p 335

85. South Beach Medical Center is preparing to open as a new 250-bed acute care hospital. This facility is located in a growing area of the city and is projected to have 85% occupancy within 3 years. To determine the number of employees needed in the HIM department, the director must first
    A. determine employee salary ranges.
    B. develop a departmental organizational chart.
    C. collect data from hospitals that are of comparable size.
    D. identify the departmental functions to be performed.

REFERENCE: Davis and LaCour, pp 415–416
               LaTour, Eichenwald-Maki, and Oachs, pp 722–723
               McWay, pp 339–340

86. A national HIM publication routinely requests that practitioners submit statistics from their facility regarding department functions. These are then summarized and published in graphic form, providing a tool for which of the following activities?
    A. benchmarking
    B. work standards
    C. job evaluation
    D. job redesign

REFERENCE: Davis and LaCour, pp 65, 363–364
               LaTour, Eichenwald-Maki, and Oachs, p 808
               McWay, pp 179, 188

87. In project management, the series of specific tasks that determine the overall project duration is referred to as
    A. project network.
    B. critical path.
    C. risk analysis.
    D. project definition.

REFERENCE: LaTour, Eichenwald-Maki, and Oachs, p 844

88. The formalized road map that describes how your institution executes the chosen strategy defines
    A. operations improvement.
    B. strategic thinking.
    C. operational mission.
    D. strategic planning.

REFERENCE: LaTour, Eichenwald-Maki, and Oachs, p 866

89. Which of the following is a tool for strategic thinking?
    A. storytelling
    B. driving force
    C. innovations
    D. critical issues

REFERENCE: LaTour, Eichenwald-Maki, and Oachs, pp 866–868

90. Which of the following helps the organization prioritize investment opportunities?
    A. return on investment
    B. profitability index
    C. net present value
    D. internal rate of return

REFERENCE: LaTour, Eichenwald-Maki, and Oachs, p 792

91. Which of the following emphasizes the work climate in which harmony and cohesion promote good work?
    A. effectiveness
    B. chain of command
    C. scalar chain
    D. esprit de corps

REFERENCE: LaTour, Eichenwald-Maki, and Oachs, p 686

92. Which of the following is often characterized as a manager's version of a pilot's cockpit as it contains all the critical information for leading the organization?
    A. balanced scorecard
    B. revenge effect
    C. executive dashboard
    D. groupthink

REFERENCE: LaTour, Eichenwald-Maki, and Oachs, p 692

93. The statement "Managers must understand the informal organization of workers (groups, group sentiments, team work), the need of workers to be listened to and to participate in the design of their work" is characteristic of which of the following schools of management?
    A. Classical School of Administration
    B. Human Relations School
    C. Scientific Management School
    D. Decision-making School

REFERENCE: LaTour, Eichenwald-Maki, and Oachs, pp 686–687, 689–690, 712
               McWay, pp 343, 386, 389–391, 712
               Shortell and Kaluzny, pp 16–17

94. Units that provide support services to the organization, such as human resources, finances, and information systems, are referred to as
    A. line managers.
    B. integrated delivery systems.
    C. matrix organization.
    D. staff departments.

REFERENCE: LaTour, Eichenwald-Maki, and Oachs, p 690
               Shortell and Kaluzny, p 79

95. In Maslow's "hierarchy or needs," the term that describes the need for a positive self-image or self-respect, and the need for recognition and respect from others best describes
    A. belonging needs.
    B. security needs.
    C. esteem needs.
    D. self-actualization needs.

REFERENCE: LaTour, Eichenwald-Maki, and Oachs, pp 687, 712
              McWay, pp 340–341
              Shortell and Kaluzny, pp 97–98

96. The Occupational Safety and Health Act of 1970, the Americans with Disability Act, and the Vocational Rehabilitation Act are all federal legislation designed to
    A. prevent sexual harassment.
    B. ensure equal pay for equal work.
    C. keep the workplace safe and accessible to all employees and customers.
    D. protect child labor.

REFERENCE: Abdelhak, p 577
              Davis and LaCour, pp 263–266, 311, 451
              LaTour, Eichenwald-Maki, and Oachs, pp 721, 722, 728
              McWay, pp 367–373

97. Which of the following methods of performance appraisal requires the supervisor to document exceptional behavior by the employee?
    A. Behaviorally Anchored Rating
    B. Graphic Rating Scales
    C. Goal Setting
    D. Critical Incident Method

REFERENCE: Abdelhak, pp 594–595

98. The HIM employee is consistently late for work. Her supervisor has given her an oral warning. According to the definition of progressive discipline, what would the next step be?
    A. written warning and reprimand
    B. meeting with the supervisor of her supervisor
    C. suspension
    D. termination

REFERENCE: Abdelhak, p 601
              LaTour, Eichenwald-Maki, and Oachs, pp 240, 755
              McWay, p 378

99. There are several methods used to evaluate jobs. Which of the following is the simplest but the least precise?
    A. factor comparison
    B. job ranking
    C. job grading
    D. point system

REFERENCE: Abdelhak, pp 605-606
              LaTour, Eichenwald-Maki, and Oachs, p 755

100. An example of a communication network that is suitable to use when you have to communicate with several people who have no need to communicate directly with each other describes
    A. wheel.
    B. chain.
    C. circle.
    D. a "Y" pattern.

REFERENCE: Shortell & Kaluzny, p 181

101. A type of job evaluation that requires the identification of essential factors or elements common to all jobs and the comparison of jobs on the basis of rating those elements (not the job as a whole), refers to
   A. job ranking.
   B. job grading.
   C. factor comparison.
   D. point system.

REFERENCE: Abdelhak, p 607
               LaTour, Eichenwald-Maki, and Oachs, p 755

102. The mechanism that provides a communication and problem-solving tool for employees to express a complaint that management has violated one of its own policies, and caused adverse consequences to the employee, refers to
   A. employee discipline.
   B. the grievance process.
   C. involuntary retirement.
   D. employee counseling.

REFERENCE: Abdelhak, p 601
               LaTour, Eichenwald-Maki, and Oachs, p 756
               McWay, pp 378–379

103. The National Labor Relations Act (NLRA), which serves as the foundation for U.S. labor laws and collective bargaining, is also known as
   A. the Equal Pay Act.
   B. the Fair Labor Standards Act.
   C. the Family and Medical Leave Act.
   D. the Wagner Act.

REFERENCE: Abdelhak, p 578
               LaTour, Eichenwald-Maki, and Oachs, p 722
               McWay, p 367

104. Which of the following examples would NOT be considered "reasonable accommodation" under the Americans with Disabilities Act?
   A. completely renovating an entire department to accommodate a disabled employee
   B. providing qualified readers or interpreters
   C. reassigning a current employee to a vacant position
   D. acquiring or modifying equipment

REFERENCE: Abdelhak, p 576
               Davis and LaCour, p 451
               LaTour, Eichenwald-Maki, and Oachs, p 742
               McWay, pp 335, 367, 370

105. An amendment to the Civil Rights Act of 1964 that extends the 180-day statute of limitations previously applied to the filing of an equal-pay lawsuit refers to the
   A. Americans with Disabilities Act.
   B. Lilly Ledbetter Fair Pay Act.
   C. Age Discrimination in Employment Act.
   D. Family and Medical Leave Act.

REFERENCE: Abdelhak, p 573
               McWay, pp 367, 374

106. Which of the following is NOT a main objective of reengineering?
   A. to improve quality
   B. to increase revenue
   C. to increase cost
   D. to reduce risk

REFERENCE: Abdelhak, p 645
               LaTour, Eichenwald-Maki, and Oachs, pp 35, 688

Answer Key for Organization and Management

ANSWER   EXPLANATION

NOTE: Explanations are provided for those questions that require mathematical calculations and questions that are not clearly explained in the references that are cited.

1. D

2. B   The reference pages indicated do not answer the question directly. The references relate to discussions of the organizational structure and design. Based on that information, assumptions regarding organizational relationships (vertical, lateral, matrix, etc.) can be made.

3. C

4. D   Remember to convert the hours to minutes.
          725×12 minutes $= 8,700$ minutes
          $1,280$ hours $\times 60$ minutes $= 76,800$ minutes
          $8,700$ minutes on coding $/ 76,800$ minutes worked $= 11.3\%$ spent on coding

5. D

6. B   This is clearly a problem of not understanding the procedures of the tasks; therefore, reviewing the job description probably will not be of much help. This rules out answers A and C. This also does not seem to be a problem that would require an in-service, thereby ruling out answer D. Therefore, the best solution is to review the procedures with her and have the analysis clerk monitor her progress to ensure that she fully understands the procedures.

7. A

8. C

9. B   Answers A and C describe a standard. Answer D describes a rule.

10. C

11. D

12. B   Formula: Total actual work units $\times 100/$ Standard work units $=$ variance percent
          $(30 + 40 + 25 + 35) \times 100 = 13,000$ $13,000/200 = 65\%$

13. B

14. B   The hours must first be converted to minutes.
          7 hours $\times 60 = 420$ minutes
          420 minutes $\times 0.20 = 84$ minutes

15. A

16. C

17. C

18. B

19. D $950 \times 20 = 19,000$; $142,500 / 19,000 = 7.5$ FTEs

20. B

21. A

22. C

23. C   20 charts $\times$ 5 days $= 100$ per week $\times$ 4 weeks $= 400$
          A standard of 400 charts coded over 4 weeks per coder.
          Coder 3 has coded only 320 charts over the 4 weeks.

24. B

25. D

26. D

27. C   It is the physician's responsibility to ensure that a patient has consented to a surgical procedure.

Answer Key for Organization and Management

ANSWER   EXPLANATION

28. A

29. D

30. C   Although a CEO is involved in all of the options given, only the organizational objectives are completed annually. The mission statement is reviewed to ensure that the organizational objectives are consistent with it, but it is not revised annually. Strategic goals and objectives are completed on a long-term basis, not annually.

31. B

32. C

33. A   In order to determine which vendor to choose, each vendor's scores are added. The vendor that scores the highest for all three criteria is chosen. Calculations: Multiply the weight for each criterion by the rating. After this is done, each column is totaled. Vendor A scores 38; Vendor B, 25; Vendor C, 37; Vendor D, 27.

34. C   Costs = \$6,000 + \$1,500 + \$500 = \$8,000.
Benefits = \$10,000. (That is the increase in reimbursement.)
10,000 / 8,000 = 1.25. Benefits/Costs Ratio = 1.25. (This also known as the cost–benefit figure.)
In other words, for every dollar invested in the encoding system, it will have a return of \$1.25 after one year.

35. B

36. C

37. D

38. B $\$7.10 \times 0.04 = 0.284 + \$7.10 = \$7.384$

39. D

40. A

41. B

42. D $2,000 \times \$13.50 = \$27,000; \$27,000 / 225,333 = 0.1198$, rounded to 0.12

43. B   The formula for budget variance percent is actual minus budget divided by budget.
675 − 495 = 180
(180 × 100) / 495 = 36%

44. B

45. A   To determine the number of employees needed for a specific job, first determine how much time the work requires. In this case, we know we will have an additional 120 records per day and each record will average about 15 minutes. To figure the amount of total time, multiply 120 × 15 = 1,800 minutes. Compute this to hours by dividing by 60 (60 minutes in an hour): 1,800/60 = 30 hours. Based on the 8-hour day, divide 30 hours by 8 = 3.75 FTEs.

46. D

47. A

48. D

49. D

50. A

51. C

52. D

53. B

54. A

55. B

56. B   A Gantt chart is a scheduling tool.

57. A

Answer Key for Organization and Management

ANSWER   EXPLANATION

58. A

59. D

60. B

61. D   One must be familiar with the various labor laws to ensure that an interviewee is not asked questions that could be considered discriminating or illegal.

62. C $25,800 - 24,300 = 1,500; 1,500 / 24,300 = 0.0617 \times 100 = 6.17\%$

63. A

64. D   Formula: initial investment/annual cash flow = payback period $32,000/$8,000 = 4 years

65. B

66. B

67. C   Currently, each FTE files 55.5 charts (500 / 9 = 55.5).
- Since there will be 150 more charts per day needing filing (150/55.5 = 2.70), you will need 2.70 FTEs for filing the extra charts.
- Add current 9 FTE to the 2.70 FTE increase needed = 11.7 FTE.
- Divide by the increase of 2.7 FTE by the 11.7 total FTE needed to get the percentage increase in FTE. (2.7 / 11.7 = 23% increase).

For an anticipated increase from 500 to 650 you need to increase your filing FTE staff by 23%.

68. D

69. D

70. B

71. D

72. C

73. C

74. B

75. C

76. C

77. B

78. A

79. D

80. A

81. D

82. A

83. C   Personal experience is subjective. A, B, and D rely on objective measurement of job performance.

84. B   Wrists should be in a neutral position.

85. D

86. A

87. B

88. D

89. A

90. B

91. D

92. C

93. B

94. D

95. C

96. C

Answer Key for Organization and Management

	ANSWER	EXPLANATION
97.	D	
98.	A	
99.	B	
100.	A	
101.	C	
102.	B	
103.	D	
104.	A	
105.	B	
106.	C	

REFERENCES

Abdelhak, M., Grostick, S., Hanken, M. A., & Jacobs, E. (2012). *Health information: Management of a strategic resource* (4th ed.). Philadelphia: W. B. Saunders.

Davis, N., & LaCour, M. (2014). *Health information technology* (3rd ed.). Philadelphia: W. B. Saunders.

LaTour, K., Eichenwald-Maki, S., and Oachs, P. (2013). *Health information management: Concepts, principles, and practice* (4th ed.). Chicago: American Health Information Management Association (AHIMA).

McLean, R. (2003). *Financial management in health care organizations.* Clifton Park, NY: Delmar Cengage Learning.

McWay, D. (2014). *Today's health information management: An integrated approach* (2nd ed.). Clifton Park, NY: Delmar Cengage Learning.

Shortell, S., & Kaluzny, A. (2012). *Health care management: Organization design and behavior* (6th ed.). Clifton Park, NY: Delmar Cengage Learning.

Competency Domains for Organization and Management

Question	RHIA Domain	RHIT Domain
1–106	4	
1–24		1

XVI. Human Resources

Mary Spivey Teslow, MLIS, RHIA

Use the following information to answer questions 1–3.

The staff in the Human Resources Department is proposing a computer-based training program for 200 employees and needs to prepare a budget for the time and cost of the training.
- The training program will be 30 minutes in length.
- The employees can take the training online at any time.
- There are 200 employees to be trained.
- The rate of pay for 50 of the employees is $15.50 per hour.
- The rate of pay for 50 employees is $12.00 per hour.
- The rate of pay for the other 100 employees is $18.00.

1. How many employee clock hours will be needed to complete the training?
   A. 200 hours
   B. 150 hours
   C. 100 hours
   D. 50 hours

REFERENCE: Davis and LaCour, pp 466–468
                Horton, p 138
                Koch, pp 55–56
                Liebler and McConnell, pp 243, 385–387

2. How much should the training staff request in the budget for doing the computer-based training program?
   A. $3,175.00
   B. $1,975.00
   C. $1,887.50
   D. $1,587.50

REFERENCE: Davis and LaCour, pp 466–468
                Horton, p 138
                Koch, pp 55–56
                Liebler and McConnell, pp 243, 385–387

3. What would be the average cost for training an individual employee?
   A. $7.94
   B. $9.00
   C. $15.50
   D. $15.87

REFERENCE: Davis and LaCour, pp 466–468
                Horton, p 138
                Koch, pp 55–56

4. At Great Plains Regional Hospital, record processing takes approximately 18 minutes. If there are 15,620 discharges for the month, how many personnel hours are needed for this volume of work?
   A. 2,891
   B. 4,686
   C. 5,496
   D. 3,394

REFERENCE: Abdelhak, p 584
                Davis and LaCour, pp 424–426
                Horton, pp 148–149
                Koch, pp 55–56
                LaTour, Eichenwald-Maki, and Oachs, p 724
                Liebler and McConnell, pp 243, 385–387
                McConnell, pp 350–351

5. The advantages of teams or committees over individuals in complex situations include all of the following EXCEPT:
   A. Decision making is accomplished more quickly.
   B. Complex problems can be better assessed.
   C. Authority can be counterbalanced.
   D. Coordination and cooperation can be increased.

REFERENCE: McWay, pp 380–381
               Sayles, pp 1082–1083

6. Mallory, the coding supervisor, must determine the number of full-time employees (FTEs) needed to code 600 discharges per week. It takes an average of 20 minutes to code each record and each coder will work 40 hours per week. How many coders are needed?
   A. 6.0   C. 12.0
   B. 5.0   D. 4.5

REFERENCE: Abdelhak, p 584
               Davis and LaCour, pp 415–416
               Horton, p 148
               Koch, pp 55–56
               LaTour, Eichenwald-Maki, and Oachs, p 806
               Liebler and McConnell, p 243
               McConnell, pp 350–351

7. Under the Americans with Disabilities Act (ADA), prior to employment, it is illegal to require a
   A. math aptitude test.   C. coding proficiency test.
   B. typing skill test.   D. physical exam.

REFERENCE: Abdelhak, pp 575–576
               McWay, p 370
               Sayles, p 836

8. Jason, an HIM educator, plans to lecture on department design and the legislative act or agency that was created to ensure that workers have a safe and healthy work environment. Which of the following legal issue will he describe?
   A. OSHA Act   C. Taft–Hartley Law
   B. Wagner Act   D. Labor Management Relations Act

REFERENCE: Abdelhak, p 577
               LaTour, Eichenwald-Maki, and Oachs, p 722
               McWay, p 373
               Sayles, p 1231

9. Dana has prepared a performance appraisal for one of her employees. As the HIM director reviews the evaluation, he notes that the employee received an overall rating of "needs improvement." After reading the comments, the director asks Dana to document specific performance improvement recommendations. Dana is unable to do so because she is basing her assessment on her memory of incidents that have occurred over the past year. The director suggests that Dana reassess the employee's evaluation because, ideally, performance appraisals should occur
   A. at the end of the 90-day probationary period.
   B. when the employee needs counseling.
   C. on a periodic basis.
   D. once a year.

REFERENCE: Abdelhak, pp 590–594
               Davis and LaCour, pp 443–445
               LaTour, Eichenwald-Maki, and Oachs, p 814
               McConnell, p 205
               McWay, p 376
               Sayles, pp 1101–1102

10. Trevor is a new scanning technician. To fulfill your responsibility as a supervisor and to help him learn and complete his work correctly, the best training resource to use would be a
   A. job description.
   B. method.
   C. policy.
   D. procedure.

REFERENCE: Abdelhak, p 646
               LaTour, Eichenwald-Maki, and Oachs, p 804
               Sayles, pp 407–409

11. Gregg is a recent graduate who has applied for a Trauma Registry position at a Chicago hospital while he prepares to apply to graduate school. In making the decision, he considers the offer of $15 per hour for a 40-hour week, benefits of 27.5% of his salary, and tuition waivers of six credits per year at $145. He calculated that his total compensation, rounded to the nearest dollar, would be
   A. $40,650.
   B. $39,563.
   C. $38,599.
   D. $31,030.

REFERENCE: Koch, pp 55–56

12. Yanique is a new supervisor at a mental health facility. She discovers that one of her employees has shared her password with a coworker. This action violates policies and procedures and is the first occasion of difficulty with this employee. Disciplinary action should be taken by
   A. waiting for another occurrence to act.
   B. referring the action to Human Resources.
   C. asking for guidance from Human Resources and then acting.
   D. immediately dismissing the employee.

REFERENCE: Abdelhak, pp 601–603
               LaTour, Eichenwald-Maki, and Oachs, pp 755–758
               Liebler and McConnell, pp 425–426
               McWay, pp 302–303

13. Conflict is inevitable. What is the LEAST effective way to manage conflict?
    A. Do not intervene: creative solutions often come from conflict.
    B. Encourage the parties to compromise by each willing to lose part of their position.
    B. Limit or control interaction when emotions are intense.
    C. Use an objective third party to seek a constructive outcome for both parties.

REFERENCE: LaTour, Eichenwald-Maki, and Oachs, p 756
               Liebler and McConnell, p 333
               McWay, p 342
               Sayles, pp 735, 1103–1105

14. The HIPAA Privacy and Security Rule requires that training be documented. What methods of documenting training efforts need to be used?
    A. retention of training aids and handouts
    B. meeting handouts and minutes
    C. training content, training dates, and attendee names
    D. signed confidentiality statements

REFERENCE: AHIMA Practice Brief

15. Holly is the day supervisor who works from 7:00 AM to 4:00 PM. Kim is the evening supervisor who works from 2:00 PM to 11:00 PM. Sarah is a transcriptionist who works from 10:00 AM to 7:00 PM, which overlaps the day and evening shifts. Sarah asked Holly, the day supervisor, if she could leave early for personal reasons. Holly said Sarah could leave early if Kim, the evening supervisor, agrees. Which theory of management does this situation violate?
    A. span of control   C. specialization of labor
    B. formal theory of authority   D. unity of command

REFERENCE: Davis and LaCour, p 419
               LaTour, Eichenwald-Maki, and Oachs, p 686
               Liebler and McConnell, p 130
               McConnell, pp 56–57

16. You are preparing a training program for specific functional areas of the department (e.g., coding, transcription, etc.). Which of the following is the primary factor to consider in developing an effective training program?
    A. credentials of the employees
    B. objectives of each functional area
    C. cost of training the employees
    D. number of employees to be trained

REFERENCE: Abdelhak, p 607
               Davis and LaCour, p 466
               LaTour, Eichenwald-Maki, and Oachs, pp 717, 733–735, 740
               McWay, p 365
               Sayles, p 1099

17. Grace Holt, RHIA, is the HIM Department Manager. She is reviewing interviewing techniques with Maria Hernandez, RHIT, as she prepares to interview for a new analyst. Grace recommends that Maria should
    A. ask questions that encourage a "yes" or "no" response.
    B. politely interrupt occasionally to seek clarification.
    C. talk down to the applicant to show authority.
    D. phrase questions so the expected answer is encouraged.

REFERENCE: Abdelhak, pp 591–592
               Davis and LaCour, pp 448–449
               McConnell, pp 139–141
               Sayles, pp 1096–1097

18. Your job description states that as Assistant Director of the HIM Department, you will supervise day-to-day operations for the record processing, transcription, and release of information areas. What principle of management is described?
    A. specialization   C. span of control
    B. centralized authority   D. delegation

REFERENCE: Davis and LaCour, p 419
               LaTour, Eichenwald-Maki, and Oachs, p 690
               Liebler and McConnell, pp 131–132
               McConnell, p 57

19. Rachel's work performance has diminished over the last 2 weeks. In addition, she has uncharacteristic mood swings and has exhibited difficulty concentrating. She is also having difficulties with tardiness and attendance. As her supervisor, you meet with Rachel to discuss your concerns. She reveals that she is struggling financially. What action should you take?
    A. Assure her that as long as she can perform her job acceptably, her personal life is none of your concern.
    B. Put her on probation.
    C. Refer her to the Employee Assistance Program.
    D. Terminate her.

REFERENCE: Abdelhak, p 601
               McConnell, pp 244–245

20. Nancy arrives for work Monday through Friday any time between 7:00 and 9:00 AM, is on the job until at least 3:00 PM, and then may leave any time between 3:00 and 6:00 PM. Nancy's schedule is an example of
    A. the 8/80 work week.
    B. the staggered work hours program.
    C. variable work schedule.
    D. flextime.

REFERENCE: Abdelhak, pp 568–599
               LaTour and Eichenwald-Maki, p 727

21. Use the following statistics from Utah Home Health to calculate the absenteeism rate.

Month: January	
Number of employees	20
Number of workdays	22
Total work days lost	25

   A. 0.44%   C. 5.8%
   B. 5.68%   D. 0.568%

REFERENCE: Horton, pp 16–19
                        McWay, p 221

22. As an HIM supervisor, one of your employees reports that a coworker has returned from lunch on numerous occasions with the smell of alcohol on his breath. What is the best approach in handling this problem?
   A. Confront the employee and place him on suspension for 1 week.
   B. Terminate the employee immediately.
   C. Ignore the report because it is hearsay.
   D. Handle the situation as you would any other disease that affects an employee's work.

REFERENCE: Abdelhak, p 601
                        McConnell, pp 243–245

23. Gary's primary concern is job continuity and adequate health insurance for his large family. What level of Maslow's hierarchy of needs does Gary operate from?
   A. physiological   C. esteem
   B. self-actualization   D. safety

REFERENCE: LaTour, Eichenwald-Maki, and Oachs, pp 687, 689
                        McConnell, pp 180–182
                        McWay, pp 340–341

24. Employers may be able to demonstrate that age is a reasonable requirement for a position. Such an exception to the Age Discrimination in Employment Act (ADEA) is called a
   A. job description essential.
   B. bona fide occupational qualification.
   C. essential element for employment.
   D. there is no such exception to ADEA.

REFERENCE: Abdelhak, pp 576–577
                        McConnell, pp 456–457
                        McWay, p 370

25. Julian supervises the department's coding section. He notices that the coding technician is working 30 additional minutes each day before clocking in at her scheduled starting time. After discussing her timecard with her, he discovers that she is starting work early in order to check the unbilled account report. Under which act are you required to pay her for all hours worked?
    A. ERISA
    B. Fair Labor Standards Act
    C. National Labor Relations Act
    D. Equal Pay Act

REFERENCE: Abdelhak, p 578
                LaTour, Eichenwald-Maki, and Oachs, p 754
                McConnell, pp 551–553
                McWay, p 374
                Sayles, p 1207

26. Puget Sound Health System has set hiring goals and taken steps to guarantee equal employment opportunities for members of protected groups (e.g., American Indians, veterans, etc.). It is complying with
    A. Affirmative Action.
    B. Equal Pay Act.
    C. Minority Hiring Act.
    D. Civil Rights Act.

REFERENCE: Abdelhak, pp 574–575
                McConnell, pp 453–454
                McWay, p 374

27. Southwest Health System has numerous semiretired staff. The Human Resources Department has provided training regarding the Age Discrimination in Employment Act (ADEA). They emphasized that it protects employees and applicants between what ages?
    A. 50 and 75
    B. 45 and 99
    C. 62 and 85
    D. 40 and 70

REFERENCE: Abdelhak, pp 576–577
                LaTour, Eichenwald-Maki, and Oachs, p 894
                McConnell, pp 456–457
                McWay, p 370
                Sayles, p 835

28. Which of the following HIPAA components would the general New Employee Orientation training most likely cover?
    A. marketing issues
    B. business associate agreements
    C. physical/workstation security
    D. job-specific training (e.g., patient's right to amend record)

REFERENCE: AHIMA Practice Brief

29. Krista combined her HIM and legal education and is now a Risk Manager. An employee has a complaint that may be considered a grievance. She should listen to the employee and then
    A. put the complaint aside to see if other employees complain about the same issue.
    B. deal with the issue as if it were a bona fide grievance.
    C. deal with the complaint only if the employee seldom complains.
    D. ignore the complaint until it is in writing.

REFERENCE: Abdelhak, pp 603–604
                LaTour, Eichenwald-Maki, and Oachs, p 756
                McWay, pp 378–379
                Sayles, p 1106

30. Human Resources provide training for new supervisors. It includes discussion of the Equal Pay Act, which was passed to eliminate discrimination based on which of the following?
    A. merit of the employee
    B. seniority of the employee
    C. employee gender
    D. personal productivity, such as in an incentive compensation system

    REFERENCE: Abdelhak, p 578
                   Davis and LaCour, pp 448–450
                   McConnell, p 456
                   McWay, p 374
                   Sayles, p 835

31. The transcription area has an opening for a transcriptionist with demonstrated skill in medical and surgical reports. Which of the following types of tests should be administered?
    A. skill   C. intelligence
    B. personality   D. stress

    REFERENCE: Abdelhak, p 591
                   Davis and LaCour, pp 449–450
                   LaTour, Eichenwald-Maki, and Oachs, p 775
                   McConnell, p 135
                   McWay, p 363

32. As manager of release of information, you supervise an employee who has been a correspondence clerk for many years. Her performance has gradually diminished and has become substandard. What method would most likely prove to be INEFFECTIVE in assisting this employee in improving her performance?
    A. threatening to fire the employee
    B. asking the employee to cross-train with other employees
    C. delegation of special assignments
    D. creating an action plan with the employee

    REFERENCE: Abdelhak, pp 601–602
                   LaTour, Eichenwald-Maki, and Oachs, pp 775–776
                   McConnell, pp 224–225
                   McWay, p 376

33. Rebecca, the revenue cycle manager, has received permission to check references for the candidate she would like to add to her team. Which of the following questions is her previous employer least likely to answer?
    A. What was her previous position?
    B. What was her previous salary?
    C. What was their personal impressions of her?
    D. What was the reason for her leaving her previous position?

    REFERENCE: Abdelhak, p 591
                   LaTour, Eichenwald-Maki, and Oachs, p 726
                   McWay, p 363

34. After receiving a completed requisitions to fill positions within the HIM Department, Human Resources can be most effective in recruiting qualified applicants with the assistance of a
    A. departmental organizational chart.
    B. current job description.
    C. salary schedule.
    D. employee benefits handbook.

REFERENCE: Abdelhak, pp 587–588
               Davis and LaCour, pp 401–402
               LaTour, Eichenwald-Maki, and Oachs, pp 723–724
               Liebler and McConnell, pp 437–441
               McConnell, p 259
               McWay, p 376

35. You are interviewing a candidate for a position for handling subpoenas in the release of information section. Which of the following is the LEAST appropriate information to ask an interviewee to provide?
    A. Do you have transportation for attendance at depositions and court?
    B. Please share an experience where you had to determine applicable state law.
    C. Please provide a copy of your most recent CE certificate and AHIMA membership.
    D. Do you have family responsibilities that would keep you from remaining at a trial?

REFERENCE: LaTour, Eichenwald-Maki, and Oachs, pp 725–726
               McConnell, pp 136–137
               Sayles, p 1097

36. Samantha is the evening discharge analysis clerk. As the evening supervisor, you personally trained her regarding the correct job procedures and policies. Within the last two months, Samantha has received an oral and written warning for failure to follow job procedures. Your facility utilizes a progressive discipline system. What is the next appropriate step?
    A. demotion   C. oral reprimand from the evening supervisor
    B. suspension   D. written warning from the director of the department

REFERENCE: Abdelhak, pp 602–603
               LaTour, Eichenwald-Maki, and Oachs, pp 755–756
               Liebler and McConnell, pp 415–416
               McConnell, pp 215–219
               McWay, pp 302–303
               Sayles, p 1103

37. Which of the following acts describes the act that requires employers to make reasonable accommodations in the workplace for individuals to perform essential job functions?
    A. Age Discrimination Act
    B. Americans with Disabilities Act
    C. Rehabilitation Act
    D. Equal Opportunity Employment Act

REFERENCE: Abdelhak, pp 575–576
               LaTour, Eichenwald-Maki, and Oachs, p 721
               Liebler and McConnell, pp 455–456
               McConnell, pp 457–458
               McWay, p 378

38. Eva Pulaski supervises the electronic document management (EDM) section. She is preparing a report that includes a graphic that displays data over time and provides an excellent visualization of quality and quantity trends. This style of a report is called a(n)
    A. Pareto chart.
    B. correlation analysis.
    C. run or control chart.
    D. scatter diagram.

REFERENCE: Abdelhak, pp 382–385
                      Koch, pp 247–278
                      LaTour, Eichenwald-Maki, and Oachs, pp 824–825
                      Liebler and McConnell, p 216
                      McWay, p 223
                      Sayles, pp 581–582, 1246

39. Kari works 40 hours per week at Rio Grande Radiology, which pays time-and-a-half for overtime and double-time for holidays. During the past week, Kari took six hours of unpaid personal leave and worked an eight-hour holiday. How many hours will Kari be paid?
    A. 34
    B. 42
    C. 48
    D. 50

REFERENCE: McConnell, pp 448–451
                      Koch, pp 55–56

40. Natalie was an orientation counselor in college and knows that a well-designed program can help those new to a setting feel comfortable. As a new manager, she continues her commitment and contributes to new employee orientation. Which of the following statements about orientation programs is NOT true?
    A. A good orientation program can substitute for a job-specific departmental training.
    B. The most meaningful training program includes a peer "show and tell" format.
    C. The orientation assists the employee in learning about the workplace culture.
    D. Proper training can enhance employee satisfaction.

REFERENCE: Abdelhak, pp 593–594
                      Davis and LaCour, pp 460–465
                      LaTour, Eichenwald-Maki, and Oachs, pp 721, 731–733
                      McWay, pp 286–290
                      Sayles, pp 1096, 1099–1100

41. Gina is the HIPAA Privacy and Security Officer and primary trainer for a regional health system. In determining how a person in a position in a department uses health information, she must certainly review the
    A. past performance evaluations of persons in the position.
    B. position or job description.
    C. facility policy on protecting health information.
    D. facility policy and procedure on documenting training.

REFERENCE: AHIMA Practice Brief
                      LaTour, Eichenwald-Maki, and Oachs, p 723
                      McWay, p 336
                      Sayles, pp 1100, 1121

42. Mary Ellen Smith has been an excellent biller for the past 5 years. Lately, you have noticed that she has the highest error rate and the lowest productivity rate of the entire billing section. She also seems to be distracted and unhappy. You have a conversation with her and she confides that she is having many "personal problems" that are causing her enormous stress. As her supervisor, you
   A. accept this explanation and determine that it is probably a temporary situation.
   B. issue a verbal warning to Mary Ellen to shape up.
   C. issue a written warning with a date to review her progress.
   D. refer her to the Employee Assistance Program.

   REFERENCE: Abdelhak, p 601
                  McConnell, pp 244–245

43. At Orientation a new employee receives the Employee Handbook. All of the following information about the Employee Handbook is true, EXCEPT that
   A. it provides a contractual obligation to continued employment.
   B. it provides policies and procedures developed by management.
   C. a receipt must be documented in writing.
   D. it must be reviewed periodically by legal counsel to avoid legal risk.

   REFERENCE: Abdelhak, pp 588–589
                  Davis and LaCour, p 460
                  LaTour, Eichenwald-Maki, and Oachs, pp 721, 731

44. Fareeda's methods improvement objectives are to use an organized approach to determine how to accomplish a task with less effort in less time or at a lower cost while maintaining or improving the quality of the outcome. Frequently, methods improvement is referred to as
   A. benchmarking.   C. work simplification.
   B. work distribution.   D. data quality improvement.

   REFERENCE: Abdelhak, pp 623–624
                  McWay, p 338

45. You work in a unionized organization and have filed a grievance. Which of the following will most likely take place?
   A. You can be terminated for registering a grievance.
   B. The grievance procedure regulations stipulated in the union contract will be followed.
   C. The facility policies and procedures for prompt and fair action on any grievance will be followed.
   D. The time from complaint to resolution should be no longer than 90 days.

   REFERENCE: Abdelhak, pp 603–604
                  LaTour, Eichenwald-Maki, and Oachs, p 756
                  McWay, p 378
                  Sayles, p 1106

46. Bay Area Home Care utilizes a discipline system that provides for stronger penalties for each successive repeat offense. They are most likely using
    A. corrective discipline.
    C. progressive discipline.
    B. preventive discipline.
    D. terminating discipline.

REFERENCE: Abdelhak, pp 601–603
                LaTour, Eichenwald-Maki, and Oachs, p 755
                Liebler and McConnell, pp 413–416
                McConnell, p 219
                McWay, p 378
                Sayles, pp 1102–1103

47. When analyzing discipline problems, which of the following should be considered?
    A. the prior performance of the employee in question
    B. the frequency of the problem
    C. the seriousness of the problem
    D. all of the above

REFERENCE: Abdelhak, pp 601–603
                Liebler and McConnell, pp 413–416
                McConnell, pp 225–227
                McWay, p 378
                Sayles, p 1122

48 Chris and Amy, two coders on your team, have come to you complaining that Jane, the discharge clerk, is deliberately holding back charts, causing a coding backlog. You are not sure Jane is really the cause of this problem because Chris and Amy have a history of blaming others for their work-related delays. To determine if Jane is truly a "problem employee" it would be best to first
    A. determine the source of the conflict.
    B. discretely ask other employees if they are having similar problems with Jane.
    C. request assistance from the Human Resources Department.
    D. observe Jane's interaction with others.

REFERENCE: Abdelhak, pp 600–603
                LaTour, Eichenwald-Maki, and Oachs, p 755
                McWay, p 342
                Sayles, pp 1103–1105

49. There is an opening for a coder in a 150-bed acute care hospital. The position requires someone who can code from a wide variety of medical records using both ICD and CPT. Of the following candidates interviewing for this position, which would be the most appropriate to hire?
    A. a high-school graduate who has applied for entry into the 2-year college RHIT program
    B. a recent graduate of a 4-year HIM program, RHIA eligible, who hopes to become a department manager within 1 year
    C. a graduate of a 2-year community college HIT program, RHIT eligible, with 1 year of outpatient coding experience
    D. an RHIA with 5 years of supervisory experience in medical records who recently moved to this city and can find no other available position as a supervisor at this time

REFERENCE: Abdelhak, pp 591–593
                LaTour, Eichenwald-Maki, and Oachs, p 725
                McWay, p 363
                Sayles, pp 1095–1097

50. Employers are required to report the status of employees to the federal government. You need an ICD-10 trainer for six months. You plan to hire an ICD-10-10 trainer with the skills to perform the training. This employee would likely be reported as
    A. an independent contractor.
    B. a leased employee.
    C. a full-time employee.
    D. a part-time employee.

REFERENCE: Davis and LaCour, pp 416, 450–451
               LaTour, Eichenwald-Maki, and Oachs, pp 722, 804, 857, 876
               Leibler and McConnell, p 181
               McWay, p 357

51. One of your new employees has just completed orientation, receiving basic HIPAA training. You are now providing more specific training related to her job. She asks whether the information she provided during the hiring process, as well as benefits claims, are also protected under HIPAA. Which of the following can you assure her that the Human Resources Department protects?
    A. all personal health information (PHI)
    B. benefits enrollment
    C. Employee Assistance Program contacts
    D. OSHA information

REFERENCE: Abdelhak, p 577
               LaTour, Eichenwald-Maki, and Oachs, pp 756–757
               McConnell, pp 272, 477
               McWay, p 375

The following questions represent advanced competencies.

52. The employee selection process increasingly involves a background check. All of the following are true EXCEPT
    A. that it requires the employee's consent.
    B. that the extent depends on the level of the employee's authority.
    C. it may include criminal and credit checks.
    D. it is most useful in selecting the best candidate.

REFERENCE: LaTour, Eichenwald-Maki, and Oachs, p 726
               Liebler and McConnell, pp 513–514
               McWay, pp 363–364

53. Emma Miller, RHIA, interviewed one applicant for the new position of data analyst and subsequently hired the applicant. During the 20-minute interview, she told the applicant about the department and hospital and what the job entailed. Much to Emma's disappointment, this newly hired employee did not work out. What went wrong?
    A. Emma asked too many questions during the interview.
    B. Emma should not have told the applicant anything about the hospital because that is the responsibility of Human Resources.
    C. Emma failed to interview enough applicants.
    D. Emma did not allow enough time for the interview.

REFERENCE: Abdelhak, pp 590–593
               LaTour, Eichenwald-Maki, and Oachs, pp 725–726
               McConnell, pp 129–130
               Sayles, pp 1095–1097

54. University Health Systems is focusing on fostering a learning environment in the organization. Which of the following characteristics is NOT required?
    A. academic organization
    B. formal and on-the-job training
    C. reflection on learning
    D. intentional career development

REFERENCE: Abdelhak, p 607
               McWay, p 365

55. One of the most common rater biases that affect an employee's evaluation is the "halo effect," which suggests that the supervisor
    A. rates everyone as average.
    B. is too lenient or too strict in rating employee performance.
    C. rates the employee on the basis of a strong like or dislike of the person.
    D. bases the employee evaluation on behavior in the most recent period rather than the entire evaluation period.

REFERENCE: Abdelhak, pp 598–599
               McConnell, p 199

56. Elizabeth is the manager of the state cancer registry. In developing a training "to-do list," she is reviewing the staff and what general training and specialized training topics would be necessary. What tool would be most helpful in organizing this information?
    A. Gantt chart to show who gets trained when
    B. spreadsheet with grids identifying who needs what type of training
    C. a "train-the-trainers" training manual to help in consistency in training
    D. documentation of previous orientation training to see what has already been covered

REFERENCE: AHIMA Practice Brief

57. To ensure consistency of coverage among trainers, you may want to develop
    A. training manuals.
    B. meeting handouts and minutes.
    C. signed confidentiality statements acknowledging receipt and understanding of any training attended.
    D. ongoing training to keep the issues in front of the workforce.

REFERENCE: AHIMA Practice Brief

58. Mark Beck is a new graduate preparing for an interview. In school, he had the opportunity to role-play a technique that requires applicants to give specific examples of how they have performed a specific task or handled a specific problem in the past. This technique is becoming more popular and is known as a(n)
    A. audition interview.   C. structured interview.
    B. behavioral interview.   D. targeted interview.

REFERENCE: Abdelhak, pp 591–593
                 LaTour, Eichenwald-Maki, and Oachs, p 726
                 Sayles, pp 1096–1097

59. Which of the following is NOT an advantage of committee meetings?
    A. Group judgment improves decision making.
    B. Group process stimulates creativity.
    C. Committees enhance acceptance.
    D. Committees are economical.

REFERENCE: Liebler and McConnell, pp 290–295
                 McConnell, p 326

60. All of the following principles are illustrated in an organizational chart EXCEPT
    A. chain of authority.
    B. unity of command.
    C. unity of direction.
    D. span of control.

REFERENCE: Davis and LaCour, pp 417–420
                 LaTour, Eichenwald-Maki, and Oachs, pp 686, 690
                 Liebler and McConnell, pp 150–151

61. As the manager of the billing department, Jessica has heard from her employees that rumors have been circulating throughout the hospital concerning centralization and layoffs. At a meeting with the CFO, all departments were asked to cut back 15%. What should Jessica tell her employees?
    A. nothing, because it would only depress them
    B. that no one in the HIM department will be laid off
    C. share with employees the facts because she knows them from the meeting
    D. tell one employee who likes to spread rumors so employees will learn from each other

REFERENCE: Abdelhak, p 593
                 Davis and LaCour, pp 474–475
                 LaTour, Eichenwald-Maki, and Oachs, pp 697–698
                 McConnell, pp 304–346
                 McWay, pp 340–343

62. Which appraisal method places the employees into a set of ordered groups (e.g., top 10%, above average 20%, middle 40%) on the basis of a global measure?
    A. critical incident method
    B. behaviorally anchored ranking scales
    C. Management by Objectives
    D. forced ranking

REFERENCE: Abdelhak, pp 595–596
               McConnell, pp 189–191

63. There are a variety of approaches to career development. Which of the following is NOT one of the recognized strategies?
    A. Supervisors may identify employee potential and set goals, particularly in performance evaluations.
    B. Mentors have a formal relationship with the proteges, providing expert advice based on personal career experience.
    C. Coaches focus on the learning process, guiding the employee in developing knowledge and skills.
    D. HR recruiters refer employees for new opportunities within the organization.

REFERENCE: Abdelhak, pp 608–609
               LaTour, Eichenwald-Maki, and Oachs, pp 751–752
               McWay, pp 379–380

64. A union is engaged in an organizing campaign in a hospital facility. Which activity should management personnel AVOID during this time?
    A. telling employees that they are free to join or not to join any organization without threat to their status with the facility
    B. telling employees of the disadvantages that may result from belonging to a union
    C. promising employees a pay increase or promotion if they vote against the union
    D. telling employees the benefits they presently enjoy

REFERENCE: Abdelhak, pp 578–580
               McConnell, pp 505–507

65. Kimberly Wolf wants a Mercedes and the position of Vice President of Information Services. She feels that achieving these goals will provide her with a sense of achievement, prestige, and reputation in the eyes of others. At what level of Maslow's hierarchy of needs is she operating?
    A. esteem   C. self-actualization
    B. safety   D. basic physiological

REFERENCE: LaTour, Eichenwald-Maki, and Oachs, p 687
               McConnell, pp 180–181
               McWay, pp 340–341

66. Research has shown that productivity increases with all of the following interventions EXCEPT when
    A. employees are rewarded for extra output.
    B. it becomes the primary goal of management.
    C. it is measured.
    D. the office environment is reengineered.

REFERENCE: Abdelhak, p 621
               LaTour, Eichenwald-Maki, and Oachs, pp 262, 687, 689, 741, 750, 754, 852

67. Human Resource managers increasingly advise which of the following as the best approach for obtaining a legally sound and reliable reference?
    A. a telephone reference from a personal friend of the applicant
    B. a written reference from a former supervisor of the applicant
    C. a telephone reference from a former supervisor of the applicant
    D. a written reference from the HR department of the applicant's former employer

REFERENCE: Abdelhak, p 591
                LaTour, Eichenwald-Maki, and Oachs, p 726
                McConnell, p 139
                McWay, p 363

68. In your new position as Director of Health Information Services, you have noticed that department supervisors arbitrarily allow employees to make up missed time due to absences. You decide that you need a policy to reinforce the attendance policy and cut down on tardiness and absences. Which policy statement would support your overall departmental goals?
    A. Advance approval is required for changes in work schedules and depend upon departmental operations.
    B. Sick days can be used in lieu of time missed due to tardiness or absences.
    C. No make-up time for absences and tardiness is allowed.
    D. Changes in work schedules must be approved in advance and depend upon departmental operations.

REFERENCE: Abdelhak, pp 645–646
                Davis and LaCour, pp 435–436
                McConnell, pp 240–243
                McWay, p 326
                Sayles, pp 407–409

69. As HIM Director, you receive a call from the CEO informing you that she has received a complaint from a patient. The patient reported that one of the coders in your department revealed his diagnosis to his neighbor. What action is recommended?
    A. Gather all the facts prior to meeting with the employee.
    B. Give the employee a written warning.
    C. Terminate the employee immediately for violation of the confidentiality policy.
    D. Immediately call a departmental meeting to discuss the importance of maintaining confidentiality.

REFERENCE: Abdelhak, pp 601–602
                McConnell, p 226
                McWay, p 337

70. Miranda has decided to accept a position as a manager in a large health system. A key factor was the opportunity to work for a transformational leader. She recognizes all but one of the following characteristics observed that the Health Information Director is a transformational leader. Which of the following characteristics would be least likely to support her decision?
    A. risk taking   C. charisma
    B. mentoring   D. dependency

REFERENCE: Davis and LaCour, pp 481–482
                LaTour, Eichenwald-Maki, and Oachs, p 691
                McWay, p 340

71. Human Resources has recently provided training for and implemented a new performance appraisal system that includes input from managers, peers, and staff. This approach is typically known as
    A. 360-degree evaluation.
    C. holistic appraisal.
    B. group appraisal.
    D. multifactor evaluation.

REFERENCE: LaTour, Eichenwald-Maki, and Oachs, p 755
              McWay, p 337

72. Employee turnover is expensive and stressful on staff and reflects poorly on managers. The best defense against employee dissatisfaction is
    A. the employee handbook.
    B. open and honest communication.
    C. written policies and procedures.
    D. weekly departmental meetings.

REFERENCE: LaTour, Eichenwald-Maki, and Oachs, pp 758, 776
              Liebler and McConnell, pp 491–496
              McConnell, pp 149–150
              McWay, p 365

73. Human Resources use a systematic procedure to determine the relative worth of a position to the organization. When this approach is used, compensation for the position is most likely based on
    A. job evaluation.
    C. job survey.
    B. job planning.
    D. job ranking.

REFERENCE: LaTour, Eichenwald-Maki, and Oachs, p 755
              Liebler and McConnell, p 195
              McWay, p 334

74. Summer is the document imaging manager. She has had a meeting with the scanning clerks. They are complaining that the pay rate for their position is too low in their facility. What would be the best way to deal with this complaint?
    A. Submit a request for merit raises for all scanning clerks.
    B. Work with HR on a job evaluation and current wage and salary survey.
    C. Explain that health care cost containment means little money for raises.
    D. Listen to the complaint and recommend applying for a higher position.

REFERENCE: Abdelhak, pp 606–607
              LaTour, Eichenwald-Maki, and Oachs, pp 722, 752, 754
              McConnell, p 256
              McWay, p 334

75. The teaching method selected by an instructor influences the student's ability to understand the material. Instructor-led classrooms work best when
    A. in-depth training and interaction are desired.
    B. there are three shifts of employees to train.
    C. you want to minimize the cost for training.
    D. employees from all departments must be trained.

REFERENCE: AHIMA Practice Brief
               LaTour, Eichenwald-Maki, and Oachs, p 744

76. Which of the following scenarios best describes job enrichment as a motivational technique?
    A. Anna is an effective data analyst. In addition to her regular job duties, her supervisor has assigned her to special projects and committee assignments.
    B. Becky prefers to work where she can be active and have personal contacts. The supervisor rotates her through all clerical jobs in the department so that she can have variety in her work.
    C. Cheryl's job keeps her fully occupied all day. In fact, she frequently has to rush to get the work completed daily. Cheryl's supervisor decides to remove some responsibility from her job so she has less stress.
    D. Derek has worked in the department for several years. His supervisor decided to combine several jobs and add other tasks to enable Derek to use his knowledge and skills gained in school. With these increased responsibilities he is increasing his chances of being promoted.

REFERENCE: McConnell, pp 187–188
               McWay, p 341

77. Amanda, an EHR project manager, wants to increase her implementation staff's problem-solving skills. Which of the following approaches is likely to have the best and most long-lasting results?
    A. hiring a consultant to assess the EHR implementation strategies
    B. providing training to develop an EHR implementation work team
    C. taking a field trip to a neighboring facility known for project management
    D. request that Human Resources provide an online module teaching program solving skills

REFERENCE: LaTour, Eichenwald-Maki, and Oachs, pp 471, 744
               Liebler and McConnell, pp 358–360
               McWay, pp 380–381

78. According to Frederick Herzberg, challenging work, recognition of workers and their accomplishments, and employee self-improvement are examples of
    A. maintenance factors.
    B. needs.
    C. motivators.
    D. hygienic factors.

REFERENCE: Liebler and McConnell, p 370
               McConnell, pp 177–179
               McWay, p 431

79. Tina, the Coding Supervisor at Highlands Hospital, has heard rumors that her facility is starting a coding training program. Rumor also has it that the HIM Director is trying to recruit the coding supervisor from a neighboring hospital to head up the training position. Tina makes the following statement to the assistant director: "I'm obviously not good enough for the training position. Perhaps I should resign." How should the assistant director respond?
    A. ignore Tina's statement
    B. refer Tina to the Employee Assistance Program
    C. assist Tina in developing her career goals
    D. guarantee Tina that she will be considered for the position

REFERENCE: Abdelhak, pp 607–609
                       LaTour, Eichenwald-Maki, and Oachs, pp 750–751
                       Liebler and McConnell, p 240
                       McWay, p 365

80. HIM professionals should be prepared with a clear statement of their department's functions and value that can be delivered during a brief encounter. This is typically called a/an
    A. e-alert   C. public relations pitch
    B. elevator speech   D. value proposition

REFERENCE: McConnell, p 375

81. Your organization's employees consist of a mixture of women and men. The women are of all ages, some are single mothers, others are married women with no children, and still others are women who care for older parents at home. The men also have varying personal lifestyles. Human Resources have designed a new benefit program that allows employees to choose from an array of benefits based on their own needs or lifestyle. The new benefit program is called a(n)
    A. prepaid benefit plan.
    B. cafeteria benefit plan.
    C. flexible benefit plan.
    D. employee-driven benefit plan.

REFERENCE: Abdelhak, pp 568–569

82. As telework becomes more common, HIM supervisors will increasingly need to evaluate employees for these virtual office opportunities. Typical criteria include all the following EXCEPT that the employee
    A. is computer literate.
    B. independently identifies required work products.
    C. successfully plans a work production schedule.
    D. checks in frequently with the supervisor.

REFERENCE: McWay, pp 381–382
                       LaTour, Eichenwald-Maki, and Oachs, pp 722, 752 754, 762

83. In your department, employee performance is rated using a continuous scale range of unsatisfactory through average to outstanding. Some other departments use a discrete system in which the supervisor assigns "fails to meet standards," "meets standards," and "exceeds standards." Both systems being used are
   A. rating scales.
   B. checklists.
   C. critical incident methods.
   D. ranking methods.

REFERENCE: Abdelhak, pp 595–598
               McConnell, pp 194–195

84. Virginia is the Record Processing Coordinator, which is a lead position. She has an excellent work record and is able to assist in most work areas of the department. She knows that she could easily get another job within the hospital for the asking. Recently, she has been arriving late and has been uncooperative in dealing with others. As her immediate supervisor, what is the BEST first step in dealing with this situation?
   A. Institute progressive discipline.
   B. Ignore the situation and hope she will return to being a good employee.
   C. Counsel her by encouraging self-analysis and problem-solving processes.
   D. Suggest that she transfer to another department.

REFERENCE: Abdelhak, pp 601–603
               McConnell, p 220
               McWay, pp 377–378

85. Health care is known for rapid change. Melissa, an RHIA who has just been hired as a systems analyst in Information Technology, understands the importance of change management and being a positive change agent. Which of the following approaches would be LEAST likely to support her approach?
   A. being available to listen to staff
   B. holding on to the vision
   C. measuring and celebrating success
   D. easing up on delegating

REFERENCE: LaTour, Eichenwald-Maki, and Oachs, pp 708, 712–713
               Liebler and McConnell, pp 48–49
               McWay, pp 344–345
               Sayles, pp 583–584, 592

86. HIM professionals increasingly participate on project teams. Tuckman has developed a model describing predictable stages. Which of the following reflects the stage where teams may experience disequilibrium?
   A. forming
   B. storming
   C. norming
   D. performing

REFERENCE: Liebler and McConnell, pp 352–354
               Sayles, p 1092
               Umiker, pp 119–120

87. Rita Mizner, MBA, RHIA, is Director of Information Services for Mt. Sinai Medical Center. She is well respected for a management style that empowers her staff. All of the following are characteristics of effective delegation, EXCEPT
    A. explaining exactly what needs to be done.
    B. agreeing on performance standards.
    C. providing necessary resources.
    D. retaining authority to make key decisions.

REFERENCE: LaTour, Eichenwald-Maki, and Oachs, pp 690, 750–751
               McConnell, p 180
               McWay, pp 377–378
               Sayles, p 1100

88. Tara is an RHIA who works at a large academic medical center. Her salary of $37,540 is paid 60% from research grants as clinical trial coordinator and 40% by HIM as a database manager. The hospital's fringe benefit rate is 23%. How much must the HIM director include in the budget (rounded to the nearest dollar) to cover Sarah's database management role?
    A. $15,016   C. $22,524
    B. $18,470   D. $27,705

REFERENCE: Koch, pp 138–139
               Horton, pp 136–137

89. Christina is a pharmacy tech who recently earned her RHIA. She is interviewing to become a representative of an international pharmaceutical firm. She would work from home, login to the corporate website several times a day, and make calls on various pharmacies in her territory. She would visit headquarters about once a quarter. This proposed work arrangement can best be described as
    A. flextime.   C. consulting.
    B. outsourcing.   D. telecommuting.

REFERENCE: LaTour, Eichenwald-Maki, and Oachs, pp 261, 728–730
               Liebler and McConnell, pp 147–150
               McWay, p 381

90. Which of the following employees is exempt under the Fair Labor Standards Act?
    A. an RHIA who performs record analysis and coding 90% of the time and who supervises three employees
    B. an RHIT who manages the Health Information Services department and is involved with planning and decision-making activities 90% of the time
    C. the department secretary who spends 100% of her time performing clerical duties for the Director of Health Information Services
    D. a file clerk who spends 100% of the time on filing activities

REFERENCE: Abdelhak, p 578
               Davis and LaCour, p 422
               LaTour, Eichenwald-Maki, and Oachs, pp 728, 754
               McConnell, pp 446–448
               McWay, pp 373–374

91. Charles Jones is employed as a regional coding consultant by a corporate hospital chain. In the organization chart, this position would be
    A. shown as a line position.
    B. shown as a staff position.
    C. not shown, because it is a consulting position.
    D. not shown, because this function is outsourced.

REFERENCE: Liebler and McConnell, pp 134–136
               McConnell, pp 51–52

92. Keith is director at a medical center that includes a daycare center and has several employees who have young children. He knows that it is important to be familiar with the provisions of the Family Medical Leave Act (FMLA), which includes all the following provisions EXCEPT
    A. ensuring any job the employee is qualified for upon return.
    B. that both men and women qualify under the FMLA.
    C. that it covers leave to care for a spouse, child, or parent.
    D. that it provides up to 12 weeks of unpaid leave annually.

REFERENCE: Abdelhak, p 578
               LaTour, Eichenwald-Maki, and Oachs, pp 722, 915
               Liebler and McConnell, p 156
               McWay, p 374

93. Ty Ngynn is Assistant Director in Information Services. He has made an appointment with the Director of Human Resources to discuss his recent trip to the state HIM meeting with his Director, Wendy Richards. During the trip, Wendy repeatedly asked Ty to her room, suggesting they work on new plans for the department. When Ty declined, Wendy suggested it might not be worthwhile for him to attend future state meetings. The HR Director should
    A. explain that off-site events are outside the scope of the HR Department.
    B. provide Ty with additional training on resisting unwanted advances.
    C. take the complaint seriously and begin a sexual harassment investigation.
    D. explain that it is the Director's right to select who attends professional meetings.

REFERENCE: McWay, p 369
               Abdelhak, p 575
               Liebler and McConnell, pp 456–457

94. Which of the following types of members is best for a committee?
    A. individuals of equal rank and authority
    B. a diverse group with widely varied rank and authority
    C. a blend of managers and entry level staff
    D. There is no clear benefit to one form or another.

REFERENCE: Liebler and McConnell, pp 297–298

95. As a new RHIA and coding manager, how likely is it that you will participate on committees?
    A. Infrequently until you are promoted to a higher position.
    B. You should expect committee participation to be a regular part of your job.
    C. Occasionally, mostly with your staff.
    D. It depends on whether your organization chooses to use the committee structure.

REFERENCE: Liebler and McConnell, pp 327–328
               Umiker, p 446

96. Niagra Falls Health Center needs occasional help in coding to remain current. Rena, the coding manager, is seeking an individual who is available evenings and weekends and will be responsible for his or her own actions. At a regional HIM meeting, Rena announces that she is looking for a(n)
    A. consultant.
    B. statutory employee.
    C. part-time employee.
    D. independent contractor.

REFERENCE: Leibler and McConnell, p 181
               McWay, p 358
               Umiker, p 446

97. Under the Immigration Reform and Control Act, all of the following apply EXCEPT
    A. undocumented workers may not be hired.
    B. U.S. citizens must be given preference.
    C. noncitizens may not be discriminated against.
    D. applicant must have I-9 documentation.

REFERENCE: Abdelhak, p 577
               McConnell, p 462
               McWay, p 358
               Umiker, p 446

98. Using Donabedian's framework for quality assessment (structure, process, and outcome), which of the following is an appropriate human resource outcome?
    A. absenteeism rate
    B. organizational climate
    C. salary and benefit compared with competitors
    D. None, Donabedian is a clinical framework.

REFERENCE: Abdelhak, pp 444–445
               LaTour, Eichenwald-Maki, and Oachs, pp 653, 627

99. Nina is participating in Human Resources training for new supervisors and has a question for the presenter. "I have an employee who is at the top of the pay scale for her position. Do I still need to do a performance evaluation?" The presenter most likely answers
    A. "Yes, at this stage, she should be asked to participate in evaluating other staff."
    B. "Yes, every employee deserves to know how he or she is performing and to set goals."
    C. "No, once no salary increase can be provided, an evaluation is not necessary."
    D. "Maybe, it is typically an optional process at this stage of employment."

REFERENCE: Abdelhak, pp 594–595
               LaTour, Eichenwald-Maki, and Oachs, p 755
               McWay, pp 376–377

100. Postage charges for Health Information Services have increased over the last quarter. As the Director, you have seen mail envelopes that have been meter-stamped that did not appear to be official hospital business. The best course of action is to
    A. remove the postage meter from the department.
    B. keep a watchful eye to see who is using the postage meter improperly.
    C. call a department meeting and issue employee warnings.
    D. put one person in charge of the meter.

REFERENCE: McConnell, pp 58–59
               McWay, pp 376–377

Answer Key for Human Resources

ANSWER   EXPLANATION

NOTE: *Explanations are provided for those questions that require mathematical calculations and questions that are not clearly explained in the references that are cited.*

1.   C $200 \times 30/60 = 100$ hours total

2.   D

50 employees × $15.50 per hour × ½ hour	= 387.50
50 employees × $12.00 per hour × ½ hour	= 300.00
100 employees × $18.00 per hour × ½ hour	= 900.00
$387.50 + $300.00 + $900.00	= $1,587.50

3.   A   Calculate by time: $1,587.50 total cost for training/100 hours needed to train = $15.88 per hour/2 to get cost for ½ hour of training = 7.938 =$7.94

OR

Calculate by employee: $1,587.50/200 employees = 7.938 =$7.94

4.   B   To determine the number of hours needed to perform a volume of work or "service units," in this case discharges (15,620) are multiplied by the "time standard" (18 minutes) and then divided by the number of minutes per hour (60).
$(15,620 \times 18) = 281,160$ divided by 60 = 4,686.

5.   D

6.   B   To determine the number of employees needed for a specific position, you must first determine how much time is being spent on work currently being done. The "service units," in this case discharges (600), are multiplied by the "time factor," 20 minutes. $(600 \times 20 = 12,000$ minutes) Because this problem's time factor is in minutes, you must also compute the number of available minutes per week. The "actual hours" in this case, 40 hours, is multiplied by 60 (60 minutes per hour) $(40 \times 60 = 2,400)$. The earned time, 12,000 minutes, is then divided by the actual minutes, 2,400, to determine the number of employees needed to perform a specific job duty. So, 12,000 divided by 2,400 = 5.

7.   D

8.   A

9.   C   Dana should be assessing employee performance on an ongoing basis. Without proper documentation, an evaluation of "needs improvement" will be difficult to justify.

10.   D

11.   A   Calculation: $15.00 × 2,080 hours per year = $31,200 × 27.5% = $8,580
Tuition waiver = 6 credits at $145 = $870
Therefore, $31,200, + $8,580 + $870 = $40,650

12.   C

13.   A

14.   C   You are required to document the training content, dates, and attendees.

15.   D

16.   B

17.   B

18.   C

19.   C

20.   D

Answer Key for Human Resources

ANSWER		EXPLANATION

21.　B　To calculate the absenteeism rate, use the following formula as suggested by the U.S. Department of Labor:

$$\frac{\text{Worker-days lost during period} \times 100}{(\text{Avg. number of workers})\ (\text{Number of days in period})} \qquad \frac{25 \times 100}{20 \times 22} = 5.68\%$$

22.　D

23.　D

24.　B

25.　B

26.　A

27.　D

28.　C　Physical/workstation security training would be appropriate for all employees in general orientation training. Answers A and B are higher level functions that would not be performed by all new employees. Answer D. Job-specific training would be better suited to training in the department in which the employee will work.

29.　B

30.　C

31.　A

32.　A

33.　C

34.　B　Job descriptions should be reviewed and updated before beginning the hiring process.

35.　D

36.　B

37.　B

38.　C

39.　B　Kari took 6 hours unpaid leave (40 – 6 = 34), but worked a holiday at double-time (8 × 2 = 16). Because 8 hours of the holiday are already figured in the work week, add an additional 8 hours for holiday pay. So, 34 + 8 = 42.

40.　A

41.　B　A well-written job description includes what and how health information is used in a position. The job description would be the document Gina would review for choosing appropriate training levels for staff members in different positions.

42.　D

43.　A

44.　C

45.　B　It is illegal for an organization to fire an employee for filing a grievance. The union contract stipulates the policy and procedures for resolving grievances. You would need to refer to the union contract for any specific time boundaries.

46.　C

47.　D

48.　A

49.　C

50.　A

Answer Key for Human Resources

	ANSWER	EXPLANATION
51.	A	
52.	B	
53.	C	
54.	A	
55.	C	
56.	B	A spreadsheet with grids identifying who needs what type of training would help in defining the department privacy and security training plan.
57.	A	Training manuals would help ensure consistency of coverage of the materials among trainers. B and C serve to help in documenting the training that was given. D. In addition to initial training, the security rule requires ongoing training/reminders.
58.	B	
59.	D	Employee salary expense is significant.
60.	C	All three are among Fayol's 14 principles, though unity of direction refers to all workers being aligned toward one single outcome.
61.	C	Managers should not attempt to "water down" information, even if it is bad news. Fueling the grapevine can also lead to additional misinformation. Managers should make every effort to communicate factual information to their employees in a calm and timely manner.
62.	D	
63.	D	
64.	C	
65.	A	
66.	D	
67.	C	Increasing legal challenges have made this an area best left to HR professionals.
68.	D	
69.	A	Even though a serious incident such as this could result in termination of an employee, it is important to gather all the facts prior to meeting with the employee to substantiate any claims.
70.	D	
71.	A	
72.	B	Weekly department meetings, having an employee handbook, and written policies and procedures are all part of the necessary open and honest communication.
73.	A	
74.	B	A common and easy solution to this problem is to ignore the complaint, although this will not solve the problem; it will only prolong it. If the clerks complain that their job rate is too low, a job evaluation seeks to determine the position's relative worth to maintain pay equity within the organization and a wage and salary survey helps in determining the market value of the position.

Answer Key for Human Resources

ANSWER	EXPLANATION

75.   B   In-depth training and interaction are best obtained in an instructor-led classroom style of training. Answers B, C, and D are disadvantages of instructor-led training. Instructor-led training becomes expensive and time intensive when scheduling and training many shifts of employees from all departments.

76.   A   Job enrichment involves assigning more challenging tasks and responsibilities without combining jobs, which is called job enlargement. Switching job tasks among employees is called job rotation. All of these are attempts to diversify work and motivate employees. Redesigning a job by removing responsibility, however, would probably not be a motivational factor.

77.   B

78.   C

79.   C

80.   B

81.   B

82.   B

83.   A

84.   C

85.   D

86.   C

87.   D   To be effective, authority needs to be delegated along with responsibility.

88.   B   Calculations: $37,540 × 123% = $46,174.20

         HIM pays 40% or $46,174.20 × .40 = $18,469.68, rounded to $18,470

89.   D

90.   B

91.   B

92.   A

93.   C

94.   A

95.   C

96.   D

97.   B

98.   A

99.   B

100.   D   Although putting one person in charge of the meter may not stop the abuse of the postage meter, it is the best first course of action to take. Answers A and C are too drastic, and answer B is not efficient use of a manager's time.

REFERENCES

Abdelhak, M., Grostick, S., Hanken, M. A., & Jacobs, E. (Eds.). (2011). *Health information: Management of a strategic resource* (4th ed.). Philadelphia: W. B. Saunders.

AHIMA Practice Brief HIPAA Privacy and Security Training. (Journal of AHIMA 84, no.10 (October 2013):). Chicago: American Health Information Management Association. (Updated.) Retrieved from http://www.ahima.org, October 8, 2013.

Davis, N., & LaCour, M. (2014). *Introduction to health information technology* (3rd ed.). Philadelphia: W. B. Saunders.

Horton, L. (2010). *Calculating and reporting health care statistics* (3rd ed.). Chicago: American Health Information Management Association (AHIMA).

Koch, P. G. (2008). *Basic allied health statistics and analysis* (3rd ed.). Clifton Park, NY: Delmar Cengage Learning.

LaTour, Eichenwald-Maki, and Oachs (2013). *Health information management: Concepts, principles and practice* (4th ed.). Chicago: American Health Information Management Association (AHIMA).

Liebler, J. G., & McConnell, C. R. (2012). *Management principles for health professionals* (6th ed.). Sudbury, MA: Jones & Bartlett.

McConnell, C. *The effective health care supervisor* (6th ed.). Sudbury, MA: Jones & Bartlett.

McWay, D. C. (2014). *Today's health information management, an integrated approach* (2nd ed.). Clifton Park, NY: Delmar Cengage Learning.

Sayles, N. B. (2013). *Health information technology: An applied approach* (4th ed.). Chicago: American Health Information Management Association (AHIMA).

Human Resources Competencies

Question	RHIA Domain Competencies					
	1	2	3	4	5	6
1–100				X		

Question	RHIT Domain Competencies							
	1	2	3	4	5	6	7	
1	X							
2	X							
3	X							
4	X							
5	X							
6	X							
7						X		
8						X		
9	X							
10	X							
11	X							
12						X		
13	X							
14						X		
15	X							
16	X							
17	X							
18	X							
19	X							
20	X							
21	X							
22						X		
23	X							
24						X		
25		X						
26						X		
27						X		
28						X		
29						X		
30						X		
31	X							
32	X							
33	X							
34	X							
35						X		
36	X							
37						X		
38				X				
39				X				
40	X							
41						X		
42						X		
43	X							
44					X			
45						X		
46						X		
47	X							
48	X							
49		X						
50	X							
51						X		

XVII. Mock Examination

Patricia J. Schnering, RHIA, CCS

Debra W. Cook, MAEd, RHIA

Sheila Carlon, PhD, RHIA, FAHIMA

NOTE:

If you are taking the mock for the RHIT examination, you may choose to complete the first 150 questions. The mock for the RHIA examination has 180 questions to complete. In timing your speed at answering questions, allow about 1.35 minutes per question. For example, if you are taking the entire mock exam in one sitting, you should allow about 4 hours and 3 minutes (180 questions × 1.35 minutes for a total of 243 minutes = 4 hours and 3 minutes).

GULFSIDE HEALTHCARE CENTER AVERAGE CLINIC WAITING TIME BY TIME BLOCK DECEMBER 2013				
TIME BLOCK	PEDIATRICS	OBSTETRICS	CARDIOLOGY	ORTHOPEDICS
8:00–11:00	12	18	10	9
11:01–2:00	8	10	8	14
2:01–5:00	10	7	7	12

1. Each month, the staff of the clinic with the lowest overall waiting time is awarded a free dessert in the Gulfside Healthcare Center cafeteria. Take a look at the information listed above. The winner will be selected based on
   A   demonstrative clinical data.
   B.   comparative aggregate data.
   C.   objective individual data.
   D.   duplicate thematic data.

REFERENCE: Abdelhak, pp 380–382
                LaTour, Eichenwald-Maki, and Oachs, pp 138, 242
                McWay (2014), p 208

2. A union campaign is being conducted at your facility. As a department manager, it is appropriate for you to tell employees that
   A.   a strike is inevitable if the union wins.
   B.   wages will increase if the union is defeated.
   C.   you need the names of those involved in union activities.
   D.   you are opposed to the union.

REFERENCE: Abdelhak, pp 579–580
                Sayles, p 835

3. As the Coding Supervisor, your job description includes working with agents who have been charged with detecting and correcting overpayments made to your hospital in the Medicare Fee for Service program. You will need to develop a professional relationship with
   A.   the OIG.
   B.   MEDPAR representatives.
   C.   QIO physicians.
   D.   recovery audit contractors.

REFERENCE: Green and Bowie, pp 325–326
                McWay (2010), pp 312–315
                Sayles, p 309

4. Employing the SOAP style of progress notes, choose the "assessment" statement from the following:
   A. Patient states low back pain with sciatica is as severe as it was on admission.
   B. Patient moving about very cautiously appears to be in pain.
   C. Adjust pain medication; begin physical therapy tomorrow.
   D. Sciatica unimproved with hot pack therapy.

REFERENCE: Abdelhak, p 119
               Green and Bowie, pp 90–92
               LaTour, Eichenwald-Maki, and Oachs, pp 256–257
               Sayles, p 126

5. In preparation for an EHR, you are conducting a total facility inventory of all forms currently used. You must name each form for bar coding and indexing. The unnamed document in front of you includes a checklist for assessing an obstetric patient's lochia, fundus, and perineum. The document type you give to this form is
   A. prenatal record.   C. delivery room record.
   B. labor record.   D. postpartum record.

REFERENCE: Abdelhak, p 113
               Green and Bowie, p 182

SAMPLE MS-DRG REPORT		
MS-DRG IDENTIFIER	RELATIVE WEIGHT	NUMBER OF PATIENTS WITH THIS MS-DRG
A	1.234	12
B	3.122	10
C	2.165	19
D	5.118	16

6. Based on the MS-DRG report above, what is the case-mix index for this facility?
   A. 0.204193   C. 11.639
   B. 2.965807   D. 57

REFERENCE: Green and Bowie, pp 316–317
               LaTour, Eichenwald-Maki, and Oachs, pp 470, 496–498
               McWay (2014), p 165
               Sayles, p 499

7. The special form or view that plays the central role in planning and providing care at skilled nursing, psychiatric, and rehabilitation facilities is the
   A. interdisciplinary patient care plan.
   B. medical history and review of systems.
   C. interval summary.
   D. problem list.

REFERENCE: Abdelhak, p 142
               LaTour, Eichenwald-Maki, and Oachs, p 254
               Sayles, pp 111–112, 114

8. Four patients were discharged from Crestview Hospital yesterday. A final progress note is an appropriate discharge summary for
   A. Howard, who died within 24 hours after his admission for a second heart attack in 2 weeks.
   B. Jackson, who had no comorbidities or complications during this admission for replacement of a pacemaker battery.
   C. Fieldstone, who was admitted just 15 days following a heart attack for the acute onset of chest pain.
   D. Babson, who delivered a healthy 8-pound boy without complications for either mother or child, and was discharged within 36 hours of admission.

REFERENCE: Abdelhak, p 113
Green and Bowie, pp 142–144
LaTour, Eichenwald-Maki, and Oachs, p 251

Use the information in the tables below to answer the next two questions.

Make Me Better Clinic (MMBC) provides well child visits and childhood immunizations for four insurance companies. Data on the services they provided and the reimbursement they received from the four companies are listed in the two tables below.

Table 1 Well Child Visits

INSURANCE COMPANY	NUMBER OF WELL CHILD VISITS	REIMBURSEMENT FROM PAYER
Lifecare	259	$ 31,196.55
Getwell	786	$100,859.52
SureHealth	462	$ 54,631.50
BeHealthy	219	$ 26,991.75

Table 2 Immunizations

INSURANCE COMPANY	NUMBER OF IMMUNIZATIONS	TOTAL REIMBURSEMENT FROM PAYER
Lifecare	412	2,175.36
Getwell	1,465	9,053.70
SureHealth	609	3,580.92
BeHealthy	417	2,118.36

9. MMBC receives the best reimbursement for well child visits from
   A. Lifecare.   C. SureHealth.
   B. Getwell.   D. BeHealthy.

REFERENCE: Math Calculation

10. Most of the children who are seen at MMBC will have a well child visit and two immunizations. If you add the reimbursement for two immunizations to the reimbursement for each well child visit, which insurance company benefits MMBC most?
   A. Lifecare   C. SureHealth
   B. Getwell   D. BeHealthy

REFERENCE: Math Calculation

11. You are calculating the fee schedule payment amount for physician services covered under Medicare Part B. You already have the relative value unit figure. The only other information you need is
   A. the facility's case-mix index.   C. the facility's base rate.
   B. a national conversion factor.   D. MS-DRG relative weights.

REFERENCE: Green, pp 795–796
                LaTour, Eichenwald-Maki, and Oachs, p 434
                Sayles, p 272

KEY WEST HOSPITAL FOUR HIGHEST MS-DRGs							
MS-DRG A		MS-DRG B		MS-DRG C		MS-DRG D	
CMS WEIGHT	NUMBER OF PATIENTS WITH MS-DRG A	CMS WEIGHT	NUMBER OF PATIENTS WITH MS-DRG B	CMS WEIGHT	NUMBER OF PATIENTS WITH MS-DRG C	CMS WEIGHT	NUMBER OF PATIENTS WITH MS-DRG D
2.023	323	0.987	489	1.925	402	1.243	386

12. Key West Hospital collected the data displayed above concerning its four highest volume MS-DRGs. Which MS-DRG generated the most revenue for the hospital?
   A. MS-DRG A   C. MS-DRG C
   B. MS-DRG B   D. MS-DRG D

REFERENCE: Abdelhak, p 661
                LaTour, Eichenwald-Maki, and Oachs, pp 433, 496–497
                Sayles, pp 266, 270

13. In reviewing a health record for coding purposes, the coder notes that the patient was put on Keflex post-surgery. There is no mention of a postoperative complication in the attending physician's discharge summary. Before querying the doctor, the coder will seek to confirm the infection by reviewing the
   A. lab report.   C. operative report.
   B. nurses' notes.   D. pathology report.

REFERENCE: Green, pp 14–16
                LaTour, Eichenwald-Maki, and Oachs, p 442
                Sayles, p 85

14. Stan works in an acute care general hospital, Fran works for a skilled nursing facility, Ann is employed at an assisted living facility, and Dan works for a home care provider. Which people are employed in facilities that may seek Joint Commission accreditation?
   A. only Stan and Fran   C. only Fran and Dan
   B. only Stan and Dan   D. Dan, Stan, and Fran

REFERENCE: Abdelhak, p 14
                LaTour, Eichenwald-Maki, and Oachs, pp 11, 76
                McWay (2014), pp 52–53
                Sayles, pp 645–646

15. Sunset Beach Clinic allows patients to communicate by e-mail to ask questions regarding their treatment and request appointment changes. E-mails and text messages are
   A. considered health care business records and are subject to the same regulations as records created in face-to-face patient encounters.
   B. considered proof of patient contact and should be summarized in a progress note in the patient record.
   C. generally maintained in a facility's electronic mail system until the next face-to-face patient encounter.
   D. not typically maintained or documented as patient encounters.

REFERENCE: McWay (2010), pp 281–285
               Sayles and Trawick, p 377

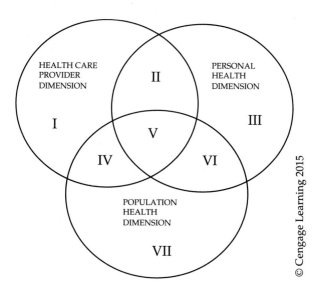

16. The proposed National Healthcare Information Network (NHIN) dimensions are graphically depicted in the diagram above. Roman numerals are added to allow for the identification of specific areas. Where would information concerning a patient's health insurance be located on this chart?
   A. I   C. III
   B. II   D. V

REFERENCE: Sayles, pp 984–986

17. The facility's policy for physician's verbal orders in accordance with state law and regulations needs updating. The first area of investigation is the qualifications of those individuals who have been authorized to record verbal orders. For this information you will consult the
    A. policy and procedure manual.
    B. hospital's Quality Management Plan.
    C. data dictionary.
    D. hospital bylaws, rules, and regulations.

REFERENCE: Green and Bowie, pp 14–16
               LaTour, Eichenwald-Maki, and Oachs, pp 247–248
               McWay (2014), p 23
               Sayles, p 676

18. Parker has type 1 diabetes with hypertension that is currently controlled with medication. Parker was admitted through the ED for an emergency appendectomy. Following surgery, the patient developed an infection at the wound site that was treated with antibiotics. When making decisions about sequencing the codes for this case, the coder should rely on definitions found in the
    A. UHDDS.   C. CMS Coding Guidelines.
    B. Coding Clinic.   D. Federal Register.

REFERENCE: AHA, pp 30–33
               Optum (2014), pp 390–391

19. Parker has type 1 diabetes with hypertension that is currently controlled with medication. Parker was admitted through the ED for an emergency appendectomy. Following surgery, the patient developed an infection at the wound site that was treated with antibiotics. Parker's principal diagnosis is the
    A. complications of hypertension.
    B. comorbidity of the wound infection.
    C. comorbidity of type 1 diabetes.
    D. acute appendicitis.

REFERENCE: AHA, pp 30–33
               Eichenwald-Maki and Oachs, pp 196, 932

20. Dr. Reed tried to explain wound care to Mr. Baker prior to discharge, but Baker (who is 104 and moderately senile) just could not seem to understand or remember what the doctor said. Mr. Baker's daughter was with him, so Dr. Reed explained Mr. Baker's aftercare to his daughter. Dr. Reed should document discharge instructions
    A. in the discharge summary.
    B. on a patient instructions form signed by Dr. Reed and Mr. Baker and filed in Mr. Baker's medical record.
    C. in the discharge summary and on a patient instructions form signed by Dr. Reed and Mr. Baker and filed in Baker's medical record.
    D. in the discharge summary and on a patient instructions form signed by Dr. Reed and Mr. Baker's daughter and filed in Mr. Baker's medical record.

REFERENCE: Abdelhak, p 113
               Green and Bowie, pp 143–145
               LaTour, Eichenwald-Maki, and Oachs, pp 251–253
               McWay (2010), pp 274–275
               Sayles, pp 93–94

21. The physician has documented the final diagnoses as acute myocardial infarction, COPD, CHF, hypertension, atrial fibrillation, and status-post cholecystectomy. The following conditions should be reported:

I10	Essential Hypertension, benign
I10	Essential Hypertension, unspecified
I11	Hypertension, heart disease, unspecified as to malignant or benign, with heart failure
I21.3	Acute myocardial infarction, unspecified site, initial episode of care
I48.91	Atrial fibrillation
I50.9	Congestive heart failure, unspecified
J44.9	Chronic obstructive pulmonary disease
Z90.89	Acquired absence of gallbladder

   A. I21.3, J44.9, I21.3, I48.91, Z90.89
   B. I11, J44.9, I50.9, I10, I48.91
   C. I11, J44.9, I50.9, I10, I48.91, Z90.89
   D. I11, J44.9, I50.9, I10, I48.91

REFERENCE: AHA, pp 34–36, 387–389, 395, 403–404, 429

22. Mary is 6 weeks postmastectomy for carcinoma of the breast. She is admitted for chemotherapy. What is the correct sequencing of the codes?

C50.911	Malignant neoplasm of the breast
Z85.3	Personal history of malignant neoplasm of breast
Z51.11	Encounter for antineoplastic chemotherapy
Z08	Follow-up exam after surgery

   A. Z51.11, C50.911   C. Z08, Z51.11
   B. Z51.11, Z85.3   D. Z85.3

REFERENCE: AHA, pp 439, 452, 456–457, 459, 461
                Optum, p 368

23. Which of the following is coded as an adverse effect in ICD-9-CM?
   A. tinnitus due to allergic reaction after administration of eardrops
   B. mental retardation due to intracranial abscess
   C. rejection of transplanted kidney
   D. nonfunctioning pacemaker due to defective soldering

REFERENCE: AHA, pp 513–518, 521–522
                Optum (1), p 382

24. Which of the following scenarios identifies a pathologic fracture?
   A. greenstick fracture secondary to fall from a bed
   B. compression fracture of the skull after being hit with a baseball bat
   C. vertebral fracture with cord compression following a car accident
   D. compression fracture of the vertebrae as a result of bone metastasis

REFERENCE: AHA, pp 299–300, 489
                Optum (1), p 375

25. If the same condition is described as both acute and chronic and separate subentries exist in the ICD-10-CM alphabetic index at the same indentation level,
    A. they should both be coded, acute sequenced first.
    B. they should both be coded, chronic sequenced first.
    C. only the acute condition should be coded.
    D. only the chronic condition should be coded.

REFERENCE: AHA, pp 58–59
               Optum (1), p 363

26. Which of the following statements is true?
    A. A surgical procedure may include one or more surgical operations.
    B. The terms *surgical operation* and *surgical procedure* are synonymous.
    C. A surgical operation may include one or more surgical procedures.
    D. The term *surgical procedure* is an incorrect term and should not be used.

REFERENCE: Koch, p 180
               LaTour, Eichenwald-Maki, and Oachs, p 496
               Sayles, p 498

27. Which of the following would be coded as a poisoning?
    A. Coumadin intoxication due to a cumulative effect
    B. idiosyncratic reaction to Artane
    C. interaction between Aldomet and a vasodilating agent
    D. reaction between Coumadin and an over-the-counter medication

REFERENCE: AHA, pp 514–518
               Optum (1), p 382

28. Which of the following diagnoses or procedures would prevent the normal delivery code, O80, from being assigned?
    A. occiput presentation   C. episiotomy
    B. single liveborn   D. low forceps

REFERENCE: AHA, pp 316, 319, 336
               Optum (1), p 377

29. Which of the following are considered a (late effect) sequela regardless of time?
    A. congenital defect   C. nonhealing fracture
    B. nonunion   D. poisoning

REFERENCE: AHA, pp 15, 60–62, 303, 484–485, 499
               Optum (1), p 364

30. Four people were seen in your emergency department yesterday. Which one will be coded as a poisoning?

    • Josh was diagnosed with digitalis intoxication.
    • Ben had an allergic reaction to a dye administered for a pyelogram.
    • Bryan developed syncope after taking Contac pills with a double scotch.
    • Matthew had an idiosyncratic reaction between two properly administered prescription drugs.

    A. Josh   C. Bryan
    B. Ben   D. Matthew

REFERENCE: AHA, pp 514–518
               Optum (1), p 382

31. Patient is admitted for elective cholecystectomy for treatment of chronic cholecystitis with cholelithiasis. Prior to administration of general anesthesia, patient suffers cerebral thrombosis. Surgery is subsequently canceled. Code and sequence the coding from the following codes.

I66.9	Cerebral thrombosis without cerebral infarction
K80.10	Chronic cholecystitis with cholelithiasis
Z53.09	Surgery canceled, contraindication
I97.821	Iatrogenic cerebrovascular infarction or hemorrhage
0FT40ZZ	Cholecystectomy, total

A. I97.821, K80.10, 0FT40ZZ
C. I97.821, I66.9, Z53.09
B. K80.10, I66.9, Z53.09
D. I66.9, Z53.09

REFERENCE: AHA, pp 126, 249, 398–401

32. The discharge diagnosis for this inpatient encounter is rule out myocardial infarction. The coder would assign
A. a code for a myocardial infarction.
B. a code for the patient's symptoms.
C. a code for an impending myocardial infarction.
D. no code for this condition.

REFERENCE: AHA, pp 38, 58
Optum (1), p 364

33. Staging
A. refers to the monitoring of incidence and trends associated with a disease.
B. is continued medical surveillance of a case.
C. is a system for documenting the extent or spread of cancer.
D. designates the degree of differentiation of cells.

REFERENCE: Abdelhak, p 488
AHA, pp 299–300, 489
LaTour, Eichenwald-Maki, and Oates, pp 371, 949
Sayles, p 439

34. Which of these conditions are always considered "present on admission" (POA)?
A. congenital conditions
B. E codes
C. acute conditions
D. possible, probable, or suspected conditions

REFERENCE: AHA, pp 571–574
LaTour, Eichenwald-Maki, and Oachs, pp 443, 921, 940
Sayles, p 439

35. In your state, it is legal for minors to seek medical treatment for a sexually transmitted disease without parental consent. When this occurs, who would be expected to authorize the release of the medical information documented in this episode of care to the patient's insurers?
A. the patient
B. a court-appointed guardian on behalf of the patient
C. the custodial parent of the patient
D. the patient's doctor on behalf of the patient

REFERENCE: Eichenwald-Maki and Oachs, p 317
McWay (2010), p 186

36. A patient is admitted through the emergency department. Three days after admission, the physician documents uncontrolled diabetes mellitus. What is the "present on admission" (POA) indicator for uncontrolled diabetes mellitus?

A. "Y"   C. "W"
B. "U"   D. "N"

REFERENCE: AHA, pp 571–574
                    Optum (1), p 168
                    Sayles, pp 270, 1238

37. The patient had a thrombectomy, without catheter, of the peroneal artery, by leg incision.

34203	Embolectomy or thrombectomy, with or without catheter; popliteal-tibioperoneal artery, by leg incision
35226	Repair blood vessel, direct; lower extremity
35302	Thromboendarterectomy, including patch graft if performed; superficial femoral artery
37799	Unlisted procedure, vascular surgery

A. 34203   C. 35302
B. 37799   D. 35226

REFERENCE: Bowie and Schaffer (2013), pp 274–275
                    Green, p 606
                    Johnson and Linker, p 17

38. Patient was seen for excision of two interdigital neuromas from the left foot.

28080	Excision, interdigital (Morton) neuroma, single, each
64774	Excision of neuroma; cutaneous nerve, surgically identifiable
64776	Excision of neuroma; digital nerve, one or both, same digit

A. 64774   C. 28080
B. 64776   D. 28080, 28080

REFERENCE: AMA CPT (2014)

39. Patient was seen in the Emergency Department with lacerations on the left arm. Two lacerations, one 7 cm and one 9 cm, were closed with layered sutures.

12002	Simple repair of superficial wounds of scalp, neck, axillae, external genitalia, trunk and/or extremities (including hands and feet); 2.6–7.5 cm
12004	Simple repair of superficial wounds of scalp, neck, axillae, external genitalia, trunk and/or extremities (including hands and feet); 7.6–12.5 cm
12035	Layer closure of wounds of scalp, axillae, trunk and/or extremities (excluding hands and feet); 12.6–20.0 cm
12045	Layer closure of wounds of neck, hands, feet and/or external genitalia; 12.6–20.0 cm

A. 12045   C. 12002, 12004
B. 12035   D. 12004

REFERENCE: Green, pp 252–255

40. Office visit for 43-year-old male, new patient, with no complaints. Patient is applying for life insurance and requests a physical examination. A detailed health and family history was obtained and a basic physical was done. Physician completed life insurance physical form at patient's request. Blood and urine were collected.

99381	Initial comprehensive preventive medicine evaluation and management of an individual including an age and gender appropriate history, examination, counseling/anticipatory guidance/risk factor reduction interventions, and the ordering of appropriate immunization(s), laboratory/diagnostic procedures, new patient; infant (age under 1 year)
99386	Initial comprehensive preventive medicine evaluation and management of an individual including a comprehensive history, a comprehensive examination, counseling/anticipatory guidance/risk factor reduction interventions, and the ordering of appropriate immunization(s), laboratory/diagnostic procedures, new patient; 40–64 years
99396	Periodic comprehensive preventive medicine reevaluation and management of an individual including an age and gender appropriate history, examination, counseling/anticipatory guidance/risk factor reduction interventions, and the ordering of appropriate immunization(s), laboratory/diagnostic procedures, established patient; 40–64 years
99450	Basic life and/or disability examination that includes completion of a medical history following a life insurance pro forma

A. 99450
B. 99386
C. 99396
D. 99381

REFERENCE: AMA CPT (2014), p 40
Bowie and Schaffer (2013), pp 37–39, 61–64
Green, pp 435–437
Johnson and Linker, pp 149–154

41. Patient was seen today for regular hemodialysis. No problems reported, tolerated procedure well.

90935	Hemodialysis procedure with single physician evaluation
90937	Hemodialysis procedure requiring repeated evaluations(s) with or without substantial revision of dialysis prescription
90945	Dialysis procedure other than hemodialysis (e.g., peritoneal dialysis, hemofiltration, or other continuous renal replacement therapies), with single physician evaluation
+99354	Prolonged physician service in the office or other outpatient setting requiring direct (face-to-face) contact beyond the usual service; first hour (list separately in addition to code for office or other outpatient Evaluation and Management service)

A. 90937
B. 99354
C. 90945
D. 90935

REFERENCE: Bowie and Schaffer (2013), pp 429–431
Green, pp 808–810
Johnson and Linker, pp 432–433
Smith, p 229

42. An established patient was seen by the physician in the office for DTaP vaccine and Hib.

90471	Immunization administration (includes percutaneous, intradermal, subcutaneous, intramuscular injections); one vaccine (single or combination vaccine/toxoid)
90700	Diphtheria, tetanus toxoids, and acellular pertussis vaccine (DTaP), when administered to individuals younger than 7 years, for intramuscular use
90720	Diphtheria, tetanus toxoids, and whole cell pertussis vaccine and Hemophilus influenza B vaccine (DTP-Hib), for intramuscular use
90721	Diphtheria, tetanus toxoids, and acellular pertussis vaccine and Hemophilus influenza B vaccine (DTaP-Hib), for intramuscular use
90748	Hepatitis B and Hemophilus influenza b vaccine (HepB-Hib), for intramuscular use
99211	Office or other outpatient visit for the evaluation and management of an established patient, which may not require the presence of a physician. Usually, the presenting problem(s) are minimal. Typically, 5 minutes are spent performing or supervising these services.

A. 90721

B. 90720, 90471

C. 90700, 90748, 99211

D. 90471, 90721

REFERENCE: AMA CPT (2014), pp 522–527
               Green, pp 802–804
               Johnson and Linker, p 429
               Smith, pp 226–227

43. A patient with lung cancer and bone metastasis is seen for complex treatment planning by a radiation oncologist.

77263	Therapeutic radiology treatment planning; complex
77290	Therapeutic radiology simulation-aided field setting; complex
77315	Teletherapy, isodose plan (whether hand or computer calculated); complex (mantle or inverted Y, tangential ports, the use of wedges, compensators, complex blocking, rotational beam, or special beam considerations)
77334	Treatment devices, design and construction; complex (irregular blocks, special shields, compensators, wedges, molds, or casts)

A. 77315

B. 77263

C. 77290

D. 77334

REFERENCE: AMA CPT (2014), pp 420–421
               Bowie and Schaffer (2013), pp 404–408
               Green, pp 753–756
               Johnson and Linker, p 403
               Smith, pp 179–180

44. A 4-year-old had a repair of an incarcerated inguinal hernia. This is the first time this child had been treated for this condition.

49496	Repair initial inguinal hernia full-term infant, under age 6 months, or preterm infant over 50 weeks' post conception age and under 6 months at the time of surgery, with or without hydrocelectomy; incarcerated or strangulated
49501	Repair initial inguinal hernia, age 6 months to under 5 years, with or without hydrocelectomy; incarcerated or strangulated
49521	Repair recurrent inguinal hernia, any age; incarcerated or strangulated
49553	Repair initial femoral hernia, any age; incarcerated or strangulated

A. 49553
B. 49496

C. 49521
D. 49501

REFERENCE:　Bowie and Schaffer (2013), pp 274–275
Green, pp 625–626
Johnson and Linker, pp 192–193
Smith, pp 126–128

45. A quantitative drug assay was performed for a patient to determine digoxin level.

80050	General health panel
80101	Drug screen, qualitative; single drug class method (e.g., immunoassay, enzyme assay), each drug class
80162	Digoxin (therapeutic drug assay, quantitative examination)
80166	Doxepin (therapeutic drug assay, quantitative examination)

A. 80101
B. 80050

C. 80166
D. 80162

REFERENCE:　Bowie and Schaffer (2013), p 419
Green, p 779
Johnson and Linker, p 418

46. Provide the CPT code for anesthesia services for the transvenous insertion of a pacemaker.

00530	Anesthesia for permanent transvenous pacemaker insertion
00560	Anesthesia for procedures on heart, pericardial sac, and great vessels of chest; without pump oxygenator
33202	Insertion of epicardial electrode(s); open incision
33206	Insertion or replacement of permanent pacemaker with transvenous electrode(s); atrial

A. 00560
B. 33202, 00530

C. 00530
D. 33206, 00560

REFERENCE:　Bowie and Schaffer (2013), pp 188–195
Green, pp 482–484
Johnson and Linker, pp 175–178

47. The transcriptionists have collected data on the number and types of problems with the dictation equipment. The best tool to display the data they collected is a
   A. flowchart.
   B. Pareto chart.
   C. Gantt chart.
   D. PERT chart.

REFERENCE: LaTour, Eichenwald-Maki, and Oachs, p 823
                McWay (2014), pp 212–215
                Sayles, pp 591–592, 1233

48. Based on the information below, what was the net death rate at Seaside Hospital in January?

SEASIDE HOSPITAL SELECTED STATISTICS JANUARY				
Admissions	Discharged to Home	Discharge Transfers	Deaths <48 hours	Deaths >48 hours
280	212	28	8	6

   A. 2.4%
   B. 2.8%
   C. 3.8%
   D. 5.8%

REFERENCE: Horton, pp 75–76
                Koch, pp 120–121
                LaTour, Eichenwald-Maki, and Oachs, p 393
                Sayles, pp 489–490, 1229

49. The formula used to calculate the percentage of ambulatory care visits made with same day appointments is
   A. $\dfrac{\text{number of patients seen with same day appointments for a period} \times 100}{\text{number of patients seen with advance appointments for the same period}}$
   B. $\dfrac{\text{number of patients seen with advance appointments for a period} \times 100}{\text{number of patients seen with same day appointments for the same period}}$
   C. $\dfrac{\text{number of patients seen with same day appointments for a period} \times 100}{\text{number of patients seen in the same period}}$
   D. $\dfrac{\text{number of patients seen with advance appointments for a period} \times 100}{\text{number of patients seen in the same period}}$

REFERENCE: Horton, pp 14–18
                Koch, p 178
                LaTour, Eichenwald-Maki, and Oachs, pp 493, 881
                McWay (2014), pp 210–211
                Sayles, 1242

50. An HIM Department Budget Report for May shows a payroll budget of $25,000 and an actual payroll expense of $22,345. The percentage of budget variance for the month is
   A. $2,655.
   B. 11%.
   C. $265.
   D. 0.9%.

REFERENCE: LaTour, Eichenwald-Maki, and Oachs, pp 787–788

51. Diverticulitis large bowel with abscess; right hemicolectomy with colostomy performed.

K57.90	Diverticulosis of colon (without mention of hemorrhage)
K57.92	Diverticulitis of colon (without mention of hemorrhage)
K63.0	Abscess of intestine
0DTK0ZZ	Open and other right hemicolectomy
0DTL0ZZ	Open and other resection of transverse colon
0D1K0Z4	Exteriorization of large intestine (loop colostomy)

    A. K57.90, 0DTL0ZZ, 0D1K0Z4
    B. K57.92, 0DTK0ZZ, 0D1K0Z4
    C. K57.92, K63.0, 0DTK0ZZ
    D. K57.92, K63.0, 0DTL0ZZ

REFERENCE: AHA, pp 243–244, 247–248

52. Your facility is engaged in a research project concerning patients newly diagnosed with type 2 diabetes. The researchers notice older patients have a longer length of stay than younger patients. They have seen a
    A. positive correlation between age and length of stay.
    B. negative correlation between age and length of stay.
    C. causal relationship between age and length of stay.
    D. homologous relationship between age and length of stay.

REFERENCE: Koch, pp 274–248
                 LaTour, Eichenwald-Maki, and Oachs, p 536
                 McWay (2014), pp 215–216
                 Sayles, p 529

53. Johnston City was set upon by a swarm of killer bees. All 5,000 residents are at risk of a bee attack. If 25 residents were attacked by the bees, the incidence of bee attacks
    A. is 5 in 1,000.   C. is 25 in 1,000.
    B. is 5 in 5,000.   D. cannot be determined at this time.

REFERENCE: Abdelhak, p 378
                 Koch, p 205
                 LaTour, Eichenwald-Maki, and Oachs, p 506
                 McWay, pp 215–217
                 Sayles, p 516

54. A 335-bed hospital opened a new wing on June 1 of a nonleap year, increasing its bed count to 350 beds. The total bed count days for the year at the hospital was
    A. 122,275.
    B. 125,485.
    C. 127,750.
    D. The answer cannot be calculated with the information provided.

REFERENCE: Koch, p 86
                 LaTour, Eichenwald-Maki, and Oachs, p 488
                 Sayles, p 483

55. A patient who was admitted to the hospital on January 14 and discharged on March 2 in a nonleap year has a length of stay of
    A. 45 days.   C. 47 days.
    B. 46 days.   D. 48 days.

REFERENCE: Koch, p 102
               LaTour, Eichenwald-Maki, and Oachs, p 489
               Sayles, p 485

56. Release of information has increased its use of part-time prn clerical support in order to respond to increased requests for release of information. The budget variance report will reflect
    A. the increase in the cost of part-time clerical support for ROI but not the increase in revenue from this area.
    B. the increase in revenue from increased volume in ROI but not the increased costs of part-time clerical support.
    C. both the increases in revenue and increased costs for clerical support in ROI.
    D. neither the increased costs nor increased revenue, as temporary changes are rarely reflected on variance reports.

REFERENCE: Abdelhak, pp 676–677
               LaTour, Eichenwald-Maki, and Oachs, p 787

57. You are heading a research study that includes a patient questionnaire. Five of the questions will be answered using the following scale:

1	Strongly disagree
2	Disagree
3	No opinion
4	Agree
5	Strongly agree

You would like to display the study in your report. If you'd like to include responses to all five questions on one display, you should use a
    A. stacked bar graph.   C. frequency table.
    B. pie chart.   D. frequency polygon.

REFERENCE: Abdelhak, p 382
               LaTour, Eichenwald-Maki, and Oachs, p 513
               McWay (2014), pp 212–215

58. Your HMO manager has requested a report on the number of patient visits per year for preschool children. Which of the age groupings below will you use for your report?

A. 0–1 year	B. <12 months	C. >12 months	D. 0–2 years
1–2 years	12–24 months	12–24 months	3–4 years
2–3 years	25–37 months	25–37 months	5 years
3–4 years	38–50 months	38–50 months	
4–5 years	51–63 months	<51 months	

REFERENCE: Koch, p 260
               LaTour, Eichenwald-Maki, and Oachs, p 508
               Sayles, p 520

59. Collins Family Hospital had a bed count of 150 for the first 6 months of the year. On June 1, it added 15 beds when it opened a new wing. If you are given the average length of stay for the year, can you calculate the annual bed turnover rate? How?
    A. Yes, using the direct method.
    B. Yes, using the indirect method.
    C. Yes, using the Joint Commission method.
    D. No, there is insufficient data to complete the calculation.

REFERENCE: Abdelhak, p 378
               Horton, pp 52–53
               Koch, pp 185–186
               LaTour, Eichenwald-Maki, and Oachs, p 488
               Sayles, p 484

60. In a research study that includes a patient questionnaire, five of the questions will be answered using the following scale:

1	Strongly disagree
2	Disagree
3	No opinion
4	Agree
5	Strongly agree

The data collected using this scale are called
    A. cardinal data.   C. nominal data.
    B. ordinal data.   D. continuous data.

REFERENCE: Abdelhak, p 380
               Horton, p 197
               Koch, p 13
               LaTour, Eichenwald-Maki, and Oachs, pp 482–483, 522
               McWay (2014), p 212
               Sui, p 293

61. Gail Smith has presented to the ER in a coma with injuries sustained in a motor vehicle accident. According to her sister, Gail has had a recent medical history taken at the public health department. The physician on call is grateful that she can access this patient information using the area's
    A. EDMS system.
    B. CPOE.
    C. expert system.
    D. RHIO.

REFERENCE: Green and Bowie, p 112
               Sayles, p 326

62. The patient's family asked the attending physician to keep the patient in the hospital for a few days more until they could make arrangements for the patient's home care. Because the patient no longer meets criteria for continued stay, if the physician complies with the family's request, this would be considered
    A. the best utilization of the hospital's resources.
    B. an inappropriate use of hospital resources.
    C. a compassionate use of the hospital's resources.
    D. appropriate provided it is limited to a few days.

REFERENCE: Abdelhak, p 467
               LaTour, Eichenwald-Maki, and Oachs, pp 15–16, 430
               Sayles, pp 609–611

63. The state is considering the closure of the Arcadia Hospital. In reviewing the hospital statistics, which indicator will best help state officials determine whether closure is warranted?
    A. daily census   C. inpatient service days
    B. percentage of occupancy   D. average length of stay

REFERENCE: Koch, p 84
               LaTour, Eichenwald-Maki, and Oachs, pp 486–488
               Sayles, p 480

64. The census taken at midnight on August 1 showed 99 patients remaining in the hospital. On August 2, four patients were admitted, there was one fetal death, one DOA, and seven patients were discharged. One of these patients was admitted in the morning and remained only 8 hours. How many inpatient service days were rendered on August 2?
    A. 94   C. 96
    B. 95   D. 97

REFERENCE: Abdelhak, p 379
               Koch, pp 64–67
               LaTour, Eichenwald-Maki, and Oachs, pp 486–488
               Sayles, p 480

65. You are implementing a quality improvement plan that utilizes the PDSA cycle. If you correctly implement PDSA, which phase of the project will take the most of your time?
    A. P   C. S
    B. D   D. A

REFERENCE: LaTour, Eichenwald-Maki, and Oachs, pp 419–420
               McWay (2014), pp 184–185

66. A run or line chart would be most useful for collecting data on
    A. waiting time in the Pediatrics Clinic.
    B. patient satisfaction with the food.
    C. delays in scheduling elective surgical procedures.
    D. medication errors and their causes.

REFERENCE: Koch, pp 274–275
               LaTour, Eichenwald-Maki, and Oachs, p 824
               McWay (2014), pp 213–214
               Sayles, p 582

Number of Visits and Wait Times in the ER

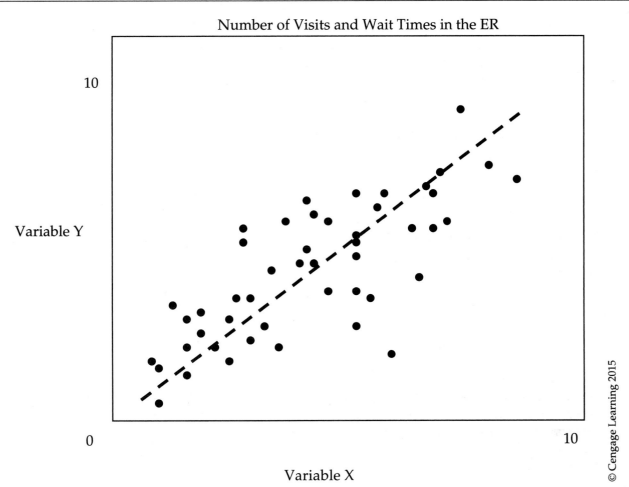

Variable X

67. The ER staff has collected the data on the number of visits and corresponding wait times in the ER. The data are displayed on the chart shown above. Based on this information, what kind of correlation do you see between the number of visits (Variable X) and the wait times (Variable Y)?
   A. a positive correlation between Variable X and Variable Y
   B. a negative correlation between Variable X and Variable Y
   C. a conjunctive correlation between Variable X and Variable Y
   D. a causative correlation between Variable X and Variable Y

REFERENCE: Koch, pp 247–248
              LaTour, Eichenwald-Maki, and Oachs, p 536
              McWay (2014), pp 215–217
              Sayles, pp 591, 529

68. Fred is recovering nicely, so he asks Dr. Jones if he can go home for the weekend. Dr. Jones approves a two-night leave of absence (LOA). Chances are Fred is a patient in
    A. an acute care facility; his LOA will decrease the month's average daily inpatient census.
    B. a long-term care facility; his LOA will increase the month's percentage of occupancy.
    C. an acute care facility; his LOA will increase the month's total discharge days.
    D. a long-term care facility; his LOA will decrease the month's total inpatient service days.

REFERENCE: Horton, p 27
               Koch, pp 111–112

69. Community Hospital reported an average LOS in December of 3.7 days with a standard deviation of 23. This information indicates that
    A. there was a small variation in the LOS at Community Hospital.
    B. there was a large variation in the LOS at Community Hospital.
    C. most of the patients at Community Hospital stay 3 to 4 days.
    D. patients stay longer at Community than at most hospitals.

REFERENCE: Koch, pp 246–247
               LaTour, Eichenwald-Maki, and Oachs, pp 517–520
               McWay (2014), p 206

70. Four HIT students are working on a LOS project at their clinical site. To describe the variability of the data, Smithson suggests using range because it is the most exact. Donaldson wants to use the mean because it is easy to calculate. Franklin recommends variance because it is the most popular measure of variability. Howell proposes the use of standard deviation because it is the most preferred and has better interpretive uses. Who made the best suggestion?
    A. Smithson   C. Franklin
    B. Donaldson   D. Howell

REFERENCE: Koch, p 246
               LaTour, Eichenwald-Maki, and Oachs, pp 519–521
               McWay (2014), pp 213–215
               Sayles, pp 540–542, 544, 552

71. Sun City reported 12 cases of chronic heart disease in a population of 8,000 in 2008. In 2011, Sun City reported there were still 12 cases of chronic heart disease, but its population had decreased to 6,000. This represents an increase in the
    A. prevalence of chronic heart disease in Sun City.
    B. incidence of chronic heart disease in Sun City.
    C. reliability of reporting chronic heart disease in Sun City.
    D. occurrence of chronic heart disease in Sun City.

REFERENCE: Koch, pp 145–146, 205
               LaTour, Eichenwald-Maki, and Oachs, p 506
               McWay, pp 210
               Sayles, pp 516–517

72. Community Hospital Administration decided to change the number of adult and children beds from 300 to 375 effective July 1. The total number of inpatient service days for adults and children for the year was 111,963. What was the percentage of occupancy rate for adults and children for the entire year?

    A. 0.9%
    B. 45.4%
    C. 90.8%
    D. 91.0%

REFERENCE: Horton, pp 49–50
               Koch, pp 91–92
               LaTour, Eichenwald-Maki, and Oachs, p 488
               Sayles, pp 483–484

73. When checking the census data at South Beach Women's Center, you see that just yesterday, there were four sets of triplets, five sets of twins, and eight single births. Yesterday, South Beach Women's Center had

    A. 17 deliveries.
    B. 25 deliveries.
    C. 30 deliveries.
    D. 39 deliveries.

REFERENCE: Horton, p 124
               Koch, p 140

74. In preparing the retention schedule for health records, the most concrete guidance in determining when records may be destroyed will be

    A. the average readmission rate for the facility.
    B. the available options for inactive records.
    C. the statute of limitations in your state.
    D. Joint Commission and AOA standards regarding minimum retention periods.

REFERENCE: LaTour, Eichenwald-Maki, and Oachs, pp 274–275
               Sayles, p 346

The Credentialing Committee reviewed Dr. Hernandez's application for renewal of his medical staff privileges. They noted that Dr. Hernandez had a high incidence of nosocomial infections after hip replacement surgery. The committee recommended renewal of Dr. Hernandez's general medical staff privileges but suspended his permission to perform hip replacement surgery until he completed an AMA-approved course on infection control and successfully demonstrated improved technique to the department chair.

75. The Credentialing Committee discovered the problems with Dr. Hernandez's hip replacements by

    A. sampling and reviewing Dr. Hernandez's patient records.
    B. reviewing Dr. Hernandez's physician profile.
    C. querying the National Physician Data Bank.
    D. interviewing the Chief of Surgery.

REFERENCE: Abdelhak, pp 464–465
               LaTour, Eichenwald-Maki, and Oachs, pp 330–331, 664–666
               McWay (2010), pp 70–71
               Sayles, pp 834–835

76. You are starting your new job as the sole HIM professional at a small psychiatric practice. The practice uses DSM for billing purposes. You find this "theoretically" reasonable because DSM
    A. is a widely used and accepted classification system.
    B. codes are also valid ICD-10-CM codes.
    C. codes are also valid CPT codes.
    D. is the industry standard for psychiatric billing systems.

REFERENCE: Green and Bowie, p 307
              LaTour, Eichenwald-Maki, and Oachs, pp 388–389
              Sayles, pp 208–210, 395

77. As the Information Security Officer at your facility, you have been asked to provide examples of the physical safeguards used to manage data security measures throughout the organization. Which of the following would you provide?
    A. audit controls   C. chain-of-trust partner agreements
    B. entity authentication   D. workstation use and location

REFERENCE: Green and Bowie, pp 270–271
              LaTour, Eichenwald-Maki, and Oachs, pp 330, 947
              Sayles, pp 1055–1056

78. The MS-DRG weight in a particular case is 2.0671 and the hospital's payment rate is $3,027. How much would the hospital receive as reimbursement in this case?
    A. $3,027.00   C. $6,257.11
    B. $5,094.10   D. $960.00

REFERENCE: Abdelhak, p 661
              LaTour, Eichenwald-Maki, and Oachs, pp 432–433
              Sayles, pp 449–450

79. A patient's husband slipped and fell in your HIM reception area and now he is suing the facility. You have to prepare detailed written answers to a long list of questions and send them to your hospital attorney. You will spend the afternoon working on
    A. affidavits.   C. interrogatories.
    B. allocutions.   D. depositions.

REFERENCE: Abdelhak, pp 541–542
              LaTour, Eichenwald-Maki, and Oachs, p 925
              McWay (2010), pp 34, 40, 57

Use the information on errors in indexing of scanned material that you have collected and presented in the table below to answer the next two questions.

TYPE OF MATERIAL	NUMBER SCANNED	NUMBER INDEXING ERRORS
CONSULTATION REPORTS	2,879	431
LAB SLIPS	15,242	458
CORRESPONDENCE	1,426	114
OTHER	6,271	313

80. If you want to begin with the type of material that has the highest error rate, you will start by working on problems with
   A. consultation reports.
   B. lab slips.
   C. correspondence.
   D. other.

REFERENCE: Abdelhak, pp 619–621, 623
               Koch, p 48

81. Referring again to the data collected on scanning errors, if you want to work on the type of material with the highest volume, you will work on problems with
   A. consultation reports.
   B. lab slips.
   C. correspondence.
   D. other.

REFERENCE: Abdelhak, p 378
               Koch, p 48

82. You are providing an educational session to new hires at your hospital. You tell the new employees that hospital records may be used as evidence in court even though hearsay laws bar the use of most evidence that does not represent personal knowledge of the witness. That is because the hospital record
   A. is written rather than spoken.
   B. was kept in the regular course of business.
   C. has not been tampered with in any way.
   D. is accurate and complete.

REFERENCE: Abdelhak, p 525
               LaTour, Eichenwald-Maki, and Oachs, pp 86–87, 142–143, 241, 264, 282
               McWay (2010), pp 51–52
               McWay (2014), pp 58–59, 68, 126
               Sayles, pp 35, 42, 131, 391, 733, 787–788

83. Which of the following responsibilities would you expect to find on the job description of a facility's Information Security Officer but NOT on the job description of Chief Privacy Officer?
    A. Cooperate with the Office of Civil Rights in compliance investigations.
    B. Conduct audit trails to monitor inappropriate access to system information.
    C. Oversee the patient's right to inspect, amend, and restrict access to protected health information.
    D. Monitor the facility's business associate agreements.

REFERENCE: Green and Bowie, pp 42, 280
              LaTour, Eichenwald-Maki, and Oachs, pp 99–101, 134, 208, 360
              McWay (2014), p 40
              Sayles, pp 1041, 1043, 1056–1057

84. Sally is a HIM professional with many years of experience. Unlike some of her colleagues, Sally loves the challenge of adapting to change. She is happy that HIPAA empowers the Secretary of DHHS to adopt standards for electronically maintained health information. Sally hopes that the standardization under HIPAA will make it easier to design safeguards for electronic data, to protect against unauthorized access, to
    A. make and use copies of the data, and to guard against unauthorized data integration.
    B. protect electronic records from corruption, and to prosecute hackers under federal law.
    C. prevent the corruption of electronically stored data, and to protect the integrity of the information itself.
    D. submit revisions of claims as they are denied, and to track third-party payers.

REFERENCE: Abdelhak, p 209
              LaTour, Eichenwald-Maki, and Oachs, pp 17, 99–101, 132, 134, 161–163 187, 208, 229, 343
              Sayles, pp 1041, 1229

85. An 11-year-old female is brought to the emergency room with a compound, comminuted fracture of the right tibia and fibula. Her mother was very seriously injured in the same accident and is unconscious. What should be done?
    A. Nothing, until consent can be obtained from the nearest relative.
    B. The mother can be treated under implied consent but not the child.
    C. The hospital should quickly seek a court-appointed guardian for the child.
    D. Both patients can be treated under implied consent.

REFERENCE: Sayles, p 102

86. A pharmacist at your facility was caught running a drug ring. The pharmacist filled orders of valuable medications with cheap outdated ones purchased on the Internet and then sold the good drugs for profit. Patients have been injured and the lawsuits are starting. Unfortunately, your facility is going to be held responsible for the pharmacist's negligent acts under the doctrine of
    A. adjudicus res.   C. respondeat superior.
    B. res ipsa loquitur.   D. stare decisis.

REFERENCE: LaTour, Eichenwald-Maki, and Oachs, p 331
              McWay (2010), p 85

87. A patient was treated for meningitis at age 3 (15 years ago). The patient is now 18. The patient's attorney is requesting information on the admission. You tell the clerk the information is
    A. no longer available because your facility retains information for 10 years after the last patient visit.
    B. available, but the attorney will have to obtain a court order before you will release it.
    C. available, but the patient's parents will have to sign a consent for you to release it.
    D. available, and the patient may sign consent to release the information in the record.

REFERENCE: Abdelhak, pp 196–197
               LaTour, Eichenwald-Maki, and Oachs, p 317

88. A patient has written to request a copy of his own record. When the clerk checked the record, it was noted that the patient was last admitted to the psychiatric unit of the facility. You advise the clerk to
    A. comply with the request immediately.
    B. contact the patient's attending physician before complying.
    C. ignore the request and advise you if it is repeated.
    D. ask the patient to send the required fee prior to the release.

REFERENCE: Abdelhak, pp 538–539
               Green and Bowie, pp 294–295
               LaTour, Eichenwald-Maki, and Oachs, pp 314, 319
               Sayles, p 800

89. Your HIS Department receives an authorization for Sara May's medical history to be sent to her attorney, but the expiration date noted on the authorization has passed. What action is appropriate according to HIPAA privacy rules?
    A. Do not honor because the authorization is invalid.
    B. Contact the patient to get permission to respond.
    C. Contact the attending physician for permission to respond.
    D. Honor the authorization since the patient obviously approves of the release.

REFERENCE: LaTour, Eichenwald-Maki, and Oachs, pp 618–619
               Sayles, pp 788, 810–812

90. The hospital's strategic plan calls for having the entire health record content recorded in discrete form within the next 10 years. Which system will the HIM Director most likely recommend in the early stages of the project as a transition strategy?
    A. electronic document management system
    B. clinical data repository system
    C. CPOE system
    D. speech recognition system

REFERENCE: Abdelhak, p 196
               McWay (2014), pp 302–303
               Sayles and Trawick, p 153

91. As the Information Security Officer at your facility, you have been asked to provide examples of technical security safeguards adopted as a result of HIPAA legislation. Which of the following would you provide?
    A. audit controls
    B. evidence of security awareness training
    C. surge protectors
    D. workstation use and location

REFERENCE: Green and Bowie, p 283
              LaTour, Eichnewald-Maki, and Oachs, pp 133–134, 332
              McWay (2014), p 292
              Sayles, p 1057

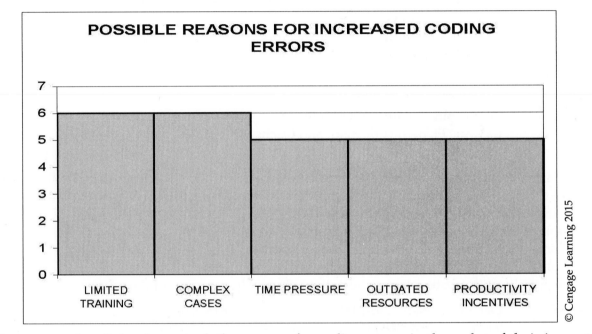

92. After your coders helped you rank the reasons for coding errors in the order of their importance, you then plotted the results on the chart above. The results of your work surprise you because
    A. you expected the coders to put more emphasis on time pressure.
    B. you thought limited training was the primary reason for the errors.
    C. the rankings show surprising disagreement on the issue.
    D. the results appear to violate the Pareto principle.

REFERENCE: LaTour, Eichenwald-Maki, and Oachs, p 823
              McWay (2014), pp 148–149, 274
              Sayles, pp 591–592

93. Joanie Howell presents to Dr. Franklin requesting rhinoplasty. Because Howell is covered by Medicare, Dr. Franklin must provide Howell with
    A. a Notice of Exclusion, because rhinoplasty is not a Medicare covered service.
    B. an Advance Beneficiary Notice, because rhinoplasty is not a Medicare covered service.
    C. a Notice of Exclusion, because Howell's rhinoplasty may not be medically necessary.
    D. an Advance Beneficiary Notice, because Howell's rhinoplasty may not be medically necessary.

REFERENCE: Green and Rowell, pp 463–465
                LaTour, Eichenwald-Maki, and Oachs, pp 449, 894
                Sayles, p 295

94. A 19-year-old former patient faxes a request to your facility requesting the release of his medical records of all episodes of care to the Army. The release of information clerk should
    A. send the records as requested.
    B. inform the young man that specific reports must be identified in his request.
    C. send a letter informing him that faxed requests are not accepted.
    D. deny the request.

REFERENCE: Abdelhak, p 539
                LaTour, Eichenwald-Maki, and Oachs, pp 285, 316–317
                Sayles, p 102

95. A 16-year-old male was treated at your facility for a closed head injury. The patient's 18-year-old wife accompanied him to the hospital and signed the consent for admission and treatment because of the patient's incapacity at the time. The patient has requested that copies of his medical records be sent to his attorney. Who should sign the authorization to release the records?
    A. the patient
    B. either of the patient's parents
    C. the patient's parent or legal guardian
    D. the patient's wife

REFERENCE: Abdelhak, p 538
                LaTour, Eichenwald-Maki, and Oachs, pp 243, 316–317
                Sayles, p 102

96. When a patient is admitted because of a primary neoplasm with metastasis and treatment is directed toward the secondary neoplasm only,
    A. code only the primary neoplasm as the principal diagnosis.
    B. the primary neoplasm is coded as the principal diagnosis, and the secondary neoplasm is coded as an additional diagnosis.
    C. the secondary diagnosis is coded as the principal diagnosis, and the primary neoplasm is coded as an additional diagnosis.
    D. code only the secondary neoplasm as the principal diagnosis.

REFERENCE: AHA, pp 447–449
                Optum (1), p 367

97. A patient initially consulted with Dr. Vasseur at the request of Dr. Meche, the patient's primary care physician. Dr. Vasseur examined the patient, prescribed medication, and ordered tests. Additional visits to Dr. Vasseur's office for continuing care would be assigned from which E/M section?
    A. office and other outpatient services, new patient
    B. office and other outpatient services, established patient
    C. office or other outpatient consultations, new or established patient
    D. confirmatory consultations, new or established patient

REFERENCE: Frisch, pp 77–82
               Johnson and Linker, pp 153–154

98. A transcription unit has been asked to tally the number of times they have to leave sections of a report blank for various reasons (poor dictation technique, background noise, etc.). The quality improvement tool most likely to help collect these data would be
    A. force field analysis.   C. flowchart.
    B. decision matrix.   D. check sheet.

REFERENCE: Johns, pp 619–620
               LaTour, Eichenwald-Maki, and Oachs, p 823
               Sayles, p 578

99. As the Director of a Health Information Technology Program, your community college has been selected to participate in the workforce development of electronic health record specialists as outlined by ARRA and HITECH. In order to keep abreast of changes in this program, you will need to regularly access the Web site of which governmental agency?
    A. ONC
    B. CMS
    C. OSHA
    D. CDC

REFERENCE: LaTour, Eichenwald-Maki, and Oachs, pp 17, 35, 83, 195
               Sayles, p 25

100. The Chief of Staff, Chief of Medicine, President of the Governing Body, and most departmental managers have already completed CQI training. Unfortunately, the hospital administrator has not been to training, refuses to get involved with CQI, and refuses to let the administrative departmental staff get training.
    A. This level of involvement is enough to meet Joint Commission standards.
    B. The Joint Commission only expects involvement from clinical staff.
    C. This will not do because it violates Joint Commission standards and CQI philosophy.
    D. If you can talk him into training his staff, you can let him skip the training.

REFERENCE: LaTour, Eichenwald-Maki, and Oachs, pp 658, 819
               McWay (2014), pp 52–53
               Sayles, pp 567, 572

RECORD COMPLETION INFORMATION FOR DECEMBER				
INCOMPLETE RECORDS	DELINQUENT RECORDS	AVERAGE MONTHLY DISCHARGES	AVERAGE MONTHLY OPERATIVE PROCEDURES	DELINQUENT OPERATIVE REPORTS
604	304	845	526	14

101. Use the information provided in the table above to calculate the delinquent rate. The delinquent rate

    A. cannot be determined.
    B. is 36%.
    C. is 50%.
    D. is 71%.

REFERENCE: Abdelhak, p 128
                  Green and Bowie, p 84
                  LaTour, Eichenwald-Maki, and Oachs, p 652
                  Sayles, p 567

102. The percentage of records delinquent due to the absence of an operative report

    A. is 1.7%.
    B. is 2.7%.
    C. is 4.6%.
    D. cannot be determined from the information given.

REFERENCE: Abdelhak, p 128
                  Green and Bowie, p 84
                  LaTour, Eichenwald-Maki, and Oachs, p 652

103. The purpose of the Correct Coding Initiative is to

    A. increase fines and penalties for bundling services into comprehensive CPT codes.
    B. restrict Medicare reimbursement to hospitals for ancillary services.
    C. teach coders how to unbundle codes.
    D. detect and prevent payment for improperly coded services.

REFERENCE: LaTour, Eichenwald-Maki, and Oachs, pp 447–448
                  Sayles, p 289

104. Access to radiologic images has been improved through the use of which of the following?

    A. LOINC
    B. PACS
    C. EDMS
    D. CPOE

REFERENCE: Abdelhak, p 229
                  LaTour, Eichenwald, and Oachs, pp 124, 249
                  Sayles, p 914
                  Sayles and Trawick, pp 229–230

105. The difference between an Institutional Review Board (IRB) and a hospital's Ethics Committee is that
    A. the IRB focuses on patient care only, and the Ethics Committee addresses both patient care and business practices.
    B. the Ethics Committee reviews ethics complaints, and the IRB focuses on developing policies and procedures.
    C. the IRB deals with the ethical treatment of human research subjects, and the Ethics Committee covers a wide range of issues.
    D. the IRB is made up entirely of patient care providers, and the Ethics Committee is multidisciplinary.

REFERENCE: LaTour, Eichenwald-Maki, and Oachs, pp 558, 580, 608, 913
            McWay (2014), pp 241–248
            Sayles, p 752

106. A common goal of the Office of the National Coordinator for Health Information Technology, RHIOs, and a national infrastructure for information is
    A. translating images into a digital format.
    B. sharing information among providers.
    C. transferring health information within a hospital system.
    D. promoting telemedicine.

REFERENCE: LaTour, Eichenwald-Maki, and Oachs, pp 17, 83, 117, 137, 204, 212
            Sayles, pp 34, 162
            Sayles and Trawick, pp 336–367

107. According to CPT, a biopsy of the breast that involves removal of only a portion of the lesion for pathologic examination is
    A. percutaneous.   C. excisional.
    B. incisional.   D. punch.

REFERENCE: Johnson and Linker, pp 224–225

108. Your facility would like to improve physician documentation in order to allow improved coding. As coding supervisor, you have found it very effective to provide the physicians with
    A. a copy of the facility coding guidelines, along with written information on improved documentation.
    B. the UHDDS and information on where each data element is collected and/or verified in your facility.
    C. regular in-service presentations on documentation, including its importance and tips for improvement.
    D. feedback on specific instances when improved documentation would improve coding.

REFERENCE: Abdelhak, pp 197–199
            LaTour, Eichenwald-Maki, and Oachs, pp 243, 442, 470
            Sales, pp 121, 292–293, 306–307

109. A piece of objective data collected upon initial assessment of the patient is the
    A. review of systems.   C. chief complaint.
    B. history of present illness. D. vital signs.

REFERENCE: Abdelhak, pp 108–109
            Green and Bowie, pp 145–148
            LaTour, Eichenwald-Maki, and Oachs, pp 245–246

110. You are the Director of Coding and Billing at a large group practice. The Practice Manager stops by your office on his way to a planning meeting to ask about the timeline for complying with HITECH requirements to adopt meaningful use EHR technology. You reply that the incentives began in 2011 and end in 2014. You remind him that by 2015, sanctions for noncompliance will appear in the form of
    A. downward adjustments to Medicare reimbursement.
    B. withdrawal of permission to treat Medicare and Medicaid patients.
    C. a mandatory action plan for implementing a meaningful use EHR.
    D. monetary fines up to $100,000.

REFERENCE: LaTour, Eichenwald, and Maki, pp 264–265
             McWay (2014), p 305
             Sayles, pp 954, 987

111. A number of key elements for your facility's computerized patient record are still input by clerical staff from handwritten data entry sheets. You are concerned about the transfer of data. If the vital signs stored in the database are not what were originally recorded, the impact on patient care could be severe. You are concerned about the
    A. stability of the data.   C. legitimacy of the data.
    B. validity of the data.   D. reliability of the data.

REFERENCE: Abdelhak, pp 410–411
             Green and Bowie, p 257
             Koch, p 249
             LaTour, Eichenwald-Maki, and Oachs, pp 90, 129, 205–206, 382, 385, 956
             McWay (2014), p 143
             Sayles, p 462

112. ORYX is a program that was developed by
    A. CMS to track Medicare costs.
    B. Joint Commission to link patient outcomes to accreditation.
    C. NIH to track communicable diseases.
    D. AMA to allow for rapid CPT updates.

REFERENCE: Green and Bowie, p 30
             LaTour, Eichenwald-Maki, and Oachs, pp 21, 201, 906, 936
             McWay (2014), p 188
             Sayles, pp 155–156

113. In preparation for conversion to a computerized patient record, a committee at your facility is defining each of the data elements in a patient record to determine which elements should be required and to set parameters for each element. The committee is working on the data
    A. edits.   C. dictionary.
    B. reasonableness. D. feasibility.

REFERENCE: Abdelhak, pp 502–503
             Eichenwald-Maki and Peterson, pp 37–38
             Green and Bowie, pp 250–253
             LaTour, Eichenwald-Maki, and Oachs, pp 202, 368, 383, 907
             McWay (2014), p 262
             Sayles, pp 882, 954, 987

114. An effective means of protecting the security of computerized health information would be to
    A. require all facility employees to change their passwords at least once a month.
    B. write detailed procedures for the entry of data into the computerized information system.
    C. install a system that would require fingerprint scanning and recognition for data access.
    D. develop clear policies on data security that are supported by the top management of the facility.

REFERENCE: Abdelhak, pp 285–288
              LaTour, Eichenwald-Maki, and Oachs, pp 129, 134, 160, 172, 204, 316, 318, 319, 328, 336, 343–344
              McWay (2014), pp 291–293
              Sayles, pp 12, 131, 415, 794, 829–830

115. In reviewing the policies on release of information in respect to the privacy rules, you note that it is still acceptable to allow release of protected health information without patient permission to
    A. the patient's spouse.
    B. a health care provider interested in the case.
    C. the quality assurance committee for review purposes.
    D. a third-party payer with a direct interest in the case.

REFERENCE: LaTour, Eichenwald-Maki, and Oachs, pp 314, 318–319
              Sayles, p 799

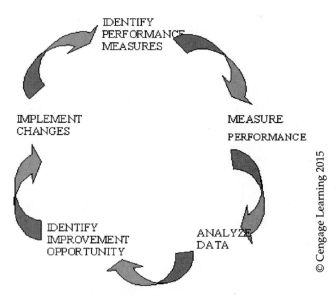

116. Your facility has a team that has been working to develop a strong performance improvement model, and they have come up with the model shown above. The team asks if you see anything missing from the model. You tell them they
    A. are missing a step requiring regular employee input into the process.
    B. are missing a step requiring reporting to the board of directors.
    C. are missing a step requiring ongoing monitoring and reassessment.
    D. aren't missing any steps; the model is a good one.

REFERENCE: LaTour, Eichenwald-Maki, and Oachs, pp 659–660
              McWay (2014), p 185
              Sayles, p 799

117. Part of your job description is to educate physicians regarding proper documentation policies and standards. You are the
    A. Information Security Manager.
    B. Clinical Data Specialist.
    C. Health Information Manager.
    D. Risk Manager.

REFERENCE: Green and Bowie, pp 98–99
LaTour, Eichenwald-Maki, and Oachs, pp 67, 902
Sayles, p 936

118. Your hospital has purchased a number of outpatient facilities. You have been assigned to chair an interdisciplinary committee that will write record retention policies for the new corporation. You begin by telling the committee their primary consideration when making retention decisions must be
    A. space considerations.
    B. statutory requirements.
    C. provider preferences.
    D. professional standards.

REFERENCE: Abdelhak, pp 196–197
LaTour, Eichenwald-Maki, and Oachs, pp 284–285, 288, 311–312
McWay (2014), pp 136–138
Sayles, pp 788–789

119. A major drug company wants to promote a fundraiser targeting patients with congestive heart failure. The drug company representative has requested a list of patients treated at your facility. As privacy and security officer, you tell them that
    A. they just need to send a written request for the list.
    B. a prior authorization is required before any PHI can be released.
    C. you will need to confer with the medical director.
    D. if the fundraising was conducted by a business associate without authorization, and the funds were to benefit your facility (the covered entity), that you could disclose the information.

REFERENCE: LaTour, Eichenwald-Maki, and Oachs, p 318
Sayles, pp 827–828, 836, 1050, 1160

120. Your facility is storing scanned records for long-term storage on optical disk. The Risk Management Committee's Disaster Task Force has recommended that copies of the disks be stored at a facility across town. The administrator is concerned that records may be altered on the disks stored off-site. You tell the administrator
    A. this is a legitimate concern; it should be addressed in the contract written with the storage facility.
    B. this is not a concern because WORM technology makes it impossible to alter the documents.
    C. this is a legitimate concern; perhaps the committee should consider storing duplicates in two locations in this facility.
    D. this is not a concern; there is really no need to make and store duplicate disks as they are difficult to damage.

REFERENCE: Abdelhak, pp 190–191
LaTour, Eichenwald-Maki, and Oachs, pp 87, 278
Sayles, pp 346, 1032

121. The Pharmacy and Therapeutics Committee has asked you to find out more about a computerized order entry system that calculates drug dosages based on patient parameters (weight, age, etc.) and even suggests the best drug given the patient's diagnosis and current treatment. The committee is asking for information on a(n)

    A. application system.
    B. clinical decision support system.
    C. ordering system.
    D. practice parameters system.

REFERENCE: Abdelhak, pp 179–180
            LaTour, Eichenwald-Maki, and Oachs, pp 94–95, 115, 118, 125–127
            Sayles, pp 915, 964–965

122. A portion of a deficiency slip is reproduced below. This patient was discharged yesterday. Your greatest concern regarding deficiencies on this record would be the missing

Physician: Hunter, J. T.				
Missing Signatures				**Missing Reports**
X	History			Diagnoses/Procedure
	Physical			History
	Consultative Report			Physical
X	Operative Report			Consultation Report
	Discharge Summary		X	Operative Report
	X-ray Report			Discharge Summary
	Other			X-ray Report
				Others

    A. signature on the physical exam.
    B. signature on the discharge summary.
    C. diagnoses and procedures.
    D. operative report.

REFERENCE: Abdelhak, p 129
            Green and Bowie, pp 99, 165

123. In the past, Joint Commission standards have focused on promoting the use of a facility approved abbreviation list to be used by hospital care providers. With the advent of the Commission's national patient safety goals, the focus has shifted to the

    A. prohibited use of any abbreviations.
    B. flagrant use of specialty-specific abbreviations.
    C. use of prohibited or "dangerous" abbreviations.
    D. use of abbreviations used in the final diagnoses.

REFERENCE: Abdelhak, p 117
            Sayles, pp 72–74, 406, 786

124. Annual costs for the only Release of Information Clerk at Jacksonville Beach Healthcare Center (salary and benefits) are $36,429. The monthly cost for the copier used solely for ROI is $89 (supplies and repairs). It costs the department $0.95 on average for ROI mailings (envelopes and postage). There were 687 requests filled for ROI last month. The cost per request for release of information last month was

    A. $4.42.
    B. $4.55.
    C. $4.63.
    D. $5.50.

REFERENCE: Horton, p 140

125. The decision makers in the HIM department have decided to use the decision analysis matrix method to select coding software. Use of this method will help ensure
    A. all alternatives/vendors are evaluated subjectively.
    B. the personalities of individual vendors will not influence the decision.
    C. consistent criteria are used to evaluate the alternatives/vendors.
    D. the level of software support will be considered in the decision.

REFERENCE: Abdelhak, p 626
             LaTour, Eichenwald-Maki, and Oachs, pp 601–602
             Sayles, p 759

126. Many of the departments in your facility create and modify forms often. A major key to forms control in this setting is
    A. consistent formatting of each page of each form.
    B. capturing every data item required by UHDDS.
    C. giving each form or view an identifiable name, number, and revision date.
    D. providing instructions when necessary for appropriate data fields.

REFERENCE: Abdelhak, pp 119–120
             Green and Bowie, pp 201–202
             LaTour, Eichenwald-Maki, and Oachs, pp 335, 337
             McWay (2014), pp 131–132
             Sayles, p 357

Record #	Patient Last Name	Date of Birth	Date of Service
32-15-65	Smith	02/3/76	3/20/2011
02-45-77	Cook	09/12/86	10/21/2011
10-88-48	Baker	01/23/24	11/14/2011

127. Which means of data modeling is illustrated in the table shown above?
    A. entity-relationship model   C. data management model
    B. object-oriented model   D. relational data model

REFERENCE: Abdelhak, pp 268–270
             LaTour, Eichenwald-Maki, and Oachs, pp 128–129
             Sayles, pp 879–881, 900, 992–993

128. Which of the following is the unique identifier in the database illustrated in the table for question 127?
    A. record number   C. date of birth
    B. patient's last name   D. date of service

REFERENCE: Abdelhak, p 190
             LaTour, Eichenwald-Maki, and Oachs, p 129
             Sayles, pp 880–881

129. Stage I of meaningful use focuses on data capture and sharing. Which of the following is included in the menu set of objectives for eligible hospitals in this stage?
   A. Use CPOE for medication orders
   B. Smoking cessation counseling for MI patients
   C. Appropriate use of HL-7 standards
   D. Establish critical pathways for complex, high-dollar cases

REFERENCE: HealthIT.hhs.gov
   LaTour, Eichenwald-Maki, and Oachs, pp 204–212, 219–221, 856–857
   McWay (2010), pp 305–309
   Sayles, p 144

130. As supervisor of the cancer registry, you report the registry's annual caseload to administration. The most efficient way to retrieve this information would be to use
   A. patient abstracts.
   B. patient index.
   C. accession register.
   D. follow-up files.

REFERENCE: Johns, p 487
   LaTour, Eichenwald-Maki, and Oachs, p 371
   Sayles, p 439

131. A supervisor reviews a job to determine the required content, skills, knowledge, abilities, and responsibilities for the position. The tasks are grouped and lines of responsibility and authority are defined. The supervisor is writing a job
   A. description.
   B. analysis.
   C. process.
   D. detail.

REFERENCE: Abdelhak, pp 586–587
   LaTour, Eichenwald-Maki, and Oachs, p 723
   McWay (2014), p 334
   Sayles, p 1121

132. The emergency department staff has complained that the clerical staff in your department is delaying stat reports. You decide to meet with your staff and develop a cause and effect diagram to determine possible reasons for the delay. You have explained the issue to your staff and have set up a blank cause and effect diagram. The next step is to
   A. discuss the importance of prompt delivery of stat reports.
   B. determine whether there are internal conflicts in the area.
   C. brainstorm possible reasons for delays in delivering the reports.
   D. design a new system that will support prompt report delivery.

REFERENCE: Abdelhak, p 455
   LaTour, Eichenwald-Maki, and Oachs, pp 821–822
   McWay (2014), p 179
   Sayles, p 585

133. As your meeting with the clerical staff on the stat report continues, one clerk suggests a possible reason for the delays is a lack of training concerning the nature of stat reports. On the cause and effect diagram, this would most appropriately be listed under
   A. personnel.
   B. equipment.
   C. materials.
   D. methods.

REFERENCE: Abdelhak, p 455
   LaTour, Eichenwald-Maki, and Oachs, pp 822–823
   McWay (2014), p 179
   Sayles, p 528

	Rule 1	Rule 2	Rule 3	Rule 4
Condition 1				
Condition 1				
Condition 1				
Condition 1				
Action1				
Action 2				
Action 3				
Action 4				

134. You stop by the office to meet a friend for lunch. Looking on her desk, you see the grid above. Your friend is trying to
    A. plan a conversion.
    B. design a system.
    C. analyze a workflow.
    D. make a decision.

REFERENCE: Abdelhak, pp 626–627
              LaTour, Eichenwald-Maki, and Oachs, p 695

SAINT JOSEPH HOSPITAL CODING PRODUCTIVITY WEEK ENDING JANUARY 4, 2012			
EMPLOYEE NUMBER	INPATIENT	OUTPATIENT PROCEDURE	EMERGENCY OR OBSERVATION
425	120	35	16
426	48	89	95
427	80	92	4
428	65	109	16

135. The performance standard for coders is 28–33 workload units per day. Workload units are calculated as follows:
        Inpatient record = 1 workload unit
        Outpatient surgical procedure records = 0.75 workload units
        Outpatient observation/emergency records = 0.50 workload units
    One week's productivity information is shown in the table above. What percentage of the coders is meeting the productivity standards?
    A. 100%
    B. 75%
    C. 50%
    D. 25%

REFERENCE: Abdelhak, p 619
              McWay (2014), p 221

136. The coding supervisor tends to deal with issues as they come up, prioritizing only when problems are pressing or appear to be important to upper management. This crisis manager is particularly weak in which management function?
    A. planning
    B. organizing
    C. controlling
    D. budgeting

REFERENCE: Abdelhak, p 616
             LaTour, Eichenwald-Maki, and Oachs, pp 686, 690
             McWay (2014), p 338

137. As a new HIM manager, you recognize that employee development is a necessary investment for the long-term survival and growth of the organization. Your goal is to design and implement a staff development program for your employees, so one of your first steps is to
    A.   implement training programs that emphasize teamwork.
    B.   establish a budget for all hospital employee training.
    C.   survey the HIM employees to assess their need for new skills or knowledge.
    D.   establish HIPAA training programs hospital-wide.

REFERENCE: Abdelhak, p 585
             LaTour, Eichenwald-Maki, and Oachs, pp 736, 739
             McWay (2014), pp 290, 303–304
             Sayles, pp 1106–1111

138. Now that the EHR has been fully implemented, you are ready to move old records to basement storage. You are ordering shelving for those old paper files. You have 18,000 records. The files average is three files per filing inch. The shelf units you have selected have six shelves that will hold 34 inches per shelf. You will have to plan for a 20% expansion rate to accommodate miscellaneous paper records over the next 10 years. How many shelving units should you order?
    A. 30
    B. 31
    C. 35
    D. 36

REFERENCE: Green and Bowie, pp 218–219
             LaTour, Eichenwald-Maki, and Oachs, p 274
             Sayles, pp 338–339

139. Postage charges in the Health Information Department have increased during the last quarter. The department director has seen metered envelopes in the mail bin that do not appear to be those used for departmental business. The best course of action for the director would be to
    A. remove the postage meter from the department.
    B. keep a watchful eye on the meter and who uses it.
    C. issue employee warnings at the next departmental meeting.
    D. assign responsibility for the postage meter to one employee.

REFERENCE: LaTour, Eichenwald-Maki, and Oachs, p 750
             McWay (2014), p 335

140. A clerk's work performance has diminished dramatically during the past 2 weeks. The supervisor initiates a discussion with the clerk, during which the clerk reveals that he recently accepted that he has an alcohol addiction. The clerk states an intention to quit drinking completely. The supervisor should
    A. terminate the clerk if it can be proved that alcohol was used on the job.
    B. suspend the clerk if alcohol has diminished the clerk's job performance.
    C. give the clerk a leave of absence until these problems can be resolved.
    D. refer the clerk to the facility's Employee Assistance Program.

REFERENCE: Abdelhak, p 602
McWay (2014), pp 376–377

141. Everyone in the Health Information Department has been working overtime to complete a major record conversion. The supervisor will have to plan for overtime pay for all personnel who are not
    A. hourly employees.
    B. salaried exempt employees.
    C. salaried nonexempt employees.
    D. temporary employees.

REFERENCE: Abdelhak, p 578
LaTour, Eichenwald-Maki, and Oachs, p 728
McWay (2014), pp 364–365

142. The coder works 7.5 hours per day. If a time standard is determined from sample observations to be 2.50 minutes per record for coding emergency room records, what is the daily standard for the number of records coded when a 15% fatigue factor is allowed?
    A. 153 records per day
    B. 180 records per day
    C. 192 records per day
    D. 200 records per day

REFERENCE: Horton, pp 135–140
McWay (2014), pp 221–226

143. The correspondence section of your department receives an average of 50 requests per day for release of information. It takes an average of 30 minutes to fulfill each request. Using 6.5 productive hours per day as your standard, calculate the staffing needs for the correspondence section.
    A. 3.8 FTE
    B. 2.5 FTE
    C. 3 FTE
    D. 4 FTE

REFERENCE: Horton, pp 14, 18
Koch, p 55

144. Your hospital takes advantage of the 8/80 exemption for health care facilities. Assuming that no employee worked more than 8 hours in a day, which of the employees listed in the table below will be paid overtime this pay period?

EMPLOYEE NUMBER	SCHEDULED HOURS PER WEEK	ACTUAL HOURS THIS WEEK	ACTUAL HOURS LAST WEEK
101	40	42	40
102	40	38	42
103	30	40	40
104	20	22	24
105	40	40	48

    A. Employees 101 and 105
    B. Employees 101, 102, and 105
    C. Employees 101, 104, and 105
    D. Employees 101, 103, 104, and 105

REFERENCE: Abdelhak, p 578

145. During the work sampling of a file clerk's activity, it is noted that the employee is speaking on the telephone during 76 of 300 observations. How much of the employee's time is spent on the phone if the employee works 7 hours a day?
    A. 1.77 hours
    B. 3.28%
    C. 3.94 hours
    D. 9.2%

REFERENCE: Horton, p 14
               Koch, pp 52–54

146. You are conducting an educational session on benchmarking. You tell your audience that the key to benchmarking is to use the comparison to
    A. implement your QI process.
    B. make recommendations for improvement.
    C. improve your department's processes.
    D. compare your department with another.

REFERENCE: Abdelhak, p 452
               LaTour, Eichenwald-Maki, and Oachs, p 708
               McWay (2014), p 179
               Sayles, pp 449, 1222

147. In conducting an educational session for your staff about implementing a benchmarking program, you tell your staff that when an organization uses benchmarking, it is important to compare your facility's outcomes to
    A. nationally known facilities.
    B. larger facilities.
    C. facilities within your corporation.
    D. facilities with superior performance.

REFERENCE: Abdelhak, p 452
               LaTour, Eichenwald-Maki, and Oachs, p 708
               McWay (2014), p 179
               Sayles, pp 449, 1222

148. You supervise five clerical employees who will be moving when a new wing of your facility is completed. When you meet with the architect to plan their space, you will ask for
A. 200 square feet of space for your clerical staff.
B. 250 square feet of space for your clerical staff.
C. 300 square feet of space for your clerical staff.
D. 350 square feet of space for your clerical staff.

REFERENCE: Abdelhak, pp 647–649

149. How long will it take to complete the project described below?

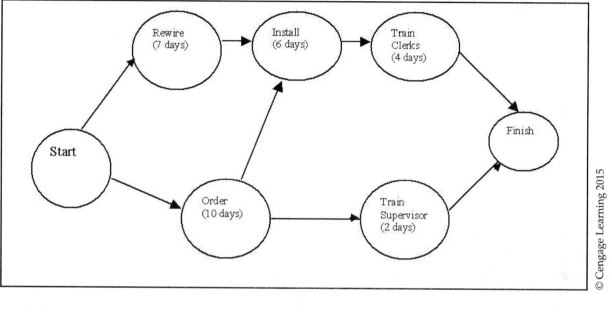

A. 12 days   C. 20 days
B. 17 days   D. 29 days

REFERENCE: Abdelhak, pp 638–640
McWay (2014), pp 345–346

150. The file clerks in your department's main file area report that they are able to locate 400 out of 450 requested records during the past month. There are a total of 4,500 records in the main file. What is the area's accuracy rate?
A. 1.1%   C. 10.0%
B. 8.9%   D. 88.9%

REFERENCE: Calculation

END OF THE RHIT MOCK EXAMINATION

FOR THE RHIA MOCK EXAMINATION CONTINUE TESTING AND COMPLETE THE REMAINING 30 QUESTIONS.

151. Encoding software was installed at your hospital 2 years ago. The coders are well trained on it and like using it. It functions well and only requires ICD code updates yearly. In terms of the Information Systems Life Cycle phases, the coding system is likely in the
   A. design phase.
   B. implementation phase.
   C. operation and maintenance phase.
   D. obsolescence or decline phase.

REFERENCE: Abdelhak, pp 303–307
   LaTour, Eichenwald-Maki, and Oachs, p 105
   McWay (2014), p 286

152. A clerical-level employee reports an incident in which the clerk felt the first-line supervisor discriminated on the basis of the clerk's gender. The best action for you to take at this time is to
   A. thoroughly investigate the matter and document your findings.
   B. talk with the first-line supervisor to determine what happened.
   C. ask the other clerical level staff if they have had similar experiences.
   D. ask the clerk to provide objective evidence of the discrimination.

REFERENCE: Abdelhak, pp 601–603
   LaTour, Eichenwald-Maki, and Oachs, p 756

153. A section of a job description states that the incumbent will handle day-to-day operations in the transcription and release of information areas. This section defines the
   A. skills required to perform the job.
   B. time required for each function.
   C. authority associated with the job.
   D. scope of responsibility in the job.

REFERENCE: Abdelhak, pp 587–588
   LaTour, Eichenwald-Maki, and Oachs, p 723
   McWay (2014), p 334

154. There are 15 employees in your department. There were 21 working days last month. There were a total of 12 lost workdays last month due to absenteeism of all types. The absenteeism rate for your department last month was
   A. 21%.
   B. 57%.
   C. 4%.
   D. 5%.

REFERENCE: Calculation

155. You have been the supervisor in quality management at Naples Hospital for almost a year now and your appraisal is right around the corner. Your director has asked the members of your staff and the physicians on the committees you service to complete forms that will provide input into the appraisal process. In addition, you have been asked to formally assess your own progress in this new position. It is time–consuming and more than a little intimidating, but you suppose it will provide you with some good insights into the quality of your work. Because you are, after all, the supervisor in QM, it is only fair that you participate fully in your facility's commitment to

A. participative evaluation.   C. conductive evaluation.

B. 360-degree evaluation.   D. managed evaluation.

REFERENCE: Abdelhak pp 594–599

                 LaTour, Eichenwald-Maki, and Oachs, p 755

                 McWay (2014), pp 300–301

                 Sayles, p 1102

156. You are a new supervisor in the HIM department and find it difficult to deal with performance issues. Laney, an employee in the Release of Information section, has been late several times this month. She has already been given a verbal warning. She was late again today. According to the progressive discipline process, your next step will be to

A. reinforce the institution's policies.

B. reissue the verbal warning.

C. suspend the employee.

D. issue a written warning.

REFERENCE: Abdelhak, pp 601–603

                 LaTour, Eichenwald-Maki, and Oachs, pp 755–756

                 McWay (2014), p 378

                 Sayles, p 1103

157. The CFO of your facility asks you to prepare a budget for the fiscal year based on the past volume and expected capacity for the coming year. This process is an example of using the "_____" budgeting method.

A. rolling budget   C. flexible or statistics budget

B. fixed budget   D. zero-based budget

REFERENCE: Abdelhak, p 797

                 LaTour, Eichenwald-Maki, and Oachs, p 785

158. The committee that is preparing your acute care hospital for an electronic health record is planning for an imaging system for record archiving in the immediate future. They are looking for a solution for data interfacing or integration of the imaging system into other computer systems. You recommend

A. data dictionary guidelines.

B. Health Level 7 standards.

C. Regional Health Information Organization guidelines.

D. Joint Commission standards.

REFERENCE: Abdelhak, pp 168–170

                 LaTour, Eichenwald-Maki, and Oachs, p 206

                 Johns, pp 996 168–169, 894

159. Your facility has decided to purchase an integrated patient information system. Your part in the initial work plan is to develop system specifications that will ultimately be sent out to vendors who will potentially submit a bid on your system. You are working on the systems specs that will become part of the
    A. CPR.
    B. IRB.
    C. RFP.
    D. CRS.

REFERENCE: Abdelhak, pp 337–346
              LaTour, Eichenwald-Maki, and Oachs, pp 105–106
              McWay (2014), p 401
              Sayles, pp 862, 1117

160. Reference checks are conducted on potential employees to help assess the applicant's fit with the position and also to
    A. confirm the accuracy of information provided on the application.
    B. uncover skills the applicant may have neglected to report.
    C. get another opinion on the applicant's emotional stability.
    D. alert the past employer that the applicant is job hunting.

REFERENCE: Abdelhak, pp 590–593
              LaTour, Eichenwald-Maki, and Oachs, p 720
              McWay (2014), p 363
              Sayles, p 1097

161. In order to perform their jobs, facility employees should have full and timely access only to the information they need to complete the task at hand. This is similar to HIPAA's provision for
    A. a Notice of Privacy Practices (NOPP).
    B. amending a record.
    C. accessing need to know information only.
    D. an informed consent.

REFERENCE: Abdelhak, p 529
              LaTour, Eichenwald-Maki, and Oachs, p 273
              Sayles, pp 54, 756, 1037, 1062

162. Authentication is one of the components necessary to produce a legal document in an EHR. This means
    A. tracking changes in the EHR system.
    B. establishing access controls for individual employees.
    C. creating audit trails.
    D. identifying who created a document and when.

REFERENCE: Abdelhak, p 191
              LaTour, Eichenwald-Maki, and Oachs, pp 264, 334
              Sayles, pp 366, 974, 1184

Patients with diabetes participated in a study to determine the effectiveness of a new drug, Glucodown.

The drug was taken at bedtime. The drug company expected patients taking Glucodown to have a normal early morning fasting blood sugar level. The null hypothesis for the study follows.

There will be no difference in fasting early morning blood sugar levels between patients taking Glucodown and patients taking a placebo.

Half the patients were given Glucodown. Half were given a placebo.

Early morning fasting blood sugar levels are reported below.

Patient	STUDY GROUP (patients receiving Glucodown)					CONTROL GROUP (patients receiving placebo)				
	1	2	3	4	5	6	7	8	9	10
Day 1	102	89	114	95	114	143	160	128	128	106
Day 2	100	83	112	98	99	147	165	111	125	110
Day 3	106	84	103	99	95	139	156	106	115	111
Day 4	100	86	114	102	98	150	168	110	128	114
Day 5	98	88	109	98	91	142	159	102	122	110

163. Based on this information, you would expect the researchers to
    A. accept the null hypothesis.
    B. reject the null hypothesis.
    C. restate the null hypothesis.
    D. draw no conclusions.

REFERENCE: Abdelhak, p 389
             LaTour, Eichenwald-Maki, and Oachs, pp 528, 532–536, 571–573, 935

164. The researchers in the previous question wonder if there is any relationship between patient age and average fasting blood sugar. The best data display tool the researchers could use to look for a possible relationship would be a
    A. Pareto diagram.
    B. line graph.
    C. scatter diagram.
    D. cause and effect diagram.

REFERENCE: Abdelhak, pp 382–385
             LaTour, Eichenwald-Maki, and Oachs, p 824
             Sayles, pp 529, 591

165. You have been asked to reduce your department's operating budget by 20%. In order to do so, you will have to effect reductions in your largest budget line. You will have to make cuts in
    A. equipment.
    B. personnel.
    C. supplies.
    D. contracts.

REFERENCE: Abdelhak, pp 676–677
             LaTour, Eichenwald-Maki, and Oachs, p 786
             Sayles, p 1090

166. Take a look at the comparison of the two life cycles below.

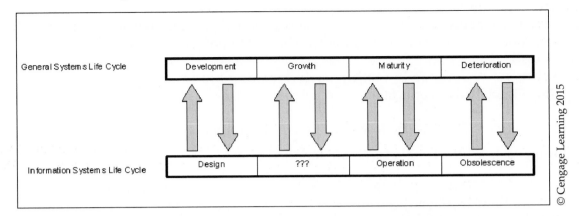

Look at the cell in the Information Systems Life Cycle that is filled with question marks. Which of the following should replace those question marks to make a complete, correct comparison?
A. Growth
B. Installation
C. Implementation
D. Reevaluation

REFERENCE: Abdelhak, pp 340–307
LaTour, Eichenwald-Maki, and Oachs, p 105
McWay (2014), pp 286–288
Sayles, pp 857, 900

167. The use of "public" and "private" keys is part of what type of data protection?
A. Firewalls
B. Biometrics
C. Encryption
D. Phishing

REFERENCE: Abdelhak, p 289
LaTour, Eichenwald-Maki, and Oachs, p 100
Sayles, pp 1042–1043

168. In your job as Chief Security Officer, you are evaluating software programs that will support your policy on sound terminal controls within your facility. One of the features you include in your request for information to vendors is
A. auto log off.
B. encryption.
C. voice recognition feature.
D. unique identifier for log-on.

REFERENCE: Sayles, p 1021
Sayles and Trawick, pp 310, 319

169. The most sophisticated level of interoperability of an EHR and other such systems is the
_____ level.
   A. basic
   B. functional
   C. semantic
   D. exchange

REFERENCE: Abdelhak, pp 218–219
             LaTour, Eichenwald-Maki, and Oachs, p 397

170. As the Project Manager for the upcoming EHR implementation, you ask your assistant to develop
a work breakdown structure (WBS). Critical to implementations and project success, the WBS
   A. lists steps needed to complete the project.
   B. determines dependencies among project tasks.
   C. describes project responsibilities.
   D. defines the project's critical path.

REFERENCE: Abdelhak, p 639
             LaTour, Eichenwald-Maki, and Oachs, p 842

171. As the HIM manager in charge of your department's budget, you are mandated to report on
variances of more than 6% either positive or negative to your Chief Financial Officer and include
the reasons for the variance and any action plans necessary. Based on the table below for the
December variance report, what category would you be required to report on to the CFO?

Variance Report for December			
Description	December Budget	December Actual	Variance
Office Supplies	5,120	5,550	(430)
Contract Services	8,500	8,340	160
Travel	3,500	3,700	(200)
Education	2,500	2,400	100

   A. office supplies   C.   travel
   B. contract services   D.   education

REFERENCE: Abdelhak, p 676
             LaTour, Eichenwald-Maki, and Oachs, pp 786–788
             McWay (2014), p 398

172. Evidence-based management and decision making is an emerging model now used to make more
informed decisions. The premise of this model is
   A. using intuition based on previous experience.
   B. using a decision tree with branches that show the alternatives.
   C. using the best clinical and research practices available.
   D. using an alternative that meets minimum requirements.

REFERENCE: Abdelhak, p 444
             LaTour, Eichenwald-Maki, and Oachs, p 128
             Sayles, pp 685, 962

Document Imaging Implementation						
Beginning Date:	December 2012		**Planning Date:**	October	2012	
Activity	**Assigned:**	**October 2012**	**November 2012**	**December 2012**	**January 9, 2013**	**February 9, 2013**
Kickoff	Team	•				
RFP	PM	•				
System Anal	PM	•				
Design	ITS		•			
RFP eval	Team			•		
Select Vendor	Team			•		
Purchase	CFO/ITS				•	
Build System	ITS				•	
Implement	Team					•

173. As a member of the project team for document imaging implementation, you were asked to provide the information in the grid above. This is an example of a
    A. PERT diagram.
    B. Gantt chart.
    C. PMBOK chart.
    D. work flow diagram.

REFERENCE: Abdelhak, p 640
                LaTour, Eichenwald-Maki, and Oachs, p 107

174. A tool that is used to illustrate the various applications, support structures, and sequencing of implementation phases for a system is a
    A. work flow diagram.
    B. migration path.
    C. milestone chart.
    D. PERTT diagram.

REFERENCE: LaTour, Eichenwald-Maki, and Oachs, pp 119–121
                Sayles, pp 1005–1007

175. A _____ uses a private tunnel through the Internet as a transport medium between locations for secure access and transmission.
    A. TCPIP protocol
    B. firewall
    C. hub
    D. VPN

REFERENCE: Abdelhak, pp 283–284
                LaTour, Eichenwald-Maki, and Oachs, p 33
                Sayles, p 219
                Sayles and Trawick, p 382

176. A technique that uncovers new information from existing information by probing data sets is known as
    A. data mining.
    C. neural network analysis.
    B. systems query language (SQL).
    D. data warehousing.

REFERENCE: Abdelhak, p 292
                LaTour, Eichenwald-Maki, and Oachs, pp 86, 539, 569, 908
                Sayles, pp 381, 887, 925

177. Your HIM department is moving to a new location and in order to arrange your employees and functions for optimal work flow efficiency and to decide which employees need to be placed close to each other, the tool you decide to use is a
    A. data flow diagram.
    C. proximity chart or movement diagram.
    B. PERT chart.
    D. flow process chart.

REFERENCE: LaTour, Eichenwald-Maki, and Oachs, p 821

178. A *p* value of less than 0.05 is what researchers commonly use to reject the null hypothesis. A smaller *p* value may place interpretation of the results of the study at risk for a
    A. sampling error.
    C. type 1 (a) error.
    B. stratification error.
    D. type 2 (b) error.

REFERENCE: Abdelhak, p 389
                LaTour, Eichenwald-Maki, and Oachs, pp 579–580

179. Which of the following employees would be considered exempt under the Fair Labor Standards Act?
    A. the head of the Department of Health Information Services who is involved in decision making and planning 90% of the time
    B. the coding supervisor who has responsibility for three employees and performs analysis and coding 80% of the time
    C. the departmental secretary who is responsible for performing a variety of clerical and administrative tasks
    D. the sole employee in the physician's workroom who has responsibility for maintaining and tracking medical record deficiencies

REFERENCE: Abdelhak, p 578
                McWay (2014), p 367

180. In order to prevent the accidental introduction of a virus into your facility's local area network, your facility has a policy that strictly prohibits
    A. doing personal work on the computer system, even during personal time.
    B. sharing disks from one workstation to another within the facility.
    C. downloading executable files from electronic bulletin boards.
    D. sending or receiving e-mail from addresses that have not been authorized.

REFERENCES: LaTour, Eichenwald-Maki, and Oachs, pp 383–384
                Sayles, pp 577, 934–935, 1037, 1256
                Sayles and Trawick, pp 326, 379

END OF RHIA MOCK EXAMINATION

Answer Key for the Mock Examination

ANSWER | EXPLANATION

1. B
2. D
3. D
4. D Progress note elements written in the acronym "SOAP" style are:
   S-subjective; records what the patient states is the problem
   O-objective; records what the practitioner identifies through history, physical examination, and diagnostic tests
   A-assessment; combines the subjective and objective into a conclusion
   P-plan; what approach is going to be taken to resolve the problem
5. D
6. B Calculation: $\underline{169.051 \text{ total relative weight}}$ = 2.965807
            57 total patients seen

7. A The interdisciplinary care plan is the foundation around which patient care is organized. It contains input from the unique perspective of each discipline involved. It includes an assessment, statement of goals, identification of specific activities, or strategies to achieve those goals and periodic assessment of goal attainment.

8. D
9. B Calculations: Reimbursement from payor for one well child visit equals total reimbursement divided by number of visits to the clinic.

INSURANCE COMPANY	NUMBER OF WELL CHILD VISITS	REIMBURSEMENT FROM PAYER FOR WELL CHILD VISITS	REIMBURSEMENT FROM PAYER FOR ONE WELL CHILD VISIT (TOTAL REIMBURSEMENT/ NUMBER OF VISITS)
Lifecare	259	$31,196.55	$120.45
Getwell	786	$100,859.52	$128.32
SureHealth	462	$54,631.50	$118.25
BeHealthy	219	$26,991.75	$123.25

Answer Key for the Mock Examination

ANSWER   EXPLANATION

10. B   CALCULATIONS:

Reimbursement for one well child visit = total reimbursement divided by number of visits.

Reimbursements for two immunizations = total reimbursement divided by number of immunizations x 2.

Total reimbursement for one average visit = reimbursement for one well child visit + reimbursement for two immunizations.

INSURANCE COMPANY	REIMBURSEMENT FOR ONE WELL CHILD VISIT	REIMBURSEMENT FOR TWO IMMUNIZATIONS [(TOTAL REIMBURSEMENT/NUMBER OF IMMUNIZATIONS) x 2]	TOTAL REIMBURSEMENT FOR ONE AVERAGE VISIT (REIMBURSEMENT FOR ONE WELL CHILD VISIT + REIMBURSEMENT FOR TWO IMMUNIZATIONS)
Lifecare	$120.45	$10.56	$131.01
Getwell	$128.32	$12.36	$140.68
SureHealth	$118.25	$11.76	$130.01
BeHealthy	$123.25	$10.16	$133.41

11. B

12. C   Calculations: MS-DRG A $2.023 \times 323 = 653.43$

MS-DRG B $0.987 \times 489 = 485.65$

MS-DRG C $1.925 \times 402 = 773.85$

MS-DRG D $1.243 \times 386 = 479.80$

13. A

14. D

15. A

16. B

17. D

18. A

19. D

20. D

21. B

22. A   The cancer is coded as a current condition as long as the patient is receiving adjunct therapy.

23. A

24. D

25. A

26. C   A surgical operation is one or more surgical procedures performed at one time for one patient using a common approach or for a common purpose.

27. D

28. D

29. B

Answer Key for the Mock Examination

ANSWER	EXPLANATION

30. C The condition should be coded as a poisoning when there is an interaction of an over-the-counter drug and alcohol. Answers A, B, and D are adverse effects of a correctly administered prescription drug.

31. B

32. A When a diagnosis is preceded by the phrase "rule out" in the inpatient setting, the condition is coded as though it is confirmed.

33. C *Staging* is a term used to refer to the progression of cancer. In accessing most types of cancer, a method (staging) is used to determine how far the cancer has progressed. The cancer is described in terms of how large the main tumor is, the degree to which it has invaded surrounding tissue, and the extent to which it has spread to lymph glands or other areas of the body. Staging not only helps to assess outlook but also the most appropriate treatment.

34. A

35. A

36. D Not all of the components of the combination code were POA.
"Y" = yes, present on admission.
"U"= no information in the record.
"W"= clinically undetermined.
"N" = no, not present on admission.

37. A

38. D Look up in CPT codebook index under foot, neuroma.

39. B The sizes of the layered wound repairs of the same body area are added together in order to select the correct CPT code.

40. A The codes in this subsection are used to report evaluations for life or disability insurance baseline information.

41. D *Dialysis* is the main term to be referenced in the CPT manual index.

42. D If the immunization is the only service that the patient receives, then two codes are used to report the service. The immunization administration code is first and then the code for the vaccine/toxoid.

43. B

44. D

45. D

46. C

47. B

48. A Calculation: $\dfrac{(6 \times 100)}{(212 + 28 + 6)} = 2.4\%$

49. C

50. B Calculation: $\$2{,}655 \times 100$ divided by $\$25{,}000 = 10.6 = 11\%$

51. C

52. A

53. A

54. B Calculation: $(335 \times 151) + (350 \times 214) = 125{,}485$

55. C Calculation: $31 - 14 + 28 + 2 = 47$ days

56. A

57. C

Answer Key for the Mock Examination

ANSWER   EXPLANATION

58. B
59. D
60. B
61. D
62. B
63. B
64. D   Calculation: Remaining at midnight 8/1   99
                        Admissions   +4
                        Discharges   −7
                        In and Out Same Day   +1
                        Inpatient Service Days 8/2   97
         Fetal Deaths and DOA have no impact on inpatient service days.
65. A
66. A
67. A
68. D
69. B
70. D
71. A
72. C   Calculation: $\dfrac{(111{,}963 \times 100)}{(300 \times 181) + (375 \times 184)} = 90.8\%$
73. A   Multiple births are still considered one delivery for statistical purposes.
74. C
75. B
76. B
77. D
78. C   Calculation: $3,027 × 2.0671 = $6,257.11
79. C
80. A   Calculation: (431 × 100) / 2,879 = 14.97%
                        (458 × 100) / 15,242 = 3%
                        (114 × 100) / 1,426 = 8%
                        (313 × 100) / 6,271 = 5%
         The highest percentage of error is in consultation reports.
81. B   The highest volume (number) of errors is in lab slips.
82. B
83. B
84. C
85. D
86. C
87. D
88. B
89. A
90. A   Many hospitals use the EDMS as a transition strategy to support their EHR effort.
91. A
92. D
93. D

Answer Key for the Mock Examination

ANSWER	EXPLANATION
94. A	
95. A	
96. C	
97. B	Consultation codes can no longer be coded when the physician has taken an active part in the continued care of the patient.
98. D	
99. A	
100. C	It is the responsibility of organizational leaders to participate in the QI process.
101. B	Calculation: (304 × 100) / 845 = 36%
102. C	Calculation: (14 × 100) / 526 = 2.66% or 2.7%
103. D	
104. B	Picture archiving and communication systems provide a means to store and rapidly access digitized file images.
105. C	
106. B	Health information exchange is a term used to refer to a "plan in which health information is shared among providers."
107. B	
108. D	
109. D	
110. A	
111. B	
112. B	
113. C	
114. D	
115. C	
116. C	
117. C	
118. B	
119. B	
120. B	
121. B	
122. D	
123. C	The Joint Commission requires hospitals to prohibit abbreviations that have caused confusion or problems in their handwritten form (e.g., "U" for unit, which can be mistaken for "0" (zero) or "4"). Spelling out "unit" is preferred.
124. D	Calculations:

- $36,429 annual labor costs / 12 = $3,035.75 cost per month
- $3,035.75 + $89 copier cost = $3,124.75 monthly costs/687
- ROI last month = 4.548 or $4.55 unit cost (not counting mailing)
- $4.55 + 0.95 average mailing cost = $5.50 per ROI

125. C	
126. C	
127. D	
128. A	
129. C	
130. C	
131. A	

Answer Key for the Mock Examination

ANSWER EXPLANATION

132. C

133. A

134. D

135. A   employee # 425: 120 + (35 × 0.75) + (16 × 0.5) = 154.25
       154.25/5 = 30.85 average work units per day
     employee # 426: 48 + (89 × 0.75) + (95 × 0.5) = 162.25
       162.25/5 = 32.45 average work units per day
     employee # 427: 80 + (92 × 0.75) + (4 × 0.5) = 151
       151/5 = 30.2 average work units per day
     employee # 428: 65 + (109 × 0.75) + (16 × 0.5) = 154.75
       154.75 = 30.95 average work units per day

136. A

137. C

138. D   Calculation: (You can only purchase whole shelf units.)
     34 × 3 = 102 records per shelf
     102 × 6 = 612 records per filing unit
     18,000 × 0.20 = 3,600 records for projected expansion
     18,000 + 3,600 = 21,600 total records
     21,600/612 = 35.29 = 36 total filing units needed

139. D

140. D

141. B

142. A   Calculation: 7.5 hours × 60 minutes per hour = 450 minutes per day
     450 × 15% = 67.5   450 − 67.5 = 382.5   382.5/2.5 = 153

143. A   Calculation: 50 × 30 = 1,500   1,500/60 = 25   25/6.5 = 3.8

144. A   Although employees 103 and 104 worked more hours than scheduled, they still did not work overtime using the 8/80 rules.

145. A   Calculation: 76/300 = 0.253   0.253 × 7 hours = 1.77 hours

146. C   Benchmarking involves comparing your department to other departments or organizations known to be excellent in one or more areas. The success of benchmarking involves finding out how the other department functions and then incorporating their ideas into your department.

147. D

148. C   Generally, allow 60 sq ft per employee. However, as time progresses, less area is being allotted for personal space.

149. C

150. D   Calculation: (400 × 100)/450 = 88.9%

151. C

152. A

153. D

154. C   Calculation: (12 × 100) / (15 × 21) = 3.80 = 4%

155. B

156. D

157. B

158. B

Answer Key for the Mock Examination

ANSWER	EXPLANATION
159. C	
160. A	
161. C	
162. D	
163. B	
164. C	
165. B	
166. C	
167. C	Central registries would not be covered under HIPAA if they do not bill for patient care services. In these cases, the general norms for data security and confidentiality should be followed.
168. A	
169. C	
170. A	
171. C	
172. C	
173. B	
174. B	
175. D	
176. A	
177. D	
178. A	
179. A	
180. C	

REFERENCES

Abdelhak, M., Grostick, S., Hanken, M. A., & Jacobs, E. (Eds.). (2012). *Health information: Management of a strategic resource* (4th ed.). Philadelphia: Elsevier.

American Medical Association (AMA). (2013). *Physicians' current procedural terminology: CPT 2014, professional edition.* Chicago: Author.

American Medical Association (AMA). (2010). *Principles of CPT coding* (6th ed.). Chicago: Author.

Green, M. A., & Bowie, M. J. (2011). *Essentials of health information management: Principles and practice* (2nd. ed.). Clifton Park, NY: Delmar Cengage Learning.

Horton, L. (2011). *Calculating and reporting health care statistics* (4th ed.). Chicago: American Health Information Management Association (AHIMA).

Koch, G. (2008). *Basic allied health statistics and analysis* (3rd ed.). Clifton Park, NY: Delmar Cengage Learning.

Johnson, S. L., & Linker, R. (2013). *Understanding medical coding: A comprehensive guide* (3rd ed.). Clifton Park, NY: Delmar Cengage Learning.

LaTour, S., Eichenwald-Maki, S., and Oachs, P. (2013). *Health information management: Concepts, principles and practice* (4th ed.). Chicago: American Health Information Management Association (AHIMA).

McWay, D. C. (2010). *Legal and ethical aspects of health information management* (3rd ed.). Clifton Park, NY: Delmar Cengage Learning.

McWay, D. C. (2014). *Today's health information management: An integrated approach* (2nd ed.). Clifton Park, NY: Delmar Cengage Learning.

Optum Learning (2014). *Detailed instruction for appropriate ICD-10-CM coding.* West Valley City, UT: OptumInsight, Inc.

Sayles, N. B. (2013). *Health information technology: An applied approach* (4th ed.). Chicago: American Health Information Management Association (AHIMA).

Sayles N. B., & Trawick, K. (2010). *Introduction to computer systems for health information technology.* Chicago: American Health Information Management Association (AHIMA).

RHIA AND RHIT COMPETENCIES BY QUESTION FOR MOCK EXAMINATION

Question	RHIA Domain Competencies						RHIT Domain Competencies						
	1	2	3	4	5	6	1	2	3	4	5	6	7
1		X					X						
2						X						X	
3			X										X
4	X						X						
5			X					X					
6	X						X						
7	X						X						
8	X						X						
9	X												X
10	X												X
11	X												X
12	X												X
13	X							X					
14	X								X				
15						X					X		
16			X							X			
17						X				X			
18	X							X					
19	X							X					
20	X						X						
21	X							X					
22	X							X					
23	X							X					
24	X							X					
25	X							X					
26	X						X						
27	X							X					
28	X							X					
29	X							X					
30	X							X					
31	X							X					
32	X							X					
33	X						X						
34	X							X					
35						X						X	
36	X							X					
37	X							X					
38	X							X					
39	X							X					
40	X							X					

Question	RHIA Domain Competencies							RHIT Domain Competencies						
	1	2	3	4	5	6		1	2	3	4	5	6	7
41	X							X						
42	X							X						
43	X							X						
44	X							X						
45	X							X						
46	X							X						
47		X										X		
48		X										X		
49		X										X		
50				X								X		
51			X								X			
52		X										X		
53		X										X		
54		X						X						
55		X						X						
56				X				X						
57		X										X		
58		X										X		
59		X						X						
60		X										X		
61						X					X			
62						X				X				
63		X								X				
64		X						X						
65		X										X		
66		X										X		
67		X										X		
68		X						X						
69		X						X						
70		X										X		
71		X										X		
72		X						X						
73		X						X						
74						X							X	
75						X						X		
76	X													X
77				X							X			
78	X													X
79						X							X	

RHIA AND RHIT COMPETENCIES BY QUESTION FOR MOCK EXAMINATION

Question	RHIA Domain Competencies							RHIT Domain Competencies						
	1	2	3	4	5	6		1	2	3	4	5	6	7
80		X						X						
81		X						X						
82						X							X	
83					X					X				
84					X								X	
85						X							X	
86						X							X	
87					X								X	
88					X								X	
89					X								X	
90			X								X			
91					X							X		
92		X										X		
93	X													X
94					X								X	
95					X								X	
96	X								X					
97	X								X					
98		X									X			
99			X								X			
100					X						X			
101		X						X						
102		X						X						
103	X									X				
104			X								X			
105					X								X	
106			X								X			
107	X									X				
108	X									X				
109	X							X						
110					X						X			
111			X								X			
112	X									X				
113			X					X						
114					X						X			
115					X								X	
116		X										X		
117				X						X				

RHIA AND RHIT COMPETENCIES BY QUESTION FOR MOCK EXAMINATION

Question	RHIA Domain Competencies							RHIT Domain Competencies						
	1	2	3	4	5	6		1	2	3	4	5	6	7
118						X				X				
119				X									X	
120			X								X			
121			X								X			
122					X					X				
123					X					X				
124				X				X						
125		X									X			
126			X					X						
127			X					X						
128			X					X						
129			X					X						
130			X								X			
131				X				X						
132		X										X		
133		X										X		
134				X								X		
135				X								X		
136				X				X						
137				X				X						
138			X					X						
139				X								X		
140				X									X	
141				X				X						
142				X				X						
143				X				X						
144				X								X		
145				X				X						
146				X								X		
147				X								X		
148				X								X		
149				X								X		
150				X				X						
							END OF RHIT EXAMINATION							

Continue on for RHIA Mock Examination

Question	RHIA Domain Competencies					
	1	2	3	4	5	6
151			X			
152				X		
153				X		
154				X		
155				X		
156				X		
157				X		
158			X			
159			X			
160				X		
161					X	
162			X			
163		X				
164				X		
165				X		
166			X			
167				X		
168					X	
169		X				
170				X		
171				X		
172				X		
173				X		
174		X				
175		X				
176		X				
177			X			
178				X		
179			X			
180					X	

RHIA COMPETENCIES BY QUESTION FOR MOCK EXAMINATION

EVALUATION FORM FOR THE BOOK

As we have learned through quality improvement concepts, there is always the opportunity to do something better. Therefore, if you have suggestions for improving the book, please let us know. We invite your input and feedback.

Please rate each of the following aspects of this book on a scale of 1 to 5, where: **5 is excellent, 4 is above average, 3 is average, 2 is below average, and 1 is poor.**

Depth/completeness of coverage	5	4	3	2	1
Organization of material	5	4	3	2	1
Study tips	5	4	3	2	1
Appropriate level of writing	5	4	3	2	1
Cover design and attractiveness	5	4	3	2	1
Overall design and layout of book	5	4	3	2	1
Overall satisfaction with book	5	4	3	2	1

Would you recommend this book to future graduates studying for the RHIA-RHIT examination?

What can we do to make these products better for you to use? _____

_____

_____

_____

_____

_____

_____

Please attach additional comments if you have further suggestions. Thank you!

Attention: Patricia J. Schnering
c/o Delmar Cengage Learning
Executive Woods
5 Maxwell Drive
Clifton Park, NY 12065

Email your comments and questions to the author at: *PJSPRG@AOL.COM*

WITHDRAWN